D1642255

WIRELESS HORIZON

WIRELESS HORIZON

Strategy and Competition in the Worldwide Mobile Marketplace

Dan Steinbock

AMACOM
American Management Association
New York · Atlanta · Brussels · Buenos Aires · Chicago · London · Mexico City
San Francisco · Shanghai · Tokyo · Toronto · Washington, D.C.

Special discounts on bulk quantities of AMACOM books are available to corporations, professional associations, and other organizations. For details, contact Special Sales Department, AMACOM, a division of American Management Association, 1601 Broadway, New York, NY 10019.
Tel.: 212-903-8316. Fax: 212-903-8083.
Web site: www.amacombooks.org

This publication is designed to provide accurate and authoritative information in regard to the subject matter covered. It is sold with the understanding that the publisher is not engaged in rendering legal, accounting, or other professional service. If legal advice or other expert assistance is required, the services of a competent professional person should be sought.

Library of Congress Cataloging-in-Publication Data

Steinbock, Dan.
        Wireless horizon : strategy and competition in the worldwide mobile marketplace / Dan Steinbock.
            p. cm.
        Includes bibliographical references and index.
        ISBN 0-8144-0714-5
        1. Wireless communication systems—History.   2. Cellular telephone services industry—History.   3. Telecommunication—History.   I. Title.

HE9713 .S73 2003
384.5′3—dc21   2002006684

Printing number

10   9   8   7   6   5   4   3   2   1

Contents

Acknowledgments

The research and writing of *Wireless Horizon* has taken several years. I initiated the research in the Nordic countries, but gradually I expanded research cooperation from northern Europe to the core clusters and lead markets in Western Europe, the United States, Japan, and China. Due to my emphasis of *global* frameworks of strategic management, I am particularly indebted to the classic works on globalization by professors Christopher A. Bartlett and Sumantra Ghoshal, Theodore Levitt, Jean-Pierre Jeannet, and Jay R. Galbraith—as well as the pioneering insights of Kenichi Ohmae, Michael E. Porter, and AnnaLee Saxenian. Additionally, on the issues of innovation, strategy, and policy, I owe gratitude to professors James M. Utterback, Clayton M. Christensen, Richard R. Nelson, Alfred D. Chandler, Jr., as well as to the classic works by Joe S. Bain and Richard Foster. In the issues of spectrum auctions, I am indebted to Eli M. Noam, director of Columbia Institute for Tele-Information, and Professor Lawrence Lessig, the founder of the Stanford Center for Internet and Safety.

At Nokia, I owe special thanks to quite a few industry executives whose studies and lectures have contributed to *Wireless Horizon,* including Jorma Ollila, Pekka Ala-Pietilä, Martti Alahuhta, Yrjö Neuvo, as well as Kari-Pekka Wilska. The assistance of Lauri Kivinen, senior VP of Nokia's corporate communications, was critical with many research materials. Since the rise of GSM in the early 1990s, the Nordic public-sector policies in wireless communications have provided a competitive model for the EC directives and worldwide telecom reforms. In this regard, I am indebted to Olli-Pekka Heinonen, former minister of Finland's Ministry of Transport and Communications, which recently has cooperated with the Japanese authorities to promote the launch of the 3G infrastructure. Furthermore, I am grateful for interviews with several politicians who, in the 1990s, contributed to the Finnish success in wireless communications, including Esko Aho, a Centrist party leader; Harri Holkeri, a veteran Conservative politician and president of the U.N. General Assembly (2000–2001); and Martti Ahtisaari, under-secretary general of the U.N. and president of Finland (1994–2000).

Through the 1990s, the Clinton-Gore administration pioneered the information infrastructure public policies in the United States and worldwide. I am most grateful for the interview with Ira Magaziner, senior adviser of the administration and the architect of public e-commerce policies. Furthermore,

I am indebted to information exchange with President Clinton's Council of Economic Advisers (CEA), which, in late 2000, released an important policy document on the impending 3G era and the U.S. competitive advantage.

Equipment manufacturers and network operators have historically played a central role in the expansion of the mobile business. Along with the Nokians, I am grateful for a large number of industry practitioners at Ericsson, Motorola, Qualcomm, and other leading global mobile vendors. I am particularly indebted to Donna Campbell, director of Ericsson CyberLab in New York. Also, I would like to extend thanks to Lars-Göran Hedin, director of publications and editorial services at Ericsson corporate communications in Stockholm; and in New York, Sandra Hetzler, investor relations program manager; and Anna Dimert, head of corporate communications at Ericsson Inc. At Motorola University, and Motorola Archives, quite a few people have provided reports, studies, and presentations on Motorola's history and its 3G visions. In that regard, I am indebted to Eric A. Schuster of Motorola Archives, as well as Kathi Ann Brown, the author of the history of Motorola and the Cellular Telecommunications & Internet Association (CTIA). At Qualcomm Inc., I am particularly grateful for Julie Cunningham, senior VP of investor relations.

In addition to mobile players, I am indebted to those digital economy leaders that have only recently diversified into mobile communications. Among these companies, I would like to thank Nathan Myhrvold, technology director of Microsoft Corp., and Jenna Fiorito, VP of business development at AOL's wireless division. Consulting for Intel Corp.'s Wireless Communications and Computing Group (WCCG), I want to thank Daniel Craig and the talented experts of the wireless team. Finally, I owe a gratitude to investor relations and other representatives at Lucent Technologies, Siemens, Samsung, Sony, Palm, Handspring, Research In Motion (RIM), and Microsoft's Pocket PC group for their research assistance. Finally, I owe a gratitude to Neil Budde, senior VP of The Wall Street Journal Interactive, especially in issues pertaining to product development in the Internet era.

Prior to undertaking my wireless research, I served as a strategy consultant for Telecom Italia, whose mobile subsidiary pioneered the first large-scale markets in Europe. In 2000–2001, I consulted for Sonera (formerly Telecom Finland), a pioneer of mobile services and mobile e-commerce worldwide. At Sonera, I am grateful for the presentations of Kaj-Erik Relander, former president and CEO. At the Swedish Telia, I am indebted to Tero Laaksonen, former managing director of Telia Finland, and Kenneth Karlberg, CEO Telia Mobile. At the Norwegian Telenor, I found great assistance from Dag Melgaards, senior press officer; Eli Hall, head of Telenor's Telemuseum; and Anne Solberg, the museum's senior documentarist. Among the larger operators, I am indebted for a wide variety of contacts at Vodafone-Mannesmann, Telecom Italia, Deutsche Telekom, Telefonica, France Telecom, BT, AT&T Wireless, Verizon Wireless, Sprint PCS, China Telecom, and several other leading operators. I owe a gratitude to Clayton Foster, director of product strategy and development at AT&T Wireless, particularly for his views on the operators' issues in the United States. I would like to express my special gratitude to Tats Shukunami, president of NTT DoCoMo USA (Washington, D.C. division), whose assistance and personal views on the global strategy of the Japanese 3G pioneer greatly assisted my research efforts. By 2000 and 2001, the entire industry talked about 3G, but only NTT DoCoMo managed to create a profitable service concept. In this regard, I have also gained a lot from the studies of Jeffrey L. Funk at Kobe University's Research Institute for Economics and Business— just as the contributions of Bertil Thorngren, director of the Center for Information and Communications Research (CIC) at the Stockholm School of Economics, have shaped my views on the technology evolution of the industry.

In addition to wireless equipment manufacturers and network operators, I am grateful for a number of trade associations, particularly CTIA, Internet Advertising Bureau (IAB), and Wireless Advertising Association (WAA). In this context, I am most grateful to Thomas Sugrue, chief of the FCC wireless bureau, as well as Michael Altschul, senior VP and general counsel of CTIA.

I am also indebted to the numerous mobile startups specializing in wireless software, content/aggregation, and commerce. They include the Finnish pioneers from Markus Wartiovaara of Razorfish to Mikko Myyryläinen of Contra Integrated; in the United States, they range from Jason Devitt of Vindigo to Peter Semmelhack of Antenna Software. The full list of these companies is too broad to print, but it includes dozens of new ventures in the United States, Western Europe, and Asia-Pacific. I would also like to thank Bo Harald, executive VP of network banking and payments at Nordea, the worldwide pioneer of mobile banking, and the first chairman of the Mobey Forum, a financial industry–driven forum. And I would like to mention Eric Goldberg, president and founder of Crossover Technologies and a cofounder of New York New Media Association (NYNMA), who provided me with a better understanding on the role of the U.S. software development community as a critical resource for the changing mobile business. Since the late 1990s, my cooperation with Nordic venture capital firms resulted in consulting for Finnish and Swedish new media ventures, many of them suppliers or subcontractors of Nokia and Ericsson, or pioneering operators, such as Sonera, Telia, and Telenor, seeking access into the international technology sector through joint ventures or strategic alliances in the United States.

Through research, consulting, and instruction, then, I have had a unique window to monitor developments in the United States, Western Europe, and the Nordic countries, as well as Japan and China. As I have examined the trials and errors of Nordic firms in their heroic efforts to access and conquer markets in Western Europe, the United States and Asia-Pacific, I have also consulted for the Organisation for Economic Cooperation and Development (OECD) and the European Commission on the differences between the (U.S.-based) Internet pioneers and the (Europe-based) mobile pioneers, as well as innovation systems in the United States and in Europe. In this regard, I would like to thank Erkki Liikanen (commissioner, European Commission for Enterprise and Information Society) and Dr. Tassos Belessiotis, head of EC's Competitive Analysis and Benchmarking. As I have managed the mobile Internet program and organized the 3G conference of the Columbia Institute for Tele-Information (CITI), I also had an opportunity to exchange views and learn from industry practitioners, trade associations, regulators, industry analysts, and academic researchers.

I am indebted to numerous analyses, studies, reports, and assessments by the world's leading investment banks and consulting firms. Among many, I would like to thank Alan F. Riffkin, Vik Mehta, Barry Kaplan, and Candice Hwa of Goldman, Sachs & Co.; William Farrell and Angela Dean at Morgan Stanley Dean Witter; John Bensche, Jennifer Cooke Ritter, and Tim Luke of Lehman Brothers; Peter C. Friedland of WR Hambrecht + Co.; NiQ Lai, head of the Asia Telecom Research Group at Credit Suisse First Boston Corp.; Marianne Wolk of Robertson Stephens, Inc.; Seyonne Kang of J.P. Morgan H&Q; Matthew Hoffman and Timothy O'Neil of Wit SoundView; and Carolina Junqueira of Booz Allen Hamilton. Among market research companies (and in addition to the UMTS Forum studies), I've had the opportunity to explore many interesting studies by a wide variety of excellent firms, including Ovum, EMC, Datamonitor, IDC, Gartner Group, Herschel Shosteck Associates, Total Romtec, Durlacher, Strategy Analytics, McKinsey & Co., Forrester Research, and Jupiter Media Metrix.

My thoughts have been shaped by debates with my Finnish and international students in the Helsinki School of Economics (HSE). As director of HSE's Centre of International Business Research (CIBR), I have been inspired by Professor Reijo Luostarinen, director of the international business faculty and a pioneer researcher of challengers in small and open economies worldwide. I remain in gratitude to Christopher H. Sterling, professor of telecommunications at the George Washington University, who has somehow always found time to comment on my various questions and inquiries. Finally, the completion of *Wireless Horizon* would not have been possible without the support of a number of people at AMACOM Books—including Neil Levine, senior acquisitions editor; Mike Sivilli, associate editor; Andy Ambraziejus, managing editor; Lydia Lewis, production manager; Irene Majuk, director of trade publicity and sales promotion; Therese Mausser, director of subsidiary rights and international sales; and Kama Timbrell, senior publicist. Most of all, I owe gratitude to Cara Anselmo who served as the publisher's reader and managed to translate complicated ideas into readable prose.

The conclusions are mine alone. I have no doubts that the very same issues could be framed quite differently. But in order to understand the competitive logic and globalization in mobile communications, the structure and objectives of *Wireless Horizon* make a lot of sense. By the same token, this framework allows one to depict a century of worldwide mobile rivalries in a concise manner—without violating the richness of the material.

At a more personal level, this book has been a unique experience in terms of its own time and place. It was completed amid the anguish of New Yorkers seeking their family members, bomb threats in the streets and offices of midtown Manhattan, blocked streets, lingering fires in a downtown human crematorium, and visits to the cemetery. It was written in perhaps the most "global city" in the world, among strangers who have become friends, agony that has turned into determination, and dreams of a better life. Months after the hell and the ashes, I dedicate *Wireless Horizon* to the victims and heroes of September 11, 2001—and, at a personal level, to Kaneez, who made it all less difficult, helping to move on, yet never to forget.

Dan Steinbock
New York City, March 11, 2002

Preface

As I rushed out to donate blood on September 11, 2001, New York City was amid the most painful tragedy in its history. A massive black cloud hovered over downtown. It bespoke of death and devastation. Thousands of office workers were trying to find transportation. Cops were everywhere. People supported each other. Some were covered in white dust. Some were bleeding. Some were in shock. Jeeps rushed along Second Avenue. Fighter jets roared in the emptiness of the bright blue sky. Amid this Dantean inferno, anybody who happened to have a cell phone was talking. "I'm all right, I'm all right." "I love you, honey." "I made it, but the rest of the office and the Tower—it's gone, all of it." "God have mercy on us all. . . . "

In scores of emotionally searing interviews conducted by the New York City Fire Department for an internal inquiry, the agency's most senior commanders said later that they had little reliable radio communication that morning, could not keep track of all the firefighters who entered the towers, and were unable to reach them as the threat of a collapse became unmistakable. "So poor were communications," reported *The New York Times,* "that on one side of the trade center complex, in the city's emergency management headquarters, a city engineer warned officials that the towers were at risk of 'near imminent collapse,' but those he told could not reach the highest-ranking fire chief by radio. Instead, a messenger was sent across acres, dodging flaming debris and falling bodies, to deliver this assessment in person. He arrived with the news less than a minute before the first tower fell."[1]

During and after the terrorist attacks of that fatal Tuesday, wireless phones and pagers were not only a convenience; they provided a vital mode of communication for firefighters, cops, doctors, chaplains, paramedics, fleet mechanics, and support staff who responded to the catastrophe without having to be asked. These cell phones were even used by the hijacked flight passengers to warn the nation and to send their last words to the families. Where cell phones failed, some people turned to wireless data devices. Most users relied on basic voice services. They wanted to hear their loved ones. They wanted to know that their children, parents, relatives, or friends were safe and sound. After a while, the cell phone acquired a more therapeutic function as people used voice communications to share their experiences and find consolation.

These user experiences were not the ones promoted before September

11, or during the slowdown in the U.S. technology sector or the European 3G license auctions. In the late 1990s, the industry focus had been on the perceived rosy future of wireless data services, which, to some extent, had already taken off in the most developed markets, including those of Japan and northern Europe.

On February 26, 1993—some eight years before the tragedy of the Twin Towers—four militant terrorists had detonated a bomb in the underground parking lot of the World Trade Center. That attack caused six deaths, and more than 1,000 people were injured. At the time, only emergency services were able to use wireless communications. However, very few victims had access to cell phones or pagers. In the Nordic countries, the digital mobile networks, which were driven by consumer mass markets, had been introduced around 1991 and 1992—years before the launch of similar services in America.

But the vital function of wireless communications was not discovered only in the 1990s. At the turn of the 1940s, Paul W. Galvin, the founder of Motorola, Inc., prodded the Army and his associates to recognize the wireless potential:

> I wonder how many of you realize the importance of radio as a deciding factor in who is going to win the war? What is it that gives the vicious efficiency to vehicles of destruction in modern mechanized warfare? It is radio. What is today revolutionizing aircraft, naval, and antiaircraft tactics and strategy? It is radio and radar. It is our job—the industry's job—to deliver these precious and important instruments.[2]

In the subsequent years, Motorola's Walkie-Talkies were used throughout Europe and the Pacific to provide critical communications links at Anzio, Guadalcanal, Iwo Jima, and Normandy. Historically, the vital function of wireless communications was acknowledged even earlier. On April 14, 1912, the liner *SS Titanic*, on her maiden voyage to New York, struck an iceberg. Sweeping regulations were enacted to govern all ships at sea.[3]

In effect, one might go even further. During the Civil War, field telegraphs were deployed to establish temporary telegraph stations linking adjacent troops during battle conditions. Wireless technology has evolved in emergency situations and military crises. For more than a century, wireless communications has served a vital function in human communications, just as it has been subject to changing public policies and worldwide competition for industrial leadership. Like the Internet, wireless communications was "born global" and holds a promise for a "worldwide wireless" of sorts. But the Internet evolved in the largely unregulated computing industry, was privatized at the turn of the 1990s, and commercialized with the first browsers a few years later. Instead, the wireless business originated from pioneering tests by

Guglielmo Marconi in the late-nineteenth century. Though a century old, the wireless business remained a niche market until the late 1980s. It was important and promising, but marginal vis-à-vis the primary revenue sources of the world's largest telecom operators. Only with the rise of the digital cellular have the industry's strategic stakes climbed dramatically in terms of accumulated investment and profitability, locational advantage, and employment. As the mobile leaders prepared for the 3G era in 2001, GSM* first pioneered in the Nordic countries, has become the most popular standard worldwide. In 1992, the number of GSM subscribers worldwide amounted to only 23 million. By early 2001, the figure had soared to 707 million—and today, it exceeds 1 billion.

By the late 1990s, this realization of the rapidly growing economic importance of the industry boosted the stock prices of leading equipment vendors, such as Nokia and Ericsson, and leading operators, such as Vodafone-Mannesmann and NTT DoCoMo. Between 1980 and 1994, during the PC revolution, more than 580 technology companies went public and created more than $240 billion in net market capitalization. By January 1999—in just half a decade—the Internet grew from a $34 billion industry, by market value measures, to one worth $257 billion.[4] Unsurprisingly, these developments went hand in hand with pioneering efforts to couple two high-growth industries: mobile communications and the Internet. In the summer of 2000, wireless stocks peaked, then followed the downfall. Nokia's market cap high of $260 billion declined rapidly with the rest of the market, declining to less than $60 billion by the fall of 2001. Others fared far worse. The U.S. technology sector was swept by consolidation. Leading European operators were taxed excessively by disproportionate 3G license fees. In the early 1990s, the business had experienced comparable birth pains as part of the transition to the 2G era, but because the industry was smaller then, risks were lower and potential rewards were higher. In the long term, the industry is poised for a new era of incremental growth. But along with winners, there will be losers.

As far back as the late 1890s, Marconi's success in wireless experiments served as a catalyst to many profitable innovations of the twentieth century, including radio, television, radiation, and satellite communications, just as it contributed to the race across the cellular platforms in the early twenty-first century. In the past century, these developments have evolved in three basic stages: pure science, commercialization in specialized markets, and large-scale consumer mass markets. Through the first two cellular eras (i.e., analog and

---

*The wireless business, even more than the technology sector in general, is haunted by acronyms and technical jargon. At times, the terms enlighten; at other times, they promote specific technologies (such as GSM), products and services, or fleeting strategic coalitions. With the privatization of standards-making activities and the declining role of public-sector consortia, these developments are probably inevitable. Instead of replicating the critical definitions from one chapter to another, I have included all of them in a separate Glossary at the end of the book.

digital), the hardware business, for most practical purposes, was about handsets, base stations, and switching stations. But even this was about to change with the 3G transition, in which value migrated from hardware to software.

Wireless Horizon is about the policies, strategies, and innovations that have made the industry leaders in the mobile business from the late-nineteenth century to the present. It also outlines success drivers beyond the 3G era.

The book tells the story of the wireless business in four parts. Part I presents the central argument of the book, the quest for the wireless horizon. Chapter 1 focuses on the rivalry for the productivity frontier and global* leverage in the mobile business. It presents the triangle framework, including the driving forces of strategic advantage—that is, macro drivers (e.g., new public policies, innovation systems, and competitive clusters) and micro drivers (e.g., firm-level leadership in products, operations, and markets). This framework illustrates the *dynamics* of the business through three critical phases: monopoly, transition, and competition. In the course of these eras, the industry has proceeded from domestication to globalization. Chapter 2 focuses on the globalization of technology innovation in the wireless business. It traces the industry evolution from pure science to Marconi's commercial innovation, from the pre-cellular technologies to the cellular platforms (i.e., analog, digital, multimedia, and broadband). In contrast to conventional wisdom, the argument is that technology innovation serves as the catalyst for the industry, but it does not "determine" the nature of competition. Today, all leading industry giants are "technology agnostic." None are committed to any singular technology. All cultivate technologies that "work." While, then, understanding technology innovation is critical to get a better idea of the industry evolution, it is even more important to analyze how these new enabling technologies—through new products and services—have been incorporated as part of the dynamic industry and firm value chains.

The sections that follow concentrate on how technology innovation has been adopted into the value systems, which strategic groups of companies have played the driving role, and finally, why certain geographic locations have been so central to this evolution and others have not. None of these determinants are directly related to only technology innovation. Yet all have shaped the winners and losers of the business, from Marconi in 1895 to NTT DoCoMo in 2001.

Part II is about network operators, from national monopolies to those companies that emerged following market liberalization. It examines the geography of wireless competition focusing on the geographical concentrations that

*In ordinary language, the terms *worldwide* and *global* are often used interchangeably as synonyms. In the present work, however, there is a significant difference between the two terms. *Worldwide* is a neutral term for the geography of the globe, whereas *global* refers to efforts to leverage a firm-level domestic strategy across the globe, or across the core clusters or lead markets.

truly count in the struggle for *global* leadership—the core clusters and lead markets of the United States, Western Europe (particularly Nordic countries), and Asia-Pacific (primarily Japan and China). In each case, this part concentrates on the dynamics of evolution from the pre-cellular era to the present and beyond, as well as on the eclipse of old telecom monopolies by their more agile successors. The network operators include U.S.-based AT&T Wireless and the new and more competitive entities, Western Europe's Vodafone, the small but technologically progressive Nordic operators, Japan's NTT Do-CoMo, and many others. This part also includes a detailed study of China's explosive high-volume market.

Part III concentrates on the leading equipment manufacturers—Motorola, Ericsson, Nokia, and Qualcomm—as well as their major contractors. Among industry players, the mobile vendors were the first to globalize their operations through competition. Historically, they have served as industry catalysts. This part also includes the most recent layer of the changing industry value chain, focusing on the leading enablers and service providers, including the great IT giants (e.g., Microsoft, Intel, America Online, and others). The chapters explore two conflicting visions of digital convergence. While the European-based mobile leaders are moving from voice to data communications, the U.S.-based IT leaders are shifting from data to voice communications. The first strategic group advocates vertical coordination to incorporate new technology innovation; the second promotes horizontalization to promote innovation. In this confrontation between two groups of firms, the strategic trade-offs are formidable, and the financial stakes are extraordinary. The conflicting visions and the intensity of the rivalry, is magnified by regional differences.

Finally, Part IV provides a comprehensive assessment of the industry evolution while setting the triangle frameworks of *Wireless Horizon* into historical context.

Until recently, there have been few managerial studies in these fields. Although the business is worldwide by nature, the few existing works tend to focus on technology or industry developments in one region or another. Such an examination is unsatisfactory, to say the least. After all, success in the United States no longer offers assurance of leadership in worldwide markets. It is vital to embrace a *global* perspective in order to provide truly useful managerial lessons. That, precisely, is the objective of *Wireless Horizon*—to serve as a managerial roadmap for industry practitioners, policy authorities, technology observers, trade specialists, investment analysts, market researchers, and general business readers in the United States and worldwide. The ongoing globalization necessitates an approach that incorporates developments in *all* core clusters and lead markets.

Like any other business, the wireless industry has evolved in place, but also in time. *Wireless Horizon* draws from history, but it is not a history. Rather, evolution, particularly through disruption or other dynamic influences that may shape industry structure, is key. Both the strategist and the historian want to remember the past; but the strategist, in addition, wants to change the future. This perspective has guided the writing of *Wireless Horizon*. It rests on efforts to better understand the winning policies, strategies, and innovations in the mobile business through evolution and geography.

In the wireless industry, the leading companies no longer compete against each other in multiple country markets. Rather, they compete *and* cooperate in a worldwide theater with global strategies. *Wireless Horizon* tells the story of this "global chessboard." It identifies the central players and their changing importance, while demonstrating how they compete. To regulators and policy implementers, the book serves as a guide to successes and failures in terms of public policies. To entrenched industry leaders in the United States, Europe, and the Asia-Pacific region, *Wireless Horizon* offers lessons on how incumbents can take advantage of disruptive business models in order to *sustain* and *renew* their strategic advantages. To industry start-ups, it provides a roadmap on how new attackers can take advantage of the very same models to *overthrow* old advantages and to create new ones—through global innovation, differentiation, and cost leadership. *Wireless Horizon* describes the past and the present—but only to subvert the future.

Part I

Quest for Wireless Horizon

*W*ireless Horizon tells the story of the wireless business in four parts. Part I presents the central argument of the book, the quest for wireless horizon. Part II is about industry evolution and network operators, from national monopolies to market liberalization. Part III concentrates on the leading equipment manufacturers (Motorola, Ericsson, Nokia, Qualcomm), contractors, as well as enablers and service providers. Part IV provides a comprehensive assessment of globalization in the wireless industry.

The sections that follow concentrate on how technology innovation has been adopted into the value systems, which strategic groups of companies have played the driving role and, finally, why certain geographic locations have been so central to this evolution and others have not.

Part I comprises two chapters. Chapter 1 focuses on globalization drivers. It examines the rivalry for productivity frontier and global leverage in the wireless business. It illustrates the triangle framework (including the driving forces of success) through three critical phases: monopoly, transition, and competition. In the course of these eras, the industry has proceeded from domestication to globalization. Chapter 2 focuses on the globalization of technology innovation in the wireless business. It traces industry evolution from pure science to Marconi's commercial innovation, from the pre-cellular technologies to the cellular platforms (analog, digital, multimedia, and broadband).

Chapter 1

Globalization Drivers

By all relevant accounts, the past century, particularly the last two to three decades, has been a period of tumultuous expansion and innovation, regulatory chaos, and market-driven explosion in wireless communications. There has been a distinct rationale to this progression in public policies, industrial innovation, and industry competition. This logic is that of productivity frontier— more precisely, that of *globalizing* productivity frontier. *Wireless Horizon* is neither a history of the wireless industry nor an account of developments in all wireless markets. As suggested by the subtitle, it is about strategy and competition in the worldwide mobile marketplace. The focus is only on the most *successful* strategies, policies, and innovations in the most developed markets— all of which have been rapidly globalizing since the 1980s.

Productivity Frontier

In competitive markets, macro developments in the economy and society account for the infrastructure that the competitors face, but these macro structures do not determine the winners and losers. Some companies manage to thrive even in unattractive environments and industries, just as some manage to fail in attractive ones. In such competitive conditions, it is the micro developments that often dictate success and failure.

Three Ways to Superior Performance

At firm level, a company can outperform its rivals only if it establishes a difference that it can preserve, sustain, and renew. To achieve this objective, companies tend to rely on three kinds of generic strategies: differentiation, cost, and innovation,[1] or a combination of the three. A company must deliver greater value to customers, create comparable value at a lower cost, find new ways of value creation, or succeed in a combination of the three. Delivering greater value allows a company to charge higher average unit prices (differentiation). Greater efficiency results in lower average unit costs (cost). Finding new ways of value creation enables the company to establish a new base for differentiation, cost, or both (innovation). Cost strategies reflect operational effectiveness.

These companies perform similar activities *better* than their rivals.[2] Differentiation means performing *different* activities from those of rivals or performing similar activities in *different ways*. Finally, innovation allows companies to discover *new* kinds of activities, which typically enables a company to achieve the benefits of differentiation, cost, or both.[3]

Productivity frontier is a hypothetical limit that constitutes the sum of all existing "best practices" at any given historical moment. When a company improves its differentiation, cost, or innovation, it moves closer to the frontier, which may be considered the joint function of relative differentiation, cost, and innovation (see Exhibit 1-1). This hypothetical frontier can be depicted schematically. Like competition, it is in constant flux. It ceaselessly shifts outward, with new technologies, inputs, management approaches, products, and services. In mobile communications, this is the story of the wireless productivity frontier, or what might also be termed wireless horizon. Whether a company attacks rivalry through differentiation, cost, or innovation, it seeks to embrace wireless horizon. Like a ship in the sea, it can never embrace the horizon; it can only reach for it. Wireless horizon holds the key to the logic of wireless competition, just as it plays a central role in *all* industries in which innovation is a critical element of success. Consequently, the lessons of this history have implications for other comparable industries.

Innovation has significant strategic implications for all industries, but it plays a critical role in wireless communications, due to successive waves of technology innovation (R&D, standards). Still, *technology* innovation alone has

Exhibit 1-1. Toward the global productivity frontier.

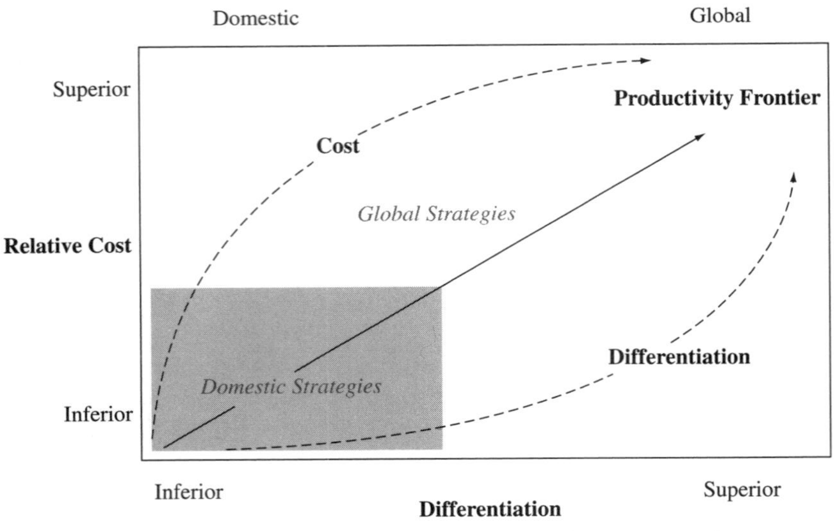

not determined the winners and losers. In effect, examples abound of more complex, precipitating conditions. In the early 1920s, for instance, police departments in the United States and England were testing the one-way wireless. Both possessed the requisite competences, but only U.S. departments proved willing to pioneer mobile communications. Or take the launch of the analog cellular at the turn of the 1980s. It was developed in the United States, but pioneered first in Japan and then in the Nordic countries. Yet, commercialization took off very slowly in Tokyo, but rapidly in the Nordic countries, and thereafter in the U.S. as well. Technology innovation is necessary to stay close to the productivity frontier, but it does not guarantee a victory in industry competition.

Like all innovation, technology innovation in the wireless business has evolved in specific locations that have served as centers of upstream activities (core clusters), and downstream activities (lead markets), or both. Until the end of the 1G era, the United States was *the* key cluster and lead market in mobile communications. Today, Finland is one of the core clusters due to its highly advanced R&D, but it is not a lead market in terms of revenues; it lacks adequate scale economies. Conversely, France is one of Europe's lead markets, due to its substantial population base, but it is not a core cluster. Despite several powerful rivals, including Alcatel and France Telecom, the key production facilities and most advanced R&D sites are not located in France. Technology innovation has been critical to stay close to the productivity frontier, but it has proceeded differently in different locations—not just because of technology advancements, but because of the geographic advantages and the industry environment.

Globalization of Productivity Frontier

Over time, wireless business has evolved from a single domestic cluster and market (the United States in the immediate postwar era) to multiple core clusters and lead markets (the United States, Western Europe, Japan, and China). Since the late 1980s, *globalization* of wireless horizon has required that the winners excel not only in differentiation, cost, or innovation. They must also be able to exploit this excellence through *global leverage*. In the past, economies of scale made the winners and the losers. Today, that is no longer sufficient. Economies of scope define success and failure. If, for instance, a company has a relatively low cost position, but it is confined to domestic markets and cannot employ leverage, it will fall behind industry leaders in *global* cost position (see Exhibit 1-1).

Until the emergence of the cellular platforms, the productivity frontier, core clusters, and lead markets were largely *domestic*. Since then, the industry has been driven by the powerful forces of *globalization*. Concurrently, the economies of scope underlying the productivity frontier have been dramatically extended via global leverage—from the singular home base to multiple locations worldwide. For decades, mobile communications evolved in the shadow of fixed-line telecommunications. Due to regulation, markets were neither global nor competitive but national monopolies. Economies of scope were limited to a single country; and most, if not all revenues were made in that one country. Consequently, the larger the country size, the greater the potential economies of scale. After two decades of telecom reforms, markets are rapidly globalizing and increasingly competitive; national monopolies are eroding. Today, any equipment manufacturer that hopes to join the top-tier players must have a presence in 80–140 countries; and the leading vendors make close to 99 percent of their revenues outside their home base. Consequently, the home base no longer determines potential scale economies; globalization does. Inherited scale economies no longer make winners; competitive scope economies do.

In the absence of globalization, industry leadership is no longer possible. That changes the rules of the game. It is one thing to employ differentiation in the domestic market, and quite another to practice a comparable strategy regionally, or worldwide. As industry environments change, strategies must accommodate change. For decades, this has been self-evident in small and open economies. Due to the small size of their inherent scale economies, the Nordic countries, for instance, are dependent on exports and foreign sales because the domestic base is saturated relatively fast and provides minimal revenues. If these countries fail to globalize, they will suffer. In their case, the small size has been a powerful motive to globalize and to look outward. In big countries, competitive incentives are very different. Due to their large inherent scale economies, great powers—such as the United States and China—have not been as dependent on exports and foreign sales because the domestic base provides a vast population base and maximum revenues. When they have failed to globalize, they have still thrived. Large size has served as a powerful disincentive to globalization and to look inward.

Today, all players must globalize and look outward, in both large and small countries. No company can any longer ignore globalization. The precellular era originated from national markets. The 1G era promoted regionalization. The 2G era gave rise to globalization. In the 3G era, leading operators, vendors, contractors, and enablers are all global operations—and it is the triangle framework that illustrates the evolution that led to the contemporary industry environment.

The Triangle Framework

The globalizing logic can be illustrated with a triangle framework and a dual (macro/micro) perspective (see Exhibit 1-2). It has proceeded from domestica-

Exhibit 1-2. The triangle framework.

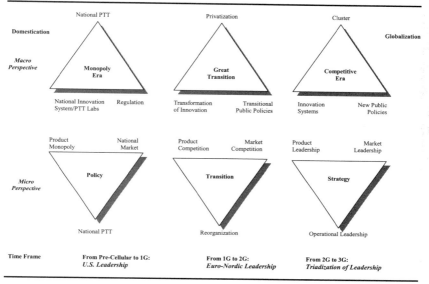

tion to globalization in three historical stages: monopoly, transition, and competition.

The Macro Perspective: From Domestication to Globalization

A decade or two ago, most country markets were ruled by the national PTT, which *was* the telecom industry before the arrival of the new public policies (*macro* perspective). Today, most country markets are dominated by competitive entities that have emerged with the new and more market-driven public policies (*micro* perspective).

The Monopoly Stage: Singular PTT

The *monopoly stage* emerged with Marconi and the pre-cellular era and lasted until the early 1G era. In terms of technology innovation, it began with wireless telegraphy, evolved with one- and two-way mobile communications as well as FM transition, peaking with the nascent analog cellular. In terms of market development, the stage began in the maritime sector and evolved with emergency services and the war years. It climaxed with industrial services and the first corporate and consumer markets in mobile communications. Most demand was still original demand. During this era, the national PTTs enjoyed a natural monopoly in telecom services. Regulation served as a valve that contained dynamic change. Public policies guided industry developments, which were confined to domestic markets. Advancements in cellular technologies and platform evolution were influenced by the national innovation system, the sophistication of R&D in the national PTT laboratories, and particularly the nature of the supply chain, which was organized differently in different regions. In the mobile business, the United States was the leader, the center of innovation, and the most progressive market. AT&T provided the most advanced model for national PTTs across the globe, and the example of "Ma Bell" directly or indirectly influenced the most sophisticated telecom businesses worldwide.

The Great Transition: New Public Policies

In contrast to the first stage, which endured almost a century, the second one—the *great transition*—lasted only one to two decades, depending on the country market. In the most advanced markets, it began with regulatory reforms in the early 1980s (privatization of British Telecommunications in the U.K., breakup of AT&T in the United States, deregulation in the Nordic countries, privatization of NTT in Japan). In most markets, it ended with the global telecom reform by 1998. Defined via wireless innovation, it started in the early 1G era, ending during the 2G era. In terms of market development, it emerged in the public-operator market but evolved with corporate markets and reached record heights with mass consumer markets in the most advanced countries; concurrently, the role of replacement demand began to rise, even if original demand still reigned. During this era, the national PTT lost its natural monopoly in most country markets. Regulators were isolated from national PTTs, which were privatized, which usually translated to years of restructuring and reorganization. As national regulatory regimes lost their bargaining power, deregulation shifted that power to competition policy authorities, who became subject to supranational forces regionally (NAFTA in North America, EU in Europe, APEC in Asia) and while initializing efforts at global "harmonization." The significance of the national innovation system remained important in basic research and infrastructure, but not in the rivalry for more specialized assets and capabilities. Innovation shifted from the national PTT to a slate of competitive players, vis-à-vis new suppliers (contractors of the leading vendors) and a new generation of more market-driven operators. Through foreign direct investment (FDI), the system of innovation *itself* became the subject of accelerating internationalization. The old "Ma Bell" PTT model split into Triad models: the competitive but inward-oriented market in the United States, the innovative and globally driven cluster in the northern Europe, the technologically sophisticated but relatively insular market in Japan, as well as the technologically primitive but massive marketplace in China, where coastal regions were opened for rapidly escalating inflows of FDI.

The Competitive Stage: Industry Specialization

In the most advanced country markets, the third stage evolved by the 2G era in the 1990s. This stage may be named the *competitive era* because, in most country markets, industry competition replaced the old monopoly model, even if the former PTT often remained a dominant carrier. It paralleled the rise of rudimentary data communications, such as short message service (SMS) in the most sophisticated GSM markets and the rise of CDMA, as well as its subsequent adoption as the core technology in the evolving multimedia cellular. The stage also coincided with the impending convergence of mobile and Internet industries. In terms of market development, it evolved in mass consumer markets, which were becoming increasingly global, with accelerating global segmentation, and the shift from original demand to replacement demand.

Today, strategies guide industry developments, which mobile leaders have expanded and leveraged worldwide. In the course of the past two decades, privatization and liberalization have disenabled the old monopolistic code, while deregulation has intensified dynamic change. Innovation has become increasingly responsive and specialized in terms of cellular advancements, standards, and technology development. The more competitive the industry value system, the greater are the incentives and rewards for innovative start-ups and challengers. In this era, leadership is no longer a monopolistic birthright. Instead, companies must *win* leadership in operations, products, and markets. In the past, vendors and operators had competed through gradual and evolutionary globalization; now many players are forced to globalize in order to compete. At the same time, the absolute and relative leadership of the United States in mobile communications has fragmented along the most advanced clusters and the lead markets in Western Europe, Nordic countries, and Asia-Pacific, particularly Japan and China.

New Public Policies

The great transition did not follow "naturally" from the monopoly era, which would have continued without the development and implementation of new public policies.[4] Over time, the role of regulators has declined, the role of competition policy authorities and supranational entities continues to accelerate, while industrial policies remain significant in many country markets (see Exhibit 1-3).[5] The market share of the national PTTs has eroded as these former giants have refocused from broad markets to narrower segments, which has often led to self-imposed or market-driven breakups and new IPOs. However, as innovation has become the basis of competition, the impact of these approaches has not been entirely benevolent.

In most country markets worldwide, the *sequence* of the phases has been similar, but the *timing* has differed. These differences illustrate the success drivers of the mobile leaders.

Separation of Regulatory Authority. Prior to new public policies, the national PTT was both a competitor (in wired and wireless services) *and* the

Exhibit 1-3. New public policies: from regulation to competition policy.

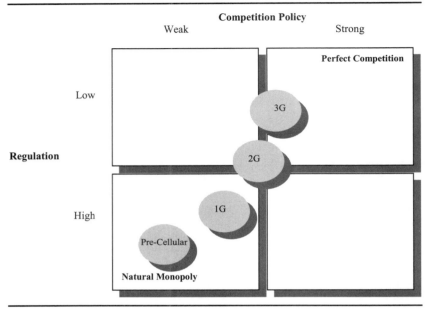

regulator of that rivalry. These arrangements provided fertile ground for conflicts of interest. Competition, however, evolved more quickly in the United States than in the nations that made up the two other poles of the Triad model for two reasons. First, AT&T was organized as a private-sector corporation under public oversight, whereas in Western Europe and Japan national PTTs were public-sector entities. Second, in the United States, regulatory powers were separated forty to fifty years before similar measures were taken in many Triad countries, where national PTTs enjoyed natural monopoly and regulatory power well into the 1980s and 1990s.

   Privatization. The privatization of the PTT and the establishment of the mobile operation as a separate entity occurred at about the same time in the most advanced Triad nations. In the United States, the breakup of AT&T took place in 1984. A year later, NTT was privatized in Japan. The Thatcher government had already allowed the privatization of British Telecommunications in 1981, and other European countries emulated the model. Despite similarity in the timing, however, the process and impact of privatization has been quite different in different countries. In the United States, the divestiture resulted in distinct local and mobile services in which ownership shifted to the Baby Bells. Despite privatization and deregulation, NTT DoCoMo continued to control more than 50 percent of the mobile market in Japan at the beginning of 2002. In Western Europe, some countries, such as the U.K., engaged in rapid privatization, whereas others adopted a piecemeal approach that has taken years. In Finland, for instance, Sonera's privatization was initiated in the late 1980s, but the government still held a majority stake in early 2002. Due to these delays, the market capitalization of the operator declined from $50 billion to less than $3 billion in 2000–2002.

      Licensing Policies. Different countries have engaged in different licensing policies which have been intertwined with issues of spectrum policy and technology standards (compare Chapter 2). In the 1970s, AT&T was still thought to have a monopoly in mobile services in the United States. Following various duopoly scenarios (wireline versus wireless rivals), the divestiture of the Bell System shifted licensing struggles to the Baby Bells. In Japan, the privatization of NTT in 1985 and the incorporation of NTT DoCoMo around 1992 gave rise to mobile rivals, but DoCoMo's new competitive strategies turned its first-mover lead into more sustainable advantages. In the U.K., the licensing of mobile competitors occurred before similar measures in other major European economies, while the Brits opted for TACS, a standard that was a derivative of America's AMPS. The Nordic countries developed a more open standard (NMT), which provided a conceptual bridge into GSM, the winning platform of the digital cellular. But despite aggressive deregulation, most Nordic PTTs enjoyed competition as little as did their more powerful European counterparts. In Sweden, Comvik challenged the domestic PTT, but failed due to its proprietary analog standard. In Finland, Radiolinja—the first GSM operation worldwide—launched its operations before it had been granted a license because it expected the Finnish PTT (future Sonera) to abuse its regulatory powers. It was this bold strategy that allowed the new operator to establish a foothold in the digital cellular, prior to the PTT doing so.

      Similar policy measures have had different industry consequences in the most advanced mobile markets. As the triangle framework demonstrates, technology transitions have boosted industry developments, but it is the interplay of macro drivers (public policies, as well as clusters, competition, and innovation) and micro drivers (firm strategies, as well as leadership in products, operations, and markets) that have been and become truly critical. At first, however, these originated from the crack in the monopoly constellation—i.e., the supply chain arrangements of the national PTT.

The Micro Perspective: From Ventel to Wintel

Through a century, the most remarkable changes in the mobile business have originated from shifts and transitions in or of the full industry value chain. As a *firm*, each company in the wireless industry has its own value chains; as *industry* players, all take part in the broader industry value system. Achieving, sustaining, or renewing strategic advantage depends not just on an individual firm's value chain, but on its role in the broader value system. These systems are not static; they change over time. In the wireless business, the *organization of the interface between the network operator (national carrier or PTT) and its supply chain (equipment manufacturer)* served as the prime catalyst of industry evolution until the 1990s. In the past, vendors and operators have competed through gradual globalization; today, many players are forced to globalize in order to compete. Moreover, vendors and operators were no longer the sole agents of change at the eve of the 3G transition. The bargaining power of new players in the value chain—contractors, platform coalitions, software and chip players, content aggregators, and service houses—was on the rise.

Unlike the equipment manufacturers, most network operators were regulated since the late nineteenth century to the late twentieth century. As monopolies, many failed to embrace new technologies and public policies. Also, the very nature of the operators' value activities posed challenges to globalization. In contrast to vendors that manufacture relatively uniform products, operators' business has relied on more diverse services. In one case, the business has been driven by globalization; in another, by localization. Yet the real issue has not been "globalization versus localization," but the *co*-evolution and *co*-existence of each in different stages of the value chain. In contrast to the bolder vendors, the operators relied on domestic strategies and often perceived internationalization as a threat rather than an opportunity. The 2G era forced them to change. With the completion of global telecom reforms by 1998, the most advanced operators—from the large big-country players (AT&T) to the small small-country players (Finland's Sonera) had initiated—or tried to initiate—regional and international strategies. In most cases, the bold, strategic intent failed. Some had been privatized but were not allowed to internationalize for regulatory reasons until the end of the 1990s (NTT DoCoMo). Only the largest and the boldest, such as Vodafone and Mannesmann, engaged in efforts at truly worldwide strategies.

The Monopoly Era: Rise and Decline of National PTTs

From the pre-cellular era, the industry value system (see Exhibit 1-4) in most country markets was either synonymous with the national PTT or comprised network operators, which were owned and operated by the national PTTs, as well as equipment manufacturers, which served as supply chains. In most country markets, a single national telecom entity—a private monopoly or a public monopoly—*was* the industry. From the supply chain to the customer relationships, this PTT dominated the business through vertical integration or control. In the more monopolistic models (old-style PTTs in Western Europe), the relationships between the vendors and the PTTs were exclusive and preferential. This arrangement locked the two in proprietary standards and domestic markets. In regulated markets, it enabled monopoly rents; in liberalized markets, it rendered the network operator vulnerable to attacks by new entrants. Through most of the pre-cellular and the early part of the 1G era, the

Exhibit 1-4. Wireless value system: co-evolution and co-specialization.

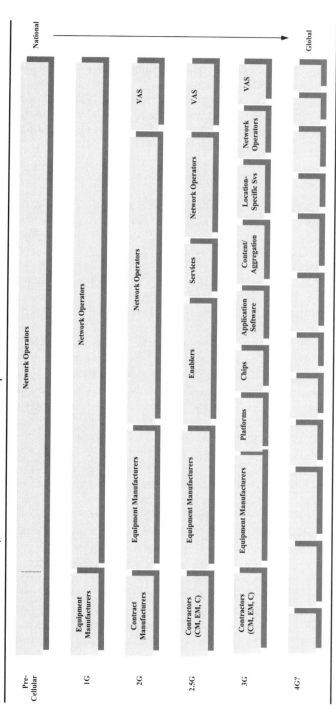

	National → Global
Pre-Cellular	Network Operators
1G	Equipment Manufacturers / Network Operators
2G	Contract Manufacturers / Equipment Manufacturers / Network Operators / VAS
2.5G	Contractors (CM, EM, C) / Equipment Manufacturers / Enablers / Services / Network Operators / VAS
3G	Contractors (CM, EM, C) / Equipment Manufacturers / Platforms / Chips / Application Software / Content/Aggregation / Location-Specific Svs / Network Operators / VAS
4G?	

Key: CM Contract manufacturer
     EM Electronics manufacturer
     VAS Value-added services

industry value system was synonymous with the national PTT. In the United States, the supply chain remained vertically integrated (i.e., AT&T/Western Electric) until the mid-1950s. In Japan, the supply chain was both competitive and cooperative (i.e., NTT and its exclusive family of suppliers). In Nordic countries, it was largely competitive (e.g., national PTTs and independent vendors). The national PTT had product monopoly, just as it controlled the national market. Unsurprisingly, the most developed markets have also been the most competitive markets worldwide.

The Great Transition: Decline of PTTs, Rise of Vendors

During the 2G era, the two key industry players—equipment manufacturers and network operators—boosted specialization by focusing on their core competencies, particularly in the more competitive country markets. In the case of network operators, global telecom reform opened competition in activities that were once the monopoly of the operators, giving rise to new service providers. These players did not own the network but served as resellers. In the U.K., such changes evolved with rapid market liberalization in the early 1980s. In Nordic countries, the Finnish Radiolinja built digital networks even before official permission, forcing the regulators and dominant operator to accept the *fait accompli*. At first vendors, such as Nokia and Ericsson, served as catalysts of globalization; a few years later, a new generation of ambitious operators, such as Vodafone, followed in their footsteps. Rivalry was no longer confined to domestic markets. Regulation no longer contained change. Public policies no longer guided industry developments, and the domestic players began to eye markets beyond domestic boundaries. In the mobile business, the dynamics of competition split among the Triad regions. The United States remained the most lucrative analog market until the mid-1990s, but fell behind new challengers in digital cellular. Western Europe, particularly the Nordic countries, captured innovation leadership. In Japan, NTT had pioneered analog cellular and was among the first to commercialize digital cellular, but the market remained more insular than those in northern Europe. In China, the telecom infrastructure was built to prepare for the growth years. A single model for worldwide markets no longer existed.

Network operators continued to exercise substantial bargaining power, but they could no longer control the full value chain. Together with equipment manufacturers, they dominated their respective industries in most country markets. As national regulatory regimes were swept by regionalization, the joint bargaining power of operators and vendors began to dissolve as well. This power stemmed from closed and homogeneous national markets. It was a poor match for open and heterogeneous markets, where multinational companies reigned instead of national monopolies. These competitive circumstances were very different in computing, an industry that has never suffered the heavy regulatory burden of telecommunications; yet one that would converge *into* mobile communications via multimedia cellular. Through the post-war era, the vertically integrated IBM enjoyed monopoly power, which began to erode only in the early 1970s, as DEC's minicomputers captured a niche of the mainframe business, while institutional customers were replaced by business markets. A more disruptive change followed in the early 1980s with the PC revolution, which built on the shift from business markets to consumer mass markets. In this industry transformation, two small suppliers, Microsoft and Intel, captured the driving role, first through licensing rights and later through market power in microprocessors (Intel) and operating systems and application software (Microsoft). In the absence of heavy regulation, the "Wintel" duopoly contributed to the fall of IBM, the old vertical giant, and established a horizontal industry structure (see Chapter 14).

With the expansion and succession of cellular platforms, something similar took place in the wireless industry. Until the 1990s, this occurred primarily *at the domestic level*, due to national regulatory regimes. In the most developed markets, the interplay of vendors and operators generated a de facto duopoly that might be termed "Ventel" (*ven*dors and *tel*ecom operators).

- AT&T and Motorola in the United States
- Nordic vendors and operators (Ericsson and Telia in Sweden, Nokia and Sonera in Finland)
- Large European PTTs (Deutsche Telekom, France Telecom, British Telecommunications, Telecom Italia) and the more competitive challengers (Vodafone, Mannesmann), and their preferred suppliers (Siemens for Deutsche Telekom, Alcatel for France Telecom)
- NTT and its historical "family" of suppliers (including NEC) in Japan

Though highly influential in their respective country markets, the bargaining power of these Ventel pairs was confined to that national market. In contrast to large-country vendors, which operated in lucrative high-volume markets, small-country vendors coped with low-profit and small-volume markets. The more competitive they were, the greater was their incentive to internationalize. In effect, Ericsson had first internationalized at the turn of the nineteenth century in telecom equipment markets, while Nokia reached a comparable point only in the late 1980s, when it had to internationalize fast to keep up with the rivals. To large-country vendors, foreign markets represented an incremental addition to core profit flows. To small-country vendors, these markets *were* the core profit flows. These companies could survive through scope only. Success in foreign markets was a matter of life or death. As a result, small-country vendors were the first to take advantage of global leverage in infrastructure equipment and handsets.

Competition: Decline of Vendors, Rise of Enablers?

At the end of the 1990s, Finland, with its relatively highest wireless and Internet penetration worldwide, became the first country to experience an explosion in short message service (SMS). Without multimedia and broadband capabilities, the service was primitive, but it attracted volumes of users precipitating the rush of the pioneering country markets to introduce the first 2.5G/ 3G services. Until the end of the 1990s, mobile vendors and, to a lesser degree, network operators dominated application software in the industry value chain. With the eclipse of the domestic Ventel pairs and the rise of regional, international, and finally global competition, these two strategic groups no longer *controlled* the enabling function in software and services. So began the rivalry to *coordinate* these activities.

Recently, the division of competitive dynamics *across* Triad regions has intensified rapidly. In the United States, the convergence of voice and data, coupled with a highly competitive industry environment, has provided new opportunities for challengers and startups. In Europe, the industry thrust has moved from the small Nordic countries to the large-scale markets (U.K., Italy, Germany, France), even as original demand (the first cell phone purchases) has given way to replacement demand (the second or third cell phone purchases, multiple cell ownership). Unlike the European technology-driven vendors and operators, Japan's NTT DoCoMo was able to develop the first service concept for the new and more competitive era. On the other hand, the European mobile leaders have been more successful in globalization than DoCoMo and its Japanese rivals, at least until recently. Unsurprisingly, then, Japanese players demonstrate eagerness to leapfrog into the 4G era, whereas the European incumbents would prefer to enjoy their entrenched positions in and through a prolonged 3G era. Recently, these Triad nations have been augmented with new entities in Asia-Pacific, including the "tiger nations" and particularly China. By the summer of 2001, the size of the subscriber base in China exceeded that of United States, for the first time in the history of wireless communications. Because of China's low penetration, the growth and future of the mobile business is now intertwined with the Chinese customer base and the "next big market"—possibly India.

By the 3G transition, European-based mobile leaders, who moved from voice to data, struggled to retain vertical control through technology coalitions. Meanwhile, U.S.-based IT leaders, who were moving from data to voice, struggled to horizontalize the industry value system by capturing control in chips (Intel), software (Microsoft), and content aggregation (America Online). Neither mobile leaders nor IT leaders, however, could any longer control the full value chain, which provided ample opportunities for new start-ups and challengers. Vendors and operators initiated this "wireless gold rush" in the late 1990s, but it was the enablers who stood to gain the most in the long term. With the arrival of the 3G era, *the key issue was not which firm could control the industry value chain, but which strategic group could coordinate the full value chain.*

Organizational Capabilities

From the mid-1940s until the 1990s, public policies dictated the pace of competition and globalization in the mobile business. Mobile markets were largely regulated and domestic. As a result, countries that engaged in telecom reforms relatively early were able to boost their opportunities and capture significant positions in the industry. Geographic advantages made strategic advantages possible. With the completion of the worldwide telecom reforms at the end of the 1990s, industry conditions changed. The mobile business has become increasingly competitive rather than regulated, increasingly global rather than domestic. Concurrently, the importance of country-based advantages has been reduced, while the importance of firm-based advantages has increased. In the past, public policies accounted for successes or failures; today, it is firm-level strategy particularly organizational capabilities, which make or break companies.

Globalization in Stages

The industry has become increasingly open and global by nature, but substantial differences exist among players in terms of their positions in the value system. The key issue for many globalizing firms is how they should organize the expanding international operations. In 1972, two pioneer researchers of internationalization, Stopford and Wells, presented a "stages model" to explore the structural evolution of multinational companies (MNCs) in the course of their globalization (see Exhibit 1-5).[6] In this framework, firms often first manage their international operations through an international division. Foreign sales still play a relatively small role in total sales, and product diversity re-

Exhibit 1-5. International structural stages model (Stopford-Wells).

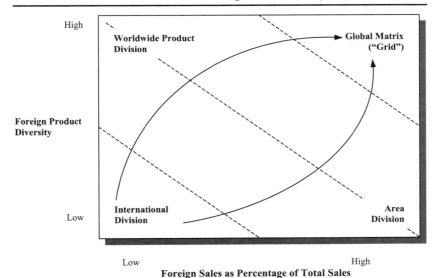

SOURCE: Based on Stopford and Wells (1972).

mains low. Subsequently, MNCs tend to exploit one of two alternative paths to expand in overseas markets. Some expand foreign sales without increasing product diversity. These firms embrace the "area division" structure. Others increase product diversity without expanding foreign sales. They adopt the "worldwide product division" structure. Finally, the third ones manage to expand foreign sales *and* increase product diversity. They favor a "global matrix" structure.

Leading Vendors

Consider the top-tier vendors. In 2000, the proportions of foreign revenues of the two Nordic leaders, Ericsson (98 percent) and Nokia (99 percent), were almost identical, whereas those of the two U.S. leaders, Motorola (52 percent) and Qualcomm (65 percent), were not that different either. But the numbers do not tell the full story. It is vital to understand the strategic paths that produced these figures.

Motorola. In the 1G era, the U.S.-based Motorola was the industry leader. In 1983, 1992, and 2000, its foreign sales accounted for 26 percent, 44 percent, 52 percent, respectively, of the total sales. Unlike its Nordic rivals, it was headquartered in a large country market, which ensured the kind of scale economies small-country vendors could only dream of. Unlike its more focused rivals, Motorola also remained a diversified electronics conglomerate, with a diverse product portfolio. And at closer inspection, its U.K. sales played a substantial role in the total, accounting for some 12 percent even in 2000. Indeed, the vendor obtained some 60 percent of its revenues in just two countries (the United States, the U.K.), even if it had manufacturing operations and sales offices in more than forty countries.

Ericsson. The Nordic rivals were far more global than Motorola. In 2000, Ericsson operated in more than 140 countries worldwide. But unlike Nokia, Ericsson achieved its first telecom internationalization well before World War I. The second wave was initiated in the 1960s; in the next two decades, Ericsson's digital switch served as its calling card to access new foreign markets. With the onset of the cellular era, the Swedish vendor already obtained 81 percent of its revenues in foreign markets.

Nokia. In 2000, Nokia sold its products in more than 130 countries, had manufacturing plants in ten countries, and R&D centers in fifteen countries. But unlike Ericsson, Nokia was the latecomer in the business and got into telecom and mobile segments only in the 1960s and 1970s. In contrast to these diversified electronics players, Nokia had not integrated into semiconductors. It focused its activities on mobile communications. In 1983 and 1992, its foreign revenues accounted for 50 percent and 80 percent of the total, respectively. But these figures refer to many nonwireless businesses, most of which the vendor divested in the early 1990s; mobile revenues remained tiny. In 1992, Nokia

Telecommunications (the precursor of Nokia Networks) accounted for 17 percent and Mobira (the precursor of Nokia Mobile Phones) 20 percent of total revenues. As Nokia focused on mobile communications, the proportion of foreign revenues soared to 99 percent.

Unlike Ericsson, where most employees no longer worked in the Nordic home base, almost 50 percent of Nokia's production facilities remained in Finland. Ericsson had globalized like the U.S.–based Motorola, but to far greater degree. Nokia had globalized like its Japanese models.

Qualcomm. Qualcomm's internationalization differed from that of all incumbents. The company was created a century after Ericsson and Nokia, and more than half a century after Motorola. It operated in a large-scale home base, but it was a challenger, not an incumbent. As a latecomer, it was disadvantaged in competition that built upon existing strengths and legacies and had locked in most of the worldwide distribution outlets. When the R&D maverick initiated its activities in 1987, it had no overseas sales. By 2001, it obtained some 65 percent of its revenues from foreign markets and had offices in some seventeen countries. The creation and establishment of CDMA drove Qualcomm's success in business *and* in globalization. Like Motorola, however, it operated primarily in two countries. Whereas the U.K. was Motorola's ancillary market, South Korea served as Qualcomm's ally. In 2001, the U.S. vendor still obtained some 35 percent of its revenues from South Korea, which had greatly benefited from the explosion of CDMA in Asia-Pacific.

Each vendor has had its own development path. In the past, these typically began with international division, proceeding to worldwide product on area division and, with the most advanced players like Ericsson, global matrix. Today, speed and scope are vital. As the mobile paths of Qualcomm and Nokia illustrate, development has become more rapid, is based on distinctive strengths, and builds on faster globalization.

Leading Operators

The story of the competitive circumstances of the operators is quite different. In 1999, the top-four mobile operators, in terms of revenues, were NTT DoCoMo ($35.1 billion), Vodafone Group ($9.7 billion), China Telecom ($8.0 billion), and Telecom Italia Mobile ($7.5 billion).[7] Vodafone Group included Vodafone in the U.K. and Mannesmann in Germany. In the first case, 77 percent and in the second 54 percent of total sales, respectively, originated from foreign markets. In 2000, the combined Vodafone Group gained some 67 percent of its revenues overseas. Despite DoCoMo's "global service strategy," the proportion of foreign revenues was not significant in 2000 (less than 10 percent). At China Telecom and TIM, the role of foreign revenues was insignificant. Indeed, most major network operators were former national PTTs, which concentrated on domestic markets until global telecom reforms while nurturing customer relationships that were highly localized. The proportion of foreign revenues in the most progressive Nordic operators was not that different. At the peak of its failed internationalization effort, foreign markets accounted for 40 percent of total revenues at Sonera. Among operators, it was an above-the-average accomplishment. For instance, Telia, Sweden's operator, obtained only 14 percent of its revenues in overseas markets in 2000. The focus of operators remained largely domestic. Even the boldest global strategies were initiated only in the 1990s.

Globalization of Organizational Capabilities

As clusters and markets have multiplied, the winning companies have developed appropriate organizational capabilities to manage this transformation. During the great transition, much of the bargaining power in the mobile ecosystem migrated from operators to vendors. In the early stages of the competitive era, some of this power seems to be migrating to enablers, which focus on software and services.

Within companies, any component of the value chain may become a subject of globalization. These components include support activities (firm infrastructure, human resource management, technology development, procurement) as well as upstream (logistics, manufacturing, new product development) and downstream primary activities (distribution, marketing and sales, service). For the sake of convenience, these may be reduced into the three subsets of key determinants in the triangle framework: products, operations, and markets. The better the company can leverage these determinants worldwide, the closer it can get to the productivity frontier and the greater its achievement in the quest for global leverage.

Once the postwar multinational companies had established a number of subsidiaries in foreign markets, many researchers' interest shifted from the stages model of internationalization to the structure and management of the headquarters-subsidiary relationship. Market multiplication required new kinds of organizational capabilities. To overcome the challenge of globalization, different companies have employed different generic strategies, including differentiation, cost, and innovation (see Exhibit 1-1). Each of these strategies has its tradeoffs. Historically, MNCs have built upon multilocal (differentiation through local responsiveness), international (worldwide innovation), and global cost efficiency (cost) strategies, which have rested on *singular* advantages (differentiation through local responsiveness, *or* worldwide innovation, *or* cost-efficiencies).[8] Neither the sequence nor the timing of these historical phases corresponds to those in the wireless industry. In the mobile business, the organizational arrangements between the national PTTs and vendors drove the business until the 1980s; in the 1990s, vendors took leadership in globalization; whereas more recently the IT enablers have concentrated on developing their organizational capabilities for globalization.

From Differentiation to Multilocal Strategies

The first *multilocal* strategies (Unilever, ICI, Philips, and Nestle) evolved in Europe, in the early twentieth century. In the mobile business, the most growth-driven national PTTs engaged in multilocal strategies toward the end of the 1G era, while some vendors acquired, created joint ventures with, or bought stakes in overseas operators. Due to their domestic mission (AT&T, European PTTs) or regulatory prohibitions (Japan's NTT), most operators did not venture into the foreign markets. Only in the 2G era did the more aggressive operators launch internationalization strategies, which were initially multilocal. In the U.K., Vodafone exemplified the new-generation operators. On the downstream side of the value chain, the recent smaller players—new service providers, resellers, online community developers, and the like—have engaged in domestic operations or multilocal strategies.

From Innovation to International Strategies

In the aftermath of World War II, the *international* strategies (Kraft, Pfizer, Procter & Gamble, General Electric) evolved in the United States, where these American firms focused on creating and exploiting innovations on a worldwide basis. In the mobile business, vendors of the 1G era exemplified international strategies, particularly Ericsson and Motorola. In both cases, foreign markets were arenas for the extension of domestic innovations. However, Ericsson operated in a greater number of markets and had more subsidiaries than Motorola. In turn, the U.S.–based vendor invested significantly into foreign subsidiaries and worked hard to become a good "corporate citizen" in the foreign markets. Similar efforts toward international strategies were made among operators. In the United States, AT&T and certain Baby Bells rushed to foreign markets after the divestiture, particularly toward the end of the analog years. The new operators were nearly all run by consortia with American or British partners who contributed far more to the start-up than their equity shares would indicate, often including interim decision-making personnel.[9] In other words, this know-how was not just about technology innovation; it was about product and service development, operations and logistics, and strategic market management. As the European players learned how to compete, the industry was transitioning into the 2G era. As with the center of innovation migrating to Western Europe, U.S. operators were the laggards in digital cellular.

From Cost to Global Efficiency Strategies

In the 1960s and 1970s, Japanese firms developed *global efficiency* strategies (Toyota, Canon, Komatsu, Matsushita) focused on developing global efficiency. In the wireless business, these cost-efficient strategies are trade-offs that maximize the benefits of cost leadership at the expense of differentiation and, thus, are premised on standardized products and operations. Among the vendors, Nokia's global focus evolved from the lessons of Japanese challengers. A "pure" global strategy may have been appealing for cultural reasons as well. In contrast to the tiny Finland, Japan comprises a larger market; yet both countries have highly homogeneous demographics (homogenous ethnic, linguistic, and religious characteristics). Unlike its Japanese models, however, Nokia has been far more international in its strategic posture and has struggled to develop responsiveness to local conditions. Among operators, it is difficult to pinpoint examples of pure global cost-efficient strategies, which characterize the upstream side of the value chain, where standardization is easier, rather than the downstream side, where customization is more common.

The first strategies—multinational, international, global integration—have built upon *singular* strategic advantages, including the innovation-driven international strategies that have been typical to the new strategic groups that entered the mobility business in the late 1990s. Intel, Microsoft, and the new generation of mobile hardware, software, and other service providers exemplify this trend. On the content aggregation side, America Online's mixed success indicates that, in the long run, only strategic partnerships provide adequate localization and globalization. By the 1990s, these old singular worldwide strategies no longer matched the environmental requirements. Instead of building on a single fundamental strategic advantage, a new generation of worldwide companies, as well as those incumbent leaders that were able to thrive in the changing environment, have sought to develop *multiple* strategic advantages. Organizationally, these translocal companies are highly distributed and specialized in terms of their assets and responsibilities. Decisions and information flow among interdependent units. In contrast to the centralized global cost structure, translocal organization is highly integrated.

From Differentiation to Translocal Strategies

Among mobile vendors, Nokia attempted to cultivate a translocal strategy at the end of the 1990s. Due to its high degree of globalization, it had to be increasingly responsive in world markets to deter domestic and highly focused differentiation strategies. It struggled to keep up with innovation by manufacturing all prevailing standards, creating technology coalitions, and building internal venture capital mechanisms and R&D activities. At the same time, it had to be highly cost-efficient to avoid divesting its manufacturing capabilities, as many of the second- and third-tier mobile vendors did in the 3G transition. To achieve these three objectives in a small Nordic country where taxation and structural unemployment were relatively high was no small feat. By the close of 2001, these circumstances prompted Jorma Ollila, Nokia's CEO and chairman, to suggest that Nokia might move its headquarters out of its native Finland. More than 40 percent of the staff remained in Finland, but sales in the country were barely more than 1 percent, leading to a situation that was "unbearable in the long run." Essentially, Nokia gave the government five years to consider the taxation situation before deciding if it will move its headquarters.[10]

Globalization Incentives: Large and Small Countries

The wireless industry is one of the few technology and telecom segments in which *small*-country firms have managed to evolve into worldwide giants. In comparison to many other industries, telecommunications has been regulated for a long time. As a result, countries that were early to implement new public policies (privatization, liberalization, deregulation) have enjoyed first-mover advantages. In the pre-cellular and 1G eras, most leading players were large-country competitors. Since the 2G era, small-country rivals have challenged industry incumbents. The ultimate winners will be companies that can translate these first- or early-mover benefits into *sustainable* competitive advantage.

Today, major rivals may look similar, but they have evolved in very different competitive circumstances, particularly the *large*- and *small*-country rivals.

In Finland, Reijo Luostarinen, a pioneer of globalization research, has emphasized the incentive function of small size, openness, and peripheral location.[11] In the late 1980s, global strategies for small and medium-sized companies had been largely ignored in research literature, as Matti Alahuhta, Nokia's senior executive, realized.[12] More recently, globalization research in large countries has focused on the subject, as well. Take the case of developed OECD countries. In the large-countries, large-scale markets are a birthright, the management mentality tends to be more insular, and the headquarters is often located in the market center. As a result, scale often suffices for scope and incentives promote domestication rather than globalization. In small countries, firms evolve in small-scale markets, the management mentality tends to be open, and the headquarters tends to be located in the periphery of the market center. Scope must be achieved for scale and incentives work for globalization rather than domestication.

Globalization of Large-Country Firms. In the 1G era, large countries with developed cellular markets had an almost automatic comparative advantage. Due to the indigenous large-scale markets, rapid saturation did not suppress their growth. Scale sufficed for scope. In the 2G era, this comparative advantage evolved into a competitive disadvantage. With globalization, large-scale domestic markets no longer sufficed for industry dominance. With fewer incentives to globalize, large-country players ignored scope for scale. By the 3G transition, the large-country leaders paid for their complacency.

Globalization of Small-Country Firms. In the 1G era, small countries with developed cellular markets had a nearly automatic comparative disadvantage. Due to small-scale home base, rapid saturation suppressed growth and foreign markets, which were dominated by national PTTs. Scale was insufficient, scope was beyond means. With globalization, this disadvantage evolved into a competitive advantage. With greater incentives to globalize, small-country players had more to gain and less to lose in globalization. They achieved scale through scope. What was once their dilemma has now become the name of the game.

Globalization of Markets

In the mid-1980s, Kenichi Ohmae, McKinney's influential business strategist, argued that worldwide industry leaders had to maintain a strong position in the key developed markets: the United States, Western Europe, and Japan.

> The Triad is where the main action is. Corporations still wrapped up in the 'United Nations' approach, seeking a market presence in each of the 150 countries of the world, often find their resources suddenly depleted . . . This Triad is where the major markets are; it is where the competitive threat comes from; it is where new technologies will originate . . . The prime objective of every corporation must be to become a true insider in all three regions.[13]

As these three Triad regions accounted for some 80 percent of the world's output, they held an equally dominant role in most industries. Any company with global ambitions had to become an "insider" in the evolving tripolar world of economic power. The rule of the thumb was to be strong in at least two regions and have representation in the third. Today, the increasing significance of China brings a new factor into the regional balance, which is often called "Triad Plus." Prior to the great transition, wireless communications was often synonymous with the national PTT and its natural monopoly in a given domestic market. Today, leading vendors, operators, contractors, and enablers compete and cooperate in a worldwide theater with global strategies, engaging in a game of "global chess" with two qualifications. First, U.S. leadership continued for a longer period of time without substantial erosion, due to the technology catch-up. Second, China's role is exceptionally important in the mobile business since most advanced markets have been saturated and are driven by replacement demand, whereas China's penetration in 2002 was still very low and driven by original demand.

The Pre-Cellular Era: U.S. Superiority

After World War II, AT&T pioneered the first wireless services in the United States, when the Mobile Telephone Service (MTS) was introduced in a handful of urban centers. In 1964, AT&T launched a more refined service concept, Improved Mobile Telephone Service (IMTS), but one that would continue to serve primarily niche segments. During these pre-cellular decades, the United States enjoyed absolute and relative superiority in wireless communications. American firms, primarily AT&T, a few vendors, and the smaller radio common carriers (RCCs) defined the best practices in the rudimentary mobile markets. The rest of the world struggled to catch up. In 1983—at the peak of the pre-cellular era—Western Europe, due to the initially relatively high but declining Nordic numbers in absolute terms, still enjoyed the highest worldwide penetration (74.6 percent) against Asia-Pacific, primarily Japan (23.6 percent), and the U.S. (1.8 percent). A year later, when AMPS was introduced in the United States, it soon achieved the highest relative penetration worldwide. (See Exhibit 1-6 and Exhibit 1-7 for market shares by geographic regions, starting with the pre-cellular era to the present.)

The 1G Era: U.S. Leadership

In any given country market, the existing cellular environment typically comprises a mix of analog and digital systems with different networks. The developments can be examined in terms of regional advantage in the cellular markets. As the available data ranges from the early 1980s to 2000, it is possible to trace the gradual evolution of cumulative markets shares. The years *1983, 1991,* and *2000* serve as appropriate landmarks for the transitional points in the cellular platforms—that is, the *peaks of the pre-cellular, 1G,* and *2G stages,* respectively. After all, the subsequent year witnessed the commercialization of the next-generation services—analog cellular in 1984, digital cellular in 1992, and multimedia cellular in 2001.

At the peak of the 1G era (1991), North America had more than half of the worldwide mobile subscribers (53.9 percent), not least because of the AMPS triumph. Western Europe had less than one-third (27.8 percent), and Asia-Pacific less than one-fifth (16.0 percent). Other geographic segments—Americas (1.6 percent), Middle East (0.5 percent), Africa (0.1 percent), and Eastern Europe (0.1 percent)—were relatively insignificant. During these early years of the wireless industry, certain small countries (Nordic countries in Western Europe) still achieved extraordinary market shares, due to relatively small penetration worldwide.

In the Americas, the United States held superior market power. Brief relative expansions took place in Canada, Puerto Rico, and Chile. In Western Europe, Nordic countries enjoyed magnificent market shares amid the transition to the 1G era, but in every case—in Sweden, Norway, Denmark, and Finland—these shares shrank rapidly toward the end of the phase. By the mid-1980s, the U.K. possessed the highest relative share in Western Europe, not least because of the early deregulation of British Telecommunications. In Asia-

(text continues on page 28)

Exhibit 1-6. Market shares by region (1983–2000).

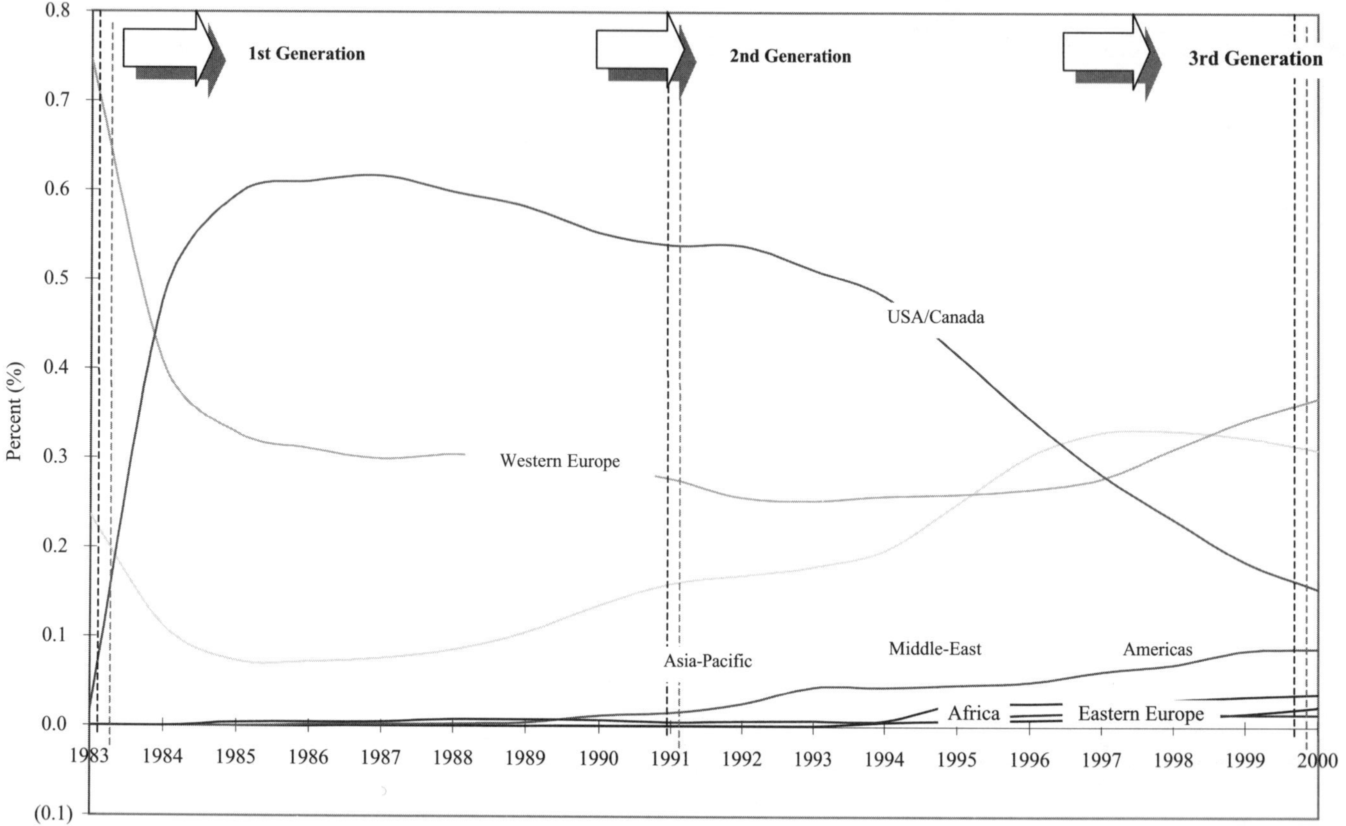

SOURCE: Data based on EMC, industry estimates.

Exhibit 1-7. Peaks of cellular eras: geographic regions (1983–2000).

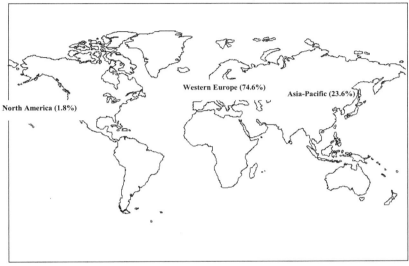

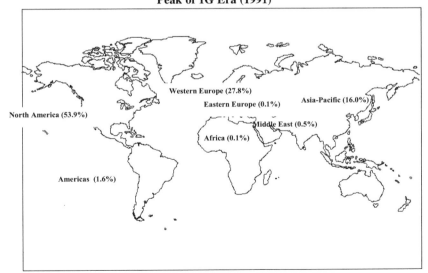

(continues)

Exhibit 1-7. (Continued).

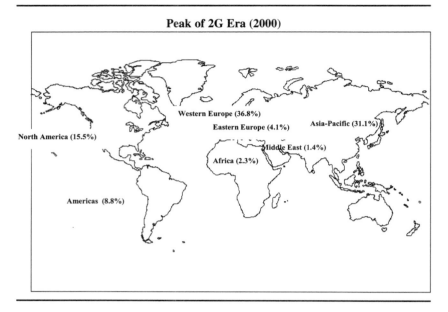

Pacific, Japan's early lead quickly eroded. NTT favored proprietary technologies rather than open specifications and it was not allowed to compete in foreign markets, due to esoteric Japanese regulations. Toward the end of the 1G era, Australia's relative penetration rose rapidly. In Eastern Europe, absolute penetration numbers were low until the end of the Cold War. As a result, Hungary's activity in wireless communications translated to a substantial lead until the rise of digital cellular.

The 2G Era: Western European Leadership

Amid the transition to the 2G era in 1992, the United States was the most lucrative country market and had the largest worldwide penetration. With digitalization, rapid growth migrated first to Nordic countries, then to Western Europe. As the European Commission made GSM mandatory in Europe, the regional wireless leaders—the Nordic vendors as well as a new generation of aggressive operators that were eager to challenge national PTTs—seized GSM to extend their domestic advantages on a global basis. In the United States, these developments initially went unnoticed because Motorola, the leading vendor of the 1G era, enjoyed high profitability until the mid-1990s. When the "American Samurai" finally awakened, the Samurai was lost. Motorola would spend the second half of the 1990s catching up with the Nordic vendors—with little success. With the popularity of analog cellular rapidly declining, European countries accelerated the transition to GSM. The United States failed to lead the developments because multiple standards fragmented the marketplace, while hindering globalization. As U.S. industry representatives were painfully aware, the standards and exports issues were inextricably intertwined:

> . . . while various U.S. companies have sold into other countries, in many cases they had to modify their equipment in order to comply or come close to complying with European-types of standards, particularly on the network side . . . I am all for competition and open markets, but the fact that U.S. manufacturers and companies are not willing to settle on one standard, hurts the U.S.'s global position. The U.S. is 35 to 50 percent of the world market, so the non-U.S. companies are willing to build to U.S. standards, but unless U.S. companies are willing to build to the different worldwide standards or maybe, ultimately, a single worldwide standard, it will hurt the U.S.[14]

In the late 1990s, the Triad regions in wireless competition—North America, Europe, and Asia and the Pacific Rim—grew to include China. At the peak of the 2G era (2000), Western Europe had the most substantial worldwide penetration (36.8 percent) versus Asia-Pacific (31.1 percent), whereas the United States had fallen well behind (15.5 percent). While other geographic segments—Americas (8.8 percent), Eastern Europe (4.1 percent), Africa (2.3 percent), Middle East (1.4 percent)—remained significantly smaller, their proportionate shares had climbed substantially. In regional market shares, 1997 was the milestone year, when North America lost its penetration leadership to Western Europe. Unsurprisingly, Motorola's growth period ended a year before, whereas AT&T's new high-volume, penetration-pricing strategies were implemented only a year later.

The 3G Era: Triad Plus Leadership

In 2002, worldwide revenue was expected to remain barely $1 billion, but by 2010 the share of Asia-Pacific would amount to $119 billion, followed by Europe ($103 billion), North America ($68 billion), rest of the world ($31 billion), and Latin America ($18 billion). Demand figures mimicked those of revenue (see Exhibit 1-8). In 2002, there were barely 2.6 million 3G users worldwide. But by 2010, the share of Asia-Pacific was estimated at 241 million followed by Europe (196 million), North America (129 million), rest of the world (64 million), and Latin America (38 million).[15] The convergence of mobility and the Internet meant new opportunities for American players, but lingering problems—namely, lack of adequate spectrum, fragmented markets, and leg-

Exhibit 1-8. 3G subscribers by region (2001–2010).

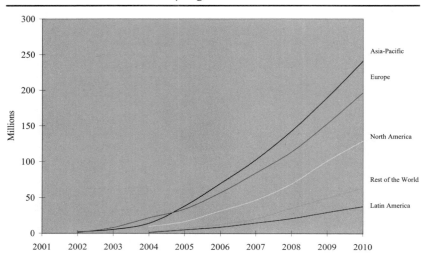

SOURCE: UMTS Forum.

acy technologies—constrained the catch-up. The future of the business belonged to China. At the end of July 2001, this vast nation had 120.6 million
mobile phone users as it overtook the United States as the largest cellular
market worldwide.[16]

Until the emergence of the cellular platforms, the productivity frontier
and the key markets were largely domestic. Since the late 1980s and early
1990s, the industry has been swept by globalization. Concurrently, the economies of scope underlying the productivity frontier have been dramatically extended from the single home base to multiple locations worldwide.

Chapter 2

Globalization of Technology Innovation

On a summer morning in 1895, in a valley to the southwest of Bologna along the river Po, three young men waited excitedly. One worked with a transmitter in an attic. Two stood on the top of a hill with a receiving apparatus.[1]

For months, Guglielmo Marconi, a twenty-year-old Italian, had labored at home, turning the Villa Griffone into a research laboratory. Obsessed with electromagnetic waves, the inventor had been inspired by the great scientists of his era, Heinrich Hertz and Augusto Righi. But unlike his academic idols, he believed that innovations could transmit messages across great distances without the use of wire. The young Italian shut himself into the long triangular-shaped attic at the Villa Griffone and conducted wireless experiments. At the time, many scientists across the world were conducting similar short-range wireless transmissions. Unlike these researchers, he was not driven by pure invention but commercial innovation.

One morning, Marconi, his older brother Alfonso, and a young tenant named Mignani participated in still another experiment. The innovator began to transmit his message—three dots designating the letter *S* in Morse code—to the spot where his two assistants waited. At a farmhouse almost a mile from the villa, Mignani watched the homemade receiving apparatus. "When you see the little hammer move three times," Marconi told him, referring to his vibration detection machine, "give the signal." The little hammer began to move. Once, then again, and again. In the past, Mignani had waved a handkerchief to signal a successful test completion. Now the distance was too great, so the two young men had agreed on another signal. Mignani fired his rifle into the sky.

As the shot rang out, only Marconi really understood what had just taken place. The demonstration proved that electric waves could be transmitted at a significant distance, if the power of the transmitter was appropriately increased. The lone rifle shot in the Italian countryside would give rise to an industry that held a promise of worldwide markets.

Starting in the maritime sector, Marconi developed the first viable business models for the wireless telegraph. In the pre-cellular era, market evolution shifted from industrial services to nascent business markets and experimenta-

31

tion in consumer markets. With the cellular platforms, the market momentum evolved from corporate services to mass consumer markets. Concurrently, functionalities have evolved dramatically from the primitive pre-cellular technologies to analog, digital, and today's multimedia cellular—just as they would develop into broadband platforms in the future (see Exhibit 2-1).

From Science to Innovation

Through successive waves of mobile innovation, sustaining developments have boosted incumbent leaders, whereas disruptive change has provided ample opportunities for challengers and new entrants to redefine competitive rules.[2] In the long term, all of these developments have been accelerated by globaliza-

Exhibit 2-1. From Marconi to 4G: technologies, markets, and innovation.

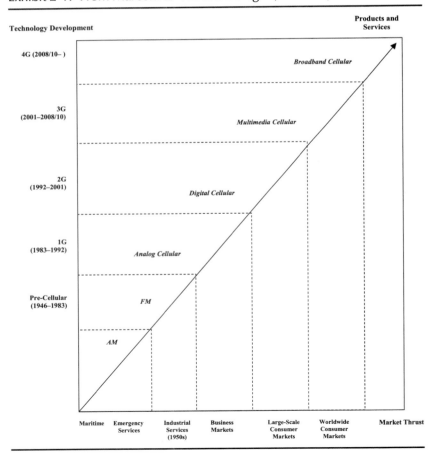

tion. The disruptive moments, however, have been relatively rare and brief. Overall, they comprise some half-dozen transitions:

- Commercialization of wireless telegraphy by Marconi
- Emergence of AM wireless communications
- Transition to FM communications and pre-cellular service platforms in America
- Adoption of successive cellular standards (e.g., rise of AMPS, the explosive growth of GSM and digital cellular, emergence of CDMA and its role as the core 3G technology, future transition to broadband cellular)

Marconi initiated these transitions, but the science of wireless has many fathers—and mothers. As the hub of the eighteenth- and nineteenth-century industrial revolutions, Britain's leadership was also reflected in its advanced national innovation system, including specialized research on wireless technologies. Far from occurring in a vacuum, however, the invention of wireless communication had quite a few forerunners in the scientific centers of the era, Britain and Germany.[3]

The Science of Wireless

Electric transmission without the use of wires had been observed in the eighteenth century. In 1831, Michael Faraday formulated the law of electromagnetic induction, which built upon the discovery of electromagnetism by a Dane, Christian Oersted. This led to research on the applicability of electromagnetism to long-distance communication. Joseph Henry, an American scientist who had invented the first efficient electromagnet, helped Samuel Morse build a telegraph relay that allowed long-distance operation and became a substitute for human transportation such as messengers, the Pony Express, and clipper ships. Physical mobility was no match for wireless mobility.[4]

The linkage between national security interests and the wireless potential accelerated during the American Civil War, which witnessed military use of electrical communication. These maneuvers underscored awareness of the mismatch between conventional wireline techniques (i.e., wireline telegraphy, later telephony), which were suited for permanent installations, and wartime communication needs, which required more flexible and mobile wireless techniques. Similarly, in naval communication, telegraph lines were out of the question.[5]

Dr. Mahlon Loomis, a Virginian dentist, was granted a U.S. patent on July 30, 1872 for an "Improvement in Telegraphing." Inspired by Benjamin Franklin, the inventor used kites as antennae. Intrigued by the military implications of wireless, the U.S. Navy sponsored the dentist's experiments, while Congress chartered the Loomis Aerial Telegraph Company. One congressman, pleading Loomis's case in the House, said, "He entertains a dream, and it may be only a dream, a wild dream that when his proposition comes to be fully applied, it may light and warm your houses. . . ."[6]

Three years after the invention of the telephone in 1876, London-born David Hughes took what some consider the first mobile telephone call.[7] Alexander Graham Bell himself, a telephony pioneer, succeeded in sending a message by telephone from one ship to another about a mile away. Then scientific initiative shifted from the United States and Britain to Germany. If France had been the center of world science in the early-nineteenth century, Germany overtook that role in the late-nineteenth century. German scientists were particularly intrigued by the technical and commercial potential of wireless communication. In 1887 and 1888, Heinrich Hertz conducted experiments that led to the discovery of "Hertzian" waves. Although inventors such as Thomas Edison had observed the effects of these radio waves as early as the 1870s, what *caused* the waves had not been explained. Hertz confirmed that the "signal" was propagated by waves that had similar properties to light.[8]

Marconi's Commercial Innovation

The European academic pioneers of wireless communication had been pure scientists who were intrigued by the wireless phenomena, whereas Marconi, like his American predecessors, was more excited about the industrial potential of wireless telegraphy. To Marconi, wireless horizon meant bringing all parts of the world together, through commerce and mass communications. He defined the *science* of wireless by the achievements of Europeans and the *industry* of wireless by the Americans' contributions:

> By the time I was twenty, I was fairly well acquainted with the published results of the work of the most distinguished scientists who had occupied themselves with the subject of electric waves; men such as Hertz, Branly, Lodge, Righi, and many others . . . By availing myself of previous knowledge and working out theories already formulated, I did nothing but follow in the footsteps of Howe, Watt, Edison, Stephenson, and many other illustrious inventors.[9]

When Hertz died in 1894, Augustus Righi, a professor of physics at Bologna University and a friend of the wealthy Marconi family, wrote an obituary that fired Marconi's imagination. What if he deployed these waves for "wireless" telegraphy? It was a revolutionary idea. After replicating some of Hertz's experiments in Bologna, Marconi set out to increase the distance over which radio waves were transmitted and received. In late 1895, he transmitted wireless signals across a distance of more than a mile, an event that many historians mark as the birth of radio.[10]

When the Italian Ministry of Posts and Telegraphs (PTT) proved indifferent to Marconi's experiments, he left with his mother for London's City, the capital of the world's leading maritime nation and greatest trading empire. Marconi hoped that the British would understand the long-term business potential of wireless, just as he was eager to secure ownership rights through patents. A. A. Campbell-Swinton, a leading engineer in electrical communication, introduced him to William Preece, engineer-in-chief of the General Post Office (GPO), who offered him support. By June 1896, Marconi submitted a revised, full specification for the world's first wireless patent for a system of telegraphy using Hertzian waves.

From FM to Mobile Services

If Marconi's wireless telegraph dominated the first two decades of the twentieth century, a distinction can be made between the ensuing pioneer phase (1921–1945), which was dominated by conventional amplitude modulation (AM) techniques, and the commercial phase (1946–1968), which was driven by frequency modulation (FM) techniques.[11] AM communications were pioneered in Detroit's police department in the aftermath of Prohibition and motorization. These developments also boosted the fortunes of a relatively small car-radio vendor, which was later renamed Motorola. By March 1933, the police engaged in the first experiments in two-way radio communications, in New Jersey. The FM era, however, began with Edwin H. Armstrong, a brilliant electrical engineer and inventor.

Genesis of FM Communications

Armstrong's mission was influenced by academic research as well as military connections, particularly a stint in the U.S. Army Signal Corps. Through a struggle to control radio patents, Armstrong persisted in his research, seeking to eliminate static, the last major problem of radio. By the late 1920s he had decided that the only solution was to design an entirely new system, in which the carrier-wave frequency would be modulated while its amplitude was held constant. In 1933, Armstrong introduced a wideband FM system that gave clear reception in field tests, even through violent storms, and offered the highest fidelity sound yet heard in radio. Two years later, he took the nascent radio industry into a new era with the first public demonstration for the Institute of Radio Engineers in New York City:

Music was projected with a "liveness" rarely if ever heard before from a radio "music box." . . . The secret lay in the achievement of a signal-to-noise ratio of 100-to-1 or better, as against 30-to-1 on the best AM stations. . . . Armstrong was not satisfied with a 100-

> to-1 ratio, and he shortly succeeded in raising this to 1000-to-1.... By all rules that had been drilled into radio engineers for nearly a quarter of a century this was ... fantastic.[12]

Compared to contemporary AM radio, the dynamic range of FM was tripled. Furthermore, FM needed much less power than AM, which paved the way for vehicular transmitters and sensitive receivers. Despite the great potential of FM, another three decades elapsed before it truly proliferated.[13]

Electronics Revolution

After World War II, American technological leadership was across-the-board. The U.S. lead in capital-intensive, mass-production sectors had emerged at the end of the nineteenth century when the United States overtook the United Kingdom. But there was no early lead in American high-tech preeminence. The U.S. dominance in sectors such as pharmaceuticals, aerospace, and electronics was a new phenomenon.[14] America was *the* center of the wireless business. It was the core cluster and it was the lead market. It had the most advanced R&D (Bell Labs), as well as the largest and most efficient production facilities (AT&T). The cellular concept became known at the end of the 1940s, but the key constituent technologies took years to evolve. The new cellular paradigm built upon an intricate interplay between intrinsic and supporting technologies, which became possible with the electronics revolution.

In 1947, the transistor was invented by three American physicists (John Bardeen, Walter H. Brattain, and William B. Shockley) at the Bell Telephone Laboratories. Seven years later, Texas Instruments—the future supplier of mobile vendors, such as Nokia—became the first company to commercially produce silicon transistors, which soon replaced vacuum tubes in many applications. The small size, low heat generation, high reliability, and relatively small power requirements of the transistors enabled the miniaturization of complex circuitry required by computers and telecommunications equipment. In 1958, TI's Jack Kilby invented the integrated circuit, which superseded individual transistors a decade later. Then in 1971, Intel Corp. introduced its first microprocessor. Originally designed for a desktop calculator, the 4004 was soon improved and placed into all fields of electronics. Along with Intel, Motorola was a pioneer in microprocessors and semiconductors. Through AT&T and Motorola, the electronics revolution diffused rapidly into the nation's evolving mobile communications industry, which Intel entered only much later—toward the end of the 1990s.

Early Mobile Telephone Services

Through the war years, popular developments in radio and wireless had been constrained by military pursuits. But in 1945, the Federal Communications Commission (FCC) began to explore spectrum allocations for a variety of uses in industrial services, especially private mobile radio, including taxicab radio systems. These efforts were soon followed by the first experiments in mobile consumer services. On June 17, 1946 in Saint Louis, Missouri, AT&T and Southwestern Bell introduced the first American commercial wireless service, Mobile Telephone Service (MTS), for private customers.[15] The service was soon extended to twenty-five cities across the United States. The MTS concept relied on several key elements, including the following:

- Narrowband FM channel
- Automatic trunking
- Direct dialing
- Full-duplex service

These and other critical "modern" features served as the intrinsic technologies of the pre-cellular era. The first larger-scale commercial applications evolved between 1962 and 1964, as the Improved Mobile Telephone Service (IMTS) was tested in field trials in Harrisburg, Pennsylvania. A year later, a commercial service had been introduced in many metropolitan centers. As its name suggests, IMTS was an enhanced, not radically new version of the original MTS. It proved the viability of wireless telephony and legitimized the FCC's plans to scale up this technology to larger systems. Though designed and packaged to emulate the convenience of traditional wireline telephony, the service was hardly without problems. Still, it served as the model for and precursor of analog cellular.[16]

Advanced Mobile Phone Service

Through the pre-cellular era, wireless communications had been haunted by the dilemma of how to provide service to as many customers as possible using a limited resource. A new era emerged in the late 1960s with the development of the first analog systems. At the time, U.S. telecommunications remained synonymous with AT&T. While industry observers expected a rapid rise in wireless services, they also anticipated these services to be a mere extension of AT&T's wireline monopoly. After all, the FCC's Cellular Docket allocated the new mobile spectrum exclusively to *wire*line telephone companies, and the Bell System covered 85 percent of the U.S. population and most major metropolitan areas.

AT&T refined the cellular concept into the Advanced Mobile Phone Service (AMPS) architecture, which was predicated on monopoly service and centralized control. Only the Bell companies had the requisite competence and capabilities to build and operate the system. Although costs remained high, AT&T was determined to attack them by scaling up production. A large market and high pent-up demand would allow high volume, which was expected to reduce costs rapidly. FM communications was not proprietary and the 1956 antitrust decree had opened competition in the manufacture of mobile terminals, which was expected to stimulate production efficiencies and declining prices. It was this eroding monopoly environment that gave rise to the AMPS cellular architecture. The intrinsic characteristics of the AMPS concept were designed to match AT&T's *organizational* competences and capabilities rather than existing (or future) *market* needs. Emulating the natural monopoly, the design effected:

- A complex and costly, top-heavy network architecture, which overlaid the wireline network
- A "big machine" approach to system control, whereby processing was centralized in large and expensive switches
- A "least common denominator" radio link technology, which was fraught with problems[17]

Fit for the purposes of the Bell System, the AMPS concept was pragmatic, realistic, and crude. Even worse, it emerged at a time when the supporting technologies were about to be swept by the electronics revolution. The concept was dated at birth. With AT&T's impending breakup, a monopoly design would no longer be viable. The new environment required more competitive solutions. And the electronics revolution would demolish the supporting technologies underlying the AMPS concept. While AT&T initiated cellular trials, the same supporting technologies and centralized design that made possible AMPS service were about to be swept by a digital tornado and distributed design.

Cellular Platforms

Since the early 1980s, the wireless business has developed explosively through successive technology platforms that have given rise to analog (1G), digital (2G), and multimedia (3G) cellular and are currently leading to broadband (4G) cellular. The origins of all these platforms stem from the late 1930s, when Bell Laboratories initiated research on wireless communications. The breakthrough came a decade later.

Cellular Concept

In 1947, only a year after the first commercial mobile service test in St. Louis, the cellular concept emerged "from nowhere." It was embodied in an internal Bell Labs memorandum, "Mobile Telephony—Wide Area Coverage," by D. H. Ring, with major input from his Bell Labs colleague W. R. Young.[18] This classic paper reflected an evolving paradigm among the Bell scientists. Based on a novel concept for a new intrinsic technology, the paper suggested that it might be possible to build a high-capacity land mobile radio-telephone system that could provide wide area coverage with a modest allocation of frequencies. It identified key elements of the cellular concept, including the idea of using low-power transmitters for small areas (the term "cell" came into common use twenty years later) to permit significant frequency reuse within the service area.[19]

The genesis of the cellular concept was not a disruptive event but one steeped in the old sustaining model.[20] But unlike the MTS concept, which built on a highly *centralized* design, the cellular concept relied on a highly *distributed* design and different intrinsic technologies. These technologies, in approximate order of importance, were:

■ The cellular system architecture (including frequency reuse within a relatively small geographic area, low-power transmitters, automated central system control, and "handoff").

■ Cellular geometry (consisting of hexagonal-shaped coverage zones—or cells—and design software to simulate RF propagation and facilitate system layout)

■ Cell splitting (putting new cell sites between previous ones, to increase capacity as the system becomes loaded)

■ Channel trunking (combined with low-cost frequency synthesizers as well as low-cost crystals with new levels of precision for generating reference frequencies)

These cellular systems were made possible by a number of supportive technologies that initially were developed for other purposes:[21]

■ Solid-state electronic technologies (e.g., microprocessors, integrated circuits)[22]
■ Digital telephone switching to connect to the telephone network
■ Improved high-capacity batteries (especially for portable units)
■ Characterization of frequency propagation (especially in urban environments)

The Ring memo was not yet a system design, but it demarcated the field for additional areas of research to verify whether the concept could be implemented. To move from theory to practice, AT&T petitioned the FCC for additional frequencies for mobile radio service. Instead, the Commission reserved it for the emerging television industry. These spectrum decisions precipitated three decades of regulatory stumbling and political intrigue, which contributed to the subsequent erosion of U.S. advantages and catch-up by Nordic countries and Japan. Without spectrum to realize dramatic improvements in wireless communications, research on cellular systems was no longer a priority at Bell Labs.[23] The diffusion of information, coupled with international telecom cooperation, provided a catalyst to a new generation of researchers in the Nordic countries and Japan.[24]

Even though Bell Labs came up with the cellular concept, the development of the concept gradually migrated to Motorola. To AT&T, wireless meant an ancillary service with low-profit potential; to Motorola, it meant a core service with high-profit potential, at least in the long term. In the first case, wireless communication threatened AT&T's lucrative fixed-line properties. In the case of Motorola, the cannibalization threat worked against rivals.

With each subsequent cellular platform, the core technologies have substantially increased spectrum capacity. Spectrum policies, however, have often failed the technologies they were designed to exploit.

Spectrum Policies

Spectrum policies have been driven by several successive paradigms (e.g., occupancy, administrative, auction, and open access). Toward the late 1990s, new and emerging digital technologies enabled new ways of thinking about spectrum use that had not been possible in an analog world (see Exhibit 2-2). At the eve of the 3G transition, current systems only reinforced the entrenched positions of the industry incumbents, while limiting the strategic options of potential attackers and challengers. With the 3G transition, even the larger countries became frustrated with auctions. The prime reason was not that the auctions failed to fulfill the equalizing objectives, but that they taxed the licensees excessively.

Technological advances intensified the debate, which also reflected the strategic repositioning of industry incumbents after the erosion of U.S. leadership and the migration of innovation to Western Europe and the Nordic countries. In Europe and Japan, regulators allocated a single spectrum across the region and the nation, respectively. Greater access to 3G spectrum has allowed them to introduce data services well before U.S. operators. This edge has contributed to the erosion of first-mover advantages in and value migration from the United States. In the U.S., the FCC developed a piecemeal approach for 3G services, which compelled the operators to build their strategies from a patchwork of different spectrum frequencies. Skeptical of the FCC's success in freeing up more spectrum, operators pushed the Commission to lift spectrum caps. This problem was one of the key motivations behind the Clinton administration's order that government agencies and the private sector work with the FCC to release new spectrum.[25]

With 3G and increasing globalization, the debate entered a new stage, where entry barriers were no longer just national but involved geographic

Exhibit 2-2. Struggle for spectrum.

The radio spectrum comprises electromagnetic radio frequencies that are used for everything from the transmitting of AM radio to the broadcasting of television and cellular phones (from 3 kHz to 300 GHz). In the wireless business, the classic problem has been how to provide service to as many users as possible using a limited resource. In past decades, technology has substantially contributed to enhanced spectrum capacity, particularly via cellular platforms. In addition to the spectrum and the installed user base (e.g., emergency, industrial, corporate, and consumer services), other stakeholders (TV and radio broadcasters, government, defense forces) hold substantial chunks of the spectrum. While the identity of the spectrum owners tends to be similar in different regions, the stakes they own differ. The greater the role of commercial service providers among these stakeholders, the greater is the available proportion of spectrum for commercial purposes. In the United States, the long battles over spectrum policy originate from the rise of the powerful TV lobby in the 1950s and 1960s, the strong historical role of defense forces, as well as regulatory hierarchies.

Eli Noam has distinguished three successive paradigms (occupancy, administrative, auction) and an emerging fourth one (open access). With the triangle framework, these paradigms can be periodized on the basis of the U.S. experiences as well as those of the key triad regions (Western Europe, Nordic countries, and Japan).

Occupancy Stage: The Pre-*Titanic* Spectrum (1912). Based on occupancy, the first stage was relatively brief. Due to congestion, transmissions were bound to collide as radio amateurs, early broadcasters, radiotelegraph operators, and the U.S. Navy all congregated on the air. The stage was characterized by a wide variety of R&D projects, increasing investments, uncertainty, and risk. In terms of geographic advantages, it coincided with Marconi's era, the rise of wireless telegraphy, and the migration of European pioneership to the United States. It came to an end with the disaster of the *Titanic* in April 1912 and subsequent regulation.

Administrative Stage: From the *Titanic* to the Early 1980s. After the sinking of the *Titanic,* the occupancy model was replaced by the administrative stage, which endured through the 1980s licensing conflicts. Frequencies were allocated by public policies. In some countries, the reception of signals was also licensed. This was the orthodoxy that emerged in the late 1920s with the expansion of the Federal Radio Commission (FRC) and Federal Communications Commission (FCC). Fights over new allocation were battles over rising entry barriers. Innovation suffered, new entrants were barred, foreign interests were excluded. The U.S. leadership in the wireless coincides with the emergence and rise of the regulatory era, just as the erosion of America's leadership parallels the decline of this era. Throughout this period, mobile interests were considered secondary to those of the powerful broadcast lobby in the United States. The crisis was acknowledged in the late 1960s, but the system was tested only with the rollout of analog cellular services in the early 1980s, when it fell apart.

Auction Stage: Early 1980s to the Internet Revolution. As spectrum was deemed a scarce and thereby highly valuable resource, Ronald Coase argued for a

(continues)

Exhibit 2-2. (Continued).

---

new system of policies in which spectrum would be allocated into property rights and sold to the highest bidder. The old administrative paradigm was replaced by the U.S. license lotteries, a bizarre system that glutted the FCC, with almost a half million "applications." Coase's auction paradigm replaced the old administrative model. Initially, broadcasters fought it, but the rise of cable operators split the TV group in two, while mobile technology led to an explosion of demand for over-the-air capacity. The new paradigm pleased the political establishment, providing it with vast new resources, but it translated into even higher entry barriers and higher cost burdens. While regulators were aware of the auction tradeoffs, the idea of "free" revenue generation appealed to the political community.

Open Access: Toward the 4G Era. Amid the impending 3G transition, the pressure for reform was rising in the United States. A 1997 FCC staff paper urged the Commission to attempt "substantial replication in the spectrum context of the freedoms inherent in property rights [to] allow competition to function more effectively, much as it does in those sectors of the economy where basic inputs are privately owned." Reportedly, wireless operators tried to kill the report altogether. In March 2001, the formal comment filed at the FCC called for liberating the airwaves, limiting federal regulation to interference rules and standard competition policy. The future belonged to some form of "open access" solution.

By spring 2001, regulators had delayed the spectrum auctions in the United States, hoping to drive up prices. One auction garnered $18 billion in fees from carriers such as Verizon Wireless. After the prices skyrocketed in the U.K., many potential new entrants lost interest in the European UMTS market. Incumbent operators in the U.K., Germany, and Italy bore an excessive 85% of the license costs across Europe. In February 2002, FCC launched a spectrum policy task force to ensure that spectrum could be put to the "highest and best use in a timely manner."

For More Information on the Spectrum Policy Debate

R. Coase, "The Federal Communication Commission," *Journal of Law & Economics II* (1959), pp. 1–40. This work is an introduction to the auction paradigm.

T. Hazlett, "Assigning Property Rights to Radio Spectrum Users: Why Did FCC License Auctions Take 67 Years?" *Journal of Law & Economics* 41 (1998). A critical analysis of the regulatory barriers in the U.S.

E. M. Noam, "Spectrum Auctions: Yesterday's Heresy, Today's Orthodoxy, Tomorrow's Anachronism. Taking the Next Step to Open Spectrum Access," *Journal of Law and Economics* 41 (1998). Noam argues that spectrum auctions are likely to become "technologically obsolete, economically inefficient, and legally unconstitutional."

L. Lessig, *The Future of Ideas: The Fate of the Commons in a Connected World* (New York: Random House, 2001). Chapter 5 is a carefully referenced introduction to the debate.

---

advantages between large- and small-country players. The greater the spectrum value, the more it raised the entry barriers, which kept new entrants and challengers at bay while constraining growth and fostering consolidation rather than competition. Instead of equalizing the playing field, market size and auctions have boosted the inherited geographic advantages by reinforcing the bargaining power of the largest operators (which just happen to be large-country operators) at the expense of the smaller ones (which just happen to be small-country operators). In these circumstances, small countries have employed beauty contests to support their indigenous players.

At the 2001 Cellular Telecommunications & Internet Association (CTIA) convention, Motorola CEO Christopher Galvin suggested that perhaps regulators should make the spectrums available for free, referring to the railroad build-outs of the mid-1800s, during which land was given to the railway companies. "Imagine what would have happened to the building of the United States if railways would have had to pay for the land," he said. "The United States would have stopped at Chicago."[26]

Multiple Access Schemes

Since the early 1980s, the cellular concept has changed little, but its execution has resulted in three successive technology generations. The three cellular generations—1G, 2G, and 3G—coincide with three different "multiple access schemes": frequency division multiple access (FDMA), time division multiple access (TDMA), and code division multiple access (CDMA).

Frequency Division Multiple Access

In FDMA, the total system bandwidth is divided into frequency channels that are allocated to the users. From the invention of radio until the rise of 2G, this was the most common analog system (AMPS in the United States, NMT in Nordic countries, TACS in the U.K.). In FDMA, only one subscriber at a time is assigned to a channel. The channel cannot be accessed by other conversations until the subscriber's call is finished or the original call is handed off to a different channel. A full-duplex FDMA transmission demands two channels, one for transmission and the other for receiving. Compared to other multiple access schemes, FDMA is the most inefficient.

Time Division Multiple Access

In TDMA, each frequency channel is divided into time slots and each user is allocated a time slot, which improves spectrum capacity. This solution evolved as frequency capacity approached its limits and networks grew congested. Just as FDMA dominated the 1G analog cellular, TDMA has dominated the 2G digital cellular with three different versions:

- North American TDMA (IS-136) or D-AMPS
- European TDMA (GSM)
- Japanese TDMA (PDC/PHS)

Code Division Multiple Access

Once named the "most beautiful woman in the world," movie star Hedy Lamarr is generally credited as co-originator of the idea of spread spectrum transmission. She and her pianist, George Antheil (a composer dubbed "the bad boy of music"), were issued a patent for the technique during World War II.[27] They discovered the technique using a player piano to control the frequency hops, and envisioned it as a way to provide secure communications during wartime. The beauty and the bad boy never made any money off the invention and their patent eventually expired. Sylvania introduced a similar concept in the 1950s and coined the term "spread spectrum." In CDMA, multiple access is created by assigning each user a pseudo-random code, which differentiates each call from the many other calls that are simultaneously carried over the same spectrum. Based on spread spectrum technology, CDMA has had a long history in military applications because it allows for highly encrypted signals. Spectrum capacity is improved with CDMA because all users occupy all channels at the same time. CDMA's "soft handoff" allows terminals to communicate with several base stations at the same time.

These multiple access schemes can be compared to different communication strategies at a cocktail party. In the TDMA scenario, each guest would have to restrict his or her talk to a specific time slot, while everyone else kept quiet. The system is manageable, but requires complex rules, rigid timing, and an authoritarian tyrant who keeps constant control. In the CDMA scenario, everyone can talk at once but must use different languages. The guests listen for messages in their own languages and ignore other sounds as background noise. The system permits each guest to speak freely but requires constant control of the volume of the guests.

Since the early 1980s, the cellular evolution has been based on successive innovation waves. In each case, variations of a given multiple access scheme have reigned over rivals. In the 1G era, the dominant role belonged to FDMA; in the 2G era, to TDMA; and in the 3G era, to CDMA. With each wave of innovation—or, more narrowly, technology platform—the interplay between the technology and the changing marketplace, not the technology *per se,* has resulted in an industry transformation.

The Pre-Cellular Era

In Japan and the Nordic countries, telecom authorities harbored few doubts about the need for their cellular system and its feasibility. In the United States, public policy implementers perceived the competitive environment very differently. For an entire decade—from 1958 to 1968—AT&T lobbied the FCC to convince regulators of the importance and feasibility of the new cellular system. Reluctant to allocate new spectrum to unproven demand, the FCC gave in to pressure only after congestion started to put strain on other mobile communications services.[28] This action, in turn, resulted in the acceleration of wireless activities and the first test in 1978. Commercial launch, however, materialized only five years later. At Bell Labs, the researchers had come up with the cellular concept in 1947; it was commercialized in 1983. Technology issues explain only some of these delays—much of it comprised self-inflicted regulatory failures.

From the 1920s to the end of the 1980s, the United States dominated wireless communications. With the advent of the 1G era, the Nordic countries and Japan caught up in terms of technological capabilities. Both regions pioneered the analog era before the United States. Although the first substantial analog systems were introduced in 1981, broad-scale market evolution took several years. At the peak of the pre-cellular era (1983), Japan's proprietary system held a fourth of the worldwide market; NTT's proprietary standard (100 percent) accounted for the share (see Exhibit 2-3, and compare with Exhibit 1-7 in Chapter 1). Struggling with regulatory delays, North America's emerging AMPS had an insignificant share (1.8 percent) of the worldwide market. In Western Europe, the Nordic NMT dominated three-fourths of the worldwide market. This leadership was the result of Nordic superiority, based on the joint Nordic standard NMT (94 percent) and, to lesser extent, the Swedish Comvik (6 percent), which had emerged as a challenge to Sweden's PTT, Televerket. Unlike NMT, Comvik and Japan's NTT relied on proprietary systems. Other regions had no penetration yet.

The 1G Era: Analog Cellular

Since the 1980s, these platform generations—or, more broadly, waves of innovation—have evolved from one dominant standard to the next, and each technology has significantly improved spectrum capacity. Standards, as Jeffrey L. Funk has noted, have had a "dramatic effect on competition."[29] Launched in the early 1980s, the nascent 1G systems relied on analog transmission for voice communication. Several systems emerged worldwide, but only three proved enduring. The underlying concepts originated from two key standards—AMPS in the United States and the Nordic NMT. These mobile systems were launched in the Nordic countries in 1981, in the United States in 1983, and in the U.K. in 1985. The growth of the analog systems continued well into the mid-1990s worldwide. At Nokia's nascent mobile arm, Mobira, marketers and top management had pushed European countries to adopt NMT, which had also been promoted by Finland's Ministry of Trade and Industry.[30] But Nordic hopes for a European NMT faded by 1983 and 1984, when regional heavy-

Exhibit 2-3. Peaks of cellular eras: technology standards and geographic regions (1983–2001).

Peak of Pre-Cellular Era (1983)

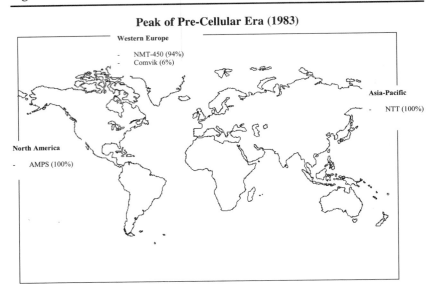

Peak of 1G Era (1991)

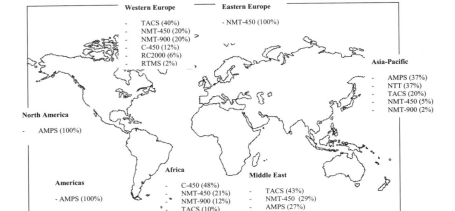

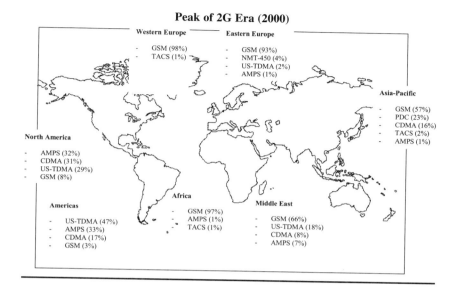

Peak of 2G Era (2000)

Western Europe
- GSM (98%)
- TACS (1%)

Eastern Europe
- GSM (93%)
- NMT-450 (4%)
- US-TDMA (2%)
- AMPS (1%)

Asia-Pacific
- GSM (57%)
- PDC (23%)
- CDMA (16%)
- TACS (2%)
- AMPS (1%)

North America
- AMPS (32%)
- CDMA (31%)
- US-TDMA (29%)
- GSM (8%)

Americas
- US-TDMA (47%)
- AMPS (33%)
- CDMA (17%)
- GSM (3%)

Africa
- GSM (97%)
- AMPS (1%)
- TACS (1%)

Middle East
- GSM (66%)
- US-TDMA (18%)
- CDMA (8%)
- AMPS (7%)

weights—the U.K., France, Germany, and Italy—introduced different standards. The U.S. players benefited from a singular standard (AMPS), whereas the European players developed proprietary systems that fragmented the market.

■ **Advanced Mobile Phone System.** AMPS relied on the old FDMA technology in the 800 MHz to 900 MHz frequency band (and more recently in the 1800–2000 MHz band). At the end of the 1990s, AMPS was the most popular analog system and, after GSM, the second-largest cellular system overall worldwide with some 50 million subscribers, mainly in North America.

■ **Nordic Mobile Telephone.** NMT originated from Nordic cooperation that started in the late 1960s. It was developed by telecom authorities, operators, and equipment manufacturers and introduced in 1981. At first, it relied on the 450 MHz band and later, due to congestion, the 900 MHz band. In the late 1990s, it remained in use by 4.5 million people in forty countries, including the Nordic countries, as well as emerging and transitional economies in Asia, Russia, and Eastern Europe.

■ **Total Access Communications System.** A British derivative of the American AMPS, Total Access Communications System (TACS) was developed from AMPS for operation in both the 800 and 900 MHz ranges. It was first used in the United Kingdom in 1985, in the aftermath of privatization and deregulation in the British telecom marketplace. Some other parts of the 900 MHz frequency have often been used for the so-called extended version (ETACS). Toward the end of the 1990s, there were still 15 million TACS users worldwide.

■ **Proprietary Systems.** In addition to these three standards—AMPS, NMT, and TACS—a large variety of proprietary systems existed for analog cellular and others that were rarely sold outside the home country, particularly in France, Germany, Italy, and Japan. Initially, some of these systems enjoyed monopolistic benefits in their home base. Typically, they were developed by national PTTs, often in cooperation with their exclusive or preferred suppliers. Based on domesticated systems, they were poorly adaptable to international-ization, not to speak of globalization. Most were harvested by the onset of the 2G era.

At the peak of the 1G era (1991), AMPS ruled in North America, the largest market area that represented more than half (53.9 percent) of global demand (as shown in Exhibit 2-3). The United States was the most lucrative country market worldwide and this triumph would endure to the mid-1990s. American vendors and operators owned the best products and services and the most efficient operations, just as they featured the most advanced innovation and the most sophisticated customers. Western Europe accounted more than a fourth of the worldwide market. TACS, the derivative of AMPS, dominated two-fifths of this region (40 percent), as did the Nordic NMT and its upgraded version (40 percent collectively). The rest of market share belonged to proprie-tary standards that were harvested before the 2G era. Asia-Pacific had less than one-fifth of the world market (16 percent); it was divided between AMPS (37 percent), NTT (37 percent), as well as TACS (20 percent). However, the Nor-dic NMT (7 percent) managed to create a foothold in Asia-Pacific markets as well. In terms of the worldwide market, other regional segments were rela-tively insignificant. But they reflected future competition in the 2G era. In the Americas, the U.S. AMPS standard dominated. In the Middle East, Anglo-Saxon standards had almost three-thirds of the market, while the rest belonged to the Nordic NMT. In Africa, C-450 possessed half of the market, whereas Nordic NMT had a third and the Anglo-Saxon standards less than a fifth. To some degree, these proportions illustrated the coming digital rivalries between GSM and its U.S. counterparts (US-TDMA, CDMA).

The 2G Era: Digital Cellular

Amid the 1G era, the key players—primarily equipment manufacturers and some network operators—were already developing the first digital systems, which were introduced commercially in the early 1990s. Just as analog cellular (AMPS, NMT) had many advantages over the pre-cellular systems (MTS, IMTS), digital cellular offered increased capacity thanks to its more efficient usage of the spectrum. Because of lower-power operation, digital networks resulted in smaller and lighter handsets, which had longer battery life. Through encryption, digital systems provided greater security for voice and data. In addition to voice communications, digital transmission also allowed data transfer through the radio spectrum, which enabled new data-driven services, including short message service (SMS). Toward the end of the 1990s, the growth of SMS exploded in the advanced markets, such as the Nordic countries.

The 1G era had witnessed the rise of three major systems worldwide, as well as several proprietary standards, which failed to attract more than national interest. With the 2G era, half a dozen systems emerged worldwide, but ultimately only two or three of these attracted more than national or regional significance. The most important standard emerged in Western Europe, initially in the Nordic markets. Impressed with the rapid regionalization of the Nordic NMT standard, the European Commission (EC) decided to support a slate of initiatives designed to replicate the triumph of NMT at a pan-European level. These initiatives were crafted together with major telecom operators and equipment manufacturers. The objective was to promote regional harmonization of cellular networks. In practice, the goal was technical and political as well; it would reinforce European integration. In the late 1980s, the EC saw GSM as a unifying force that would allow the players to integrate the European mobile markets. But the EC also employed GSM as a hammer to crack down the old PTTs and their national monopolies, thereby boosting competition in Europe's country markets. Finally, the EC expected the competition to result in consolidation, which would eventually result in regionwide players that could challenge industry leaders in the United States and the Asia-Pacific market. For most practical purposes, the logic proved valid.

Launched in 1989, the European Telecommunications Standards Institute (ETSI) played a central role in GSM standardization. Relying on TDMA, GSM operated in the 900, 1800, and 1900 MHz frequency bands. A Finnish mobile operator, Radiolinja, launched the first GSM network in 1991. After decades of playing catch-up, the Europe-based players employed GSM to overthrow U.S. industry leadership, but the start was not easy. The story of the GSM success conceals the competitive ferment during the launch of the first digital networks in the early 1990s—as well as the political motives. At the end of the 1990s, the GSM standard ruled in Europe and, to the surprise of its advocates, proliferated worldwide, beating TDMA, CDMA, as well as PDC/PHS.

■ **TDMA IS-136.** Introduced in late 1991, TDMA IS-136 (also known as US-TDMA) served as the digital enhancement of analog AMPS used in the 800 and 1900 MHz frequency bands. Initially referred to as D-AMPS, it was launched to protect the substantial investments of the service providers in AMPS. After all, these operators had envisioned a transition from AMPS to D-AMPS by overlaying their existing networks with a TDMA architecture, using the same frequencies and radio channels. By the end of the 1990s, digital AMPS services had been launched in some seventy countries worldwide, and

22 million TDMA handsets were in circulation. The dominant markets were the Americas and parts of Asia.

■ **CDMA IS-95.** This standard comprised a slate of digital communication techniques that increased capacity. CDMA was pioneered and commercially developed by Qualcomm. Commercially introduced in 1995, it became one of the world's fastest-growing wireless technologies. In 1999, there were almost 29 million CDMA subscribers, mainly in Asia-Pacific and the Americas. South Korea was the largest single CDMA IS-95 market worldwide with almost 60 percent of these CDMA subscribers worldwide. That year, the ITU selected CDMA as the industry standard for the new 3G wireless systems. By 2002, Qualcomm estimated that more than 100 million consumers worldwide were relying on CDMA for voice communications and leading-edge data services.

■ **Personal Digital Cellular.** Initially called Japan Digital Cellular, PDC was based on the TDMA technology, like GSM and TDMA IS-136, and operated in the 800 and 1500 MHz frequency bands. At the end of the 1990s, PDC was the second largest digital standard worldwide for mobile systems. Like the proprietary systems of the 1G era, PDC had been developed, launched, and used exclusively in Japan since 1994. During the next half decade, the number of NTT DoCoMo's PDC users soared from 2 million to almost 45 million. In contrast to its European and U.S. counterparts, the Japanese operator had developed a strong service concept. However, the system could not be leveraged globally.

■ **Personal Handyphone System.** Launched by NTT in Japan in 1995, the Personal Handyphone System (PHS) was a digital system that reflected aspects of both cellular and cordless technologies. With low handset costs, monthly fees, and calling rates, PHS was introduced as a low-cost alternative to cellular. By the spring of 1999, there were 5.77 million PHS subscribers in Japan. It was a domestic niche product. In 1999, DDI (later KDDI), the rival of NTT DoCoMo, took over NTT's unprofitable PHS terminal and launched a high-speed data service over the PHS network.

Despite the extraordinary leadership of the U.S.-based AMPS standard, digitalization transformed the industry. Around 1990–1991, GSM dominated more than 99.3 percent of these earliest digital cellular markets, whereas US-TDMA had only 0.7 percent. Certainly, first-mover advantages did not promise sustainable advantages. But they did secure a substantial lead in regional advantages, through network effects. And it was this dynamic lead that the European players managed to exploit to the maximum in the coming years. To the U.S. players, the result was, simply put, catastrophic.

At the peak of the 2G era (2000), Western Europe had almost two-fifths (36.8 percent) of the worldwide market. In this market, GSM had triumphed (98 percent) against TACS (1 percent). Asia-Pacific had almost a third (31.1

percent) of the worldwide market. In this rapidly growing region, GSM was now dominant (57 percent), against Japan's PDC (23 percent) and various Anglo-Saxon standards (CDMA 16 percent, TACS 2 percent, AMPS 1 percent). Only one technology generation before, the United States had controlled more than half of the market; now it had less than one-sixth (15.5 percent). Regulatory delays, multiple standards, and strategic complacency devastated America's promising lead in the mobile business. While Europeans initiated migration to the digital in 1992, the old analog AMPS remained the most popular standard in the U.S. market, with 32 percent market share. CDMA (31 percent) captured almost a third and beat US-TDMA (29 percent). Prior to the 2G era, GSM had secured a foothold in Asia-Pacific; now the Euro standard did the same in the U.S. market, attaining 8 percent of the marketplace. The market share of the Americas (8.8 percent) had risen rapidly to less than one-tenth of the worldwide market. Due to the U.S. influence, the role of GSM remained low (3 percent), whereas U.S. analog AMPS (33 percent) and digital standards (US-TDMA 47 percent, CDMA 17 percent) dominated. The remaining regional markets—Eastern Europe, Middle East, and Africa—had less than a tenth (8.8 percent) of the worldwide market. In each case, however, GSM had a dominant role (93 percent in Eastern Europe, 97 percent in Africa, 66 percent in Middle East).

These years coincided with market globalization, which caused the annual production of mobile units to soar from a few million in the early 1990s to close to 400 million units in 2001. In the United States, the missed opportunities translated to billions of dollars in lost revenues.

The 3G Era: Multimedia Cellular

In the past, the transition of platforms in wireless communications had been largely an intra-industry affair. With the convergence of mobility and the Internet, the opposition between European-based mobile leaders and U.S.-based IT leaders was magnified by differences in evolution. In mobile communications, the industry had advanced from the pre-cellular era to analog and digital cellular and was amid the transition to multimedia cellular. In the IT world, the industry had evolved from mainframes, minicomputers, and personal computers to Internet-enabled systems, which were amid mobilization. Mobile leaders were transitioning from voice to data; IT leaders from data to voice.[31] New and disruptive developments were certainly not over with the 3G era. For instance, speech recognition heralded more far-reaching developments. Dr. Gordon Moore, Intel's first chairman, thought that this technology could potentially revolutionize many consumer-oriented applications: "Once the computer can really recognize speech in context, it is essentially going to understand speech. Maybe it is 20 years away or maybe it is closer than that. But that one application is going to have a big impact."[32]

Industry evolution proceeded to a new stage as the cellular concept was swept by the Internet concept.

Internet Concept and UMTS (3G)

The cellular concept guided the evolution of technology platforms until the end of the digital cellular. With the coming of the 3G era, the Internet concept emerged as a new dominant amalgam of intrinsic technologies, with new components:

- Internetworks (a set of interconnected communication networks)
- Common protocols governing addressing, routing, and error-checking of information packets
- Packet switching (whereby information on the network is formed into packets from multiple, simultaneous users, then sent and reassembled at destinations using sequencing and routing information contained within the packets)
- Switches, or routers, at each node of each network that control the routing of packets[33]

While the wireless business was a century old, the *globalization* of the standardization activities was initiated only toward the end of the 1980s. With GSM, the European Commission had played a critical role; with 3G, that role belonged to the International Telecommunications Union (ITU). In the 1G and 2G eras, cellular systems had been designed for national and, at best, regional networks. And many standards were still based on proprietary rather than open system specifications. Except for the Nordic markets, they possessed limited roaming capabilities. During those years, the ITU issued technical recommendations on how these early generation systems should work with each other, but it did not issue standards for them. In the 1G era, a single standard in the United States contributed to the AMPS triumph, whereas multiple standards in Europe reinforced market fragmentation. These lessons did not go unnoticed at ITU.

In the late 1980s, ITU began to develop 3G systems that emphasized the need for harmonized frequency spectrum and radio interface standards worldwide. The goal was to achieve a global standard for the 3G era, through an initiative called International Mobile Telecommunications-2000 (IMT-2000).[34] In the United States, regulators, operators, and equipment manufacturers termed the initiative 3G, for third generation. In Europe, these high-speed systems came to be called Universal Mobile Telecommunications System (UMTS), a concept developed by ETSI with the European Radiocommunications Committee (ERC), which coordinated regulatory issues. The ITU defined the distinctive characteristics of IMT-2000, which included:

- A high degree of commonality of design worldwide
- Compatibility of services within IMT-2000 and with the fixed networks
- High quality
- A small terminal for worldwide use
- Worldwide roaming capability
- Capability for multimedia applications and a wide range of services and terminals[35]

Regional Coalitions and the 3G Struggle

While no single mobile player could any longer develop and control an entire technology platform, strategic groups did try to shape development paths to their favor. Converging interests prompted such alignments in the late 1990s, through regional strategic coalitions.

EU and Japan: Two Out of Three Ain't Too Bad

The ITU expected the platform to give rise to 2 billion users worldwide by the year 2010. The first 3G services were expected to launch commercially in 2001, with widespread global deployments by 2005. The struggle for the 3G future began almost two decades before.[36] As long as the mobile business was domestic and regulated, network operators often enjoyed the greatest bargaining power. With deregulation in the most advanced markets and increasing internationalization, this power began to migrate toward vendors. At Nokia, the first R&D projects evolved around 1987. The door to the future went through the European Telecommunication Standards Institute (ETSI), where Nokia's representatives began to shape 3G in the vendor's favor. Toward the end of the 1990s, a single regional trading block would not suffice for a standards victory in the impending 3G rivalry, whereas two blocks out of three might be adequate. Neither the Nordic nor the Japanese players would win alone; in the 3G rivalry, they needed each other.

In February 1997 Nokia's CDMA converts concluded that Europe could thrive in competition against the United States, but only as Japan's partner. Conversely, the Nokians thought that Europe would *not* succeed in competition against the Japanese, even if they had U.S. partners. For decades, Nokia and Ericsson had competed with each other. Now they joined forces to persuade the Japanese into a compromise. NTT, the monopolistic parent, did not want to collaborate with the GSM giants, whereas DoCoMo, its competitive mobile subsidiary, was eager to cooperate with Nokia and Ericsson. In May 1997, the Nordic and Japanese sides began talks, but they also found competition in the quest for the wireless horizon.

Qualcomm and Trade War Threats

In 1997, U.S. manufacturers, led by Qualcomm, announced that they would develop a technology for the 3G cell phones. To neutralize the U.S.

initiative, Nokia and Ericsson rushed to publicize their agreement. In August 1997, NTT DoCoMo's legendary CEO Kouji Ohboshi and R&D chief Minoru Kuramoto visited Finland and promised to join the Nokia-Ericsson camp. A month later Siemens and its partners, Alcatel of France and Canada-based Nortel, announced their own proposal (TD-CDMA) for Europe's new standard. Siemens's objective was an alliance between Europe and the U.S. that would force the Japanese to compromise. Motorola and other major equipment vendors joined the new alliance. Despite EC efforts to intermediate, the conflict only got worse. In January 1998, ETSI voted for the standard. Nokia and Ericsson earned 61 percent of the votes, but a win would have required 71 percent. After behind-the-scenes talks, Nokia, Ericsson, and Siemens prepared a compromise and ETSI agreed on a 3G mobile standard, UTRA (UMTS Terrestrial Radio Access), which built on both W-CDMA and TDMA-CDMA proposals.[37] The European standards struggle was over and the United States had been played out from the 3G competition. Or so it seemed.

As Europeans and the Japanese were busy negotiating, Qualcomm initiated collaboration with Microsoft, via Wireless Knowledge. The joint venture made the leading mobile vendors uneasy. Now Qualcomm argued that 3G rivalry needed a *single* standard. The European CDMA and its own technology (cdma2000) would have to be combined, or ITU would choose one or the other. After the EC support to the ETSI decision in December 1998, EU Commissioner Martin Bangeman received a letter from the U.S. government, threatening the EU with a trade war. The ITU published a press release in which it expressed its concern for a "holy war" that could destroy the dream of the 3G mobile communications. Meanwhile Bangemann managed to appease the U.S. government.

Toward Flexible Reconciliation

In mid-February 1999, the Trans-Atlantic Business Dialogue (TABD) had a conference in Washington, D.C. T-Mobile, a major German operator, crafted a compromise proposal that suggested a 3G "umbrella" solution based on CDMA and covering major technologies. Operators could make their own informed choices. The idea of a uniform single standard was out; the idea of a single flexible standard was in. The TABD solution was formalized at the ITU conference in Fortaleza, Brazil, in March 1999. The key players decided to develop IMT-2000 into a single flexible standard with a choice of multiple access methods including CDMA, TDMA, and combined TDMA/CDMA.[38] A month later, the U.S. government sent one more verbal note to the EU Commission, but the standards struggle was over and trade wars had been avoided. At the end of 2001, the old *de facto* Japanese-Finnish alignment turned into a *de jure* alliance.[39]

By early 2002, GSM remained the leading cellular technology.[40] In each national market, the competitive circumstances were somewhat different, depending on the unique mix of the development path. Moreover, the integration of the cellular *and* the Internet concept (i.e., intrinsic, sustaining technologies) would take years. In this regard, 3G was a *transitional* phase rather than an endpoint. Truly pervasive mobile computing would evolve only in the 4G era. Moreover, the pioneer 3G experiences did not reflect explosive growth trends. Even in Japan, users were slow to adopt new phones.

Globalization of R&D*

In the pre-cellular era, wireless technology development was synonymous with the activities of Bell Labs. At the macro-level, national innovation systems played an important role during the monopoly era, when most wireless R&D remained within the national PTTs and their preferred or competitive vendors. With the great transition and the competitive era, vendors captured R&D leadership. Temporally, these three eras—monopoly, transition, competition—were separated by just a few years; in terms of organizational capabilities, they were centuries apart. Globalization transformed the organization of R&D operations within the leading industry players. In the past, R&D activities had been domestic, closed, and highly centralized; today, they are global, networked, and highly distributed. If Bell Labs represented the highpoint of domestic centralization, Motorola's R&D in the 1980s provided a transitional structure, just as Nokia's R&D toward the late 1990s reflected increasing global networking.[41]

Motorola's Centralized and International R&D

In 1940, Motorola founder Paul Galvin hired Daniel E. Noble, a pioneer in FM radio communications and semiconductor technology, as director of research. In 1946, Noble budgeted in excess of $1 million for research and assigned more than 240 engineers to development projects focusing on new technologies, products, and manufacturing processes. The venture into semiconductors was a bold strategic choice. "If you don't like my decision," Galvin told the board, "you can get rid of me; but you can't change my decision."[42] Motorola's R&D drew from defense, consumer electronics, and semiconductors. The details of Bell Labs' cellular system design became public with AT&T's 1971 proposal to the FCC. Two years later, Motorola's own development of the cellular systems concept became public, with the presentation of "The DynaTAC Concept" to the FCC.

In the pre-cellular era, Bell Labs offered a model of traditional R&D. It served domestic markets, was highly centralized, and formed a relatively closed unit in the vertically integrated AT&T. During the 1G era, Motorola's

---

*This account draws from Dan Steinbock (2003), "Globalization of Wireless R&D," unpublished manuscript.

R&D served primarily domestic markets, but it gradually reached further through leverage. It remained relatively centralized, and although it was still somewhat insular, it began to cultivate more market-driven relationships with the internal organization and the external environment. By the 1990s, Nordic and Japanese firms captured R&D leadership, but only Nordic vendors managed to *globalize* it. Their concept of R&D was almost the reverse of the model adopted early on by Motorola.

Nokia's Global R&D Networks

At year-end 2000, Nokia had more than 19,300 research and development employees, representing 32 percent of its total personnel.[43] By 2002, Nokia's worldwide R&D network consisted of three major circles of networked activities. The primary R&D concentrations were in Nordic countries, Western Europe, and Asia-Pacific. The United States was the key site for Internet capabilities. The Nokia Research Center (NRC) had more than fifty R&D centers in fifteen countries, representing all central Triad locations. The network emulated the basic manufacturing configuration (see Exhibit 2-4). Many key resources could be found in close proximity to Nokia's critical production sites. Typically, home-base-augmenting sites were located in regional clusters of scientific excellence. In contrast, home-base-exploiting sites were located

Exhibit 2-4. Globalization of R&D capabilities.

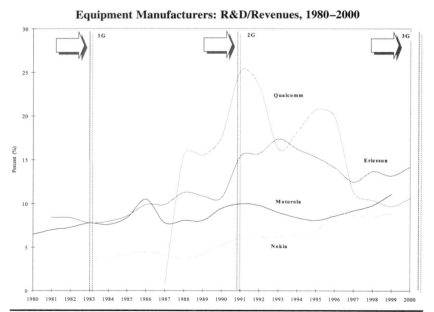

Equipment Manufacturers: R&D/Revenues, 1980–2000

Source: Company reports.

close to large markets and manufacturing facilities to commercialize new products rapidly in foreign markets. Between home-base-augmenting R&D sites and the NRC, technology-related information reigned. Between home-base-exploiting sites, information on markets and manufacturing counted the most.[44]

By the 3G transition, the prevailing R&D operation in the mobile business had become the reverse of the old Bell Labs model. It was global instead of domestic, networked instead of centralized, and outward-looking instead of inward-looking. Amid the transition, industry thrust migrated from vendors toward software, as reflected by Microsoft's entry into the mobile business. Irrespective of the outcome of this struggle, the shifts in R&D management were irreversible. This transition from central to distributed R&D characterizes the developments in cellular R&D, in which the reign of the national PTTs and their suppliers reflected R&D practices until the 1G era. The rise of the mobile vendors in the 1990s illustrated these very same practices until the 3G era.

Top-Tier Mobile R&D: From Early 1980s to 2000

The R&D expenditures of the mobile leaders are not directly comparable. Two of them (Nokia, Qualcomm) have been relatively focused on mobile communications, while the remaining two (Motorola, Ericsson) have been more diversified. In all, the absolute investments accelerated dramatically between the early 1980s and the 3G transition. But in relative terms (i.e., R&D as a percentage of net sales), trends differ illustrating different priorities (see Exhibit 2-4).

In relative terms, Nokia's R&D stayed below 4 percent of net sales through most of the 1980s. In the first half of the 1990s, Nokia's R&D climbed from 6 percent to 6.9 percent, soaring to 8.9 percent by the end of the decade. These investments had been steadily increasing, but they were, in relative terms, behind those of other top-tier mobile leaders, including Ericsson, Motorola, and Qualcomm. Between 1981 and 1990, Ericsson's absolute R&D almost quadrupled, while relative R&D increased from 8 percent to more than 10 percent. In the 1990s, Ericsson's absolute R&D investments grew almost eightfold, while relative R&D peaked at 17.4 percent. In 2000, these expenditures accounted for 14.2 percent of Ericsson's revenues; at Nokia, this proportion was barely 9 percent. In absolute terms, Ericsson invested in R&D three times more than Nokia (Ericsson's definition of R&D, however, was considered relatively broad). In contrast to its rivals, Nokia built on downstream activities, including branding, segmentation, and design. Consequently, solid R&D figures tell less about the sources of its strategic advantages.

At Motorola, R&D expenditures grew steadily from $200 million in 1980 to $3.5 billion in 1999. In the 1980s, its relative R&D increased with the growth of the economy, peaking at 10.5 percent in 1986. But even as the vendor experienced its most lucrative years in the early 1990s, its relative R&D declined from 10 percent to 8.1 percent. As Ericsson almost doubled its R&D fraction, Motorola kept reducing it. The U.S. vendor began to invest proportionally more only in the latter half of the 1990s, but this was too little too late. By 2000, Motorola's relative R&D fraction was 2 percent more than Nokia's but 2 percent less than Ericsson's. The story is quite different at the entrepreneurial Qualcomm, where revenues climbed from $0.5 million in 1987 to $340 million in 2000. The fluctuations of R&D corresponded closely to the role of CDMA and the wireless segment in Qualcomm's business portfolio. Relative R&D soared from less than 1 percent to more than 25 percent in 1991, when the R&D maverick was establishing the role of CDMA in the United States. The percentage varied between 16 percent and 23 percent until 1996, when Qualcomm still pushed the standard internationally while building its manufacturing capabilities. Only at the end of the decade did the relative R&D decline to 10 percent or 11 percent.

The 4G Era: Broadband Cellular

Amid the 3G transition, researchers of the leading mobile players were already laying the groundwork for what some called 4G and others termed an undefined "wireless world," which is expected to become operational between 2008 and 2011.

Toward Seamless Convergence

In March 2001, a slate of leading European mobile vendors—Alcatel, L.M. Ericsson, Nokia, and Siemens—founded the new Wireless World Research Forum (WWRF). The organizers stressed that WWRF membership was open, but the list of the founders did not include network operators or software leaders. The goal of the new body was to "secure momentum, strategic orientation, and impact for the research on wireless communications beyond 3G," as Martin Haardt of Siemens put it.[45] WWRF was not the only arena of scientists, researchers, and industry practitioners seeking to define the post-3G specifications, but it reflected a wide variety of R&D efforts driving the 4G era—which will be characterized by broadband cellular communications.

The transition to 4G will not imply a change in interface technology, as did the shift from 2G (GSM in Europe) to 3G (UMTS in Europe). Instead, 4G promises to integrate different modes of wireless communication, from indoor networks such as wireless LANs and Bluetooth, to cellular signals, radio and TV broadcasting, as well as satellite communications. The ideal is a *seamless convergence* in which users of mobile devices would roam freely from one standard to another—pervasive and ubiquitous computing.[46] WWRF has sought to put such a technical view into a wider context that encompasses:

■ A user-centered approach, looking at the new ways in which users will interact with the wireless systems

■ New services and applications that become possible with the new technologies

■ New business models that may prevail in the future, overcoming the now-traditional user/service provider/network provider hierarchy

The major innovative thrust is expected to come from new ways of interacting within the system or among systems. An example for a vision of the Wireless World is the emerging need to bridge the real and the personal virtual world and to continuously stay in contact with both. The researchers were willing to define the objective—the Wireless World—but not the way to get there.

R&D Beyond 3G

Around 2001 and 2002, visions for future systems were developed in a number of bodies and interest groups, including standardization bodies, arenas for network operators, and equipment manufacturers. While each group had a different agenda, most shared a relatively harmonized view on next-generation networking. Some activities were at a global system level, seeking to embrace the entire system beyond 3G.[47] At the broadest level, the WWFR sought to synthesize these activities into three frameworks:

■ "MultiSphere," a reference framework relying on a user-centered approach, which shows the Wireless World as a succession of concentric spheres (from The Book of Visions 2000)

■ "Building Blocks of the Wireless World," a collection of system elements and functions believed to play a prominent part in the systems of the Wireless World

■ "Timeline," a view of the coming of the Wireless World and the actions that the WWRF is planning to undertake

Driven by 3G horizontalization, future vertical applications and services are expected to draw together a multitude of wireless technologies in an ad hoc manner. Those elements surround the user through a number of concentric circles, from the personal area network (PAN), which represents the user's closest interaction with the Wireless World, to the outmost sphere of the cyberworld furthest from the immediate real world. The building blocks consist of the major system elements expected to illustrate and make up the emerging Wireless World. Research into items considered crucial to the Wireless World was initiated in the late 1990s (for example, the 5th Framework Program of the European Commission). Prototypes are expected to become available in 2003. System development and integration would evolve at the end of 2006, leading to first commercial deployment around 2011.

Impending Struggle for 4G

Many of the components required to implement the Wireless World are expected to evolve from previous systems. Yet the definition of the 4G era indicates a paradigm shift. Instead of "standards" as these are understood currently, it would be based on policies, rules, and principles. The distinction is subtle but vital. It may well be in the interest of the incumbent leaders and mobile pioneers, but not necessarily in the interest of new entrants and IT leaders (who were not among the founders of the WWRF). If the evolution were to be "incrementalized," as the distinction indicates, it might reduce the potential for disruption and thereby industry transformation. Such a paradigm would reflect well the old voice business, which favored sustaining developments, but it would reflect poorly the emerging data business (from mainframes to minicomputers, PCs, Internet-enabled systems, and mobile Internet devices), in which disruptive change has been customary, if brief in temporal terms.

In the long term, the Japanese players in particular have struggled to speed up the transition from 3G to 4G.[48] With the phenomenal success of 2G services, and even before 3G services were under way, NTT DoCoMo Chairman Kouji Ohboshi made public his eagerness to push 4G development: "I would like to introduce 4G in about 2007."[49] Japanese players hope to lead breakthrough developments in 4G and begin standardizing the technology by 2005, while targeting commercialization of 4G technologies by 2010. With its highly successful i-mode, NTT DoCoMo hit the jackpot in Japan, but old regulatory rules have continued to hinder its internationalization. By December 2001, Masanobu Fujioka, general manager of Nippon Ericsson, expected 4G spectrum allocation to begin as early as 2005.[50] In late spring 2002, NTT DoCoMo announced trials for its 4G technology in Japan, initiating feasibility trials. Reportedly, the company expected to have maximum transmission speeds of 100M bits/s, which was more than *200 times* faster than the recently introduced 3G systems.

The longer the wait, the longer the European players would benefit from their regional superiority in 3G, and the greater the opportunities for the U.S. Internet leaders to develop mobile competences and capabilities, as well as disruptive tactics to overthrow European incumbents. NTT DoCoMo could establish a significant global position only by treating 3G as a transitional phase.

The pre-cellular and 1G era had been about America's dominance. The 2G era was about Euro-Nordic mobile leaders. The 3G era started with accelerating specialization and fragmentation of the industry value chain in Western Europe, Japan, the United States, and China. The 4G era is being initiated with great dreams of pervasive computing, R&D collaboration, and joint ventures (see Exhibit 2-5)—but the closer the implementation, the tougher would be the efforts at dominance and control, as so many times before over the past 130 years of mobile evolution.

In the wireless business, the standardization process has never been only about technology innovation. Nor has it ever been about market efficiency alone. It has always been permeated by the politics of standards, international trade and dynamic competition.

Exhibit 2-5. Toward a homogeneous global network.

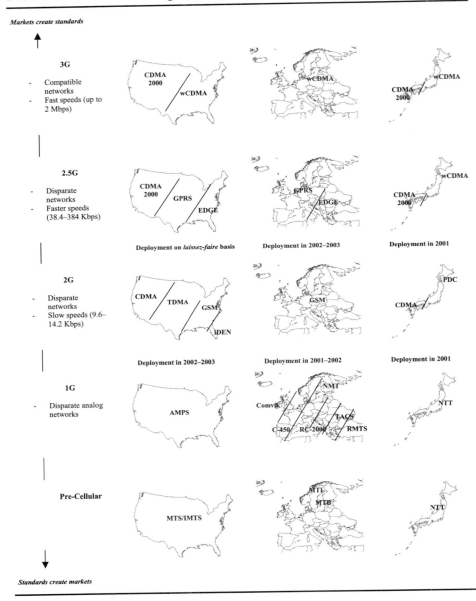

Markets create standards

3G
- Compatible networks
- Fast speeds (up to 2 Mbps)

2.5G
- Disparate networks
- Faster speeds (38.4–384 Kbps)

Deployment on *laissez-faire* basis   Deployment in 2002–2003   Deployment in 2001

2G
- Disparate networks
- Slow speeds (9.6–14.2 Kbps)

Deployment in 2002–2003   Deployment in 2001–2002   Deployment in 2001

1G
- Disparate analog networks

Pre-Cellular

Standards create markets

Part II

Network Operators: From National Monopolies to Market Liberalization

The next five chapters describe the successive waves of technology innovation that have shaped and formed mobile value systems, the strategic groups that have played the key role, as well as those geographic locations that have been central to this evolution. Part II focuses on network operators, from national monopolies to companies that emerged with market liberalization. It explores the geography of wireless competition, particularly the core clusters and lead markets in the United States, Western Europe and Nordic countries, and Asia-Pacific (i.e., Japan and China). It focuses on the dynamics of evolution from the pre-cellular era to the present and beyond, as well as the eclipse of old telecom monopolies and their more agile successors.

The chapters have been framed according to the successive waves of wireless evolution. Chapter 3 tells the story of the pre-cellular era, from Marconi's commercial innovation to early U.S. leadership, as demonstrated by the nation's police departments, FM communications during World War II, as well as postwar mobile telephone services. Chapter 4 examines the rise and decline of U.S. leadership, from AMPS and the 1G era to digitalization and the 3G transition. Chapter 5 concentrates on the Euro-Nordic pioneers, focusing on the GSM triumph and Nordic innovation, from digital cellular to multimedia cellular. Chapter 6 tells the story of Japan's mobile communications, concentrating on the regulatory barriers and the struggle for globalization. Chapter 7 examines the impetus for evolution in the vast Chinese market, which illustrates the future of the wireless business.

Chapter 3

The Pre-Cellular Era: From Marconi to U.S. Leadership

At the turn of the twentieth century, Marconi's wireless telegraphy dominated mobile communications. Innovation accelerated in the early 1920s, when emergency services in the United States initiated efforts to move wireless communications from the sea to the ground. With the shift to one-way and two-way mobile communications, the industry thrust migrated from Western Europe to North America. In the 1920s, the combination of motorization and Prohibition turned police departments into wireless pioneers. But it was the rise of FM communications and the military uses of Handie-Talkies and Walkie-Talkies during World War II that created a favorable environment for the emergence of a large-scale wireless industry. In the postwar era, rapid industry developments served as catalysts for new technology advances, including the development of the cellular concept, the opening of AT&T's supply chain, the growth of Motorola and other companies, the early markets in private mobile radio (PMR), and the first consumer services (i.e., MTS and IMTS).

Marconi and Market Creation

In the United States, the railroad, the telegraph, and telecommunications played key roles in the technology revolution of the late nineteenth century. These industries provided the fast, dependable transportation and communication that was essential to high-volume production and distribution, or what Alfred D. Chandler, Jr. has called "the hallmark of large modern manufacturing or marketing enterprises."[1] They were also the first modern business enterprises to appear in the United States in the sense that they required a large number of full-time managers to coordinate, control, and evaluate the activities of a number of dispersed operating units. If the new technologies, products, and services built upon unprecedented scale, the companies behind them also enabled extraordinary scope. By the 1880s, American consumer products first burst their formerly regional bounds. In the aftermath of the Civil War and Reconstruction, the states were one nation, politically. Concurrently, the new communications technologies extended the geographically limited markets by incorporating the entire nation into a veritable mass market.

At first, many people were skeptical about the value of the telegraph and the telephone, which Alexander Graham Bell developed in 1876. In contrast to consumers and businesses, emergency services readily acknowledged the vital function of these new technologies, which were designed to deliver timely information. Only a year after the Bell invention, police departments were among the first organizations to use telephones extensively.[2] The value of the wireless was acknowledged far more readily than that of the telephone. In the United States, the wireless was an essential part of the communications revolution. In 1835, Samuel F.B. Morse demonstrated the principle of the electromagnetic telegraph. The first commercially successful telegraph line was introduced between Washington, D.C. and Baltimore in 1844. When Western Union was founded in 1851, more than fifty telegraph companies operated in the United States. During the Civil War, the telegraph itself became mobile. Field telegraphs were deployed as movable instruments to establish temporary telegraph stations linking adjacent troops during battle conditions. There were no doubts over the vital function of the wireless in emergency situations and military crises.

Most accounts of the wireless business and its evolution stress supply-side factors, particularly technology innovation. Necessary but not adequate, these determinants explain little of *market* evolution, or demand-side factors, not to mention the subtle interplay of supply and demand in mobile communications. In the wireless business, technology change typically has reshaped existing markets and resulted in new ones, which have influenced innovation. Furthermore, subsequent wireless markets (as opposed to technologies) have not been mutually exclusive; they have been layered upon each other. The emergency services, for instance, prompted pioneering in industrial services, which led to the business markets, which in turn triggered the expansion of the consumer markets. Conversely, when the industry thrust shifted to corporate markets in the analog era, the prevailing dominant designs (particularly in terminals and infrastructure) reshaped emergency services.

Historically, the evolution of wireless markets originates from Marconi's era. Soon after the invention of the wireless in the late-nineteenth century came the first efforts to commercialize the new technology. Following his first successful radio system in 1897, Marconi, unlike most of his scientific precursors, set out to transform the invention into a *commercially* viable business. It was Marconi who initiated wireless *market* creation in the maritime sector and naval communications, primarily in the United States and the developed markets of Western Europe. He was not the "father of the wireless." Like most inventions, the wireless telegraph had multiple founding fathers (and mothers!). However, Marconi did give rise to the *business* of wireless—just as he pioneered the first wireless markets.

Creation of First Wireless Markets

By the late 1890s, Marconi had a revolutionary idea, but no customers; these had to be *created*. Technology innovation had to be coupled with market diffusion, through commercialization. There was nothing automatic about this process. It was entrepreneurial by nature. To some extent, these pioneer years of the wireless business are reminiscent of American success in early mass marketing.[3] Like the pioneers of Coca-Cola, General Motors, A&P, or Sears, Marconi was motivated by an entrepreneurial drive and vision, which were essential to create and organize market development. First-mover advantages (coupled with Marconi's shrewd business model and efforts to secure patent benefits) were expected to result in lucrative profits, while serving as barriers against potential entrants. In addition, new players were forced to emulate the first mover's strategy, in which case they suffered from differentiation challenges (Marconi had already established a positive reputation and created the first customer relationships), or relative cost disadvantages (only a new and disruptive innovation could obsolete Marconi's sustaining business models). Furthermore, the long-term success of Marconi's wireless empire depended on the ability to manage organizational capabilities and environmental change over time.

There were also substantial differences between Marconi and the legends of American marketing. Today, mobility is primarily about global mass consumer markets. That was not the case in Marconi's era. His enterprise operated in government and institutional markets (state and political administrations, admiralties), and later in industrial services (naval communications). Indeed, these efforts differed from those of the classic American marketers in two respects. First, while the strategy of profit through volume was the keystone of many successful U.S. marketing companies, Marconi's business model built profitability with national governments, defense forces, and maritime sectors in several developed economies. Second, because mass production was not central to Marconi's operation, mass marketing was not required either. Of course, volume advantages were real and substantial in his business as well, but these did not pertain to mass-manufacturing or mass-marketing capabilities.

Due to heavy telecom regulation worldwide from the late-nineteenth century to the late-twentieth century, the dual nature of the wireless business—driven initially by public sector and today by the private sector—resulted in complicated industry arrangements. As long as national governments and PTTs drove technology innovation and industry evolution, *public policies* rather than private strategies determined the winners and the losers. Business was domestic and as much about politics as about markets. Since the 1980s, the roles of these drivers have gradually been reversed in the marketplace. Today, *firm strategies* rather than public policies dictate the winners and the losers. Business is increasingly global and market-driven. Political considerations still play a substantial role, because of the importance of the industry for economic growth and national defense, military, and security policies—as witnessed by U.S. and worldwide mobile developments after September 11, 2001.

At the turn of the nineteenth century, Marconi knew that being an innovator was only part of the game. In the wireless business, one also had to be an astute politician, an entrepreneur with one eye constantly scanning for new opportunities, a street-smart fund-raiser and PR person, a shrewd coalition-builder, and an inspiring leader. To stimulate demand, Marconi initiated talks with governments, defense forces, and national telegraph and telecom authorities (the precursors of the national PTTs)—first in Western Europe and later in the United States.

Wireless and the PTTs: An Uneasy Alliance

Since the Italian Ministry of Posts and Telegraphs was indifferent to Marconi's experiments, the young innovator left to raise capital in London's City, the financial center for the world's leading maritime nation and the greatest trading empire at the turn of the nineteenth century. Marconi thought that the British might understand better the long-term business potential of the wireless. In London, he was introduced to William Preece, engineer-in-chief of the General Post Office (GPO). In late 1896, Marconi demonstrated his system to the British GPO and the armed services. Along with governments, defense forces and the maritime sector, the national post, and telecom and telegraph administrations became the first customers of the wireless vendors.

As long as Marconi's demonstrations and landmark trials covered only distances of one to four kilometers, Preece tolerated the Italian. In private, the Brit was more of a skeptic and had little faith in the competitive threat of the wireless. When, in 1897, Marconi's trial extended the range to fourteen kilometers, Preece thought that day wireless might substitute *his* business. Why should he fund a rival? Marconi had to look for new financiers. When the Office argued that even a ship-to-shore service required a license, it prompted the first wireless regulatory dispute. For an entire century, this uneasy relationship between the wireless and the Post Office (and its successors, the national PTTs) would endure with occasional eruptions—until the global telecom reform in 1998, which ensured market liberalization.

Birth of an Industry: Courting Admiralties and Shipping Companies

In July 1897, the Wireless Telegraph & Signal Company was registered in the U.K. Because commercial success depended on extending the range of transmission, Marconi soon trebled it. Capital expenditures allowed R&D efforts, which translated to a rising rate of innovation. But incremental advancements required growing investments. To boost innovation, Marconi would have to expand business. And to grow his business, he would have to improve the technology. In December 1898, his company opened the world's first wireless factory at Chelmsford in Essex. He was still preoccupied with demonstrations to prove that the wireless could be used to protect lives at sea by means of ship-to-shore communication.

In the United States, wireless communication was quickly put to practical use, especially to communicate with remote mobile units (ships, airplanes) and less accessible locations (islands), where laying wires was not considered practical. During these early years, wireless proved most popular in emergency services. The first installations included the establishment of wireless communication with a lightship off the coast of Fire Island, New York, in 1899 and the linking of five Hawaiian Islands by radiotelegraph two years later. Like in Western Europe, radio communication was particularly useful in the maritime sector. By 1901, the United States Navy established a wireless system for ship-to-shore communication. Trials with two-way systems followed in the mid-1910s. The first commercial radiotelephone service was launched between the United States and Europe in 1927.[4]

When Marconi transmitted the first international wireless message across the English Channel, his customer was the French government, which appointed naval and military officers to conduct tests between the land and French warships. These deals prompted the British Admiralty to ask Marconi to fit three Royal Navy ships with wireless for its first use during naval maneuvers. After reporting on yacht races in The America's Cup, Marconi had less success with trials on warships. He did register a subsidiary, The Marconi Wireless Telegraph Company of America, which later became Radio Corporation of America, RCA. He also formed The Marconi International Marine Communication Company, which proved to be even more important vis-à-vis market evolution.

Until 1898, Marconi's customers had been governments and national PTTs, but now he attempted sectoral deals. To make use of the new opportunities in shipping, The Marconi International Marine Communication Company undertook *all* maritime work. At the turn of the nineteenth century, intercontinental transport was marine. When Marconi commercialized the wireless invention, he essentially connected ships at sea. This achievement held the promise of a new and equally magnificent market. What if these pioneer services could be taken from the seas to the ground, as well?

Market Creation: Naval Communication

Before World War I, early radio pioneers built their business models on navy contracts. Although radio initially failed to transmit speech effectively, it had a far greater range for wireless telegraphy than photophone, and it could penetrate rain, fog, and even buildings. As radio development substituted the photophone, the primary initial application was for naval communication. Through the 1910s, all intercontinental transport remained marine, and the primary opportunities and clients were in the shipping and maritime segments.

Between 1915 and 1916, the United States War Department began a research program to develop ship-to-ship and ship-to-shore communication. Though the results came too late to shape the war events, an experimental ship-to-shore radiotelephone service was established in 1919 for ships along the eastern seaboard. A decade later, a commercial service was initiated for ships on the Atlantic.[5]

Marconi's first order was from Lloyds of London for communication to lightships. In 1900, it was followed by The Royal Navy's order for thirty-two wireless sets for a total cost of £6,000 with an annual royalty payment of £3,200. This business model—an initial payment for equipment and an ongoing revenue flow—became so central to Marconi's wireless strategy that he replicated it in his dealings with the French government and shipping firms worldwide.[6] The model built on a commercial version of public monopoly to achieve economic rents. As long as it was not threatened by new and disruptive technologies, it served him well. In his next project, Marconi became the first person to bridge the Atlantic by wireless. In a substantial technological and financial gamble, he made Nova Scotia the North American terminus of the first transatlantic radio communications service. The service linked the Old World and New World by the wireless. Despite the huge gamble, this technological achievement represented only incremental progress in terms of customer creation. To ensure a satisfactory cash flow, Marconi continued to rely on his lucrative contracts with the Admiralty, Lloyds, and various shipping companies.

By 1903, Marconi's company had built a number of stations on shore. Concurrently, many merchant ships had been fitted with its wireless sets, which had to be rented from the company and were operated by Marconi's personnel. The latter could communicate with operators using apparatus from rival companies only during emergencies. The shrewd arrangements and exclusive rights enhanced Marconi's growing maritime business. As the company began to generate lucrative profits, the number of its critics grew. To put an end to what they perceived as a ruthless drive for monopoly, the Germans called for an international conference, but failed to overthrow the Italian's international empire. Marconi's business arrangements made life difficult for challengers and new entrants. The model originated from first-mover advantages, but ultimately it was not sustainable. Marconi's company retained its edge only through ceaseless innovation. With new and more efficient substitutes, the wireless empire, like its successors (internationally driven operators and vendors), was doomed. As companies have chased the wireless frontier, success has often bred failure—through the complacency of industry leaders, the disruptive potential of new technologies, and the rise of successful challengers and startups.

Rise of Regulation: The *Titanic* Tragedy

In 1909, Marconi shared the credit when 1,700 lives were saved through wireless distress calls as two liners collided and one of them sank off the coast of the United States. A year later, Marconi again enjoyed success when the wireless was used for the first time to apprehend a dangerous criminal. Concurrently, it became mandatory for very large ships to be equipped with wireless and have at least one operator. These reforms were not adequate. On April 14, 1912, the liner *S.S. Titanic*, on her maiden voyage to New York, struck an iceberg less than a minute after it was sighted by the lookout. The "CQD" (General Distress Call) was not made until thirty-five minutes later. Some fifty-eight miles to the southeast of the *Titanic*, the *Carpathia*'s wireless operator was about to retire when he happened to contact the *Titanic*. The *Titanic* requested urgent aid. Upon arrival at the scene, the *Carpathia* found only emptiness except for the lifeboats. Some 1,500 lives were lost, including one of the two Marconi wireless operators, whose distress signals brought rescue to more than 700 survivors.

Disaster investigations led to a call for an International Radio-Telegraphic Convention in 1912, which established regulations and procedures governing wireless services aboard ships and shore stations. In November 1913, the "Safety of Life at Sea" Conference in London was a landmark event in wireless communications. Sweeping regulations that would govern all ships at sea, whether motor propelled or sailed, were put into effect.[7] National governments initiated regulatory efforts to create order amid confusion and interference in unregulated radio experimenting. In the United States, the Radio Act of 1912 required station and operator licenses and assigned some spectrum blocks to existing users. The objective was pragmatic, but the execution contributed to new problems; practically any person who filed for an operating license received one.

This pattern of noble intentions, regulatory delays, and chaotic results set the scene for regulatory policies for decades to come in U.S. mobile communications.

Marconi's International Wireless Empire

By 1912, the Marconi company had manufactured almost 1,000 wireless sets—twice as many as Telefunken, its close rival. The firm provided both the equipment and the operators. That year, the number of overseas companies in Marconi's international operation (see Exhibit 3-1) increased to thirteen. In some countries, including the United States, Canada, France, Argentina, Russia, Italy, and Spain, these companies had registered significant stocks. The most successful were the British Marconi Wireless Telegraph Company, with a capital investment of £1.5 million, and the American Society, with a registered stock of $10 million. Marconi also had headquarters in more than half a dozen major cities worldwide. Additionally, a network of dozens of stations covered all continents, from North and South America to Europe, Asia-Pacific, Africa, and Australia. Marconi never hid his disappointment that Italian finan-

Exhibit 3-1. Marconi's wireless empire: headquarters of international companies (1912).

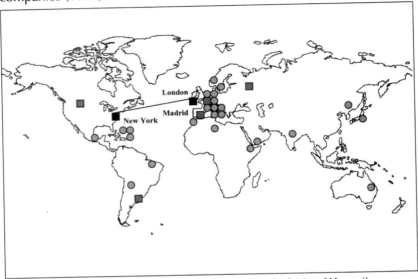

In 1912, New York and London were the two most lucrative subsidiaries of Marconi's international wireless empire. Other major headquarters connected the core operation with Continental Europe (Bruxelles, Paris, Rome, Madrid), Russia (Petrograd), and Latin America (Buenos Aires).

In addition to the headquarters of Marconi's companies, a network of stations ranged around the work, including Aden, Algeria, Australia, the Azores, Belgium, Brazil, French Guiana, Burma, China, France, Germany, Holland, India, Japan, Mexico, Morocco, Norway, Sweden, Uruguay, the West Indies with Curacao, Jamaica, Trinidad and Tobago, Zanzibar.

In Marconi's home base, Italy, these stations included Asinara, Bari, Capo Mele, Capo Sperone, Maddalena, Forte Spurio, Monte Cappuccini, Monte San Giuliano, Ponza, Reggio, Santa Maria de Leuca, Venice, and Viesti.

ciers had not been more forthcoming in their support. "If I had been listened to, Italy would have had the chance of becoming the virtual owner of the large organization I had set up, freeing herself from the stranglehold of the foreign Cable Companies."[8]

Like its successors, Marconi's corporation sought worldwide leverage. From the late 1890s, its objective was to leverage the competencies of the parent's core capabilities in lead markets. Innovation was developed at the center (the United States and the key European operations) and transferred to overseas units. With a shrewd business model, Marconi's company had initially enjoyed near-monopolistic advantages and a configuration of assets and capabilities that fit its environment. Similarly, it had developed the kind of overseas operations that fit the overseas trade of its era. The success of the model was dependent on the development and diffusion of knowledge from and through the center.

When Guglielmo Marconi died in Rome on July 20, 1937, wireless stations closed down and transmitters all over the world fell silent in a gesture of respect to the wireless pioneer. Some fifteen to twenty years before, his innovation had traveled from the sea to the streets of Detroit. But it was not "Ma Bell" that first developed the mobile market. As the Mafia learned to use cars for smuggling, the police seized the wireless as an antidote. In the United States, the cops were the true wireless pioneers.

From AM and FM Communications to Wireless Services

The early decades of the wireless invention witnessed efforts to extend the mobile business into consumer markets. With Lee de Forest's first transmission to an automobile in 1906, the car had to be stationary to receive its message, so the transmission was of little practical use. But the message itself demonstrated substantial industry foresight: "How do you like your first wireless ride? The fire department, steamships, and railways ought to adopt the same method of communication."[9] Concurrently, Abraham White, the president of De Forest Wireless published a news release that went even further: "Hereafter we hope it will be possible for businessmen, even while automobiling, to be kept in constant touch."[10] The vision was sound, but White's firms failed.

Prior to early *civilian* use of mobile telephones, telephone companies had manufactured portable telephones for internal use, for example, to test lines. These had also been used by the armed forces in fixed systems. During the 1890s, L.M. Ericsson had developed several types of transportable telephones which were bought by Swedish defense forces.[11] In 1910, Lars Magnus Ericsson, founder of L.M. Ericsson, a leading Swedish equipment manufacturer, and his wife Hilda began to develop a car phone. The horseless carriage served as an early "telepoint" application because telephone calls could be made from the car. Instead of access by radio, Hilda used two long sticks, like fishing rods to hook them over a pair of telephone wires. Lars Magnus cranked the dynamo handle of the telephone, which produced a signal to an operator in the nearest exchange.[12] The Ericssons had not come up with mobile telephony, but they had pioneered a rudimentary form of personal mobility, which provided telephone service from a stationary car.

Cops as Innovators

Apparently, the first version of a truly mobile radiotelephone was developed in 1924 by Bell Laboratories. Unlike telephone, wireless communications found practical uses rapidly. But AT&T did not pioneer land mobile in the United States. The development of wireless service was a marginal objective for Bell

System planners and engineers. Like the relationship between Marconi and Preece, wireless innovation and AT&T did not go well together. The Bell System had little interest in developing technologies, products, and services that might cannibalize its lucrative revenue base. Due to AT&T's *de facto* monopoly in wired communications, its ambivalence was soon shared by regulatory regimes. The earliest efforts toward wireless communications among people and vehicles were taken by police departments, which struggled with the consequences of motorization and Prohibition.

The first land mobile systems had been employed by public safety agencies. The earliest use of electronic communications in law enforcement may have occurred in 1845, when the New York Police Department used a telegraph system to link signal boxes for patrolmen with their station houses. In 1920, the first radio station was issued to the NYPD. A year later, Detroit's police pioneered experiments in wireless communications.

Detroit's Wireless Pioneers

Detroit's first nonmilitia peace officers were appointed in 1801 and a night watch patrol was established three years later. The Metropolitan Police Department followed only in 1865. In the beginning, the police were watchmen, patrolling neighborhoods and business districts on foot. The closeness of the cop on the beat with the community reinforced the bond between the two. But foot patrol was difficult to supervise and beat officers spent much of their tours inside warm stores with friendly merchants. In 1810, there were only 750 residents in Detroit, which covered just three square miles. By 1870, the physical size of the city had quadrupled, and the population had increased to almost 80,000. With rapid expansion, even motivated police officers found it impossible to cover their areas in a single tour of duty. Furthermore, critical time lapses existed between the incident and the arrival of the beat officer. To alleviate the transportation problems, the police department used open farm wagons and later, bicycles, to disperse and collect patrol officers.

The rapid growth of the city strained human resources, which prompted the department to resort to motorization. The horseless carriage was actually born in Europe, and the first American gasoline car was built in Springfield, Massachusetts. Detroit's early automobile pioneers had to compete with carmakers in Cleveland, Toledo, Buffalo, Hartford, St. Louis, and elsewhere. In 1909—before Detroit evolved into the leading automobile cluster worldwide—the police commissioner began to use the automobile for police work. With the "Roaring Twenties," foot patrols and bicycles were no longer a match for speeding automobiles. Prohibition provided gangsters with a lucrative business, which also allowed them to purchase high-powered cars and prompted the police to put cops on wheels across the country. Still, dispatching the cars remained a problem. In 1917, the Detroit Police Department began to test motorized patrol units across the city using a "booth car" system. The booth was a small building equipped with a potbelly stove, a coal bin, and a telephone. One officer stayed at the booth with the car, the other patrolled the beat by foot. This practice, however, left the officer and the car out of contact with the police department for hours at a time.[13]

Playing Violins and Catching Criminals

If a ship like the *Titanic* could call for help across many miles, wondered William P. Rutledge, Detroit's police superintendent and later commissioner, why not a roving patrol car? After all, the automobile had given the criminal an advantage in speed that could not be overcome by police cars controlled by telephones. In 1921, the Detroit Police Department installed the first land-mobile radiotelephone systems for police car dispatch and became the first to test voice transmission. Like the later paging systems, the new systems offered one-way transmission, so patrolmen had to stop at a wireline telephone station to call back in. Police calls were interspersed with a regular commercial program. Both voice and radio telegraph were tried, but the basic problem of receiver instability and lack of sensitivity limited the coverage.[14] Detroit's police department also battled with the Department of Commerce, which was reluctant to authorize police radio. After six years of futile experimentation and bureaucratic struggle, the accumulated frustration caused the cops to lock up the radio room. That very year, Robert Batts, a future Motorolan, convinced the Detroit police commissioner that he could solve the problem of car radio reception. With the creation of the Federal Radio Commission (FRC) in 1927, Detroit reactivated its radio tests, and the first operational one-way mobile radio system, KOP, went on the air in April 1928.

Substantial technical obstacles remained. The vacuum tubes of the radio receiver were fragile and required extensive cushioning. Six-volt batteries had to be mounted on the running boards to support the electrical systems. The battery had to be replaced every four hours. Funding grew problematic because the city council was reluctant to spend public dollars on an unproven endeavor. Regulatory conflicts increased, as well. The FRC refused to renew the department's radio license several times because it failed to live up to requirements that KOP broadcast "entertainment during regular hours, with police calls interspersed as required." After one such refusal, Commissioner Rutledge asked, "Do we have to play a violin solo before we dispatch the police to catch a criminal?"[15] Well, actually, they did. As the first radio broadcasting stations cooperated with police to carry bulletins to police cars, phrases like "Calling all cars!" were interspersed with entertainment and commercial programming. The experiment was considered successful, and in 1924, *The Detroit News* called for more radio dispatched cars: "The motor car has been a big asset to criminals, because it permitted a quick getaway. But the radio is swifter than any motor vehicle ever invented. . . . The police department now has three radio-equipped flyers. It should have more. The motorized bandits would soon learn that Detroit had become a trap for them and they would move on to some town with less modern ideas."[16]

When two seven-passenger cars known as "cruisers" were equipped with new radio receivers, the radio-dispatched police car became a permanent fixture in Detroit. Meanwhile, the Detroit Police Radio System drew worldwide publicity, and visitors arrived from all over the world to inspect the system. Other city police departments planned radio systems, and like Detroit, they were forced to build their own receivers. In the end of 1930, seventy-five radio cars had been equipped and were credited with more than 20,000 arrests. By 1931, all New York Police Department cars were equipped to receive radio messages from three transmitting stations. One-way mobile radio communications was a dramatic improvement, but obstacles remained. Officers had to stop at a phone or call box to acknowledge a radio dispatch. They could not coordinate law-enforcement activities with other officers. And they were unable to request assistance.

From One-Way AM to Two-Way FM Communications

In March 1933, the first two-way radio communications were established in the police department of Bayonne, New Jersey. The Detroit department implemented two-way communications only a few months later. By 1934, there were 194 municipal police radio systems and fifty-eight state police radio stations in the United States, which served more than 5,000 radio-equipped police cars.[17] During these early years, the combination of a powerful transmitter and a sensitive transmitter confined the first systems to "push-to-talk" transmission, and the bulky radio equipment filled the entire trunk of the car. The ordinary radio listener could manipulate the antenna to improve the signal, but the wireless user was vulnerable to fluctuations in channel conditions, which seemed impossible to tame—until Edwin H. Armstrong and the new FM era.

Motorola's Entry Into Police Radio Communications

In 1926, national radio sales reached half a billion dollars in the United States. The future looked bright for manufacturers who struggled to keep pace with the public's seemingly insatiable appetite for radios. The auto radio also marked the first use of the Motorola trademark. Radio stocks boosted the exchanges until the Great Crash of 1929. Even the Depression increased the nation's appetite for entertainment and, thereby, car radios. In 1932, 143,000 sets were sold across the country. Because of complicated installation procedures, poor audio quality, and high costs, the car radio remained something of a rarity. Paul Galvin, the founder of Motorola, challenged his employees to design a simplified auto radio that could be installed in most automobiles at a reasonable price. By the mid-1930s, the Motorola auto radios were endorsed by radio and film stars. The company was prompted to enter the home radio business, as well. These developments were triggered by Motorola's experiments with police radio. In 1936, the FCC allocated the first permanent radio channels for police communications, while Galvin Manufacturing introduced its first AM mobile radio receiver, the Police Cruisers. The following year, the company launched its first station transmitting equipment. "There was a need," noted Galvin, "and I could see it was a market nobody owned."[18]

The invention of FM coincided with Motorola's official entry into police radio communications in 1937, which initiated its industry leadership. By 1940, most police systems in the United States had converted to FM.[19] The demand for two-way radios rose. "Not only law enforcement agencies," recalls a veteran industry observer, "but the utilities industry, truckers, taxicabs, forest rangers, and other operations began using such radios once the FCC allowed their use for emergencies."[20] Paul Galvin hired professor Dan Noble as chief of R&D at Motorola. In the late 1930s, Noble had developed the first two-way FM mobile system for the Connecticut State Police. For its part, the FRC loosened its cautious grip on licensing the airwaves in the early 1930s, setting aside a few specially designated police frequencies. So began Motorola's cooperation with police departments. Recalls Elmer Wavering, who devoted his time to Motorola's car radio line and, in 1939, became the head of the company's Special Police Radio Department:

> ... it was 1933 or 1934, that we signed a contract with the Chicago Police Department for one of the first two-way radio communications systems in the world. When Chicago went on the air with their two-way police communications ... almost immediately we were deluged with calls from large cities and even from some of the states adjacent to the Chicago area about two-way communications. From that original impulse we received contracts from four states very close together with Illinois, Iowa, Missouri, and I think Wisconsin ... and then we expanded eventually to the whole country.[21]

Eventually, the experimental one-way police radio department grew into the massive Motorola Communications Sector. But the rise of police radio in the United States was not just about technology innovation. A valid argument could be made that it was actually about *service* innovation. Initially, the very same Motorolans who had been so adept at marketing and installing the company's over-the-counter entertainment radio were over their heads with the police radio. The latter innovation was too sophisticated for the off-the-shelf orientation of most wholesalers. As one astute observer said to Galvin, "You're selling a black box; you should be selling a black box with an assistant, with someone to maintain it."[22] In 1940, Galvin adopted a radically new approach. Motorola's police radio line would be sold *directly* to the customer, cutting out the distributor completely. The principal advantage of factory-direct sales was the company's ability to maintain control over its product. Direct sales brought order to an otherwise chaotic marketing process. Like so many times before, what began as a divergent idea quickly evolved into accepted industry wisdom.

Early Regulation: Broad Mandate, Conflicting Objectives

Although Motorola converted car radios for police use, this enterprise remained largely informal because of regulatory barriers. At first, industry participants hoped that the FRC would overcome policy-created obstacles in the launch of the private-sector radio. Still, an influential FRC report cautioned that "no consideration can be given to the authorization of such a service until a sufficient number of frequencies becomes available."[23] In 1932, spectrum scarcity was already a substantial constraint. Through the next seventy years, the spectrum issue would resurface with every wireless debate.

With the exception of requests from the progressive urban police departments, the demand for radio communications grew slowly nationwide. Equipment remained relatively expensive, hard to maintain, occasionally unreliable due to the level of technology, and limited in use value. In the mid-1930s, law enforcement officials established the Associated Police Communications Officers (APCO) to pressure Washington with a collective voice for reasonable rules and expanded frequency assignments. Only then—after more than a decade of ambivalence and regulatory stumbling by the FCR—did the newly formed Federal Communications Commission (FCC) began to set standards, issue regulations, and allocate spectrum to a growing number of interested police jurisdictions. The federal government gave the new agency a broad public interest mandate as license awards became subject to "public interest, convenience, and necessity." Due to its extraordinary breadth, the mandate could be adapted to a wide variety of new circumstances; but by the same token, it gave rise to highly conflicting interpretations. Founded as part of Roosevelt's New Deal, the commission promoted social change while constraining monopolistic concentration. The objectives of social equity and economic efficiency proved difficult to reconcile. Radio users such as taxi services or a tow truck dispatchers required little spectrum to conduct their business. By comparison, radiotelephone used large frequency blocks to serve just a few people.

Mobile radio was used increasingly by police in the 1930s. Gradually, it spread to fire departments and other emergency services. The FCC, with its mandate to regulate wired telephone business *and* to manage the radio spectrum, controlled the presumably scarce and therefore highly valuable resource. Wired telephone business was synonymous with the powerful Bell System. Wireless business was a marginal niche with intriguing long-term opportunities, but relatively low cash prospects. The ambivalence of AT&T over mobile communications soon extended to the FCC, which was extremely cautious in allocating the radio frequency spectrum. The commission insisted on complicated licenses and tightly regulated use of the airwaves. Priority was granted to emergency services, government agencies, utility companies, and other services that the FCC deemed helpful to the most people. Starting in 1940, the growth of two-way land-mobile radio took off rapidly. That year, there were only a few thousand licensed mobile transmitters. The number increased to 86,000 in 1948; 695,000 in 1958; and 1.4 million in 1963.[24]

From the very beginning, the FCC fueled public debate, private frustration, lobbying, and trade protests within the mobile business. However, the industry was still in its precommercial phase. The industry and the regulators avoided a major confrontation until the postwar era. Things would get much worse before they would get any better.

The Impact of World War II

The outbreak of World War I stimulated new advances in the wireless industry. In 1914, an estimated 2,000 to 3,000 wireless sets were in use worldwide. Britain dominated this new market, along with the international cable telegraph market. With the war, amateur experiments were stopped and the Admiralty took over production at Marconi's Chelmsford works. However, the technology did not meet the British army's requirements for portability and reliability. Today, handsets weigh less than one hundred grams. During World War I, Marconi's smallest equipment weighted eighty-six pounds (thirty-eight kg), while other sets required four to five horses to carry them. One set, which was intended for aircraft, weighed 200 pounds (ninety kg). Another, for airships, weighed 500 pounds (220 kg). Still, by 1916, the British army was equipped with trench sets, one of the first "transportable" designs, even if only one of these spark transmitters could be used on each divisional front.[25]

The Triumph of FM Handie-Talkies and Walkie-Talkies

When World War II broke out in Europe in 1939, the focus of the British radio receiver industry on the war effort resulted in the design and production of radar. The manufacturing of two-way radio sets was an extension of skills and capabilities in domestic radio receivers. American forces took advantage of expertise at General Electric and Motorola. Convinced that a major military conflict was inevitable (well before American entry into the war and without a government contract), Galvin directed the company's resources to the development of a light and portable two-way radio to replace the primitive and cumbersome radio equipment. In 1940 and 1941, Bell Labs and Western Electric were commissioned to develop mobile communications systems for military vehicles, including tanks and military aircraft. As U.S. defense forces opted for the FM, great advances were made in size, weight, cost, performance, and reliability. The mobile communications of the U.S. forces were simply "beyond anything either the enemy or the other allied nations possessed."[26]

With World War II, most manufacturers of commercial (AM) radio sets converted their production to supply military requirements (mainly FM). An enduring result of the war years was commercial FM mass-manufacturing capability. In late 1940, a Motorola engineering team produced prototypes of the five-pound *Handie-Talkie* radio, an AM unit with a one-mile range. A year later, the United States Army awarded Motorola a small contract, and by the end of the war, the company manufactured more than 100,000 units. The shortcomings of the SCR-536 *Handie-Talkie* radio, especially short-range and static interference, led the company to continue R&D of another product early in the war. The signal corps needed a long-range portable radio for frontline troops to integrate radio communications among artillery, armored, and infantry divisions. Beating the rival manufacturers, the Galvin SCR-300, a high-frequency FM unit, was the superior entry. With it a thirty-five-pound backpack and a range of ten miles or more, it could be tuned to various frequencies and had stable frequency calibration. These Walkie-Talkies were used throughout Europe and the Pacific and provided critical radio links at Anzio, Guadalcanal, Iwo Jima, and Normandy (see Exhibit 3-2).

Expansion of the U.S. Radio Industry

With the wartime demand for added production, U.S. radio industry employment expanded fivefold between 1941 and 1945, while aggregate net earnings increased twentyfold. Radio technology and products became more sophisticated. Significant technological advances included standardization of components; miniaturization and the consequent reduction in the size and weight of equipment; and the increasing use of scientific talent to design equipment and manufacturing processes. At the end of the war, the radio industry had become aware of the magnificent commercial value of applying radio technologies to consumer and industrial products. Furthermore, it had acquired expertise and capabilities in manufacturing large quantities of sophisticated electronic equipment at relatively low cost. In the coming decades, these factors—the commercial potential and mass production capabilities of the radio—transformed the radio business into the electronics industry.

Following WW II, many servicemen returned to civilian life with knowledge of radio technology and an appreciation of its value and convenience. Surplus military radio equipment, particularly the Motorola *Handie-Talkie*, entered civilian life as taxi dispatch radios. The FCC gave taxicab companies one experimental radio channel. One of the earliest postwar taxicab radio systems was installed for Checker Cab in Beaumont, Texas. In the evolution of two-way radio business, this was the first opportunity to sell radio not on its public safety merits, but on its commercial market benefits. Industry practitioners saw the moment in evangelical terms. As one Motorolan summed up the company's pitch to taxicab owners:

Exhibit 3-2. Radio communications during the war years.

The SCR-536 *Handie-Talkie* portable radios became the chief communications venues for soldiers, squads, and platoons on the front lines. Other FM communications radios included the SCR-509 and 510 models, and the SCR-609 radios, used in jeeps, tanks, and other vehicles or as portable units.

During World War II, the SCR-300 radios were being carried backpack-style, as well as mounted in the turrets of tanks, and in reconnaissance planes.

Radio would be the answer to the cab companies' prayers. Telephone line charges for cab stands would disappear. Income per cab would soar. They would no longer be tied to a fixed cab location or be forced to cruise the high customer areas.[27]

Wireless business in America was about to enter a new era—that of service *commercialization*.

Commercialization of Wireless Service

Between 1940 and 1948, the number of wireless users in the United States soared from a few thousand to 86,000. As the numbers climbed, regulators attempted to facilitate market expansion. By 1945, the FCC began to explore spectrum allocations for a wide variety of uses in industrial services:

- Police and fire departments
- Forestry services
- Electric, gas, and water utilities
- Transportation services, including taxis, railroads, buses, streetcars, and trucks

A year later, AT&T enabled the first trucker mobile call, which was soon expanded. These explorations precipitated the expansion of the industrial services market, which would be swept by corporate users in the 1980s, by mass consumer markets in the 1990s, and by global mass consumer markets during the 3G transition. In 1949, the FCC officially recognized mobile radio as a new class of service, even though most users were not yet interconnected to the telephone network.[28] The typical wireless user was not a consumer, but a dispatch worker in a private mobile system. The Cold War contributed to the growth of two-way radio by increasing investment in civil defense and general emergency preparedness. These actions encouraged the FCC to make more room on the airwaves and loosen licensing restrictions—which, in turn, provided another boost to Motorola's expansion.

Private Mobile Radio

In the aftermath of World War II, Motorola set out to dominate the business segments in which it already had experience, from two-way radio systems to microwave radio systems. In 1944, the company had already created the first experimental system to use frequencies above one hundred MHz in Miami, Florida. In 1948, the *Dispatcher* line of two-way FM radio communications equipment took advantage of the additional radio spectrum for industry and business. The spectrum allowed the company to boost the commercial and industrial market for two-way radios for public safety systems, especially in police, fire, and medical services. Eventually, commercial transportation customers included railroads, taxis, trucks, and bus fleets. New customers comprised oil companies and natural gas and electric power utilities, rural industries (farming, forestry, and lumber), material handling and warehousing industries, and the construction industry. By 1952, 350,000 two-way mobile radios were in use; Motorola had manufactured half of them. The company also supplied more than two-thirds of the operating microwave systems in the United States.[29]

Americans were not alone in developing the private mobile radio (PMR) market. However, the pace of industry evolution was fastest in the United States, which also provided the greatest economies of scale.[30] Until the arrival of the junction transistors, handportable equipment had not been practical in wireless communications. By the mid-1960s, The British Pye manufactured the first UHF pocket-size phones in Europe, and similar products became available in the United States. The pace and the extent of PMR adoption varied significantly in different countries, often depending on attitudes of regulators and potential user groups. In the United States, the FCC embraced a fairly liberal licensing philosophy, while customer segments were eager to adopt new and more efficient technologies. By 1977, PMR penetration was almost 70 percent higher in the United States than in Sweden, which was the leading European country in these services at the time. Used for short information exchanges or critical mission communications, PMR calls were typically brief. The PMR networks were capable of providing telephone services, but spectrum shortage did not allow real wireless *communication*. These services became the next objective—a difficult one, as the coming years would demonstrate.

Commercial Mobile Telephone Services

On June 17, 1946, in Saint Louis, Missouri, AT&T and Southwestern Bell introduced the first American commercial mobile radiotelephone service to private customers. The Mobile Telephone Service (MTS) used newly issued vehicle licenses granted to Southwestern Bell by the FCC; they operated on six channels in the 150 MHz band with a sixty kHz channel spacing. The service was soon extended to twenty-five cities across the United States. Unlike past services, the interconnection of wireless users to the public telephone landline network allowed calls *from fixed stations to mobile users*. These systems were based on FM transmission and used a wide-area architecture, with a single powerful transmitter offering coverage to fifty miles or more. A year later, AT&T began to provide radiotelephone service between New York and Boston. The beginning was cumbersome. As one industry observer noted, "Service in those early days was very basic, the mobile subscriber was assigned to use one specific channel, and calls from mobile units were made by raising the operator by voice and saying aloud the number being called. Mobile units were assigned distinctive telephone numbers based upon the coded channel designator upon which they were permitted to operate. . . . All conversations meant pushing the button to talk, releasing it to listen."[31]

Ultimately, AT&T considered the system a failure. At the beginning of the St. Louis experiment, however, it asked for more frequencies from the FCC. The request precipitated a long struggle for more capacity and a long-standing confrontation between mobile and broadcast interests, which—from the mid-1950s to the early 1980s—went hand in hand with the government's

AT&T antitrust investigations. In the course of two decades, wireless technology improved steadily, and demand for mobile services grew far more rapidly than supply. Concurrently, the FCC decisions gave rise to the UHF TV industry, which failed to use the spectrum optimally.

Improved Mobile Telephone Services

Through incremental advancements, the MTS of 1946 evolved into the *Improved* Mobile Telephone Service (IMTS), which underwent field trials in Harrisburg, Pennsylvania, from 1962 to 1964. A commercial service was introduced in many metropolitan centers, forcing the FCC to engage in substantial spectrum allocation. It was the IMTS that first introduced the mobile into *larger*-scale consumer markets (automatic trunking radio systems enabled greater efficiencies, which allowed more users). The IMTS proved the viability of mobile telephony, just as it seemed to legitimize the FCC's plans to scale up this technology to larger systems.[32]

As soon as the wireless was launched in major U.S. cities, waiting lists proliferated and systems became oversubscribed. In the old dispatch-type mobile systems, communication lasted only a few seconds. In the mobile system, a normal phone call could run for minutes. As the usage per customer was ten to fifteen times more than that for a dispatch circuit, the number of users who could share a single channel was reduced. Similarly, the quality of wireless service deteriorated rapidly. By 1976, only 545 subscribers in New York City had Bell System mobiles, while 3,700 remained on a waiting list. More than 20 million people had only twelve available channels.[33] Nationwide, 44,000 Bell subscribers used AT&T's services, but 20,000 people were placed on five- to ten-year waiting lists.[34] Some seven years later, there were 150,000 mobile telephones in the United States, but they used low-technology systems and could not expand due to a lack of available frequency channels. The few privileged users were provided with a very poor service.

Designed and packaged to emulate the convenience of traditional wireline telephony, the service, despite many problems, served as a model for and precursor of analog cellular.

Chapter 4

The 1G Era: Rise and Decline of U.S. Leadership

After World War II, the United States was *the* critical country market for most industries worldwide. In the wireless business, the United States was both the core cluster and the lead market. The early lead did not ensure sustainable strategic advantages at the national level or at the individual firm level among network operators and equipment manufacturers. As economies in other parts of the world completed their postwar reconstruction efforts, the United States lost its singular leadership. Itemizing the historical trends of the past policies, Benjamin M. Friedman, an influential economist, noted in 1988 that:

> The collapse of our international competitiveness during the first half of the 1980s was spectacular in both speed and extent. One industry after another, laboring under an increasingly overvalued dollar, withered before the force of foreign competition—cars, motorcycles, bicycles, steel, textiles, shoes, electronic equipment, televisions and radios, cameras, personal computers, toasters, telephones, lawnmowers, pianos. The list of industries that suffered severely from foreign competition reads like the chamber of commerce directory. And in the markets for some newer products, like videocassette recorders, we did not become a producer at all.[1]

The erosion of U.S. leadership in wireless communications exemplifies these broad trends. The industry was not included in Friedman's list because, at the time, it was still emerging and appeared to be thriving. The United States enjoyed a single standard and its operators and vendors were the industry leaders. But as the 1G era faded into history, so did these competitive advantages. Analog systems continued to thrive until the mid-1990s, but success bred complacency. At the end of the decade, the erosion of U.S. strategic advantages was rapid and steep. With the triumph of the GSM standard in the 1990s, industry leadership migrated to Western Europe. The U.S. retained its position as the most lucrative country market, but the widest population base migrated to China.

From Monopoly to Competition

The outbreak of World War I stimulated the emergence of the wireless industry. During World War II, U.S. defense forces opted for the FM transmission, and great advances were made in equipment weight, size, cost, performance, and reliability. The wireless communications of the U.S. forces were "beyond anything either the enemy or the other allied nations possessed."[2] During the next three decades, the United States lost this lead. As long as regulators reigned, the monopoly of AT&T remained intact, broadcast interests prevailed, and the wireless business—despite a promising start and strategic advantages—was confined to niche segments. Changes were suppressed until antitrust practitioners intervened.

Regulatory Turmoil

As bargaining power migrated from the FCC to the antitrust department of the Department of Justice, the vertically integrated AT&T began to crumble, wireless claims were taken into account along with those of broadcast interests, and the wireless business grew rapidly. The same years saw the proliferation of industry groups requesting spectrum for two-way mobile radio. These user segments included police; fire departments; forestry and conservation; electric, gas, and water utilities; transit utilities, including bus and streetcar operators; special emergency services; miscellaneous radio services, including motion pictures and relay press; and railroad radio. In May 1945, land mobile radio was an amalgam of service categories, including railroad, bus, truck, taxi, and three categories of common carrier radio (general, urban, and highway). Only after the *General Mobile Radio* proceeding in 1949 did the FCC officially recognize mobile radio as a new class of service. This classification finally permitted land mobile radio to be made available to small businesses, through an allocation to the radio common carriers (RCCs). At the same time, automobile telephone service was authorized, although development had originated in 1940.[3] That year, the FCC also created the Citizens Band (CB) Radio Service.[4] These simple push-to-talk sets were really an old-fashioned AM radio, a kind of wireless Model T that prepared Americans for cellular communications.

During World War II, wireless communications had ensured a U.S. military advantage. In peacetime, the preconditions of the FM triumph contributed to regulatory failures. In terms of quality, FM surpassed AM by an order of magnitude; in terms of spectrum it required far more bandwidth than AM.[5] Large blocks of spectrum would be needed for large metropolitan areas, such as New York and Los Angeles. Additionally, the earliest mobile offerings, the Mobile Telephone Service (MTS), suffered from gross inefficiencies. Between 1945 and the mid-1960s, the spectrum efficiency of analog FM was quadrupled, but only through seemingly endless regulatory struggles. These confrontations originated from and were perpetuated by the long-standing conflict between broadcast and wireless interests, with regulators in the middle. It was hardly a struggle of equals, but one between the wireless David and the broadcast Goliath.

In the postwar era, the United States allowed the powerful new medium of television to evolve through competition. The ensuing success translated to extraordinary bargaining power, which meant regulatory obstacles against the expansion of the mobile business. In contrast, Western Europe and Japan subjected broadcasting to regulation. These differing evolutionary trajectories had substantial repercussions in the wireless business. In the United States, the broadcasters, along with the Department of Defense, captured substantial chunks of the spectrum. In Western Europe and Japan, they did not. As the nascent mobile technologies evolved and the first cellular platforms became commercialized, adequate spectrum was available in Western Europe and Japan but not in the United States.

Broadcasters Versus Wireless Interests

Through the war years, developments in radio and the wireless had been suppressed by military pursuits. By 1945, the FCC explored spectrum allocations for a variety of uses in industrial services, especially private mobile radio, including taxicab radio systems. The MTS followed shortly thereafter. By the early 1950s, wireless systems in the United States were driven by a variety of sectors, notably police, fire, emergency, public utility, forest, business, industry, and local government communications. However, the basic frequency allocation to these systems had been established in the 1940s and barely changed until the late 1960s. The results were predictable. Despite a quadrupling of spectrum utilization, the growth in demand exceeded technological capabilities to cope with increasing congestion.[6] While wireless interests struggled for recognition in the late 1940s and 1950s, network television penetrated America. The new medium required substantial amounts of spectrum. As a perceptive observer noted:

> Each TV channel represented about three times the total spectrum of all pre-cellular mobile telephone frequencies. On the other hand, each TV channel provided service to millions of people, while a mobile telephone circuit benefited only an elite few. Measured by the utilitarian yardstick of 'the greatest good to the greatest number,' TV was viewed as a superior service. For the next two decades, the spectrum allocation policies of the FCC would be strongly skewed to the broadcasters.[7]

The first proposal for a large-capacity mobile telephone system by Bell engineers was presented in 1947, only a year after the introduction of MTS. But this proposition, along with many subsequent ones, was ignored.[8] In 1957, the FCC initiated an inquiry on additional spectrum, but little came out of it. By 1964, the Commission acknowledged the important contribution of land mobile services to the U.S. economy. But it also continued to resist allocating additional spectrum in the proposed new range for land mobile systems. Such a reallocation, argued the FCC, would encroach upon the seventy channels that had already been committed to UHF television, which—as it turned out—developed far more slowly than the Commission anticipated. The FCC was compelled to assign a study group to examine relief for mobile radio congestion. Regulators hoped that a new technology solution would allow them to avoid a political confrontation with the broadcast interests. But the Advisory Committee for Land Mobile Radio Services saw no such solution on the immediate horizon. Even with the "cellular concept," new spectrum allocations would be necessary.

From "Spectrum Mismanagement" to Cellular Docket

After two decades of industry frustration and policy stalemates, the confrontation between mobile and broadcast interests climaxed in 1968, when a House of Representatives select committee initiated hearings on the "crisis in land mobile communications." The TV interests had been allocated 87 percent of the available spectrum below 960 MHz. Mobile communication as a whole had received only 4 percent, and less than 0.5 percent had been allocated for mobile telephony. As the House committee called for "usable frequency spectrum to be allocated without delay," a Presidential Task Force Report on Communications Policy ensued, blaming the chronic congestion and poor service in mobile communications on "spectrum mismanagement by the FCC."[9] Prompted by these developments, the FCC proposed the reallocation of UHF channels 70–83. Reportedly, it was political muscle—Motorola's FCC lobbyists and then-CEO Robert Galvin's role in the 1968 presidential campaign—that accounted for the regulatory approach adopted in the "Cellular Docket" (18262).[10] These proceedings created the formal preconditions for the rise of the cellular business in America, which took another fifteen years.

At the Department of Justice, the Cellular Docket was regarded as an excellent instrument that provided the FCC with a historical opportunity to expand the role of competition in the communications industry. The DOJ urged the FCC to adopt a policy that would stimulate competition in the equipment manufacturing market by forbidding the wireline common carriers (i.e., the Bell wireless providers) from "owning, manufacturing, supplying, or maintaining user mobile equipment." The DOJ suggested that similar prescriptions could be imposed in the base station market.[11] The proposals, along with market-driven emphasis on innovation, arrived in Washington, D.C. only a decade later. Meanwhile, similar principles served as essential elements in Nordic cooperation, which accelerated rapidly, while in the United States, regulators, politicians, and lobbyists struggled to define the nascent business.

In one of the most contentious proceedings in the history of the FCC, the wireless interests were led by AT&T, GTE, Motorola, the National Association of Manufacturers, the American Petroleum Institute, the American Automobile Association, and a host of lesser-known organizations and industrial interests. They were confronted by the Big Three networks (CBS, NBC, and ABC) and a number of smaller independent TV stations. The FCC concluded that the congestion crisis could be resolved only by allocating additional spectrum. The First Report and Order of May 1970 resulted in new allocations to wireless services, but they did not alleviate the underlying problems. At the same time, the role and nature of public policy players were changing. While regulatory struggles dwindled and the role of the FCC receded, industry struggles escalated and the role of the Department of Justice expanded.

Antitrust Gains Ground

At the end of the 1940s, the Bell engineers had identified the basic elements of the cellular concept, but the technology remained crude and spectrum was not available. In 1970, the First Report and the Cellular Docket established the wireless claim to spectrum, but partitioning prompted an industry struggle. In 1982, the FCC released another docket instituting licensing procedures, and the actual licensing began a year later. A total of thirty-five years passed between the emergence of the cellular concept and the FCC cellular licensing in 1983. As Ericsson's historians note, America's first commercial cellular system "wasn't the first in the world. It wasn't even the second or third. In spite of all the pioneering work done in the U.S., America was now about two years behind the Europeans, who had seized and exploited the American technological advances."[12] Many of these delays were self-inflicted wounds. Until the late 1960s, the only countervailing force to regulation comprised the antitrust division of the Department of Justice, which, since the 1910s, had struggled to limit AT&T's monopoly power. Essentially, the DOJ saw the mobile business as an instrument to promote competition in U.S. telecommunications—just as the European and Japanese regulators did later.

In all three lead markets—the United States, Western Europe, and Japan—the regulatory regimes initially supported the old telecom giants or did little to "rock the boat." In contrast, competition policy authorities, as well as Europe's pan-regional policymakers, which had embraced more competitive approaches, used the emerging mobile business to demolish the old PTT natural monopoly. This focus on competition rather than regulation began in the United States, where antitrust policies had been established in the 1890s. In Western Europe and Japan, competition authorities emerged only in the aftermath of World War II and, from the 1950s to 1970s, played a relatively insignificant role in actual industry rivalries.

Rise of Non-Bell Challengers (RCCs)

The St. Louis experiment had hardly started when the Bell System asked the FCC for more frequencies. Two years later, the Commission did allocate a few more channels, but it gave half to entities other than telephone companies, which wanted to provide mobile telephone service. These radio common carriers (RCCs) were the first FCC-created competition for the Bell System. They also precipitated the EC efforts to use mobile services to promote competition from mobile start-ups and challengers. The growth of the RCCs built on the launch of automatic dialing.[13] However, their rise had less to do with technology evolution than with public policies—particularly two catalysts, each with different objectives and institutional ramifications. One originated from the long-standing antitrust crusade by the Department of Justice against AT&T's alleged monopolistic practices. Another stemmed from the struggle of the mobile industry for spectrum. With the 1956 settlement, the former created preconditions for a new U.S. growth industry. But over several decades of delays and inertia, the spectrum mess mitigated what the antitrust authorities accomplished.

In 1913, the so-called Kingsbury Commitment had defused the first attempt at competition within the Bell System. Between 1949 and 1956, an antitrust suit of the Department of Justice led to a consent decree by the DOJ and AT&T, which retained its *de facto* monopoly. The decree acknowledged the inherent competition in mobile radio communications, as opposed to the public utility characteristics of traditional telecommunications. The Bell System was also forced to divest its mobile radio production. In the wireless business, the settlement had two significant consequences, which both contributed to the reorganization of industry and business practices:

- It legitimized the non-Bell operators, the RCCs.
- It prompted the breakup of the Bell System's supply chain.

Despite AT&T's pleadings, the FCC authorized independent operators to provide mobile telephone service in the late 1940s. Telecommunication was still regarded as a "natural monopoly," but mobile radiotelephony was not. Accordingly, the FCC supported competition in wireless communications. In addition to breaking up the Bell supply chain, the settlement solidified the position of the RCCs in the industry. On both counts, the U.S. decision precipitated similar decisions in Western Europe by twenty-five to thirty years. Yet due to regulatory inertia, the industry was not able to benefit from the first-mover advantage.

Through the 1950s and 1960s, the incumbent Bell companies and RCCs engaged in different generic strategies. Excelling in technology innovation, the Bell progenitors concentrated on industrywide low-cost strategies that provided basic telephone service to the masses. Little attention was given to more differentiated mobile services. Excelling in marketing innovation, the RCCs were small entrepreneurs involved in several related businesses (e.g., telephone answering services, private radio systems for taxicab and delivery companies, maritime and air-to-ground services, and "beeper" paging services). As a strategic group of companies, the RCCs were more sales-oriented than the telephone companies. Some became rich in the paging business. Unlike the Bell System companies, which enjoyed a *de facto* monopoly in their respective markets, the RCCs were highly independent of each other.[14] By 1978, the RCCs had some 80,000 wireless subscribers, twice as many as the Bell System incumbents.

The list of leading network operators worldwide demonstrates the diversity of national systems in the pre-cellular era (see Exhibit 4-1). Most major countries in Europe and leading Nordic countries had quite different systems from those of the United States and Canada. The price of mobile equipment extended from a high of $4,100 to $4,500 in West Germany to a low of $1,000 to $2,000 in Sweden. Prices in the United States occupied an intermediate zone of $2,100 to $2,500. Monthly rental fees in the leading European markets

Exhibit 4-1. Leading vendors and operators (circa mid-1970s).

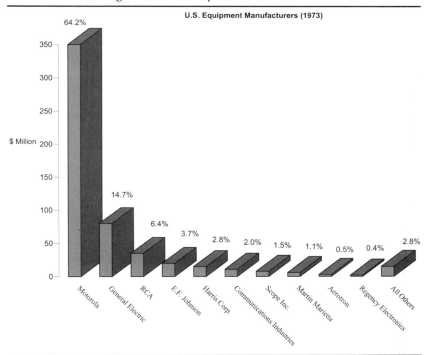

SOURCE: Data from "Go Ahead Signal: The FCC Has Given One to Mobile Communications," *Barron's*, June 10, 1974 (Paul Kagan & Associates).

(continues)

Exhibit 4-1. (Continued).

OVERVIEW OF OPERATIONAL FEATURES OF PRESENT AND PLANNED PUBLIC MOBILE RADIO SYSTEMS

	Present Moderate Capacity Systems								Planned High-Capacity Systems		
Country	United States	West Germany	France	Italy	Canada	United Kingdom	Netherlands	Sweden	Sweden	United States	Japan
System	IMTS	B-Network	Paris (I–IV)	IMTP	MTS	ILRP	Mobilephone	MTD	MTC	MCMTS (Cellular)	MCMTS (Cellular)
Mode of Operation	Automatic	Automatic	Automatic	Automatic	Manual	Manual	Manual	Manual	Automatic	Automatic	Automatic
Two-way Direct Dial Automatic Connect	Yes	Yes	Yes	Yes	No	No	No	No	No	Yes	Yes
Special Land to Mobile Paging Channel(s)	No	Yes	Yes	Yes	No	Yes	No	Yes	Yes	Yes	Yes
Channel Selection	Automatic	Automatic	Automatic	Automatic	Manual	Manual	Manual	Manual	Automatic	Automatic	Automatic
Marked-Idle Free Channels	Yes	Yes	—	Yes	No	No	No	No	No	Yes	Yes
Selective Call Addressing	Yes	Yes	Yes	Yes	Yes & No	Yes	Yes & No	Yes & No	Yes	Yes	Yes
Call Privacy	Yes	Yes	Yes	Yes	Yes & No	Yes	No	Yes	Yes	Yes	Yes
Automatic Identification	Yes	Yes	Yes	Yes	No	No	Optional	No	Yes	Yes	Yes
Call Timing and Billing	Automatic	Automatic	Automatic	Automatic	Operator	Semi-Auto	Operator	Operator	Automatic	Automatic	Automatic
Automatic Mobile Location and Call Hand-Off Between Cells or Zones	No	No	No	No	No	No	No	No	Maybe	Yes	Yes
Mobile Equipment Price	$2100–$2500	$4100–$4500	$2800	$2000	$1500–$2500	$1500	$1000–$2000	$1000–$2000	—	$1000	—
Mobile Service & Equip. Mo. Rental Fee	$100–$120	$110	$121	$134	$30–60	—	$40	$113	—	$50–$80	—

SOURCE: IEEE Vehicular Technology Conference Record (1976), "Public Mobile Telephone—A Comparative Analysis of Systems Worldwide," R. L. Lagace & H. L. Pastan Arthur D. Little, Inc.).

were not that different from those in the United States ($100–$120) but were higher than those in smaller European countries. To some extent, these trends precipitated those to come.

Breakup of the Bell Supply Chain: The Role of Western Electric

A year after Alexander Graham Bell patented the telephone in 1876, he founded the Bell Telephone Company. As early as 1879, Theodore Vail—one of his managers and the creator of the Bell System—declared that AT&T's objective was "one system, one policy, universal service." From the late-nineteenth century to the 1984 divestiture, AT&T's annual reports reiterated the commitment to provide "the best possible service at the lowest possible cost."[15] The nucleus of the Bell System was already in place in 1880, when the American Bell Telephone Company purchased the Western Electric Company of Chicago, which was Western Union's telephone supplying subsidiary. Two years later, American Bell agreed to purchase all of its telephone equipment from Western Electric, while the latter company agreed to supply only American Bell and its licensees. This arrangement gave rise to a vertically integrated Bell System—that is, AT&T coupled with Western Electric Manufacturing Company. In contrast to the Nordic and Japanese models, the value chain in the United States allowed for only a single supplier of telecom equipment.

Founded as an electric-equipment shop in Cleveland in 1869, Western Electric was popular among inventors. Before the 1930s, the Bell System had a single supply chain, was characterized by tight vertical integration, and was confined to the domestic market.[16] Over time, two exceptions confirmed the rule of the integrated system. Outside AT&T, some independents did evolve, such as GTE, but they were confined to small telecom services markets. Similarly, Motorola's postwar expansion in equipment manufacturing was possible only because it concentrated on wireless communications, a specialized niche segment at the time. Western Electric was AT&T's largest entity and, at its peak, operated twenty-three major plants across the United States.

Although Motorola had pioneered the FM era in mobile communications and reaped substantial first-mover advantages, AT&T's vertical integration constrained the vendor's expansion. In 1956, AT&T and the Department of Justice settled another antimonopoly suit. AT&T agreed not to expand its business beyond telephones and transmitting information, while Bell Laboratories and Western Electric would not enter such fields as computers and business machines. Relying on the Bell System specifications, Motorola and other players (e.g., Secode, ITT-Kellogg) invaded the industry segment to make AT&T's next generation of radiotelephone equipment.

With the Carterfone decision (1968–1972), the FCC determined that any equipment could be connected to the Bell network if it had been certified as safe to use.

From AT&T Monopoly to Duopolies

In 1968, AT&T had some 34,000 wireless subscribers nationwide, about 50 percent of the total market. But it was no longer alone in the business. The Bell System had more than 100 million telephones in the wireline network. The remaining 50 percent of U.S. subscribers belonged to some 500 RCCs. Traditional telecom markets were maturing and promised only slow growth. New wireless markets barely existed, but they promised explosive growth. Individually, none of the RCCs could compete with AT&T, but collectively, they had almost as many subscribers as the giant. The RCCs may have been regarded as antiquated "mom and pop" operations by the Bell System and the FCC, but the Department of Justice considered their entrepreneurship a healthy antidote to AT&T's monopolistic instincts.

In 1970, U.S. telecommunications, for most practical purposes, was still synonymous with AT&T. While industry observers expected a rapid rise in the new mobile services, they also anticipated these services to be a mere extension of AT&T's wireline monopoly. In 1971, the FCC acknowledged the role of the RCCs by redefining the eligibility requirements for cellular providers and opening the allocations to "any qualified common carrier." However, since the plan allowed for just a single license per region, it would ensure AT&T's control of all major metropolitan markets. By 1975, the FCC reversed its earlier decision to extend the legal monopoly of the wireline carriers into the cellular market. It concluded that "any qualified entity, in addition to wireline carriers, will be permitted to apply for authorization to develop and eventually operate cellular radio systems."[17] Mobile communications in the United States was no longer the extension of AT&T's natural monopoly in telecommunications.

The FCC decisions were brought to the Court of Appeals. In a 1976 decision, the court affirmed the allocation of 40 MHz for development of the cellular system and 30 MHz for private mobile service, including a new class of entrepreneurial operators called Special Mobile Radio services (SMRs). As the RCCs took their case to the courts, AT&T and Motorola initially aligned against the RCCs. The alliance was not solid. While Motorola expected to be the market leader for the mobile units, it continued to compete for parity with AT&T as the supplier of cellular systems. The latent conflict exploded in the mid-1970s, when AT&T announced its plan to test the cellular system in Chicago with contractors such as E. F. Johnson Co. and Oki Electric, a Japanese vendor. Stunned by its exclusion, Motorola attacked the cellular allocation, joined the RCC interests, accelerated R&D on its own systems design, and by 1977, joined a large RCC in developing a second cellular system.

Even as the Bell System struggled with rapidly changing public policies, technology evolution was eroding AT&T's historical monopoly advantages. In the early 1970s, the Bells still enjoyed a monopoly on critical intrinsic technologies. As proprietary technologies were standardized and prices fell, the RCCs could set up and operate cellular systems. The number of RCC paging subscribers soared from 50,000 to more than 600,000 between 1971 and 1978. The nation's fascination with paging systems had made the leading RCCs wealthy. In the process, the attitude of the FCC was changing as well.

During the last two decades of the twentieth century, FCC mobile policies reflected the three eras of monopoly, transition, and competition, supporting monopoly, then duopoly, and finally *de facto* consolidation. At first, the Commission supported AT&T's monopoly in mobile communications. By 1980, it opposed AT&T's single-operator monopoly concept, as well as the RCCs' insistence on an unlimited number of competitors. Instead, the Commission supported two systems per market, each with half the spectrum. While the FCC accepted AT&T's arguments that smaller systems were less efficient and more costly, it opted for the principle of competition under increasing technology uncertainty and complexity.[18] In each market, one license would be set aside for the local wireline telephone company (Bell) while the other would be retained for the "nonwireline carriers" (RCCs). The FCC expected these arrangements to streamline the licensing process, in which application costs would discourage potential small entrants. These expectations did not materialize. Rather, a chaotic licensing process led to a chaotic auction process, which eventually gave way to consolidation.

The Failure of Success: From Analog to Digital Cellular

After the 1956 consent decree, AT&T's exclusive supply chain with Western Electric faded to history. As vendors had to compete for Ma Bell's attention, Motorola and others soon established their position in the industry value chain. By 1973, the leading U.S. equipment manufacturers generated more than $550 million in annual revenue (see again Exhibit 4-1). The list was heavy at the top. Motorola dominated, with revenues of $350 million and a market share of 64 percent. General Electric followed, with revenues of $80 million and a 15 percent market share. Four leading vendors controlled some 89 percent of the marketplace. Not a single Japanese or European manufacturer was among these vendors—yet.

The Breakup of AT&T: The License Game

In 1974, a lawsuit charged AT&T with monopolizing the market for telephone equipment and long-distance service. This suit led to a 1982 decision that called for a divestiture. The Justice Department's antitrust action led to the breakup of the company on January 1, 1984. Two years later, AT&T's breakup resulted in seven separate and independent regional Bell operating companies (RBOCs). The RBOCs were restricted to local services, whereas the new AT&T retained its long-distance and customer premises equipment operations, as well as Western Electric and part of Bell Laboratories. Only telephone equipment was fully deregulated. The settlement also allowed AT&T to enter other electronic businesses, including computers (see Exhibit 4-2).

As part of its divestiture in 1984, AT&T had retained its cellular hardware division and released its cellular service group to the Baby Bells. Cellular was considered a niche business, not a future cash cow. In 1980, the carrier commissioned a study that dramatically underestimated the future demand for cellular. In 2000, it anticipated that there would be only 900,000 U.S. cellular subscribers, whereas, in reality, the user base would amount to more than *100 million* at the time. As former AT&T executive Sam Ginn later put it, the company was "more interested in the Yellow Pages at the time than wireless."[19] Thus, Ma Bell renounced the very technology its own labs had spawned and effectively gave away AT&T's claim to cellular. Instead, the wireline licenses fell to the RBOCs after the divestiture.

Exhibit 4-2. U.S. wireless industry: from AT&T monopoly to consolidation (1946–2000).

The Pre-1984 Era: AT&T's Monopoly	The Post-1984 Era: Regulation-Driven Competition	The Pre-3G Era: Consolidation-Driven Competition
- AT&T enjoys "natural monopoly" in U.S. telecommunications.	- The breakup of AT&T results in several strategic groups in long-distance and local telecom.	- As the "new" AT&T fails to slow market erosion, focus strategies result in breakup speculation.
- AT&T's wireless subsidiary enjoys comparable monopoly in mobile communications.	- Most members of these groups have a wireless subsidiary.	- Investors and markets force former Bell subsidiaries to consolidate.
- In the postwar era, RCCs establish foothold in mobile services, but they are too small to pose a threat to AT&T.	- Some RCCs have evolved into larger independent operations while growth prospects attract new start-ups.	- RCCs and Bell subsidiaries merge, acquire, divest, and partner with each other to achieve scale economies.
- Distinct boundaries exist between these three strategic groups	- Boundaries between the strategic groups begin to blur.	- Market-driven forces generate new strategic groups.
- AT&T's mobile subsidiary is the sole competitor.	- Wireline operators (Baby Bells) and wireless operators (RCCs) do battle, giving rise to national and international players.	- Operators consolidate into multinational entities.

The Old Bell System	Regional Bell Operating Companies (RBOCs)	New Market-Driven Wireless Giants	
Illinois Bell		**Companies**	**Subscribers (Million)**
Indiana Bell	**Long Distance**		
Michigan Bell		Verizon Wireless	27.5
Ohio Bell	☐ AT&T		
Wisconsin Bell	☐ MCI	Cingular	19.7
	☐ Sprint		
Bell of Pennsylvania		AT&T	15.2
C&P Companies			
New Jersey Bell	**Local Telcos**	Sprint PCS	9.5
South Central Bell	☐ Ameritech	Nextel	6.7
Southern Bell	☐ Bell Atlantic		
	☐ BellSouth	ALLTEL	6.3
New York Telephone	☐ NYNEX		
New England Telephone	☐ Pacific Telesis	Voicestream	3.9
	☐ Southwestern Bell		
Nevada Bell	☐ US West	U.S. Cellular	3.1
Pacific Telephone			
Southwestern Bell		Total	109.5%
Mountain Bell		Top-4	65.7%
Northwestern Bell		Top-8	83.9%
Pacific Northwest Bell			

Along with GTE, the nation's largest independent operator, the seven regional RBOCs seized 87 percent of the top-30 MSAs[20] licenses. Unlike the seven Baby Bells, AT&T was given leverage to compete in the interexchange carrier (IXC) and broader information markets. The RBOCs were required to launch a separate wireless subsidiary. The reorganization did not hinder wireline rollout plans. In May 1984, the FCC lacked the appropriate resources to evaluate the high number of bids, so it resorted to a lottery with all awards beyond the top-30 MSAs. In practice, this meant negotiation games between bidders, extended delays, and rising criticism of the FCC procedures. After the second and the third round, the FCC abandoned the basic criteria of previous evaluations—technical merit, financial viability, and advance financial commitments—and opted for a simple lottery with the remaining low-value licenses. Now negotiation games were replaced by opportunistic speculation as initial bidders were seldom the ultimate owners. By the end of 1984, some twenty-five wireline systems were in operation versus only nine nonwireline operators. This imbalance changed by the end of 1986, when most of the top-90 markets had two competing systems.

Advanced Mobile Phone Service

In May 1978, the Bahrain Telephone Company may have been operating the first commercial cellular telephone system. Two months later, Advanced Mobile Phone Service was initiated in the United States. In AT&T Labs Research in Newark, New Jersey, and in Chicago, Bell and AT&T jointly rolled out analog cellular telephone service. A half year later, a market trial began with paying customers who leased car-mounted telephones. The "service test" relied on the newly allocated 800 MHz band. Somewhat surprisingly, the Bell System bypassed its traditional supply chain by purchasing an additional 1,000 mobile phones from Oki for the lease phase; it placed orders from Motorola and E. F. Johnson for the remaining 2,100 radios.

In 1981, the FCC finalized the rules for awarding licenses. It invited applications for the first round of licenses in the thirty largest MSAs. Since the first round comprised the most valuable licenses in the United States, the competition was intense. In October 1983, Ameritech, one of the Baby Bells, initiated U.S. commercial cellular service in Chicago. Cellular service evolved from this AT&T model, along with Motorola's analog system, DynaTAC[21], introduced commercially in Baltimore and Washington D.C. by Cellular One on December 16, 1983. This launch heralded Motorola's decade-long leadership in the 1G business. The earliest use of AMPS and cellular licensing coincided with the breakup of AT&T.

U.S. players had lost first-mover advantages due to three decades of spectrum debates. They were now about to lose another decade in a licensing turmoil. When the FCC began sorting out applications for cellular operating licenses in the top-30 U.S. markets in 1982, Ericsson's veterans followed the events with puzzled smiles, noting that "the office of the Secretary of the FCC, at 1919 M Street, began to look like an explosion in a paper factory. The weight of the boxes could have been measured by the ton, as elegantly dressed lawyers worked hand-in-hand with teamsters in coveralls to deliver applications for cellular licenses in the top-30 markets. Applications arrived by truck, by semi-trailer, by armored car, by a caravan of men, each carrying a box of documents (on their heads?) and by more conventional means."[22]

Despite industry chaos, Motorola enjoyed product leadership. As early as 1982, it offered the world's broadest cellular product line. According to estimates of the Finnish Mobira (the precursor of Nokia), Motorola had 22 percent of the market in the mid-1980s, whereas Mobira was in fourth place with 13 percent and Ericsson in sixth with 6 percent.

The technical limitations of AMPS soon prohibited further expansion.[23] A Narrowband Analog Mobile Phone Service (NAMPS) was developed as a transient solution to the problem of low calling capacity.[24] But incremental enhancements did not resolve the fundamental problems. After years of delays, AMPS had been introduced at a time when, in purely technical terms, it was about to become obsolete. Even as AT&T, Motorola, and others were blinded by the success of AMPS in one country, new European operators and ambitious vendors were driven by the future potential of GSM *worldwide*. Furthermore, not only were American players falling behind in technology progression; they were also repeating the Europeans' mistake in the impending 2G era. In the 1980s, Western Europe had been ridden by multiple standards, which fragmented the market, whereas in the U.S., AMPS unified the marketplace. In the 1990s, GSM unified the European marketplace, whereas in the United States, several digital platforms (TDMA, GSM, CDMA, iDEN) were added. The result was predictable. Multiple standards fragmented the U.S. marketplace. The story of McCaw Cellular, the operator that first created a national footprint, served as a model for a new generation of U.S. operators seeking to unify a market that regulators allowed to fragment.

From McCaw Cellular to AT&T Wireless

Craig McCaw was the son of John Elroy McCaw, Seattle's pioneer entrepreneur in radio and cable. After McCaw senior committed suicide in 1969, his widow and four sons were left with the debt-ridden empire, and eventually only a single small cable system called Centralia. Embracing his father's opportunistic strategy, Craig McCaw, while still a student at Stanford, took over McCaw Communications while securing loans against Centralia to buy cable companies. It was then that the young and bold entrepreneur developed his own rapid growth formula. Following a completed acquisition, he cut costs, improved programming, and raised subscription rates. Right before cable deregulation, he agreed to a partnership with Affiliated Publications, which owned the *Boston Globe*, to purchase cable systems before the prices soared.[25] Initially, McCaw focused on cable properties, but in 1974, he diversified into RCCs as well. Different industry, same growth formula.

Building a Nationwide Footprint: "Sign 'em Quick, Close 'em Slow"

With the arrival of the 1G era in the United States, McCaw managed to secure several early FCC-granted franchises. Like so many early cable entrepreneurs, McCaw struggled under heavy debt, but survived with Affiliated's resources. He soon embraced the new economics of cable, where a growing cash flow created tremendous buying leverage. He would buy a system at its undervalued price. Then he would bring in professional management to improve service. Thereafter, he could raise rates and find more customers to boost cash flow. And finally, he would get a new loan and use new funds to purchase another system. In other words, he bought cheap, improved service, commanded price premium, added customers, borrowed more—and started a virtuous cycle again. At the same time, he turned deal making into an art through his motto "Sign 'em quick, close 'em slow." The idea was to obtain effective control of the franchise fast, but delay the moment when he would have to pay cash to complete the sale. These lessons came in handy when he began to leverage future growth in cellular operations.

In early 1980, even before the FCC decided how to issue cellular licenses, McCaw formed a partnership named Northwest Mobile Telephone, in order to obtain a substantial share of the licenses. As a history major, he saw the fixed phone as an evolutionary relic, locked in the pre-Marconi era of calling a location rather than communicating with a person:

> With cellular telephony, we saw an enormous gap between what was and what should be. I mean, [the fixed phone system] makes absolutely no sense . . . As we, both individually and collectively as a society, avail ourselves more and more of the flexibility of mobile communications, we may begin to associate a telephone number more with a person than with a place. We will no longer have one number in our home, another in our office and another in our car. We will have one number where we can be reached at nearly any time.[26]

Anticipating that the FCC would issue two licenses in each market, McCaw expected the cellular licensing process to resemble the licensing of television in the late 1940s and 1950s, with comparative hearings. Industry foresight prepared McCaw's strategy, but when the FCC dropped comparative hearings for a simple lottery in 1983, cellular was about to become a speculator's game. McCaw turned to Michael Milken and junk bonds in order to acquire licenses. During his time at Drexel Burnham Lambert, Milken channeled some $26 billion into MCI, McCaw, Metromedia, Viacom, TCI, Time Warner, Turner Broadcasting, Cablevision Systems, News Corp., and other cable, telecom, wireless, publishing, and entertainment businesses. In 1986, McCaw's executives met Milken in Beverly Hills where the "junk bond king" introduced more radical financial instruments. "Your problem is," he said to McCaw's men, "you went to veterinarians when you wanted brain surgery."[27]

As the debt burden climbed, McCaw opted for cellular, divested the cable business, and offered 12 percent of McCaw Cellular to the public. Merging the old McCaw Communications into McCaw Cellular, he engaged in bolder license acquisitions. After all, cable TV and cellular had many affinities. Both were network industries that were regulated by the FCC. Both involved transmitters and towers, assigned radio spectrum, and had common engineering issues (including signal interference). And they were often supported by the same lenders and brokers. From McCaw's perspective, the incumbent telecom giants entirely misjudged the future of the cellular. Too focused on the current long-distance market, they ignored the future.

Opportunism and Back Doors

With the end of the "booming eighties," both the cable and cellular industries faced consolidation. When Affiliated spun off its stake to its shareholders in 1989, McCaw Cellular's debt had soared to 87 percent. To secure the business, Craig McCaw sold a 22 percent stake to British Telecommunications while selling the southeastern cellular systems to Contel. A year later, he acquired a 52 percent stake in LIN Broadcasting for $3.4 billion, which gave his company entry into several key markets, including New York, Los Angeles, and Dallas. The stake was critical to McCaw's strategy, which struggled to achieve a nationwide footprint. Meanwhile, he developed his own common-sense guidance for service innovation. In a company newsletter, his first message was entitled "What We Stand For":

> *Keep It Simple:* Simple solutions solve complex problems. Complex solutions rarely accomplish anything.
> *Be Humble:* If you think you're great, you're probably not.
> *Pursue Excellence:* The pursuit of excellence is what gives real meaning to life.
> *Stay Close to the Customer:* Otherwise, when we're gone, nobody will notice (or care).
> *Employ Good Judgment:* It's one of the few things man does better than machines.
> *Consider the Future:* Short-term gratification is just that, SHORT-TERM.

> *Hire Great People:* If you don't surround yourself with great people, you're a turkey.
>
> If you follow the above, you'll have fun and enjoy more spare time.

It was vintage McCaw: clear, blunt, direct. It was also the operator's version of the vendor's rules of conduct, as codified by Motorola and later Nokia.

Amid the recession of 1990–1991, McCaw reduced debt by offering a debt-for-equity swap and selling cellular interests in eighteen Midwestern markets to BellSouth, a cellular-hungry Baby Bell. Continuing his acquisition and disposal binge, McCaw also bid successfully for advanced paging service licenses in 1994. These tactics were not about corporate continuity in a mature stage; they were about opportunistic strategy in the emerging and growth stages of industry evolution. Flexibility, not rigidity; maneuvering, not steering; options, not lock-in—McCaw refined these views into a form of art:

> Never go through the front door unless you've got a back door, and the hardest thing to get people to do is to not commit themselves to one course of action. . . . [to think] about what you're going to do next. Playing chess with my father, I give him credit for that. I mean, if you haven't thought three moves ahead and what if he does this, and what if that happens, and what if that happens, in today's world you can't predict what's going to happen. . . . You can take chances, but you never, ever play the game without an out. Maybe that's from being a history major, [studying] everybody in history who has failed to have a back door, whether it's Hitler, Napoleon, and down the list. If you take a chance, always have a back door. That's the fun of it.[28]

In 1993, AT&T announced a definitive merger agreement with McCaw Cellular Communications Inc., then the largest provider of cellular service in the United States. The deal was completed amid legal wrangling and valued at $12.6 billion. Formerly based in Washington, D.C., McCaw's last reported sales were $2.2 billion in fiscal 1993. The acquisition was renamed AT&T Wireless. It was taken over by Daniel R. Hesse, who arrived at wireless services after a stint in AT&T's equipment arm. Between 1984 and 1994, AT&T had been out of the wireless game; now it was back in. Despite the strong brand, AT&T Wireless was just a patchwork of small operations. Most importantly, it lacked clout with AT&T's home office in New Jersey, which had rejected attempts to create a national calling plan that would eliminate roaming fees, fearing it would hurt the flagship long-distance business. Once Hesse gained approval, he revamped the company, taking away all regional authority and making it a national organization.

In the mid-1980s, AT&T barely noticed the potential of cellular. By 1994, AT&T's then-CEO Bob Allen said he wanted to put a cellular phone in everyone's pocket and provide customers with a seamless, national network. In this effort, the Digital One Rate Plan was the key.

The Digital One Rate Plan

Price homogenization was the great theme in the wireless industry in 1998. Nextel Communications was the first wireless operator to offer no roaming charges. Similarly, Sprint tested the market for no roaming and no long-distance charges by offering optional features such as Home Rate USA and Toll Free USA for $4.99 and $19.99 per month, respectively, starting in early 1998. But AT&T revolutionized the conventional pricing scenario with the launch of Digital One Rate, which provided a flat rate for all calls from anywhere to anywhere in the United States, on or off its analog or digital cellular network. It also enticed other carriers to introduce their own versions of "one rate" all-inclusive plans. The voice communications service industry was moving closer to wireline substitution as cellular carriers slashed roaming and long-distance charges and local airtime rates continued to decline. These new, differentiated rate plans had an important effect on the industry overall as the Yankee Group's Wireless Price Index declined by 40 percent since 1995.

Compared to international developments, the plan was neither unique nor pioneering. Instead, it was reminiscent of NTT DoCoMo's new mass-market strategy in the mid-1990s and Vodafone's streamlined pricing solutions of the early decade—all of which drew from the Nordic tariff policies of the 1980s. In addition to standards-driven regional insularity, this extraordinary delay prevented the U.S. players from employing one of their most potent competitive weapons: *service pricing*. As one industry representative noted:

> When you enter a lot of these countries, regulatory issues are the first ones you deal with. After that, price competitiveness is by far our strongest advantage. We can outprice the Europeans and Japanese one-on-one. Now, if Japan wants to give away its equipment there is nothing we can do. The same for the Europeans—they are kicking our butt right now in cellular because they have economies of scale advantages. But one-on-one we are about half as expensive as the Europeans, and in the end would you rather get caught in the government morass or be the lowest-cost provider. I think that in the long run the sustainable cost advantage is to be the low-cost provider.[29]

AT&T Wireless and NTT DoCoMo

In September 1995—some eleven years after the divestiture decision and a year before the highly anticipated Telecommunications Act of 1996—AT&T engaged in a voluntary breakup by restructuring into three separate companies: a services company, which retained the AT&T name; a products and systems company, later named Lucent Technologies; and a computer company, which reassumed the NCR name. By the end of 1996, both Lucent and NCR had been spun off. This breakup finally cut the cord between the successor (AT&T Wireless) of the old national PTT (AT&T) and the vertically integrated equipment manufacturer (Lucent). Yet AT&T's strategy was adrift. Only with the arrival of C. Michael Armstrong in late 1997 did the "new AT&T" take shape. Up till that point, the fate of wireless communications was dictated by efforts to incorporate the old giant's distinct businesses as well as its enduring effort to employ wireless to secure a local presence—a tactic that used to make strategic sense but was a losing proposition financially.[30]

In May 1999, AT&T acquired Vanguard Cellular, one of the largest independent operators of cellular telephone systems in the United States. A month later, the carrier announced plans to create a new wireless company, AT&T Wireless Group, and a new class of AT&T common stock that would track the performance of the wireless enterprise. At the end of 1999, Hesse was passed over for the top spot at AT&T's new Wireless Group, which led to his departure. John Zeglis, AT&T's president and longtime general counsel, got the CEO position.

In October 2000, AT&T announced a strategic restructuring plan to create a family of four new AT&T companies out of each of the major business units (wireless, broadband, business, and consumer). Meanwhile AT&T and NTT DoCoMo announced the formation of a strategic alliance to develop the next generation of mobile multimedia services. In the process, NTT DoCoMo invested nearly $10 billion (16 percent) in AT&T Wireless. By 2002, AT&T Wireless, with almost 20 million subscribers, was the third-largest U.S. mobile operator, behind Verizon Wireless and Cingular Wireless, an SBC-BellSouth joint venture. And it provided service nationwide.

Struggle for the 3G Era

In 1993, Congress created the statutory classification of Commercial Mobile Radio Service (CMRS) to promote the consistent regulation of mobile services that are similar in nature. At the same time, Congress established the promotion of competition as a fundamental goal for CMRS policy formation and regulation. This was progress, but the impact would require time. And since digital cellular arrived late in the United States, American companies fell further behind in their efforts to stay close to the productivity frontier. Of course, industry expansion was extraordinary, but it could have been even *more* extraordinary.

Industry Consolidation, Market Expansion

Between the mid-1980s and 2000, the number of cellular subscribers soared from 92,000 to 97 million. Through these years, the United States was the most lucrative cellular market worldwide (see Exhibit 4-3). In July 2001, the subscriber base in the U.S. market exceeded 120 million (though China was about to become the largest market worldwide). In the past fifteen years, total six-month revenues in the United States had soared from $178 million to $24.6 billion, while cumulative capital investments climbed from $355 million to $76.7 billion. At the same time, investments per subscriber declined from $3,873 to $790, while average revenue per subscriber (ARPU) decreased consistently from $1,944 to $240. These figures reflect the industry transition from low differentiation and low volume to high differentiation and high volume. With the 3G convergence, the shift from voice to data coincided with another change, where usage rather than penetrationbecame the paramount revenue criteria. In 2000, the industry witnessed the first signs of a reversal that was expected to become more common with data communications, as ARPU actually increased to $254. In the year 2000, the CMRS industry continued to experience increased competition and innovation as evidenced by lower prices for consumers and greater diversity of service offerings. Between 1987 and 1998, the average monthly bill fell from $97 to $39. More recently, increasing use of new services has increased the bill to $45. Through analog and digital cellular, industry expansion has translated to substantial employment as well. In 1985, the industry employed only 1,400 people; in 2000, it employed 160,000.

Mobile Telephony

The process of carriers building nationwide footprints continued to be a significant trend in the sector as operators filled in gaps in their coverage through mergers, acquisitions, and license swaps. In parallel with the process of footprint building, mobile operators deployed their networks in an increasing number of markets, expanding their digital coverage and developing innovative pricing plans. At the end of 2000, Verizon Wireless was the nation's largest mobile carrier, with almost 28 million subscribers. Cingular, the joint venture between SBC and BellSouth, had the second position with 20 million users. The old industry leader, AT&T Wireless, ranked fourth with 15 million subscribers.

(text continues on page 108)

Exhibit 4-3. CTIA's semiannual mobile telephone industry survey (1985–2000).

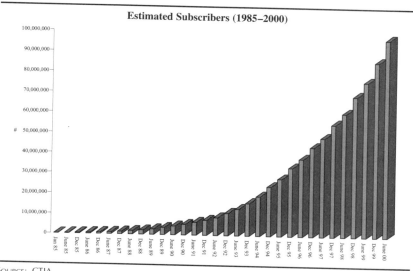

SOURCE: CTIA.

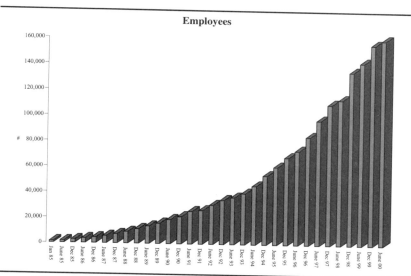

SOURCE: CTIA.

(continues)

Exhibit 4-3. (Continued).

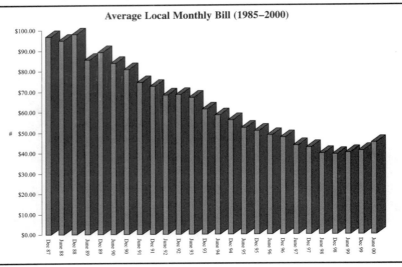

Average Local Monthly Bill (1985–2000)

SOURCE: CTIA.

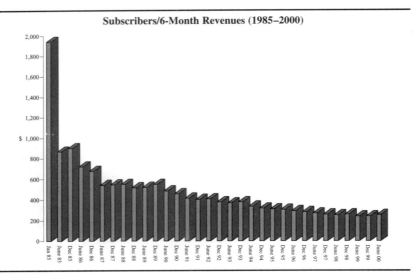

Subscribers/6-Month Revenues (1985–2000)

SOURCE: CTIA.

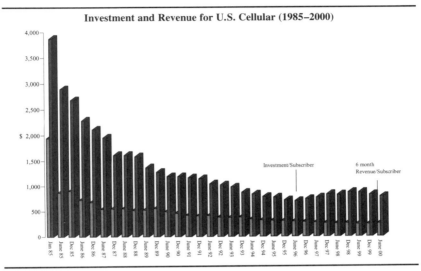

Investment and Revenue for U.S. Cellular (1985–2000)

SOURCE: CTIA.

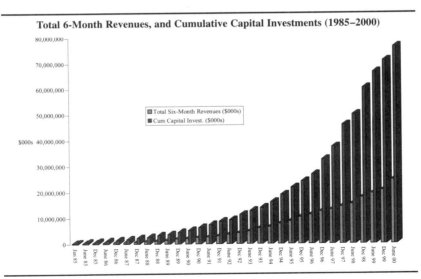

Total 6-Month Revenues, and Cumulative Capital Investments (1985–2000)

SOURCE: CTIA.

The mobile telephony sector generated more than $52.5 billion in revenues, increased subscribers from 86.0 million to 109.5 million, and produced a nationwide penetration rate of roughly 39 percent. Broadband PCS carriers and digital SMR providers continued to deploy their networks. The number of rivals ensured relatively high competitive intensity. Almost 91 percent of the total U.S. population (i.e., 259 million people) had access to three or more different operators (cellular, broadband PCS, and/or digital SMR providers) offering mobile service in the counties in which they lived. About 75 percent of the U.S. population (i.e., 214 million people) lived in areas with five or more mobile telephone operators competing to offer service. And 47 percent of the population (i.e., 133 million) could choose from at least six different mobile telephone operators. The belated digitalization of the mobile sector continued unabated. In contrast to Europe's unified GSM market, U.S. industry players employed CDMA, TDMA, and Integrated Digital Enhanced Network (iDEN). By 2001, however, GSM advanced rapidly in the United States as well. The number of digital customers increased and the number of analog customers decreased. At the end of 2000, digital customers made up 62 percent of the industry total.

Mobile Data

By 2000, the mobile data sector continued its transition from paging/messaging to mobile Internet access services. Numerous companies, including paging/messaging carriers, mobile telephone carriers, handheld personal digital assistant (PDA) manufacturers, and dedicated data network operators, offered a myriad of mobile Internet access products on a variety of mobile devices. Starting in late 1999, seven major mobile operators began offering mobile data services, including wireless web, short message service (SMS), and e-mail, on mobile telephone handsets. Four of those seven operators reported mobile Internet usage and had a combined total of 2.5 million mobile Internet users. In April 2002, AT&T also began offering "mMode," a U.S. version of the highly popular i-mode offered by DoCoMo.

Toward Resurgence

"Today, I am pleased to sign an Executive Memorandum that will help ensure that America maintains its leadership in two of the most important technologies driving the U.S. economy—wireless telecommunications and the Internet," said President Bill Clinton in October 2000. "I am directing federal agencies to work with the Federal Communications Commission and the private sector to identify the radio spectrum needed for the 'third generation' of wireless technology. These so-called 3G systems will allow Americans to have mobile, high-speed access to the Internet and new telecommunications services anytime, anywhere."[31]

The tone of the statement was reminiscent of the early days of the 1992 campaign and the first Clinton term. During the 1992 campaign, Bill Clinton and Al Gore vowed to rebuild America. One of their policy priorities had been the creation of "a national information network to link every home, business, lab, classroom, and library by the year 2015. . . . To expand access to information, we will put public records, databases, libraries, and educational material online for public use."[32] Clinton and Gore set out to formulate and implement the National Information Infrastructure (NII) initiative in 1993, the Global Information Infrastructure (GII) initiative in 1994, and even the Global Framework for Electronic Commerce (1997).[33] As the duo shaped institutional preconditions for the Internet revolution worldwide, these policy initiatives, and the accompanying public/private partnerships, boosted and U.S. economic growth and solidified links among science, technology policy, and economic policy. Indeed, President Clinton saw the coming of the 3G era as an extension of the Internet revolution:

> If the United States does not move quickly to allocate this spectrum, there is a danger that the U.S. could lose market share in the industries of the twenty-first century. If we do this right, it will help ensure continued economic growth, the creation of new high-tech jobs, and the creation of exciting new Internet and telecommunications services.[34]

But the efforts that resulted in the dotcom explosion from 1995 to 2000 were quite different from next-generation mobile services. They focused on the *wired* Internet, not the *wireless* Internet. U.S. leadership had been lost in the mobile business around the mid-1990s. The presidential directive portrayed a real concern, but not a compelling reality. Furthermore, the implementation of the first commercial cellular systems had taken almost thirty-six years, from the initial elucidation of the cellular concept at Bell Labs in 1947 to the launch of the first commercial systems in Chicago and Washington/Baltimore in 1983. These postponements resulted from a flawed regulatory process that has suppressed the efforts of U.S. firms to retain, recapture, and renew strategic advantages for decades.

Starting in the early 1990s, things began to change again. The promotion of competition as the basic objective for CMRS policy formation and regulation was a great advance, but its full impact will take time. Even more important, it cannot undo the self-inflicted wounds in policies, strategies, and innovation; nor can it restore the first-mover advantages that were lost in the 1990s and must be won anew. The advent of 2G prompted U.S. policy and regulatory interests to take on the market-driven objectives that Nordic countries initiated in the late 1960s and implemented through deregulation and liberalization in the early 1980s. U.S. companies bidding for major overseas sales contracts needed appropriate and expeditious support from the U.S. government. Such support was a major component of the Clinton administration's national export strategy. "Advocacy is important because foreign competitors in international markets often resort to political or economic pressures to assist their firms marketing abroad," noted a 1998 study.[35]

The long-term evolution of the mobile business in the United States (see Exhibit 4-4) has been smoother and more pragmatic than in Western Europe and Japan. Industry objectives have been neither exclusively political nor driven by R&D concerns alone. Rather, "whatever works" has been the prime catalyst of the industry. It was not pragmatism that failed the U.S. mobile cluster and markets between the 1950s and the early 1990s, but public policies

Exhibit 4-4. U.S. singular leadership and beyond.

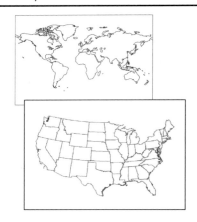

MONOPOLY ERA

National PTT
- AT&T's monopoly from late 1880s to 1984 breakup.
- Private-sector monopoly; vertically integrated supply chain.
- Rise of cellular platforms coincides with transition of public policies.

NIS/PTT Labs
- From 1911 to AT&T breakup, U.S. mobile innovation primarily at Bell Labs.
- Starting in the 1950s, augmented with Motorola and several other players.
- Innovation within firms; insular "Big Science" orientation.

Old Public Policies
- Regulation-ensured AT&T monopoly until "land-mobile crisis" of 1968; broadcast and defense interests dictate spectrum policies.
- Consent decrees of 1913 and 1956, independent mobile operators (RCCs), opening of supply chain (1956).
- Regional roaming, high pricing (CPP), licensing turmoil.

TRANSITION ERA

Privatization
- Between 1984 and 1996, Bell breakup.
- Transition to competition; vertically disintegrated value system.
- Triumph of 1G coincides with privatization; CDMA fragments market.

Transformation of Innovation
- Turmoil at Bell Labs.
- Mobile innovation migrates to Motorola and other vendors.
- Innovation within firms, and public-private partnerships, tech coalitions, and academia-industry alliances; eclipse of "Big Science," rise of market-oriented R&D.

Transitional Public Policies
- Deregulation over regulation.
- With AT&T's demise, rising significance of competition policy over regulation.
- Incompatible technologies constrain roaming; CPP not overthrown; licensing turmoil.

COMPETITIVE ERA

Cluster
- U.S. operators internationalize slowly; overseas operators' FDI in the U.S.; Motorola loses industry leadership.
- Convergence developments prompt entry of IT leaders.
- CDMA becomes the core of the 3G standard.

Innovation Systems
- Market-driven innovation proliferates.
- Leadership in innovation splits between the European-based mobile leaders and U.S.-based IT leaders.
- Innovation increasingly externalized, vis-à-vis tech coalitions.

New Public Policies
- Deregulation reigns, but the role of defense interests constrains spectrum allocations.
- FCC promotes and DOJ permits increasing consolidation, compensating for mistaken policies (roaming, CPP, licensing).
- Efforts to promote 3G transition end with new administration; after 9/11, security interests influence policies.

that did not facilitate competition, were poorly designed, and lacked consistency. These concerns were reflected in a 1998 industry study, which argued that high-level U.S. government officials did not or could not, due to policy restrictions, support U.S. companies to the same extent that European and Asian governments supported their equipment manufacturers.

From the pre-cellular era to the end of the analog era, U.S. leadership in mobile communications paralleled the monopoly era in telecommunications. As long as regulation reigned at the expense of competition, domestic public policies drove the business. Through these phases, geography was destiny, and country markets dominated. The larger and the more advanced the marketplace, the more powerful were the domestic industry leaders. Business activities were shaped by economies of scale and competition in a singular location, not by economies of scope or competition across multiple locations. With the 1990s, these roles were reversed. Today, success in wireless communications is driven by business, not geography. Even small country markets generate competitive global players.

In February 2002, the U.S. Cellular Telecommunications & Internet Association (CTIA) convened the first meeting of its newly formed Wireless Internet Caucus Leadership Council, launching an industrywide initiative to address the hurdles that faced the U.S. market in wireless data and mobile Internet products and services. Even though U.S. players were still laggards in the 3G transition, they were not doomed to remain so. Some were willing to make bold initiatives. Sprint CEO William Esrey set summer 2002 for the launch of the new 3G service. AT&T Wireless was planning to offer services sometime in 2002 as well, and Cingular Wireless in early 2004. The convergence of mobility and the Internet resulted in new opportunities. However, all of these operators were bleeding as well. With the stocks of AT&T Wireless and Nextel in the single digits and the IPOs of Cingular and Verizon Wireless on ice, speculation was rampant that, as *The Wall Street Journal* reported, "consolidation among the big six national wireless operators is imminent. The drive for bulk is being spurred by slowing subscriber growth, stratospheric costs associated with upgrading to higher-speed networks, and fierce competition forcing companies to offer customers more for less."[36] The forces of consolidation, however, were far from recent. "Over the past twenty years, the telecommunications industry has been fractured and transformed," notes Bruce Wasserstein, whose analysis of telecom and mobile M&A waves parallels the arrival of new public policies and the three stages of monopoly, transition, and competition.[37]

Consolidation has been part of industry evolution in all central Triad regions. In the United States, old-style public policies delayed it for decades, despite the noble rhetoric of free-market objectives. Regulatory barriers have proved detrimental to U.S. mobile policies, industry competition, and innovation systems. It was the regulatory zeal to force domestication and fragmentation on the globalizing and consolidating marketplace that effectively dismantled America's competitive advantage in the mobile business between the late 1940s and the 1980s. As regulators have reviewed their policies and digital convergence led to the entry of America's powerful IT leaders, future prospects look far more promising. But decades were lost for self-inflicted wounds.

Chapter 5

The 2G Era: Euro-Nordic Pioneers

"Wherever two or three Norwegians, Swedes, Danes, or Finns are congregated," wrote A. R. Bennett in 1895, " you may be certain that they always, in addition to a church and a school, will construct a telephone switchboard."[1] While the Swedes and the Finns have played key roles in the Nordic pioneership, the Norwegians and the Danes have never been that far behind. The real competitive difference originates from the fact that the latter two countries have not possessed flagship companies, such as Ericsson or Nokia, which have driven national success in Sweden and Finland, respectively.

From World War I through the 1G era, the United States was the core cluster and lead market in the wireless business. By the turn of the 1980s, wireless vendors and operators in Nordic countries had not only caught up with the United States, but were engaged in efforts that would ultimately allow them to take over its leadership. The excellence of Nordic operators and vendors built upon a long history of telecom innovation. But to overcome the inherent limitations of their tiny markets, the Nordic players would have to achieve global leverage.

The Nordic Model

Due to their competitive innovation, Nordic firms have not only imitated industry leaders; they have excelled over U.S. firms and others in upgrading and innovation. In the case of the productivity frontier, Nordic players have turned their inherent weakness (small scale) into a source of strength (incentive for scope). While U.S. leaders have concentrated on differentiation or cost leadership strategies, the smaller Nordic players have been flexible enough to reach for both simultaneously. Finally, the third determinant—early, extensive internationalization by Nordic players—is intertwined with the issue of productivity frontier because it is scope that has allowed the Nordic companies to achieve scale. Unlike their rivals, Nordic firms do not possess a vast domestic market. Rather, their tiny home base has necessitated scale through scope.

In the late nineteenth century, the drivers of the Nordic model—com-

113

petitive innovation, high quality and low cost, scale through scope—typified only the leading Nordic markets, not the U.S., continental, or Japanese models. By the late-twentieth century, these drivers permeated the entire globalizing business.

Emergence of the Nordic Model: Toward Open Specifications

Over time, particularly with the rise of the cellular platform, these determinants—the early quest for competitive innovation, productivity frontier, and internationalization—have promoted open specifications in northern Europe. The early victory over Bell necessitated competitive innovation and avoidance of lock-in with a singular supply chain. In Finland, additionally, political autonomy vis-à-vis Russia nurtured efforts at competitive local telcos. In turn, high quality and cost leadership have been easier to realize through market-driven value chains. Finally, internationalization, if it is to be competitive and efficient, requires open specifications, which are more responsive to local conditions. In contrast to popular myths, it was not just or even primarily "Nordic egalitarianism" that created this drive toward openness (the conduct of Nordic PTTs has often been as monopolistic as that of the large national PTTs in continental Europe). Rather, it was the competitive necessity to achieve scale through scope that accounted for their penchant for open specifications.

Victory Over Bell: Competitive Innovation

In 1876, Alexander Graham Bell applied for a U.S. patent on the telephone. That same year, Nordic countries followed in these footsteps. In Stockholm, Lars Magnus Ericsson opened a telegraph repair shop. Soon thereafter, Ericsson began to upgrade and innovate by moving from phone repair to manufacturing. The great telephony breakthrough in Sweden took place in 1880, when the U.S. Bell Company, relying on equipment made in the United States, built the first telephone networks in Stockholm and several other key cities. The showdown ensued in 1881, when the city of Gävle on the Baltic coast called for bids to supply a local telephone system. The testers found Ericsson's telephones "simpler, stronger, and more attractive."[2]

The Swedish innovator and the nascent Swedish PTT were certainly not alone in the pioneering activities. The Norwegians, Danes, and Finns followed. Finland's first telephone connection, for instance, was built in December 1877 in Helsinki. Despite their sophistication in the new telecom business, the Finns, unlike the Swedes, did not possess a flagship company. The extraordinary success of the cluster had historical roots that originated from Russia's rule in the late-nineteenth century, as well as more contemporary drivers, stemming from Nokia's strategy. Despite persistent myths, these determinants had little to do with competition until the 1980s and 1990s, with the emergence of Finland's wireless valley (see Exhibit 5-1).

High Quality and Low Cost

The last two decades of the nineteenth century were very productive years at Telefonaktiebolaget LM Ericsson. Unlike the first bulky telephone prototypes, the Swedish manufacturing firm sought a light, attractive appearance without sacrificing technical performance. To Ericsson himself, *designer skills* and *technical insight* were not mutually exclusive, but complementary:

Exhibit 5-1. Emergence of Finland's wireless valley.

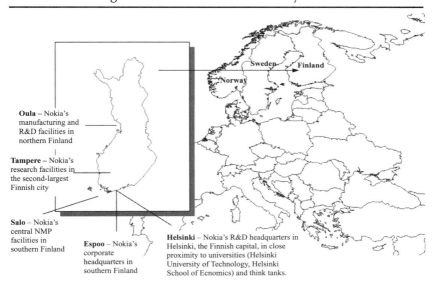

Oula – Nokia's manufacturing and R&D facilities in northern Finland

Tampere – Nokia's research facilities in the second-largest Finnish city

Salo – Nokia's central NMP facilities in southern Finland

Espoo – Nokia's corporate headquarters in southern Finland

Helsinki – Nokia's R&D headquarters in Helsinki, the Finnish capital, in close proximity to universities (Helsinki University of Technology, Helsinki School of Ecnomics) and think tanks.

In the late 1990s, many observers attributed the success of Finland's mobile cluster to competition. That was a myth. True, the number of Finnish local telcos once peaked at more than 800, but this was well before World War II and far ahead the emergence of the cellular business in Finland.

Through the 19th century, until the Bolshevik revolution and Finland's independence declaration, the country was part of the Russian Empire. Through these eras, communications played a crucial role in military efforts. Due to defense and security considerations, the precursors of Finland's wireless cluster emerged first in the key coastal cities – during Sweden's reign, in Turku; during Russia's reign, in Helsinki. Telegraph was highly centralized and "born international," hence its critical role in the administration of the Tsarist empire in the late 19th century. In contrast, telephone was decentralized and "born local." Unlike the telegraph, it served individuals, consumers, households, and small businesses. The Russian authorities could allow certain autonomy in local telephone communications, but the telegraph was a matter of national security. The Finns seized the political opportunities offered by a new technology and the ensuing regulatory uncertainty, and pushed the control of telecommunications from St. Petersburg to Helsinki. *That* initiated industry efforts, which, ultimately, made Helsinki the center of the Finnish mobile cluster. With Nokia's drastic growth in the postwar era, many productive facilities were later located outside the coastal cities of the south (Salo, Tampere, Oulu).

Historically, the success of Finland's Wireless Valley in the 1990s originated from geopolitics (Finland's special relationship with Tsarist Russia and Soviet Union), public policies (Nordic cooperation, EU strategies and Finnish liberalization in the 1970s and 1980s). At firm-level, necessary preconditions included first-mover advantages (strategies of mobile vendors and operators, particularly Nokia's role in war repatriation in the 1950s, diversification into electronics in the 1960s, as well as mobile and telecom segments in the 1970s).

> In his eyes, an invention was not an end in itself but only a means.
> His inventions may be said to represent stages in a constantly pro-
> ceeding energetic effort to develop and improve the branch of
> electrotechnique to which he had devoted himself. . . . Ericsson's
> work at the drawing board was lightened to a high degree by his
> thorough knowledge of the trade. . . . He could visualize to the last
> detail how the instrument engaging his thoughts for the moment
> should be built up, so that it could be produced in the most simple
> and efficient manner.[3]

High quality and high performance with simple yet efficient manufacturing practices—these characteristics became an integral part of L.M. Ericsson's
reputation and, later, the hallmark of Nordic mobile pioneers. In the United
States, a vast and lucrative market has favored substantial specialization. For
decades, most companies have engaged in differentiation *or* low-cost strategies,
while foreign markets have held little pull. In the Nordic countries, the competitive telcos have excelled in quality *and* cost leadership, while the small
domestic home base has served as a powerful push motive for internationalization.

The Nordic concept of high quality coupled with low cost has not been
confined to equipment manufacturers; it pertained to the operators as well.
Because of their egalitarian public service mission, the operators were forced
to compete for a small customer base while keeping price levels relatively low.
As early as in 1883, Henrik Tore Cedergren, a close friend of Ericsson,
launched Stockholms Allmänna Telefonaktiebolag (SAT), a private operating
company, which competed alongside the state-owned PTT in Sweden. Some
thirty-five years later—in 1918—SAT merged into L.M. Ericsson. With his
vision of "a telephone in each home in Stockholm," Cedergren wanted to make
the telephone available at a reasonable cost. The concept evolved as a response
to the rates charged by the Swedish Bell companies, which he considered close
to prohibitive.

Scale Through Scope: Early Internationalization

Because of their vast home base, U.S. companies, until recently, have been
able to achieve scale even while ignoring scope. In contrast, the Nordic firms
could achieve scale only through scope. For the U.S. vendors and operators
and for many large-country European firms, internationalization has been an
afterthought. For Nordic competitors, it was a necessary condition for survival.
For many vendors, it was also a regulatory stipulation. For instance, Ericsson
could not sell equipment to the Swedish market. In Sweden, public switching
equipment and telephones were manufactured by Telai, which was owned by
the Swedish PTT; Ericsson manufactured exclusively for foreign markets.[4]

Furthermore, Swedish business managers have historically cherished an international orientation, and Sweden has given rise to more multinationals than any other Nordic country.[5] This mind-set reinforced Ericsson's early internationalization and Nordic views on competition, deregulation, and standards. But in wireless communications, these countries lagged behind U.S. developments until the 1960s and 1970s.

The Pre-Cellular Era: Swedish Catch-Up

Though the Bell teams initiated the cellular concept, they were not alone in building the new cellular systems. The Nordic catch-up followed soon after the adoption of one-way wireless by Detroit's police department. In 1933—only some twelve years after the pioneering work in Detroit—the Swedes engaged in similar experiments with police radio in Gothenburg. From 1935 onwards, there was a regular service with a number of radio cars (see Exhibit 5-2). Transmission took place on shortwave frequencies and radio telegraphy was employed. As the Swedes made a concerted effort to keep abreast of technical developments in radio, World War II increased the pace of these initiatives and the demand for wireless communications.

In most of Western Europe, the end of World War II served as a catalyst for a renewed interest in European unity. Finding themselves between the socialist East and the capitalist West, Nordic countries struggled for a "third way" that would do justice to their mixed economies. In 1945, the Nordic Social Democrats drafted a far-reaching declaration on Nordic cooperation.[6] The explosion of the cellular business was one result of these Nordic initiatives. From the introduction of dispatch radio services, the major Nordic countries—Sweden, Finland, Denmark, and Norway—adopted an unusually progressive attitude toward wireless communications. The use of the wireless was heavily promoted and the use of the available spectrum was encouraged. The Nordic topography favored mobile communications, due to the dispersion of much of the population in remote places. Efforts to develop a common network and to standardize the technology triggered Nordic cooperation, in which the early pioneering built on the Swedish experiences.

From Swedish Pioneer Systems to Consolidation of Equipment Manufacturers

In the late 1940s, when plans for wireless telephony trials began to mature, Sture Lauhren and Ragnar Berglund, two engineers of Televerket—the Swedish PTT (today Telia)—were given the task of designing a mobile system. Late in 1950, Televerket installed a trial system in Stockholm, MTL (Mobile Telephone Lauhren). A year later, these efforts resulted in the world's first automatic wireless telephone system. In 1961, another trial was set up for Berglund's new system, MTB (Mobile Telephone Berglund). Following

Exhibit 5-2. From Swedish catch-up to the first Nordic mobile system.

In 1933, the Swedes engaged in mobile experiments with police radio in Gothenburg...

... and Stockholm. And from 1935 onwards there was a regular service with a number of radio cars.

Lauhrén's fully automatic mobile telephone system built on a relay technique triggering international interest.

In 1951, an experimental installation was set up in Stockholm.

By the mid-1950s, Berglund presented his "tone code principle," in which a particular selection tone was exclusively identified with the mobile station.

In 1971, the Nordic countries introduced the first MDT system, a manual version of the first Nordic NMT system – more than 12 years prior to the U.S. launch of the first commercial cellular system in 1983.

Source: Photos by Telemuseum, Sweden. Police radio photo by the Swedish Museum of Police.

successful trials, MTB systems were installed for commercial use in the mid-1960s, in Stockholm, Gothenburg, and Malmö. While these systems were used side by side, the need for a *countrywide* wireless telephone system became increasingly urgent. The expansion of coverage was costly. Similarly, increasing subscriber density in the cities required substantial chunks of spectrum. The Swedish engineers and regulators soon understood that the existing technologies were leading to a dead end.

Concurrently, two Nordic equipment manufacturers—Ericsson in Sweden and Nokia in Finland—were diversifying into electronics and mobile communications. In 1961, Svenska Radio Aktiebolaget (SRA), a subsidiary of L.M. Ericsson, reorganized to focus on radio systems and divested in consumer goods markets. In addition to the nascent industrial wireless markets (towing, taxi, and trucking services), SRA sold to the police and armed forces. In Finland, Nokia was evolving into a comparable flagship company. In 1933, the Nordic wireless pioneers had been behind U.S. wireless companies; in the 1970s, they caught up. With the digital transition in the early 1990s, *they* became the pioneers.

Progressive Public Policies

In the postwar era, the strategies and policies of the Nordic countries proved superior to those of the United States on two counts. First, Nordic telecom authorities formulated and implemented liberal policies and excelled in coordination. Second, they aggressively promoted the early adoption of new wireless technologies. In Sweden, the early systems (MTL, MTB) were followed by a third one, a manual system (MTC). In the late 1970s, MTC was seen as an interim solution before the introduction to the cellular. But while these Nordic experiments were innovative and progressive, the countries were small, and wireless markets lacked economies of scale. Without adequate scope, even the most progressive Nordic players would not be able to scale up their operations.

In larger European markets, the national PTTs introduced their wireless systems after the Nordic countries. In contrast to the Nordic pioneers, European telecom monopolies favored exclusive supply chains and indigenous contractors. These contributed to high costs and inefficiencies, which in turn delayed and marginalized the adoption of the new wireless technologies. Nordic cooperation resulted in a model that was precisely the reverse. Nordic PTTs did not favor their own national suppliers. The prices of terminals and services were kept low to promote adoption and affordable use in accordance with the public service mission. The Nordic telecom authorities, PTTs, and vendors nurtured a very different vision of the wireless than that of the PTTs in larger European countries. The Nordic players envisioned an industry that built upon open and nonproprietary solutions.

Public Service, Market Drivers

In 1964, the Swedes formed a study group chaired by Carl-Gösta Åsdal
to clear out the commercial, economic, and political aspects of future wireless
services. Three years later, its report, "Land Wireless Radio Communication,"
recommended the development of three services (mobile telephone, paging,
land-mobile radio) for use in vehicles.[7] Televerket approved the report in 1967,
and development began the next year. These activities coincided with increasing Nordic cooperation in telecommunications. Historically, Swedish government had been Ericsson's key customer. As the leading Nordic country,
Sweden served as a model for Denmark, Finland, and Norway, as well as *their*
telecom administrations, operators, and vendors. In a Nordic conference two
years later, Åsdal proposed that mobile telephony become part of Nordic cooperation. With the creation of the Nordic Mobile Telephone Group (*Nordiska
Mobil Telefongruppen*, or NMT), the task was to develop a new, Pan-Nordic
automatic mobile telephone system. It began by outlining system requirements
based more on market needs than technical parameters:

- Fully automatic operation and charging
- System and terminal compatibility between all four countries
- Full roaming capability between all Nordic countries
- Wireless to wireless calls, in addition to wireless-fixed and fixed-wire-
  less
- Sufficient capacity to last many years
- High reliability, particularly for signaling features such as call charging
  and number transmission
- Use similar to a conventional fixed telephone, with the same facilities
- Low-cost infrastructure and wireless
- Conversations protected against interception
- Open specifications with no exclusive supplier rights

These specifications were not geared to foster profitability, but to support
the public-service mission of the Nordic PTTs, which integrated wireless operations with the rest of their activities. Because the price for fixed subscriptions was relatively low, revenues were dependent on adequate traffic levels
and cost-leadership strategies. Unsurprisingly, the Nordic PTTs also saw Ericsson's AXE switching system "as the nodal point in such a system, a node
which would be the interface with the national network, but which would also
provide the system's intelligence."[8]

Regulators and engineers expected the project to take about a decade to
complete because of the required R&D and the expected availability of new
developments in microelectronics. "The group's vision was to transform wireless phones *from a luxury item to a tool for everyone* [author's italics]," recalls Åke
Lundqvist, formerly president of Ericsson Radio Systems.[9] In the interim, the

NMT group recommended the establishment of manual mobile systems in the Nordic countries to cover growing demand *and* to develop the market. These systems would be harmonized, follow common specifications, and use identical sets of frequencies *regionwide.*[10] The group also recommended that mobile stations (terminals installed in vehicles) should not be owned by the PTTs, but by the subscribers who would purchase them from manufacturers in a competitive market. The terminal solution forced open standards upon the mobile vendors, which accelerated competition and eroded the monopoly power of the Nordic PTTs. This, in turn, boosted the expansion of Nordic equipment manufacturers *worldwide.*

From Regional Success to Global Triumph: NMT and GSM

A converging set of determinants caused the Nordic countries to take the lead in the emerging cellular services. In the early 1980s, Sweden, for instance, had the world's highest relative penetration in computers and telecommunications. Dispersed populations made the wireless value proposition cost-efficient compared to fixed services. Because of relatively high income levels, tariffs did not pose an obstacle. From the beginning, the licensing regimes took a liberal tact, stressing market-driven solutions and public service mission. Finally, the Nordic PTTs did not subsidize cellular services. Early terminal prices were high but affordable in the target groups.[11]

Toward a Nordic Standard

As Nordic PTTs embraced the proposal, the Swedish initiative turned from a *national* matter into a *regionwide* effort. Before the late 1960s, Nordic PTTs had shared similar approaches and objectives in the mobile R&D, but each had catered largely to a domestic market. Due to the inherent homogenity of the Nordic countries (population, religion, mixed economies, culture), as well as the escalation of cross-border activities, regionalization occurred rather effortlessly. By the same token, it leveraged the underlying assumptions of the Swedish technology solutions and policy preferences (open specifications, low-cost pricing, competitive suppliers, roaming) across northern Europe. Prior to 1969, the Swedish PTT and Ericsson had a home base in Sweden; now their home base covered all Nordic countries. Concurrently, scale economies extended over entire northern Europe. The European Commission made note of the success of the Nordic standard (NMT), saw it as a means to promote competition in the monopolistic telecom sector, and threw its political weight behind the emerging digital standard, GSM. The United States dominated information technology. The Japanese ruled over consumer electronics. The EC wanted to ensure that the wireless profits would stay in Europe.

Regionalization: Nordic Mobile Telephone

The first NMT system was not adopted in the Nordic countries, but in Saudi Arabia in the summer of 1981. Sweden and Norway launched it in the autumn, and it was introduced in Finland and Denmark the following year. Initially, the technology configuration reflected the driving role of the Swedish cluster. All four Nordic countries chose the Ericsson AXE switch, but base stations were bought from four separate suppliers. In October 1982, the roaming function allowed NMT telephones to be used in all Nordic countries. The success of NMT boosted the early expansion of Ericsson and Nokia in infrastructure and handsets. But instead of being content with a regional base, SRA and Ericsson sought new markets by making agility their strength. "One of our greatest competitive advantages was our ability to make quick decisions," recalls Åke Lundqvist.[12] Both the technology *and* the organizational capabilities made AXE a success in the United States. In the early 1980s, the SRA/Ericsson system was chosen in some forty of the 130 requests for tender from nonwireline operators (who were allocated half of the licenses). Growth resulted in rapid expansion at SRA, which was taken over in full by Ericsson in 1983 and renamed Ericsson Radio Systems AB (ERA).

By October 1985, NMT had 30,000 Finnish subscribers and 200,000 more throughout Scandinavia. The four major Nordic countries—Sweden, Finland, Norway, and Denmark—were the first in Europe to introduce commercial wireless telephone services using cellular technology. The public service mission inherent in the policy choices (i.e., liberalization and deregulation) prepared the pioneering Nordic companies for mass-market competition in the 1990s. Because consumer needs had been considered during the planning of the network, mobile phones moved quickly from business markets to consumer markets. The competitive superiority of the Nordic model as compared with the U.S. approach became relatively clear—including public policies, roaming as an instrument of scale economies, competitive suppliers, selection of frequency bands, critical differences in tariffs, and—most important—the penchant for open specifications.[13]

As long as the Nordic vendors were dealing with high differentiation and low-volume capabilities, they could respond to price competition. When digital cellular pushed the industry toward low differentiation and high-volume capabilities, they found it harder to compete with low-cost producers.

Learning Low-Cost Manufacturing

In the 1980s, the wireless industry was still a low-volume, high-cost business. But even before the 2G era, things began to change. With the impending migration from business markets to consumer markets, Nordic players had to learn the art of low-cost manufacturing. As a latecomer in the mobile *phone* business, Ericsson struggled to catch up, as did Qualcomm in the United States. Ericsson first got a taste of the new production pressures at Kumla in the late 1980s. As the terminals became smaller and lighter, production volume soared. With the first order for Curt by Panasonic, Ericsson's factory began a rapid growth.[14] Until 1988, prices in the NMT markets remained relatively high, which allowed Ericsson to profit in the mobile phone business. But price cuts of some 30 percent at Motorola in response to the Japanese challenge (and to squeeze out smaller rivals) caused havoc at Ericsson. The new era belonged to a new generation of more entrepreneurial and market-driven operators—the kind of carriers that Nokia embraced, not the old PTTs that were Ericsson's clients.

At ERA, the awakening came in 1987, when Panasonic decided not to introduce its own handheld into the NMT 900 market. In the past, Ericsson and Panasonic had worked together. Now their cooperation intensified, which forced Ericsson's production at Kumla to catch up with Panasonic's standards in quality, price, and productivity. In the old days, the products entailed high-labor content, plenty of space within the phone casing, relatively high prices, and small quantities. Changes began around 1984, and project teams were launched between 1985 and 1988 to collaborate with Lund's product development. The Swedes entered a new era.

> The Kumla factory in the mid-1980s was a typical Ericsson production unit. Production was seen largely as something separate and self-contained, with its own management and its own accounting. The product development people developed a new design, and the drawings and specifications were sent up to the responsible production unit, which set up the necessary tools and machines—and announced the cost of the product. The product went on the market, sales were made—with luck—and production orders were sent in.[15]

Toward the late 1980s, Ericsson needed a large factory that would make fewer products, but in great quantities. As Ericsson established a business relationship with Elcoteq, a Finnish supplier that would greatly benefit from Nokia's growth in the 1990s, it was in for a new surprise: The Finns were selling handsets to Ericsson, at a profit, at a price 35 percent below the manufacturing cost at Kumla.[16] After a slate of restructurings, Kumla's four different units were brought under a single management in 1991, when it was making about 200,000 phones. Soon rising volumes necessitated subcontracting because low-cost manufacturing capabilities became vital.

In the early 1G era, NMT held substantial potential, and some Scandinavians hoped it would evolve into a Pan-European standard. In the end, it proved a regional success. By the end of the 1990s, NMT remained in use by about 4.5 million people in some forty countries, including the Nordic countries, Asia, Russia, and other Eastern European countries. It failed as a world standard, but it showed the way toward one.

The GSM Triumph

GSM became the first dominant, commercially operated digital cellular system as a result of intensive technology innovation *and* politico-regulatory initiatives. The need for such a unified European cellular standard was recognized by the French PTT and the German Bundespost as early as 1981. With the gradual unification of the European markets at the end of the 1980s, the European Conference of Postal and Telecommunications Administrations (CEPT), which comprised the telecom administrations of twenty-six European countries, decided to develop a common standard for digital mobile telephony. In 1982, CEPT formed a new standards group, Group Special Mobile, specifically for radio and telephone systems in Europe. Today, this standard is known as Global System for Mobile Communications (GSM). Created in 1989, European Telecommunications Standards Institute (ETSI) played an important role in the standardization of the GSM. In contrast to U.S. regulators, the European Commission, relying on a Pan-European political initiative, joined the telecom operators and equipment manufacturers to promote regional harmonization of cellular networks. In Europe, GSM became a *mandatory* standard.

GSM, European Integration, and Nordic Leadership

Despite old-style industrial policies, the general thrust of the early EEC integration was free and open trade. In the late 1980s, the concept of GSM matched the European Commission's objectives of providing comprehensive Pan-European services and standards, as well as the EC's willingness to transform European telecommunications from domestic monopolies into a fully competitive environment. To avoid political confrontation, the EC initiatives were introduced in a piecemeal fashion, from the liberalization of equipment to value-added services. But the ultimate objective was competition in network operation and basic voice service by 1998.

Directives of the European Commission

In September 1987, most European cellular operators that signed the GSM memorandum of understanding still operated as monopoly suppliers of all telecom services in their respective countries. These PTTs were domestic, vertically integrated, hierarchic giants that owned and operated the networks, provision of services, and usually equipment manufacturing. They were also charged with regulation. The arrangements cultivated vested interests because the PTTs competed *and* regulated competition. Initially, most players considered the emerging cellular industry a threat rather than an opportunity. But times were changing. The old competitive environment began to crumble with the EC directives.[17] As the role of the national PTTs and telecom authorities declined, that of regionwide competition policy increased.

The first GSM specification was completed in 1988, allowing manufacturers to start producing equipment. The first test systems were taken into operation three years later, and commercial operations followed in 1992. At Ericsson, these years prompted an intense debate on the mission of the company. "A common view was that phones were consumer products that were best left to the Japanese," recalls Åke Lundqvist. "But we killed the myth that Ericsson could not make consumer products. Being able to offer a complete product portfolio, including phones, and having expertise in all aspects of the system were also significant advantages."[18] This view prevailed from the late 1980s until the turmoil of 2000 and 2001, when the unit was merged with Sony's operation.

In 1991, the Finnish wireless operator, Radiolinja, launched the first GSM network (see Exhibit 5-3). Only four years earlier, Finnish voters had elected the largest non-Socialist majority since 1930, and Harri Holkeri, a veteran conservative politician, was appointed prime minister, becoming the first Conservative prime minister since World War II. That gave a powerful boost to deregulation. He was Finland's prime minister until 1991, during the critical years that boosted deregulation and prepared for Nokia's expansion. According

Exhibit 5-3. The first GSM call.

Founded in 1988, Radiolinja was a mobile communications provider by the Finnet Group, a speculative venture that sought a license to operate a second GSM network. The Finnish PTT strongly opposed granting the license, arguing that the construction of two rival GSM networks in a small country would mean duplication of investments and dilution of economic efficiencies. Despite intrigues, the Finnish GSM growth took off in mid-1994 and exploded two years later.

"At the time, we certainly had no idea of the explosion that would follow," Harri Holkeri, a veteran Finnish Prime Minister, acknowledges. "Commercially, the business went through a Death Valley before it became profitable. We demolished a monopoly, which gave way to a duopoly, which has now given room for more players. *That* gave Nokia an opportunity to exploit its full capacity at home. Today Nokia is a global player, but wasn't then. The Nokians have acknowledged that it was the early deregulation that provided them first-mover technology advantages vis-à-vis rivals, including U.S. players. Deregulation allowed Nokia to exploit its home base as a test laboratory."

SOURCE: Steinbock, D. (2001), Interview with Harri Holkeri, the president of the 55th session of the U.N. General Assembly, at the United Nations, New York City, May 10, 2001.
Photo: Radiolinja.

to Holkeri: "In those days, we decided, after tough talks with the social democrats and conservatives that our regulatory regime must be overhauled. 'Nothing is holy anymore', that's what we used to say at the time." By August 1997,
Nokia supplied GSM systems to fifty-nine operators in thirty-one countries.
Its triumph had become synonymous with that of the GSM, and vice versa.
Despite its GSM success, the Finnish vendor was technology-agnostic and, by
1994, became the first manufacturer to launch a series of handportable
phones—the Nokia 2100 family—for all major digital standards (e.g., GSM,
TDMA, PCN, Japan Digital Cellular).

By 1999, GSM was the dominant cellular standard, with more than 45
percent of mobile subscribers worldwide. The GSM-driven expansion provided the foundation for the explosive growth of Nokia and the Finnish mobile
cluster, which soon became known as "Finland's Wireless Valley."[19]

Old PTTs and New Operators: From Engineering to Marketing

Even prior to the GSM triumph, the rules of the game changed dramatically as the business migrated from regulation to deregulation in the most
developed country markets.[20] In the past, the PTT authorities had been the
vendors' key customers. Starting with deregulation in the U.K. in the early
1980s and the breakup of AT&T in the United States, compliance-driven
PTTs faded in history. A new generation of marketing-driven operators favored integrated turnkey solutions on common platforms. Order and delivery
cycles became less predictable and far more competitive. These changes added
to competitive pressures, but also brought about attractive new opportunities.
Adapting to the new rules required substantial changes in organizational capabilities. In national PTTs (i.e., Europe's large-country operators), engineers
accounted for 56 percent of staff (among the service-driven Nordic PTTs,
about 50 percent). Among the new operators, however, engineers accounted
for less than a fifth of the staff. The focus was on marketing, sales, and service,
which accounted for most of the staff (35 percent in marketing/sales, 25 percent in customer services), as opposed to 20 percent in national PTTs and 32
percent in Nordic operators. New operators also put more stress on IT than the
old PTTs or service-driven PTTs; comprehensive management information
systems were critical to cellular applications.[21] Even though traditional PTTs
and new operators were in the same industry, they could not have been more
different vis-à-vis organizational capabilities. Nokia, in particular, aligned with
the new generation of operators.

Globalization of Operators

In the industry value chain, vendors were the first to engage in global strategies. They were soon followed by a new generation of operators. The first

firms to be privatized and deregulated were also the first to internationalize. The first wave of internationalization took place toward the end of the 1980s and early 1990s. Most players were U.S.-based Baby Bells. In the home base, they faced heavy regulation; growth was in the foreign markets. As the Baby Bells engaged in international strategies, they also contributed to rising entry barriers. The second wave of internationalization evolved toward the end of the 1990s. In the late analog phase, Baby Bells leveraged their domestic know-how in foreign markets. In the late digital phase, European-based operators and some U.S. carriers extended *their* domestic expertise into international markets. In both cases, then, experience was traded for access, but in the late 1990s, the financial and strategic stakes were different by an order of magnitude. At the same time, internationalization contributed to regionalization.

First Wave of Internationalization

Through the 1G era, the industry thrust remained in the United States. This did not automatically reflect on the internationalization of U.S.-based carriers. Due to the century-long monopoly era, domestic leadership in a major Triad nation did not coincide with internationalization. In contrast to ITT, AT&T had not engaged in substantial operations in foreign markets until the divestiture of 1984. *After* the breakup, it rushed overseas. Having lost its lucrative domestic monopoly, it went for growth markets with gusto. But this strategic reorientation was too little too late. Before the end of the Cold War, AT&T also faced substantial challenges in lead markets including China, where political rather than market considerations doomed the company's belated triumph. Aside from Motorola and other major vendors, the industry comprised the RCCs. These were too small, weak, and too fragmented to internationalize. Most important, the worldwide telecom industry remained regulated and dominated by the national PTTs. As the new public policies were still an anathema in the traditional telecom world of the early 1980s, the first movers in deregulation, privatization, and liberalization—the U.K., the United States, the Nordic countries, and a handful of other nations—were not the rule but the exception. Even if vendors and operators *could* internationalize in these pioneer country-markets, they were *prohibited* from effective entry in many lead markets.

The early internationalization of competitive operators rested on three requirements. First, the monopoly era had to fade away in the core clusters *and* the lead markets, in order to enable new organizational capabilities while allowing for market entry. Second, the worst turmoil of the great transition had to subside to support internationalization efforts in foreign markets. Third, global telecom reforms had to be initiated in the lead markets. In the absence of new public policies, the internationalizing operators would not have been able to establish a foothold in lead markets because there would have been no market terrain to hold onto.

Baby Bells: Trading Experience for Access

The first wave of internationalization among network operators began primarily in the United States, where the breakup of AT&T resulted in the proliferation of industry players in local telecom markets. Despite industry turmoil, the Baby Bells still possessed the most advanced technologies, products, and services, as well as the most effective operations. They also emerged in the most competitive market worldwide. While the 1984 breakup restricted their domestic scope into local operations, comparable barriers did not exist for foreign market entry. As the industry turmoil lessened in the United States and telecom reforms accelerated in lead markets, a number of relatively successful Baby Bells leveraged their expertise in lead markets and in markets that were introducing competition. The first wave of internationalization rested on strategic coalitions (particularly joint ventures). Through these partnerships, the Baby Bells essentially traded experience for access.

The Baby Bells' international conquest followed the deregulation trail. With the integration objectives of the European Commission, Western Europe was the first to promote competition, followed by Asia-Pacific and later Latin America. This early wave of internationalization started around 1989 and lasted until the mid-1990s. It coincided with industry consolidation in the analog cellular and ended with the large-scale adoption of the digital cellular.

Rising Entry Barriers

With more than 43 percent of worldwide penetration, the United States enjoyed the highest market share among the top-eight country markets in 1994. That year, North America still had almost 50 percent of the worldwide subscribers. Two other major first-mover nations—the U.K. and Japan—both had more than 6 percent, whereas Germany, Italy, and Australia each had between 3 and 5 percent. China had less than 3 percent. In 1994, other countries held about 25 percent of the market total. These market figures did not translate to corresponding ones in international strategies. In China, the cellular infrastructure was still being built. In Germany, Italy, and Australia, the leading operators were former national PTTs, which engaged in domestic strategies. In Japan, NTT DoCoMo was subject to regulations that prohibited internationalization. Nordic country markets had given rise to highly advanced operators, but ones that lacked appropriate scale. In the mid-1990s, that left only two countries to compete for internationalization: the United States and the U.K.

The leading players (see Exhibit 5-4) were the U.S.-based AT&T and Baby Bells, and the U.K.-based Cable & Wireless, whose parents enjoyed $7 billion to $10 billion in annual revenues. Additionally, there were smaller new entrants, such as Vodafone ($1.3 billion), and niche players such as Millicom ($81 million). The list also included leading vendors, such as Motorola

(text continues on page 132)

Exhibit 5-4. Leading international cellular operators.
Mid 1990s

OPERATOR	Annual Revs.	North America	Western Europe	Eastern Europe	Latin America	Asia-Pacific	Africa and Middle East
Vodafone (UK)	$1,263	na	France, Germany, Greece, Malta, Netherlands, Sweden	na	na	Australia, Fiji, Hong Kong, India	na
Airtouch (US)		United States	Belgium, Germany, Italy, Spain, Sweden	Poland, Romania	Puerto Rico	India, Japan, South Korea	na
Bell South (US)		United States	Denmark, France, Germany	na	Argentina, Chile, Uruguay, Venezuela	Australia, India, New Zealand	Israel
Cable & Wireless (UK)	$6,978	na	France, Germany	Belorus, Bulgaria, Kazakhstan	Colombia, Trinidad, several Caribbean properties	Australia, Hong Kong, Japan, Macau, Pakistan, Singapore, Soloman Isl.	Bahrain, Oman, South Africa, Yemen
US West (US)	$10,953	United States	France, UK	Czech Rep., Hungary, Poland, Russia, Slovakia	na	India, Japan, Malaysia	na
Bell Atlantic (US)		United States	Italy	Czech Rep., Slovakia	Mexico	New Zealand	na
Nynex (US)		United States	Greece	na	na	India	na
SBC (US)		United States	France	na	Chile	South Korea	South Africa
Millicom (US/Sweden)	$81	United States	Sweden	Lithuania, Russia	Bolivia, Colombia, Costa Rica, El Salvador, Guatemala, Paraguay	India, Pakistan, Philippines, Sri Lanka, Vietnam	Ghana, Mauritius
Motorola (US)	$22,245	na	na	Lithuania	Argentina, Chile, Dominican Rep., Mexico, Nicaragua, Uruguay	na	Israel
AT&T (US)	$4,246 (1996)	United States	na	na	Colombia, Ecuador, Venezuela	Hong Kong, India	na

(continues)

Exhibit 5-4. (Continued).
ca 2001

OPERATOR	Annual Revs.	North America	Western Europe	Eastern Europe	Latin America	Asia Pacific	Africa and Middle East
Vodafone (UK)	$21,250	United States, Canada	Belgium, France, Germany, Greece, Ireland, Italy, Malta, Netherlands, Portugal, Spain, Sweden, Switzerland, UK	Albania, Hungary, Poland, Romania, Czech Republic, Slovakia	Argentina, Dominican Rep., Mexico, Venezuela	Australia, China, Fiji, Japan, New Zealand, Indonesia, Philippines, Taiwan	Egypt, Kenya, South Africa
Cingular (US)	$12,647	United States, Canada	Belgium, Denmark, France, Germany	na	Argentina, Brazil, Chile, Colombia, Ecuador, Guatemala, Mexico, Nicaragua, Peru, Uruguay, Venezuela	India, Taiwan	Israel, South Africa
AT&T (US)	$10,448	United States, Canada	na	Czech Republic, Slovakia		India, Taiwan	na
Nextel Int'l (US)	$330	United States, Canada	na	na	Argentina, Brazil, Mexico, Peru	Japan, Philippines	na
Leap Wireless Int'l (US)	$50	United States	Iceland, Ireland	Croatia, Georgia, Slovenia	Bolivia, Haiti	na	Cote d'Ivoire, Ghana

Cable & Wireless (UK)	$11,480	United States	UK	na	Dominican Rep., Panama, several Caribbean properties	Fiji, Japan, Singapore	Bahrain
NTT DoCoMo (Japan)	$36,963	United States	Netherlands	na	Brazil	Hong Kong, Japan	na
France Telecom (France)	$31,714	na	France, Germany, UK, Italy	na	na	na	Egypt
Deutsche Telekom (Germany)	$38,556	United States	Austria, France, Germany, Netherlands, Spain, UK	Poland	na	na	na
Telefonica Moviles (Spain)		na	Spain	na	Brazil, El Salvador, Guatemala	na	Morocco
Sonera (Finland)	$1,937	Canada	Finland, Sweden, Spain, Turkey	Estonia, Hungary, Latvia, Lithuania, Russia	na	na	na
Telia (Sweden)	$5,742	na	Norway, Sweden	Estonia, Latvia	Brazil	Hong Kong, Philippines	Namibia, Uganda
Telecom Italia Mobile (Italy)	$7,466	na	France, Greece, Italy, Netherlands, Turkey		Brazil, Peru, Venezuela	na	
KPN (Netherlands)	$5,519	na	Belgium, Germany, Ireland, Netherlands	Czech Republic, Ukraine			
Millicom Int'l (US/ Sweden)	na	na	UK	Russia	Argentina, Bolivia, Colombia, El Salvador, Guatemala, Honduras, Paraguay, Peru	Singapore, Cambodia, India, Mauritius, Pakistan, Philippines, Sri Lanka, Vietnam, Sumatra, Laos	Ghana, Senegal, Tanzania, Sierra Leone, Congo

($22,245 million), but manufacturers saw services as a sideline and were about to divest these properties.

In the early half of the 1990s, a typical "new" international leader, such as AirTouch or BellSouth, used its home base (the United States) in order to gain leverage worldwide. AirTouch focused on Western Europe for some time and added Asian properties later. BellSouth was successful in Western Europe but was more willing to take greater risks, including in Latin America. After winning a PCN license in the U.K. market, US West expanded its footprint in Eastern Europe. Southwestern Bell (later SBC) bid actively in certain European countries, but as a late mover failed to secure the necessary political clout for the partnerships. Unlike other Baby Bells, Nynex and Ameritech engaged in fewer international pursuits. The leading operators applied their international strategy in some dozen major Triad countries. In contrast, a typical "old" international leader, such as Cable & Wireless, built its empire on the European base and existing relationships in Asia-Pacific, while seeking new footholds in emerging and transitional economies. Hungry entrants, such as Vodafone, used the early deregulation of their home base to expand more quickly than incumbents, first in continental Europe, then in Asia-Pacific, and finally in the United States.

Initially, the Baby Bells considered any opportunity a viable opportunity. BellSouth, for instance, maintained a team of almost 150 specialized international staff to write bids and assist with start-ups. With more bid opportunities and greater geographic scope, the incumbent international players became more discriminating. At about the same time, they initiated joint ventures with new competitors for licenses, mainly drawn from the national PTTs in Europe.[22] Cable & Wireless and Millicom had the most licenses. However, the Baby Bells positioned themselves in the most lucrative markets. As new public policies kicked in across Western Europe, the former national PTTs began to expand internationally. In one way or another, each sought to leverage its special competencies in new markets. Nordic operators rushed to the expanding Baltic sphere and won licenses in Western Europe, while the Swedish Telia was willing to purchase international licenses (as would the Finnish Sonera a few years later). Spain's Telefonica began to expand into Latin America. Deutsche Telekom made some efforts to expand into Asia and even the United States.

Only half a decade later, the competitive realities were quite different.

Second Wave of Internationalization: Triadization

At the eve of the 3G transition, the balance between the United States and "other countries" had been reversed with regard to market penetration (see Exhibit 5-4). Now a broad variety of nations worldwide represented two-fifths of the worldwide market penetration. The United States still enjoyed the greatest share worldwide, but it had been reduced to 14 percent and would soon be behind China (11 percent), where subscribership grew explosively. Japan's proportionate role had grown to 8 percent, whereas the top-four European markets (Germany, Italy, U.K., France) had each 4–6 percent of the total market, followed by Korea (4 percent), the pioneering CDMA cluster. With globalization, penetration rates demonstrated increasing equalization worldwide. As a result, the new international leaders were no longer as homogeneous as they had been only half a decade before. That they were not more heterogeneous had to do with entry barriers, which grew with market explosion and financial stakes.

In the past, market access had been difficult because of regulatory obstacles. Now the height of entry barriers served increasingly as a deterrent. Big was beautiful. A size that, in the mid-1990s, had ensured market access to leading international players barely opened the worldwide doors only half a decade later. By 2001, international strategy required annual revenues of $11 billion to $22 billion. The independent corporate names of distinct Baby Bells had become extinct. Some had become subsidiaries of foreign-based global operators, such as Vodafone (Bell Atlantic, Nynex, GTE). Others, such as Cingular (BellSouth, SBC), had survived through mergers and joint ventures. Still others, such as AT&T (acquisition of McCaw Cellular), simply bought their way into the big leagues. Between 1999 and 2001, this list of cellular dragons came to include several former national PTTs, as well, starting with the powerful NTT DoCoMo ($37 billion in annual revenues), Europe's changing telecom monopolies (Deutsche Telekom, France Telecom), and more focused mobile plays (Telecom Italia Mobile, Telefonica Moviles). In addition, the service-oriented mobile operators of the Nordic countries were too small to count (from $2 billion to $6 billion) in M&A games but were strategically important because of their advanced R&D positions.

Amid the 3G transition, a leading global operator, such as Vodafone, operated in all Triad Plus regions (Western Europe, United States, Asia, China). It had a dominant presence in at least two Triad regions (Europe and United States, in Vodafone's case) and operated in more than thirty Triad countries. Additionally, it was present in emerging and transitional economies, which possessed promising future markets. It was no longer engaged in an international strategy; it operated globally. In this regard, Vodafone was the model. The remaining U.S. players were the primary followers, while the largest of the former national PTTs struggled to secure a position in the worldwide markets.

In relation to the technical standards issues, the operators were the technology-agnostics of the industry, years before the "single flexible standard." Starting with the first wave of internationalization, the U.S. Baby Bells got involved in GSM systems, and some even ran NMT 450 analog systems. Meanwhile, Cable & Wireless from the U.K. operated many AMPS systems as did several other European-based operators.

Vodafone: Globalization of Network Operations

In 2001, Vodafone was the largest mobile operator worldwide with interests in wireless networks in twenty-eight countries across five continents. The Group had a staff of more than 100,000 and served more than 95 million proportionate customers worldwide. Its objective was to be the world's leading wireless telecom and information provider, generating more customers, more services, and more value than any of its competitors. Vodafone's global strategy embraced voice, data, and Internet-based services, focusing on customer satisfaction. The strategy was expected to enable Vodafone to bring a wider and richer range of services to its customers by capitalizing on new technology developments.

Industry Foresight

Vodafone's beginnings parallel the explosion of cellular platforms in Europe. It was launched in 1983 as a joint venture between Racal Electronics, a British electronics firm, and Millicom, a U.S.-based telecom company. Gerald Whent, chairman of Racal's Radio Group, convinced the parent to bid for the private-sector U.K. cellular license. Based in Newbury, the company had fewer than fifty employees. The product was expensive (£3,000) and heavy (4.8 kilos) at first, but price and the size decreased rapidly over the years. The network was prohibited by license from selling directly to the public. So Vodac, a wholly-owned subsidiary, was formed in 1984 to be the service provider. This configuration of network and service providers set a pattern for wireless value chains in many Western European nations. At the end of 1985, the analog network had 19,000 customers in the U.K. Both Vodafone and Cellnet, the other licensee, were about to be swamped with demand.

From the beginning, Vodafone (*voice*, *da*ta) was committed to the convergence of voice and data, fifteen to twenty years before the actual multimedia convergence. The operator built its vision on a quest for global leverage. In 1987, Gerald Whent committed Vodafone to aggressively develop mobile telephony internationally. The operator began to participate in consortia formed to bid for licenses, while identifying opportunities for acquisitions. This path of rapid external growth consistently outstripped projections of the original business plan.

In 1988, Racal Telecomms Division accounted for a third of Racal's profits. As it demonstrated its success and profitability, Racal offered 20 percent of Vodafone to the public in London and New York, while the rest of the company would be spun off three years later, as Vodafone Group.

Low Price, High Volume: Scale Through Scope

As the first digital systems were tested in the core clusters of Western Europe and Nordic countries, Racal entered the second phase of its evolution, which began with increasing shifts in strategy and organization. Racal and Vodafone were separated in what was then the largest de-merger in U.K. corporate history, while a new and independent entity, the Vodafone Group, was listed on the London and New York Stock Exchanges.[23] In the past, Vodafone and Cellnet, a joint venture of British Telecom (now BT Group) and Securicor, had enjoyed a duopoly in the U.K. When regulators decided not to impose price controls, profitability was ensured. In 1993, a new wireless provider, One 2 One, launched a digital network in London. Vodafone responded by launching its own GSM network.

After Vodafone and Telecom Finland (today Sonera) made the world's first international roaming call, Vodafone's digital GSM service was launched, the first in the U.K. A few months later in 1992, Vodafone and Telecom Finland signed the world's first international GSM roaming agreement. The cooperation prepared the British operator for very different cooperation with Nokia, a Ventel arrangement that was far more extensive in terms of scope. Like Nokia, Vodafone was a hungry challenger, not a former monopoly. It was not driven by national politics, hierarchical, or domestically focused. It was the spearhead of a new generation of operators, an attacker rather than an established leader. It was driven by market responsiveness, flexible and agile, and internationally-oriented.

Concurrently, Vodafone introduced new tariffs for the consumer market. This action illustrates the new strategy that Vodafone was developing for global leverage. LowCall, a low user tariff, offered a reduction of 40 percent on the existing business tariff. The pricing solution—the Nordic low-cost, high-volume service orientation—was critical to the success of digital cellular in Western Europe in the early 1990s. In Japan, it formed the foundation of NTT DoCoMo's mass-market-driven strategy around mid-decade. Due to the delays in digitalization, it arrived in the United States as AT&T's innovative pricing scheme only in 1998. It surfaced again in China around 2000 and 2001 to facilitate the growth of the world's largest user base (China Mobile, China Unicom, China Telecom). In 1992, this scheme was still perceived as risky and untested, even bold in the large-scale markets of Western Europe. In contrast to Telecom Finland and other Nordic PTTs, which operated in domestic and at best regional markets, Vodafone expected to achieve scale through scope—it leveraged the tariff structure internationally.

Envisioned in the late 1980s, Vodafone's internationalization took off in 1993, when the company obtained interests in wireless networks in Australia, Greece, Hong Kong, Malta, and Scandinavia. It was an early mover but hardly among the first movers. It followed in the footsteps of the U.S. Baby Bells. By 1995, more than 500 specialist retail outlets and seven High Street chains connected mobile phones to the Vodafone network. The quest for domestic mass markets via retail was coupled with the search for scope through international partnerships. The leverage of strategy was accompanied by a shift in organizational capabilities. The parent formed an international division—Vodafone Group International—to acquire licenses and supervise overseas interests. By 1998, these also included the New Zealand GSM network and Misrfone consortium (30 percent), which was awarded the license to build a second mobile network in Egypt. Even as it developed its low-tariff policy on the basis of the Nordic model, Vodafone continued to build new solutions (prepaid, bundled services) to facilitate market expansion.[24]

Through the 1G era, Vodafone nurtured international dreams but remained primarily a domestic operation.

M&A Fever

In the first half of the 1990s, Vodafone had engaged in international partnerships and purchased stakes in foreign operations. As its foreign subsidiaries multiplied, the old organizational capabilities no longer sufficed. A simple international division was not adequate for the operator's properties, which were rapidly proliferating. As Whent left operational activities and a new strategic leadership stepped in, Vodafone refocused its organization, streamlining distribution and international properties. Such changes were necessary to rationalize the existing assets but insufficient to manage the future ones. In the late 1990s, Vodafone moved from internationalization to globalization. That required an area structure, especially as the company prepared to swallow a slate of world's largest international operators, including AirTouch Communications, Bell Atlantic, and Mannesmann.

In January 1997, one era changed to another when Christopher "Chris" Gent stepped in as Vodafone's CEO. A smooth succession was paralleled by a drastic transition in organizational capabilities, particularly in distribution. After the six wholly owned service providers were reduced to three (Vodafone Corporate, Vodafone Retail, and Vodafone Connect), the numbers of billing and customer care systems were rationalized, while brands, retail interiors, and tariffs were streamlined. These rationalization measures extended to tariff policies as well. Instead of pushing novel technologies and complicated pricing offerings, Vodafone promoted simple, convenient, and affordable policies by introducing its "Pay As You Talk" digital package, which offered no bills, no credit check, no fixed-term contract, and advanced digital services.

Until the summer of 1999, Vodafone had been a regional giant, cultivating an international base. In January, it connected the five millionth customer in the U.K. In March, the number of worldwide Vodafone Group customers surpassed 10 million. These figures grew exponentially in June 1999, with the merger of Vodafone Group Plc and AirTouch Communications Inc, the cellular arm of Pacific Telesis. This growth-hungry Baby Bell later fused with SBC. After Bell Atlantic made a $45 billion bid for AirTouch, Vodafone acquired the operator for some $60 billion. Before the merger, Vodafone and AirTouch were leaders in wireless services in their respective home markets in the U.K. and the United States. Now the two formed the "largest mobile communications company in the world" to serve as an "engine for growth in the twenty-first century."[25] A few months later, Bell Atlantic and Vodafone AirTouch decided to create a new wireless business with a national footprint—a single brand and a common digital technology composed of the U.S. wireless assets of the two giants. Bell Atlantic had been one of the most ambitious Baby Bells; it internationalized in the early 1990s and had tried to purchase cable giant TCI. Instead, it spend $25.6 billion to buy Nynex in 1997, and two years later it acquired GTE, a giant independent telco, in a $53 billion deal.

The merger with Bell Atlantic strengthened Vodafone's corporate bases along the Anglo-Saxon axis of Western Europe and North America. It was underpinned by a new strategic objective that was no longer international, but global by nature.

> Commitment to being the world's leading wireless communications company, providing more customers with more services and more value from their mobile terminals than any other.[26]

In the United States, the British operator employed four strong operators—AirTouch, Bell Atlantic, Nynex, and GTE—to achieve an extensive national entity. In Europe, the U.K., and Germany, along with Italy and France, were the two critical country markets. As Vodafone AirTouch had secured a powerful base in the United States, it initiated talks with Mannesmann AG, the German giant.[27] In 1999, Mannesmann's entry into the U.K. alerted Vodafone. To deter the threat *and* solidify a base in Germany, the operator launched a hostile bid and acquired Mannesmann in a $180 billion stock deal. In February 2000, the transaction of Mannesmann, the German mobile whale, almost doubled the size of the Vodafone Group.[28]

The Vodafone Group had now become the largest mobile operator in the world and one of the top-ten companies worldwide, by market capitalization. Its core operations were in Europe, where it had a customer base of over 32 million, and telecom interests in fourteen countries. The region represented 54 percent of the Group's worldwide base. In the United States, it combined its wireless properties with those of Bell Atlantic and GTE to form Verizon Wireless, the market leader in the United States. Finally, there was the newly formed U.K., Middle East, and Africa region. A few months later, its geographical division of operations was reorganized into five regions: Continental Europe, the Americas and Asia-Pacific, the U.K., the Middle East, and Africa. Vodafone Group continued to solidify its European interests with new acquisitions while signing strategic alliances in Hong Kong and expanding its stakes in Japan Telecom and its J-Phone mobile phone operations by buying out rival BT.

Vodafone's strategy rested on the three pillars of global focus, innovation, and service. First, it leveraged its focus strategy by concentrating on wireless communications globally. Second, through mobile focus, it sought scale through scope. It extended the reach, range, and penetration of wireless services to as many customers as possible in as many geographic territories throughout the world as could sustain viable and profitable operating environments. And third, it stayed close to the productivity frontier in order to develop attractive services. By June 2001, Vodafone's worldwide base included more than 93.1 million registered customers, while the venture base covered over 202.6 million registered customers. At the turn of the 1990s, Nokia and Vodafone had still been relatively small operations compared to the incumbents, Motorola in handsets and the Baby Bells in mobile networks. A decade later, the maverick challengers were the industry leaders.

3G Transition: Erosion of Nordic Leadership

Over the 1990s, the Nordic pioneers led in products, operations, and markets. At the same time, Nordic home bases offered the world-class benchmarks for generic strategies, public policies, and innovation (see Exhibit 5-5). In each of these three areas, the failures of policymakers and regulators, as well as industry practitioners in the United States, allowed the Nordic triumph. But the success did not emerge out of the blue. It had a long history and provided an alternative model for the mobile business, one driven by the quest for competitive innovation, productivity frontier, and internationalization. In the pre-cellular era, the Nordic model expanded from Sweden to other Nordic countries and then regionally. In the 1G era, the NMT triumph attracted the attention of the European Commission, which made GSM mandatory to crack open the old European PTT monopolies, while promoting competition and integration in Europe. The impending explosion in mobile communications, in turn, changed the very agents of this transformation. Both operators—new leaders such as Vodafone rather than incumbent PTTs—and vendors—new giants including Nokia and Ericsson, rather than the exclusive supply chains of the incumbent PTTs—had to transform their organizational capabilities to manage the new high-volume markets. At the same time, they had to differentiate themselves from competition in products and services, which were rapidly turning into commodities.

This evolution reflected the feat of the Nordic way in mobile communications, starting with the cooperation of Nordic countries in the late 1960s and peaking with the Nordic success in the 1990s. This high point illustrated an eclipse, as well. In the late 1940s, the Bell Labs researchers had come up with the cellular concept. It was *their* great accomplishment, but without appropriate instruments (i.e., strategies or policies) to *innovate* this invention, it also reflected the peak of the old AT&T era. Employing the U.S. innovation, the Nordic countries developed the requisite policies and strategies for mobile communications.

As the Nordic model made open specifications the rule of the game, it

Exhibit 5-5. Euro-Nordic innovation: Triad leadership.

MONOPOLY ERA

National PTT
- National PTT monopolies reign from 1880s to early 1980s.
- In large Western European countries, public-sector monopoly and vertical integration; in some Nordic countries more competitive local telcos and international vendors.
- Rise of cellular platforms coincides with deregulation and European integration.

NIS/PTT Labs
- Euro-Nordic pioneership builds on mobile innovation by few Euro-Nordic vendors and PTTs.
- In late 1960s, Nordic innovation promotes open and market-driven specifications.
- Innovation within firms and in public-private research centers.

Old Public Policies
- Regulation-ensured PTT monopoly until EC directives in late 1980s. Broadcast regulation, minimal defense interests; spectrum policies dictated by public service mission.
- Large-country PTTs favor closed specifications; Nordic PTTs and vendors advocate international roaming, low pricing (CPP), and liberal licensing policies.
- Large-country PTTs driven by industrial policies and "national champion" ideals; small-country PTTs more internationalist; Nordic vendors the first to internationalize.

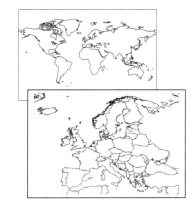

TRANSITION ERA

Privatization
- Between 1981 (U.K.) and 1998, privatization of Euro PTTs promotes competition through deregulation
- Vertically disintegrated value system, fewer new challengers and start-ups than in U.S.
- Rise of 2G coincides with deregulation and privatization; EC decides to make GSM mandatory; CDMA fails to penetrate Euro fortress.

Transformation of Innovation
- Turmoil of PTT Labs less tumultuous than in U.S.; greater continuity.
- Leadership in mobile innovation migrates to Nordic vendors; in early 1990s their R&D is domestic and centralized; in late 1990s, globally networked.
- Innovation within firms, and through public-private partnerships, tech coalitions, and academia-industry alliances.

Transitional Public Policies
- Deregulation over regulation; in spectrum policies, increasing financial stakes.
- EC's Pan-European efforts coincide with proliferation of market-driven PTTs and vendors.
- Through GSM, Nordic open specifications coincide with Europe's development path.
- EC directives nurture growth of a new generation of international operators (Vodafone); large-country vendors emulate best practices of Nordic vendors.

COMPETITIVE ERA

Cluster
- Due to GSM triumph, Euro operators and vendors are best positioned for 3G era, but not for mobile Internet; early WAP debacle.
- Defensive posture against entry of U.S. IT leaders.
- With CDMA core 3G standard, loss of European tech edge.

Innovation Systems
- Market-driven innovation proliferates; globally networked innovation among Nordic leaders.
- Leadership in innovation splits between European-based mobile leaders and U.S.-based IT leaders.
- Innovation externalized, vis-à-vis tech coalitions.

New Public Policies
- Deregulation rules; short-sighted licensing policies in spectrum allocations lead to industry slowdown.
- Slowdown promotes consolidation, at the terms of the large-country players.
- Due to market-driven public policies, importance of EC declines, that of EC competition policy increases.

---

also triggered a curious dialectic that would eventually become its own gravedigger. These specs abhorred exclusivity and special privileges. They were perfectly in line with the quest for competitive innovation, productivity frontier, and internationalization. But the quest was *global* by nature. It thrived in scale, whether this was inherited (large-country firms that dominated domestic markets) or created (small-country firms that came to dominate global markets). In some cases, scale was indigenous to the market. In the United States, Baby Bells and vendors like Motorola enjoyed such an advantage. In other cases, scale was gained through scope. Ericsson and Nokia achieved such a feat through global products, efficient operations, and market multiplication, but Nordic operators did not.

Equipment manufacturers were able to achieve such scale through scope, but network operators were not. Vendors operated in an upstream business that could be globalized; operators were in a downstream business that required high localization. Even at the peak of their success in the late 1990s, Nordic vendors, such as Nokia and Ericsson, thrived, but operators, including Telia and Sonera, stumbled. Although these operators were more competitive and service-oriented than their counterparts in continental Europe, they were incumbent PTTs, as well. They were more agile and more flexible because they were smaller and smarter, but they were still dinosaurs. Their privatization was too slow for dynamic markets. The home base could not give rise to capital-intensive challengers that could have taken their attacks across the globe, and the business was inherently highly localized.

As the triangle framework would have it, industry leadership in competitive wireless markets requires leadership in products, operations, and markets. Until the mid-1990s, the worldwide mobile markets were essentially corporate markets, even if the Nordic cluster had already moved toward consumer markets. But by the end of this growth decade, the business was all about globalizing consumer mass markets. Nordic vendors managed this transition as long as they were able to change with the markets. And by the end of the 1990s, Nokia and Ericsson obtained more than 98–99 percent of their revenues *outside* of their home base. In contrast, Nordic operators, even the most international leaders, could not capture more than 10–35 percent of their revenues outside the home base. In other words, the Nordic model had triggered a new industry thrust that made scale and scope critical to leadership in products and operations. As the gentle dinosaurs of Northern Europe completed their pioneership during the growth decade, they made the struggle for globalization the central driver in the industry evolution. The unintended consequence of this transformation was the fact that the Nordic leaders also opened a new entry opportunity for the large Asian operators, vendors, contractors, and consumer-electronics giants. And, through convergence developments, they opened still another door for the industry leaders in software, microprocessors, and online services in the United States. By the same token, the Nordic dinosaurs, as Groucho Marx might say, included themselves out. Unlike the United States, the larger European countries, Japan, or China, Nordic countries simply lacked the kind of scale that was required to optimize the very strategies and policies they had developed.

This critical shift became apparent in European market evolution toward the end of the 1990s. As the small Nordic countries had already achieved the highest penetration rates, scale migrated to major EU countries, which, except for Italy, still had low penetration rates. Conversely, small Nordic countries had become largely saturated and had low market potential. Therefore, high-growth prospects were now in the major EU markets, not in northern Europe. In the handset shipments, for instance, the high volume was entirely in the major EU markets. And due to industry globalization, the great European markets paled in comparison to those in Asia-Pacific. At the end of 1999, Italy's cellular market exceeded a subscriber base of 30 million users, while U.K. and Germany each had some 24 million and France about 20 million. Behind these top European markets, Spain had 15 million cellular subscribers. In other words, these top-five Euro-markets represented a total of 113.1 million users. Only a year later, China alone had in excess of *120 million* subscribers. Most importantly, the cellular penetration varied around 35 percent to 40 percent in the top European markets, but in China it was still in the single-digit sphere.

In the past, pioneership had made the difference, but by 2000, scale and scope—the total market size—was more important. At regional level, the EU might have promoted new, market-driven mechanisms of facilitation in public policies, but this would have required institutional reform, one that would take into account the interests of both large and small European nations. In February 2002, Paavo Lipponen, the Finnish prime minister, accused the EU's larger nations of seeking to sideline smaller member states as the union prepared a new round of institutional reform. While the polemic went far further than the narrow mobile business, it held particular significance to the industry and the role of the small Nordic countries in that industry. As larger EU nations held to inherited comparative advantages, they were suppressing the dynamics of technology-intensive competitive advantages. In the long run, this served neither smaller nor larger EU nations.

In 1993, the United States Congress established the promotion of competition as a fundamental goal for Commercial Mobile Radio Services (CMRS) policy formation and regulation. The U.S. approach to regulation was not as liberal as that in Nordic countries, but the effort to make *competition* the guiding light for policymakers and regulators was certainly reminiscent of Nordic principles that had evolved with deregulation and liberalization in the early 1980s. In Japan, similar efforts evolved in parallel with the United States. As CMRS competition emerged as a common denominator for industry practitioners, regulators, and policymakers in the United States, Kouji Ohboshi implemented a drastic reversal in NTT DoCoMo's strategy. To stretch the point, one might argue that, by the mid-1990s, all the leading Triad country markets in the mobile business had been "Nordicized." Each was implementing—or at least had initiated—new public policies involving privatization, liberalization, and deregulation. All had made competition the common denominator of policies, strategies, and innovation. In each case, industry leaders were developing strategies that were permeated by highly differentiated, high-volume, mass-market postures. Other players followed, both laggards and future challengers. With the completion of EC's liberalization agenda and the finalization of global telecom reforms, almost all country markets had opted for the "Nordic way" by the end of the 1990s. In the case of China, an additional incentive involved the membership in the World Trade Organization in 2001, which required such regulatory reforms.

From the late-nineteenth century to the end of the twentieth century, the epicenter of the mobile business had been either in Western Europe or North America. Amid the 3G transition, that was no longer the case. High volume and high growth were now the prime movers of the great markets. Industry thrust was about to migrate to Asia-Pacific. In the short term, that meant Japan. In the long term, it meant China. Those industry players who enjoyed the greatest foresight understood these competitive realities in the early 1980s. Those that did not were forced to understand them around 2000 and 2001, when industry consolidation compelled lesser players to divest and joint venture their manufacturing capabilities to new and emerging Asian producers—and when those leaders that had not secured an adequate position in China began to crumble.

Chapter 6

The 3G Era: Japan's Service Innovation

In 2000, the explosive boom in worldwide mobile communications suddenly changed into a widespread industry slowdown except in Asian growth markets. As the "twin drivers" of mobility and the Internet crashed with the U.S. tech consolidation and the 3G debt burden of the leading European operators, the success of NTT DoCoMo attracted increasing industry attention. To some industry observers, the Japanese carrier came out of the blue. In reality, it had pioneered the analog cellular and been an early mover in the digital cellular, yet it had failed twice to exploit this success. The Japanese operator pioneered the 3G era with a strategy that was almost the reverse of those of its counterparts in Western Europe and the United States. But even this model had weaknesses.

The Great Technology Catch-Up

In the United States, Bell's invention initiated the rapid expansion of telecommunications, starting in 1876. Nordic countries followed within months. So did Japan. In northern Europe, the catch-up built on an alternative business model through an emphasis on quality and cost, as well as ceaseless upgrading and innovation. This model was premised on relatively low domestic regulation and high globalization. In Japan, the early openness as well as imitation and upgrading were soon replaced by models that originated from a more closed, homogeneous society and economy, which encouraged domestic regulation and low globalization.

Ma Bell in Japan

As Japanese tariff walls rose to foster the growth of domestic industries, many American and European companies, including Western Electric, the supply chain of the Bell System since 1881, initiated production in Japan. In effect, the ensuing Nippon Electric Company (NEC) was Japan's first joint venture

with a U.S. company. The majority stake (54 percent) belonged to Western
Electric and the remaining shares were locally owned. The fate of this venture
illustrates the eagerness of the Japanese authorities to acquire Western technology. Unlike the Chinese a century later, however, the Japanese firms and regulators were not about to trade technology for access.

Within less than two years of the Bell invention, Japan's Ministry of Industry imported the Bell telephone. Shortly thereafter, the Osaka Police Department used the new device, and the government ministries in Tokyo began
to operate phones for limited office purposes. At the factory of the Ministry of
Industry, engineers tried to replicate the imported sets with primitive equipment. Dissatisfied with these results, the government authorities decided to
rely more on foreign producers to meet domestic needs. Having been dispatched to the United States and Europe to report on telecom companies and
their systems, Dr. Oi Saitaro of the Ministry of Communications recommended
that the government adopt some of Western Electric's telephone systems.[1]
Through Japan's history of modernization, this episode typified the Japanese
pattern of acquiring knowledge from the West by means of:

- Reverse engineering and reproduction
- Frequent dispatching of experts or study missions to the West for field
  research
- The active role of government (and its various agencies) as a scanner/
  locator and experimenter of cutting-edge foreign technologies, as well
  as a promoter of absorption and adoption, once foreign technologies
  were found to be promising and critical[2]

The Nordic model, too, has relied on experts and study missions, but
these have comprised both senior executives and government representatives.
Similarly, it stressed imitation, but more as an instrument of upgrading and
innovation. Finally, it emphasized the role of companies and public/private
partnerships rather than government labs.

The NEC episode precipitated a brief boom of *inward* foreign direct investment in Japan, starting in 1899 when the Japanese Civil and Commercial
Codes were liberalized to accommodate the new rights of foreign investors.
That period came to an end with the rise of militarism and imperial expansion
from 1930 to 1945. Only after World War II could Japan concentrate on catching up to the technology gap vis-à-vis advanced Western industries.

In contrast to the Nordic model, in which the national PTTs remained
more open and market-driven than the European PTTs, Japan's telecommunications was heavily regulated, closed, and engineering-driven until the privatization of NTT in 1985. But there were two Trojan horses in the system. First,
NTT's supplier arrangements promoted catch-up before World War II and in
the postwar era. Second, the convergence of computing and consumer electronics, in which Japan has enjoyed great historical strengths, and telecommu-

nications, in which the natural monopoly has suppressed advancements, forced Japanese mobile communications to change from within—but not until the incorporation of NTT DoCoMo, in the early 1990s.

NTT's Technology Catch-Up

In 1868, Japan's Ministry of Industry established a government-owned factory to produce telegraph equipment. Through this factory and other initiatives, the Japanese public sector gave rise to many future vendors, including Toshiba, Oki, NEC, Fujitsu, and Hitachi. In 1885, the Ministry of Communications assumed responsibility for telegraph and later telephone services from the Ministry of Industry. Focusing on the development and management of communication networks, the Ministry of Industry left the equipment manufacturing to a small group of private-sector firms. Over time, a close relationship evolved between the Ministry and these suppliers, including senior personnel transfers. In practice, the cooperative relationship between a large monopoly procurer and user of equipment and a closed group of suppliers meant a kind of "controlled competition." Until 1952, Japan's Ministry of Communications was the procurer and user; thereafter this role shifted to NTT.[3]

By the 1920s, NEC, which was still partly owned by Western Electric, was the Ministry of Communications' dominant supplier. In the 1930s, NEC retained a strong position but faced increasing competition from Oki, Fujitsu, and Hitachi. Meanwhile, depression, a financial crisis, and nationalism reduced Japanese dependence on foreign technology and boosted domestic technological capabilities. Due to the Cold War, the United States tolerated Japan's protectionism, which enabled the country to build up industries by importing the relevant technology through licensing agreements, while restricting inward foreign direct investment to a minimum. Imported technology was regarded as "raw material" to be transformed into "finished technologies," and, ultimately, exported back to world markets.[4] This pattern of catch-up was also typical to mobile communications, but it did not result in Japan's leadership in *worldwide* markets.

In 1944, there were a million telephone subscribers in Japan. After World War II, that number fell to 400,000. This reduction led to the establishment of NTT, in consultation with the Supreme Commander for the Allied Powers. NTT was created to reconstruct the Japanese telecom facilities and to develop the required technology for domestic use and production. The reorganization emulated the U.S. model—AT&T—but because of a different strategic environment and organizational capabilities, the results were quite different.[5] As a public corporation, NTT was reminiscent of AT&T. But the old organizational relationships that had evolved in the era of controlled competition continued to shape Japanese telecommunications, particularly through the special relationship between NTT and its family of suppliers. Indeed, Takeshi Kajii, former president of NEC, was named NTT's first president.

In 1952, the Ministry of Postal Affairs was renamed the Ministry of Posts and Telecommunications (MPT) and given regulatory responsibility in some telecom segments. The Ministry of Telecommunications, for all practical purposes, was transferred to NTT, which was granted a monopoly over telegraph and telephone services. Like its European counterparts, NTT would contain and regulate competition. It was charged with rebuilding Japan's war-ravaged phone system and confined to the domestic market. Another company, Kokusai Denshin Denwa (the precursor of KDDI Corp.), was created in 1953 to handle international telecommunications. The decision to split domestic and international telecom activities had a rationale at the heyday of regulation, when markets were primarily domestic by nature. But in the long term, this policy decision sentenced NTT to relative isolation.

While Japan's PTT achieved extraordinary control of the domestic market, it lost the opportunity for global leverage, which later became the success formula for Japan's global technology leaders. Unlike the great postwar pioneers of Japanese consumer electronics, such as Sony and Matsushita, which emulated America's best practices and kept an eye on global markets, NTT remained introverted, was forbidden to internationalize, and focused on the domestic marketplace until 1992.

NEC: Internationalization Through Diversification

With a group of investors, Kunihiko Iwadare formed Nippon Electric Company (NEC) in a joint venture with Western Electric in 1899. Starting as an importer of telephone equipment, NEC became a maker of equipment and a major supplier to Japan's Ministry of Communications. As NEC began manufacturing telephones, equipment, and switchboards, it used Western Electric's technology to achieve competencies in radio communications. In 1925, Western Electric sold its stake in NEC. With weakening technological linkages between NEC and its former parent, the Japanese vendor was compelled to strengthen its technology competencies in segments in which it previously had sought assistance from Western Electric. Also, the Japanese military's growing demand for radio-related equipment speeded the development of NEC's radio capabilities. With rising nationalism at home, the company affiliated with the Sumitomo *keiretsu* (industrial group) in the 1930s.

At the same time, NEC initiated research on microwave communications. "More than 80 percent of [Japan's] land consists of mountainous terrain, so the laying of cables is expensive and, moreover, installation is difficult and time-consuming," recalled Koji Kobayashi, a former chairman of NEC, and a young engineer in the early 1930s. "Given these factors, microwave links appeared to be the best solution for a quickly completed nationwide communications network, and pioneering efforts were made to utilize microwave systems."[6] By 1950, the Ministry of Telecommunications opted for microwave systems for nationwide telephone and TV relay networks, while the Ministry's laboratories initiated an extensive R&D program, in which vendors were invited to join. Meanwhile, postwar reconstruction also boosted fortunes at NEC, which benefited from informal personal networks with the Ministry of Communications and NTT.

After NTT was formed in 1952, NEC became one of its four leading suppliers. In the aftermath of World War II, reconstruction of Japan's national telecom systems resulted in strong demand from NTT for NEC's products. In the 1950s and 1960s, NTT's business represented more than 50 percent of NEC's sales. Having accumulated the requisite know-how and capabilities, the vendor also expanded overseas and diversified into related segments in the 1950s and 1960s, including transistors, electronic switches, computers, and satellite communications. In this way, it was NTT that "made" NEC, through its "Den Den Family," the traditional Japanese supply chain. Kobayashi underscored this fact in a 1967 memo:

> Since NEC's founding the primary mission of our company has . . . been to make communications equipment for our number one customer, formerly the Ministry of Communications and now NTT . . . Before the war almost three-quarters of our sales were to the Ministry of Communications . . . Even today nearly half of our sales are still to . . . NTT.[7]

NEC came to age in the 1960s, when ITT sold its stake in the company. Two years later, when the Japanese supplier began to sell microwave technology to ITT, the deal was widely perceived as evidence of the Japanese company's technological maturity. It also allowed NEC to loosen the restrictions that Western Electric and ITT had placed on NEC's exports to third markets. That, in turn, facilitated NEC's efforts to accelerate growth by expanding into foreign markets. By the late 1960s, NEC claimed to be the world's leading exporter of microwave communications systems. It no longer won orders only in developing countries. In 1968, NEC made a significant microwave deal with U.S. defense forces and, three years later, with AT&T's New York subsidiary. Meanwhile, from 1939–1985, NEC's domestic revenues declined from 91 percent to 65 percent of the total.[8]

In major industrialized countries, the markets were developed and often monopolized by indigenous equipment vendors. If NEC could not get through the door directly, it would work indirectly. It began exporting to developing countries, which it used as a springboard to more developed markets. Until the late 1960s, most of NEC's revenues had originated from Japan's telecom market. Thereafter, diversification into related segments resulted in new sources of revenues, which ensured high growth, in contrast to NTT's low-growth but stable cash cow. NEC used telecommunications to access new business markets, and it used new business markets to find access into new geographic markets. These new markets enabled global leverage that proved relatively insignificant in mobile communications due to NTT's confinement to the domestic base. Over time, NEC also became a major player in switches, base stations, system interconnections, and mobile phones.

The Challenge That Never Materialized

Japan's land mobile radio communications evolved out of systems that were originally developed for the country's extensive fishing fleet and harbor traffic. After the introduction of the first primitive marine mobile system in 1923, Japanese fishing and transport vessels remained the primary users.[9] On land, private companies provided many mobile communications systems, but it took until 1948 that the first more significant mobile radio system was launched in the public sector. After the pioneering police radio system, other emergency services in Japan followed, including fire and flood protection. Development of mobile phones began with the marine telephone, which was introduced in 1953. Operating in the 150 MHz band, the system was soon expanded and, by the mid-1970s, it serviced all coastal areas of Japan. In addition to shipboard telephones, Japan had a system of railroad telephones on its long-distance trains. The service was launched in the late 1950s and operated in the 400 MHz band. Despite the importance of these two sectors, their users represented a limited market niche.

The First Mobile Telephone Systems

In 1961, the NTT secretariat planned a mobile telephone system for automobiles. Prototype testing began three years later. By the mid-1960's, the Ministry of Posts and Telecommunications, which was responsible for radio frequency management, began planning spectrum allocation in 400 MHz band, even as U.S. regulators found themselves in a "land mobile crisis." In 1967, the research phase was over, and NTT had developed a system similar to AT&T's IMTS.[10] NTT also proposed a nationwide cellular radio system and initiated studies on such a system.[11] Concurrently, Japanese researchers began to contribute to cellular R&D. They had become active contributors and innovators, especially in the design of commercial cellular systems.[12] Among other things, Bell's presentations concerning the Cellular Docket relied upon cellular research by Japan.[13] In 1968, NTT began offering paging services. By the mid-1980s, field tests were carried out in the Tokyo metropolitan area and successfully completed two years later.[14]

The great postwar catch-up in mobile communications was over.[15] In Japanese technologies, products and services were on par with those in the United

States. The pace of growth in mobile stations was extraordinary. In 1970, there had been barely 160,000 such stations. By the mid-1970s, there were an estimated 329,000 land mobile radio stations. Almost half of the stations belonged to taxi services (43 percent) while a fourth belonged to emergency services (i.e., police and fire departments), utilities (i.e., electric power), and national railroads.[16] Even as a cellular system was being planned, the existing mobile communications relied primarily on simple paging devices, particularly a one-way paging system called Pocket Bell, which NTT introduced in Tokyo in 1968. The popular device took off in other cities as well. In 1975, more than 395,000 Pocket Bells were in use. The high quality of the public telephone system boosted demand. By early 1977, some 640,000 subscribers were served in forty-two cities, more than in any other country worldwide including the United States, which had introduced paging a decade before Japan and had twice the national population. The demand remained explosive and ran some 100,000 units ahead of supply.

By the close of the 1970s, Japan's telecom regulatory agency, the Ministry of Posts and Telecommunications gave permission to NTT to establish cellular mobile services using a variant of AMPS, which had been developed by NEC. In December 1979, the operator introduced a car telephone service in the twenty-three districts of Tokyo in the 800 MHz frequency band and later spread the service throughout Japan. Though a latecomer in the business, Japan was the first country to enter the 1G era.

NTT's Mobile Vendors: "Controlled Competition"

From the 1920s to the mid-1980s, controlled competition reigned in Japanese telecommunications. It differed from the U.S. and Nordic models. In the United States, AT&T and its supply chain were vertically integrated until the mid-1950s. In the Nordic countries, the supply chain relationship relied more on market competition. Furthermore, the PTTs could use both domestic and foreign suppliers. Nationality did not count; world-class standards did. Compared to these models, the Japanese approach represented a middle ground. The relationship between NTT and its suppliers was neither vertically integrated nor nonintegrated; it was cooperative but exclusive. The wireless business remained an exclusive domain of Japanese firms through the intense catch-up efforts in the pre-cellular and 1G eras.

In 1974, only $400,000 of land mobile radio equipment (less than 2 percent of the total) in Japan comprised imports. All of this was from the United States. As Japan caught up with the U.S. productivity frontier in the wireless, the market, though developed, offered few opportunities to non-Japanese players.[17] Conversely, the potential U.S. market for Japanese mobile equipment was lucrative and accessible. The asymmetry of access and the accompanying bilateral tension surfaced in 1975, when AT&T did not award the contract for the first 135 cellular transceivers to one of the more traditional U.S. vendors, but to Oki Electronics, a Japanese NTT supplier with a U.S. subsidiary. Oki reportedly had offered to supply the items for some 40 percent less than the rival U.S. bidders. The fears of a U.S. marketing executive illustrated a widespread unease:

> In television and comparable areas, the consumer at least could make his own choice between foreign and domestic products. But with the [cellular] market, it is up to AT&T. If AT&T sticks with foreign suppliers, we're dead.[18]

After all, AT&T was still synonymous with U.S. telecommunications. Following the Oki debate in the late 1970s, an American observer of the mobile industry described the business between the two nations as an asymmetric reciprocity:

> This quick and significant penetration of the U.S. market by low-bidding Japanese firms, plus the expectations of American firms being effectively excluded from the Japanese market, is consistent with growing images of a semiofficial lockout on one side and Japanese government-endorsed dumping on the other. The U.S. electronics trade journals have depicted this situation as another Japanese invasion. Fears have not been radically diminished by AT&T's even more recent decision to award manufacturing contracts to two American firms along with Oki.[19]

In certain industry segments, NTT's close R&D relationships with prime suppliers did seem to be the result of controlled markets. Take, for instance, pagers. After conducting initial research on the Pocket Bell system, NTT encouraged production research among three vendors (NEC, Toshiba, and Matsushita) and sought to divide the paging market equally among them. By the mid-1970s, NTT controlled the entire Japanese market and there were no imports in the $14 million paging industry.[20] The success of Japanese challengers in foreign markets, however, boosted debate on access into the Japanese markets. In 1982, Motorola lowered its pager prices by a third to respond to Japanese competition. Arguing that its rivals were selling pagers at prices below the manufacturing cost to gain market share, the U.S. vendor also filed a formal complaint with the U.S. International Trade Commission and won the case. Cultivating NTT as a customer, Motorola worked closely with the U.S. Trade Representative. In the long term, Japanese mobile vendors, which focused almost exclusively to domestic markets, were vulnerable to such attacks by leading non-Japanese vendors, which thrived on global leverage.

Cellular Platforms: From Domestic Monopoly to Internationalization

By the 1970s, Japanese success stories, such as Sony and Matsushita, did not exemplify "Japan, Inc.," a monolith corporation combining the muscle of business and government. In many ways, *NTT* did. As the end-user, it purchased about 85 percent of all communications equipment. It controlled sales and influenced suppliers. Furthermore, NTT and the government favored a "buy Japanese" policy, which kept foreign attackers at bay.[21] On the other hand, the American debate was heavily colored by fears of "Japanese invasion." But in the early 1980s, Oki was not Motorola's problem; neither was NEC nor the other Japanese suppliers. In mobile communications, the real problem was the decline of the U.S. productivity frontier in the wireless vis-à-vis other Triad country markets. The U.S. debate failed to distinguish between Japanese electronics and computers and Japanese telecommunications. In the former case, competition, openness, and globalization were the rule. In the latter case, monopoly, closedness, and domestication were the rule. It is only recently that this distinction has become better understood in the U.S. debate. Indeed, there have long been two Japans—the one that has been highly competitive and outward-looking, and another, almost invisible until recently, that has been highly uncompetitive.[22] NEC started in the domestic Japan, but later moved into the competitive, globalizing Japan. Starting in 1992, NTT DoCoMo followed in its footsteps.

Of course, NTT's vendors often saw themselves as pioneers in computers *and* telecommunications. In 1977, for instance, CEO Koji Kobayashi first publicly articulated NEC's vision of "C&C"—the convergence of computers and communications.[23] Concurrently, NTT pioneered the first commercial mobile service, while NEC's accumulated competencies in radio and microwave communications were extended into mobile communications. But in mobility, the vendor remained captive to its most lucrative customer, NTT, which could not internationalize. The vision was prescient. But the execution of the vision was not allowed in Japanese wireless.

Due to a historical idiosyncrasy, the onset of the analog cellular era coincided with the collapse of America's international competitiveness during the first half of the 1980s. The demise was spectacular in speed and extent as one industry after another fell under the force of foreign competition. Japanese challengers were blamed for the eclipse of U.S. industries. The fear was real but exaggerated. In wireless communications, many observers expected Japanese challengers to demolish U.S. industry leadership. In practice, this would have meant threats against the leading operators (AT&T, Baby Bells, and independents) and vendors (Motorola and others). These expectations escalated as the demand migrated from business markets toward mass consumer markets, which many had come to consider a Japanese territory. "In 1979 when Mobira was established," recalls Kari-Pekka Wilska, Nokia's future chief of Americas, "we were told: You boys will die when the Japanese enter these markets . . . they will kill you when NMT starts . . . in 1985 you will be chewed up and spat out."[24]

However, NTT was forbidden to engage in internationalization despite its monopoly power in the domestic market. Because the operator rather than the vendors enjoyed bargaining power in the analog era, NTT's domestication shaped the strategies of its suppliers, through resource dependency.

The 1G Era: Toward Liberalization

Between 1952 and 1985, NTT excelled in technology innovation, in so far as it achieved public objectives (eliminated telephone installation backlog, installed nationwide direct dialing); acquired, adapted, and improved technological knowledge from abroad; and proved to be one of the most innovation-driven national carriers worldwide. But even in this regard, competition proved a better discipline. In the mid-1980s, NTT had invested some 2.5 percent of its revenues into R&D. By 1992, after privatization and increasing competition, it was forced to increase these investments to 4.6 percent. NTT's old monopolistic inclinations were fading, but very slowly.

Privatization of NTT

Despite its role in pioneering the 1G era, NTT failed to exploit the lead. It could not prepare for a regional system (like Nordic NMT in the 1G era) or an open standards design (like PC clones in the 1980s or GSM in the 2G era). Instead, it opted for a closed model that allowed the operator to establish mobile leadership in Japan but discouraged global strategies. This strategic posture was in line with Japanese regulation, which explicitly forbade NTT from internationalizing; but it was entirely out of line with long-run industry trends. Due to the monopoly structure, NTT did not differ from the national PTTs in Western Europe. Driven by an engineering mind-set, technology innovation thrived, but marketing lingered. Service barely existed and price premiums were excessive. Users had a limited number of terminals and these were available only for rental.

In 1979, NTT was the first to launch an analog cellular system. Nationwide coverage became available in 1984. Because the technology was proprietary and the usage expensive, it attracted few customers until years later when competition was introduced and rates were lowered. This was the Nordic model turned on its head: closed, pricey, and unpopular. Japanese vendors did supply cellular terminals in overseas markets (for instance, handportables for AMPS and TACS), but its customers were marginal in worldwide terms, for example, in the Middle East and Australia. Furthermore, the rapid ascent of the GSM resulted in substitution with systems manufactured in the Nordic countries. Japan had little impact on technical developments and fell behind the European monopolies in market evolution. By 1989, the Japanese network had attracted 180,000 to 200,000 subscribers, which translated to a penetration of 0.14 percent, in contrast to 2.5 percent in Sweden and Finland and about 1.4 percent in the United States. It was a lousy end for a great beginning.

Between 1982 and 1984, legislative efforts accelerated in the Japanese Diet, which moved ahead to partly privatize NTT and to introduce competition in long-distance and local services. The NTT Corporation Act focused on privatization issues, while the Telecommunications Business Act set new regulatory ground rules for competition.[25] At the same time, wireless carriers proliferated as well. In 1986, NTT initiated in-flight phone service and a year later a mobile phone service. A decade later, the number of wireless carriers had soared to ninety. In the aftermath of industry consolidation and the phase out of the Personal Handyphone System (PHS) standard, the number of the carriers decreased to twenty-two in 2000. The number of foreign investors in Japan grew rapidly. In wireless communications, NTT was the sole operator until the late 1980s, when competition was allowed and two new operators entered the industry. IDO (Nippon Idou Tsushin Corporation) and DDI (Daini Denden) provided service based on JTACS.[26] These so-called new common carriers (NCCs) differed from their counterparts in the United States (e.g., MCI, Sprint) and the U.K. (e.g., Mercury) in that the former had a large number of corporate shareholders.[27] However, the market remained restricted. For example, handsets were not for sale and could only be rented from one of three service providers. Tariffs were high.

In effect, through the 1G era, the number of terminals grew slowly until the marketplace was opened to competition, from 151,000 in 1987 to 1.4 million in 1991. During the 2G era, the number of terminals soared from 1.7 million in 1992 to more than 56 million in 2000.[28] The anticipated increases in revenues and jobs contributed to efforts of the industry practitioners and government regulators to speed up the 3G developments and to establish a powerful position by the 4G era. Despite consensus on broad objectives, there was a deep disagreement on the necessary *means* between NTT and NTT DoCoMo.

NTT's Suppliers: After Privatization

Even before privatization, NTT had begun to open its procurement to foreign companies and other Japanese firms. Still, the traditional supply chain (the "Den Den Family") had a vested interest in opposing divestiture. Until 1985, the closed group of NTT suppliers consisted primarily of four companies: NEC, Fujitsu, Hitachi, and Oki. Through controlled competition, these companies cooperated with NTT and each other, in joint development. At the same time, they engaged in competition against each other, in order to sell the jointly developed equipment to NTT. All, however, could expect to receive a significant share of NTT's order. Building upon the competencies they accumulated in telecommunications, these suppliers were able to enter in semiconductors and computers, as well. When Japan's Ministry of International Trade and Industry (MITI) established its first cooperative projects to cultivate computer expertise in Japanese companies, NTT's suppliers—Hitachi, NEC, and Fujitsu—assumed the leadership role. Although MITI also included Toshiba and Mitsubishi Electric in most of its projects, these companies were in a weaker position relative to the members of the "NTT family."[29]

NTT and its family of suppliers had cooperative relationships. But the list of suppliers was select and limited, making these relationships exclusive. NTT was forbidden to operate in foreign markets. The supply chain was domestic by nature. Until 1985, controlled competition nurtured a cozy relationship. What made the relationship inferior to the Nordic model and poorly adapted to industry globalization was the fact that it was neither competitive nor able to globalize. Controlled competition did enable the leading Japanese companies to build competencies in computers, communications, and semiconductors. In contrast to the high-tech segments, which were competitive and export driven, the nature of the supply relationship in telecommunications constrained the strategic flexibility of the vendors. Adapting to their tasks, they became neither competitive internationally nor driven by foreign markets.

The 2G Era: Globalization Gap

By 2000, Japan had the second largest cellular market worldwide. A year later, it introduced the world's first 3G system. These first-mover advantages originated from strategic decisions and investments at the turn of the 1990s. Despite advanced R&D, *commercial* cellular growth had started slowly in Japan.

From Protected Bays to Open Seas

Having learned from the attacks of Japanese companies in various high-tech industries during the 1970s and 1980s, equipment manufacturers in the United States and Western Europe anticipated the challenge of Japanese vendors in their wireless markets. In 1987, Jorma Nieminen, Nokia-Mobira's then-CEO, expected cutthroat competition: "Mobira faces open competition and lacks shelter from pressures from any direction. As in open sea sailing, when you confront a storm, you have to be able to face it. There will be no available shelter."[30] But to the surprise of the European and Nordic vendors, no storm arose from the East.

Why the Follower Geese Did Not Fly

After the mid-1950s, many Japanese industry leaders, particularly those thriving in consumer electronics, employed an approach that later became known as the "flying geese" paradigm in the West. A variation of the catch-up model, this paradigm envisioned a series of interactions between the lead country (the "lead goose") and the challenger (the "follower goose") countries.[31] The paradigm offered an evolutionary vision of how an initially disadvantaged or nonexistent industry could be developed into an advantaged industry through a sequence of imports and competence assimilation, domestic production protection through intense competition, exports, outward foreign direct investment (FDI), and technological self-reliance. This was the path of Sony and Matsushita in consumer electronics.

In telecommunications, the evolutionary path was different, except for the early historical phase of imports and knowledge adaptation. The first Japanese-American joint venture, NEC, illustrated these efforts to acquire, improve, and then export Western technology. In the Japanese high-tech sector, the phase was followed by intense domestic rivalry, which prepared companies for the worldwide markets in the 1950s and 1960s. In the next two decades, Japanese companies challenged and overthrew industry giants in a variety of industries with exports and outward FDI. But in the wireless industry, progression was arrested in the second phase. There was no domestic competition, and by law, NTT was not allowed to enter worldwide markets. International activities were the preserve of KDD (formerly Kokusai Denshin Denwa), NTT's counterpart which had been created in 1953 to handle international phone service.[32] Even before privatization, the Ministry of Posts and Telecommunications saw KDD as a constraint to limit NTT's revenue and power. In the post-privatized environment, KDD remained the Ministry's "favored son." NTT and its suppliers were confined to the Japanese home base. Until privatization, the overwhelming majority of the vendors' sales came from NTT. The Japanese wireless attack did not fail to materialize because Japanese vendors could not compete, but because they were not allowed to compete.

By the end of the 2G era, NTT DoCoMo struggled to access worldwide markets. Its confinement to domestic markets did not *entirely* prevent it from globalization. In R&D (and more recently in procurement), the company engaged in joint development projects with industry leaders, such as Nortel, IBM Japan, DEC, Ericsson, and AT&T. Through many of its subsidiaries (particularly NTT International, founded in 1985), AT&T has offered telecom consulting and engineering services outside Japan, which started with a $1.6 billion Thai contract in 1992. Finally, the operator established several strategic alliances, including one with Microsoft. Although aspects of these activities may characterize traditional multinational and international companies, all represent a very low degree of internationalization and do not reflect global or translocal strategies.[33]

What Is Bad for Big Geese Is Very Bad for Little Geese

In 2001, NEC had 150,000 employees. It operated a network of sixty plants and more than 300 sales offices in Japan, as well as subsidiaries and affiliates in forty countries. In 2001, Japan's mobile phone market gained momentum as NTT DoCoMo's i-mode mobile phone services expanded, and IT investment in Japan at length showed signs of recovery. Concurrently, NEC attributed the increase of its total sales partially to "brisk domestic sales of mobile phones."[34] After the peak years of the Internet revolution, NEC generated more than $43 billion in revenues. Unlike the leading mobile vendors, however, its net profit margin had been very slim through the 1990s, at 0.2 percent to 2 percent. Erosion in semiconductors and increasing competition in PC manufacturing contributed to these low numbers. At the end of the decade, NEC lost its status as the world's largest semiconductor maker to Intel. In the late 1990s, it took control of Packard Bell. Yet, its market value amounted to just $5.2 billion.

Having started its corporate existence as NTT's supplier, NEC had diversified beyond telecommunications in the 1960s, and redefined itself as a PC maker in the 1980s. At the turn of the millennium, it recast itself as a provider of Internet products and services. Eager to sharpen its focus, NEC realigned its vast tech empire into three groups. NEC Solutions made computer hardware and offered software and consulting services. NEC Electron Devices was a top semiconductor manufacturer. Only the third group reflected its historical past: NEC Networks supplied computer and telecom networking equipment. Having implemented wide-ranging structural reforms in organizational capabilities, NEC President Koji Nishigaki had a vision for NEC's future in which the mobile played a role:

> NEC Networks aims to become a global number one in optical networking systems, high-quality IP (Internet protocol) networks, next-generation mobile phone systems, and mobile handsets. Indeed, NEC's achievements to date make it a strong contender. . . . NEC is a step ahead in developing infrastructure and mobile handset technology for next-generation mobile phones. In particular, NEC has already supplied systems and handsets to NTT DoCoMo, which is leading the way in commercializing 3G mobile phone technology.[35]

In parallel with diversification and internationalization, the role of telecom products and services steadily declined in total revenues. Prior to its move beyond Japan, NEC had obtained 80 percent to 90 percent of its revenues in Japan, from NTT. By 2001, NEC Networks accounted for 31 percent of total sales. But there was another catch to the projections in the mobility business. As long as NTT DoCoMo itself was confined to the Japanese marketplace, NEC's supply function would remain captive of its prime client's needs. The vendor's geographic diversification illustrated the globalization gap. In contrast to Nokia and Ericsson, which garnered 98 percent to 99 percent of their total sales outside the home base, NEC obtained only 20 percent of its total revenues outside Japan (and 7 percent of these foreign sales originated from the United States). Even at Motorola, the relative role of foreign revenues was twice as high.

Through NTT DoCoMo's competitive circumstances, NEC shared the pain of the globalization gap. If the follower geese did not fly, the little geese hardly got off the ground.

From NTT to DoCoMo

In 1991, NTT established a subsidiary to adopt its various wireless segments. Under the leadership of NTT executive Kouji Ohboshi, NTT Mobile Communications Network—which soon adopted the DoCoMo nickname (short for "Do Communications Over the Mobile Network" and is also a play on the Japanese word for "anywhere")—launched its operations a year later. A maverick executive, Kouji Ohboshi was sent to run DoCoMo, then an unprofitable unit.

Ohboshi's Strategy: Early Years

Instead of turning the mobile operator into a replica of NTT, Ohboshi decided to make it the reverse of the parent: market-driven, competitive, and hungry for internationalization. Business was no longer as usual. Like the large-country PTTs in Europe and the pre-cellular AT&T in the United States, NTT's executives saw wireless as a luxury service; hence the high prices and low volumes, which effectively undid Japanese pioneership in mobility. In contrast, Ohboshi thought like the leaders of the Nordic PTTs. He saw wireless as an affordable mass-consumer service; hence the low prices and high volumes, which would boost Japanese pioneership in mobility. His vision went even further. The Nordic vendors had pioneered mobility worldwide, whereas operators had failed to create requisite scope internationally. Japan's population was five times greater than that of all Nordic countries combined. Ohboshi was determined to exploit this home base advantage to initiate globalization at NTT DoCoMo.

The number of DoCoMo's subscribers exceeded 3.5 million, or half the market of mobile phone users. At the same time, the operator's pager business peaked, then began a long-term decline. But the rising volumes of the mobile phone market soon made up for the losses.[36] With more than a million analog mobile phone users in 1992, DoCoMo shared the Japanese cellular market with two new telecom companies, DDI and IDO, which was later bought by DDI. Initially, paging was more popular than mobile phones, with DoCoMo winning more than 3 million customers. In 1993, the operator launched a digital mobile service based on Personal Digital Cellular (PDC). The system was incompatible with the digital standards in Europe and the United States.[37]

Three years after the creation of NTT DoCoMo, liberalization of the Japanese cellular market boosted growth. As three or four new carriers entered in each regional block, the handset market was liberalized. In the past, Japanese consumers had to lease mobile phones from the network operators; now they could purchase them at retail stores. Internationally, these developments lagged behind those in rival country markets. In the United States and the Nordic countries, comparable measures had been implemented a decade before. Concurrently, prices began a dramatic decline with PDC services, while tariffs were tailored to match users' needs. Ohboshi's independent thinking did not go unnoticed at the NTT headquarters, which expected the maverick's bold dreams to crash in 1994, when the government opened Japan's mobile-phone market to new competitors and let consumers buy phones. A year later, competition accelerated again with the launch of PHS. Based on neither a cellular nor a cordless technology, it was a combination of both. With lower handset costs, monthly fees and calling rates, PHS had been introduced as a low-cost alternative to cellular.[38]

By the spring of 1999, there were some 41.5 million PDC users and some 5.8 million PHS subscribers in Japan. PHS was a niche product, but PDC was the second largest digital standard worldwide, even though it remained stuck within domestic boundaries. Deregulation did not break DoCoMo, but made it. The stalemate circumstances between the growth-hungry mobile subsidiary and its powerful parent NTT set the context for a future struggle over succession and control. Ohboshi wanted to get rid of the parent's stake in DoCoMo. And the parent returned the favor. It wanted to get rid of Ohboshi.

Struggle for Succession and Control

In 1997, Asia's financial crisis was felt in Japan. As regulatory failures were widely perceived as contributing to the stagnation of the economy, the spotlight turned toward DoCoMo's parent. Japan's Fair Trade Commission ordered NTT to reduce its 95 percent ownership of the wireless subsidiary. Meanwhile, NTT failed to get rid of Ohboshi. A year later, Keiji Tachikawa, then considered an NTT loyalist, succeeded the sixty-five-year-old Ohboshi as DoCoMo president.

As chairman, Ohboshi was expected to stay quietly in the background. But that did not suit him. In spring, DoCoMo and its bankers discussed whether DoCoMo should invest in a Brazilian mobile-phone operator as part of a plan to spread DoCoMo's technology abroad. Tachikawa declared that DoCoMo was not interested, but Ohboshi thought they could handle the risk. President and chairman denied allegations of friction, but observers talked about it. Later that year, DoCoMo made the Brazilian investment, which triggered the operator's efforts to capture minority stakes in the central Triad players. As NTT agreed to let DoCoMo go public on the Tokyo Stock Exchange, it dispatched Hitoshi Tajima to DoCoMo, in part to help keep an eye on Mr. Ohboshi. As the parent's PR chief, Tajima had played a critical role in minimizing damage after the so-called Recruit scandal. He was to lead Do-CoMo's IPO. In October 1998, NTT sold 30 percent of its DoCoMo stock to the public, raising $18 billion. It was one of the largest share offerings in history, but the key role belonged to DoCoMo executives and their advisers from Goldman Sachs. In the IPO process, two men closely connected to Japan's then-prime minister, Keizo Obuchi, held lucrative DoCoMo shares. Well before the scandal erupted, Tajima slashed his own throat with a kitchen knife. Whether it had to do with personal and family issues, the suicide contributed to the controversy, while strengthening Ohboshi's position in the DoCoMo power struggle.[39]

Meanwhile, the number of DoCoMo's subscribers increased to 15 million, despite the economic turmoil in the Pacific Rim. Unsurprisingly, international markets discovered the Japanese operator. In 1998, DoCoMo's much-awaited IPO raised more than $18 million, while NTT's stake in DoCoMo was cut to 67 percent. At the same time, multistandard rivalries entered the Japanese market, in which DDI became the first carrier to introduce a CDMA-based network. Though DoCoMo still relied on PDC, it reinforced efforts to develop and standardize a wideband version of CDMA, aligning with the Nordic vendors. Even in its home base, NTT DoCoMo was increasingly challenged by an emerging coalition of forces (see Exhibit 6-1). By 2001, KDDI (formerly DDI) had become the second-largest telecom player in Japan with $18 billion in revenues. A year earlier, the company had expanded dramatically as it acquired rivals KDD (NTT's international counterpart) and IDO. KDDI had 14 million mobile phone subscribers, including more than 5 million subscribers to its mobile Internet service, Ezweb.

Increasing Competition and Standards Wars

One of the Nokians' greatest surprises in the late 1980s and the 1990s was the weak performance of Japanese competitors in the 2G rivalry. Initially, Japanese players hoped to use the proprietary PDC standard to cover the Asian markets, in order to respond to Europe's GSM challenge. These hopes crashed with the burst of the bubble economy, just as the R&D of the PDC exhausted the resources of Japanese mobile manufacturers. Through the 2G rivalry, Japanese consumer electronics giants, such as Panasonic, Sony, and NEC, failed to gain more than niche shares in the mobile markets. Despite their GSM success, however, the Finns had been unable to penetrate the Japanese markets. Nokia had competed in Japanese markets with mobile phones, but not with networks. At first, its PDC sales rose rapidly and the market share increased to 12 percent by the mid-1990s. By the end of the decade, it had declined to 5 percent. In Europe, even the most lightweight phones weighed more than 100 grams. Nokia's new models were about 92 grams. In the Japan, the market leaders, such as Panasonic, sold phones that weighed less than 70 grams. "We underestimated

Exhibit 6-1. Japan's cellular industry (1983–2000).

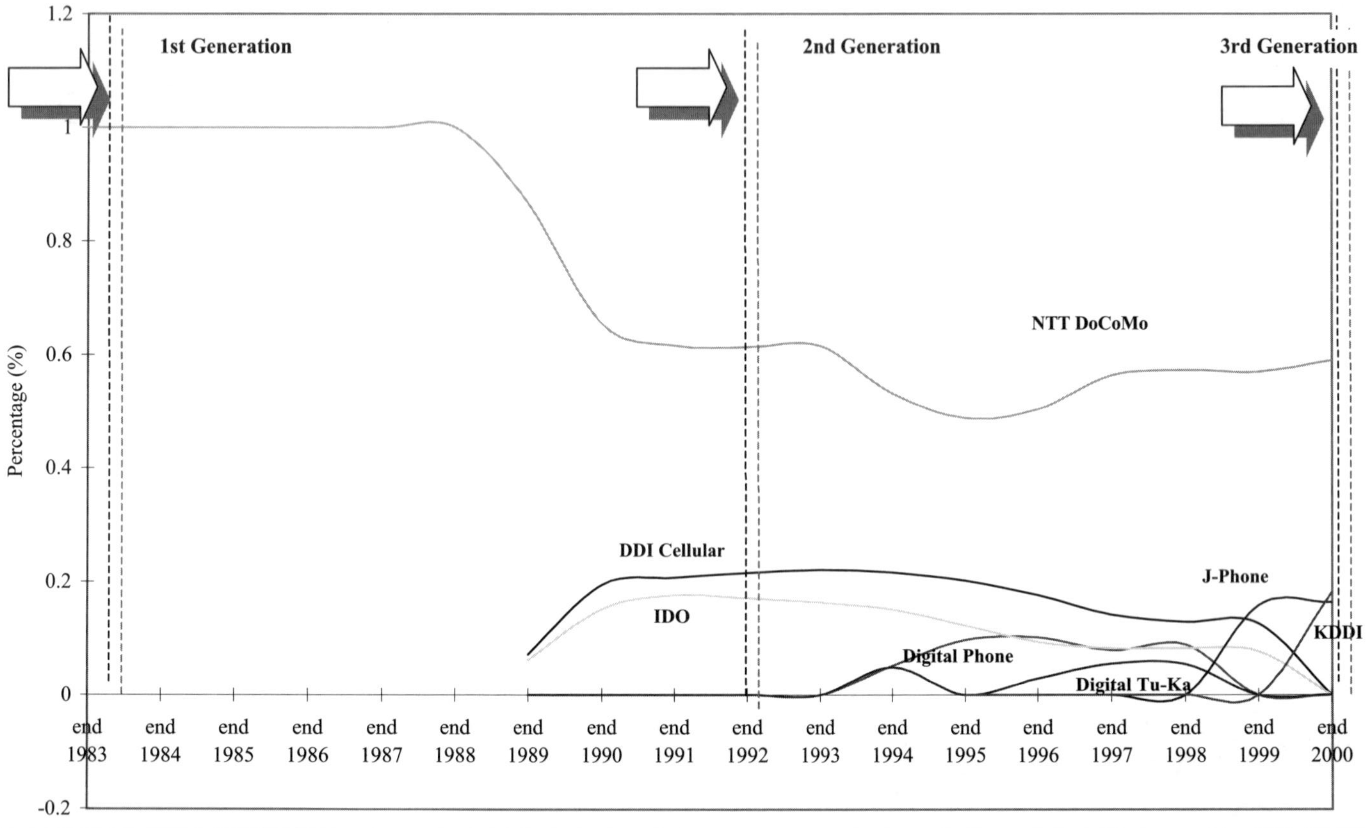

the significance of the smallness and lightness," admitted Olav Stang, chief of Nokia's Japanese activities, in early 1999.[40]

By 2001, the standards wars had arrived in Japan, as well, through foreign stakes.[41] The battlefront was divided between W-CDMA (NTT DoCoMo, J-Phone), which was supported by the European players, and CDMA2000 (KDDI), which had been designed by Qualcomm. Having pioneered CDMA in the Japanese marketplace, KDDI argued that CDMA2000 network was more cost-efficient than W-CDMA.[42] On the other hand, J-Phone—a Japanese vendor in which Vodafone had acquired a controlling stake—stressed W-CDMA's global appeal, arguing that it would provide global economies of scale that would lower network and handset costs. In particular, the cost of manufacturing GSM phones would be 25 to 30 percent lower than manufacturing similar PDC phones in the 2G game, due to superior global economies of scale. J-Phone expected this difference to be duplicated in 3G between W-CDMA, a global *de facto* platform, and CDMA2000, a minority platform. In the late 1990s, Japanese and European companies agreed to work together on developing W-CDMA as a global 3G standard. At the time, this cooperation gave the impression of similarity between the networks. But despite similar designations, the European and DoCoMo's W-CDMA network differed somewhat in terms of software architecture. When DoCoMo prepared to launch its 3G service, the leading European vendors (Nokia, Ericsson) were not among DoCoMo's list of handset suppliers. This difference was expected to narrow when Asian and global operators began overlaying 3G networks.

Until the end of the 1990s, Japan's proprietary standards confined local players to the domestic market. This solution, which reflected NTT's old monopoly background, was intertwined with the operator's globalization gap.

NTT DoCoMo's Global Strategy

The historical genesis of Japan's mobile communications goes back to the late-nineteenth century, the first American-Japanese joint venture (NEC), and the business relationship between the national PTT and its family of suppliers. After the devastation of World War II, Japan's NTT caught up with America's technology leadership and became the pioneer of analog cellular, just as it was among the early movers in digital cellular. In both cases, NTT could not exploit its R&D leadership in worldwide markets. Only with the incorporation of NTT DoCoMo in 1991 did this change. In the latter half of the decade, DoCoMo demonstrated the viability and strength of its service concept. And in 2001, it became the first major operator to pioneer and commercialize the 3G infrastructure.

NTT DoCoMo remained a member of the powerful NTT Group, which oversaw its operations (see Exhibit 6-2). The two shared basic R&D. In turn, DoCoMo oversaw eight regional NTT DoCoMo Group units located throughout Japan. It had subsidiaries in Japan as well as Europe, the United States, and Brazil. It had four key businesses:

- Mobile phones (including cellular service, packet communication service, satellite mobile communications service, in-flight telephone service, and equipment sales in each of these areas)
- PHS (encompassing PHS service and PHS equipment sales)
- Paging (encompassing paging services and paging equipment sales)
- Miscellaneous (including international dialing service)

The mobile phone segment, particularly i-mode, accounted for DoCoMo's explosive success at the close of the 1990s.

Explosive Growth: i-mode and Service Concept

"In Japan, DoCoMo's wireless web phones are all the rage," reported *Fortune* in September 2000. The story focused on the efforts of the mobile operator to take its cutting-edge technology global:

Exhibit 6-2. NTT DoCoMo organization chart.

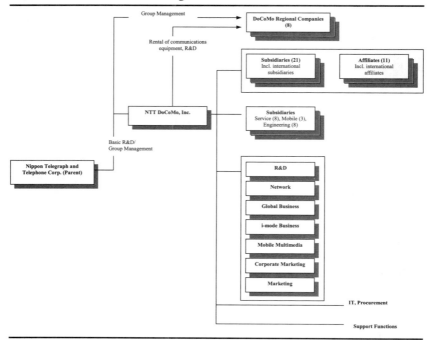

When it launched its wireless web service less than two years ago, Japan's NTT DoCoMo had no idea what kind of stir it would cause. Today the cellular giant has ten million customers who use their sleek i-mode phones to scan the Web. And that number is growing by 50,000 a day. DoCoMo's i-mode phones have the potential to become the biggest consumer phenomenon to emerge from Japan since Sony's Walkman in the early 1980s.

The world will soon find out whether that prediction is true: DoCoMo is set to bring its cutting-edge mobile web technology to the U.S. and Europe. And the phone company's huge success in Japan should give it a technological and marketing edge over global competitors like AT&T and Vodafone. Small wonder that the industry considers DoCoMo the most important company to watch in the coming huge battle for the mobile Internet market.[43]

The story was entitled provocatively, "Today, Tokyo; Tomorrow, the World." Unfortunately, globalization was not just a matter of leveraging scale, but of leveraging scale through *scope.*

Between 1997 and 2001, DoCoMo's i-mode users soared from fewer than 11 million to more than 36 million. Despite increasing competition, DoCoMo's market share actually increased from less than 53 percent to more than 59 percent in Japan. At the same time, churn rate remained less than 2 percent, which was a remarkable accomplishment. As anticipated, the decline of the average revenue per user (ARPU) toward the end of the voice era ended with the data services.

Starting with Ohboshi's new strategy in the early 1990s, Japan's cellular phone market had grown explosively. By May 2001, the nation had 62 million subscribers, almost half its entire population. Following the shift from analog to digital, NTT DoCoMo pioneered the development of nonvoice mobile communications with DoPa, Japan's first "packet" communications service. Anticipating that the cellular phone market would soon become saturated, DoCoMo built on the success of DoPa and developed innovative mobile data communications services for consumer markets. After its launch in 1999, i-mode rapidly achieved an unparalleled level of acceptance. Two years after its launch, it continued to grow in popularity, thanks to expanding offerings and low fees (see Exhibit 6-3). By May 2001, i-mode was an integral part of the business and personal lives of almost 30 million NTT DoCoMo customers. Unlike the European players, NTT DoCoMo's i-mode succeeded because—as Jeffrey L. Funk has argued—it kept things simple: "The mobile Internet contents must be simple, due to the small screens and keypads found on mobile phones."[44]

With i-mode, Japanese cellular phone users had easy access to more than 40,000 Internet sites, as well as specialized services such as e-mail, online shopping and banking, ticket reservations, and restaurant advice. i-mode empowered users to do much more than just talk. It offered them digital intelligence with easy dialing and simple web access from their mobile phones, while keeping them connected to the Internet at all times (i.e., an "always on" connection). NTT DoCoMo's i-mode business model synchronized the *entire* i-mode value chain, in order to develop ever-better mobile service for subscribers. Instead of perceiving wireless and the Internet as separate technologies, DoCoMo saw them through a unitary vision. The company had adopted a wireless communications model using variations of *de facto* Internet standards such as HTML. By basing it content on iHTML, a subset of HTML, it gave its customers access to the existing network of conventional web servers and therefore provided them with seamless web service. At the same time, its use of iHTML greatly simplified the creation of i-mode sites for its content providers.[45]

In fall 2001, NTT DoCoMo's launched Freedom of Multimedia Access (FOMA) service in Japan, the pioneering 3G platform worldwide. It provided voice transmission quality on a par with fixed-line communications, with minimal interference and noise, while supporting diverse multimedia content (see Exhibit 6-3). Based on the W-CDMA system, FOMA fueled the evolution of i-mode, other web-connection services, and innovative applications. It supported full-motion video image transmission, music and game distribution, and other high-speed, large-capacity data communications. It enabled users to connect with "anyone, anytime, anywhere." With a maximum downlink speed of 384 Kbps, forty times faster than conventional wireless data communications, FOMA delivered high-quality video as well as enhanced voice clarity. To paraphrase ads for palm computers in the United States, NTT DoCoMo's FOMA *literally* put the world of mobile multimedia "in the palm of your hand." From initial installation points in the Tokyo area and parts of Yokohama and Kawasaki in late 2001, NTT DoCoMo was steadily expanding the FOMA network to ensure optimum communications quality throughout Japan.

NTT DoCoMo's financials reflected its growth; its number of employees tripled from 1995 to 2001, from fewer than 6,000 to more than 18,000. Concurrently, revenues quadrupled to $37 billion and net profit margin soared from 2 percent to almost 9 percent. Despite Japan's stagnating economy, NTT DoCoMo's margin grew in excess of 33 percent, while the subscriber base continued to increase. But too much of a good thing can be a bad thing: the operator's growth led to a problem with its parent, the powerful NTT, which was still 45 percent owned by the Japanese government. Policymakers, regulators, and senior executives at NTT and DoCoMo were faced with a dilemma. If the mobile subsidiary were to remain with the parent, it could serve as Ma NTT's life-support system. If, conversely, the operator were unleashed, it could evolve into a global giant. Naturally, NTT and DoCoMo held reverse views on the preferred outcome. Norio Wada, NTT's second-leading executive, thought bigger was better. With its formidable R&D facilities and skilled work force, a united NTT could help lift the country out of its slump. "It's best to remain a group, since we have the resources to deal with the drastic changes hitting the telecommunications industry," Wada argued. As for DoCoMo, the argument was simple: "We want control."[46] DoCoMo's chairman, Kouji Ohboshi, had spent a decade resisting integration, which conflicted with the 1992 incorporation that promoted competition through a fully autonomous DoCoMo. In January 2002, DoCoMo was the world's second-leading mobile operator after the British Vodafone Group. Yet it remained 64 percent owned by NTT. "Japan has been stagnant because of regulations and monopolies," Ohboshi argued.[47]

Exhibit 6-3. From i-mode to FOMA.

(a) NTT DoCoMo's i-mode concept.

New Platform and User-Friendly Portal
Introduced in February 1999, i-mode was depicted as a new platform for mobile communications. It took off very fast, attracting some 30 million subscribers by the close of 2001. Through i-mode, cellular phone users got easy access to more than 40,000 Internet sites, as well as specialized services such as e-mail, online shopping and banking, ticket reservations, and restaurant advice. Users could access sites from anywhere in Japan and at relatively low rates. The charges were based on the volume of data transmitted, not on the amount of time spent connected.

i-mode and Value Chain Collaboration
NTT DoCoMo synchronized the *entire* i-mode value chain in order to develop ever-better mobile service for subscribers. The company believed that close collaboration with equipment manufacturers, content providers, and other platforms ensured that wireless technology, content quality, and users' experience would evolve at the same optimal pace.

Simple, Affordable Pricing
To sign up for i-mode, a cellular subscriber with a standard voice transmission arrangement simply needed to request a packet transmission service contract along with a basic i-mode contract. Customers paid a low monthly fee of 300 yen ($2.48), which comprised a 200 yen ($1.65) packet transmission charge, and a 100 yen ($0.83) fee for i-mode service. In addition, users paid low variable packet fees, based on the volume of data transmitted as well as flat monthly fees ranging from 100 yen ($0.83) to 300 yen ($2.48) for each content provider site to which they subscribe.

i-mode Network Structure

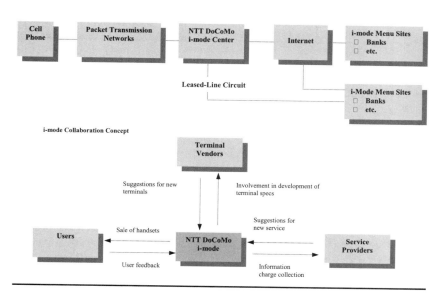

(continues)

Exhibit 6-3. (Continued).

(b) NTT DoCoMo's FOMA concept.

High Data Rate					
INTERACTIVE	**POINT TO POINT**	**ONE WAY**	**ONE-WAY INFO ("PULL")**	**MULTIPOINT**	**MULTIPOINT**
Video Conferencing	Remote Medical Diagnosis	Video Catalog Shopping	Video on Demand	Digital Info Delivery	Mobile TV
Videophone	Video Mail	Remote Education	Mobile Video Player	Advanced Car Navigation	
	Web		"Karaoke"	Digital Info Delivery	Mobile Radio
Mobile Banking	Voice Mail	Digital News-paper/Publishing	Mobile Audio Player		
Telephone	E-Mail			Digital Info Deliver	
	Short Message				
Low Data Rate					

	Video
	Still Image
	Audio Data
	Text Data
	Speech

SOURCE: Based on company reports.

According to the Japan Electronics and Information Technology Industries Association (JEITI), Japan's domestic sales of mobile phones fell more than 34 percent to 3.1 million handsets, in 2001. The decline was attributed to saturation, reduced adoption of Internet-capable phones, and a slower economy overall. As the hypergrowth stagnated, underlying tensions began to surface as well. With its high stakes, the behind-the-scenes drama certainly had elements of a Shakespearean drama. Yet, the more rapidly DoCoMo grew, the firmer became the grip of NTT.

Efforts at Global Strategy

At first, i-mode had been a pet project of Ohboshi. When DoCoMo launched the mobile Internet service in February 1999, NTT underestimated the maverick's prescience once again. Not only did i-mode become highly popular in Japan; it also attracted wide international attention. Unlike the European WAP, the Japanese "had got 3G right." While NTT downplayed Ohboshi's role, the chairman published a book on managing high-growth companies. In *The NTT Phenomenon*, he explained how DoCoMo developed its i-mode service, how it planned to export its success around the world, and its vision for the 3G era. Ohboshi saw the experience instructive in terms of "leading the broadband revolution."[48] Meanwhile, Tachikawa, who was officially portrayed as the strategist behind DoCoMo's success, engaged the operator in the international expansion. In the organization, Yoshinori Uda was in charge of the company's global business operations.

In 2000 and 2001, NTT DoCoMo built alliances with mobile phone carriers and other telecom companies around the world, "to ensure i-Mode's future as the *de facto* global standard." To push these new data services, the Japanese operator initiated a slate of strategic partnerships in Japan and, more importantly, in foreign markets. The two co-evolved: i-mode's hypergrowth boosted NTT DoCoMo's international ambitions, while the efforts to build presence in the lead markets of Western Europe and the United States attracted international attention to DoCoMo and i-mode. The international alliances started with a 1999 joint venture in Japan with Microsoft (known as Mobimagic), which was followed by a 19 percent stake in the telecom unit of Hong Kong's Hutchison Whampoa. In 2000, DoCoMo became the largest shareholder in America Online Japan, in which it acquired a 42 percent stake. It had been working with KG Telecom of Taiwan on a joint mobile Internet project and had been planning a quick launch of i-mode–based mobile multimedia services. In Europe, it joined Hutchison Whampoa and Dutch KPN in an alliance to bid on next-generation mobile phone licenses in Europe. It paid $4.5 billion for a 15 percent stake in KPN's wireless unit, KPN Mobile, to promote multimedia services and launch an i-mode-like service in the Netherlands, Germany, and Belgium. It also teamed up with Telecom Italia Mobile to introduce i-mode services in Europe. In the United States, it paid $9.8 billion for a 16 percent stake in AT&T Wireless. Many of these investments in overseas mobile units caused significant losses and writedowns at DoCoMo, including the investment in AT&T ($6.5 billion) and KPN Mobile ($2.7 billion). In April 2002, AT&T debuted "inMode," a U.S. version of DoCoMo's i-mode. Its success or failure would serve as a critical market signal of the expandability of the Japanese offering, and it hoped to provide the operator with i-mode technology and know-how to boost the mobile multimedia business.[49]

NTT DoCoMo envisioned a future in which people around the world would benefit from borderless global communications, live-action video on mobile terminals, and even mobile control of home and office appliances. The purposeful efforts at a "global strategy" did not make up a worldwide empire, but they did provide a slate of footholds to build one over time. In the analog and digital cellular eras, NTT had failed to seize leadership in worldwide mobile markets. In 2001, DoCoMo was determined to export the success of i-mode in Japan into overseas markets. But like the great Japanese consumer electronics giants, it had a long-term perspective. In the 3G era, it would still thrive primarily in the Japanese markets. It had different and far bolder ambitions for the 4G era.

According to the parent NTT, DoCoMo had stumbled with its foreign investments and the new 3G service. In reality, the operator had moved relatively quickly after years of insularity, even as the parent's stake made its internationalization more difficult. Similarly, no new-generation services had invaded the markets overnight, and the 3G shift was likely to be even slower, due to substantial changes in the transition from digital to multimedia cellular. Ambivalent about the future developments, regulators and policymakers were buying time by leaving NTT intact. After all, NTT, with its more than 220,000 employees (DoCoMo included), continued to garner over $92 billion in sales. Japan's stagnating economy suffered from increasing unemployment, whereas NTT promised stability. Why rock the boat? AT&T had been broken up in 1984 and 1996, and, by 2002, was undergoing its third breakup. The once-massive giant survived only through its small, distinct clones. This idea of competition as a destructive force had a long history in Japan, starting with the "controlled competition" of the supply chain in the domestic telecom sector. However, the notion of contained competition nurtured political dependency, which often surfaced in political deals and corruption.

By early 2000, DoCoMo's growing market power in Japan led to pressure from regulators, who worried that it was stifling competition. These concerns supported the idea of an independent DoCoMo. In May, the telecom ministry demanded that NTT submit a plan for reducing its stakes in DoCoMo and in NTT's international unit. Meanwhile, the tech sector consolidation and 3G transition hurt Japanese players, and both DoCoMo and NTT saw their shares plummet. Also, technical glitches forced Tachikawa to delay the launch of 3G service for four months. These twin problems in the subsidiary and the parent suppressed efforts to reorganize NTT. In November, DoCoMo took a $2.1 billion writedown on its overseas investments, whereas NTT expected to post a net loss of $2.7 billion for the year. Both underestimated the losses. In April 2002, NTT booked a net loss of $6.7 billion, the biggest in its history. It intended to venture its profitability by cutting 17,000 jobs (8 percent of the total) over the next three years. Initially, the fluctuating fortunes appeared to turn the tide in NTT's favor, in the short term. Fearing increasing instability and unemployment, Japanese policymakers granted NTT a year to submit a divestiture plan. The year could be critical. Ohboshi planned to retire in June 2002. Thereafter, Tachikawa could become chairman, return to NTT, or retire, which would allow NTT to hire its own candidate to lead an independent DoCoMo. Meanwhile, Vodafone prepared to compete with DoCoMo by acquiring Japan's third-leading mobile operator. At age 69, Ohboshi, the persistent rebel, called NTT a "cozy club" that kept its members happy but overlooked Japan's broader interests.[50]

Exhibit 6-4 is a summary of the Japanese path to 3G innovation—from

Exhibit 6-4. Japanese 3G innovation: Triad leadership.

MONOPOLY ERA

National PTT
- ☐ Public-sector monopoly, comparable to those in large European countries, from 1880s to NTT's privatization in 1985.
- ☐ Vertically integrated except for cooperative supply-chain arrangements.
- ☐ Rise of cellular platforms coincides with triumph of Japanese consumer electronics.

NIS/PTT Labs
- ☐ Mobile innovation by a family of vendors and NTT's centralized research labs.
- ☐ Catch-up with U.S. innovation by early 1970s.
- ☐ Stress on research rather than commercialization; proprietary rather than open specifications.

Old Public Policies
- ☐ In postwar era, U.S. authorities fail to turn NTT into an AT&T clone; regulated broadcasting, minimal defense interests, spectrum policies dictated by public mission.
- ☐ Industry policies for domestic markets (national roaming, high tariffs, noncompetitive licensing).
- ☐ NTT forbidden to internationalize; vendors diversify to internationalize.

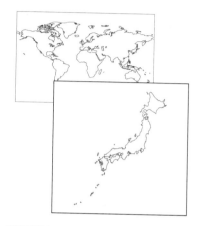

TRANSITION ERA

Privatization
- ☐ NTT's privatization in 1985; incorporation of NTT DoCoMo in 1992. Stress on competition and deregulation, but effects not yet shown.
- ☐ Vertically disintegrated value system; new industry players, but NTT controls industry evolution.
- ☐ Rise of 2G coincides with NTT's privatization, incorporation, and deregulation and privatization; foreign players arrive.

Transformation of Innovation
- ☐ Labs remain domestic and centralized.
- ☐ Digital pioneership, but again weak commercialization and proprietary standards.
- ☐ Innovation takes place within firms, international activities accelerate.

Transitional Public Policies
- ☐ Deregulation accelerates; spectrum policies subject to public mission.
- ☐ Roaming, pricing, and licensing policies crafted for domestic market.
- ☐ NTT still driven by old-style policies; internationalization is discouraged.

COMPETITIVE ERA

Cluster
- ☐ After NTT's incorporation, new leadership and new Nordic-style managerial approaches; competition and deregulation increase; DoCoMo's first viable business models for multimedia cellular.
- ☐ Aggressive first-mover strategies with 3G, efforts to leapfrog early into 4G.
- ☐ DoCoMo's marketing-driven "global service" strategy, with emphasis on low prices, high quality, large volumes; minority stakes in Triad locations.

Innovation Systems
- ☐ Standard homogenization contributes to Asian players' cost-effective strategies.
- ☐ DoCoMo joints international tech coalitions, but holds onto its i-mode concept.
- ☐ Efforts to export i-mode into overseas markets.

New Public Policies
- ☐ Deregulation intensifies; spectrum allocations become subject to commercial considerations; no license taxes, no industry slowdown.
- ☐ Despite competition, DoCoMo boosts its market share.
- ☐ Through W-CDMA, open specifications arrive in Japanese market; new public policies permit increasing FDI by foreign players.
- ☐ Due to Japan's stagnation, NTT tries to capture corporate control at DoCoMo.

the monopoly era through transition and to the present-day competitive environment.

NTT represented the past. Without DoCoMo, it was a crown without jewels. With DoCoMo, it was the king without clothes. NTT DoCoMo represented the future. With NTT, it was constrained from expansion in business and geography, at best. DoCoMo was about hope for a future that could become a reality in Japan more quickly than in other Triad regions. But it had to be able to globalize as well—and that was impossible with NTT's leash.

Chapter 7

The Future: The China Card

In the 1910s, Marconi's empire dominated wireless telegraphy. From the 1920s to the late 1970s, the United States enjoyed leadership in mobile communications. With the 2G era, the center of wireless innovation migrated from America to Western Europe, particularly the Nordic countries. Toward the end of the 1990s, Japan's NTT DoCoMo captured industry leadership in the 3G services. The future of the wireless industry, however, was not in the United States, northern Europe, or Japan—but in China.

Joining the Global Chessboard

The importance of China has as much to do with trade as with politics. Liberal reforms in the world's most populous country have created a massive potential market for the wireless industry. Meanwhile, access has served as a bargaining chip, as China has traded market share for advanced technologies. In the past, these policies opened Chinese markets for the mobile leaders. In the future, they are expected to shift innovation toward China, which could have substantial implications for the global chessboard, in wireless communications and across a wide variety of industries. Whoever has access to the world's largest developing mobile market has a foothold in future success. After all, some 5 million Chinese a month—the entire population of Finland—were taking out new subscriptions in early 2002. The struggle for access to this market began more than twenty years before.

The first milestone in the changing global chessboard took place on August 14, 2001, when China overtook the United States as the largest cellular phone market worldwide. But competition for the wireless future began more than two decades before that, when Deng Xiaoping and the reformers of the Communist party resumed full diplomatic relations with the United States.

The Long March to Reforms

For most of the past two millennia, China was the world's economic superpower. In 1820, it contributed about a third of global gross domestic product. Then it slid into more than a century of decline. The Communists promised

170

to reverse the trend, which they actually intensified. The Mao regime proclaimed the People's Republic of China in October 1949, with Beijing as the new capital and Zhou Enlai as premier. A year later, China's share of the global economy fell to 5 percent. For three decades, the nation would live in cultural isolation and outside the global chessboard. In an attempt to restructure the primarily agrarian economy, Mao undertook the "Great Leap Forward" campaign in 1958, which led to the abandonment of farming activities and widespread famine in which more than 20 million people died. As the failure of the industrialization campaign touched off a power struggle within the Communist party, Mao, starting in 1966, exploited a "Cultural Revolution" to crush opposition. Another two decades were lost in a great leap backward.

By 1971, the Nixon administration, eager to exploit the continued Sino-Soviet rift, initiated reconciliation efforts. Despite occasional waves of new suppression, reform-minded Deng Xiaoping was appointed deputy premier, chief of staff of the army, and member of the Central Committee of the Politburo in 1977.[1] As reformists surfaced in the party apparatus, Beijing and Washington announced full diplomatic relations on January 1, 1979. In a matter of months, the massive Chinese market opened its doors to the outside world, after half a century of isolation. In 1981, Motorola received its first orders from China, and as it rushed to build a presence, the European rivals hurried in its footsteps.

As Deng protégé Hu Yaobang was appointed party chairman in 1981, old Communist doctrines were buried and sweeping economic changes were set in motion. Rejecting the Marxist tenets that had slowed modernization, Chinese leaders began to import Western technology and management techniques. In 1999, the United States and China signed the bilateral World Trade Organization (WTO) agreement in Beijing. Thirteen years in the making, the agreement was a major advance for China toward WTO membership, which would legitimize the nation's new role as a global power and stimulate exports.[2] In 2002, China was expected to initiate an unprecedented range of reforms and measures to open its market as a member of the WTO. Business visionaries such as Kenichi Ohmae saw world trade at the dawn of a new era:

During the next two decades, China will become a thoroughly new type of political and economic entity. It will be brutally competitive in both the political sphere and the marketplace, innovative and resilient in the face of turbulence, and more dominant as an international political and economic power than any nation except the United States. This is the sort of change that takes place about once every century—comparable to the emergence of the United States as a world power at the beginning of the twentieth century.[3]

Signs of dissonance were appearing as well.[4] Still, none of these circumstances or reports cast doubt over the fact that China has evolved into world's leading powerhouse of wireless communications.

Trading Technology for Access

This Janus-faced bargain between China's need for sophisticated technologies in exchange for foreign direct investment (FDI) dictated Chinese policies vis-à-vis the leading mobile vendors and operators that were willing to trade access for technology competences and capabilities. As the vast nation opened its doors to these equipment manufacturers, it allowed them to translate exports into investments and presence, while negotiating on behalf of indigenous industry interests.

During the past two decades, this FDI has undergone substantial shifts in terms of entry modes, industry selection, project location, investment size, and operational phase. Overall, foreign investors have followed an evolutionary approach by incrementally increasing—and occasionally temporarily decreasing—their resource and financial commitments to local operations. Over the years, all investors have engaged in more proactive postures and risk taking in the Chinese market.[5]

Through these years of growth and turmoil, China has traded technology for access.

First Phase: Testing the Waters

Before opening its doors, China had developed its own industrial infrastructure, mainly on the basis of a nonequity foreign (advanced) technology transfer.[6] Officially, China opened its doors to FDI in 1979, with a new joint venture law that opened the first phase of investment flows (1979–1985). Concurrently, the Chinese government established special economic zones (SEZs) in Shenzhen, Zhuhai, and Shantou in Guangdong province and Xiamen in Fujian province, and it designated the entire province of Hainan as an SEZ. The objective was to better effect reform, open the domestic market to the outside world, and stimulate economic development. In 1984, China opened fourteen coastal cities to overseas investment. A year later, these open coastal areas were further expanded. By design, the cities were to play dual roles. As "windows," they opened China to the outside world; as "radiators," they spread economic development. In both cases, they built up the export-oriented economy.

During this first phase, foreign investment focused on small-scale assembling and processing for export. International multinationals were still testing the market rather than building manufacturing (not to speak of R&D) facilities. In absolute terms, FDI remained below $1.7 billion per year. Yet it was during this phase that the mobile leaders established their first footholds in China.

Resource commitments remained low. The objective was to create presence and monitor developments.

Second Phase: Accelerating Activities

After the initial boom years ended with rising inflation and lack of legal clarity regarding foreign investment, the Chinese government introduced regulations, which led to a rapid recovery in FDI and the second investment phase (1986–1989). Political clouds signaled new economic volatility. The removal of Hu Yaobang, a reformist hero, as party chairman in 1987 reflected a hard-line resurgence within the party. After the death of Hu in April 1989, the ideological struggle spilled into the streets of the capital. In May, student demonstrators occupied Beijing's Tiananmen Square, calling for democratic reforms. Less than a month later, the demonstrations were crushed in a bloody crackdown as troops and tanks moved into the square and fired on protesters, killing several hundred. In the aftermath of the "Tiananmen Massacre," as the media labeled the crisis, many foreign—particularly U.S.—investors distanced themselves from China, ending the second investment phase.

Unlike its predecessor, the second phase had resulted in extensive FDI, up until the Tiananmen crisis. More than 70 percent of FDI projects concentrated on manufacturing industries. Annual FDI flows doubled to $3.4 billion in 1989. In the mid-1980s, the improved investment climate and promise of greater stability, coupled with the breakup of the Bell System in the United States and the subsequent interest in foreign growth markets, boosted the investments of Motorola and AT&T in China. These developments came to a standstill after Tiananmen Square, when U.S. companies and others minimized their role in China. In the mobile business, this milestone event reduced the first-mover advantages of U.S. players while providing an opportunity for European players, particularly Ericsson and to a lesser degree Nokia, to fill a vacuum.

Third Phase: Adjusting and Consolidating

In 1990, the Chinese government issued a new joint venture law that was followed by new tax laws and sped-up market-oriented reforms. The government termed this a "socialist market economy" strategy. The idea was to reattract those investors that had fled after the Tiananmen crisis. Two years later, investment surged. A new wave of FDI focused on large infrastructure and manufacturing projects. These measures were accompanied by further market access. The third FDI phase involved surging foreign investment through most of the 1990s, while investment flows entered a new period of adjustment and consolidation.

The magnitude of FDI soared early in the decade, tripling in size by 1992 and more than quadrupling by 1997. A decade before, annual FDI had been at $1.9 billion; now it climbed to $452.6 billion. Market-oriented reforms gave a powerful lift to the entrenched wireless players in China. Now Motorola could implement objectives it had outlined in the late 1980s. Lucent Technologies rushed to China as well. But U.S. vendors and operators were no longer alone.

The Watershed: The Tiananmen Crisis

In China, a combination of growing popular discontent and escalating elite power struggles may have made the events of June 4, 1989 likely.[7] Outside China, these events triggered a wide variety of responses in the ensuring months and years that would have a substantial impact on the future of mobile communications in China—and, through China, worldwide. Certainly, the co-incidence of the U.S. presidential campaign of 1992 did not help. Having accused President George H. W. Bush of "coddling dictators from Baghdad to Beijing," President Clinton came to office determined to change China's human rights practices. By leveraging America's trade and market power, Clinton, in his first term, conditioned normal trade relations with China on demonstrable improvements in the country's human rights. As Beijing refused to yield to President Clinton's pressure, the Democratic administration eventually gave in and gave up the trade/rights linkage. As one perceptive observer has noted, the combined effect of the Tiananmen crisis and the first Clinton administration had a long-term impact in China:

> Chinese increasingly view America today as a bully who habitually badgers their pride, belittles their accomplishments, transgresses their national sovereignty, and attempts to thwart the rise of their country's international influence. Perceived American self-righteousness, arrogance, "obsession" with liberty and democracy, and most of all, missionary zeal to change China's Communist regime have served to fan sentiments that range from indignation to rage.[8]

The Tiananmen crisis was a watershed event in the mobile business, as in many other industries. Taking advantage of the reduced U.S. presence, the Euro-Nordic players seized the historical opportunity boosting their operations in China.

Mobile Leaders and Chinese SEZs

Today, most of China's five special economic zones are located in the southeast (see Exhibit 7-1). Primarily geared toward exporting processed goods, these zones seek to integrate science and industry with trade, and they benefit from advantageous policies and special economic managerial systems to facilitate exports. Eager to bring in new investors, China's SEZs provide preferential conditions to foreign investment. The first positive results were gained years

Exhibit 7-1. Special economic zones (SEZs).

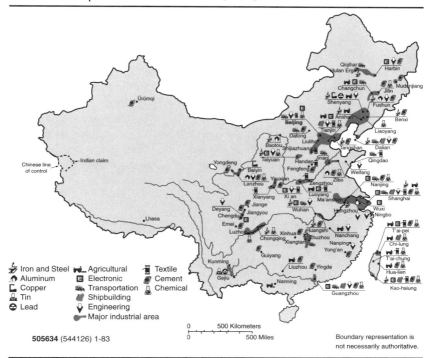

after the Tiananmen crisis, following increased access. In 1990, the Chinese government opened the Pudong New Zone in Shanghai and a number of additional cities to overseas investment. A chain of open cities extended up the Yangtze River valley, with Shanghai's Pudong as its "dragon head." After 1992, a number of border cities were opened for investment, as were all the capital cities of inland provinces and autonomous regions.[9] The seven open coastal economic zones became hotbeds for foreign investment, accounting for 80 percent of all foreign investment.[10]

Investments by mobile vendors have mirrored advancements in the general investment environment; they also represent typical *developed*-country FDI. These investment flows are critical to China's future. While firms in developing countries have favored cost leadership strategies, those in the developed countries have engaged in differentiation strategies. Generic strategies have been capital- and technology-intensive only in the latter case. Whereas China's shrewd politicians have traded minimal access for maximal technology and capital investments, mobile players have struggled to trade maximal access for minimal investments. Timing has played a critical role. Not only did the Tiananmen events shape the volume of FDI flows in China; they also precipitated the digital transition and the subsequent Euro-Nordic leadership in the 2G era.[11]

   After Deng Xiaoping's death in February 1997, Hong Kong's reversion to Chinese rule occurred relatively smoothly. The new government formulated an agenda based on the concept of "one country, two systems," preserving Hong Kong's economic freedom. A year later, Prime Minister Zhu Rongji introduced a sweeping program to privatize state-run businesses and further liberalize the nation's economy. While economic reforms have continued, tensions in Sino-U.S. relations peaked in early 2000, when the Chinese shot down a U.S. spy plane. Typically, *Business Week*'s cover story presented the U.S. dilemma over whether to contain or engage China.[12] The cover featured a Red Army soldier. Instead of a gun, the soldier held a cell phone—the new instrument in the global struggle for supremacy. In the wireless business, the crisis triggered initial impressions of "Tiananmen déjà vu" but did not prove as detrimental.

Long March:
Mobile Leaders and Investment Phases

In the past two decades, most foreign investors in China have followed an evolutionary posture, moving gradually from cautious market tests to substantial FDI. Over time, all have increased their stakes through internationalization and organizational learning.[13] In the early 1980s, most mobile vendors were opportunistic experimenters setting up few joint ventures in more developed locations. The idea was to test the degree of risk in uncharted territory. With more experience in China's industrial and institutional environment, foreign companies became strategic investors in the late 1980s and early 1990s. With increased commitments to local operations in terms of investment size and production scale, they employed wholly owned subsidiaries as an entry mode, entered capital- or technology-intensive industries, and located projects in less-developed inland provinces. The largest early entrants established multiple subunits in various geographic or product segments, seeking greater market power and superior positions nationwide. With still more accumulated experience, some world-class early entrants have become dominant local players in China. They have secured dominant market shares in their industries and generated above-average returns in the business. The host country government and customers consider them "local" because they employ domestic production and suppliers, use local management, and have a commitment to China's consumers.

   This process of localization in mobile communications was pioneered by Motorola in Europe during the 1G era. It has been emulated by all major rivals in China through the 2G era. Through years of patience and persistence, these vendors and operators have engaged in substantial investment programs and are building dominant, nationwide market positions and global businesses. By 2002, the leading global mobile vendors (Ericsson, Motorola, and Nokia) and certain second-tier suppliers (Lucent, Siemens, and several others) achieved this stage. All have established early positions and struggled against political windmills while seeking to sustain and solidify operations before the 3G era. As a result, competition has often resulted in unexpected changes. AT&T, one of the earliest entrants, moved in slowly in the pre-divestiture era, then eagerly in the post-divestiture phase. After Tiananmen, it lost its first-mover advantages. For Motorola, a vendor that had patiently built position in China, the Tiananmen crisis translated to lost opportunities, whereas Ericsson benefited from its great engineers and its impressive government relations, honed by decades of relationships with the leading national PTTs and their operators. In China, these skills were put to use at the turn of the 1990s. Nokia created a presence relatively early, but its financial crisis deferred more substantial investments. Once the vendor's cadre of senior executives was solidly in place in Helsinki, the Finns embraced the Chinese market with all the courting skills of a belated suitor. Finally, Qualcomm was able to access the market only after a long-standing lobbying effort—and because CDMA served a purpose for the Chinese regulators, who employed it to divide the vendors.

How AT&T Lost the Chinese Market

AT&T's presence in China originates in the post–World War I era. At the close of the 1970s, no other U.S. or international company matched AT&T's size and strength. It could have established a pioneer operation but did not seize the moment. AT&T's strategy failed. The U.S. policies failed. The timing failed.

The First Lost Opportunity

In 1918, International Western Electric, the manufacturing arm of AT&T, launched a telephone equipment production facility in China. In the early 1920s, the U.S. government forced the company to sell off its international business (the nucleus of ITT). Between 1949 and 1979, the Communist rule shut AT&T out of the Chinese marketplace. When the reformists captured power in China at the end of the 1970s, they invited AT&T to build the first joint venture plant in China for telephone switches. AT&T declined. Preoccupied with domestic concerns (i.e., the antitrust suit and new long-distance rivals), the U.S. operator had little understanding of the emerging Asia-Pacific markets.[14] Later, concerns about being locked out of Europe had prompted AT&T's efforts to access China, where it initiated some activities before the breakup expecting an estimated $15.7 billion of Asian telecom orders to open up for all suppliers. As John Hinds, then-VP of AT&T International, put it, Asia was the "world's biggest market after the U.S. and it's still growing faster than any other region."[15] But unlike Motorola, AT&T had not *competed* internationally for half a century.[16]

In 1984, the Justice Department's antitrust ruling forced AT&T's breakup into seven regional operating companies. Now it was AT&T's turn to rush to international markets. When AT&T set up its first representative office in Beijing in 1985, Ericsson, Nokia, and several other vendors had already arrived in the country. Despite its clout, AT&T accomplished little and expanded slowly in China. Although it established joint ventures to build fiber-optic cable and transmission equipment (in 1989), it was shut out of the lucrative switching market by NEC, Alcatel, and Siemens.

The Second Lost Opportunity

For an entire century, AT&T had dominated worldwide telecommunications. But in China, its technology investments fell behind its rivals. With the Tiananmen crisis in 1989, the United States imposed trade sanctions against China, which responded with sanctions of its own, when the State Council issued a secret directive that banned AT&T from the Chinese phone switch market. Known as Article 56, the directive mandated that future contracts for Chinese switches be reserved for Siemens AG, Alcatel-Alsthom, and NEC. This and other barriers to U.S. companies, along with a fast-growing trade deficit, prompted the Bush administration to launch a one-year investigation into China's trade practices in 1991. These talks ended in October 1992, when China agreed to eliminate some 80 percent of its import quotas and other market barriers over the next five years. AT&T made its plight and Article 56 a focal point of those talks.

As relations between the United States and China improved, the countries signed a trade liberalization agreement that lifted the directive. Again, the change in the political environment allowed AT&T to resume talks with China on market access. By now China had been saturated with rivals that had established substantial footholds. By 1992, it was the fastest-growing market for Ericsson's AXE switching system, and the Swedish vendor had 20 percent of the market. A year later, China became Motorola's largest overseas cellular market, with product sales exceeding $1.2 billion. As a latecomer, AT&T could not compete with these pioneers. So it set out to impress the Chinese with its capabilities in telecom equipment and services as well as software. After visits to AT&T's business units, manufacturing facilities, and Bell Laboratories, the members of China's State Planning Commission signed a memorandum of understanding with AT&T in February 1993. The following July, AT&T China was created.[17] With a single sweeping agreement, AT&T became an insider in China's telecom equipment market. However, rivals were already positioned. France's Alcatel-Alsthom SA had taken over former ITT operations in China; Sweden's Ericsson landed a $150 million order, the largest to date in China; other major suppliers included Japan's NEC and Fujitsu. But unlike AT&T,

none of these competitors had comprehensive operations in network gear, transmission services, and R&D. "AT&T," said Ye Qing, vice chairman of China's State Planning Commission, "offers the full range of technologies, products, services, and network experience that will benefit China well into the twenty-first century."[18]

With its might, AT&T managed to impress the Chinese. But it took a lot more to invade China's markets.

Parent's Reorganization, Launch of AT&T China: Too Little, Too Late

In June 1993, AT&T named William J. Warwick, its turnaround expert, to head its newly formed China business unit. With AT&T China, he took charge of all planning for AT&T's businesses in the region, including Hong Kong and Taiwan, and was appointed a senior VP of the corporation. "My job is to execute the memorandum of understanding we have with China," he said.[19] Warwick was allowed to run his business independently of the new Asia CEO and expand the company into a full-fledged supplier of network equipment to the Chinese government and its chief R&D collaborator. As AT&T grew serious about its presence in China, it also initiated a reorganization. The business units would report to Warwick as well as their heads in the United States. Meanwhile, AT&T China would report directly to Robert Allen, then CEO of AT&T. This "global and local" matrix strategy reflected AT&T's efforts to move closer to the customer, while emphasizing the significance of China in its operations. Though relatively new in the United States, the organizational innovation hardly matched that of Ericsson or Nokia.[20] Besides, AT&T's entry built on joint ventures, whereas its rivals were ahead in the learning curve and developing more substantial properties, often through majority investments or wholly owned subsidiaries. The Nordic firms had capitalized on AT&T's mistakes and developed organizational capabilities that AT&T did not possess.

Despite competitive realities, AT&T continued to have faith in its China card. In July 1993, AT&T announced a high-level management reorganization, reflecting the hope of AT&T chairman Robert Allen to garner at least 50 percent of AT&T 's revenue from overseas by the end of the decade. By December, struggling with slow growth in the United States, AT&T set up foreign units with their own CEOs to pursue the potentially huge new markets in Asia, Europe, and Latin America. The new CEOs had the power to establish individual country operations, set local pricing for AT&T products and services, and even hunt for mergers and joint venture opportunities to help AT&T 's global expansion.[21] It was then that the doors to China slammed close again.

Lucent's Turn

By 1995, all key vendors were increasing their FDI in China. Meanwhile, turmoil escalated at AT&T. In order to refocus on its communication services, the company engaged in a self-imposed breakup that resulted in three separate companies: a service provider (a "new" AT&T), computer vendor (NCR), and equipment manufacturer (Lucent Technologies). After the split, AT&T eliminated NCR, which had suppressed its value for years, whereas AT&T Director Henry Schacht was chosen to head Lucent, whose IPO raised $3 billion. But because foreign firms were prohibited from involvement in telecom services, AT&T found itself shut from the Chinese market, again. Lucent, however, rushed to Asia. In 1995, the vendor signed an agreement with the Chinese government to upgrade the switching systems manufacturing operation in Qingdao. The joint venture became Lucent's largest switching manufacturing center outside the United States and produced its flagship switching system, the 5ESS. A year later, the vendor made its first CDMA call in China from the Guangdong CDMA commercial trial system. When Lucent initiated operations, it took over most of the old AT&T's properties in China. Soon thereafter, it set up two new manufacturing facilities: a Qingdao Power System, its first wholly foreign owned enterprise (WFOE) in China, and Guoxin Lucent Technologies, a Shanghai joint venture.

Domestically, Lucent was flying high. In 1997 SBC Communications canceled a distribution agreement with rival Northern Telecom (Nortel) in favor of a five-year deal selling Lucent's office phone equipment. Later that year, President and COO Richard McGinn, who had joined AT&T as a salesman in the late 1960s, succeeded Schacht as CEO. Concurrently, Lucent engaged in mergers and acquisitions. By 1998 Lucent's market value surpassed AT&T's. But as a late mover, it was facing new issues in strategic positioning. While Nokia led in handsets and Ericsson dominated infrastructure, Motorola fell behind in both. Lucent saw little future in the terminal business and sold its wireless handset and defense systems units. Instead of getting into head-to-head fights with the big three vendors, it moved toward data networking, but with mixed results.[22]

In 2001, as the tech sector consolidated, Lucent began another round of restructuring. The plan included laying off about 16,000 employees, writing off inventory, consolidating facilities, and shifting more production to contract manufacturers. Concurrently, it claimed it was "gaining ground in the international marketplace, scoring wins in optical, wireless, data networking, and software in China, Australia, Brazil, Sweden, Germany, and elsewhere."[23] Lucent saw the greatest opportunities in China's mobile market where indigenous players were growing rapidly. In May 2001 two employees of Lucent and a third man were charged with conspiring to steal the company's proprietary technology and transfer it to a state-controlled Chinese company. Federal authorities said the men hoped to create a data networking company that would become the "Cisco of China."[24]

The new Lucent had businesses in more than ninety countries and territories. In 2000, its revenues amounted to almost $34 billion. But after a depressing year of tech downturn, the number of businesses declined to sixty-five countries and territories, whereas revenues were $21 billion. Faced with massive debts from overextended vendor financing, Lucent engaged in another round of restructuring, including the layoff and early retirement of 20,000 employees. When, in 2002, Patricia Russo, previously the CEO of Eastman Kodak and a former Lucent executive, was tapped as CEO, the vendor's clout was fading.

In China, Lucent had set up seven regional offices, eight joint ventures, and three wholly-owned companies, manufacturing a full array of telecom network equipment. It had over 3,500 employees in these locations. But AT&T's voluntary breakup had changed its role as China's premier R&D partner. The 1996 breakup had split AT&T into smaller entities. After the turmoil and the restructuring of 2000–2001, Lucent's staff had shrunk from 131,000 in 1995 to 77,000 in 2001. Job cuts continued by 6,000 the next year. The might that appealed to China's leaders was gone. Lucent had become just another vendor courting for an opportunity.

Motorola: Pioneering Presence in China

Toward the end of 2001, Motorola had an estimated 32 percent of the Chinese market, while Nokia was second at 30 percent. The U.S. vendor had already sold 25 million cell phones in China, where its revenues grew to $3 billion in 1999 and were expected to amount to $4.5 billion in 2000. Reportedly, it was profitable *and* reinvested back into the market. Of the leading vendors, Motorola was the first to establish an extensive presence in China, where it also became the largest investor at the end of 1996, with more than $1.2 billion in commitments. It had been among the first foreign investors in Tianjin, where it possessed a wholly-owned venture. It also had a holding company registered in China and was involved in six equity joint ventures, five cooperative projects, and dozens of other major investments.

The pace and significance of Motorola's investments went far beyond wireless communications, semiconductors, and electronics. In China, it played the role of a catalyst that was a replica of Motorola's role in South Korea, where the company began assembling chips in the late 1960s. These investments made Korea a force in the semiconductor business. As the Asian center of gravity in the technology sector moved from Korea to the "Asian tiger" economies and thereafter to China, Motorola again sought to participate in the coming boom. "By the year 2005 or 2010, China will have the world's largest electronics industry," predicted C. D. Tam, head of Motorola's semiconductor products group in the Asia-Pacific region.[25] That boded well for China's emerging mobile suppliers as well.

Entry Into China

Motorola's communications sector received its first major order from China as early as 1981. Five years later, it opened a representative office in

Beijing and leased a manufacturing facility near Tianjin. These were the peak years of Motorola's trade conflicts with Japan and its efforts to catch up with the Japanese quality difference. In the global chessboard, China was far behind Japan in economic development, but it held significant promise for the future. Historically, the year 1986 was a milestone in Motorola's presence in the Chinese market. A team led by Robert Galvin, then-chairman and the father of Christopher Galvin, his successor, toured China. Although the nation was mired in the technology of the 1940s and 1950s, Galvin's group was convinced that China was serious about modernizing its economy and made a long-term commitment. To avoid problems with the inadequate legal infrastructure and the government bureaucrats, the U.S. vendor cultivated long-term relationships with the central government and local officials. Some of these early supporters proved critical in later negotiations, including Jiang Zemin, the future Shanghai mayor and China leader.

Motorola opened a sales and marketing office while investments boosted its presence. After the company had trained people at 347 different state-owned enterprises and twenty-one universities, it obtained direct access to a great talent pool. It transferred technology, helped flood victims, built schools, and underwrote many other activities that seemed unrelated to the business. Like its later imitators, Motorola was trading market access for new technology. In 1989, the goodwill allowed Motorola to set up a 100 percent–owned semiconductor testing facility in China, the first awarded to a foreign company.[26] The U.S. giant also tackled the poorly developed Chinese retail market, setting up training centers in Beijing, Chengdu, and Shanghai, while planning another training facility for Guangzhou. Retailers learned how to display and sell mobile phones, and they made simple repairs. As Motorola obtained access, China got technology. At the same time, the epicenter of the industry migrated to Asia-Pacific.

The Tiananmen Divide: "When You're in Hot Water"

Motorola started negotiating a deal for local cellular operations in 1989, but initially, Chinese officials were not ready to award the U.S. company full ownership. They insisted that Motorola accept an American-Chinese joint venture. This was a more typical arrangement for foreign investors, but Motorola was not just any foreign investor. Before deal making, politics nabbed the spotlight. Because of the Tiananmen crisis, the balance of bargaining power shifted. China needed investors. Motorola had been a pioneer and a major investor in China, and it continued its presence even after June 1989, unlike AT&T, where the avoidance reaction was more pervasive. With its patient strategy, Motorola had been able to access the European market, and it hoped that strategy would work in China, too. Negotiations were suspended for a few months until the U.S. government clarified its guidelines for investment in China. Then Galvin returned to the talks. After the dust settled, the Tiananmen crisis caused Motorola to lose time but improve its hand at the bargaining table. "We felt the best way to help the Chinese people was to continue dialogue and engage," said C.D. Tam, the semiconductor division chief who was a key player on the negotiating team. "Motorola believed [the Tiananmen crisis] was a regrettable event but not the end of the world. China basically looked to us as a friend, and the time you need a friend most is when you're in hot water."[27]

The reasoning proved valid. As the Chinese party leaders opened the market for access, a backlash was almost inevitable. Strategic investors had to keep their eye on the prize and nurture cooperation and compromise. As the Clinton-Gore White House began to consider China a "strategic partner" rather than an unreliable adversary, Motorola initiated a new and more decisive push into China. The re-entry was no longer built upon a joint venture, but a *wholly-owned* subsidiary. When Motorola Electronics Ltd. (MEL) was incorporated in March 1992, Motorola pledged to develop some 5,000 new jobs and transfer to China the requisite technology to manufacture products for domestic and foreign consumption.

From the beginning, Motorola's business plan emphasized local production. Still, the company faced a significant quality hurdle: the need to export a percentage of its goods to meet the standard government demand for offsetting the hard currency drain caused by importing components. The solution was to quickly inculcate its new employees with a quality culture, including the concepts of "total customer satisfaction" and "Six Sigma." Within six months after starting semiconductor assembly at one temporary facility, rookie Chinese line operators achieved Six Sigma output quality, an achievement well above average. But as Motorola traded access for technology in China, it boosted the growth of future Chinese giants, while losing timing and focus at home. After the mid-1990s, the post-Tiananmen euphoria proved costly.

The Roller-Coaster of the Late 1990s

Despite its political and economic problems, China served as a magnet to advanced technology companies through the late 1990s. Motorola's cellular systems operated in twenty-three of China's twenty-seven provinces, and product sales amounted to $3.3 billion in 1995. Its first joint venture had been Leshan Radio Co., Ltd., to manufacture semiconductors. At the close of 1995, cellular networks covered the entire country and five more joint ventures were launched early the next year. Meanwhile, China embraced Motorola's paging standard. The U.S. vendor, it seemed, could do nothing wrong. Northern Telecom and Philips manufactured semiconductors in Shanghai, where Intel was building a $50 million chip assembly and testing plant. Sweden's Ericsson made telephone switches in Nanjing. IBM put together PCs in Shenzhen. Among these players, Motorola was in a class of its own. Having entered China in full force in 1987, it was about to invest another $1.9 billion to build a chipmaking plant in Tianjin, a port in northern China. The operation was expected to supply Motorola and to sell to some ten new Chinese rivals that, in 1999, captured a 5 percent share of the local market. Meanwhile, new mobile vendors and operators were rushing to the market as well. Vodafone invested $2.5 billion in China Mobile, but as a latecomer to the market, it earned only a 2 percent stake in the operator, whereas Motorola, as an early entrant, had 100 percent ownership of its China wafer factory.

By popularizing the cellular phone in China, Motorola helped the Chinese leapfrog the era of wired telecommunications. In China and Hong Kong, cell phone sales doubled in two years to reach $3.2 billion in 1995, which represented nearly 12 percent of Motorola's worldwide revenues. The potential market for the gadgets was expected to be enormous—3 million new cellular phones a year until the end of the decade. As the cell phone took off, "Motorola" became the popular generic name for this device in northern China. By 1996, the vendor still enjoyed high brand equity in cellular and dominated the Chinese market for analog handsets with an estimated 40 percent to 50 percent share. But an invasion of handset makers from Europe, Japan, and Hong Kong hammered down margins. And many of the latecomers, from Shanghai bankers to provincial entrepreneurs, were turning away from analog phones to newer digital technology. As Ericsson and Nokia pushed GSM, the most popular standard worldwide, Motorola and its backers—Nortel, Lucent, and Samsung—lobbied the Chinese to adopt the CDMA standard. But Motorola offered too little, too late. With a long-term view of the emerging mobile market, the Chinese sympathized with Motorola but had little use for narrowband CDMA, especially as 3G services were behind the door.[28]

By 1998, the Nordic vendors appeared to have wrested market leadership from Motorola.

Struggle for the Future

Because of its model of cooperative development in Chinese investments, Motorola's presence shifted from sales to manufacturing to R&D over time. In the past, the U.S. vendor's role in China had been dictated by the expected long-term market potential, not innovation. But toward the end of the 1990s, signs began to surface that Motorola's long-standing investments in resource commitments were also resulting in new asset-specific gains, especially in R&D. Investing heavily in Chinese R&D centers, Motorola developed eighteen sites and 800 researchers, and it hoped to double the staff by 2001. The payoffs included Accompli A6188, a chipset designed for Chinese characters (see Exhibit 7-2), which found an important U.S. application as a component in the PalmPilot.[29]

In August 2000, Motorola won Chinese government approval for a $1.9 billion project to make silicon chips for its mobile phones. Because the facility

Exhibit 7-2. The Motorola Accompli A6188.

Accompli A6188: The combination of phone and PDA.

[Accompli A6188] weighed 150g (battery included). It was only slightly heavier than a cellphone. Unlike most PDA/phones, which were the size of a typical mobile handset, the A6188 had slightly squarer dimensions, much like those of a PDA.

The model came with a handwriting recognition program, which recognized alphanumeric as well as Chinese characters. Although the recognition speed was slow, its accuracy was as good as that achieved by the best recognition kernels accompanying PC handwriting tablets and on Chinese Windows CE machines. English handwriting recognition was excellent as well.

"No mobile phone has captured the attention of fellow employees in our company as much as this latest model from Motorola," reported PC World Hong Kong in July 2000. "Although the A6188... lacks any glitter or an obvious 'cyber' look-and-feel on the surface, it's a pragmatic mobile phone and PDA hybrid. It's also the first mobile PDA/phone with fully localized features."

TEXT SOURCE: "TaiChi [Motorola Accompli A6188] successfully combines PDA and phone," *PCWorld Hong Kong*, July 6, 2000.
Photo Source: Motorola, Inc.

was expected to reach full production in 2002, Motorola would no longer need to import chips from a plant in Phoenix for the mobile handsets it produced in China. This new investment amounted to 5 percent of all foreign investment in China in 1999 ($40 billion). At the same time, Motorola became the leading foreign investor in China, with a total of $3.5 billion. Motorola was the country's biggest American investor. It made about 70 percent of products sold in China at its manufacturing base in Tianjin. It had poured in money to build up government connections and establish brand-name recognition. The world's largest Motorola store was not in the United States, but in Shanghai, on swanky Huaihai Zhong Road. Motorola's total R&D investment in China was expected to climb to $109 million by 2001. It was signing contracts valued at $228 million with two telcos, China Unicom and China Mobile, to service Sichuan, China's most populous province. By the end of 1999, however, government officials indicated that they might declare quotas on foreign mobile manufacturers to ensure that local manufacturers would receive 50 percent of the pie.

Through the 1990s, Motorola struggled to establish a foothold in the Chinese market, where it hoped to deter the European vendors. That hope never materialized. Unlike the U.S. firm, Nordic vendors were not hampered by Sino-U.S. relations. In June 2001, Motorola signed three contracts totaling $34.4 million to supply cellular infrastructure products to China Mobile Communications, China's largest telecom operator. In November, Motorola announced it would invest $3 billion in R&D over the next five years to expand its China operations. Even as the U.S. vendor restructured in other geographic segments, it had a total of 13,000 employees in China. After a board meeting in Beijing, the vendor formalized its heavy strategic focus on China. "Today, China dominates the growth model for the region," said Joe Guglielmi, Motorola's EVP in charge of developing software for mobile services worldwide. Although Motorola had long had investments in Penang, Malaysia, and elsewhere in Asia, it was not expanding these operations. Motorola intended to increase investment in China to $10 billion within five years. It was not about to give up the struggle for the future—but nor were its competitors.

Ericsson in China: From a Challenger to a Market Leader

Like many other Swedish multinationals, Ericsson established its first foreign affiliates well before World War I and expanded substantially in the 1970s and 1980s. In both phases, China played a strategic role in Ericsson's internationalization. As early as in 1894, when the company first registered its L.M. Ericsson trademark, it began the first deliveries to China. In effect, its historical presence in China precedes that of most vendors, including Motorola, Nokia, and Qualcomm. This role has been driven by both pull and push factors. First, due to the domestic monopoly of the Swedish PTT, Ericsson, like its counterpart ITT, was forced to create a foothold in foreign markets. Second, Sweden has traditionally been more important as a home country than as a host country to multinationals. Third, Swedish business managers have historically nurtured a more international business orientation than those of other Nordic countries.

In the 1960s, Ericsson initiated a new growth strategy that was coupled with a new wave of internationalization, including factories in Australia, the Nordic countries, and Mexico. In the beginning of the 1G era, the center of this second internationalization wave was the United States, the most lucrative country market. By the mid-1980s, Asia was rapidly increasing in importance for Ericsson.

From Market Penetration to Building Share

As Ericsson focused attention on the United States and the Asia-Pacific region, it began cultivating the markets for public networks, mainly those for mobile telephony and the fully digital version of its AXE switching system. "The People's Republic of China, where a number of orders were booked, became a large market for Ericsson in 1985,"noted the board of directors' report.[30] That year, the first AXE exchanges were in service in China and the Swedish vendor signed six delivery agreements, including a framework agreement covering delivery of AXE exchanges worth SKR 235 million in Liaoning Province.

Eager to strengthen its positions in the fastest-growing market areas, Ericsson paid particular attention to the United States, Europe, and certain country markets in Latin America and Southeast Asia. China was one of these strategic markets, but the initial experiences were not rewarding. In 1986, the vendor acknowledged that "the rate of growth [in China] has been lower than expected."[31] Like its rivals, the Swedish vendor took a long-term view of the vast market. Its first objective was penetration; only then did it begin to build share. A patient strategy was required. By the end of the 1980s, Ericsson had a substantial presence in all major Triad regions. Even as the company concentrated on penetrating the American market, it built a presence in China. By 1988, CEO Björn Svedberg proudly noted that Ericsson had "delivered the first mobile telephone system to be installed in the country, and the company recently received an order for AXE equipment that is the largest telecommunications contract ever placed by the Chinese authorities."[32] Following the installation of some 200,000 AXE lines in China, Ericsson signed a framework agreement early in 1988 covering the supply of 200,000 additional lines, along with other telecom material. The high-profile deal, which amounted to half a billion Swedish kronor, boded well for the future. While telecom growth was strongest in Europe, the market continued to expand rapidly in Southeast Asia and China, where *long*-term prospects were more promising than anywhere else.[33] In the process, Ericsson's representative office was coupled with a liaison office in Dalian, another office in Shanghai, and still another office in Guangzhou.

The Tiananmen Crisis: Threat as Opportunity

After the Tiananmen crisis, business continued as usual between China and Ericsson. By 1989, the Swedes handed over the millionth AXE line in China, where Ericsson now had a 23 percent share of the market. Typically, most installations had been made in the coastal provinces. While deliveries continued according to contracts, no new orders could be signed, due to difficulties in obtaining soft-loan financing. Deliveries were resumed after credits were granted by the Swedish government. The intervention resulted in orders for 271,000 lines by the provinces of Guandong, Xiangsu, and Liaoning. The post-Tiananmen years allowed Ericsson to boost its market presence. By 1992, China was the fastest-growing market for AXE, with a total of 1.7 million lines, 620,000 of which were installed that year. A number of contracts were signed that covered continuing deliveries to various provinces. Ericsson had a 20 percent share of the market. It had many large contracts for analog mobile telephone systems. China had also become the largest market for Ericsson's MD110 subscriber exchanges, with more than 650,000 delivered lines. The system, which accounted for 25 percent of the Chinese market, was largely manufactured within the country on license.

By 1993, Asia accounted for 13 percent of Ericsson's total sales. The vendor also received its largest-ever contract in China, an order totaling SEK 2.2 billion for AXE equipment to be installed in Guangdong province. As CEO Lars Ramqvist acknowledged, "The greater part of our sales are in Europe, but Asia—and China in particular—is the market area that is now growing most rapidly. During the year we formed a number of joint ventures in China and also inaugurated new production plants there."[34] More than half of the provinces had signed mobile systems contracts with Ericsson. With only one exception (Guandong's order for a first GSM system), the contracts involved analog systems. Ericsson had delivered mobile networks in China that had the capacity to serve more than 1.2 million subscribers. A year later, 21 percent of Ericsson's total sales came from Asia, with Japan and China accounting for a large part of the growth. The vendor now had six joint venture companies in China, including a GSM production plant in Beijing. It was a market factory that linked back to Kumla and was upgraded to full final assembly in 1996. In the process, Ericsson learned a thing or two about risk and uncertainty, while understatement developed into a form of art: The "highly successful operations in China provide cause for a certain amount of caution with respect to the future. Activities in China will be highly dependent on the country's access to international credits."[35]

Ericsson Phones in China: "Flexibility, Pragmatism, and Opportunism"

Starting at Sonab and selling loudspeakers, Lars-Olof Pehrsson had had a colorful career.[36] As he enjoyed a dinner with Ericsson's executives in Hong Kong, a huge Motorola neon sign stood overlooking the water. They all found it horrible. Soon thereafter—early in 1994—Pehrsson was hired as Ericsson's regional director for Asia-Pacific operations. Headquartered in Singapore, the company sold 100,000 phones in the region in 1993. At the time, Ericsson remained steeped in its traditional systems provider role. Pehrsson's first task was to teach the management that consumer product marketing differed drastically from the classic operator business and corporate markets. That was no easy task.

Pehrsson struggled to instill the idea of multicustomer marketing, thereby eliminating exclusive deals with selected distributors and operators. He preached that Ericsson should trade with many customers and pick the most valuable ones. As he saw it, the problems were not in the region, but inside the company. In 1994, Ericsson had a budget for 200,000 phones to be sold in China, but only 54,000 were sold. When he was asked to explain the vendor's China strategy, he used to say: "We don't have a strategy. In China it's all a matter of flexibility, pragmatism, and opportunism—nothing else."[37] The Chinese market had a huge potential. Ericsson's organizational capabilities had not been tailored for a market that was about to explode. The organization had to change.

In 1996, Ericsson's mobile unit sales soared to 1 million and the company joined the leading suppliers of GSM mobiles in China and worldwide. Before 1994, there was a lack of product and human resources to handle the massive Asia-Pacific market. But after the turmoil, this area became Ericsson's largest regional market, whose success story has been replicated in Australia, Singapore, Hong Kong, and Taiwan. This new wave of Asian operations, in turn, has solidified Ericsson's traditional markets in Malaysia, Thailand, Indonesia, and even Korea. The vendor used the lessons of these two Asian waves to enter Japan in late 1997.[38]

Increasing Direct Investment

China was the single largest market for AXE in 1995, with 9.8 million lines delivered. The volume of business, however, had not changed, due to severe price competition. Ericsson was now establishing production in China. By 1997, Ericsson's sales in Asia amounted to almost a third of its total revenues, even if the regional financial crisis was expected to slow the rate of growth somewhat. The Swedish vendor had developed a number of legs in China. It was very strong in the market for mobile systems and terminals. The world's largest GSM network run by China Telecom had in excess of 7 million subscribers; Ericsson reportedly supplied about 50 percent of the analog and digital mobile network capacity. For years, the market for telecom equipment for the fixed network had attracted large international suppliers to China, which had become Ericsson's largest single market in terms of order bookings. "On the whole," noted CEO Lars Ramqvist, "the trend of the market in Asia is uncertain and difficult to evaluate at the present time."[39] Ericsson was boosting its position by supporting local expertise in China's telecom industry, while Chinese authorities applauded the creation of a new research center in Shanghai. A year later, the center was followed by the Ericsson China Academy, which represented the vendor's largest investment to date in the development of local expertise in China.

To get closer to its Chinese customers, Ericsson distributed its knowledge and key functions into the regions, even as it concentrated heavily on local recruitment and training. At the end of 1997, it had more than 3,300 employees;

it intended to recruit another 700 persons in a year. Due to a thorough over-haul and reorganization, it was shifting from a centrally controlled organization into a highly regionalized and customer-focused organization. These capabilities would contribute to differentiation, which Ericsson hoped would boost local responsiveness. Growth was expected to be explosive and enduring. "China has 1.2 billion inhabitants, but there are only 75 million fixed telephone subscribers in the country," estimated John Gilbertson, president of Ericsson (China) Company Ltd. "Another 14 million Chinese have mobile telephones, but the demand is very great."[40]

By 1998, Asia was one of Ericsson's four market areas. While headquarters remained in Stockholm, the market area functions were moved closer to the customers. The central office for Asia-Pacific was established in Hong Kong. China again surpassed the United States as Ericsson's largest market, account-ing for 12 percent of the company's total sales. Sales were more than fourfold higher than in the other top markets (Japan and Australia). The vendor esti-mated that it held more than a 40 percent share of the market for mobile systems. While the number of mobile subscribers in China had grown to 25 million, the penetration rate was still only 2 percent. Represented throughout the country, Ericsson was now a partner, with Chinese companies, in eight joint ventures. Five of these had production facilities, while the research center was in Shanghai. As the Chinese government announced that it would give priority to suppliers with local production, Ericsson, through its joint ventures, wanted to be regarded as one.

By 2000, Ericsson's sales amounted to $29 billion, with the Asia-Pacific market accounting for 21 percent of the total. In adverse conditions, that was not adequate. As Ericsson struggled with internal problems, Western Europe lingered in industry slowdown, and the U.S. technology sector suffered from consolidation. The vendor hoped to increase its market share in China by doubling investment in the country to $5 billion within five years. In Novem-ber 2001, it announced investments in the development, production, and mar-keting sectors. Industry observers expected the Pacific region to increase the share of Ericsson's total sales from 27 percent to one-third within the next couple of years. But even as the Chinese market was exploding, Ericsson itself was swept by increasing turmoil.

Nokia in China: The Latecomer's Path

Unlike its rivals, Nokia did not have appropriate financial and managerial re-sources to build a beachhead in most markets, but it found out that this was not necessary. To establish a foothold in the *lead* markets, it was adequate to leverage limited resources by narrowing the business focus, while maximizing the coverage in the international markets. At Nokia, scope was the prime in-strument to boost scale, and China held the greatest promise in foreign growth markets. To paraphrase a well-known song: If a vendor could make it there, it could make it anywhere. Conversely, an equipment manufacturer that failed to create a presence in China was doomed. That made China critical to Nokia's future.[41]

The Early Years: Building the Chinese Operations

Even the old forest-industry Nokia had exported to Russia and China in the 1930s. In the 1960s, the company again nurtured international ambitions. But it was only in the mid-1980s that it started to build a presence in China. Without substantial competition, high entry barriers, or complex technology standards, Nokia was able to build resource commitments at lower cost. Initially, however, China was a very difficult market for a company that was more familiar with European markets.

When Topi Honkavaara, a veteran Nokian, arrived in Beijing to head the local office, Nokia's sales were less than FIM 1 million; when he left China, revenues amounted to FIM 2 billion. Known as being difficult but diligent and loyal, Honkavaara built the operation from scratch and, over time, became a China expert. Difficulties between Honkavaara and Nokia headquarters worsened in the early 1990s. Reportedly, Honkavaara and Jorma Ollila, Nokia's CEO, did not get along. Honkavaara was invited back home, demoted, and left with promises until the loyal Nokian committed suicide. In addition to being a personal tragedy, this chain of events reflected a difficult organizational transition. As Nokia renounced the old diversification strategy and focused its value activities into mobile communications, the values and culture of the old small subsidiary did not mesh with those of the new and expanding parent, which rushed to establish a far larger position in the Chinese market. The old world of exports was now history; to struggle for the future, Nokia had to secure a solid position in China—and that meant accelerating FDI flows as well as establishing a strong and highly visible presence.

The Years of Expansion: A Rush to Secure Position

With the rising popularity of the GSM standard, Nokia began to receive orders for networks from the People's Republic of China, the Philippines, and Malaysia. In October 1994, Wu Jichuan, Minister of Post and Telecommunications, made the first official GSM call in China, relying on a cell phone and network by Nokia. "In 1995, our annual revenues amounted to $200 million," acknowledged Matti Vesala, chief of Nokia Networks' production in China. "In the course of the next three years, these revenues tripled."[42] That year, Nokia signed five new GSM deals in China and expanded the Beijing network. Concurrently, the vendor announced the establishment of new factories in China and the United States, its major country market; in the future, China would take over that role. Nokia also signed two joint venture agreements in

China, one for the manufacture of accessories and another for the production of mobile phones.

In the post-Tiananmen environment, public policies contributed to market access. "China was *very* important for our business delegation," recalls Martti Ahtisaari, then-president of Finland. "Instead of taking the civil servants and the formal part of delegation to China, I asked the leader of the business delegation to pick half of the travel team. 'Pick up those you want to see there,' I told him. I left the choices to business, not to the Ministry. In China, I had a very strong delegation, including Ollila, president of Nokia. There were only three of us, but we addressed the total leadership of China, including the president, prime minister, the deputy prime minister, foreign minister speaker of the parliament, and so on. We had just a small room by Chinese standards, in a small hotel. After I'd addressed China's leaders, Pekka Hallberg spoke on the legal cooperation between Finland and China, which has been flourishing because they want to build a legal society and we want to help them out. To Nokia, China is very important. Along with the United States and Germany, China is one of its three key markets."[43]

In 1996, Nokia inaugurated a base station and mobile phone factory in China. A year later, the company won its largest order to date in China, with Fujian PTA. China had now become Nokia's third-largest market in sales, after the United States and the U.K. The growth prospects were in a class of their own. To extend its collaboration activities in Asia, Nokia established research cooperation with the Beijing University of Post and Telecommunications (BUPT). Furthermore, Nokia built contacts with several top universities, all with specific expertise in technology areas relevant to Nokia. The vendor also established an R&D facility in China. Located in Beijing, the unit focused on R&D in tomorrow's wireless and wireline technologies. In addition to forming partnerships with China's government, Nokia formed strategic alliances with foreign distributors, including CellStar and Brightpoint, the two leading distributors of wireless phones and telecom products in China.

Despite Asia's currency crisis, Nokia increased its investments in China through the end of the 1990s. In October 1998, Jorma Ollila, CEO of Nokia, and Paavo Lipponen, prime minister of Finland, visited Beijing to open Nokia's new R&D center. In the long term, Ollila thought that China might become Nokia's leading geographic segment. The vendor already had seven factories and it was building GSM networks in nine of China's twenty-three key regions. The number of Nokians in China had climbed to 3,000. China was now Nokia's second-largest market, with EUR 1.8 billion in sales, versus EUR 2 billion in the United States. In September, Nokia became the first vendor to have large-scale manufacturing facilities for complete GSM networks in China, including mobile switches, base station systems, and cellular transmission. With several manufacturing facilities in China, Nokia had delivered line capacity to more than 10 million subscribers.

The Nokia global R&D network also expanded during 1998 to include new R&D centers in China, Denmark, Germany, Hungary, and Sweden. With the help of a global cooperation network, the Finnish vendor hoped to generate quick responses to technological developments.[44] Experimental wideband W-CDMA networks were built and expanded for field testing in 1999 in China, Finland, and Japan, where the system performance would be demonstrated to existing and new customers.

The Market of the Future

Through the late 1990s, Sari Baldauf, a member of the group executive board (and a former academic specialist in international business), was responsible for Nokia's operations in China. By 2000, China had become Nokia's third most important market area in terms of employment (5,700 persons), net sales (EUR 3.1 billion), assets by location (EUR 2 billion), and capital expenditures (EUR 157 million). Like other vendors, Nokia located its technologically advanced projects in several key parts of China, primarily in the prospering coastal clusters. In each region, it had agreements with the Post and Telecommunications Administration (PTA). Each was located in the open coastal economic region.

According to its global strategy, Nokia's units were under the centralized control of the corporate headquarters in Helsinki. Nokia concentrated on standardized, "global products" for a variety of markets. Production was coordinated centrally to allow economies of scale. While Nokia's Chinese units were independent, the home office maintained integration among them. The strategy allowed Nokia to exploit experience-curve effects and location economics, but, as some critics argued, "it lacks local responsiveness, which makes it difficult to coordinate strategies and operation decisions among its international ventures."[45] In Finland, such criticism was often ignored. Yet it hit the core of Nokia's global strategy. In the long run, the Finnish vendor would have to build on innovation, even without the old GSM advantage, and cost-effectiveness. After all, indigenous Asian producers were quickly learning the cost game and differentiation, even though more than 40 percent of Nokia's production facilities remained in Finland. At Nokia, the disadvantages inherent in the strategy were addressed through cooperation, coordination, and the sharing of resources with China's industries. The vendor adopted a global product group structure to coordinate resource transfers between corporate headquarters and Chinese divisions. Each division was responsible for its own area. In the short term, these tactics would reinforce Nokia's position. In the long term, the vendor was vulnerable. It no longer possessed a technology edge in innovation, and rivals had copied its generic designs in marketing innovation. It was vulnerable to cost focus attacks. And while it could develop differentiation, local producers would have a home base advantage.

Despite Nokia's long-term strategic challenges, the Finnish vendor and Finland itself held a certain fascination among Chinese authorities. In January

2000, Olli-Pekka Heinonen, the Finnish minister of transport and communications, assisted Wu Jichuan, the minister of telecommunications of China, in the codification of telecom regulation. The Finns provided something of a model to the Chinese reform-minded authorities. Finland was the world's leading handset vendor, but only a decade before, it had been a minor regional player. Its market-driven strategies were nurtured by public authorities, and it had the world's highest mobile penetration without universal service obligations. It had a highly egalitarian culture, but liberal-minded regulators. It had welfare society values but Western capitalism. Indeed, it all sounded very much like China's SEZs. With its mixed economy, solid technology infrastructure, and high-level educational institutions, the small Nordic country provided lessons in every pillar of the triangle framework: strategy and competition, new public policies, and innovation systems. Of course, there was a critical difference. There were 5 million Finns and more than 1.2 billion Chinese. The latter enjoyed scale economies that the former could only dream of.

By 2000, Nokia's revenues in China had climbed to approximately $2.3 billion, and the vendor had invested at least $1 billion in the rapidly growing market. Between 1997 and 1998 alone, the number of cell phones in China doubled. Nokia's physical presence in the market location was vital. It already manufactured half of its Chinese products in China. And as Nokia opened access to the Chinese market, its suppliers, partners, and other software firms followed in its footsteps.[46] In November 2001, Nokia announced that it would set up an R&D center in Hangzhou, the capital city of Zhejiang province, to develop platform technologies for its 3G networks. Expecting to employ up to 500 people in three to four years, the center would focus on software development. "With this new R&D center, China will strengthen its position as part of Nokia's global R&D network. For Nokia, China is the second-largest market. We are convinced, based on the excellent cooperation [achieved] so far, that this project will be a long-term success for all parties involved," said Sauli Salo, senior VP of Mobile Core Networks, Nokia Networks. The Hangzhou R&D center would have a vital role in Nokia's global R&D network and would begin operations at the beginning of 2002. It planned to carry out R&D with a local Chinese partner company. Hangzhou was the rapidly developing capital city of Zhejiang province and home to Zhejiang University, the largest institution of higher learning in China. The presence of the university, a focus on software capabilities and high-level education, as well as the existence of a good transportation and communications infrastructure were pivotal in the location choice, said the Nokians.[47]

As a latecomer, Nokia faced tough competition in China. By the end of 1997, Nokia's market share was estimated at 22 percent, against Ericsson's 35 percent and Motorola's 26 percent. In 2000, Motorola still had 32 percent of the market, but its leadership was based on analog phones. In digital products, Nokia's share climbed to 30 percent.

Qualcomm and the Chinese Roller-Coaster

In 2001, most of China's estimated 130 million mobile phones still operated on the European-backed GSM network, while CDMA offered an alternative standard with greater cost-efficiencies and performance capabilities. But the issue of a transition to CDMA was political as well as technical. In May 1999, when U.S. warplanes dropped bombs on the Chinese embassy in Belgrade during the NATO air campaign over Yugoslavia, CDMA contract negotiations between China Unicom and foreign vendors were shelved for six months, without specific reasons for the delay. The technology issue also played a role in the lingering bilateral negotiations toward China's accession to the WTO, and there were also domestic Chinese politics and indigenous mobile rivalries.

Toward the end of the 1990s, Irwin Jacobs, Qualcomm's CEO and chairman, made it a personal mission to bring CDMA to China. Despite several close breakthroughs, these talks were an Asian equivalent of a good old Coney Island roller-coaster ride. The fluctuations of Qualcomm's stock price illustrated the ups and downs of the negotiations. In December 1999, Qualcomm's stock hit a high of $185, not least because of its expected triumph in China. Suddenly, the company became the toast of Wall Street. Then, in June 2000, Qualcomm reduced its estimates for the number of chipset orders in South Korea as wireless subscriptions there began to slip. The vendor's stock fell to $51.50. But by the fall, Qualcomm's luck turned once again. AT&T Wireless, one of the top-three U.S. wireless services providers, announced its plans to use Qualcomm's CDMA standard.

The technologies may have been novel and complex. But the political machine that handled the talks was a curious mixture of old-party bureaucracy and simple ideology, along with a subtle eye for bargaining and a reform-minded obsession with practical results. The U.S. vendor was not entirely alone in appealing repeatedly to China's top leaders; it was often backed by senior U.S. government officials. The bilateral tension in U.S.-China relations delayed the deal making, just as the trilateral tension in U.S.-China-EU relations ultimately opened doors to CDMA in China. By using the U.S.-based standard, the Chinese government could drive up competition and play U.S. and European vendors against each other. It was a foretaste of a mobile future in which China, rather than the old mobile leaders, flexed its muscles.

From the pre-cellular to the 1G era, the United States had been the leading cluster and market center in wireless communications. Starting with digital cellular, mobile innovation split into three key Triad regions: the United States, Western Europe, and Japan. By the late 1990s, this split was reinforced by a fourth core region: People's Republic of China, or more precisely, China's SEZs. In the 3G era, Triad *plus* would reign over the wireless business—and in that global chessboard, the Chinese players, at least for now, could play industry leaders against each other. The rule of *divide et impera* allowed Beijing to exploit the internal conflicts of mobile leaders, *and* those of IT leaders, *and* the convergence conflicts between these two strategic groups. In this game, the boundary between political interests and market forces was a line drawn in quicksand. It was also a game in which the position of the United States was fragile and uncertain, and could become even more so after the events of September 11, 2001.

The China Unicom Roller-Coaster: Big Guns at Beijing

At the turn of February 2000, Qualcomm's shares increased sharply on news that the R&D maverick had struck a deal to license key cellular technology in China. The stock rose 15 percent in response to reports that Qualcomm executives were meeting with their counterparts at China Unicom (China United Telecommunications). Under the deal, China Unicom licensed CDMA wireless phone technology from Qualcomm. The system was to be built by local Chinese manufacturers using the CDMA technology. Qualcomm would receive royalties on equipment sales. China Unicom hoped to use CDMA as a selling point to gain a bigger share of the roughly 40 million cell phone users in the country. At the time, China Telecom, the incumbent leader, supplied an estimated 90 percent of the market using GSM, even as the market was expected to almost double within a year. The same estimates put CDMA's share at less than 1 percent in China. Still, the key to the future was not the present penetration or number of users, but the potential user population in China. With only 51.6 million mobile phone users (a penetration rate of 5 percent), growth prospects were enormous.

By late February 2000, less than a week after China had announced it would deploy a new type of wireless communications that relied heavily on U.S. technology, the government postponed the process indefinitely. The delay, which was not made public, stunned foreign firms, some of which had already bid on the project that would build a national mobile phone network. Certain observers speculated that the move was a bargaining tactic as the U.S. Congress prepared to debate whether to support China's entry into the WTO. CDMA certainly did feature in the situation. A week before the government announcement, China Unicom had declared its intention to build a mobile network using Qualcomm's CDMA.[48] In the past, the U.S. vendor had hoped that its CDMA technology would be adopted as the wireless phone standard for all of China, but the rival GSM standard took hold in China as the Tiananmen crisis allowed European competitors to level the playing field in FDI.

Confusion and delays caused substantial harm to China Unicom, which was preparing for an impending overseas IPO. A spokesman of China Unicom claimed he was unaware of delays. "We'll have to wait and see what happens," said Leo Zhang, Qualcomm's general manager in China.[49] In 1999, Qualcomm enjoyed a record $109 billion market cap. In late 2000, it shrunk to $53 billion. That was not acceptable. Qualcomm resorted to bigger guns. After the Tiananmen Square massacre, Brent Scowcroft—national security adviser in George Bush, Sr.'s administration and one of Qualcomm's directors—secretly visited Beijing. Because China had been isolated internationally, Scowcroft's visit had earned Beijing's gratitude. Scowcroft and Qualcomm's Jacobs flew to Beijing. Scowcroft owed Qualcomm, and Beijing owed Scowcroft.

In September 2000, 68 percent of the world's 559 million digital wireless phone users communicated on GSM systems, while 13 percent used CDMA systems. Despite its technical superiority, CDMA continued to lose share to GSM. In Beijing, Scowcroft and Jacobs met with Zhu Rongji, the Chinese premier. Joining Zhu were Yang Xianzu, the chairman of China Unicom, and Wu Jichuan, the minister in charge of telecommunications, who had earlier blocked the development of CDMA in China. Scowcroft and Jacobs had two central points. First, they sought to persuade the Chinese to live up to an earlier CDMA commitment. Second, they coupled the business argument with a technical one. While GSM had the greatest penetration through the 2G era, CDMA would play the key role in the 3G era. Murphy's Law added to Qualcomm's struggles. Around mid-September, Jacobs found his laptop missing from the podium after he wrapped up questions from the Society of American Business Editors and Writers in Irvine, California. Unfortunately for Qualcomm's chief, he was surrounded by journalists and the news hit the wires quickly. The laptop contained highly sensitive information that could be of great value to "foreign governments." The debacle contributed to investors' long-standing concern over Qualcomm's precarious relationship with China.

By mid-October, China Unicom announced that it was seeking bids to build a 10-million-subscriber network using Qualcomm's current cdmaOne technology. The system was to be up and running by 2002. The U.S. vendor hoped to benefit royally from the Beijing decision. By 2004, nearly a third of China's mobile telephone customers might be using Qualcomm's cdmaOne or CDMA2000 systems, up from the current 0.5 percent. Such developments would support not just Qualcomm but a network of equipment manufacturers that licensed its CDMA technology, including Lucent, Motorola, Nortel, 3Com, and Samsung.

How CDMA Arrived in China

At the turn of 2001, Qualcomm's stock price suffered, partially because of uncertainty over its prospects in China's strategic market. China Unicom had inherited a very small CDMA network with about 200,000 subscribers when it acquired a small wireless carrier called Great Wall Telecom.[50] This time there was uncertainty about China Unicom's intention to build upon that CDMA network, and if the network were built, which variant of CDMA technology the Chinese would rely on. Wideband CDMA (W-CDMA) was partially based on Qualcomm's core patents, but it was backed by its rivals Nokia and Ericsson. The alternative was Qualcomm-patented CDMA2000. To the U.S. vendor, it was a win-win scenario. In the former case, it would win big. In the latter case it would win *really* big.

Before May 2001—at the eve of China Unicom's signing the first round of equipment contracts with foreign and domestic vendors—the Chinese government intervened and postponed the signings without giving a reason. The delay froze a $1.7 billion deal for CDMA wireless equipment from U.S.-based vendors (Motorola and Lucent), other foreign players (Samsung in South Korea, Nortel of Canada, Ericsson of Sweden, and Alcatel of France), as well as Chinese vendors (including Huawei Technologies, Shenzhen Zhongxing Telecom, Guangzhou Jinpeng, and Datang Telecom Technology). Some Chinese and foreign vendors had received assurances from Unicom that the delay was "a simple procedural issue." Others expressed concern that testy U.S.-Chinese relations were having an effect on the deal making. Less than two weeks after the delay, Chinese President Jiang Zemin told a gathering of global business leaders that Qualcomm's CDMA wireless technology would be "useful" to have in China. In the United States, this was perceived as a high-level endorsement of CDMA. Yet the vendors noted that contract signings planned for April had never taken place. Worries remained that political tensions between Washington and Beijing were hampering the deal, which could finally open the Chinese mobile market to U.S. technology and vendors. However, no concrete evidence surfaced and officials at China's Ministry of Information Industry declined to comment.

A week after the Chinese president's positive signaling, Qualcomm and the mobile vendors enjoyed a long-awaited victory as China Unicom signed contracts to purchase $1.46 billion in CDMA network equipment.[51] These signings were of critical importance in the worldwide mobile rivalry, reflecting a breakthrough into China's massive mobile market for a U.S.-backed standard. By June 2001, the U.S. Cellular Telecommunications & Internet Association (CTIA) signed a memorandum of understanding with the Chinese Institute of Communications (CIC), the preeminent telecommunications trade association in China. The agreement, signed in Beijing, recognizes that "a close cooperative relationship between the two organizations will contribute to the sound growth of the wireless communications industries of the United States and China, the two largest wireless markets in the world."[52] In the past, the United States, Western Europe, and Japan were the central lead markets; during the 3G era, China would join these three. But unlike the established lead markets, China was far from saturated. The mobile market explosion had barely begun.

In July 2001—after roller-coaster deal making and years of preliminary negotiations—Qualcomm announced its first agreements to license CDMA to two Chinese telecom equipment makers, ZTE Corp. and Great Dragon Information Technology Corp. Despite some concessions in the financial terms, the deals were a new milestone for CDMA in China. In October, China Unicom was expected to launch a nationwide CDMA network that would initially support 15 million users. Interestingly enough, it was expected to charge service fees that would be only half of those for GSM users. In a parallel step to accelerate China's rapidly growing telecom market, the government also canceled fees for installing fixed lines and setting up mobile phone accounts. Qualcomm hoped that these incentives for new competition and substitution could turn the existing GSM accounts into historical relics, while boosting the fortunes of CDMA in China. "China still has a relatively low penetration rate, meaning most of the growth is yet to come," said Jacobs, who predicted a jump in mobile users.[53]

Following in the footsteps of executives at Motorola, Ericsson, and Nokia, Qualcomm's chief visited Beijing to open a new training center. Now, in the almost twenty-year game of market access for technology, Qualcomm, too, was meeting its obligations. But that resulted in new problems. By playing favorites with Chinese vendors, the U.S. company was aggravating customers elsewhere. As it engaged in a *de facto* dual policy on royalty fees, South Korean firms found themselves paying premiums, which squeezed their profit margins. Even though the Korean market was Qualcomm's historical CDMA foothold, strategic actions in China were dragging its equipment exports. As Qualcomm shifted from a domestic player with export sales to foreign operations, its strategy became increasingly global. It could no longer subsidize strategic actions in one country market by other actions in another market, except for short-term tactical gain. Then again, such tactical headaches felt insignificant after years of struggle to access the Chinese market.

Toward Triad Plus: China's Wireless Marketplace

At the end of July 2001, China overtook the United States as the biggest cellular phone market worldwide with 120.6 million mobile phone users—against 120.1 million in the United States—after a surge of 42 percent that year. The number of subscribers in China increased by 35 million, and another 80 million cell phones were expected to be in use by the end of 2002.[54] In a geographic area roughly the same size as the United States, China had a population of 1.3 billion and a very low rate of penetration. On average, every two Europeans already had a cellular phone; in the United States, two out of five people had one. In China, barely one in ten had a cell. There was an extraordinary potential for continued expansion. Increasing competition and declining tariffs would speed growth. The low penetration rate functioned as a life-support system for the industry giants. Amid U.S. tech consolidation and Europe's 3G birth pains, China's rapid growth strengthened its attractiveness to mobile vendors, such as Motorola, Nokia, and Ericsson. These 2G top three accounted for some 75 percent of the 52 million phones manufactured in China in 2000. At the peak of the wireless boom, investment analysts predicted that mobile phone sales worldwide would reach 400 million to 500 million units. By the summer of 2001, many were projecting only 370 million to 400 million units, the first actual fall in more than two decades. In these circumstances, it was the Chinese volumes that kept the industry humming.

China's Emerging Competition

Due to a Communist past and phased reforms, new public policies arrived relatively late in China. When they finally did, change was rapid and tumultuous. In the late 1980s, the powerful Ministry of Posts and Telecommunications (MPT) still served as China's national PTT responsible for policy and regulation. In 1988, the first cellular systems had been installed in the key locations of Beijing, Shanghai, and Guangdong province, typically with the TACS technology by Motorola and Ericsson. These early networks were essentially large-city stand-alone systems because there were no roaming facilities in any of the thirty administrative authorities. In 1993—with the resurgence of FDI flows following the Tiananmen crisis—MPT set roaming standards, first within key regions and later for a national seamless service. Over the next two years, Motorola and Ericsson, the two dominant vendors of the early decade, implemented the new systems.[55] As MPT became a clearinghouse for roaming revenues, it also occupied a more formal and central policy in China's mobile communications. By 1994, all administrative authorities had operational cellular systems.[56] It was a milestone year. China's government set up China Unicom in 1994 as the first competitor of China Telecom. This was a watershed event because it marked the eclipse of the historical monopoly of the public telecommunications network and the beginning of deregulation.

Despite the popularity of TACS in the first half of the 1990s, MPT made no official decision to adopt it as a national standard. Digitalization was a different story. As the standards wars first surfaced in China, Qualcomm lobbied MPT, but the powerful Ministry opted for GSM as a national standard in 1994. The decision was a *de jure* blessing for *de facto* circumstances. As the Tiananmen crisis led to AT&T's departure from the Chinese market and Motorola reduced its personnel in China, Euro-Nordic rivals seized the opportunity and installed GSM systems. Qualcomm's advocates arrived in China too late, but that would not be the case with the 3G transition. Meanwhile, MPT prepared to coordinate the digital cellular transition. Because of low penetration, analog networks did not suffer from capacity problems. Typically, the early pressure to digitize originated from Hong Kong, the most prosperous and concentrated location, where the operators had committed to a transition from TACS to GMS or from AMPS to D-AMPS. The pressure migrated rapidly from fast-paced Hong Kong to the prosperous province of Guangdong, the richest SEZ in China with 60 million inhabitants and income levels ten times the national average. At the time of the transition, every second Chinese cell subscriber was in Guangdong, with most of the rest in Beijing and Shanghai. All subscribers required roaming with Hong Kong.

Despite its power in Chinese telecommunications, MPT did not manage the spectrum, which was controlled exclusively by the military authorities. The China National Post and Telecommunications Industry Corp. (PTIC) implemented MPT's policies. While MPT had close control over costs, each administrative authority enjoyed a degree of autonomy, including its own telecom operator. From the government's standpoint, connection charges, subscription costs, and terminal sales were an important revenue source for the local PTTs. Cellular users had to pay not just $27 per month but an initial fee of $3,500 to $4,500, which was more than ten times the average annual income at the time in China.

Until the reforms of the late 1990s, the Chinese marketplace had some affinities with the pre–NTT DoCoMo market in Japan. Mobile communications was perceived as a luxury service, which justified high tariffs. The service quality was low, volumes were small, and differentiation rudimentary. As new public policies swept the Chinese market, the catchwords of the late 1980s and early 1990s—privatization, deregulation, and liberalization—arrived in China. Until 1998, MPT owned all major industry manufacturers (PTIC) and operators (China Telecom and China Mobile). With global telecom reform, the Chinese government separated industry regulation from business activities.[57] That meant complicated reorganizations (see Exhibit 7-3a). MPT gave rise to the Ministry of Information Industry (MII) while merging with the former Ministry of Electronics Industry and part of the Ministry of Radio, Film, and TV. Subsequently, the MII spun off its manufacturing and service subsidiaries, which became state-owned enterprises. A vast organization with thirteen departments, it had been under increasing pressure from the central government (the State Council) and the public because of the promotion of competition in China and complaints about pricing policy, which many considered unreasonable. In 2001, the MII served as regulator for China's information and communications technology (ICT) sector, including telecommunications, electronics, Internet, and related technologies and services (see Exhibit 7-3b).

By the latter half of the 1990s, mobile expansion and growth came into its own in China.

Operators

Between 1995 and 2000, service revenues of Chinese operators nearly tripled from $15 billion to almost $45 billion. These were similar to figures in the United States, where service revenues grew from $16.5 billion to $45.3 billion. The markets, however, were still narrow and fragmented in China. In 2000, only two operators garnered more than $1 billion in revenues: China Mobile ($1.4 billion) and China Telecom ($1.1 billion). China Unicom's revenues exceeded $300 million. Other companies' revenues were below $100 million. The top-four operators possessed barely 7 percent of the total market.

In 1995, the number of total cell phone users had been almost insignificant compared to that of total fixed-phone users. By 2001, the discrepancy between

Exhibit 7-3. China's public sector, telecom operators, and IT industry.

(a) Ministry of Industry Information (MII) and China's licensed telecom operators.

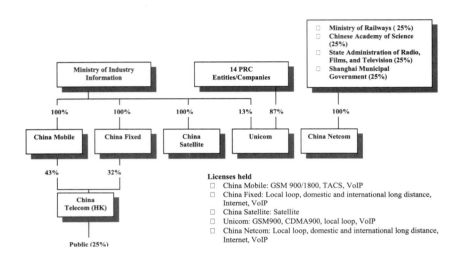

Licenses held
- China Mobile: GSM 900/1800, TACS, VoIP
- China Fixed: Local loop, domestic and international long distance, Internet, VoIP
- China Satellite: Satellite
- Unicom: GSM900, CDMA900, local loop, VoIP
- China Netcom: Local loop, domestic and international long distance, Internet, VoIP

(b) China's ICT industry

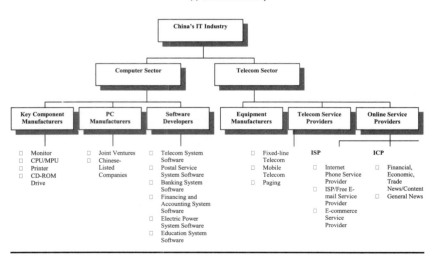

the two was rapidly leveling. The annual growth of Internet users had been even more explosive in China, peaking at more than 350 percent in 1999. A year later, the number of web users exceeded 20 million and was expected to triple by 2003. Mobile vendors had entered the Chinese marketplace in the early 1980s; service revenues emerged a decade later. The cell phone market shares reflected the difference.

In contrast to the fragmented service business, the equipment industry was highly concentrated. Motorola had 32 percent of that market, Nokia 30 percent, Siemens 15 percent, and Ericsson 13 percent. The top-four vendors controlled 90 percent of the entire Chinese marketplace. The remaining 10 percent belonged to indigenous vendors whose role was expected to grow. Between 1995 and 2001, annual telecom investments increased from less than $10 billion to some $35 billion. The cumulative annual growth of telecom investments had peaked at 70 percent in 1998, the milestone year of deregulation.

China Telecom

In February 1999, China Telecom was divided into three corporate entities: China Telecom, China Mobile, and China Satellite Telecommunications. A year later, China Telecom, China's then-largest telco, was further split into two companies. The northern section was incorporated with China Netcom Corp. and Jitong Communications Co. Ltd. to form a new telecom giant called China Netcom Group Corp. The southern section retained the name China Telecom and the current assets of that company.[58] Before its breakup in 2000, China Telecom generated $20.8 billion in total sales and employed almost 590,000 people. It was the nation's dominant provider of fixed-line local and long-distance phone services, serving about 144 million subscribers. Its nationwide fiber-optic network was backed up with satellite communications and digital microwave systems to offer data and multimedia services, including IP (Internet protocol) telecom services.

Even in 2000, China Telecom's organizational structure reflected the old national PTT, with its departments for the Communist party's "political education" and "disciplines inspection." Zhou Deqiang, president of China Telecom, used Mao's old precedent to illustrate the nature of the new economy:

> During the new long march, the working staff of China Telecom will unite as one, continuously explore and create new things so as to make new contributions for pushing ahead the informatization of the national economy and serving the reform and opening up as well as China's modernization.[59]

China Telecom launched a mobile service in the prosperous southern city of Shenzhen, neighboring Hong Kong, without a mobile license from the MII.

In December 2001, the service had attracted 70,000 subscribers, even though the users could not call outside Shenzhen. The allure of the service was in the tariff. The cost structure of the calls was on par with fixed-line calls and less than half the rates for China Mobile and China Unicom. Also, this service relied on CDMA, not rival GSM technology. Oddly enough, the MII, which had withheld a mobile license, remained the *owner* of China Telecom. Despite its year-long efforts to obtain a license, China Telecom had stumbled on the MII's reluctance to grant one in such a lucrative mobile market.[60]

China Telecom hoped to win a nationwide mobile license in 2002, which would allow it to roll out its CDMA service across China. Such a development would not only increase revenues for Qualcomm but would raise the competitive pressures faced by China Mobile and Unicom. Indeed, it was conceivable that China Telecom and the MII had reached some sort of "understanding" on the status quo. The former national PTT and its owner/regulator remained close. Of course, their objectives might have been different. China Telecom seized price wars to deter rivals. In turn, the MII saw the *de facto* market entry and CDMA as an appropriate way to harness competition. Furthermore, the network access equipment supporting the *shi hua tong* service was made by ZTE, a local manufacturer that had developed its CDMA equipment in cooperation with Qualcomm, which earned royalties from ZTE sales. Regulators saw indigenous vendors, such as ZTE, as pioneers of a truly Chinese mobile industry.

China Mobile Communications Corp.

China Mobile Communications Corp. (CMCC) has been in operation since 1987, when mobile telephony was first introduced in the Chinese mainland. In a sense, the history of mobile communications in China was synonymous with the development of China Mobile and its predecessor, the mobile communications service under China Telecom. As China restructured its telecom industry to prepare for entry into the WTO, China Mobile Communications was spun off from China Telecommunications Corp. in 2000. With about 89 million subscribers, the operator was China's leading mobile phone service provider, far ahead of China Unicom. Worldwide, only Vodafone had more subscribers. China Mobile's subsidiary in Hong Kong, served 59 million customers in thirteen provinces and planned to buy more provincial subsidiaries from its parent company.[61] China Mobile Communications was controlled by China's MII.

In 2000, China Mobile had almost 112,000 employees and subsidiaries in eighteen provinces, including autonomous regions and municipalities. It was fully owned by China Mobile Group (Hong Kong) Co. Ltd., which had subsidiaries in thirteen provinces. In 2000, China Mobile sales amounted to $5.9 billion and were growing 69 percent per year. The leading operator considered the year 2001 "a crucial one for CMCC to fulfill the strategic objective of 'striving to be a world-class communications enterprise.'"[62] In that year, China Mobile had engaged in a series of network acquisitions from its parent, funding most of the deals through multibillion-dollar equity offerings on the New York and Hong Kong markets.

China Unicom

China Unicom first consisted of sixteen groups, including the ministries of railways, electricity, and electronics. Its task was to provide cellular services and thus compete against comparable services of the local telcos. Unlike other new entrants in different industries, the operator has enjoyed certain government-conferred financial advantages (e.g., low tax rates, high depreciation rates, obligation to return only 10 percent of governmental loans). Moreover, its financial resources were diversified, in comparison to China Telecom, a state-owned company. As a new player, China Unicom has potential for more flexible organizational capabilities than the incumbents. Importantly, too, it is not subject to the universal obligation, which has allowed the company to engage in cream-skimming in areas of high demand while avoiding the necessity of providing service in high-cost rural areas. Finally, it has enjoyed certain political advantages (e.g., sponsoring ministries in State Council and dominant stock-holding companies), including close affiliation to the State Economic and Trade Commission. As one company official has put it, China Unicom "has three mouths in the Cabinet, while China Telecom has just one."[63]

China Unicom launched its first four GSM networks in mid-1995, in several key regions (Shanghai, Beijing, Tianjin, and Guangzhou in Guangdong), with the assistance of BellSouth, a U.S. Baby Bell. Unicom engaged in similar arrangements with other foreign operators (including Ameritech, Bell Canada, and Nortel) for other regions. By 2000, the Chinese government floated a minority stake in China Unicom. In 2001, the state-controlled China Unicom provided paging, long-distance, data, and mobile communications services. It was China's dominant paging company and the nation's second-largest mobile operator, right behind China Mobile Communications. Together, China Unicom and its parent, China United Telecommunications, served 31 million mobile phone customers.

From FDI to Indigenous Capabilities

In an industry that personified Joseph Schumpeter's famous notion of "creative destruction," the mobile leaders have been able and willing to destroy old technologies, products, and services in order to create room for new ones, across several technology platforms. In their home base and core cluster, these mobile leaders served as cannibals of sorts. In China, they served a very different function. They were digging their own graves. As cannibals, they had established their strengths and renewed their advantages, from one cellular era to another. But as such, they were also giving rise to a new generation of cannibals who could devour their own creators. This transition would start with low-end segments and cost focus strategies; but it would end with high-end segments and differentiation strategies. In both cases, the massive scale economies and the consequent decline in cost structure were expected to provide the key leverage. The old cannibals had embraced the future; now they would have to deal with it. They would not be able to deter the emerging Chinese giants, but they could become "like" local players, hence, their rushed localization strategies.

In the long term, Chinese policymakers hoped that indigenous vendors would become major players that could overthrow the foreign giants that gave birth to them. Certainly, the rapid rise of China's electronics giants provided a good start. Between 1979 and 2001, global mobile vendors provided a powerful lift to China's mobile communications, through exports, FDI, substantial presence, instruction, and training. In the long term, China's capacity to imitate and modify imported technology may be even more important for its technological transformation. These capabilities can make or break China's emerging "must win" market, just as they may turn contemporary Chinese suppliers, contractors, and nascent equipment manufacturers into future industry giants.[64] "The winners in China in recent years are the local suppliers," acknowledged John Gilbertson, president of Ericsson (China) Company Ltd., in 1998. "These companies have become highly skilled at building telecommunications systems and . . . with their low production costs, are now taking an increasingly firm grip on the market."[65]

As this shift has gone hand in hand with extraordinary gains in the productivity frontier, China's challenge is bound to last longer than that of Japan. Not only has FDI contributed to a high-level technology infrastructure in China, but it has provided sophisticated capabilities. Chinese firms have been quick to upgrade and innovate these capabilities with massive scale economies *and* globalization. Take, for instance, Huawei Technologies. Established only in 1988, this high-tech company was fully owned by its employees. It specialized in R&D, production, and marketing of communications equipment, providing customized network solutions for telecom carriers in fixed, mobile, and data communications networks. With total sales of $2.7 billion in 2000, Huawei achieved an increase of almost 80 percent upon the previous year's $1.5 billion. Like the Nordic mobile leaders, it had initially used partnerships with leading global players in both product development and marketing promotion. These were typically U.S. IT and mobile leaders, including Texas Instruments, IBM, Motorola, Lucent Technologies, Intel, Sun Microsystems, and others. In just few years, Huawei had set up more than forty branch offices worldwide, as well as research institutes in Silicon Valley, Bangalore, Stockholm, Moscow, Beijing, and Shanghai. After U.S. IT leaders and Euro-Nordic mobile leaders had given birth to future titans, such as Huawai, they were gradually beginning to fear them—the nascent Chinese giants operated with entirely different scale economies than Japan's Fujitsu or NEC.

Like Japan, South Korea, and the "tiger economies," Chinese SEZs have not been content with simple cost-advantage strategies but have quickly upgraded to far more innovative strategic postures. "It took the Asian tigers—Taiwan, the Philippines, Malaysia, Singapore, Thailand, and Korea—more than fifteen years to build their economies into symbols of new development," argues Kenichi Ohmae. "It is taking China only a few years to supplant them."[66] Time will tell whether this shift will be across-the-board, as this view suggests, or sectoral, as mobile evolution in China might indicate. In either scenario, Japan, South Korea, and the tiger economies face a historical challenge that will not go away—and that will hit hard the dynamic growth core of those economies (i.e., their high-tech manufacturing base).

Still another milestone was reached in November 2001. While all major wireless players suffered from the technology slowdown in the United States and the bleeding of Europe's leading operators after the 3G license auctions, China's market held a promise for the future. When China's entry to the WTO became imminent and Beijing was selected to host the 2008 Olympics, China's strong growth prospects were further heightened. A slate of new multibillion-dollar investment initiatives by the world's leading vendors resulted in November 2001. These developments were not confined to equipment vendors in the wireless business. With China's WTO entry, many multinationals struggled to speed up the adjustment of their development strategies for the country in order to diversify investments and prepare for across-the-board competition. Most strategy adjustments required the restructuring of investment in manufacturing. Some multinationals went even further by shifting their production to China, while others developed parts production and procurement networks. Multinationals' investment in R&D in China has grown rapidly since 1997, both in quantity and in coverage. Lucent planned to increase its researchers in China to about 1,500 in 2001, while Motorola set up a North Asia center. Other competitors, including Nokia, relied on more aggressive strategies. The number of employees of the Nokia China Research Center increased ten times within a year. By the end of 2000, at least twenty-nine multinationals had opened thirty-two independent R&D units. Many multinationals invested heavily in knowledge-intensive services to make China the center of their operations and management in the Asia-Pacific region.

In short, the combination of extraordinary scale and low penetration accounted for the mobile potential of the Chinese market. Exhibit 7-4 summarizes the central characteristics and worldwide significance of the Chinese growth market—from the monopoly era through transition and to the present-day competitive environment.

In the wireless business, the promise of China has grown with increasing market access as well as the saturation of wireless markets in Western Europe and the United States. New cannibals are waking up.

Exhibit 7-4. The Chinese growth market: Triad Plus leadership.

MONOPOLY ERA

National PTT
☐ Until 1979 economic reforms, centralized, political public-sector monopoly under Party rule.
☐ Vertically integrated supply chain.
☐ First cellular experiments in 1987.

NIS/PTT Labs
☐ Mobile innovation low until the arrival of U.S. and European vendors in early 1980s.
☐ Instead of spillovers, centralized system keeps expertise within China Telecom, until FDI leads to some diffusion.
☐ Policymakers hope joint ventures will lead to indigenous suppliers.

Old Public Policies
☐ Tight monopoly arrangements until early- to mid-1990s. Broadcasting tightly regulated, spectrum policies dictated by military.
☐ At first, roaming and pricing (CPP) policies confined to most prosperous cities and SEZs; coordination of national licensing policies in 1995.
☐ Initially, TDMA-based standards.

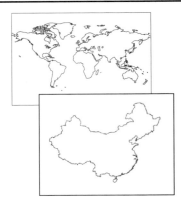

TRANSITION ERA

Privatization
☐ In late 1990s, China Telecom's breakup and ownership arrangements, driven by global telecom reforms and entry to WTO in 2001.
☐ Vertical disintegration initiated; new industry players; regulators control developments.
☐ With Euro-Nordic cellular leadership, GSM reigns.
☐ Acceleration of FDI by foreign vendors, which consolidate infrastructure and handsets markets; services highly fragmented.

Transformation of Innovation
☐ Through FDI, spillovers among indigenous suppliers and contractors.
☐ Qualcomm fails to make CDMA a national standard.
☐ Innovation takes place within firms, but increasing participation in international activities; foreign investors trade technology for access.

Transitional Public Policies
☐ Role of Ministry of Post and Telecom lessens, role of Ministry of Information Industry increases, regulators moved to MII; deregulation, military controls spectrum policies, but commercial considerations grow.
☐ Roaming, pricing, and licensing policies crafted for domestic market.
☐ CDMA enters China as an alternative standard.

COMPETITIVE ERA

Cluster
☐ China's subscriber base largest worldwide (July 2001).
☐ Competition accelerates among old and new operators.
☐ First price wars reflect the arrival of Nordic strategies (low prices, high quality, large volumes).
☐ GSM dominates China's path to 3G, challengers opt for CDMA.

Innovation Systems
☐ Mobile leaders build new R&D centers, networks, and science parks.
☐ Chinese vendors capture 10% of market and increase R&D.
☐ Chinese suppliers begin internationalization.

New Public Policies
☐ Deregulation, spectrum allocations subject to commercial considerations.
☐ Increasing FDI and new public policies boost decentralization.
☐ Standards wars arrive.

Part III

Industry Catalysts: From Equipment Manufacturers to Enablers

Part III concentrates on the leading equipment manufacturers and their contractors. Historically, they have served as industry catalysts. Chapters 8 to 11 tell the stories of the classic "Big Three" equipment manufacturers—Motorola, Ericsson, and Nokia—as well as their more recent challenger, Qualcomm. In each case, the narrative focuses on globalization through competition. Each account also offers a glimpse of a different global strategy. Motorola has engaged in an (innovation-driven) international strategy, whereas Ericsson's strategy has been more (responsive) multinational by nature. Nokia's internationalization began through multinational activities, but it has evolved toward a translocal direction. Qualcomm's rapid growth and internationalization provide intriguing lessons on how new entrants and challengers may upset the rules of the game.

Chapter 12 focuses on the contractors of the mobile vendors, which have evolved from "board stuffers" to electronic manufacturing services (EMS) providers. This part also explores the most recent layer of the changing industry value chain, focusing on the leading enablers and service providers, including the great IT giants.

Chapter 13 examines the mobilization of the digital economy, and the efforts of the mobile leaders to achieve the transition from voice to data. Chapter 14 focuses on Apple's PDA pioneership (the Newton project), the rise of palm computing, as well as the Internet vision and the industry entry of the U.S. IT leaders in software (Microsoft), microprocessors (Intel), and online services (America Online). While the mobile leaders advocate vertical coordination to incorporate new technology innovation, the IT leaders promote horizontalization to promote innovation. In this extraordinary confrontation, the strategic and financial stakes have been formidable.

Equipment Manufacturers

Before the early mobile Internet strategies, the telecom equipment market was estimated at $191 billion in 1998 (Exhibit III-1). The industry was concentrated. Among the top-20 vendors, U.S.-based firms had 46 percent of revenues, European players 40 percent, and Asian companies less than 14 percent. But by 2001 and 2002, the strategic advantages of the leading U.S. firms (i.e., Lucent, Motorola) were eroding. Among the European players, Nokia had triumphed, whereas others (e.g., Ericsson, Alcatel, and Siemens) were merging, joint venturing, or outsourcing their manufacturing capabilities. The list's Asian players were primarily Japanese (e.g., NEC, Fujitsu, and Matsushita). With the 3G transition, new Asian producers—from the established Kyocera to emerging Chinese vendors—were struggling for the top-tier positions.

Exhibit III-1. Telecom and mobile equipment sales and shares.

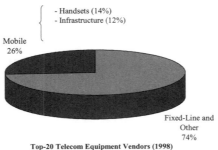

Total Telecom Equipment Sales (1998)

- Handsets (14%)
- Infrastructure (12%)

Mobile 26%

Fixed-Line and Other 74%

Top-20 Telecom Equipment Vendors (1998)

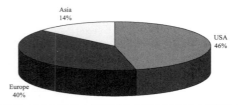

Asia 14%

USA 46%

Europe 40%

Of the total telecom equipment market, mobile handsets and infrastructure (i.e., base stations and switches), accounted for 14 percent and

12 percent of all sales, respectively, or just over one-quarter of the total market when taken together. As the value has been migrating from traditional telecommunications to mobile communications, the contribution of mobile manufacturers to total equipment sales has been rising as well. Still, the equipment segment has become highly concentrated with some dozen players accounting for the majority of sales. In 1998, mobile handsets worldwide were about 163 million units, growing by more than 50 percent over the previous year. Digital handset sales accounted for 85 percent of total sales. That year Nokia became the leading handset vendor in market share (23 percent) surpassing Motorola (20 percent) and Ericsson (15 percent), followed by Panasonic (8 percent) and Alcatel (4 percent). The "Big Three"—Nokia, Motorola, and Ericsson—controlled 58 percent of the total market against second- and third-tier players (30 percent and the remaining niche rivals).

As the 3G transition heralded new disruptive opportunities, the number of global subscribers was still expected to soar from 484 million to 1.1 billion in 1999 and 2002. The Big Three were expected to increase their market share to 60 percent in 2001, but much of this was attributed to Nokia's powerful market leadership, whereas Motorola and Ericsson were rapidly losing their sales to challengers, many of which were of Asian descent. Meanwhile excess channel inventory contributed to valuation meltdown.

Through the cellular era, equipment manufacturers, along with a slate of second- and third-tier producers and a variety of contractors (i.e., component providers, contract manufacturers, and EMS providers), have been catalysts in the wireless evolution. From the 1970s to the end of the 1990s, the industry value system was driven by the dual efforts of the PTTs and the vendors—until the entry of the IT challengers. The vendors were the first to engage in competition, and through this competition, they became the first to seek global leverage. In the case of large-country players, vendors extended and leveraged their strategies worldwide, seeking scope through scale. In the case of the small-country players, vendors have used globalization to establish necessary scale economies, seeking scale through scope.

In the pre-cellular and analog eras, Motorola had been the leading vendor worldwide. In the digital era, Nokia captured leadership in handsets and Ericsson in infrastructure. At the same time, Qualcomm surprised all by developing the core technology for the 3G era. Meanwhile, these top-tier vendors accelerated their outsourcing, which provided ample opportunities to the contractors. Digital convergence offered a strategic window to world's leading IT players, which entered the industry in the late 1990s—and launched their offensive in the spring of 2002.

Chapter 8

Motorola: The Failure of Success

Through most of the twentieth century, Motorola's name was synonymous with wireless, pagers, and personal communications. If it failed, it got back on its feet to win again. By 2001, the "American samurai" seemed to have lost its way. And its own success contributed to its defeat.

Since the late 1920s, Motorola has engaged in three basic strategies:

Entrepreneurial Strategy (1928–1946)
Electronics Strategy (1946–1996)

- Early Electronics Strategy (1946–1959)
- Internationalization of the Electronics Strategy (1959–1974)
- Quality and Globalization (1974–1997)

Reorganization and Refocus (1997–Present)

Initially, Galvin Manufacturing Corp., the precursor of Motorola, had an entrepreneurial focus. Building on its capabilities in two-way police radio, Galvin engaged in extensive defense contracting and grew rapidly. World War II provided a powerful boost that transformed the company while its product portfolio expanded rapidly. With electronics as the foundation, the manufacturer launched its R&D facilities, introduced its first pagers, and diversified into integrated circuits and semiconductors. In the postwar era, Galvin adopted a new corporate identity as Motorola. Focusing on electronics, it extended and leveraged its business strategy geographically. Toward the late 1960s, Paul Galvin's son initiated internationalization as the company entered cellular, satellite, and data communications. Internationalization accelerated until Motorola was battered by Japanese challengers. In the 1980s, this defeat led to an internal and external transformation. Internally, it prompted extensive quality programs. Externally, it triggered the company's efforts to use trade politics to contain the challengers in the global chessboard.

As a diversified electronics giant, Motorola struggled for international leadership. In the wireless business, it held absolute and relative dominance through the 1G era. This success made it complacent. Falling captive of its customers, Motorola enjoyed lucrative profits in the analog cellular until it was too late to create a sustainable position in the digital cellular. At the peak of the 1980s, George Fisher, Motorola's then-CEO, analyzed the basic challenges that the company would face:

> *What is Motorola doing today to be competitive twenty years from now?* Every organization is a victim of its own success. . . . There's a strong belief in this company that the areas in which we're the leader today won't be the areas that make us healthy twenty or thirty years from now.[1]

In the wireless business, those twenty or thirty years came in barely five years.

Entrepreneurial Opportunism

The entrepreneurial Paul V. Galvin (1895–1959) started his first business as a popcorn vendor at the age of thirteen. Born in a small midwestern town, the Irish-American cherished populist values and spoke for the Sherman Antitrust Act. Throughout his life, he "reflected the direct, no-nonsense philosophy of his small town heritage." The young Galvin even flirted with socialism, arguing that "the labor of a human being is not a commodity or article of commerce."[2] Galvin's company's values were rooted in his own life and the lives of the firm's early labor force—Chicago's first- and second-generation immigrants, who struggled to achieve the American dream through loyalty and hard work.[3]

Motorola became known for its humane and democratic work environment and, like Hewlett-Packard, a competitive but open corporate culture. Everyone, including Paul Galvin, was addressed on a first-name basis. The time clock in the plant was replaced with an employee honor system. And by 1947, Paul Galvin established a profit-sharing program for the company's 2,000 employees. Thanks to these efforts, Motorola was union-free, which ensured the kind of flexibility that its early foreign rivals did not possess, especially in Europe. Even with increasing internationalization, Motorola seized "people values" (see Exhibit 8-1) that enabled the company to succeed in serving its customers while cementing the loyalty of an increasingly heterogeneous workforce worldwide. At the same time, these values became benchmarks for Motorola's Nordic rivals, including Nokia, as they engaged in internationalization efforts of their own (as discussed in Chapter 10).

Exhibit 8-1. Paul V. Galvin: the founder of Motorola.

(a) The Founder of Motorola.

The entrepreneurial Paul V. Galvin started his first business as a popcorn vendor at age 13. His was a direct, no-nonsense philosophy of the small town heritage. Loved by his employees, he turned a small battery eliminator manufacturing company into America's postwar innovation giant.

Robert Galvin and Paul Galvin in 1956. When Galvin died in 1959, his son Robert continued as president and was named CEO in 1969.

Born in a small midwestern town, the Irish-American Galvin cherished many populist values, believing in the dignity of the labor of a human being.

Motorola's famous profit-sharing program and "People Values" reflected these values, which were embraced by its rivals, including Nokia.

(b) People Values: From Motorola to Nokia.

Motorola's "People Values" (mid-1980s)

PEOPLE VALUES

1. *To treat each employee with dignity.*
2. *To treat each employee as an individual.*
3. *To maintain an open atmosphere where direct communication with employees affords the opportunity to contribute to the maximum of their potential.*
4. *To foster unity of purpose between employees and Motorola.*
5. *To provide personal opportunities for training and development to ensure the most capable and most effective workforce.*
6. *To respect senior service.*
7. *To compensate fairly by salary, benefits, and where possible, incentives.*
8. *To promote on the basis of capability.*
9. *To practice the commonly accepted policies of equal opportunity and affirmative action.*

The "Nokia Way" (late 1990s)

To You From J.O.

Nokia's way of operating –
Connecting People

Nokia unites people
In open, honest cooperation.
It offers equal opportunities
To develop skills and know-how.

Nokia unites people
All over the world
By manufacturing innovative
Products and solutions.
Its goal is customer satisfaction.

THE MORE YOU WILL DO FOR NOKIA,
THE MORE NOKIA CAN DO
FOR YOU.

* J.O. = Jorma Ollila, CEO and Chairman of Nokia.

SOURCE: Motorola, Inc.

The Ice Cream Story

Motorola's early strategy had little to do with the kind of business or corporate strategy that MBA students learn in business schools. It was more about having an eye for opportunities, the struggle for survival, and the fleeting bliss of technology fortunes. Galvin's ice cream story had all of these elements.

In 1910, when the big snow hit Harvard, Paul Galvin sold large baskets full of ham sandwiches to passengers on the snowed-in trains. As the plows got through, the great sandwich boom ended. That summer, Galvin introduced a new product: He began selling ice cream cones on the trains. In those days, there was no air-conditioning. Ice cream was a best-seller. But competition picked up. Every boy wanted to get into the business, and in other towns along the line, groups of boys assaulted each other on the trains. To beat the competition, the boys swarmed onto the trains before they even stopped. Then came the day when one of the boys slipped and fell under the wheels, hanging onto a railing and hauling himself clear of the wheels until the train stopped. "We were out of the popcorn business before we got the declaration," recalls Galvin. Later, he would retell the story to his associates when some product or market was on its way out. "Recognize the signs," he would say. "If you're going to take a licking, take it, and get on to the next job."[4]

The ice cream story includes elements of Motorola's success—rapid entry models, industry foresight, efforts to translate pioneering technology benefits into more sustainable first-mover advantages, the inevitable pairing of great opportunities and intense competition, the high-stakes game over monopolistic profits and sustainable advantages, new product development, and ceaseless innovation. The lesson is not about cellular phones or semiconductors; nor is it about ice cream. It is not about any one industry, technology, product or service. It is about *demand.* While technologies give rise to new business models, it is the new value proposition that attracts the customers. Paul Galvin never forgot the lesson, but his successors occasionally did. Then again, they never saw that young boy hanging onto a railing.

Galvin Manufacturing Corp.: From Battery Eliminators to Radios

In the wireless industry, sustaining business models have seldom been favorable to new entrants. As a result, most challengers have established a foothold during disruptive periods of turmoil and ferment. Such an industry transition gave Paul Galvin and his brother, Joseph E. Galvin (1899–1944), their first real break. Initially, the young Galvin worked for the D&G Storage Battery Co. in Chicago, which made electric storage batteries for automobiles. In 1920, KDKA Pittsburgh began broadcasting, starting the radio revolution in America. A year later, Galvin and a partner, Ed Stewart, formed Stewart Battery Co., a consolidation of two plants. It failed, but five years later, Galvin rejoined Stewart in a new business for manufacturing "B" battery eliminators, devices that enabled battery-operated radios to be powered by household electric currents. As electricity became common in U.S. households, the partners anticipated that owners of battery-operated radios would opt for eliminators rather than buy new and more expensive models. It was this uncanny industry foresight—the ability to understand the dynamics of rapid-growth industries *and* the foresight to detect a disruptive curve—that guided Galvin from the late 1920s to the late 1950s.

In 1928, the Galvin brothers purchased the battery eliminator business from the bankrupt Stewart Storage Battery Co. and founded the Galvin Manufacturing Corporation. Because the company could not survive on eliminators alone, it entered the home radio business and manufactured standard AC sets with assorted name plates for private-label sale. This sideline became Galvin's first source of income, even though the business was dominated by major manufacturers like Atwater-Kent, Kennedy, Spartan, Majestic, Zenith, RCA, and GE. With Black Friday, October 25, 1929, the bull market ended and Galvin suddenly was stuck with a substantial inventory while the big players dumped their brand-name sets on the market at private-label prices. By Christmas, he was out of business again. And that was not all. Within just five months, he lost his mother, father, and mother-in-law. But just as everything seemed to be lost, life began anew.

From Car Radios to Police Radios

Galvin had heard about men on Long Island who made custom radio installations in cars. Instead of a garage-type operation, Galvin saw a lifetime opportunity in *mass* manufacturing package car radios. But first he had to learn the business from the scratch. "We had no sponsorship, no money, no business. The car radio idea in 1930 was very unpopular. . . . [Yet] our business attracted young men who hoped to grow up with a new industry and were willing to take a chance."[5] In the 1920s, radio's soaring popularity was matched only by the appeal of the automobile. The two seemed destined to go together. The auto radio was a rarity until the 1930s because of complicated installation, high expenditures, and a slate of technical obstacles. After remarkable "shoehorning," Galvin's men managed to install an auto radio set in Galvin's Studebaker in time for a convention of the Radio Manufacturers' Association.

Galvin focused on the product *and* the service. He challenged his employees to "put music on wheels"—to design a simple car radio that could be installed in most contemporary models at an affordable price. Motorola was not a pioneer in an early niche market. It was a first mover in the first mass markets. Since 1927, car radios had been designed, manufactured, and marketed, but these sets had been "custom" designed for a specific installation for $200 to $300. Motorola's model was designed on a commercial basis and sold for $110 to $130.[6] To overcome installation difficulties, Galvin and Elmer Wavering, who had assisted in designing the radio, started the company's first sales and service organization. In 1931, independent wholesalers remained the primary sales outlets for radio manufacturers, marketing 80 percent of all radios. Galvin's distributors remained loyal and grew with the company. By 1934, the radio industry noted the extraordinary potential of mass-produced car radios, and several larger players joined the competition. To deter the merchandising attacks, Galvin developed a relationship with the B. F. Goodrich Company, whose hundreds of stores and garages made Motorola radios available nationally and on credit. The supplementary pattern of distribution became a cornerstone relationship for the young company.

Galvin also launched the great Motorola highway advertising program. By 1936, Motorola was the market leader in auto radios. Motorola auto radios were endorsed by radio and film stars, such as Betty Grable, Jane Withers, and Rita Hayworth, and bandleaders such as Ray Noble and Lawrence Welk. Soon Americans recognized the trademark. This combination of high quality, affordable prices, and service excellence, coupled with strategic distribution alliances and shrewd mass advertising, made Motorola's early reputation. As Motorola expanded in car radios, it also entered the police radio market.

War and Transition

In 1936, the Galvin family took a six-week tour of Europe. Galvin came back from Germany convinced that war was inevitable. The impressive autobahns "have not been built just for autos, they are war roads."[7] Upon his return to the United States, Galvin moved the company into product areas that might be useful to the nation during war and had his engineers investigate military applications of radio. Motorola's new line of FM mobile police radios, initially designed and developed independently of government contracts, became the basis for a new set of Armed Forces specifications for vehicular radio applications.

In early 1940, Galvin heard about the lack of appropriate radio communications in the National Guard's war games at Camp McCoy, Wisconsin. That year, the company developed the first handheld two-way radio for the U.S. Army Signal Corps. As all of Motorola's facilities were quickly converted to military engineering and production, nonmilitary manufacturing ground to a halt. Marconi had been his own spokesman for the civilian and military use of wireless telegraphy some four decades before. Now Galvin prodded the Army and his associates into recognition of the wireless potential:

I wonder how many of you realize the importance of radio as a deciding factor in who is going to win the war? What is it that gives the vicious efficiency to vehicles of destruction in modern mechanized warfare? It is radio. What is today revolutionizing air-craft, naval, and antiaircraft tactics and strategy? It is radio and radar. It is our job—the industry's job—to deliver these precious and important instruments.[8]

As the portable SCR-536 two-way AM radio was used worldwide, the Handie-Talkie AM radio became a World War II symbol. Meanwhile, Motorola's R&D chief Daniel Noble designed the first portable FM two-way radio, the SCR-300 backpack radio, for the U.S. Army Signal Corps. Weighing thirty-five pounds, the radio had a range of ten to twenty miles and was known as the Walkie-Talkie. After the war years, these products served as a bridge to Motorola's early dominance in commercial two-way communications. In the 1930s, Galvin Manufacturing was a small player, but between 1941 and 1943, sales soared from $17 million to $78 million. Galvin knew that these results did not reflect the potential of the company in the postwar market; the production was geared for the military. "This tight and controlled market," he said, "tells us nothing about the pattern we will have to meet later on."[9]

Following VJ Day and Japan's formal surrender on September 2, 1945, the company received cancellations of war contracts. As the car radio business picked up again, it became top producer of two-way communications equipment, joined the top-10 companies in home radios, and rose rapidly in the nascent TV set business. The transition from eliminators to car and home radios had taught Galvin the significance of growth and diversification. But it was the war that allowed the company to engage in vertical integration and expand into a high-volume manufacturer.

Electronics Strategy: Fifty Years of Success

After the war, Dan Noble told Paul Galvin that the next fifty years in electronics would be related to solid-state electronics and began to speak for Motorola's own research laboratory. By 1946, Galvin's company initiated the development of a variety of promising new technologies and products. To realize these bold objectives, it budgeted more than $1 million for research, while assigning some 240 engineers to development projects focusing on new technologies, products, and manufacturing processes. In 1947, to signify the new era and clearly identify the company's products with the Motorola trademark, the Galvin Manufacturing Corp. changed its name to Motorola, Inc. (from *motor* and *victrola*), which reflected its early successes in radio, cars, and sound.

This shift from visceral entrepreneurial opportunism to a purposeful electronics strategy made Motorola's success in the next five decades. These years were punctuated by three different phases:

- **Early Electronics Strategy (1946–1959).** This earliest phase stabilized the basic outline of Motorola's electronics strategy in the U.S. home base.
- **Internationalization (1959–1974).** The second phase witnessed the extension and leverage of this strategy internationally.
- **Quest for Quality and Globalization (1974–1997).** The third phase reflected Motorola's response to the Japanese challenge.

In each case, Motorola's organizational capabilities were refined and adapted to match the requirements of the rapidly changing and globalizing environment.

Innovation, Electronics, and New Industries

Motorola entered electronics at a time when it was becoming the foundation for a variety of new industries and industry segments. Over time, the company's new core competences and accompanying core capabilities transformed the wartime contractor into a high-tech corporation. The evolving electronics strategy built on constant innovation and upgrading. Its foundation was the small R&D facility, which expanded dramatically in the postwar era. Between 1942 and 1950, Motorola grew from 1,500 employees and $31 million sales to 9,300 employees and $177 million in sales. At the eve of the Cold War, the entrepreneurial firm was a key defense contractor and was joining a pioneer group of TV manufacturers.

R&D Labs and Semiconductors

In 1958, Motorola set up a top-classified research laboratory in Phoenix, Arizona, which was the genesis of its Semiconductor Products Sector and Government Electronics Group. The diversification also boosted the Communications Sector with product innovations and development of two-way mobile and portable radiotelephones, pocket pagers, and cellular radios. As transistors were about to replace bulky and fragile vacuum tubes, Motorola, at first, focused on military electronics. The more conservative Motorolans saw the R&D operation as "Noble's Folly." But by anticipating the enormous potential of the transistor, the company became one of the world's largest manufacturers of semiconductors.

In the 1950s, Motorola contributed to U.S. efforts in the Korean War, even as it began to produce power transistors made from germanium for use in auto radios. For several years, the transistor business operated in the red, but Galvin and Noble stuck to the business by supplying its internal market for transistors (e.g., auto radios, radio communications equipment, consumer electronics) and working to become a volume supplier of semiconductor devices to large-scale markets. Today, its diversification into electronics seems almost natural, but that was not the case in the immediate postwar era. "If you don't like my decision," Galvin told the board, "you can get rid of me; but you can't change my decision."[10]

During these early years, Motorola set out to dominate those business segments in which it already had experience, from two-way radio systems to microwave radio systems. It also invested in an expansive sales organization, which was augmented by a nationwide network of independent, authorized, two-way radio service businesses. By the mid-1950s, there were more than 650 Motorola Service Stations (MSSs), each carrying a full line of parts and test equipment.[11] The MSS organization had nothing to do with technology innovation, but it did represent marketing innovation.

Leveraging the Electronics Strategy

By 1960, Motorola's net sales were at $299 million and net earnings at $13 million. It had 14,740 employees. The electronics strategy was established in the late 1940s, solidified in the 1950s, and internationalized toward the end of the 1960s.

Leadership Transition

In 1948, Motorola entered a smooth succession as Robert W. Galvin, the founder's son, was elected executive vice president.[12] By the mid-1950s, Motorola was too large for a one-man show. Father and son reshaped the entire company along product division lines. Each division would be self-contained with its own engineering, purchasing, manufacturing, and marketing departments. While this structure was already effective in some areas of the company, the two men made it a companywide policy. Each division, including Automotive, Consumer Products, Communications, Semiconductor, and Military, would be its own profit center. In terms of organizational capabilities, this was a critical moment. Decentralization was necessary for Motorola's domestic expansion, and it facilitated the vendor's early internationalization. But it also rendered Motorola vulnerable to globalization, i.e., the efficiency attack by the Japanese and the quality challenge by the Nordic rivals. With the basic strategy in place, the new posture had to be communicated to the public at large. By the mid-1950s, Motorola adopted a new corporate logo, the "batwing" M. A variety of design elements were used until 1965, when the designers finally opted for the circle surrounding the M.

When Galvin died in 1959, his son became CEO. Galvin had groomed his son for the job. The very same democratic values and respect for the individual that had characterized his father's era permeated his leadership as well.[13] The man and the son shared affinities, but the transition also meant substantial changes. The founder had turned a struggling start-up into a reputable high-tech conglomerate focusing on half a dozen product lines. The son would seek greater diversification. In the process, the ice cream story was lost.

Early Internationalization

These were the golden years at Motorola. In 1961, the company became one of the first to use the epitaxial method to mass-produce semiconductors. The Automotive Products Division began producing alternators, inaugurating Motorola as a supplier of "under the hood" electronics. Three years later, Motorola developed the first rectangular picture tube for color television. In conjunction with Ford and RCA, Motorola designed and manufactured the first eight-track tape players for the automotive market. In 1967, Motorola expanded its international business by adding manufacturing facilities in many countries, including Australia, France, Hong Kong, Israel, Malaysia, Mexico, Puerto Rico, South Korea, Taiwan, the United Kingdom, and West Germany. Joint ventures for the production of automotive and other products were established in Italy and Japan. By 1970, Motorola's net sales had climbed to $796 million and it had 36,000 employees.

These years saw the reinforcement of Motorola's tradition of a "two-in-box" management structure, a mechanism for management development and succession in which responsibilities were divided and shared by a primary and secondary chief executive officer. Prior to the 1960s, founder Paul Galvin and his son Robert had shared these obligations.[14] Galvin championed several reorganization efforts and product/market shifts, as well as a variety of participatory management, executive education, and strategic planning programs.[15] Motorola's strategic pioneership also led to a technology innovation planning process or "technology roadmap" that involved the periodic projection of future technological developments and the subsequent planning and review of progress against that projection.

Between the late 1950s and the mid-1970s, the fate of three segments—government programs and space exploration, consumer electronics, and mobile communications—paced the company's future. The combination of defense and semiconductors positioned favorably Motorola to participate in government-funded programs. The company's efforts in the miniaturization of electronic components, as well as its experience in radio communications and government projects, contributed to its long-standing role in the space race. In 1969, astronaut Neil Armstrong's first words from the moon to earth were relayed by a Motorola radio transponder aboard the Apollo 11 lunar module.

Two-Way Radio and Pager Markets

In the postwar era, the rapid growth of the two-way radio market led Motorola to intensify its focus on radio communications products. Before transistors, mobile and portable radios were heavy and bulky and required a relatively large amount of power to operate. New technologies began to fuel the business, which led to new products and services. Just as in semiconductors, these advances in radio communications prompted Motorola to build an international market for its pagers and paging systems. The Communications Product Division had initiated international expansion in the 1960s and 1970s. It eventually distributed its products in ninety-one countries and established manufacturing facilities in Toronto, Canada; Wiesbaden, West Germany; and Melbourne, Australia. Joint production ventures were established in Tel Aviv, Israel, and Bramley, South Africa.

The rapid evolution of the two-way radio and pager markets went hand in hand with Motorola's entry into the nascent cellular markets. When the FCC proposed the allocation of frequencies for a new mobile service based on small radio coverage areas (i.e., cells) in 1970, Motorola designed its DynaTAC system, which comprised both mobile and portable wireless telephones. A decade before the first commercial cell network in the United States, the vendor embraced the cellular future: "DynaTAC system will ultimately permit personal radiotelephone service to be offered to hundreds of thousands of individuals in a given city."[16] In the United States, however, it was a decade of delay, frustration, and resignation, due to regulatory obstacles. "To stay ahead of the competition," argued Martin Cooper, the Motorolan father of the first cell phone, "you had to understand the market and you had to understand the technology—and not just one technology, but a whole bunch of technologies."[17]

It was this combination of technology novelty and systemic complexity, coupled with the requisite business savvy, which would emerge as the hallmark of mobile market leaders in the cellular era.

Quality and Globalization

Because of technology innovation and accelerating globalization, the industry environment was shifting. Semiconductors remained the foundation of the electronics strategy, but the company's traditional strengths were eroding. Three trends reflect these dilemmas. First, from the late 1950s to the 1980s, Motorola's participation in government programs and space exploration, though initially highly successful, steered its capabilities away from competitive markets. These ventures ended with its Iridium debacle.[18] Second, although the company had built its reputation in consumer electronics, it was forced to exit the business by the 1970s.[19] Third, along with government space contracts and consumer electronics, Motorola had been active in wireless communications, but these markets were about to enter a period of turmoil as well. Three trends—participation in high-profile profit disasters, failure to respond to the globalization of cost-leadership strategies, and getting locked in with fading markets—would later contribute to Motorola's delays in the 2G platform technology (digital cellular) and globalization (GSM).

By the mid-1970s, Motorola's new international headquarters was opened in Schaumburg, Illinois, as the company rushed into the emerging microprocessor business while investing in M&As in computers and communications. As its organizational capabilities no longer provided a match for the novel technologies and systemic complexity, Motorola boosted its internal training and pioneered the idea of lifelong learning, which was quickly embraced by its Nordic rivals.[20] Under Galvin's leadership, no employee with more than ten years of service could be fired without his approval. These practices originated from the Depression Era. But by the 1970s, the world looked very different.

Motorola was no longer the sole pioneer; nor was it alone in emergent industries. In the past, the company had been a multinational. Now it was set for globalization. New rivals were proliferating worldwide, cycle times became shorter, and quality requirements were more stringent. Yet Motorola was instilling systems and controls that rewarded those who had ensured success in the old environment. It was an effort to face the future by looking behind. Japanese attackers such as Sony and Matsushita assailed Motorola's consumer electronics businesses with global efficiency, while building global brand awareness. Others challenged the U.S. giant's semiconductor business. "Before, we were simply reacting to ideas that the operating guys had," said Kenneth Bane, then-VP and director of corporate strategy. "[Then] we began strategizing. We began thinking about where we wanted the company to go."[21]

What made Motorola's posture different from many other U.S. companies was the fact that it was willing to pursue a global strategy in every business it competed in, to fight back. As Bob Galvin declared that he wanted the vendor to remain the leader in two-way radio communications and capture the number-one spot in semiconductors worldwide, EVP Stephen Levy pointed to the long-term impact of Japanese attacks: "We have learned our lesson from our experience in consumer electronics. Never again do we want to be caught with a strategy that relies only on the America market."[22]

Strategically, the Motorolans linked three basic principles: global leverage, sticking to electronics as the foundation of new applications, and emergent industries. Any opportunity ignored was a viable entry point for a potential competitor. The vendor was not about to cede any application to its rivals. At least that was the intention.

"The Quality of Our Products Stinks"

In 1979, Art Sundry, Motorola's top communications sales executive, announced in a company meeting: "Gentlemen, we have a problem. The quality of our products stinks."[23] That year, Motorola began to scrutinize the overall quality of its products and operations. A companywide total quality program was under way by the mid-1980s. The rise of Japanese competition necessitated the internalization of the quality movement. As part of its efforts to become the supplier of the highest-quality goods and services possible (i.e., "total customer satisfaction"), Motorola's executives initiated talks with a variety of customers, including Apple, Ford, Federal Express, and the U.S. Department of Defense. In the early 1980s, it might take three years for a new product to move from the blueprint stage to completion. One solution involved concurrent engineering (CE), a methodology of product development that led to a significant reduction in cost and development time without sacrificing the desired product specifications. While CE and other new managerial approaches were necessary and ensured short-term gains, there was little in this learning that could not be imitated and competed away in the 2G era. "Global competition, with or without the Japanese, is inescapable," observed Stephen Levy. "You can run but you can't hide."[24]

As the U.S. samurai looked East, Euro-Nordic rivals attacked from the North.

The Japanese Challenge

By the spring of 1983, Galvin thought that Motorola was poised for a new competitive era. Having just weathered a recession in the semiconductor industry, the company had suffered losses (profits slipped by 6 percent at worst) but less so than Texas Instruments and Intel (49 percent and 72 percent, respectively). Rapid expansion and corresponding increases in sales and earnings resulted in new managerial challenges that exacerbated existing problems. Meanwhile, growth-driven complacency made change more difficult. Unfortunately, the company was among the world's leading producers in those industry segments—two-way radios, cellular telephone systems, semiconductors, and microprocessor chips—that Japanese firms had "targeted" (through cooperative efforts to break into and capture a specific international market) and "dumped" (by selling products at less than "fair value" to boost market share rapidly). Testifying before the Senate Foreign Relations Committee in September 1982, Galvin argued that U.S. policy on technology trade should stress the fact that:

> . . . [America] will not accept a situation where foreign national industrial policies, based on nonmarket mechanisms and unreasonable trade practices, enable any country to disrupt U.S. markets, prevent reasonable access to its home markets, or give unjustified advantage to its firms in pursuing Third World markets.[25]

Among the internal threats, Galvin paid increasing attention to a wide variety of "structural concerns." These challenges could be reduced to problems of organizational capabilities, including:

- Problems inherent in the size and complexity of the matrix organization
- Conflicts between Motorola's customer-oriented functional managers

(i.e., downstream activities) and more technology-driven product-line managers (i.e., upstream activities)

- Absence of project champions to monitor developments through all cycles, coupled with ever-lengthening product development cycles
- Top-down and mechanistic initiatives to nurture cooperation among units
- Triumvirate CEO office, in which three leaders often had overlapping functions but conflicting views of strategy

The succession mechanism that had functioned well in the past was crumbling. "They call us three bears," noted John F. Mitchell, president and assistant COO, "and they ask, 'Why can't you be single in voice, style, and direction?'"[26] But as far as Motorola's senior executives were concerned, Japan was problem number one. The company had repeatedly been denied a chance to compete in the Japanese home market. By 1981, it mounted an advertising campaign titled "Meeting Japan's Challenge" targeting U.S. business and political leaders: "In high technology electronics, Americans are both the creators and leaders. And companies like Motorola intend to keep it that way. . . . Innovation and imagination in this field, as in others, is American. It is from this solid innovation base that we must meet Japan's challenge. . . .[27]

In the late 1980s, Motorola set out to achieve its fundamental objective— "total customer satisfaction"—by reaffirming its key beliefs, goals, and operational initiatives, which stressed the new and popular quality disciplines. Among other things, it set an ambitious companywide goal of achieving a hundredfold improvement in quality by 1992. It adopted a quality measure called "Six Sigma" that called for a defect rate of no more than 3.4 million opportunities for defects on a part (99.99966 percent defect-free). After the first Malcolm Baldrige National Quality Award, the emphasis on quality and cycle time became an inherent part of Motorola's corporate credo.

Worldwide Dispersion: Product Structure

In 1979, one-third of Motorola's sales were international. The company had made substantial long-term investments outside of the United States and had twenty-seven major facilities worldwide and some eighty-five non-U.S. sales offices. A year later, Motorola's net sales climbed to $3.1 billion and net earnings exceeded $186 million. With 71,500 employees, Motorola had extended its product base to home radios, phonographs, televisions, transistors, and semiconductor components. Facilities were dispersed worldwide, but they were not managed globally. In 1983—with the advent of mobile communications—Motorola had sold many consumer electronics businesses and moved into new markets based on new technologies. By then, the company included five geographically dispersed segments (net sales information is in parentheses):

- Semiconductor Products Sector ($1.3 billion) manufactured micropro-cessors, memory chips, and integrated circuits.

- Communications Sector ($1.5 billion) produced two-way radios, paging devices, and cellular telephones.

- Information Systems Group ($485 million) manufactured an integrated line of data transmission and distributed data processing systems.

- Automotive and Industrial Electronics Group produced fuel-injection systems, electronic engine controls, and instrumentation and electronic appliance controls.

- Government Electronics Group conducted research in satellite communications technology. (Combined sales for automotive, industrial and governments electronics was $564 million in 1983.)

The *product*-focused structure had grown from the concern that a company's obligation was to listen to its customers and that a large, highly centralized organization might not be responsive enough. In the aftermath of World War II, Motorola decentralized its operations. In the 1950s, Paul Galvin formed divisions. In the early 1960s, Bob Galvin launched product lines with product managers who handled specific marketing and engineering areas, whereas manufacturing and sales functions remained centralized. Product specialization and organizational decentralization was necessitated by increasingly multinational operations. By the early 1980s the structure, consisting of groups and sectors, was in place, along with a multilayered matrix system of management. These organizational capabilities endured until the digital transition in the mid-1990s. Motorola was strong in responsiveness but growing weaker in innovation. At the onset of the 2G era, the new globally driven Nordic challengers had found the Achilles heel of the U.S. giant—just as Asian challengers in the 3G transition would attack the weakness of U.S. and Euro-Nordic leaders (namely, their cost-efficiencies).

How Motorola Won the 1G Leadership

In 1972, Motorola delivered a proposal to the Federal Communications Commission (FCC) for a mobile and portable cellular system. A license was granted five years later for the installation and demonstration of an experimental system in the Washington, D.C./Baltimore area. In addition to equipment and service for 2,500 customers, the system provided AT&T with cellular phones for its test system in Chicago. By 1982, the company saw the cellular car telephone market as a key opportunity. It had invested more than $100 million and 1,000 work years of engineering and manufacturing resources in pursuit of this new market. In 1983, the first of Motorola's DynaTAC systems was placed into commercial operation. "During the next ten years," thought the executives, "the cellular business could represent $1 billion worth of opportunity to the company in the United States, with an equivalent potential from international cellular markets.[28]

Toward Analog Cellular

In 1983, Motorola's pioneer system in Baltimore was granted one of the first commercial operating licenses in the United States. After fifteen to twenty years and $150 million to $200 million in development, the Communications products division recorded its first domestic sale only in 1984, when its cellular telephone network—the DynaTAC cellular system—began commercial operation. That year, sales in the Communications Sector soared 27 percent to a record $2.1 billion, and operating profits improved substantially.[29] The company formed the General Systems Group while combining Motorola Computer Systems, Inc. (formerly Four-Phase Systems, Inc.) with the Cellular group. More than eighty Motorola cellular systems were in service or planned in North America, Europe, the Middle East, and Asia.

In the manufacture of portable equipment, the company focused on four critical functions: *size, weight, cost,* and *current drain* (a driving function of the size and weight of the battery). In the formal technology planning, independent of market studies and specific product development planning, the company developed five- and ten-year technology roadmaps for these four forces. After the introduction of cellular systems in the United States, there were soon three times as many Japanese as American producers of cellular phones. These challengers learned quickly to match size, weight, and drain requirements, but their attack targeted cost through price competition. When Japanese manufacturers cut their prices to half those charged by U.S. firms, Motorola appealed to the United States Trade Representative and, again, won its case.

By 1989, Motorola launched its MicroTAC personal cellular phone, the smallest and lightest portable on the market at the time (see Exhibit 8-2). It was the size of a wallet and weighed less than eleven ounces. The development and production of this phone was made possible by the technologists in the cellular and semiconductor groups as well as corporate research. However, market research was not the primary force behind MicroTAC. Like Sony's Walkman, Motorola's cell phone emerged from efforts to create new customers rather than do market research with old ones. Or as former Motorola CEO George Fisher put it in 1989:

> . . . [C]ustomers will always pull you in directions of interest to them. As a technology leader, sometimes we have to show people what we can do. The portable telephone is a good example. Motorola jumped way out in front on the car phone—so far out in front that there were pictures in magazines two or three years before the systems were actually available. We didn't have thousands of people saying, "We want portable telephones that look a certain

Exhibit 8-2. Motorola's 1G phones.

Portable radiotelephone for the DynaTAC *cellular system. In 1982, Motorola offered the world's broadest cellular product line. [Motorola Annual Report, 1982.]*

DynaTAC portable cellular telephone in Hong Kong, where Motorola was part of a joint venture that operated the system. [Motorola Annual Report, 1985.]

In 1989, Motorola introduced the MicroTAC personal cellular telephone, the smallest and lightest on the market. Like Sony's Walkman, Motorola's cell phone emerged from efforts to create new customers rather than from market research with old ones.

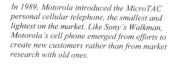

The new StarTAC wearable cellular phone. It was the world's smallest and, at 3.1 ounces, the world's lightest cellular phone. The first wearable cellular phone, it was introduced in January 1996. [Motorola Annual Report 1995.]

SOURCE: Motorola, Inc.

way and have particular kinds of features." We presented it to the world. Unfortunately, the regulatory bureaucracy slowed us down once we introduced the product. Other people were able to catch up while we were forced to sit on our hands.[30]

This boldness was typical of Motorola's cellular activities in the early analog era. Between 1989 and 1993, the number of cellular users soared from 7 million to more than 20 million, and more than half of Motorola's cellular revenues came from overseas. From the late 1980s to the mid-1990s, Motorola was the market leader. Unfortunately, MicroTAC was a marvel only in the analog world. It reflected strategic and technological capabilities of an era that was fading away.

In 1990, Motorola discontinued development of wireless infrastructure based on a TDMA standard in favor of an alternative, CDMA, which was expected to have higher capacity to carry phone calls. By 1998, the lack of TDMA equipment meant that Motorola could not supply 25 percent of the digital U.S. wireless infrastructure market. Several important customers— GTE, Southwestern Bell, BellSouth, and Metro One—dropped Motorola because of poor switching capabilities in its wireless equipment. Three years later, Motorola and Northern Telecom discontinued their joint venture for wireless equipment. The absence of a strong switch partner hurt Motorola's ability to deliver end-to-end wireless networks. Meanwhile, the company raised $800 million for the Iridium satellite system, which proved to be a financial nightmare.

In the early 1990s, 85 percent of the cell phones McCaw Cellular sold to its subscribers had been made by Motorola. By the end of 1997, fewer than 40 percent of AT&T Wireless's cell phones were Motorolas. Even as it was falling behind competition in quality, the vendor's bullying tactics caused a backlash among wholesalers, who complained that Motorola's strategy of distributing phones through only a few companies—a doomed effort to retain high margins and price premiums—made competitive purchasing impossible.[31] In 1994, Motorola still claimed some 60 percent of the U.S. market in wireless phones.[32] But the writing was on the wall.

Visions, Transition, Defeats

In the late 1980s, Robert W. Galvin remained chairman of the board, but Motorola entered a new era as George M. C. Fisher was elected president and CEO. The new management triumvirate consisted of Fisher, Gary L. Tooker, and Christopher Galvin, grandson of Paul Galvin. The three saw global expansion as the key issue for Motorola's future. "The globalization of Motorola is one of the more profound trends that has been developing within the corporation over the last few years. Non-U.S. revenues as a percentage of the total have increased from approximately 27 percent in 1985 to more than 36 percent in 1988."[33]

In the 1930s, Motorola was a pioneer in providing information by two-way radio for people on the move. The early efforts in solid-state electronics allowed the company to extend this leadership. In the 1970s, Motorola applied digital computing and control to the way information was communicated. By 1980, the company still saw *all* of its segments as branches of semiconductors: "Motorola operates predominantly in *one industry, electronic equipment and components* [author's italics].[34] Under Fisher's leadership at the turn of the 1990s, the company sought to 'build on [its] semiconductor technology and market position to be the world's premier provider of products, systems, and services for communication, computing, and control for people and machines on the move.'[35] The problem was that even the most favorable strategic positioning had little relevance if it occurred in an environment that was about to fade out. Also, Fisher himself left for Eastman Kodak Co. At Motorola, Fisher had earned his reputation for betting big on new manufacturing technologies and products. He also advocated a management system that would have flipped the organization, thus empowering the sales force.

> We want to put the salesperson at the top of the organization. The rest of us then serve the salesperson. . . . When most of these companies began, they were driven by brilliant technologists, so the organization grew up reversing the engineer and the scientist—we do at Motorola, and we always will. But . . . there's an adversarial relationship between sales and technologists. We don't know precisely how we're going to make this change.[36]

With Fisher's departure, Tooker was elected vice chairman of the board and CEO.[37] Even as clouds gathered over Motorola, he saw little need for strategic changes. Between 1990 and 1995, Motorola's revenue almost tripled, from $10.9 billion to $27 billion. Net profit margin climbed from less than 4 percent to almost 7 percent, even as the number of the employees soared almost 50 percent, from 105,000 to 142,000. Motorola witnessed the most profitable years of its history. Now it would experience the most troublesome years of its existence.

Tooker's views dominated—until there was no choice but to replace both the strategy and the strategist and to take another look at Fisher's diagnosis.

Reorganization and Refocus

In 1994, *Fortune* had declared Motorola "the company that almost everyone loves to love."[38] Soon the company that could do nothing wrong, "a big company that sizzles," was being roasted by customers, partners, suppliers, and analysts. To many investors, it became the company that almost everybody loved to hate.

Until the 1990s, the mobile business rewarded globalization strategies that stressed innovation *or* decentralization *or* cost leadership. Motorola's management reflected the first two in the 1G era. But as it fell behind the digital train, the innovation advantage was lost. Concurrently, the organizational capabilities that were left were about to fall apart.

Motorola was organized in six business groups:

- Semiconductor Products (microprocessors, memory chips, and integrated circuits)
- General Systems (cellular telephones, personal communications, and information technologies)
- Messaging, Information, and Media Products (paging and wireless data systems)
- Land Mobile Products (two-way radios and network services)
- Government and Systems Technology (satellite communications and tactical electronics)[39]
- Automotive, Energy, and Controls Group (energy products, electronic components, and systems)[40]

In the past, the independence of the six business groups—and their culture of "warring tribes"—was moderated by regional directors and the CEO office. In the early 1990s, rapid growth mitigated these influences. And in the latter half of the decade, declining fortunes unleashed the destructive forces of the warring tribes. As the Nordic players tried to globalize through innovation *and* decentralization *and* cost leadership, Motorola would fall behind in all of these areas.

The 2G Migration

Despite a tradition of anticipation and renewal, a succession mechanism that stressed continuity amid discontinuities, and a host of control mechanisms, Motorola failed to pioneer, lead, or dominate digital cellular. It underpruned for years and made critical decisions only when the game was over.

Complacency and Failure

The signs of erosion became apparent in early 1995, when AirTouch Communications, then a leading wireless operator, was supposed to have a sophisticated multimillion-dollar digital cellular system from Motorola up and running in Los Angeles. Technical problems caused lines to go dead. *Business Week* asked: "[H]as Motorola hit a bit of momentary turbulence, or is the high-flying star finally coming down to earth?" The magazine provided its own response: "While [Motorola] waits for long-term bets to pay off, profits erode."[41] The uneasiness escalated in January 1996, when the company announced that fourth-quarter earnings would fall 16 percent to $432 million. Senior executives blamed much of the slide on cellular, but problems extended from the business strategy to the corporation on the whole.

In 1992, Nokia initiated a radical focus strategy. Ericsson followed in its footsteps soon thereafter. In contrast, Motorola was still competing in a wide variety of markets, extending from tiny chips for cars to U.S. Army ground stations for airborne surveillance equipment. Meanwhile, the adversarial relationship between Motorola's technologists and marketers deepened. As a growing proportion of its products were in consumer markets, the problems grew and red flags rose on Wall Street.

In the mid-1990s, cellular accounted for 40 percent of Motorola's sales. After three years of 30 percent in annual growth, demand in the United States began to slow, even as the Nordic rivals—Ericsson and Nokia—stepped up their efforts in the American market and worldwide. As the price war hit Motorola's earnings, its market share (42 percent in 1994) began to erode. And while Motorola had bet on the promising but slowly emerging CDMA, delays allowed a challenger, Qualcomm, to capture the CDMA handset market. Between 1995 and 1998, the company's revenues climbed slowly from $27 billion to $29.4 billion, whereas its net income dived from $1.8 billion to a net loss of $962 million. A reduction of workforce from 150,000 to 133,000 was insufficient. Shareholder return averaged less than 1 percent annually, in contrast to an average of 54 percent in the previous three years. And the problems went still deeper.

Falling Behind

For years, Motorola had supplied most mobile phones to Ameritech, one of the Baby Bells. As the telco initiated digital migration in the summer of 1997, Motorola was not ready to supply the phones and Ameritech turned to Qualcomm. As AT&T initiated migration into the 2G era with its Digital One Rate plan, Motorola did not have a digital telephone to supply. The most popular models—phones that could handle both analog and digital calls at two radio frequencies—were not ready even by Christmas 1998 (a season when 40 percent of all cell phones were sold). Even though it was failing in the market, Motorola continued to bargain for price premium (StarTAC in January 1996, then the V series phone in fall 1998). Finally, it suffered from industrywide problems, including a downturn in the semiconductors and paging, as well as Asia's currency turmoil. Motorola had become slow and expensive in a business that thrived on speed and affordability. Between 1994 and 1998, Motorola's market share in the United States fell from 60 percent to 34 percent.[42] These problems were compounded by product delays, marketing miscues, and bully tactics.

The equipment business was hit as well. In spring 1998, despite its past reputation for quality, Motorola found itself amid customer complaints. It lost a $500 million contract with PrimeCo, an influential mobile operator (later part of Verizon Wireless). Subsequently, Motorola lost ground to Lucent Technologies and Northern Telecom (Nortel) in the United States and to Ericsson worldwide. Unlike these three tough rivals, Motorola still did not own a switching technology, a costly but critical component in telecommunications. It was the sole supplier of cellular service without such an end-to-end solution. As the new communications structure was put in place in summer 1998, Galvin and Merle Gilmore (president of the communications organization) tackled Motorola's troubled wireless equipment business. After the top-two executives of the group left for a start-up, Gilmore recruited Bo Hedfors, the CEO of top equipment maker Ericsson's U.S. operations. To catch up, Motorola announced bold joint ventures with Cisco Systems and Sun Microsystems, with which it hoped to develop a packet-switching technology that could shuttle voice, data, and video from the Internet to wireless devices. To realize the "broadband living experience," Lucent acquired Ascend Communications, while Nortel bought Bay Networks. By early 1999, Motorola lost its lead in the handset market to Nokia for the first time ever.

Strategic Turbulence

Panic reinforced a sense of urgency at Motorola. In 1998, the company's executives had a showdown with engineers over web browsers being built into Motorola phones. The engineers didn't see much urgency in developing web-enabled phones. But Janiece Webb and other executives insisted that Motorola should offer trial equipment by early 1999. Meanwhile, pressures grew over its production facilities, and it agreed to outsource about 15 percent of its manufacturing to Flextronics International Ltd. in a five-year, $30 billion deal. Market downturn spoiled the huge deal.[43]

Motorola had raised or secured deals worth $3 billion for its remaining investments in a slate of international wireless operators. By March 2001, it began selling these cellular stakes, expecting to net another $2 billion by the third quarter of 2001.[44] The sale decision fit with Motorola's broader focus objectives. But compared to its rivals, particularly Nokia and Ericsson, it was half a decade late. Both Nordic players had engaged in focus strategies and noncore divestitures in the early 1990s—*before* digital migration in the cellular business.[45]

"Motorola for the Digital Age"

In January 1997, Christopher B. Galvin took over as CEO and set out to find the right balance between traditional Motorola and the need for radical change. But the critics were disappointed. Motorola, they claimed, opted for nepotism.

A year later, Galvin huddled in top-secret meetings with COO Robert L. Growney to figure out how to remake Motorola into a major Internet player. The two executives understood that this required a radical change in the company's culture. The internal competition it had prided itself on was now hurting product development and customer relationships. Motorola needed a sweeping restructuring to replace its warring tribes. Motorola would combine all of the thirty units that made cell phones, wireless equipment, satellite products, and cable modems into one large communications division. The idea was to leverage resources and reduce the old adversarial culture. The goal, Galvin told the group, was to create a Motorola for the Digital Age.[46]

The Motorola Communications Enterprise established separate sectors for consumer products, industrial equipment, and systems integration. Some divisions were larger than many well-known companies. The Personal Communications Sector, for instance, became a $11 billion business that built about 65 million devices a year (according to Motorola, about half of such devices worldwide). The structure also included groups to foster relations with existing customers, develop new businesses, and address Internet-related concerns. The reorganization signaled the rise of Merle Gilmore—a close adviser to Galvin, former head of the unit that made two-way radios, and chief of Motorola's European operations—who became president of the revamped communications organization. The semiconductor business was similarly streamlined. Leadership became the measure of success. "We aspire to be number one in all of our businesses," said Galvin. "Some have been able to achieve it, and others have achieved second or third place. But every entity is seeking to be best in that segment."[47]

From Warring Tribes to Cooperation

In the old days of few competitors and low-intensity competition, "warring tribes" had resulted in high-quality engineering. But this culture of conflict and decentralization had become a burden, slowing down product development and increasing manufacturing costs, thus contributing to Motorola's slow migration from analog to digital. Under the old model, Gilmore noted, "we had four sectors that were very independent business units, each with its own technology solution, in some cases competing with customers, and not doing much portfolio management." With the new model, "we've put the pieces of the old business together, put our resources together."[48]

Some analysts viewed the reorganization as a positive signal for change management. Others remained skeptical, arguing that the changes were cosmetic. To speed up the change and enhance expectations, Galvin announced cost-cutting goals and a companywide restructuring, including slashing annual manufacturing costs by 4 percent ($750 million) and laying off 15,000 workers. As Motorola rushed to create new wireless products and markets, it bet on controversial investments in emerging industries, such as satellite communications and cable modems. It also took a charge against earnings of $1.9 billion. By mid-1999, its shares, which had sold for less than $40 the previous fall, sold for almost $100—a leap of $30 billion in market value. Motorola was benefiting from its restructuring and refocusing efforts, the revival of demand in the Asian market, and the inflated industry valuations. A large part of Galvin's restructuring was to intensify Motorola's focus on the Internet. "Being fast, smart, quick, agile—this is what will make the company different so we can avoid the issues that occurred in our past," argued Galvin.[49]

In early 2000, Motorola acquired General Instrument in a $17 billion deal. The acquisition united one of the world's best-known consumer electronics makers with one of the cable television industry's leading equipment manufacturers. Galvin vowed that the pact would make Motorola a vital participant in the emerging broadband market for interactive cable TV services.[50]

Success Drivers: Fall from Grace

By 2000, Motorola saw itself as a global leader in providing integrated communications solutions and embedded electronic solutions (see Exhibit 8-3). It operated in five business segments: Personal Communications; Semiconductors; Global Telecommunications; Commercial, Government, and Industrial; Broadband Communications; and Integrated Electronics. In the spring, Galvin was heralded as a turnaround artist who had managed to revive Motorola for the digital era. By the fall, the company lost around half of its stock market value in just six months. The consolidation of the technology sector in the United States and the costly 3G bidding in Europe contributed to these problems, but they originated from internal strategic issues and were reflected in considerable management turnover.[51]

Motorola had fallen from grace. After the monopoly era and the transition era (see Exhibit 8-4), the new competition was merciless.

The Monopoly Era

In the 1930s, Motorola built its capabilities in battery eliminators, then moved into radio. Gradually, the small contractor evolved into a manufacturer that entered American homes, cars, and police departments. Before the war era, it remained a hungry but minor supplier. Disruptive opportunities came with the use of FM communications in World War II. In the late 1940s, Motorola began substantial internal R&D, which was critical to its emerging electronics strategy and to competition in the technology sector. The initial thrust, however, was in semiconductors. In the mobile business, a new era ensued with the 1956 consent decree, which opened AT&T's supply chain (Western Electric) while boosting the expansion of the independent operators (RCCs). With the decree, cutting-edge R&D and new product development diffused from Bell Labs to Motorola as well. These early efforts and investments were rewarded in the early 1G era, when the vendor captured the dominant position in equipment manufacturing in the United States. While AT&T had dominated the first consumer service experiments (MTS and IMTS), Motorola pioneered the large-scale AMPS markets, as well as the leading products and services—primarily in the United States, but in several overseas markets, as well.

From the late 1920s until World War II, Motorola's operations were dictated by its entrepreneurial strategy. A new era began with defense contracting, which resulted in high-volume capabilities. Concurrently, the vendor developed an electronics strategy, which accounted for its magnificent expansion for fifty years, until the mid-1990s. The embrace of the strategy was accompanied by organizational decentralization, which deepened over time. In the 1970s, Motorola met the Japanese challenge, but unlike so many other U.S. leaders, it did not give up. Instead, it struggled to implement those activities that accounted for the success of the new Japanese challengers, from quality management to concurrent engineering and flexible manufacturing.

Between 1928 and World War II, Motorola expanded from a local con-

---

Exhibit 8-3. Motorola's business and geographic segments (1977–2000).

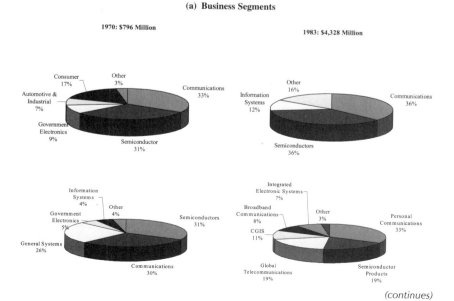

(a) **Business Segments**

1970: $796 Million

1983: $4,328 Million

(continues)

Exhibit 8-3. (Continued).

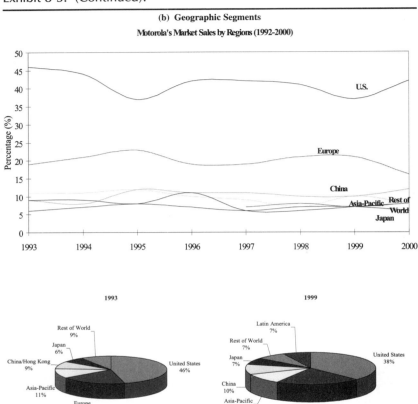

(b) Geographic Segments

Motorola's Market Sales by Regions (1992-2000)

SOURCE: Company reports.

tractor to a national player, particularly through defense contracting. After the postwar transition and increasing R&D, the electronics strategy led to internationalization. From 1959 to the mid-1970s, these activities comprised primarily exports, joint ventures, and foreign direct investment. With the Japanese challenge, Motorola boosted foreign direct investment (FDI), especially in the Asia-Pacific region.

The Transition Era

Despite substantial R&D and the first mobile efforts at corporate innovation in 1987, Motorola failed to invest appropriately in digital cellular R&D.

Exhibit 8-4. Motorola: drivers of wireless growth (1928–present).

THE MONOPOLY ERA

Products
- In 1930s, early capabilities in radio; disruptive opportunities vis-à-vis FM communications and World War II; postwar R&D.
- The 1956 consent decree opens AT&T's supply chain; expansion of RCCs
- In the early 1G era, dominant position in the United States, via AMPS.

Operations
- Defense contracting leads to high-volume capabilities; scope through scale.
- After World War II, fifty-year electronics strategy; organizational decentralization.
- Responding to Japanese challenge; total quality management internally, lobbying for aggressive trade policy externally.

Markets
- Between 1928 and WWII, transitions from a local contractor to a national player.
- Early internationalization from 1959 to the mid-1970s, primarily through exports, joint ventures, and some FDI.
- With the Japanese challenge, substantial FDI.

THE TRANSITION ERA

Products
- Despite R&D and corporate innovation, delayed transition to digital cellular.
- The Bell breakup and mistaken cellular policies cause market risk and uncertainty, while constraining digital cellular R&D.
- Due to transitional delays, AMPS triumph in U.S. endures into the mid-1990s, but Motorola falls behind in the digital cellular standards, products, and services.

Operations
- Increasing decentralization deteriorates into internal "warring tribes."
- Domestic AMPS triumph hides erosion in operational capabilities.
- Motorola's rivals reorganize and refocus activities; Motorola does not.

Markets
- Despite substantial investments overseas, Motorola's "globalization" builds primarily on the U.S./U.K. axis and a few key markets worldwide.
- None of the pull or push drivers of the European small-country vendors.
- First vendor to pioneer the Chinese market, but the Tiananmen crisis allows rivals to catch up.

THE COMPETITIVE ERA

Products
- Failure to catch-up with Euro-Nordic R&D and NPD.
- U.S. loses worldwide cluster and market leadership; Motorola's customers are no longer the most sophisticated worldwide.
- Failure to regain leadership by leapfrogging technology generations.

Operations
- Starting in 1997, explicit efforts at reorganization and refocus.
- Eclipse of electronics strategy forces senior executives to confront "warring tribes."
- Increased use of outsourcing.

Markets
- Motorola fails to develop global focus strategies in parallel with Euro-Nordic leaders.
- Motorola considers itself global, but overseas revenues are half of those of its Nordic rivals.
- Through the Tiananmen crisis, substantial presence in China, but rivals capture significant chunks of the market.

In the United States, the breakup of the Bell System caused substantial market turmoil and interfered with innovation and policy efforts to facilitate the 2G transition. Because of these technology delays, the AMPS triumph endured well into the mid-1990s in the United States, which boosted Motorola's cellular profitability through the early part of the decade. Motorola appeared to be invincible, but it had already been defeated. Seizing the disruptive opportunity inherent in the digital transition, European vendors captured industry leadership, leaving Motorola behind in digital cellular standards, products, and services.

Through the transition, the electronics strategy deepened Motorola's decentralization. Like most American companies, the vendor sought scope through scale. This structure and its slow-moving autonomous hierarchies fit the stable environment. It fit the requirements of the monopoly era, but it was no match for the transition era. Rather, industry ferment favored fast-moving, cross-functional team networks, which fit the dynamic environment. As the Nordic vendors exploited their strengths in agility and flexibility, Motorola's structure deteriorated into internal "warring tribes." Yet these delays were not perceived as such at the time. In cellular operations, the domestic triumph covered the erosion in operational capabilities. As Motorola's rivals reorganized and refocused their activities, the U.S. vendor did not. Rather, the AMPS success prepared its failure in the digital cellular market.

Motorola's stated "globalization" strategy built primarily on the axis between the United States and the U.K., as well as a few other key markets. It was not a global strategy. Strictly speaking, it was an effort to clone little Motorolas in the more valuable regions of the global chessboard. That strategy served Motorola well, but only as long as it dominated innovation worldwide. Compared to other U.S. firms, Motorola was certainly more internationally oriented and responsive to local conditions, but it had none of the pull or push drivers of the European small-country vendors. When everything was said and done, the "action" remained in the United States as far as Motorola was concerned, whereas to the Nordic vendors, access to and leadership in multiple overseas markets was a question of life or death. Furthermore, political complications involved the role of the United States as the only remaining superpower. Motorola was the first vendor to pioneer the Chinese market, but the Tiananmen crisis provided a disruptive opportunity for its rivals.

The Competitive Era

With the dawn of the competitive era in the 1990s, Motorola's efforts to catch up with Nordic R&D and new product development failed. It was complacent until the middle of the growth decade. When it finally awakened, its leadership was gone and the Nordic players already dominated most markets. It did too little too late. Motorola then aimed at the 2.5G and 3G standards, hoping to win in the next-generation products and services what it had lost in the 1990s. It did pioneer some such products (such as GPRS) in the United States, but did little to boost its full product portfolio in the United States or in worldwide markets. Besides, this was not a purposeful strategy; it was an attempt at short-term gains to develop a strategy. Unfortunately, Motorola's self-inflicted strategic wounds went hand in hand with the erosion of national competitive advantage as the United States lost its worldwide cluster and market leadership to the cellular competition. The implications were far-reaching. In the competitive era, the critical consequences pertained to the downstream side of the value chain. In brief, Motorola's cellular customers were no longer the most sophisticated worldwide; this distinction now belonged to customers in the new Nordic mobile clusters and in Japan.

In 1997, Motorola finally initiated explicit efforts to reorganize and refocus. Now the eclipse of the electronics strategy forced senior management to confront the "warring tribes." Meanwhile, efforts at efficiency resulted in increasing outsourcing. Motorola's Nordic rivals had engaged in global focus strategies in the early 1990s, whereas the U.S. vendor followed only at the end of the decade. Although Motorola considered itself global, the proportion of its overseas revenues was barely half of that of its Nordic rivals. After the Tiananmen crisis, Motorola remained a substantial presence in China, but Nokia, Ericsson, Qualcomm, and others had captured significant chunks of the market. It was no longer *the* player in China; it was one of several.

Motorola's electronics strategy was no longer effective. In the coming years, the company saw substantial high-growth opportunities in broadband, wireless, and the Internet. Its strategic focus was at three nodal points in the converging value chain: solutions on a chip, integrated embedded solutions (i.e., chips and circuit boards that power everything from automotive dashboards to toasters), and end-to-end network solutions.[52] To beat the competition, it wanted to get into the "next big thing" before rivals. Strategically, these efforts were a dead-end. Success in 2.5G technologies was not likely to reverse the vendor's fortunes because its rivals were already building a learning curve in 4G. In another effort, Motorola depicted itself as a solutions business—hence, the acquisition of Starfish Software, a specialist in linking data between mobile devices and computers. This purchase was the eleventh key alliance since January 1997, when Galvin took over. But the Nordic vendors were even further in the R&D curve and had already established subsidiaries in Silicon Valley and other key software clusters in the United States. Meanwhile, Asian cost producers followed in their footsteps, even as the IT giants entered the industry.

Motorola had fallen behind in all three fields of the productivity frontier. Its products and services were no longer the most advanced worldwide, and it had lost the home base advantage with the most sophisticated customers. Operationally, it stumbled behind the more flexible Nordic vendors, and it could not match the cost capabilities of the new Asian producers. In the United States, it had pioneered international strategy, but the new era belonged to globalization. Like Nokia or Ericsson, Motorola could renew itself for a new era. But that would require far more radical changes.

Chapter 9

L. M. Ericsson: The Switching Giant

At the end of the 1990s, Ericsson dominated the wireless infrastructure market and Nokia dominated in handsets. These core segments accounted for 70 percent or more of the two companies' respective sales. Ericsson's home base was Sweden, Nokia's was Finland. Because both companies are Nordic, they have often been regarded as similar, especially outside the Nordic markets. The perception is understandable but naïve.

In contrast to the highly focused Nokia, Ericsson made enterprise networking and communications systems, modems, components, cable, and military electronics, including radar and communications systems. Unlike Nokia, the Swedish switching giant was integrated into semiconductors. Historically, the Finnish company was a latecomer in the telecom business, whereas Ericsson entered the emerging telecom industry only months after Bell's first phone call in 1876. Nokia initiated large-scale internationalization toward the end of the 1960s, whereas Ericsson was a major multinational well before World War I. And while both firms operate in similar wireless segments (infrastructure, handsets), their customer focus has been different since the 1980s. As a latecomer, Nokia entered the business by aligning with non-PTT operators that had the least to lose and the most to gain during the years of deregulation and privatization. The Finnish vendor focused on handsets, which helped to sell infrastructure equipment. As an early mover, Ericsson had aligned with incumbent operators that had the most to lose and the least to gain. Over time, the Swedish player has proved most successful in infrastructure, which it has used to sell handsets. For years, Ericsson has been widely regarded as an excellent engineering firm with little concern for marketing, whereas Nokia's strength has been consumer mass marketing. In Ericsson's case, the primary markets have comprised government and business customers. In Nokia's case, the primary customers have been consumer mass markets.

Ericsson and Nokia have very different evolutionary contexts in terms of strategy and organizational capabilities, history, internationalization, and customers. Strategically, Ericsson has had four key phases:

Entrepreneurial Strategy (1876–1880s)
Telecom Strategy (late 1880s–1960)

Growth Through Internationalization (1960–1988)
Refocus (1988–present)

In 1876, Alexander Graham Bell applied for a U.S. patent on the telephone. Only a few months later, Lars Magnus Ericsson opened a telegraph repair shop in Stockholm. Soon Ericsson upgraded the business from phone repair to manufacturing, expanded a small enterprise into a major Swedish corporation, vertically integrated into cable manufacturing and telephone operations, and secured a foothold in the worldwide markets. In the early 1930s, Ericsson lost its corporate autonomy for three decades due to the financial speculation of Ivan "The Match King" Kreuger. When Kreuger committed suicide in 1932, one of his creditors, Sosthenes Behn's ITT, acquired a substantial stake in Ericsson. The Swedish vendor's strategy, however, did not essentially change in the subsequent decades.

In 1960s, ITT sold its interest in Ericsson to the legendary Swedish industrialists, the Wallenberg family, bringing the unit back to Swedish control and enhancing the new growth strategy. This strategy picked up dramatically in 1975, when Ericsson introduced its computer-controlled exchange (AXE), which contributed to the operators' shift from electromechanics to computer control worldwide. It was AXE that boosted Ericsson's second wave of internationalization. Buoyed by success, the company rushed to unveil the "office of the future" in the early 1980s. This diversification into computers and office furniture was based on an exciting vision that never materialized. As profits plunged, Ericsson's leadership shifted to Hans Werthen, whose mission became to "save Ericsson." The company divested its noncore properties, refocused on telecommunications, and reshaped its AXE for the emerging cellular markets. The explosive wireless market boosted Ericsson's profitability from the late 1980s to the late 1990s.

By 2001 and after substantial management turbulence, Ericsson's share price fell to a record low amid extensive layoffs and more refocusing. With industry transition to the 3G era, old strategic anomalies resurfaced.

From Lars Magnus Ericsson to the Swedish Multinational

The founder of the switching giant was born in 1846 on a small farm in the province of Värmland in Sweden. A frail and religious youth, the young Lars Magnus Ericsson was driven by a "spiritually rich" life. He lost his father when he was eleven years old and had to earn a living with his mother and two younger sisters. His two older brothers had already left home. Without formal school attendance, Ericsson began work as a day laborer and, at the age of fourteen, worked on mining projects and railway construction jobs. "Deep down," he later acknowledged, "there smoldered an ever stronger desire to learn a trade, preferably in the mechanical branch."[1]

The Birth of L. M. Ericsson

At first, the young man headed a nail manufacturing department of the Charlottenberg Works. In 1867, after two years of learning and working "like a dog," he was hired at the Öller & Company Telegraph Factory, one of Sweden's industrial giants. Established a decade earlier, the workshop was the first in the electromechanical industry in Sweden to manufacture telegraph instruments and other equipment for telegraph stations. Ericsson spent six years at the job, while studying craftsmanship and languages including German and English. Driven by his desire to get further in life, the farm boy had stumbled on the precursor of the future L. M. Ericsson. But he needed to learn more.

Between 1873 and 1875, Ericsson received two grants from the Swedish Government to study in German and Swiss factories. At Siemens & Halske's factory in Berlin, he learned about the production and processes of different telegraph instruments. At Lud Loewe & Co.'s factory, he familiarized himself with the "advantages of the American machine tools." Additionally, he worked in Munich and Berne. Having studied physics, the "best practices" of the era, and American mass manufacturing, he was ready to strike out on his own.

On April 1, 1876, Ericsson launched an electromechanical workshop in a rented kitchen in Stockholm (see Exhibit 9-1). His working capital consisted of 1,000 kronor borrowed from a single investor and his labor force was his twelve-year-old assistant. But the timing was right. In the United States, Alexander Graham Bell had just obtained the first telephone patents, which was the first step toward a telecom revolution. And the location was not too bad, either. As the Bell system in the United States began rapid internationalization, Sweden was an attractive target. Though the market was very small, the Nordic country had a relatively skilled labor force and a well-developed infrastructure.

Ericsson's dealings with early public and private customers eventually led to long-standing relationships with telegraphy, fire departments, police administration, and rail transportation. Concurrently, he brought in a former workmate from Öller's, Carl Johan Andersson, as his first and only partner. The start-up became known formally as L. M. Ericsson & Co. At first, Ericsson concentrated on the repair of telegraph instruments and other electrical devices. But as he learned more, he began to improve equipment of his *own* design. He created a dial telegraph instrument for railway systems, and designed a fire telegraph system for small communities. In the latter case, the model became an enduring prototype of systems used in Sweden and abroad. Ericsson was able to leverage his pioneership from the tiny Swedish home base into larger-scale markets, which was critical in the long term.

By 1878, Ericsson no longer repaired telephones, but manufactured them. The firm grew rapidly, supplying equipment first to Swedish phone companies and later to other European companies. In the early 1880s, Ericsson was able to deter the U.S. Bell challengers in the Swedish and Norwegian markets. Over

Exhibit 9-1. The Ericsson legend.

Between 1877 and 1880, the workshop of Lars Magnus Ericsson was located at Oxtorget, in central Stockholm (above).

At 32, Ericsson married Hilda Simonsson who became a beloved wife and an active business colleague. At the time of the photo, he was still repairing telegraph instruments (right).

Nordic Way: Low Cost and High Quality

Ericsson's first telephone instrument was produced in 1878 (above).

Ericsson pioneered in the development of desk telephone instruments. This early design originates from 1892 (right).

SOURCE: Telefonaktiebolaget L. M. Ericsson.

time, he also got into telecom services. In 1883, Henrik Tore Cedergren, Ericsson's good friend, launched Stockholms Allmänna Telefonaktiebolag (SAT), a private operating company that competed alongside the state-owned PTT. Over time, collaboration between the two companies deepened. And thirty-five years later—in 1918—SAT merged with L. M. Ericsson to form Telefon AB L. M. Ericsson.

By the 1890s, Ericsson excelled in high-quality (differentiation) and low-cost manufacturing (cost leadership) *simultaneously*. Except for Nokia, most large-country rivals have found this very difficult to accomplish. In addition, Ericsson initiated internationalization before the end of the nineteenth century.

It could achieve scale only through scope. To Ericsson and Nokia, large multi-nationals from small countries, the ability to *leverage* strategy has always been as critical as the development and implementation of the strategy itself.

Driven to Foreign Markets

According to a myth, the secret of success of Nordic leaders, such as Ericsson and Nokia, originates from "highly competitive domestic markets." While it is true that the Nordic PTTs have been more service-oriented than their counterparts in continental Europe, it does not follow that these telecom dinosaurs have not exploited their monopolies in domestic markets. In effect, Ericsson's success has had less to do with a competitive home base than with the monopolistic conduct of the Swedish PTT and the tiny size of the local market, which forced the aspiring vendor to compete elsewhere.

Early regulation stipulated that Ericsson could not sell equipment to the Swedish market, which developed telecom systems jointly with the domestic PTT. In Sweden, public switching equipment and telephones were manufactured by Teli, which was owned by the PTT, whereas Ericsson manufactured exclusively for foreign markets.[2] This arrangement was reminiscent of one adopted in the United States, in which AT&T, though privately controlled, served as a *de facto* monopoly, with Western Electric as its supply chain. In the international markets, ITT sought to replicate AT&T's domestic dominance. Indeed, both the early ITT and the early Ericsson were "driven" to foreign markets by their respective domestic monopolies. The interests of the two coincided at the turn of the 1930s, when ITT acquired a major stake in the Swedish company.

Ericsson's Early Internationalization

Ericsson differs from its rivals in the United States and in Western Europe in still another respect. Unlike large companies in large countries, it had to grow large in a small country. Without appropriate scale economies, it had to think internationally, if only to survive. Ericsson delivered its first telephone in 1878; two years later, the first telephone exchange was launched in Sweden. By 1886, the small Nordic country led the world in telephone density. After the expansion of factory facilities in Stockholm, Ericsson delivered equipment for Europe's largest telephone exchange in downtown Stockholm in 1887. Ericsson also began internationalization with export orders in 1881 from Russia and Norway. As the company registered its L. M. Ericsson trademark in 1894, it began deliveries to China as well. Only three years later, it targeted the Russian market and began manufacturing in St. Petersburg.

By the mid-1890s, Ericsson employed 500 people and had established a solid foothold in both domestic and export markets. Its core cluster and customers were in the Nordic countries, but it also operated in England, Russia, and Britain. Exports exceeded sales in the limited Swedish market and often accounted for 70 to 85 percent of invoicing.[3] In 1898, Ericsson launched a sales office in London and, while the Russian market took off, the company initiated its first invasion in the United States. In 1902, a sales office opened in New York and a factory in Buffalo followed only two years later. Before World War I, Ericsson launched factories in the U.K., Budapest, Vienna, Warsaw, and the outskirts of Paris. In the Americas, it launched a subsidiary in Mexico, where it would operate a nationwide telephone network. In Asia, it began to modernize Bangkok's telephone network. Exhibit 9-2 illustrates the company's internationalization efforts in these early years.

By the end of the 1920s, some fifty Swedish companies operated foreign production affiliates.[4] In the 1930s, the end of the growth years resulted in international protectionism, which constrained the foreign expansion of Swedish multinationals. Some companies did continue to expand, including AGA, Alfa Laval, ASEA, SKF, Swedish Match, and Ericsson. Many foreign investments were sales subsidiaries, some of which later evolved into extensive manufacturing capabilities. In addition to continental Europe, investments picked up in Latin America and the United States in the interwar period. Starting in 1923, Ericsson installed automatic exchanges based on its 500-switch system, first in Sweden, Norway, and the Netherlands. At the same time, it introduced the dial phone, and phones with plastic casing followed eight years later. In 1927, the company also acquired a radio technology firm.

Internationalization took off again after World War I and continued until the end of the ITT era. After 1918, Ericsson launched its first Nordic subsidiary in Finland and built factories in Rijen, the Netherlands, Romania, Nor-

Exhibit 9-2. Ericsson's internationalization: the early years.

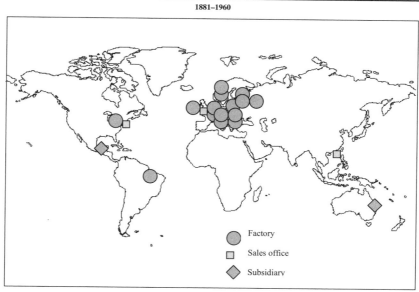

1881–1960

Factory
Sales office
Subsidiary

way, Estonia, Czechoslovakia, and on the outskirts of Stockholm. The company established franchises for telephone operations in southern Italy and Sicily. Unlike its future rivals, and along with Swedish industry, it emerged intact from World War II, thanks to Sweden's neutrality. Unlike Germany and Japan, which had to rebuild their economies, Swedish multinational companies (MNCs) were in a favorable position to supply the growing needs for industrial products throughout Europe. During the immediate postwar period, many of these MNCs managed to consolidate their international positions. Ericsson in particular benefited from its positioning.[5]

Ericsson as a Swedish Multinational

In Sweden, Ericsson has long been a leading MNC. Unlike Nokia in Finland, it has not been alone. Sweden is a small, open economy with a disproportionate number of large successful MNCs; the country has more companies among the world's leading MNC's than many larger economies. In the early 1990s, Swedish MNCs, despite the small national economy, accounted for 4 percent of the *world's* foreign direct investment (FDI) stock. Only three countries—the U.K., the Netherlands, and Switzerland—had a higher ratio of outward-FDI stock to GDP at the time. Swedish business managers, unlike those in Finland or Norway, have cultivated an international business orientation. Many contemporary Swedish MNCs established their foreign affiliates *before* World War I, although the great expansion of foreign operations really took off in the 1970s and 1980s.[6]

Ericsson belongs to an elite group of leading Swedish companies (including, among others, Alfa Laval, AGA, and SKF) that grew beyond the domestic market and became multinational toward the end of the nineteenth century and the early-twentieth century. Initially, most Swedish MNCs extended their international boundaries by leveraging their strategic advantages worldwide. Typically, these advantages were technology-related. Some emerged as a result of major innovations and the subsequent acquisition of a broader range of expertise (e.g., SKF in ball bearings, AGA in beacons, and Alfa Laval in separators). Others drew directly on abundant local raw materials (e.g., Sandvik in metal products, and Stora and SCA in pulp and paper). Still others focused on the pharmaceutical and medical-equipment sectors (e.g., Astra, Gambro, Pharmacia). Ericsson belonged to a fourth group, which built its strategic advantages on the long Swedish tradition of metal manufacturing and, over time, moved to more advanced industries (e.g., ASEA in electrical equipment and turbines, and Volvo and SAAB-Scania in transport equipment).[7] Ericsson built its expansion on incremental innovation following the Bell invention.

For most of the twentieth century, Ericsson's key telecom customers have been public telecom administrations that have paid great attention to local employment and national sovereignty. The first wave of internationalization reflects that of many other early Swedish MNCs. Prior to World War I, the main location for Swedish FDI was Europe, particularly Russia. With the Soviet revolution, investments were still directed to Europe, but increasingly to the United States and Latin America, as well. In this regard, too, Ericsson's exports and FDI were typical to many other Swedish multinationals of its era.[8]

Telecom Strategy

By the early 1930s, Ericsson and Siemens competed for the German electrical and telephone businesses. When ITT entered the rivalry, the Europe-based competitors joined in an informal alliance, which some observers thought would result in a binational giant, like Royal Dutch Shell. Just as the British-Dutch petroleum combine competed with the U.S.-based Standard Oil for worldwide markets, these observers anticipated that Ericsson and Siemens might join forces to neutralize ITT, the U.S.-based telecom power.

Colonel Sosthenes Behn founded the nucleus of his telecom empire in 1920. Over the next four decades, it grew into a powerhouse with business and political interests on several continents. In the aftermath of World War I, Behn acquired a slate of operating telephone and telegraph companies in Europe and Latin America, glued them together with cable interconnects, and bought a group of equipment factories. He named the ensuing combination the International Telephone and Telegraph (ITT), which he called "The International System," a worldwide version of the U.S.-based Bell System.[9] As Behn built his empire, he was intrigued by European telecom vendors. In the United States, AT&T controlled telecommunications; in Europe, PTTs enjoyed a natural monopoly in nation states. AT&T's supply chain was controlled by Western Electric, whose worldwide arm, International Western Electric, competed against L. M. Ericsson and Siemens & Halske. The latter two were private suppliers that provided most equipment for the European PTTs. Both were concerned about the rising power of ITT. The grandiose dreams of an alliance between the two, however, faced an obstacle—Ivar "The Match King" Kreuger, who took a small position in Ericsson in 1927 but expanded it to a controlling stake two years later. The Swede founded his empire on matches. He also liked to play with fire.

Ericsson, Siemens, and ITT: Battle for Corporate Control

Kreuger was a Swedish businessman and an international speculator whose financial machinations were widely reported at the time. Relying on Kreuger & Toll as a corporate base, he combined a variety of companies in mining, construction, ball bearings, wood pulp, and newspapers. These fortunes originated from a majority stake in some 250 factories worldwide that produced 30 billion matchboxes annually, or 75 percent of the market. Between 1923 and 1929, Kreuger sold some $148 million of International Match stock and bonds through Wall Street. Like so many other firms, Ericsson had been battered by the Depression, but it had telephone subsidiaries and manufacturing operations in several countries and continued to compete with ITT in Argentina and Mexico. As with his match empire, Kreuger planned to use his foothold as a base for industry dominance. "The telephone," he wrote to a

friend, "has the same qualities as matches. With the arrangement and management of telephone organizations, I can get State concessions and monopolies
just as I can with my little wooden soldiers."[10]

In May 1931, Kreuger approached ITT's Behn and proposed to either
sell his Ericsson holdings or exchange them for ITT paper. Because of its poor
condition, ITT could not make a cash tender; nor was its stock attractive.
Kreuger, however, sweetened the deal by offering to transfer 600,000 Ericsson
shares—a majority stake—to ITT in exchange for 400,000 shares of ITT stock
and $11 million in cash. It was a low price. Kreuger's paper empire was falling
apart and he needed cash quickly. Both parties were in poor financial condition. The deal took months to materialize. Kreuger fought for time; Behn's
empire approached solvency. Kreuger needed cash; Behn wanted the $7 mil-
lion he assumed to be in the Ericsson treasury. When the two parties reached
an impasse in February 1932, Kreuger returned to Europe. In March, he shot
himself in the heart. The suicide triggered a fire in Kreuger's match empire.
After the dust had settled, auditors found hardly any financial assets. Eventually, Behn renounced the millions of dollars in return for 600,000 Ericsson
shares. Marcus Wallenberg, the legendary Swedish banker, negotiated a deal
with ITT, which left the Swedish vendor intact to operate as an independent
entity, even if ITT continued to hold a substantial portion of its stock. The
Swedish courts reduced ITT's voting rights to a third, which made ITT a
significant minority stockholder in Ericsson.

Growth Through Internationalization

Only in 1962, three decades after the original deal, did the Wallenbergs manage
to buy out ITT. The Swedish industrialist family returned the unit to Swedish
control, with a new growth strategy. However, ITT and Ericsson continued to
share a special relationship.[11] Before World War I, the growth of Ericsson,
like that of so many other Swedish MNCs, had coincided with expanding
international trade. Depression, protectionism, and war years suppressed more
active internationalization, even though Sweden, unlike most European countries, was able to avoid direct participation in the military operations during
World War II. The outflow of FDI took off again in the 1960s, and Ericsson
was prepared for another internationalization wave (compare Exhibit 9-2).
With the launch of the European integration, continental Europe became the
most important investment location to most Swedish MNCs. To ensure market
access, Swedish industry considered it necessary to invest within the tariff
walls.[12] By 1965, some 50 percent of Ericsson employees were already employed in thirteen manufacturing subsidiaries worldwide. As the European
economies suffered from stagflation and *Eurosclerosis*, the U.S. economy still
grew at a steady pace and therefore became the main target for Swedish FDI,
which increased dramatically. In that regard, Ericsson's efforts at growth

through internationalization—particularly vis-à-vis the U.S. market—were again in line with those of Swedish multinationals of the era.[13]

When Swedish controls on international capital movements were liberalized in 1986, obstacles to outward investment were removed. As competition accelerated worldwide, some of the traditional Swedish industries declined, but those representing more advanced and complex engineering products thrived. Ericsson was among the Swedish MNCs whose foreign acquisitions increased in the 1970s and 1980s. In the early 1960s, Swedish R&D expenditure had been only 1.7 percent of the GDP, but it increased to 2.3 percent in 1981 and 3 percent in 1991. At the leading MNCs, more advanced products and services required increasing in-house R&D, first in the home base, and over time, in foreign countries.[14] From 1960, when Ericsson regained its corporate autonomy and engaged in a growth strategy, to the end of the 1980s, this internationalization again reflected that of other Swedish multinationals. If anything, it was bolder and more aggressive. It also focused increasingly on telecommunications, particularly the wireless business.

Toward Digital Switch: The Story of "X"

By 1970, the L. M. Ericsson parent company was organized in several product divisions, while a few departments and the manufacturing facilities formed a separate organization. The product divisions were responsible for development, sales, and administration, while purchasing their production from the factory organization. By its history and nature, Ericsson was an engineering company that cherished continuity and tradition. These characteristics pertained to the Telephone Exchange Division (i.e., the switching division or "X" within the company). In 1970, X was reorganized.[15] At the time, a telephone exchange had two broad functions: *switching*, or the making of connections, and *control*. The distinction became clear only over time. Strowger selector, which had no autonomous control system, had been largely overtaken by the crossbar switch, which was still electromechanical but more compact and reliable. In crossbar, separate devices (e.g., registers and markers) operated the switch and provided the control. In the 1960s, interest increased in the computerized stored program control (SPC). In the long term, the French CIT-Alcatel's E10 had the greatest potential. With E10, the control system was not new, but the switch was. At Ericsson's X, engineers were intrigued by the promise of the *digital* switch.

From AKE 13 to AXE

In 1968, Ericsson's first SPC telephone exchange was opened in Tumba, Sweden. The control system of AKE 12, its precursor, was relatively primitive and limited. Designed for large national and international transit exchanges, this improved system was named AKE 13.[16] The Swedes struggled for ideas to form a new system, not just at Ericsson but at Televerket, the Swedish Telecommunications Administration. In June 1970, Björn Lundvall, Ericsson's president, and Bertil Bjurel, director general of the Swedish PTT, formed a jointly owned company, Elemtel, that undertook design and development projects exclusively for the two parents. Among the first tasks was a project called AX—the development of a proposal for an SPC local exchange system, which would provide cost benefits. In the past, the development of the first SPC system (AKE) had been managed by Ericsson's technical departments, which had limited contact with markets. With AX specifications, the task was given to the *marketing* section of the switching division.

Soon, the small working group found itself with two different requirement specifications. Televerket's version reflected its vision of the Swedish telephone system, whereas Ericsson's had been designed in view of worldwide export. Eventually, the team found two reconciling principles. *Modularity* promised efficiency and rested on the global nature of the Ericsson specification, which sought to cover all telephone exchange markets without a cost penalty. *Ease of handling* promised local responsiveness, but required the system to be easy to design, install, maintain, and teach.

By 1972, competitors, including ITT, Japanese companies, Philips, and Western Electric, pushed products that incorporated analog switching.[17] Because crossbar would be the most popular product for years to come, a strong Ericsson lobby argued that there was no urgency to introduce a new system. Similarly, Televerket saw no great hurry at the time. In February 1972, a decision was made to develop the AX switching system along the line proposed by Ellemtel, with a target date for years later, for the first pilot exchange. By the end of 1974, the telephone industry felt the effects of the oil crisis. A year later, Ericsson introduced AXE, which promised cost-efficiency and, over time, contributed to the operators' shift from electromechanics to computer control worldwide. Still, the early years were tough.

As crossbar sales fell drastically during 1976 and 1977, AXE grew up in the highly visible public-tender spotlight. In May 1978, the world's first digital AXE exchange was cut over at Turku, in Finland. Four months earlier, digital AXE exchanges had been at the core of the largest telecom contract in history for Saudi Arabia. In the process, AXE beat Western Electric and ITT. The success of the AXE development project built upon disruptive thinking, not conventional industry wisdom.[18] Ericsson opted for marketers rather than engineers. It rejected profitable existing solutions for debatable future solutions. This was not just great intuition. In the early and mid-1970s, only two or three vendors offered digital systems; by 1978, there were nearly a dozen rivals. The quest for first-mover advantages had a central role in Ericsson's effort to translate pioneering technological advances into more sustainable competitive advantages.

To exploit new technology possibilities without having to undertake entirely new development work, Ericsson began to apply a "life cycle philosophy" to its products. After long-term evaluations of trends in technology and market requirements, the products were designed in a way that, when a certain technology became mature or a new function was needed, only limited modifications or additions were necessary. Consequently, customers could enjoy "stable" systems, while taking advantage of new technological possibilities.[19] It was an early effort to manage technology novelty and systemic complexity in an increasingly dynamic environment. With accelerating rivalry and rising stakes, new requirements emerged. Financial capabilities became part of the game. The manufacturers had to be able to arrange or supply the loans to finance the expansion of the customer's network. This soft money often proved decisive in getting a contract unless more political or military terms were involved (e.g., a package deal for arms). In addition, due to long-term vendor customer relationships, the vendors had to be able to provide service at all levels, before and after a sale. Finally, a vendor had to be able and willing to establish local manufacture in customer countries (Ericsson's crossbar, for instance, was manufactured in twenty-two countries providing a solid manufacturing base worldwide), which forced the competitive players to move early and rapidly from exports to foreign direct investment in core clusters and lead markets.[20] Ironically, the very same technology that had ensured great cost efficiencies contributed to rising entry barriers and capital intensity of the business itself.

Now AXE was Ericsson's key asset. As Ericsson president Björn Svedberg put it, "We entered the 1980s with a strong weapon—AXE—a switching system that well defends our positions in the telephone exchange technology that is important to the Ericsson Group. This product area, in which the large telecommunications administrations are our customers, has long accounted for half of the Group's sales."[21] In the early 1970s, Ericsson had about 10 percent of the worldwide market for telephone exchange equipment. At the close of the decade, it had captured more than 15 percent, due to AXE.[22] By the early 1980s, Ericsson, along with others, faced the Japanese challenge, which did not prove as powerful as feared. "The Japanese suppliers, by virtue of intensive marketing, combined in certain instances with 'unrealistic' sales terms, have won a number of bidding competitions," noted Ove Ericsson, who headed the company's public telecommunications. "However, they have not increased their market shares to the same degree as in such other industries as automobiles and home electronics."[23] The ability to deter attacks was critical because 95 percent of Ericsson's public telecommunications sales came from *outside* Sweden.

The Demise of the "Office of the Future"

By the early 1980s, Ericsson's Group structure was developed to "adapt smoothly to changed requirements from markets and the surrounding world, and to create a more flexible operating organization."[24] The company perceived itself as built upon a common technology and a common marketing organization. Competence and experience in telecommunications served as its base for broadening product and market segments. This concept was a mirror image of Motorola's postwar strategy, in which electronics rather than telecommunications served as the common foundation. In both cases, a broad enabling technology functioned as the fountain of new ideas, products, and services for individual units. Ericsson saw telecom technology as a part of information technology: methods and equipment for handling information in the form of speech, data, text, and pictures. It did not consider the organizational changes as diversification, but as a logical development of the company's inherent strength.

Before its 1982 reorganization, the Ericsson Group had been organized by products rather than markets. The new objective was to improve the group's ability to adapt smoothly to new requirements from markets and the surrounding world, and to create a more flexible organization. [25]

With the arrival of the 1G era in 1983, Ericsson's sales exceeded SEK 25 billion, and the company operated in fifty-nine countries worldwide. Some 20 percent of total sales still originated from Sweden. With the beginning of the 2G era in 1992, Ericsson operated in sixty-four countries and sales had climbed to $6.6 billion. At the same time, the portion of total sales originating from Sweden had declined to 13 percent. The Swedish vendor had changed significantly, but the globalization had barely begun.[26]

As AXE boosted a new wave of internationalization, Ericsson, buoyed by its success, rushed to unveil the "office of the future" in the early 1980s. Its visionaries predicted that, in the coming years, office equipment, computer technology, and telecommunications would converge into "integrated information systems." The diversification into computers and office furniture was an exciting vision, but it did not materialize in demand for office automation. Ericsson's timing was off, and its profits plunged. Electrolux chairman Hans Werthen was recruited to split his time between the two companies and to rescue Ericsson, which sold its computer business to Nokia in 1988 and refocused on telephone equipment. Meanwhile, the Swedish vendor dusted off its aging AXE system for the burgeoning cellular market and won key contracts.

Ericsson's Entry Into Mobile Phones

After the mid-1990s, Ericsson veterans named the story of their handset unit "the ugly duckling":

> So what about the title of the story? It doesn't have any ornithological connotations, even though one or two turkeys appear here and there. And in choosing the title we did not have the mobile telephone—that noble instrument—in mind. The "ugly duckling" of our story is rather the department in Ericsson where it all started, which grew to a division, then to a business unit, and eventually a company. That metamorphosis is our theme. Hans Christian Andersen would have liked it.[27]

Because its engineers were most comfortable with operators and business markets, Ericsson stumbled into mass consumer markets, which ultimately became *the* realm of mobile telephones. The mobile phone unit grew through trial and error. In the end, the ugly duckling found a partner named Sony. Some considered it a happy ending; many Ericssonians did not.

The Early Years

Historically, Ericsson's diversification into mobile telephones originates from a 1919 stake in the Swedish Radio Company AB (SRA), which was formed by ASEA, AGA, and L. M. Ericsson. Only two years later, the U.K.-based Marconi came in as part-owner, while AGA and ASEA sold out their interests. SRA had built radio transmitters and receivers (the Radiola radio set), TV sets, and during the 1950s, land-mobile radio systems. Civilian and military demand for land-mobile radio systems took SRA outside the Swedish market. In 1961, paging systems were included in the product portfolio. The radio and TV set operations were sold off, and SRA was restructured to expand in the defense business (radar and troop radio), along with the military and civil land-mobile radio business, which continued to turn out paging systems. By the mid-1960s, Åke Lundqvist—a key figure in Ericsson's future mobile phones—joined SRA.

The first steps toward mobile telephony in Sweden had been taken in the late 1940s. The real breakthrough occurred after increasing Nordic cooperation in the 1970s, which were followed by two decades of explosive growth. At the time, Ericsson was the majority owner of SRA, the British company in which Marconi held a minority share. In 1970, Lundqvist was appointed manager of the land-mobile radio division at SRA. The group envisioned transforming mobile phones from a luxury item to a tool for everyone. By 1970, Lundqvist took charge of the land-mobile radio division and contributed to growing exports in developing countries, including Nigeria, Egypt, and Libya. After SRA moved to its new headquarters in Kista, north of Stockholm, Lundqvist took over as SRA's managing director. Marconi's interest was reduced, and Ericsson bought out the remaining shares in 1982. The next January, SRA became a wholly owned subsidiary within Ericsson and its name was changed to Ericsson Radio Systems AB (ERA) (see Exhibit 9-3). Ericsson's entry into mobile stations had taken place a few years before.

The First Terminals

ERA's basic segments were growing and fairly profitable. In 1981, the NMT mobile telephone systems were introduced in Sweden and later in other Nordic countries. Lundqvist augmented the unit's product portfolio with terminals (mobile stations) as well (see Exhibit 9-4). For all practical purposes, the initial diversification was a result of incremental evolution, which built upon the capabilities of Sonab, the radio operations of a Swedish firm SRA had acquired in the late 1970s.

Sonab had a land-mobile station product, which could be upgraded into

Exhibit 9-3. Ericsson's mobile telephone business (1919–present).

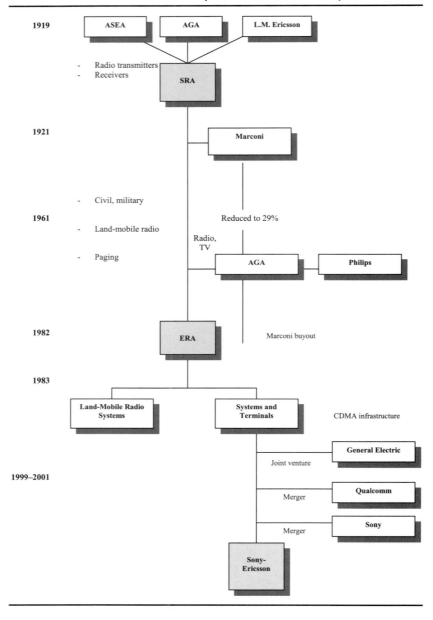

Exhibit 9-4. Ericsson's product portfolio: from terminals to smart phones.

T68, GSM & GPRS phone with color display, digital imaging and
audio capabilities and built-in Bluetooth™ wireless technology

SOURCE: Telefonaktiebolaget L.M. Ericsson.

a terminal by incorporating a telephone unit; it also had a similar in-house land-mobile radio product that could be transformed into a mobile telephone station. These early terminals had few affinities with the small, light, cheap, and stylish mobile phones of the late 1990s; rather, they were large, bulky, and expensive units for installation in vehicles.

The entry into terminals business was accompanied by an extraordinary deal. In 1977, Ericsson, in a joint venture with Philips, won a contract to build a new (fixed) telephone network in Saudi Arabia. A year later, the network was in service, which required the company to gear up very quickly for large-scale production of electronic switching systems. The contract heightened the visibility of the new digital AXE switching system. One of the Saudis' follow-up contracts included mobile telephone networks for the Kingdom's three major cities, as well as 8,000 mobile stations, which Ericsson would provide. That meant a major run for the production facilities, while a shipment of many units to a single market tied ERA's hand into Saudi Arabia. Meanwhile, the Nordic markets despaired for mobile stations. Instead of Ericsson, the Finnish Nokia-Mobira seized the opportunity.

Preparing for the 1G Era

In the early 1980s, the rapid proliferation of the first analog cellular systems in Nordic countries, the United States, and Japan boosted the fortunes of

Ericsson. In 1981, the company initiated efforts to build mobile telephone networks based on the analog NMT 450 system in three Nordic countries and Saudi Arabia. Only two years later, Ericsson received its first order for the AMPS system in the United States. Soon thereafter, its fiber-optic cables were introduced on a broad scale. As Ericsson increased efforts in the analog networks, it also entered analog mobile phones. In 1986, the company turned out its first handheld mobile phone for the NMT 900 system. That year also saw the first commercial order for AXE in the United States. By 1990, the vendor put in service the world's largest system for nationwide paging in Taiwan.

In the first half of the 1980s (following the Saudi success/failure debacle), ERA focused on putting in place the pieces of its operation.[28] In mobile radio, the company estimated Motorola to have about 40 percent of the world market and 60 percent of the business in North America. Ericsson's SRA also competed against General Electric and Philips. It had a relatively small portion of the world market, but it was the largest supplier in the Nordic countries and the Middle East. In mobile telephony, Motorola was Ericsson's foremost competitor, but the Swedish company's AXE gave it a distinct competitive advantage. Other rivals included Japanese suppliers and the Bell system in the United States. In five years, SRA's sales had risen rapidly, at an average of 30 percent annually. Most was attributable to volume increases. SRA's plans called for strong expansion, which in turn required large investments for product development and marketing (development costs alone amounted to over 10 percent of sales).[29]

With growing terminal business and nascent internationalization, Ericsson increased its investments in new product development. In 1983, the Ericsson Mobile Telephone Laboratory was inaugurated in the Ideon technology park in Lund, an old university town in Sweden. The original charter of the new mobile lab was vague and resulted in futuristic studies on "the mobile pocket phone of tomorrow." Things changed in 1985, when Nils Rydbeck was hired to head the unit.[30] Production was taking off at Kumla. A new product development operation had been created at Lund. Exports resulted in some internationalization. The organization was shuffled for growth. However, neither Ericsson nor its rivals had handheld mobiles, only relatively unsophisticated car phones and portable phones for the NMT 450 networks. The products were expensive and ridden with quality problems. Functionality reigned over beauty. Volumes were small. In 1986, only 10,000 units were produced. Demand was confined to business use, and marketing intensity was relatively low. In design, manufacturing, and marketing, Ericsson still struggled to catch up with its rivals, Motorola and Nokia-Mobira. None of the basic functions of the business—development, manufacturing, marketing, distribution, accounting, management—were in place yet. ERA sold add-ons rather than mobile stations to push systems.

In 1985—during his first year at Lund—Nils Rydbeck prepared a mighty vision, a ten-year plan for the development of a series of *handheld* mobile telephones. A year later, Flemming Örneholm took over Ericsson's "ugly duck-ling," which led to the creation of the ERA. As a systems company, the Swedish vendor was rapidly expanding as AXE established itself as a world leader. Örneholm implemented an innovation program that gave rise to a branded product line ("Harry Hotline") targeting young business professionals. Con-currently, ERA had to learn the painful basics of low-cost manufacturing to catch up with the productivity frontier. The Hotline campaign had introduced "Curt," Ericsson's first handheld wireless telephone. Designed for the new NMT 900 system standard, the model invaded the Swedish market, where it found hardly any rivals. Based on an old police radio design, the P300 was an experiment in which complex electronics, transceiver, and telephone were crammed into a single unit. After Curt's success, Ericsson named the new mod-els by female names—Olivia, Sandra, Jane, and Emma—because they were "so small and shapely" (see again Exhibit 9-5).[31]

New Wave of Internationalization

Between the 1960s and early 1980s, Ericsson's growth strategy was accompa-nied by a new wave of internationalization. In 1963, the company launched a factory outside Melbourne, Australia. In 1971, it established new factories both in the Nordic cluster (Finland, Norway) and in its long-standing Mexican market. By the early 1980s, the thrust of internationalization moved to Asia-Pacific, only to shift to the United States at the end of the decade.

Building Operations in Asia-Pacific

Establishing the handset business went hand in hand with international-ization. As a NMT system had been sold to Malaysia in 1984, Flemming Örne-holm was sent to the location to organize a sales and service department for the terminals. He hired Bengt Jordahl and Michael Leong to serve as "resident sales consultants" in Kuala Lumpur. The two men soon set up a drive-in shop and signed contracts with car sales firms. In the process, the Volvo dealer, which was losing to competition, sold cars with installed mobile telephones and won customers back. The success soon attracted competition. Although Nokia and the Japanese entered the Malaysian market, Ericsson retained a substantial market share, not least because of its first-mover advantages. Soon thereafter, a system was sold to Thailand. Again, Örneholm drew up plans for selling terminals, while Jordahl moved to Bangkok. As the veterans acknowl-edge, "Success was attributable to salesmanship and service: The products were still lousy, or at least not top of the market. But . . . repair service in those countries was cheap."[32] In 1986, a system was sold to Indonesia and, again, the Jordahl family traveled.

Successful operations in Malaysia, Thailand, and Indonesia were followed by others in Taiwan and Korea. At Ericsson, these operations had a twofold

Exhibit 9-5.   Ericsson's handhelds: from analog to digital (1987–1996)—greater performance with smaller, lighter, and cheaper models.

ERICSSON ≋   ERICSSON ≋   ERICSSON ≋   ERICSSON ≋

1987: Curt, a converted police radio design turned into an NMT 900 phone and later an ETACS mobile. The first Ericsson handheld. Known officially as the HotLine Pocket.	**1989:** Olivia. Introduced originally for NMT 900 networks, followed by versions for ETACS, AMPS, and eventually GSM. The first Ericsson GSM phone and consequently its first all-digital mobile.	**1991:** Sandra, first version in NMT 900, then ETACS, D-AMPS/AMPS, and finally GSM in 1993.	**1996:** Jane, D-AMPS, GSM, DCS, PCS1900/GSM. A "slim" version appeared in a D-AMPS 1900 model as well as a PDC version.

These models were still primarily domestic products. Also, they served as categories that could be leveraged across geographic markets on the basis of standards. As the pioneer analog model, Curt was created for the Nordic NMT 900 market in 1987. Two years later, it was leveraged across the ETACS regions. About a decade later, Jane was launched for the digital cellular. In less than two years, it was leveraged for a half dozen markets (D-AMPS, GSM, DCS, PCS 1900/GSM, D-AMPS 1900, PDC). What made Jane so different from Curt? In Curt's case, the model covered only two markets, and this leverage took a while to achieve. With the digital Jane, the leverage was threefold and was therefore accomplished more quickly. In brief, the number of leveraged product categories was increasing, while product life cycles were growing shorter.

SOURCE: Telefonaktiebolaget L.M. Ericsson.

impact. On the more obvious level, the success stories were important for in-house motivation. They increased momentum, enabled management to see the business potential, and ensured continued investment. On a less visible level, they transformed the perception of the mobile telephone unit. Initially, there was no unit strategy in the market entry; terminals were considered a nice source of minor revenue. The strategy was not particularly purposeful, either.

SRA and then ERA drifted into the terminal business. But with each overseas success story, Ericsson saw an added impact of the economies of scale on the aggregate revenues. Over time, another realization ensued. If the company could replicate the terminal business model *worldwide*, network effects would kick in and the scale economies might ensure a powerful revenue drive.

Establishing a Foothold in the United States

With the introduction of the analog cellular, Ericsson, like other mobile vendors, saw the United States as the most attractive country market in the global chessboard. It provided the greatest scale and the highest potential growth. In fact, Ericsson had done business in the United States in several phases. The first one took place with its early internationalization, when the company launched the first factory in Buffalo to manufacture telephones, switchboards, and components for the car industry. Eventually, the unit ran into trouble and was sold off in the early 1920s. Between the Depression and World War II, Ericsson relied on its traditional markets to survive, especially in the developing countries. In the postwar era, the company used its popular crossbar switching to establish a new foothold in the United States. In Galion, Ohio, the North Electric Co. introduced an Ericsson-based crossbar system that would serve independent telephone companies. In the late 1950s, North Electric became Ericsson's platform for introducing a fully electronic switch (412 L) to the United States Air Force, just as in the 1960s, Ericsson transferred to North Electric the technology of the computer-controlled AKE switching system.

As attractive as the United States was to Ericsson, it also posed a significant problem. Due to different technical standards, the Swedes could not make optimal use of the marketplace. Ericsson sold North Electric but continued technology transfer. Through the 1970s, the Swedish vendor only sold switchboards and telephone sets in the private market, and business was marginal. Competitive circumstances began to change only with the antitrust proceedings against AT&T. Rivalry—from Ericsson's standpoint—meant the proliferation of rivals, which meant more customers, which meant a lucrative market for transmission equipment. In 1980, Ericsson formed a joint venture with Atlantic Richfield, a U.S. oil corporation. Headquartered in Orange Country, California, the new Anaconda-Ericsson focused on cable manufacture, PBX switchboards, and transmission equipment. As Ericsson built its corporate presence in the United States, it also entered the financial markets with a $240 million stock issue (as ADRs) in 1983.

Eager to exploit Ericsson's growing presence in North America, SRA entered the new U.S. mobile telephone systems market in early 1982. The FCC had decided to award two operating licenses for each market, one for a Bell company, and another for a nonwireline company. By June 1982, there were 140 license applications. In forty of them, Ericsson was named as the proposed supplier for base stations and switches. Before its stock issue, Ericsson was relatively unknown in the United States. The news rocked the financial markets and stunned Motorola, which had expected to dominate the segment. In May 1983, Ericsson signed its first contract, appropriately for the city of Buffalo, the site of its production facility in America.[33] That year, the company also introduced its first AXE development center in North America in Richardson, Texas. A year later, Ericsson Inc. in the United States became a wholly-owned subsidiary.

By the end of the 1980s, Ericsson had a 30 percent market share for cellular systems in North America (United States, Canada), but it was primarily a *systems* player. Not a single Ericsson mobile telephone had been sold in the United States. By the end of 1989, Ericsson set up a joint venture with General Electric in a major strategic decision aimed at attaining a substantial U.S. market position. At first, GE had a 40 percent stake in Ericsson-GE Mobile Communications, which provided the Swedes with the U.S. market, production facility and, most importantly, a significant learning experience. Organizationally, it was not a geographic division for the Swedish mobile unit; it represented the full-scale *migration* of the Swedish unit to the United States. As Ericsson's historians acknowledge, "The new company was given worldwide responsibility for all the mobile telephone business, and for mobile data systems and wireless security systems as well—development, manufacture, and sales. It became Ericsson's world headquarters for the business, with a corporate head office in Paramus, New Jersey. Åke Lundqvist moved over as President."[34]

At Lund, an *autonomous* R&D unit proved vital. Lundqvist did not establish a new R&D facility at the GE production plant in Lynchburg, but at the Research Triangle Park near Raleigh, in North Carolina. Concurrently, he persuaded Nils Rydbeck to take charge of the new laboratories early in 1990, while Rydbeck remained responsible for R&D in Lund, as well. That year, the Lynchburg plant produced the CarPhone, a portable AMPS model. Of the total 225,000 units that year, more than 50 percent came from the former GE plant. Meanwhile, the Swedish side of the new company was named RMOT International.

Ericsson was now a worldwide player and possessed a substantial presence in all major Triad regions. In this regard, the most important development was its telecom contract with China in 1988, which was the largest ever at that time. In the 1990s, the Internet revolution in the United States prompted the Swedish vendor to solidify its presence close to the new media by opening Ericsson CyberLab in New York City.

The Refocus Strategy

With the demise of the "office of the future," Ericsson's profits plunged in the late 1980s. Strategic leadership shifted to Werthen, whose mission to "save

Ericsson" was realized by the explosive growth of the digital cellular in the 1990s. But the 3G transition led to new turmoil.

Toward the 3G Era

In 1998, manager Sven-Christer Nilsson was appointed CEO. He announced reorganization plans, including 14,000 layoffs. Only two years earlier, Ericsson and aircraft maker Saab had merged their military aviation electronics operations as Ericsson Saab Avionics. Now the new entity was dissolved. By mid-1999, Nilsson was pushed out for moving too slowly on restructuring plans. He was replaced by chairman Lars Ramqvist, who put many of the duties on president Kurt Hellström. Called "The Cowboy" because of his affinity for Harley-Davidsons, Hellström set out to simplify the Swedish vendor's managerial and accounting structure. The company continued to reshape by divesting noncore businesses, including its private radio systems, power supply, and equipment shelter operations. Ericsson's profits fell after the company was slow to market with new handset models and fixed-line business dropped. Hellström resorted to cutting costs, trimming the company's bloated workforce, and pushing new phone models to market.

In the early 1990s, the approaching digital cellular boosted Ericsson's fortunes. In the latter half of the decade, the company rushed to the emerging 3G markets while speeding development efforts in Internet capabilities—internally, through strategic alliances, and with various M&A activities. This went hand in hand with increasing presence in the U.S. market. A new era of détente with Qualcomm was part of this repositioning in the new technology space. Ericsson had fought bitterly with its U.S. rival over wireless standards and patents, but the companies settled in 1999, signing a cross-licensing deal and agreeing to push for the standardization of 3G technology based on Qualcomm's CDMA. As a part of the deal, Ericsson also purchased the infrastructure business of its U.S. rival, thus heightening its in-house CDMA capabilities.

Fierce competition and an industrywide slowdown in handset sales forced Ericsson to begin outsourcing the manufacture of its phones to third parties including Flextronics in the United States and Anima and GVC in Taiwan. The restructuring involved cutting 11,000 jobs by the end of 1999.

Ericsson's Vision, Organization, and Offerings

By the end of 2000, Ericsson had been active worldwide since the early 1880s. After three waves of internationalization, it operated in more than 140 countries and had more than 105,000 employees. More than 71,000 were located in Europe, the Middle East and Africa, while 13,500 were located in the United States and Canada. Latin America and Asia-Pacific each had 8,500, respectively. The shortage of highly skilled human capital in telecom and data industries represented a challenge to the company, which recruited around 10,000 new employees annually. In spring 2000, Kurt Hellström coined the phrase "Be first, be best, and be cost-effective," in order to facilitate the prioritization of employee efforts and resources.

With a strong R&D focus, Ericsson's annual investments in technical development averaged 15 percent of sales. The company filed 1,300 patent applications during 2000 expecting these investments to contribute to its leadership in mobile infrastructure and mobile Internet, especially as it had been committed to 3G development for more than a decade. Five business divisions were designed to allow the organization to fit the changing market and create a business structure capable of growing with new market opportunities.[35] Ericsson formed Mobile Systems in July 2000 to compete in mobile communications. The core of the division included two older entities, Segment Network Operators and Service Providers. It comprised six business units, which included the four mobile systems business units: CDMA Systems, GSM Systems, PDC Systems, and TDMA Systems. The other two business units were Transmission Mobile Systems and Special Business Operations. The division also had two product units and four core product units.

Geographically, Ericsson's operations were organized in five market areas: Western Europe; Central and Eastern Europe, the Middle East, and Africa; North America; Latin America; and Asia-Pacific (see Exhibit 9-6). Ericsson also had key functions in London. Supplying operators and service providers around the world, offerings consisted of end-to-end solutions in mobile and broadband Internet.[36] Within the network operators business segment, Ericsson used to work across business unit boundaries with respect to services. The new division was expected to focus more on the customer.

Ericsson remained the world leader in wireless infrastructure equipment, but its hold on the handsets was crumbling worldwide. As Ericsson and Sony combined their handset businesses in a joint venture (Sony Ericsson Mobile Communications), they were left behind Nokia and Motorola, while Siemens and Asian manufacturers were rapidly catching up. Katsumi Ihara, Sony Ericsson's president, swept aside concerns about potential cultural differences between the two companies. His objective was to turn the vendor into the world's leading producer within five years, even though Sony Ericsson had a market share of just 8 percent in 2001 (lower than Ericsson alone in 2000), while Nokia, the world leader, had more than 35 percent.

Ihara, however, believed that complementary strengths were the secret to the fifty-fifty joint venture. Ericsson was a specialist in wireless technology, Sony brought a deep knowledge of music, games, and entertainment as well as a consumer-end view of things. In March 2002, the new entity made a strong start with the sleek T68, the world's first color-screen phone (see again Exhibit 9-4). But it was caught off-guard by the phone's success, badly underestimating demand and, hence, producing too few. The struggle with manufacturing capabilities that had begun in late 1980s continued to haunt the company, but

Exhibit 9-6. Ericsson's organization structure (2001).

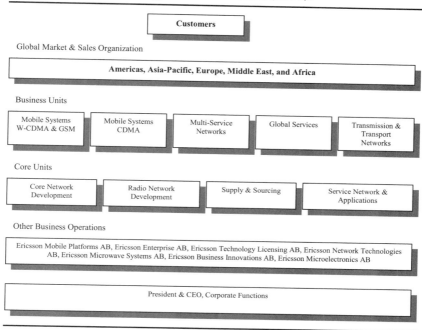

SOURCE: Company reports.

now the reasons were different. Ericsson outsourced its production, while Sony retained its own production. "Right now we are investigating what the appropriate manufacturing strategy for Sony Ericsson should be," said Ihara. The short-term financial target is to make a profit this year, after a loss of SEK 1.4 billion ($136 million) in the last quarter of 2001.[37]

At the headquarters, the Swedish vendor sought to respond to new challenges by reorganizing its product and geographic divisions, while shedding 22,000 employees. At the same time, internal debates prompted friction over corporate governance. Ericsson was still controlled by two groups, the Wallenberg family and Industrivarden (a holding company linked to Handlesbanken). Each party had about 42 percent of the voting power but a small share of the capital. In this way, Ericsson reflected a combination of "family capitalism" (old English multinationals) and "group capitalism" Japanese global challengers). The role of the Wallenbergs and the banks constrained more radical reforms in the vendor's corporate governance. Coincidentally, there were similar characteristics in Motorola's decline in the 1990s.

In August 2001, Ericsson announced sweeping changes in its management structure to focus on its five largest customers: Vodafone Group, France Telecom, Deutsche Telekom, Telefonica, and Telecom Italia Mobile. In the face of an international market downturn, the vendor named Per-Arne Sandstrom to the new COO in charge of a revised product and service structure based on the five units for large global customers. By March 2002, Ericsson continued to adjust its organization "to benefit from the ongoing globalization trend among operators and drive the technology shift to mobile and broadband Internet."

"This is an important and proactive step for us in strengthening our leading position within the telecom industry," said Kurt Hellström, president and CEO of Ericsson. "Our new organization will put even more emphasis on serving our customers, reduce complexity, and more efficiently apply our resources."[38] But even these measures were not sufficient, despite divestitures of noncore businesses, joint venture with Sony, outsourcing of manufacture of its phones to Flextronics, outsourcing of IT operations in Europe to EDS, sale of direct enterprise sales and service unit, as well as cuts of more than 20,000 jobs in 2001. In spring 2002, Ericsson posted its first annual loss in its history (about $2 billion). It intended to cut its workforce by an additional 20 percent (from 10,700 employees at the end of 2000 to 65,000 by late 2003).

Success Drivers: Eclipse of Centralized Innovaton

By 2001, Ericsson saw itself as the world's leading telecom supplier with the largest customer base, including the world's top-ten operators. The vendor provided total solutions covering everything from systems and applications to mobile phones and other communications tools. In doing so, it aspired to generate a competitive economic return for its shareholders. Despite its worldwide dispersion, the Swedish vendor nurtured a combination of three corporate values, which it considered the foundation of the Ericsson culture: professionalism, respect, and perseverance. It had a vision of an "all communicating" world.

> Voice, data, images, and video are conveniently communicated anywhere and anytime in the world, increasing both quality-of-life, productivity, and enabling a more resource-efficient world. We are one of the major progressive forces, active around the globe, driving for this advanced communication to happen. We are seen as the prime model of a networked organization with top innovators and entrepreneurs working in global teams.[39]

But there was a snake in Ericsson's all-communicating world. The very center of its success drivers (see Exhibit 9-7) was falling apart.

The Monopoly Era

Lars Magnus Ericsson launched his phone repair shop in Stockholm in 1876. The operation was soon upgraded with manufacturing capabilities, and telecom services followed with the SAT merger after the mid-1910s. At the same time, the company developed the telecom strategy that would keep it

Exhibit 9-7. Ericsson: drivers of wireless growth.

THE MONOPOLY ERA

Products
- ☐ Following Bell invention in 1876, Lars Ericsson's repair shop in Stockholm leads to manufacturing capabilities; telecom services integrated in mid-1910s.
- ☐ Early Ericsson gives rise to the Nordic model (high quality, low cost, internationalization).
- ☐ In mid-1960s, Swedish PTT regionalizes domestic mobile cluster via Nordic cooperation; in late 1970s, digital switches boost Ericsson's fortunes.

Operations
- ☐ From late 1880s until 1960, telecom strategy keeps Ericsson close to productivity frontier in fixed-line telecom.
- ☐ Advanced but small home base; scale through scope.
- ☐ In early 1960s, a new growth strategy through internationalization; at Motorola, internationalization subject to strategy; at Ericsson, internationalization reigns over strategy.

Markets
- ☐ Ericsson's first internationalization between 1880s and World War I.
- ☐ Second internationalization coincides with the new growth strategy in 1960s.
- ☐ Some joint ventures, but emphasis on long-term FDI.

THE TRANSITION ERA

Products
- ☐ Ericsson's successful digital switch serves as a foothold for other products.
- ☐ Nordic NMT builds on Ericsson's infrastructure; EC support for GSM boosts Ericsson's role in Europe.
- ☐ Introduction of mobile phones.

Operations
- ☐ Aggressive internationalization coupled with new organizational structure.
- ☐ Innovation centralized in Sweden, which provides ideal technology infrastructure and sophisticated customers.
- ☐ Heavy push to United States and Asia-Pacific results in increasing decentralization.

Markets
- ☐ Primary relationships with national PTTs.
- ☐ After the Bell breakup, Ericsson becomes leading supplier of independent operators; in Asia-Pacific it pioneers new markets.
- ☐ Ericsson follows Motorola and AT&T to China

ERICSSON

THE COMPETITIVE ERA

Products
- ☐ In 1990s, worldwide leadership in switches and a strong base in handsets; by 2001, the latter erodes and business merges with Sony's.
- ☐ Thrust of mobile innovation migrates from the United States to Sweden and Finland, which develop the most advanced mobile cluster worldwide, along with Japan.
- ☐ By late 1990s, convergence of voice and data; tech coalitions mitigate the core of Ericsson's organizational leadership—centralized innovation.

Operations
- ☐ In 1997, efforts at reorganization and refocus; increasing outsourcing.
- ☐ Erosion of old international strategy as rivals follow footsteps into same markets.
- ☐ Organizational capabilities no longer unique, but part of the cost of doing business for all leading vendors.

Markets
- ☐ Following Nokia, quest to leverage focus worldwide.
- ☐ Despite erosion in product and operational leadership, over 98% of revenues from worldwide markets.
- ☐ After Tiananmen crisis, Ericsson captures a substantial share of the Chinese infrastructure market.

close to the productivity frontier in fixed-line technologies, products, and services, while giving rise to the Nordic model (high quality, low cost, internationalization). Until the early 1950s, the Swedish mobile R&D thrived primarily in the PTT. About a decade later, R&D diffusion accelerated as Sweden's PTT promoted Nordic cooperation to develop a joint standard, which expanded the cluster from a single Nordic nation to the entire region. At first, Ericsson benefited most from these developments because they offered a sophisticated customer base for its digital switch in the 1970s.

From the late 1880s to the 1970s, Ericsson's operations were dictated by its telecom strategy. Domestic innovation and advanced technology infrastructure provided the framework for corporate strategy. But unlike its large-country rivals, the Swedish vendor had to achieve scale through scope. As ITT was bought out, Ericsson regained its full autonomy in the early 1960s, which led to a new growth strategy, almost exactly in parallel with Motorola. But at Motorola, internationalization was subject to strategy, whereas at Ericsson, internationalization reigned over strategy. The difference in strategy originated from the difference in geography. Motorola had a large, sophisticated, and lucrative home base. Ericsson's home base was not that different in terms of technology innovation or economic wealth, but it lacked the scale economies.

Ericsson's first internationalization occurred well before World War I. The second wave went hand in hand with the new growth strategy in the 1960s. It meant a push into the United States, the most lucrative and sophisticated market of the era, and Asia-Pacific, the most promising markets of the future. In the past, Ericsson had focused on exports, joint ventures, and some FDI. Now it employed joint ventures to gain access to some markets, but the emphasis was on long-term FDI.

The Transition Era

As regulated markets were replaced by deregulated competition, Ericsson's digital switch proved a success and served as a foothold in the emerging markets for other products. The Nordic NMT was developed upon Ericsson's infrastructure. In turn, the regional success led to EC support for the GSM, which meant a powerful boost to the role of the Swedish vendor in Europe. Encouraged by growth prospects worldwide, Ericsson launched a mobile phone unit to complement its soaring infrastructure sales.

Until the 1980s, Ericsson's operations were defined by its efforts to augment the old telecom strategy with internationalization. But the popularity of the digital switch, the success of NMT, and the promising forecast of future GSM sales prompted the vendor to take increasing risks to improve its operational effectiveness. Concurrently, the core of the internationalization shifted from fixed-line activities to the wireless. Innovation remained centralized and located in Sweden, which provided an ideal technology infrastructure and sophisticated customers. At the broader level, the heavy push to the United States and Asia-Pacific meant increasing organizational decentralization.

By the 1980s, AXE was Ericsson's calling card that opened market access worldwide. In the United States, the breakup of the Bell System made the vendor the preferred choice of most independent operators. This popularity, in turn, enhanced Ericsson's clout in Asia-Pacific, where it was busy pioneering new markets. Following AT&T and Motorola to China, the vendor began to explore the vast market, which it knew to be identical with future competition. When the Tiananmen crisis interfered with the growth of the U.S. mobile leaders, Ericsson quickly tapped the opportunity by increasing its activities and investments in China. This triumph of new markets was not entirely without cracks. In the long term, the most serious problem involved the nature of the business relationships. Because of its telecom history, Ericsson's primary customers were public-sector operators (former PTT monopolies), which left Nokia the crumbs—a new generation of hungry but small operators. In the early 1990s, the money was in the PTT camp. But by the end of the decade, it had shifted to the new challengers and consumer markets. With new challengers, Ericsson had fewer relationships. In mass consumer markets, its engineers felt like nerds lost in *Baywatch*.

The Competitive Era

During the 1990s, Ericsson captured worldwide leadership in switches and developed a strong base in handsets. The thrust of mobile innovation migrated from the United States to the Nordic mobile clusters, particularly Sweden and Finland, which developed the most sophisticated customers in infrastructure and handsets. But as the digital cellular peaked toward the end of the decade, infrastructure leadership eroded. The turmoil in handsets became so volatile that the vendor, after two decades of doubts and ambivalence, merged the business with Sony's mobile operation. By the late 1990s, the convergence of voice and data required new competencies, which the vendor sought to internalize through tech coalitions.

Starting in 1997, Ericsson's strategic leadership began to reorganize and refocus, while reinforcing outsourcing. Meanwhile, the very nature of technology development was changing. New technologies and system complexity substituted for old technologies and simpler systems. Existing offerings became obsolete more quickly than ever before. The eclipse of the old telecom strategy and the leading position in technology development forced senior management to seek new solutions and test new approaches. But as innovation occurred increasingly outside the company, these coalitions nullified the core of Ericsson's organizational leadership—centralized innovation.

Following Nokia, Ericsson sought increasing focus, which it would leverage globally. Despite the erosion in product and operational leadership, more than 98 percent of Ericsson's revenues originated from worldwide markets. After the Tiananmen crisis, the vendor captured a substantial chunk of the Chinese infrastructure market. But the value of its strength was eroding. Geography was no longer destiny. Successful innovation that could be translated to sustainable advantage was now key. Technology coalitions were critical to Ericsson's strategy, but they mitigated the very basis of its old international strategy, in which it dominated innovation in the Swedish base. The historical single center of innovation no longer existed; it was fragmenting into ever-smaller pieces of strategic advantages across the world. And centralized innovation without the center was like running a marathon in quicksand.

Chapter 10

Nokia's Translocal Gamble

Founded during the early industrialization of Finland, Nokia grew along with the national ambitions of a small country that had been ruled for centuries by its neighboring Sweden and Russia. Almost 140 years old, the vendor has endured Russian oppression, a Bolshevik revolution, an independence struggle, a civil war, a worldwide depression, two world wars, reparations, cyclical recessions, the collapse of Soviet trade, and the premature deaths of its key executives. Until recently, it was less known for cell phones than its rubber boots, winter tires, and toilet paper.[1] While Nokia's *global* success in the wireless industry is very recent in terms of its history, it did not happen "out of the blue."

Throughout its history, Nokia has engaged in five basic strategies:

Entrepreneurial Focus (1865–late 1890s)
Diversification (late 1890s–late 1960s)
Growth Through Internationalization (late 1960s–late 1980s)
Global Focus (1992–1997)
Translocal Focus (1997–Present)

Most recently, rapid globalization and the concomitant rise of the Internet have accelerated Nokia's efforts to build new capabilities internally (e.g., R&D, Internet, and venture capital units) and externally (e.g., some M&As and global networking). These efforts reflect an evolving translocal focus. Despite its narrow focus on handsets, infrastructure, and more recently software, Nokia is struggling to exploit several strategic advantages *simultaneously* and *worldwide*. These strategic advantages include innovation (i.e., new technology and new marketing approaches), cost (i.e., manufacturing, logistics, and new product development) and differentiation (i.e., brand, segmentation, and design). That is Nokia's translocal gamble.

The Historical Era

Fredrik Idestam, one of Nokia's two founders, came of age in the 1850s and 1860s, an era of entrepreneurialism, optimism, and new technological opportunities. During his university studies, the young engineer had a fortuitous meeting with Leo Mechelin, the Nordic country's first parlamentarian who, four decades later, played a crucial role in Finland's struggle for political independence. From the 1860s to the 1910s, Nokia's two founding fathers—Idestam, a businessman, and Mechelin, a politician—complemented each other. Nokia would be inconceivable had it not been for Mechelin's active role in government relations, board activities, and capital allocation.

Entrepreneurial Focus

Like Ericsson, Nokia originated from entrepreneurial opportunism. Additionally, both companies used imitation to upgrade and innovate. Having heard of Wilhelm Ludwig Lüders, who had created a new process to manufacture pulp in Germany, Idestam traveled to Lüders's factory in 1863 and persuaded local engineers to illustrate the workings of the mill. Lüders threw the Finn out for what he deemed industrial espionage. But Idestam had seen and heard enough. In May 1865, he received authorization to build his mill, which laid the foundation for the future Nokia. It was not the first in the business, but it was the most innovative one. After sales took off in England, Russia, and Finland, Nokia Corporation was created at the home of Leo Mechelin.[2] Like Ericsson, Nokia relied on international markets from the very beginning to capture scale economies.[3]

Diversification Strategy

By the 1890s, Nokia's tiny mill gave way to a large mill, a smaller one, a pulp factory, a large paper factory, and other industrial facilities. The company also diversified into electrical power. Nokia's products were exported first to Russia and then to Great Britain and France. In the 1930s, China became an important trading partner as well. Between 1895 and 1913, Nokia's revenues tripled from FIM 1.2 million to more than FIM 3.6 million. Despite early diversification, Nokia focused on paper products in this era (see Exhibit 10-1 for an overview of Nokia's organizational history).

Three-Firm Coalition and Soviet Reparations: The Rise of Cable

By diversifying into electrical power, Nokia was not as vulnerable to the consequences of World War I or Finland's Civil War, as were most Finnish forestry firms. Before the Great Depression, Nokia grew rapidly and revenues soared to FIM 36 million in 1928. Even the years of recession were followed by solid growth. With the Finnish Rubber Works (FRW), the Finnish Cable Works (FCW), and the old forestry business, the company had grown into a three-firm coalition. During the Second World War, Finland fought three interconnected wars, two against the Soviet Union and one against Germany. These wars shattered the old political and social order. Despite the great losses

Exhibit 10-1. Nokia's organization structure (1865–present).

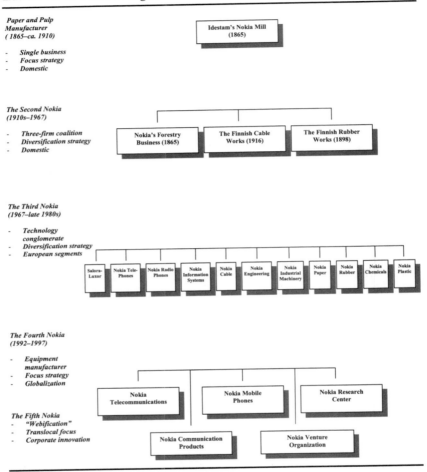

inflicted by the war, the Finns preserved their independence, but neither the nation nor Nokia would ever be the same.

After the peace treaty in 1948, Finland assumed a policy of cautious neutrality and *realpolitik*, carefully taking into account its geographical location next to the Soviet Union. Ironically, the war reparations proved very beneficial to Nokia, which played a central role as a cable supplier to the Soviets. In the coming years, more than 50 percent of the FCW's entire production went to the Soviet Union.[4] After the reparations had been paid and the capacity of the factory had been doubled, a political relationship was converted into a business relationship. With Soviet exports, Nokia's cable business, which had been a cash hole of the 1920s, became the cash cow of the company's three firm-

coalition. In the late 1950s, Finland opened its economy to Western Europe, while the country's commercial ties deepened with the Soviet Union and the Eastern Bloc. After the 1973 oil crisis, Finnish exports to the Soviet Union spared the small country from the more severe recession affecting Western markets. In both cases, Nokia benefited immensely. Reparations made its cable business, just as the 1970s Soviet trade provided a testing ground for its electronics products.[5]

The 1967 Merger: Birth of an Industrial Conglomerate

On the surface, Finland's postwar "economic miracle" was reminiscent of Stalin's and Hrustsev's early industrialization, but never achieved the high efficiencies of the Asian tigers. This success, however, came with a price. During the post–World War II era, technology transfer became far more difficult. Not only was Nokia faced with market and technological uncertainties; it also had to cope with the implications of the "special relationship" with the Soviet Union. At Kremlin, the Soviets perceived technology partnerships as political alliances and blocked Finnish participation in the Marshall Plan and the Organization for European Economic Cooperation (later the Organization for Economic Cooperation and Development, or OECD). While the Marshall Plan enabled the military losers of the war (i.e., Japan and Germany) to become the economic winners of the Cold War, Finland missed the first "technology catch-up" train.[6] Competitive necessities were subject to political realities.

From 1945 to the mid-1960s, the FRW continued to control Nokia and the FCW through its majority stakes. But this control no longer reflected the changing revenue mix of the company. In 1967—three decades after the first combination talks—Nokia's three constituent companies merged into one. The new corporate entity was an industrial conglomerate with four major business segments: forestry, rubber, cable, and electronics. As sarcastic Finnish observers put it, the new company's name, Oy Nokia Ab, came from wood processing, its management from the cable factory, and its money from the rubber industry. But it was the seemingly most insignificant segment, electronics, that renewed Nokia's competitive advantage for the new era. It also meant a strategic U-turn for the company.

The Pre-Cellular Era: Nokia, Electronics, and Telecommunications—''A Sum of Great Many Chances''

In Finland, the electronics industry originated in the 1920s, with the rise of radio manufacturing and the Finnish Broadcasting Corporation. During the war years, radio communication played a vital role. Nokia's rise as the leader of the cellular industry did not start in the 1990s but originated with the consolidation of Finnish electronics in the postwar era, which, in turn, stemmed from the company's leadership in cable since the early 1910s. The fortunes of the State Electric Works (Valtion sähköpaja), FCW, and Salora illustrate these developments. The process started with the launch of FRW in 1912 and climaxed with the creation of Nokia Mobile Phones and Nokia Networks in the 1990s (see Exhibit 10-2).

Nokia's Successful Consolidation . . .

Between 1945 and 1980, Nokia consolidated state-controlled and privately owned units of Finnish businesses that had played a crucial role in electronics, radiophones, and TV. It was not a purposeful strategy, but a com-

Exhibit 10-2. Evolution of Nokia's wireless business.

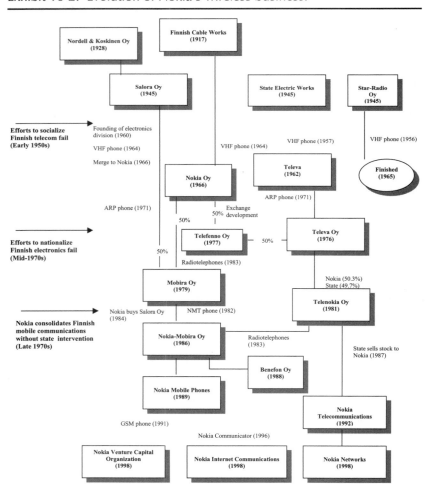

plicated series of piecemeal moves in a vaguely framed effort to invest in innovation and growth.

Televa (Key Public-Sector Player). Starting in 1945, the State Electric Works—which had been launched in 1925 as a research laboratory of the Finnish Defence Forces—served as an industry catalyst. In 1981, Televa Oy was taken over by Nokia. This purchase was the final step in Nokia's consolidation of the nascent electronic and wireless industries in Finland.

Mobira (Key Private-Sector Player). In the early 1960s, Salora Oy, a veteran radio and TV set producer, diversified into radiophone manufacturing. In the mid-1970s, Nokia's marketing activities with Salora resulted in increasing cooperation, which led to a joint venture, Mobira Oy (as in *mobi*le *ra*dio), in 1979.[7]

Nokia Electronics. In 1960, the Finnish Cable Works diversified into electronics, focusing on calculation activities, the sale and leasing of computing systems, and the manufacture of electronics equipment. Concurrently, Nokia began importing computer systems by Elliot in the U.K.and Siemens in Germany. As Nokia researched radio transmission technology, the French computer firm Machines Bull selected the company as its Finnish agent in 1962. At the same time, activities were divided into computing and electronics. With the three-firm merger five years later, the key customers of the electronics unit consisted of taxi companies, industrial concerns, shipping firms, the PTT, transport organizations, fire departments, and utilities. While this customer base mirrored that of the pre-cellular Motorola, the revenue base was tiny. To survive, Nokia had to internationalize.

. . . Due to Political Failures

Nokia's efforts to consolidate the business would not have succeeded without two critical failures by the public sector; failures that official reports neglected to mention until the end of the Cold War.[8] The first occurred in the early 1950s, when the leftist political parties, particularly the Communists, tried to socialize Finnish telecommunications. As conditions in Finland improved, these objectives were buried. The second effort took place in the 1970s, when another leftist coalition sought to nationalize the emerging Finnish electronics industry through the creation of a "national champion." Initially supported by the Socialists, Communists, and Centrists, this plan led to the so-called Valco corruption scandal, which resulted in a national debacle. Only after these two failures could Nokia consolidate the business, which it accomplished through the acquisition of Televa. Recalls Harri Holkeri, Finland's veteran conservative leader and friend to Nokia CEO Kari H. Kairamo, who played a critical role in telecom deregulation:

> Whatever the Valco debacle cost, the money that was burned in this affair was useful because it taught what market forces mean and that state bureaucracies don't manufacture TV sets. When Nokia was allowed to acquire Televa, *that* was a major political and, to a lesser degree, technological factor in the vendor's future expansion. The public sector couldn't inject the kind of capital that was needed. Nokia's consolidation of these various different firms was really a sum of great many chances. When it developed its mobile unit with Televa's technology concept, that, too, was something of a chance.[9]

There was no grand strategy behind these concentration efforts. Instead, they were guided by Nokia's determination and success in electronics, failures of the public sector's high-tech ambitions, and, toward the late 1970s, Kairamo's dogged obsession to turn Nokia into a technology business. But ultimately, it was Nordic cooperation that gave rise to and nurtured the infant wireless industry, starting in the late 1960s. Equipment manufacturers joined the process in spring 1977. Two years later, Mobira manufactured the first Nordic Mobile Telephone (NMT) base stations to Finland's PTT. With Nordic NMT cooperation, Nokia increased its radiophone activities accordingly and Mobira began to invest in NMT mobile phones and base stations while harvesting overlapping products and marketing activities. As England and Sweden launched their first networks in 1981, Mobira entered these markets, even if its most important customers were in Finland. Concurrently, Nokia consolidated the industry. As political interventions failed, market-driven efforts would rule.

Growth Through Internationalization

Nokia tenaciously stuck to its long-term strategy, which occasionally led to the loss of potential short-term profits. The problem, as Björn Westerlund, chief executive of the FCW, saw it, was that the Soviet Union, as *the* most significant customer, was building Nokia and its capabilities. Yet the Soviet economy was not market driven. When Nokia's Soviet business amounted to 20 percent of the total revenues of the FCW, Westerlund warned the senior management: "We must be cautious and not allow the proportion of Soviet business to grow too much. . . . If one day they'll say *nyet* in Kreml, we'll lose our business overnight."[10] Through the Cold War, Finnish business strategies were constrained by geopolitical exigencies. Starting with the reparations, Nokia played a critical role in Soviet trade, but unlike most Finnish firms, it was not swept by political visions and did not allow Eastern trade to monopolize its exports.

In the 1970s and 1980s, Kairamo initiated Nokia's radical growth strategy while investing in electronics. It was a bold business strategy with substantial political implications because it meant a shift from Eastern trade to Western exports. To grow, Nokia had to internationalize; to internationalize, it had to grow. Neither was possible without Western technology—which, in turn, would not please the Soviets.

Kairamo's Rebellion: From Trees to People

In 1977, when Westerlund retired, Kairamo was appointed managing director of the company (in 1986 he became its CEO). Born into a family of wealth and rebellion, the mercurial and charismatic Kari H. Kairamo (1932–1988) transformed Nokia. Traditional formalities gave way to immediacy while change and flexibility became the new catchwords. For all practical purposes, Kairamo *was* Nokia through the 1980s:

> To us, the Finns, internationalization is not an alternative to something else. Finland has quite a few resources. Briefly put, there are two of them: the people and the trees. Exports are obligatory, in the future as well. Things must be sold abroad so that living conditions will remain good domestically. This, in turn, requires that we have extensive experience in international business. . . . That's the greatest risk facing the Finns—the small amount of international business experience.[11]

In the past, Finland's success originated from comparative advantage and natural resources ("trees"). In the future, it would be about competitive advantage and human capital ("people"). To Kairamo, that meant a "kind of Japanese model." Kairamo sought a *dynamic* fit between Nokia's resources and its environment. Through leveraged fit, Nokia would anticipate and respond to future changes in the environment, just as it would employ those environmental characteristics that were currently seen as limiting to make its strategy more effective. At least that was the theory.

Struggle for Technology: Between U.S. Export Controls and the KGB

With the advent of the Reagan era, the United States prohibited technology exports to Soviet Union. As a result, Nokia was confronted with a Janus-faced dilemma. While Finland (and Nokia, in particular) served as Moscow's primary supplier of "Western technology," the future of Finnish electronics depended on U.S. technology. As NATO suspected the Finns were leaking technology to the Soviet Union, Kairamo had to convince the United States and its allies that critical technology products were not being delivered to

Kremlin. Many Western countries felt threatened by the Finns' participation in tech coalitions, which—as the skeptics, again, argued—might lead to technology secrets leaking to the Soviet Union and Eastern Europe. Only persistent diplomatic efforts enabled Finland to participate in EUREKA, the European research program in the mid-1980s. As long as Finland was constrained by its special relationship with the Soviet Union, Nokia would not be a credible partner in technology coalitions.

During the 1960s and 1970s, "Finlandization" had become a pejorative warning in the West.[12] And there's no smoke without fire. In the small Nordic country, all major foreign and sometimes even domestic policy decisions were carried out with an *a priori* assessment of the possible Soviet reaction. Every major Finnish politician of significant standing and even corporate leaders had a "friend" (read: a KGB acquaintance, or a *kotiryssä*, as the Finns put it) in the Soviet Embassy. Many Finnish politicians had few inhibitions in discussing the positive and negative aspects of their own and other political parties with KGB officials.[13] Kairamo himself was no exception. Viktor Vladimirov, a KGB general who presented himself as a loyal follower of the new party chief Yuri Andropov, later declared Kairamo to be one of the most important Finnish industrialists he had a pleasure to keep regular contact with.[14] One anecdote illustrates the precarious balancing act. In 1984, Richard N. Perle, the U.S. assistant secretary of defense for international security policy, visited Finland. In the past, Nokia had built cable factories in Russia; now Kairamo wanted to export Nokia's new DX 200 switching stations. As Kairamo served as Perle's host, he had an opportunity to talk about U.S. export controls, which were threatening Nokia's technology exports to the Soviet Union. With the assistance of Western technology, argued Perle, the Soviets saved at least five years in product development. Still, after the Finnish visit and Kairamo's persuasive diplomacy, Perle wrote a gracious letter in which he expressed his confidence that a solution could be found to minimize the harms caused by export controls to Nokia, even while securing the defense interests of the West. Later that year, the first DX 200 stations were exported to the Soviet Union.[15]

Because of politics and trade, Kairamo could neither distance himself from the Soviet Union nor approach the United States. So began his quest for a third way—European integration—a decade or two before it became ideologically faddish and politically safe in Finland. This political enterprise was intertwined with his determination to turn Nokia into an electronics giant. In fact, the idea had been discussed since the 1973 oil crisis. As Kairamo later recalled, "We came to the conclusion that we couldn't grow in Finland with cables or tires anymore. . . . We decided to keep what we had but also to put all the new money we could scrape together into high tech."[16]

The Birth of the Electronics Concern

In the late 1950s and early 1960s, Nokia shifted its focus to consumer and business electronics and modernized its basic industries. The groundwork for the shift to telecommunications was laid in the 1960s, when the electronics department initiated research into radio transmission. Realizing the future potential of semiconductor technology, the company gave rise to several "digital gurus," including Björn Westerlund and Kurt Wikstedt, who maintained good relations with universities, had a strategic vision of a digital future, and were eager to exploit new technology commercially. In 1969, Nokia was the first company to introduce standardized pulse code modulation (PCM) transmission equipment.[17] By 1985, most of the growth in Nokia's transmission systems came from PCM, which was supplied to telecom authorities. Pioneership did not ensure easy revenue, however. From the late 1950s until the mid-1970s, Nokia's electronics department was a cash trap. It took years of investments and hard effort to turn the unit into a cash cow.

The view of Kurt Wikstedt, then chief of the unit, on the significance of electronics relied on American management approaches—especially the experience curve and portfolio analysis—years before they were widely employed in Finland. "Electronics has been right for the company," acknowledged Wikstedt. "Its profitability is not as good as we'd like it to be, but this has to do with our vast investments."[18] Strategically, it made sense; financially, it was horrible, initially. Only when Wikstedt was about to retire did the unit become profitable. It had been in the red for seventeen long years. The diversified conglomerate sought financial discipline through portfolio management, which was benchmarked from General Electric. Nokia also adopted an active corporate strategy, boldly allocating capital to electronics and telecommunications. Both were perceived as "star" segments with promising growth prospects. But even in 1967, electronics still generated only 3 percent of the Nokia Group's net sales and provided work for only 460 people. In the early 1970s, most telephone exchanges remained electromechanical analog switches, but Nokia's electronics unit began developing the digital switch that eventually became the famed Nokia DX 200, a multifaceted platform that remains the basis for Nokia's network infrastructure. By stepping into the digital age early, Nokia made one of the most important strategic decisions in its corporate history.

M&As and Internationalization: From Basic Industry to Technology

In the 1960s and 1970s, the most innovative Japanese leaders had applied American insights to increasingly global industries. Now the Nokians were about to do the same in mobile communications. The company was small enough to exploit new technologies more flexibly and quickly than its mass-producer rivals. Before its M&A binge, Nokia had established footholds in international markets, even if core activities were in Europe. That boded well for globalization. Electronics played an insignificant role in this expansion. Also, Nokia's fate remained intertwined with that of the East rather than the West. Some 37 percent of its exports went to European Free Trade Association (EFTA), European Economic Community (EEC), and other OECD countries, whereas 52 percent went to the Soviet bloc countries. Things began to change with the slowdown of Finnish electronics in 1981, when the sharp expansion of telecom production precipitated promising growth prospects. Between 1983 and 1984, Nokia was transformed from a diversified conglomerate into an electronics concern, which translated to a shift from Eastern trade to Western exports. For the first time, the electronics revenues *exceeded* those from cable, forest, or rubber.[19]

Acquisitions altered Nokia's strategic and geographic focus, even as it moved production closer to customers, which meant more overseas manufacturing facilities. Less than half of Nokia's personnel was Finnish. Between 1982 and 1987, market value more than tripled from FIM 2,272 million to FIM 8,029 million. Though the largest company in Finland, Nokia remained relatively unknown in Europe. "Like its homeland, Nokia has an image problem," noted *The Wall Street Journal*. "Outside of Finland it barely has one."[20] By the spring of 1987, things looked more promising. There was even some talk that Nokia could acquire Ericsson. Nokia was intent to being *the* leading European technology conglomerate. To prepare the company for international markets, Kairamo initiated an organizational reform designed to increase flexibility and cooperation while delegating responsibility. The legendary decentralization and teamwork found today at Nokia originates from these efforts.

Like Jorma Ollila, Kairamo wanted to demolish old hierarchies that prevented the company from "listening to the customers," especially overseas. In the early 1970s, exports and foreign activities accounted for only 20 percent of total sales. By 1980, exports and foreign activities increased to more than 50 percent of total sales. Acquisitions and internationalization resulted in a thorough transformation (see Exhibit 10-3). Between 1980 and 1988, Nokia's personnel more than doubled to 44,600. At the same time, revenues quadrupled to FIM 21.8 billion. In the process, electronics (59 percent) became the primary business segment of the company, while cable (18 percent), forestry (14 percent), and rubber (8 percent) served as support segments. The more frantic the pace of change, the more uneasy the Finns felt about Nokia. Kairamo, however, had a great faith in the tech future: "European industry, as well as the cost structure of products, has become increasingly knowledge-based. . . . What is essential, then, is the continuing change and renewal; in other words, adaptability vis-à-vis new circumstances and market opportunities."[21]

Forestry created Nokia. Cable and rubber sustained Nokia. Technology would renew Nokia.

The 1G Era: Nokia-Mobira and the Booming 1980s

The initial strategic objective of Nokia-Mobira, a wholly-owned subsidiary of Nokia, was to combine resources to ensure the long-term competitiveness of the Finnish radiophone industry. Managing Director Jorma Nieminen and

Exhibit 10-3. Nokia's diversification (1967–2001).

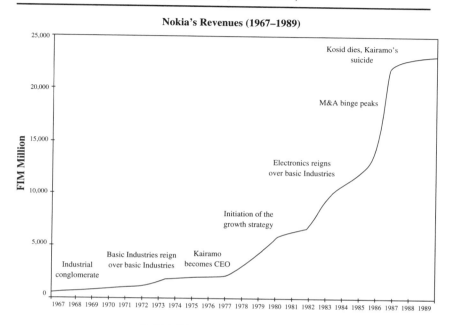

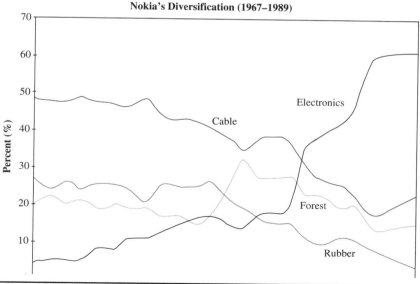

(continues)

Exhibit 10-3. (Continued).

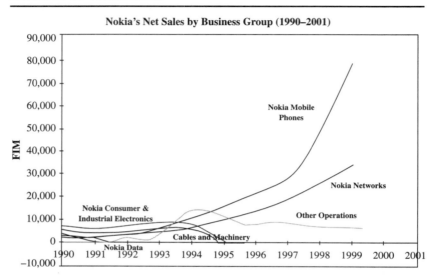

Nokia's Net Sales by Business Group (1990–2001)

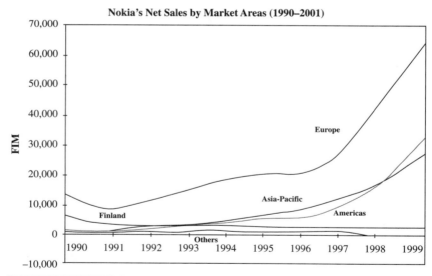

Nokia's Net Sales by Market Areas (1990–2001)

SOURCE: Company reports.

Marketing Director Kari-Pekka Wilska took charge of the company, whose revenues amounted to some FIM 50 million. Although Helsinki remained the home base, Salo was chosen as the corporate headquarters and manufacturing center of radiophones. Base stations and other PMR equipment were produced in Oulu, which soon became an integral part of the Finnish mobile cluster.[22] Through the 1980s, Nokia-Mobira designed, manufactured, and marketed mobile end-user equipment, whereas Nokia Cellular Systems focused on the system infrastructure. By the early 1990s, these two subsidiaries evolved into the famed Nokia Mobile Phones and Nokia Networks.

Established in 1979 as a joint venture with Salora, Mobira saw its fortunes soar with the joint Nordic standard. As Mobira became a part of Nokia, Telenokia's radiophone unit was moved into Mobira (refer to Exhibit 10-2) and the Finns began to develop their nascent mass-manufacturing capabilities. That year, the Nokia Telecommunications division accounted for almost 50 percent of the net sales by the entire Electronics Group.[23] In 1982—a full decade before Ollila's global focus strategy—Jorma Nieminen presented his celebrated vision of the early radiophone business as a *global* industry:

> . . . NMT represents a critically important development phase in worldwide scale. . . . It has already changed the general thinking and views on radiophones. It has become understood that NMT is only an example of the direction that must be taken. The ultimate objective must be a worldwide system that permits the indefinite communication of mobile people with each other, irrespective of the location.[24]

New markets emerged worldwide and grew rapidly. Novel technologies and increasing complexity required greater R&D expenditures. Between 1979 and 1987, revenues soared from FIM 49 million to FIM 1,084 million, while exports more than doubled to almost 75 percent. In the United States, Mobira needed a strategic partner with an existing distribution network. In 1984, Tandy proposed a joint venture to make mobile phones in Korea. The two set up a plant in South Korea to distribute phones in the United States through Tandy's Radio Shack outlets and under the Radio Shack brand name. Activities were reorganized into five units that focused on the NMT standard, the United States, Europe, Oulu, and PMR. To its surprise, Nokia-Mobira became the leading supplier of automatic cellular phones in Europe, North America, and the Far East. But sales remained relatively small in total revenues. At Nokia, the two key units—Telecommunications and Nokia-Mobira—amounted to just 7.5 percent and 6.4 percent of total net sales, respectively.

Rapid growth continued in 1987, when Nokia-Mobira grew 28 percent to $269 million, which made it the world leader, with 13.5 percent of the $800 million cellular phone market worldwide. Since competition had halved the prices of cellular phones since 1983, the company began looking for ways to shore up margins. Nokia-Mobira joined forces with France's Alcatel and West Germany's AEG to devise a system for Europe that it hoped would become an international standard for the digital cellular network of the 1990s. To ensure that Nokia could influence standards, Kairamo sought greater market share, preferably through the United States. He insisted on a single brand name—Nokia—for all products before the anticipated GSM explosion. To avoid being priced out of the growth markets, the company had to drastically improve its operational effectiveness. The United States, in particular, served as a lesson. Lamented Mobira's Marketing Director Kari-Pekka Wilska:

> Price competition is nowhere as tough as in the U.S. markets. That was the biggest surprise to me. . . . The competition is ruthless. It is cash flow thinking. . . . If the cash flow directs the business, then issues arise, including market misconduct. In the United States, the margins are totally different. . . . The business involves huge volumes, and if you fail to enter the volume business, then you'd better forget it.[25]

Disagreements led to the resignation of Jorma Nieminen as managing director of Nokia-Mobira. He recruited several senior managers to launch his own company, Benefon. Nokia-Mobira's new president, Timo Louhenkilpi, helped the company refine its organizational structure. The revised organizational chart reflected Nokia-Mobira's rapid geographic expansion along six different units: Finland, Scandinavia, North America, the U.K., Central Europe, and Far East. In the long term, these geographic segments formed the nucleus for Nokia's globalization. Nokia Cellular Systems was established as an independent company. As the company prepared for high volumes, Nokia's electronics manufacturing activities in Salo were brought under a single umbrella. Concurrently, a new mobile phone factory in Nokia's manufacturing facilities in Bochum, West Germany, was launched to meet growing demand in Continental Europe. On the downstream side, sales and marketing were reorganized in the main markets.

As Nokia established its foothold in the worldwide 1G markets in the late 1980s, two units that had played relatively minor role in the electronics group became the crown jewels of the company. By 1991, the net sales of Nokia Telecommunications totaled FIM 1.8 billion. Of these sales, public networks (i.e., national PTTs) accounted for 48 percent, cellular systems (i.e., deregulated telecom markets) for 34 percent, and dedicated networks (i.e., corporate systems) for 18 percent. Only half a decade before, national PTTs had dominated net sales, but new public policies had pushed the industry toward competition. Still, Nokia Telecommunications had to struggle with Ericsson's established relationships, whereas Nokia Mobile Phones (NMP) was Europe's largest and the world's second-largest mobile phone manufacturer by 1991. In addition to the main facility in Salo, NMP had 22 locations worldwide. It supplied phones for all analog systems worldwide and had a worldwide production and logistics network. Its net sales totaled FIM 2.5 billion. Of the net sales, mobile phones accounted for 87 percent and components only 13 percent.

Throughout the 1G era, Nokia's objective was to develop into an industry leader in products, brand, and logistics. In this process, *quality* was perceived as the prime instrument employed to bring stability and thereby contribute to managing constant change. The quality strategy precipitated the global focus strategy to the extent that it evaluated Nokia's activities on the basis of worldwide standards, not conversely.[26] "This is based on our company values as a foundation for everything we do, with operations being managed using quality tools and developing processes. This makes for speed, productivity, and customer satisfaction," noted Matti Alahuhta, NMP's president.[27] Nokia did not simply imitate the American-based Six Sigma, but encouraged its employees to apply the method and report back. Self-reflectivity, thus, was incorporated into the self-assessments.

Crash and Restructuring

As Nokia's mobile units struggled to manage hypergrowth, the parent was swept by a bitter struggle for corporate control. In 1986, Nokia remained a diversified technology conglomerate with some eleven industrial groups. The new organizational structure reflected size and complexity, as well as problems that remained invisible in Finland and abroad until the turmoil of 1988. The high-tech growth proponents of the executive board (Kairamo, Timo H. A. Koski, and others) pushed for growth and internationalization. The financial gatekeepers of the supervisory board (the chiefs of leading Finnish banks Mika Tiivola and Jaakko Lassila, as well as controversial investor Pentti Kouri) sought to contain the excesses of unmanaged growth. The banks may also have conspired to overthrow Kairamo's leadership. Such a theory has been refuted by bankers and in Nokia's authorized history. In this view, Kairamo is portrayed as a manic-depressive out of touch with realities. Nokia's former chief of R&D, Matti Otala, has given a quite different account, arguing that there was indeed a conspiracy by the banks.[28]

In April 1988, Timo H. A. Koski, then managing director of Nokia's electronics unit and Kairamo's right hand in the Nokia University project, suffered a cerebral hemorrhage on a plane in Heathrow, London. This loss portended others that followed. With his heir gone, Kairamo took charge of the Nokia University project and the company's M&A activities. Growth was no longer under control, but Nokia was still portrayed as a challenger to U.S. and Japanese players and as Europe's great Nordic hope. "Kairamo's work isn't finished," reported *The Wall Street Journal.* "He wants to dominate Europe's cellular phone business and, someday, America's, too. In fact, Nokia, whose U. S. headquarters is just under the nose of [AT&T] in Basking Ridge, New Jersey, plans to spend up to $1 billion soon to expand in the U.S., either with an acquisition or a joint venture."[29] That fall, Kairamo became convinced that the banks were willing to spin off into pieces the empire he had been building for years. The banks denied such allegations. On December 11, 1988, when board members thought Nokia's chief was about to travel to Thailand for a vacation, Kairamo hanged himself. So began Nokia's restructuring and financial roller-coaster.

The much-debated restructuring that was initiated by Simo Vuorilehto and completed by Jorma Ollila had long been in the air at Nokia. Kairamo himself had toyed with the idea of focusing and restructuring as early as 1981. Despite the depth of the recession, Nokia recovered quickly as its new CEO, Vuorilehto, streamlined its businesses. A tough-minded engineer, Vuorilehto had risen through the ranks of Finland's big pulp and paper industry. He lacked experience in electronics and did not share Kairamo's ambition to make Nokia a more international company. Under his leadership, the company moved from a buying binge to a selling binge. In just few months, some 10 percent of Nokia's revenues were gone.[30] The buying binge continued in a more focused manner with an important, strategic purchase of Technophone, a U.K. mobile phone manufacturer that had been the second in the European market after Nokia. Vuorilehto was far more cautious and conservative than Kairamo. When the two men had played together, Nokia benefited. One drove visions, the other implemented them. With visions gone, Nokia's corporate strategy focused on restructuring. With Vuorilehto in charge, many Nokians felt they were treated like trees—used and harvested.

As Vuorilehto's cadre of executives were shown the door, forty-one-year-old Jorma Ollila was appointed CEO in 1992. Under his leadership, Nokia made the strategic decision to focus on mobile communications and divest noncore operations.

Global Focus

After the elections of 1991, Finland had its first purely non-Socialist government since 1966. As Social Democrats moved to the opposition, the Centrist-Conservative Esko Aho government formulated an export-oriented economic strategy to revitalize exports and industrial production. Because of a severe recession and the collapse of the Soviet Union, Finland took several decisive steps in the early 1990s toward a new national industrial strategy, seeking to strengthen its economy and establish itself as a competitor in the global telecom and mobile industries. European integration provided the business environment that Kairamo and his executives had envisioned as a catalyst for Nokia's new expansion.

In the past, Finnish presidents were expected to be foreign policy experts because of the geopolitical position of the country. After the demise of the Soviet Union and the collapse of Soviet trade, the emphasis shifted from foreign policy to trade policy. In the early months of 1994, Martti Ahtisaari, former under-secretary general of the United Nations and a member of the Social Democratic Party, was elected president of Finland. That October, the Finnish electorate voted to accede to the EU, which Ahtisaari had strongly supported. Ahtisaari served in this job from February 1994 to February 2000—the years of Nokia's hypergrowth and globalization. To him, Finland's political integration in Europe in the 1990s was the mirror image of the country's telecom industry deregulation in the 1980s. "It was vital to liberalize in telecommunications because that contributed to our competitiveness and gave us an early position. It taught the industry to operate in a globalized world. We didn't want the industry to look too much at bilateral trade commissions." Unlike the U.S. vendors, Nokia and Ericsson achieved scale through scope. Finland, Ahtisaari thought, provided unique opportunities for public/private partnership (see Exhibit 10-4). "These opportunities had to do with the small size of our population, which is half of that in metropolitan New York." In the mid-1990s, Finland's President Martti Ahtisaari traveled more than any previous president in the nation's history. As a keen observer of international trade policy, he was familiar with recent research on industrial clusters. Finland's future depended on exports, especially forestry and telecommunications. "We planned those travels *with* Finland's industry federation," Ahtisaari acknowledged. "I'd ask, 'Where would you like to go? Which countries?' And they'd respond. We traveled a lot. We covered almost all of our target countries."[31]

In January 1995, Finland's membership in the EU signaled the beginning of the innovation stage of competitive development. Public policies contributed to and facilitated Nokia's expansion beyond the Finnish borders. But in the aftermath of the great transition, it was the vendor's strategy that ultimately determined its fate. And this strategy was crafted according to Ollila's vision, in which digital cellular played the key role. His leadership focused the operation, continued to divest noncore properties, and most important, initiated the worldwide leverage of Nokia's operations.

Toward the GSM Explosion

In August 1998, *Business Week* published a flattering cover story on Nokia. The feature opened with a parallel of the Finnish sauna and Nokia's strategy: "Behind his gentlemanly demeanor, Jorma Ollila, CEO of Nokia Corp., is a man of extremes. As his wife, Liisa Annikki, tells it, her husband fires up the Finnish sauna a good fifteen degrees warmer than she likes it, all the way to 212F—hot

Exhibit 10-4. Struggle for market access: "Give me ten Nokias."

"In the beginning of my presidency in the early months of 1994, Nokia was already growing rapidly and I had regular contact with the company," recalls Martti Ahtisaari, former President of Finland and an internationally highly regarded crisis negotiator. "We had an annual meeting with the board, with Jorma Ollila and the others. When I started as president, this was the message: 'Give me 10 Nokias.'"

The eclipse of the Cold War and the demise of the Soviet empire meant a "dramatic shift" in Europe and particularly in Finland, Ahtisaari contended. Yet there was continuity in the openness of the small country. "We Finns have always looked for free trade opportunities and tried to secure our access to our main markets. That is vital to us. Trade policy basically hasn't changed. In the past, there certainly was a close relationship between the business community and the president, but that was limited only to Soviet Union. It was not an innovative exercise."

Ahtisaari's "travel policy" was unique and unorthodox. Some criticized him for mixing too much with the Finnish industrialists. "But I didn't give a damn," says Ahtisaari. "I figured that if I didn't help them, I could not help the workers either. One of the key targets was China, where Nokia's chief Ollila joined the president.

The cover of Martti Ahtisaari's (2000) *The Kosovo Peace Process* (Helsinki: WSOY 2000)

Together with Strobe Talbott, Deputy Secretary of State, and Viktor Chernomyrdin, former Prime Minister of Russia and Special Representative of President Boris Yeltsin, Ahtisaari was the chief architect of the Kosovo peace plan in June 1999.

SOURCE: Steinbock, D. (2001) *Interview with President Martti Ahtisaari,* New York City, May 2001. On the China visit, see the Nokia section in Chapter 9.

enough to boil a pot of tea. . . . Emerging from the sauna, Ollila paused, then plunged naked into the icy lake. Ollila, a forty-seven-year-old former banker, lives by the plunge. He believes people get comfy and complacent and that it takes a dive into the unknown, or a push, to tap into their strongest instincts—those that guide survival."[32] Inadvertently, the *Business Week* story set a pattern for most Nokia profiles thereafter, from *Forbes* to *Wired.* The sauna/strategy parable would be quite dramatic if it were not for the fact that such sauna habits are quite typical to the Finnish lifestyle. But what was customary in Finland became portrayed abroad as an exotic Nordic existential gamble. Thus was born a new myth of Nokia: the underdog that came in from the cold. In reality, Nokia was then some 125 years old, and Ollila was not exactly a man of extremes.

Ollila and the New Strategy: "You Got Six Months . . ."

Initially, Ollila intended to explore engineering physics at the Helsinki University of Technology, but he switched to applied mathematics and systems theory and began to study economics in the University of Helsinki. In 1974, he earned a degree in political science while serving as chairman of the National Union of Finnish Students (SYL). Ollila, the young Centrist, aligned himself with the upper-class student radicals who spoke for a "proletarian revolution" in Finland. He was not a follower, but one of the leaders representing SYL in "peace festivals" in Moscow, East Berlin, and Havana. But he was also a pragmatist. The transition from a radical student politician to a Citibank banker and CEO of Nokia abounds with irony. A far more interesting way to look at this personal transformation is to understand it through continuity rather than change. The very same negotiating skills that Ollila showed in Finnish student politics in the early 1970s were crucial in Nokia's financial deals in the late 1980s and the technology coalitions in the late 1990s. In each case, he has ingeniously mediated between different, often hostile organizations in adverse circumstances.

In the mid-1980s, Kairamo's Nokia was one of Citibank's key clients. While an account manager at Citibank, Ollila was assigned to examine the firm at the peak of its internationalization and M&A activities. Having discovered problems in foreign activities, he argued that Nokia's organization did not match the new competitive environment and that it needed a thorough transformation. Dynamic competition required dynamic organizational capabilities. After a September 1984 meeting, Kairamo hired Ollila as VP of international operations. Two years later, Ollila, through a replacement, became company's CFO and joined the board. His new life at Nokia progressed rapidly. Under Vuorilehto, Ollila got his first taste of the mobile industry by heading the small but strategic cellular phone division in Salo. Along with investor Pentti Kouri, Antti Lagerroos, previous managing director of the cellular unit, had plotted against the group leadership. When Lagerroos was forced to leave the company, Ollila was promoted to take his place in February 1990.

In 1982, Nokia Mobile Phones exported terminals to Nordic countries. Five years later, it exported them to some twenty-four countries in Europe, North America, and Asia. NMP had been profitable during 1981 and 1982, as well as 1990 and 1992, when, at the end of Ollila's reign, the unit exported to seventy countries, and in 1994, to some 100 countries. By 1992, Nokia had doubled its share of global markets to 20 percent. The distance to corporate headquarters allowed Ollila to avoid Nokia's power struggles in the early 1990s. He focused on the GSM project, understood its potential for Nokia, and reentered the leadership arena at a more opportune time. As markets opened up, he reasoned, even small-country companies could become world players—if they had the right focus.

As Finland was hit by a severe recession, Nokia struggled to survive. In late November 1991, the owners of Nokia had many questions for Ollila. Most of them had a common denominator: *Can Nokia be saved?* If Nokia focused on mobile phones and opted for GSM technology, argued Ollila, Nokia could be saved. In mid-January 1992, he got the job. If he could turn around the company, they would let him continue. If he failed to do so, they would intervene. "What I was told by my seniors was, 'Look, you get six months to make a proposal on whether we sell it or what we do with this business.' After four months I said, 'No, we're not going to sell this one.'"[33]

"Focus, Global, Telecom-Oriented, High Value-Added"

Before the Ollila era, Vuorilehto's Nokia had FIM 15.5 billion in net sales, with the telecom and mobile groups accounting for 28 percent of the total. But brighter prospects were on the horizon. In July 1991, Finnish telecom authorities inaugurated a digital mobile network supplied by Nokia Telecommunications, while Nokia Mobile Phones presented a digital GSM car phone for mass production. Nokia was now the first company to offer digital mobile phones in all three main markets of Europe, America, and Japan. Following the boardroom shake-up in 1992, CEO Ollila and CFO Olli-Pekka Kallasvuo envisioned a new course for the company. "We had unhappy Finnish shareholders, unhappy international shareholders," Ollila has recalled. "The only thing you could do is to start building a base for very meaningful stock performance."[34]

Ollila bet Nokia's future on the GSM vision. In August 1992, he was working on a presentation for still another weekend seminar on Nokia's strategy. He quickly scribbled a title, "Nokia 2000," and four words: *Focus, Global, Telecom-Oriented, High Value-Added.*[35] The company would have to obtain new organizational capabilities, build strategic advantages upon these capabilities, and globalize. While Ollila and Kallasvuo crafted the basic elements of Nokia's winning strategy, the group executive board refined and executed it. It was this "collective mind" that made the company both visionary and efficient through the 1990s. Conversely, Ollila and senior executives were suspicious about the personalized myths that grow up around successful top managers. The following March, Ollila's first review as Nokia's president and CEO precipitated the themes of Nokia in the 1990s, including globalization, focus, divestiture of noncore operations, expansion to North America and Asia-Pacific (especially China), corporate renewal in a dynamic environment, new digital platforms, and organizational agility.[36] Despite the success of Nokia's strategy in the 1990s, it also entailed a vulnerability, which was reflected by the group executive board. While the members were highly qualified, they were all Finnish, despite the global nature of Nokia's operations. In April 2002, two new members—chief of Nokia IP Mobility and Nokia Mobile Software—joined the board. They were Finnish as well. These characteristics—highly centralized control coupled with global activities—was reminiscent of the Japanese challengers, their initial success, and their ultimate failure. Unlike the Japanese attackers, however, Nokia continued to listen to its customers.

Marketing Innovation

As it narrowed its business focus to handsets and infrastructure, Nokia, loyal to its translocal posture, aspired to exploit several strategic advantages simultaneously and worldwide, including:

- Innovation (i.e., new technology and new marketing approaches)
- Cost-efficiency (i.e., manufacturing, logistics, and new product development)
- Differentiation (i.e., brand, segmentation, and design)

In addition to technology development and logistics, global branding and product segmentation played an important role in Nokia's new strategy.

Global Branding

Along with global logistics, R&D, and segmentation, global branding played a critical role in these efforts. Through most of the 1980s, Nokia had been known as an original equipment manufacturer (OEM). It served as a supplier for several industry giants, such as IBM Corp., Control Data Systems, and Tandy in the United States, as well as Canada's Northern Telecom, Japan's Hitachi, Italy's Olivetti, Sweden's Ericsson, and British Telecom. The OEM strategy was useful as long as Nokia did not have adequate marketing experience of its own. Toward the late 1980s, the vendor revised its marketing approach. By 2002, like worldwide brand leaders such as Sony, Nike, Coca-Cola, Microsoft, and Heineken, Nokia invested boldly in building and maintaining its brand name worldwide. It adopted the logo "Nokia Connecting People" for immediate global recognition. In 1991, Ollila's team decided that Nokia would have to be marketed as a *single* brand and hired a young 3M marketing executive, Anssi Vanjoki—today a senior VP in Nokia's group executive board—to figure out how to make Nokia a household name. At the time, the leading vendors were sales machines rather than marketers. Having evolved as suppliers to national monopolies, they treated advertising as an afterthought. As Vanjoki researched the history of companies that had developed successful brands, he discovered a common denominator among such leaders as Nike, Daimler-Benz, and Philip Morris. These companies thought about the brand in every aspect of the value chain, including design, production, and distribution. The basics of Nokia's "holistic" brand strategy plan were completed by June 1991. The position statement emphasized "high technology with the human touch," a precursor of the "connecting people" theme. Building on the success of the Cityman, Freedom, and Talkman campaigns, Nokia developed its brand on five basic dimensions: high technology, Nordic design, individualism, freedom, and enduring quality. Most dimensions stressed lifestyle values, including ecological themes, which resonated with the vendor's early-adopter users.

By September 1996, the vendor had the strongest cellular brand awareness and image in Europe. There was little "new" in Nokia's branding. It was unique because it involved an *industry* in which consumer marketing was new. Like Sony, Nokia branded the entire company. In keeping with the holistic branding approach, Nokia made sure that the look and feel of its mobile phones (see Exhibit 10-5) created a "single, unified approach" across entire regions. This strategy worked well until spring 2002, when reports surfaced on defects

Exhibit 10-5. Nokia's product segmentation.

Evolution of Nokia's Product Segmentation

SOURCE: Nokia Corporation.

in some Nokia phone models. The vendor considered these reports "erroneous and misleading," arguing that they involved a component quality problem with only one display supplier and just a small proportion of Nokia models produced between October 2001 and January 2002. Despite controversy, the brand seemed to take it in stride. However, the incident did alert analysts on the potential vulnerabilities of the Nokia brand.

Product Segmentation: The "Procter & Gamble" Strategy

As the market has become increasingly segmented, the ability to master various product categories became crucial. "In a segmented consumer market with high volumes," the Nokians believed that "critical success factors include a comprehensive product portfolio, a strong and appealing brand, as well as efficient global logistics. We will continue to focus in these areas with the aim of sustained brand leadership."[37] Segmentation and design went hand in hand. Erik Anderson, a product manager who was in charge of producing the phones designed by Frank Nuovo, Nokia's chief designer, has illustrated how Nokia tackled Motorola, the king of the cell business in 1993:

> They were so strong and so powerful we could never beat them head on. We had to find another way. We had to use ingenuity, because they had wealth we could not rival. Originally, we had one phone—the phone Frank designed. And we tried to make it

that one perfect phone. By 1993 . . . I realized that making one perfect phone wasn't going to work for us. We needed to make many perfect phones, and they needed to be different. Any growing market will segment—it's an economic law of nature.[38]

The product strategy was not something new. In the 1920s, Alfred Sloan and General Motors had seized a similar segmentation strategy to overthrow Ford's Model T.[39] But Nokia's product strategy did represent something new in the *mobile* industry.

At the end of the 1990s, Nokia enjoyed strong leadership in digital cellular handsets. According to contemporary hype, this superiority stemmed from the Finnish vendor's aesthetic eye and design as the base of differentiation, while Nokia's chief designer was touted as something of a celebrity. "In general, [Frank] Nuovo favors bubbles and elliptical shapes, the aerodynamic icons of speed," wrote *The New Yorker* in 2001. But as fascinating as those bubbles and shapes may have been, in reality they did not make the Finnish vendor's success. Instead, Nokia's product leadership originated from its realization in the late 1980s that continuous product launches were necessary to catch up with market leaders, and that filling the shelves would squeeze out even strong rivals. Nokia moved toward continuous product launches because of pressure from the sales organization. As Marketing Director Kari-Pekka Wilska put it:

Nokia had fifty competitors in the early 1990s, and each was launching new products every two to three years. As a result, about twenty new products were launched each year. As Nokia's sales organization did not get any new products for two years in the late 1980s, motivation and enthusiasm decreased. That was enough to justify the increased role of design in Nokia: to highlight the role of design, to indicate that something new has been launched, and to help our sales organization to sell.[40]

The new strategy built on the realities of shortening product life cycles and the competitive necessity of leveraging new phones across regions. Certainly, the design contributed to product leadership; however, it was not aesthetics but the adoption of a Procter & Gamble strategy that showed the way. By late 1998, Nokia pumped out new models every thirty-five days. The approach was tested in Japan, where the Finnish vendor launched many of its niche systems. Just as Procter & Gamble engaged in segmentation and micromarketing to fill up the supermarket shelves, Nokia engaged heavily in segmentation to dominate categories.[41]

Leveraging Business Units Worldwide

In the early 1990s, Ollila and the board did not just refocus the company in terms of its businesses; they also repositioned it in terms of *global* growth. It was an extraordinarily bold and ambitious strategy. At the end of the 1980s, Matti Alahuhta, another member of the group executive board, had written his dissertation on global growth strategies, illustrating many central tenets of strategic thinking at Nokia's headquarters before the restructuring. Increasing global competition, coupled with accelerating development of new technologies, resulted in shorter product life cycles and higher innovation intensity. In turn, the shorter product life cycles forced companies to place more emphasis on R&D and to recognize new opportunities and exploit them more quickly and with better timing. By the late 1980s, the competitive life cycle of a cellular phone had already shrunk to less than three years. Because markets had become increasingly uniform, the winners would be companies that operated in several markets simultaneously, timed their new product development correctly, and thereby gained both higher volume and faster learning.

To make limited resources stretch around the globe, companies would have to concentrate on fewer businesses, but expand those businesses into all relevant markets worldwide. Nokia opted for a *global focus* strategy. It would concentrate on its core capabilities (i.e., Nokia Mobile Phones and Nokia Networks) while leveraging both units worldwide. And it would divest all noncore properties. During those troubling times, it was a bold strategic intent.[42] Led by the Nordic markets, the Europeans opted for GSM, which was pioneered by Nokia and Ericsson. The first GSM call was made in 1991 in Finland with a Nokia phone on a Nokia-equipped network. That same year, Nokia agreed to supply GSM networks to nine other European countries. In 1994, Nokia was the first manufacturer to launch a series of handportable phones for all major digital standards (e.g., GSM, TDMA, PCN, Japan Digital): the Nokia 2100 family. By August 1997, Nokia supplied GSM systems to fifty-nine operators in thirty-one countries. For all practical purposes, the story of GSM's commercialization is the story of Nokia's success, despite early struggles in R&D and high-volume production. In the European Commission, the triumph of the GSM standard, the Nordic cellular industry, and the global rise of Nokia and Ericsson showcased pan-European competitiveness. Those were the glory days. Organizationally, things were changing again. In the mid-1990s, a new logistics chain had ensured Nokia's success. In spring 2002, the NMP was reorganized. The new product-driven organization comprised nine distinct business units. The objective was increased agility and flexibility. Typically, the majority of the chiefs of these new entities were not Finnish. In other words, Nokia sought to distribute organizational responsibilities, as well as to boost differentiation, in order to respond to the challenges of the volatile environment.

The Translocal Gamble

In spring 2000, Ollila and Pekka Ala-Pietilä, Nokia's president, claimed that there were no limits to Nokia's determination. But only a year later, the tone was quite different: "We understand the details and the importance of getting the little things right. In short, we strive to satisfy our customer needs in a cost-efficient way." As the industry underwent a shakeout and struggled with consolidation, Nokia's chief executives sought to "make best execution an asset."[43]

Nokia Corp.'s net sales in 2000 increased by 54 percent to a total of EUR 30,376 million. Operating profit grew by 48 percent to a total of EUR 5,776 million. Operating margin was still 19 percent. In the post-Enron environment, accounting specialists estimated that if the stock options that Nokia employed to recruit and reward talent were to be accounted for as expenditures, the pro forma results would have been reduced by about 10 percent.[44] With 60,300 employees, Nokia served customers in 130 countries, had production facilities in ten countries, and carried out research and development in fifteen countries. It had a global network of distribution, sales, customer service, and other operational units. It had two basic business groups, Nokia Networks and Nokia Mobile Phones, as well as the Nokia Research Center, Nokia Communications Products, and the Nokia Ventures Organization. In 2000, Europe accounted for 52 percent of Nokia's net sales, the Americas 25 percent, and Asia-Pacific 23 percent. The ten largest markets were the United States, China, the U.K., Germany, Italy, France, Brazil, the Philippines, Australia, and Spain, together representing 64 percent of total sales.

Nokia Mobile Phones

NMP had become the world's largest mobile phone manufacturer, with a strong global brand identity. In 2000, it had 23,508 employees and sold products in more than 130 countries. It developed sophisticated mobile phones and accessories for all major analog and digital standards, including GSM, AMPS, CDMA, and TDMA. Product development was geared at "unsurpassed functional and technological design." As the size of mobile phones continued to shrink, Nokia increased its emphasis on design. It has developed many standard features, including large graphics displays, signal and battery indicators, colored covers, and ringing tones. By amortizing design costs over multiple countries, it has been able to increase profitability, while the sleek, functional designs contributed to its competitive differentiation. As NMP settled in its strategic course, sales increased from FIM 10.7 billion in 1994 to FIM 27.6 billion in 1997, and more than FIM 78.4 billion in 1999. By 2000, sales in NMP grew by 66 percent to EUR 21,887 million.

Growth in Nokia's mobile phone sales continued to exceed market growth in 2000 as a whole and in every quarter. Overall, Nokia sold 128.4 million mobile phones, representing 64 percent year-on-year growth. Replacement sales accounted for an estimated 40 percent of the 405 million total volume. This share was expected to rise to around 50 percent of total volume in 2001. Nokia's sales volume growth was clearly higher than market volume growth in all regions, most notably in Asia-Pacific and Europe. Nokia continued to strengthen its market leadership in 2000, leading to a total global market share of approximately 32 percent. With a comprehensive product portfolio that covered all consumer segments and standards, NMP was in a strong—but not necessarily unique—position to lead the development toward the mobile information society.

Nokia Networks

In 2000, Nokia Networks was a leading supplier of mobile, broadband, and IP network infrastructure products and related services. With 23,508 employees, it also developed mobile Internet applications and solutions for operators and Internet service providers. In 1990, Nokia Telecommunications still drove the company's revenue growth with FIM 2.5 billion in net sales. During the firm's restructuring phase, the group's sales were slow but steady. Between 1995 and 1999, the group's sales more than tripled from FIM 10.3 billion to FIM 33.7 billion. Sales in Nokia Networks grew by 36 percent to EUR 7,714 million. Operating margin was 17.6 percent. The group's operating profit consistently exceeded that of NMP until 1997. A year later, its profit was still strong at FIM 6.4 billion, but only a third of that of the mobile unit.

In 2000, sales increased in Nokia Ventures Organization (NVO) by 106 percent to EUR 854 million, with an operating loss of EUR 387 million. NVO developed innovative new ideas for the home environment and the corporate world, expanding Nokia's business scope. The mission of Nokia Ventures Organization was to push the limits of Nokia's growth beyond the scope of current businesses, as well as to introduce and develop new business ideas inside and outside of Nokia. Nokia Research Center drove the company's technological competitiveness and renewal through cooperation with its business groups and with universities, research institutes, and other corporations.

By late January 2002, Nokia's shares had risen about 70 percent since September 11, beating other European companies in the sector. Nonetheless, the vendor faced substantial turmoil as it was drifting on a collision course with Microsoft. In October 2001, Nokia's board of directors agreed with Jorma Ollila on the extension of his contract as chairman and the CEO of Nokia for an additional five years through 2006. Paul J. Collins, Nokia's vice chairman of the board and Ollila's longtime friend, noted that "ensuring continuity of leadership and management is particularly critical as we face an unprecedented technological transition in the mobile communication business."[45] After

the appointment, Ollila challenged Finnish government for greater cooperation, particularly in lowering the tax burden and facilitating the inflow of high-
skill foreign IT labor in Finland. "We love this country," he said. "But we must
make rational decisions on the basis of the competitive circumstances."[46] Times
were changing—again.

Success Drivers: Where Are the Core Capabilities?

In January 1999, Ollila lectured to the Finnish strategic society on "Nokia's
strategic intent." The strategy work at Nokia Group, he said, aimed at a "new
management paradigm." It was designed to cope with developments and challenges in dynamic markets. Instead of resource- or market-based strategies,
Nokia built on what Ollila called "market-making strategies." In dynamic markets, sustained competitive advantages were rare, but first-mover advantages
in next-generation or breakthrough products could make or break companies.[47]

The goal of Nokia's senior management was to combine and balance winning foresight and excellent execution. This execution thrived in voice-oriented markets, it would be far more difficult to achieve in data-oriented
communications. Data communications was the "what" of the emerging markets. If mobile leaders were to define the changing industry value drain, Nokia
was best positioned in the new terrain. If, however, they were to lose their
competitive advantage, Nokia's 2G success would not protect the vendor in
the 3G world (see Exhibit 10-6).

The Monopoly Era

Nokia had nothing to do with telecom until the postwar era. Initially a
forestry enterprise, it was essentially a three-firm coalition that operated in
forestry, rubber, and cable products and services from the 1920s to the 1960s.
Telecom interests evolved first by chance and then by design. After two wars
against the Soviet Union, reparations boosted Nokia's cable interests, which
gave rise to its diversification into electronics and telecommunications. Following Nordic cooperation in the late 1960s, investments into these segments accelerated expansion in the mobile business.

Domestically, Nokia could not consolidate Finnish mobile and electronics
interests before public-sector failures in socialization (1950s) and nationalization (1970s). Meanwhile, the Swedes initiated Nordic mobile cooperation,
which led to the NMT standard.

Until the late 1960s, Nokia's mobile operations were defined by a functional organization, corporate diversification, and R&D. Technology assets
played a minor role in strategy, while costly development occurred without
profitability. In the 1970s, the rise of Kari H. Kairamo led to a new era in
which change, flexibility, and lifelong learning were promoted. Kairamo's rapid
growth strategy shifted the strategic base from old-industry diversification

Exhibit 10-6. Nokia: drivers of wireless growth.

MONOPOLY ERA

Products
- ☐ Fredrik Idestam launches Nokia in 1865 with support of Leo Mechelin. In the 1920s to the 1960s, it is essentially a three-firm coalition operating in forestry, rubber, and cable.
- ☐ Interest in telecom evolves first by chance, and then by design when Nokia is the leading cable supplier in Soviet reparations. Interest in electronics and digitalization is triggered, which leads to telecommunications and mobility.
- ☐ Domestically, Nokia consolidates Finnish mobile and electronics interest only after public-sector failures in socialization (1950s) and nationalization (1970s). Meanwhile, Swedish PTT makes possible vis-à-vis Nordic cooperation, which results in NMT.

Operations
- ☐ Until late 1960s, Nokia's mobile operations are defined by its functional organization, diversification and R&D; technology assets play a minor role in strategy; costly development occurs without profitability.
- ☐ In the 1970s, rise of Kari H. Kairamo leads to a new era at Nokia, where change, flexibility, and lifelong learning are promoted.
- ☐ Kairamo's rapid growth strategy shifts the strategic base from old-industry diversification toward technology businesses, but unlike Ericsson, Nokia has little international experience on joint ventures or FDI.

Markets
- ☐ Nokia's first internationalization occurs before WWI, but it is export-oriented and telecom interests play no role in it.
- ☐ Second internationalization coincides with the Kairamo era and political détente, but only in the 1980s.
- ☐ Trained in the United States, Kairamo popularizes American thinking on technology and management at Nokia, which is exceptional at the time, due to Cold War influence in Finland.

NOKIA
CONNECTING PEOPLE

THE TRANSITION ERA

Products
- ☐ In the 1980s, the Nordic NMT and the fast deregulation of Finnish telecommunications provides an early boost to Nokia, which rapidly consolidates Finnish telecom, mobile, and consumer electronics interests.
- ☐ Nokia launches first successful products in infrastructure and handsets, and the strategic shift to technology permeates the new growth strategy.
- ☐ While NMT cannot invade the large European markets, EC decision to make GSM mandatory in Europe allows Nokia to push its handset operations regionwide, while reinforcing R&D in GSM.

Operations
- ☐ Between 1982 and 1988, Kairamo engages Nokia in a bold M&A wave, which shifts the corporate emphasis from old industries to technology.
- ☐ The NMT explosion steers R&D and resource allocations heavily toward telecom and mobile interests. Nokia's hypergrowth accelerates its organizational decentralization, as well as the IT-driven transition to process organization.
- ☐ The struggle for corporate governance leads to Kairamo's suicide in 1988 and four years of "Sturm und Drang" at the Nokia HQ. The transition era ends with the arrival of Jorma Ollila, and the new global focus strategy (including the efforts at global branding, logistics, process organization, segmentation, and design).

Markets
- ☐ The success of Nokia's NMT products lead to first relationships with a new generation of European challengers in network operations.
- ☐ In Europe, the United States, and Asia-Pacific, Nokia follows closely Ericsson's footsteps.
- ☐ In China, Ericsson initially leads, but the Tiananmen crisis allows Nokia to solidify its position in early 1990s.

THE COMPETITIVE ERA

Products
- ☐ In 1990s, Nokia captures worldwide leadership in handsets, while developing strong capabilities in infrastructure as well.
- ☐ Thrust of mobile innovation migrates from United States to Nordic mobile clusters, particularly to Sweden and Finland, which develop the most sophisticated customers in infrastructure and handsets.
- ☐ With the eclipse of digital cellular in late 1990s, Nokia targets a dominant position in the 3G systems, while the convergence of voice and data requires new competences, which it seeks through tech coalitions.

Operations
- ☐ Starting in 1997, Ollila initiates efforts in the "webification" of the organization; efforts at efficiency result in increased outsourcing, but core operations stay in Finland.
- ☐ The 3G transition is precipitated by Nokia's mobile Internet strategy, which leads to inflated valuations in 1997–2000 and results in deflated valuations thereafter.
- ☐ Nokia employs the existing handset and infrastructure subsidiaries, corporate innovation, and a new Internet unit to generate new technologies, products, and services, while developing tech coalitions. Because Nokia's strengths are in the downstream side of the value chain (brand, segmentation, design), the proliferation of tech coalitions do not threaten its mobile product leadership at first.

Markets
- ☐ With its global focus, Nokia leverages its strategy globally.
- ☐ Despite attacks and challengers, over 99% of revenues originate from worldwide markets.
- ☐ After Tiananmen crisis, Nokia captures a substantial portion of Chinese infrastructure market and boosts its position toward the 3G era.

---

toward technology businesses. However, unlike Ericsson, Nokia had little international experience with joint ventures or foreign direct investment (FDI). Nokia's first internationalization occurred before World War I, but it was export-oriented and did not involve telecom interests. The second internationalization coincided with the Kairamo era and political détente, but not before the 1980s. Kairamo, who was trained in the United States, popularized American thinking on technology and management at Nokia, which was exceptional at the time because of the Cold War influence in Finland.

The Transition Era

In the 1980s, the Nordic NMT and the fast deregulation of Finnish tele-communications provided an early boost to Nokia, which consolidated Finnish telecom, mobile, and consumer electronics interests. Nokia launched its first successful products in infrastructure and handsets, and the strategic shift to technology permeated its new growth strategy. NMT could not invade the large European markets, but the EC decision to make GSM mandatory in Europe allowed Nokia to promote its handset operations regionwide while reinforcing R&D in GSM. Between 1982 and 1988, Kairamo engaged in a bold M&A wave, which shifted the corporate emphasis from old industries to technology. Meanwhile, the NMT explosion steered R&D and resource allocations heavily toward telecom and mobile interests. The struggle for corporate governance led to Kairamo's suicide in 1988 and four years of "Sturm und Drang" at Nokia headquarters. The transition era ended with the arrival of Jorma Ollila and the new global focus strategy (including the efforts at global branding, logistics, segmentation, and design). By the early 1990s, Nokia's hypergrowth speeded both organizational decentralization and the IT-driven transition to a process organization.

The success of Nokia's NMT products led to its first relationships with a new generation of European challengers in network operations. In Europe, the United States, and the Asia-Pacific region, the company followed closely Ericsson's footsteps. In China, the Tiananmen crisis allowed Ericsson and Nokia to take advantage of the weakened U.S. presence and solidify their market positions in the early 1990s.

The Competitive Era

In the 1990s, Nokia captured worldwide leadership in handsets and developed a strong base in the network infrastructure. The thrust of mobile innovation migrated from the United States to the Nordic mobile clusters, and "Finland's Wireless Valley" became a test laboratory for the multinationals. Nokia targeted a dominant position in 3G systems, which would eclipse digital cellular in the late 1990s, while using technology coalitions to internalize new competences in the convergence of voice and data. In 1997, Ollila initiated the "webification" of the organization. Efforts at efficiency resulted in increased outsourcing, even if critical production facilities were kept in-house and in Finland. The 3G transition was precipitated by Nokia's mobile Internet strategy, which, along with media hype, contributed to inflated valuations from 1997 to 2000 and resulted in deflated valuations thereafter. As the transition proceeded, Nokia employed its handset and infrastructure subsidiaries, corporate innovation, and a new Internet unit to generate new technologies, products, and services. It also adopted a proactive role in tech coalitions. Unlike Ericsson, Nokia was not cannibalizing its own activities because its strengths were in the downstream side of the value chain (e.g., brand, segmentation, and design).

Nokia leveraged its strategy globally. Despite competitive attacks and challengers, more than 99 percent of revenues originated from worldwide markets. After the Tiananmen crisis, Nokia captured a substantial portion of the Chinese infrastructure market and boosted its position toward the 3G era. The externalization of R&D activities and the proliferation of tech coalitions did not threaten Nokia's mobile product leadership—as long as its core innovation coincided with that of the changing industry. The implications, however, were worrisome. Even if Nokia were able to execute its vision and succeed in its products, operations, and markets, that would not suffice if the new industry entrants redefined the rules of competition. Furthermore, what made Nokia's strategic considerations exceptionally complicated was the fact that, in seeking to retain its mobile leadership, it was actually reversing its stated strategy.

Translocal Challenge

"Nokia's $25 billion in annual sales roughly equals the entire budget of the Finnish government, which finances one of the world's most-generous welfare states," noted *The New York Times* in March 2002. "This impressive growth, now slowing somewhat in tandem with the broader world economy, has some Finns wondering if they have not, in fact, exchanged one master—the Soviet Union—for another." Concurrently, even the OECD paid attention to the increasing dependency of Finland on Nokia.[48]

Until summer 2000, Nokia's translocal strategy seemed invincible. In spring 2002, it seemed more like a gamble. Suddenly, the Finnish vendor found itself attacked on all sides. Despite its product leadership in the 2G era, Nokia was challenged by a "Wintel II" attack when Microsoft and Intel targeted mobile communications. Based on the Internet vision, Microsoft's operating systems and application software, and Intel's hardware building blocks, the Wintel duopoly advocated greater differentiation advantages worldwide while relying on extensive developer communities. The proliferation of new access devices (e.g., cell phones, PDAs, 3G laptops, 3G web tablets, info appliances) rendered the vendor's product segmentation less effective. In the 2G era, Nokia had managed to fill the supermarket shelf with its broad product variety; but as the shelves were extended in new directions, users no longer stayed with cellular products. Old loyalties became unglued. Despite Nokia's operational leadership, it also found itself challenged by primarily Asian producers. These were no longer just established Japanese players such a Sony and Matsushita, but comprised a new generation of bolder attackers from Japan and elsewhere in Asia-Pacific, among them Samsung, Kyocera, and new Chinese suppliers. In the long term, their attack rested on greater cost-efficiencies worldwide. And despite Nokia's market leadership, the vendor was challenged by a horizontal attack, which did not just target its product variety, but also its market dominance. In the past, only Nordic players had managed the "scale via scope" game; by the 3G transition, it was no longer a way to generate revenues, just a cost of doing business. Furthermore, Nokia was headquartered in a small country far away from the current market centers in the United States, large European nations, and Asia-Pacific (e.g., Japan, India, China, and the Tiger countries).

Sequestered on all three sides, Nokia could no longer count on macrodrivers, either. With new public policies, global telecom reforms had been implemented by the end of the 1990s. In the 1980s, these policies had boosted the vendor's home base advantages; by the 3G transition, they had been embraced in most developed markets. Similarly, technology advantages were gone. In the 1980s, the EC's decision to make GSM mandatory had reinforced Nokia's opportunities, even if the vendor always remained technology-agnostic and learned to manufacture all standards. By the 3G transition, the core technology was CDMA. The cutting edge in innovation was migrating from Nordic countries to the software, chip, and new media clusters in the United States. Lastly, competition was globalizing even more rapidly, with the 3G transition *and* the entry of U.S. IT leaders. And these changes translated to shifts in the division of labor across mobile clusters worldwide. As long as Nokia competed against the old-style telecom vendors, it was a challenger among less agile European giants. But as it began to compete against new-style IT leaders, it was maturing into just another agile challenger.

Chapter 11

Qualcomm: Redefining the Rules

In 1991, only trade people knew about Qualcomm (for "*quality comm*unications"), which had barely 600 employees and generated only $90.3 million in revenues, with a net loss of $8.4 million. Barely a decade later in 2000, the R&D maverick launched by Dr. Irwin Mark Jacobs was the most successful start-up in San Diego. Known worldwide, it had more than 6,300 employees, $3.2 billion in revenues, and more than $670 million in net income. In the United States, it leaped into the public eye in 1999, when its stock outgrew all other major issues on the NASDAQ and NYSE, having soared *2,621 percent*. This hypergrowth status was boosted after the spring of 2000, when mobile vendors and operators agreed on the 3G standard, in which Qualcomm's CDMA would serve as the central roadmap. The market feat came after years of patient investments for the future.

Despite its magnificent growth, Qualcomm and its senior executives were relatively invisible in the high-profile technology sector. As *Fortune* noted as late as the summer of 2000:

> Jacobs remains an enigma, even here in his hometown. He's not like Andy Grove, Scott McNealy, Larry Ellison, or Steve Jobs—public figures all. Even though Jacobs has accomplished as much as any of these Info Age barons, he's largely unknown outside the insular world of the cellular industry. San Diego itself is one reason; until recently, it has been a high-tech backwater. Another reason is that Jacobs has never worked high tech's Borscht Belt—the endless round of Silicon Valley gatherings and high-tech conferences. Instead, he has focused relentlessly on getting Qualcomm's [CDMA] established as the world's digital wireless standard.[1]

By 2001, Qualcomm made chipsets, software, global positioning systems, and satellite ground stations used in wireless communications. In the mobile business, it had pioneered the commercialization of the CDMA standard for digital wireless transmissions, while manufacturing products for digital, cellular, personal communication services, and wireless local-loop systems. It provided equipment to low-orbit satellite phone service provider Globalstar and was known for the popular Eudora e-mail software and OmniTRACS system for tracking long-haul truckers. Finally, it had designed a standard (BREW) for custom mobile-phone software and was developing a digital distribution system for cinemas worldwide.

Qualcomm did not built its empire by playing by the rules. In the 1990s, European mobile visionaries expected the future to belong to GSM. CDMA redefined the rules and turned those dreams into ashes. But as a latecomer, CDMA was disadvantaged. Had Qualcomm played by the rules, it would have been "just another" third- or fourth-tier supplier. By developing an exciting standard of its own, the company transformed the competitive environment. Understandably, technology innovation has been seen as the driver of Qualcomm's success. It was critical, but not sufficient to success. Rather, it was innovation *leveraged worldwide* that made the company so successful.

The Technology Start-Up

Dr. Irwin Mark Jacobs cofounded Qualcomm, Inc. in July 1985. Born in New Bedford, Massachusetts, he grew up in a lower-middle-class family during the Depression and World War II. The youth had an affinity for mathematics and science. After studying electrical engineering and graduating from Cornell in 1956, Jacobs went on to earn a PhD at MIT, in just three years. From 1959 to 1966, he served as an assistant/associate professor of electrical engineering at MIT. Jacobs and his wife and children then headed to San Diego, and between 1966 and 1972, he was a professor of computer science and engineering at the University of California, San Diego (see Exhibit 11-1).[2] Then the academic phase of his life was over.

The Linkabit Years: From Defense Contracts to Commercial Wireless

Jacobs and two of his friends from UCLA, Andrew Viterbi and Leonard Kleinrock, formed a part-time consulting company called Linkabit, which developed military-satellite technology. Viterbi later helped found Qualcomm,[3] whereas Kleinrock won fame as one of the founders of the Internet. One of Linkabit's earliest contracts was with DARPA (Defense Advanced Research Projects Agency). Bob Kahn, then head of DARPA, and Jacobs tried to sell the idea of packet communications, but found no interest. In San Diego, defense contracts ensured much of the early revenues of Linkabit, just as they would later boost Qualcomm's success. After all, CDMA built on technology that originated from military radio communications.

Exhibit 11-1. Irwin M. Jacobs and CDMA.

Jacobs received the highest award bestowed by the U.S. President for extraordinary achievements in the commercialization of technology, for "his vision, innovation and leadership in the field of digital wireless communications over the past 25 years." Presented by Vice President Al Gore, the ceremony was followed by a White House meeting with President Clinton. Previously, Jacobs had been awarded the Ernst & Young Information Technology Award for Global Integration by the Computerworld Smithsonian Award Program for outstanding contributions to global integration through the use of information technology.

Irwin M. Jacobs, an MIT and UCSD academic, became a technology entrepreneur in the early 1970s. By 1991, he served as chairman and CEO of Qualcomm Inc., a maverick R&D startup which was intent on making its CDMA technology the gateway to the 3G future – to the surprise of industry observers and to the chagrin of the GSM advocates.

At first, OmniTRACS business unit provided the majority of Qualcomm's total revenue. In the road transit business, Jacobs and Qualcomm were considered wireless wizards who helped bring the transportation industry into the information age. In October 1993, Fleet Owner, an influential trade publication, released a story on Jacobs – "The Man Who Changed Trucking".

Source: Qualcomm Incorporated.

Many of the first employees in these two companies were former defense industry engineers. As Linkabit grew, Jacobs left UCSD to run the digital signal processing equipment firm full-time. In 1980, he sold the company to M/A-COM, a cable television equipment company based in Massachusetts. The deal netted Jacobs an estimated $25 million. Tall and lanky, Jacobs was a fearsome basketball player who sometimes settled Linkabit engineering disputes with arm-wrestling matches. He had established a reputation as a soft-spoken but hard-driving executive. "He's mellowed out a lot since those days," said Cliff Vaughan, a sales executive with Oki Semiconductor Inc., a unit of Japan's Oki Electric Industry. Vaughan still remembers the arcane price squabbles. "He used to know everything. Now he just knows half."[4]

In 1986, General Instrument, then a leading maker of cable TV equipment, acquired M/A-COM and CommScope, another cable maker.[5] However, the founders of M/A-COM Linkabit—Jacobs, Viterbi, and five other executives—had left the company already around 1985. Jacobs retired but grew bored. According to the corporate legend, he was driving down Interstate 5 in Southern California one day in the mid-1980s, shortly after selling Linkabit. He was musing about spread spectrum. During World War II, United States Defense Forces had developed a secure wireless transmission system, CDMA (see Chapter 2). For civilian use, CDMA's main advantage was signal clarity and the efficient use of increasingly crowded bandwidth. Seeing the commercial possibilities for spread spectrum, Jacobs founded Qualcomm with Dr. Viterbi and four other partners in 1985. "It was supposed to be a way for us to take it easy and have fun at business," Qualcomm President Harvey White said.[6] The first headquarters was located above a strip mall pizza parlor in San Diego.

Initially, the company served as a contract provider of R&D services. But Jacobs thought big. His dream was to modify the CDMA system for commercial use—first in the United States, then worldwide.

From OmniTRACS to CDMA

CDMA was not the first success of the entrepreneurial Qualcomm. In 1988, the company introduced OmniTRACS, a satellite-based system that tracked the location of long-haul truckers. Qualcomm's initial expansion built on success in the road transit industry. Historically, this business reflected the thriving postwar mobile services, particularly the dispatch segments. With OmniTRACS, Jacobs sought to bring the transportation industry into the information age. The satellite-based, two-way data messaging and position reporting system helped transportation companies improve their rate of return on assets, while increasing efficiency by improving communications between drivers and dispatchers. With the defense buildup of the Reagan-Bush years, Qualcomm also engaged in expanding cooperation with Pentagon. By 1989, when the company introduced its first version of CDMA, it had defense contracts worth $15 million. But as the Cold War came to an end, so did the U.S. military buildup.

Around 1999–2000, the leading global mobile operators and vendors agreed on the 3G standard, in which Qualcomm's CDMA played a driving role. But a decade before, when Jacobs had first approached wireless carriers to pitch the new technology, few people saw the point. As far as industry leaders were concerned, the standard game was over. AT&T, Motorola, and others had already opted for the time division multiple access (TDMA) digital standard. In 1990, the Cellular Telecommunications Industry Association (CTIA) was finalizing plans to adopt TDMA as the U.S. standard for the 2G era. As far as the industry leaders were concerned, the game was over. Qualcomm was late, so why bother? "TDMA had won," Jacobs has said, "and we came along and said, 'Perhaps there's a better way.'"[7] Soon thereafter, two Baby Bells—Nynex (later part of Bell Atlantic) and Ameritech (later part of SBC Communications)—embraced CDMA, which crashed the hope for a unitary standard.

By November 1991—after the company's extensive CDMA public relation blitz but before the actual commercialization of the technology—Qualcomm was receiving license or development revenues from AT&T, Motorola, Nortel, OKI, Alps Electric, ETRI (a primary research facility for South Korea), Clarion, Nokia, and Sony. Two years later, Janice Obbuchowski, former telecom policy advisor to President Bush joined Qualcomm's board of directors. In July, the CTIA adopted CDMA as a North American standard for wireless communications, which meant that now there were two voluntary industry standards.[8] Qualcomm's great faith in its new technology and willingness to promote it heavy-handedly gained the company enemies as well.[9] Concurrently, with Loral Corporation, it unveiled plans for Globalstar, a satellite telecom system similar to the failed Iridium system.

Winning Worldwide: From Growth and Leadership to Refocus

Focused on technology development, Qualcomm was eager to expand manufacturing and marketing in the early 1990s to execute its "growth and leadership strategy." It was eager to lead the mobile business into a CDMA era. There was a problem with the scenario. With limited production capabilities, Qualcomm had no experience of manufacturing CDMA cellular products in high commercial volumes.

Quest for Mass-Manufacturing Capabilities: Toward the Sony Partnership

Toward the late 1980s and the subsequent GSM explosion, the absence of appropriate mass-manufacturing capabilities caused substantial turmoil at

Ericsson and Nokia. These two Nordic companies had already operated in the business for a decade or two. In contrast, Qualcomm was a newcomer. It had a better technology offering, but it was poorly prepared for mass production. By the early 1990s, the company was swept by turmoil and delays as it struggled to deliver its orders. It was a paradoxical endpoint for the 1G era and odd entry into the 2G era. In the long term, Qualcomm had the right technology know-how (CDMA for 3G), but it lacked the requisite manufacturing capabilities.[10]

Even as Qualcomm's OmniTRACS system became profitable at the turn of the 1990s, its overall profitability was offset by the high level of R&D associated with the commercialization of CDMA. By the end of the decade, Qualcomm's R&D amounted to 10 percent to 11 percent of sales. In 1991 and 1992, however, it soared to 23 percent to 25 percent. The company had taken extraordinary risks with its CDMA investments, which began to pay off, as demonstrated by the escalation of CDMA-related activities in 1994, including system trials by major U.S. carriers, license agreements with leading manufacturers, and an expanding CDMA development group. Jacobs also gained national recognition when he was awarded the 1994 National Medal of Technology.

In 1995, when most of the fourteen largest U.S. cellular carriers announced plans to deploy CDMA, Qualcomm celebrated its tenth anniversary. It made a public offering of 11.5 million shares of common stock, which netted $486 million. The funds were used for the establishment of manufacturing capabilities for CDMA products, vendor financing, product development, contributions to joint ventures, and general working capital. The growth and leadership strategy was now becoming a reality; in 1993, the number of employees had grown by *169 percent* to keep pace with expanding operations.

Qualcomm planned to produce a million CDMA phones and some 2,500 base stations per year to support the deployment of cellular, PCS, and WLL. It also planned to supply its licensees with a large volume of CDMA application-specific integrated circuits (ASICs), which were required to meet the growing market demand for CDMA equipment. Not only did the company rush to build its manufacturing capacity, it also used partnerships to augment this capacity. Through the Qualcomm/Sony partnership—Qualcomm Personal Electronics (QPE)—it initiated production and deliveries of the QCP-800, a new dual-mode CDMA and AMPS portable telephone. In 1996, most of the major U.S. cellular carriers upgraded to CDMA, and Qualcomm's overall revenues grew 111 percent to a total of $814 million. Concurrently, the primary source of CDMA revenues shifted from development and licensing fees to sales of Qualcomm products. With rapid deregulation and privatization, the company was also able to access new international markets. In 1996, CDMA digital wireless services were launched in markets across the United States by many major cellular and PCS service providers; now users became familiar with QPE's portable phones (see Exhibit 11-2).

Exhibit 11-2. CDMA phone portfolio (1996).

Q Phone	QCP-820	QCP-1920	QCP-2700	QCT-1000
The palm-sized CDMA digital Q phone sought to combine high voice quality and enhanced security with advanced capabilities that, over time, were expected to provide e-mail and Internet access. It aspired to provide the best of a phone, pager and answering machine in a single compact device.	The QCP-820 was a CDMA digital cellular dual-mode phone that automatically switched into analog mode where digital service was not yet available. It featured a large, four-line display area, three battery options for up to five hours of talk time and a unique dial shuttle for easy one-touch operation.	The QCP-1920 was a lightweight CDMA digital PCS phone. Like all of Qualcomm's CDMA digital phones, it provided clear, static-free connections with reduced background noise, greater privacy, fewer dropped calls and longer talk and standby times.	This was the world's first CDMA digital dual-mode dual-band phone, capable of switching seamlessly between new CDMA digital systems and older analog cellular networks. The lightweight QCP-2700 sought to deliver the best of both worlds, with high-quality digital service and access to broader coverage areas.	The QCT-1000 CDMA digital cellular fixed wireless phone (the white one in the background) could be activated immediately to provide wireline-quality voice and reliable operation through a broad range of environmental conditions. Qualcomm's QCT series also included other fixed wireless handsets and terminals for cellular, PCS and WLL service.

Source: Qualcomm Incorporated.

The shift from a R&D maverick into a CDMA manufacturer was a strategic gain, but a financial loss. Because of the high costs associated with the ramp-up manufacturing, growing investments in R&D and marketing, and shortages of key components, Qualcomm's net income actually decreased 30 percent to $21 million. To fulfill current orders and prepare for future ones, the company continued to make large investments to expand manufacturing capabilities.[11] Rapid growth and seemingly favorable environmental developments, coupled with bold ambitions for the future, allowed Qualcomm to realize a dream. "We've expanded our manufacturing," noted senior executives, "to become a *leading supplier* of wireless equipment."[12] It was an overstatement, but illustrated hopes of overachievement.

But soon realities caught up, and product delays began to haunt Qualcomm.

Product Delays: "The Path Has Not Always Been Smooth"

In December 1991, Jacobs told the industry press that all questions about CDMA "have been put to rest." In the coming years, that statement would be updated with several CDMA improvements. In January 1992, Jacobs announced that CDMA would be commercially available in twelve months, an estimate that turned out to be forty months off. "I was overly optimistic," he acknowledged later. Industry leaders grew skeptical, wondering whether the tardiness of CDMA had set back the U.S. mobile digitalization, perhaps irrevocably.[13] Not only was CDMA more than three years late in coming to market, but the operators were not yet sure if it worked any better than the existing standard. While some observers considered Qualcomm the future promise of American mobile business, others blamed Jacobs for single-handedly putting the United States behind Europeans. Neither assessment was fair, but both were understandable in the volatile environment. At first, Jacobs had claimed that CDMA could cram up to twenty to forty times as many calls onto a network as old-fashioned analog systems, whereas TDMA managed only about three times analog capacity. He also argued that CDMA would have about thirteen times the capacity of its main digital rivals, TDMA and GSM. By 1996, the sixty-three-year-old scientist defended his tactics, but acknowledged the doubts: "Every other week you wonder, 'Does it work? Will it get to market?'"[14]

In 1997, Qualcomm's earnings bounced back, and the company signed a contract to supply ground stations for Globalstar. That year, internationalization encountered the first obstacles. Russia charged a Qualcomm technician with espionage but allowed him to return to the United States. Meanwhile, manufacturing efforts, as well as rapidly escalating competition, resulted in Qualcomm's intensive brand-building effort that included print and TV advertising, event sponsorships, and other promotional activities. As consumers became more familiar with the Qualcomm name and what it represented, the company expected to build loyalty for its brand of leading-edge products.

In 1998, digitalization swept the U.S. cellular markets and Qualcomm's revenues broke the $3 billion mark. The company felt it had accomplished the goal of becoming a high volume manufacturer of phones, continued its emphasis on customer support, and further promoted brand recognition. In San Diego, the phone plant was working around the clock, and a new facility was opened in Brazil to support CDMA growth in Latin America. Qualcomm had evolved into one of the top-three digital wireless phone manufacturers in the United States. It also began installing CDMA infrastructure networks as the sole source contractor on five continents, while participating in joint projects with strategic partners. "The path has not always been smooth," acknowledged Jacobs, now chairman and CEO, and Richard Sulpizio, president and COO of Qualcomm. "We recognized certain quality issues early in the year and dealt with them proactively with our customers. We learned important lessons and we believe it strengthened our customer relationships for the long run."[15]

The Refocus Strategy

Since the turn of the 1990s, Qualcomm's strategy had been to make the company the leading provider of CDMA-based wireless communications technology, products, and services. In comparison to other mobile vendors, it had been engaged in a highly R&D-centric strategy. As the company put it in 1999:

> Qualcomm is a company full of people with big ideas. Those ideas lead to technology and products that help people communicate . . . Big ideas create big opportunities. And opportunities open the door to creating value for our customers, employees, and shareholders. That is why Qualcomm will continue to innovate and lead.[16]

As telecom giants were getting bigger and bigger, Qualcomm opted for a reverse strategy. By 2000, it was getting more and more focused and smaller, spinning off one division after another, while building a portfolio of patents, some 1,000 and growing.

Spin, Spin, Spin

Starting in 1999, Qualcomm refocused its strategy on its core competencies and capabilities. For years, it had struggled to become a "high volume manufacturer of phones." Yet, its strategic advantage was not in manufacturing or operations, but in the innovative *technology development* that had resulted in OmniTRACS and CDMA. Jacobs was a success because he was "the man who changed trucking," not because he had a successful trucking manufacturing business. Qualcomm was a success because of CDMA, not because it had excelled in the high-volume manufacturing of CDMA. If anything, the company was constantly burning cash in building manufacturing capabilities that even industry giants were increasingly outsourcing. Why? It was this insight that provided the basic criteria for its new focus strategy and, thereby, for the re-definition of the business segments. Qualcomm's growth and leadership phase was over. The company had grown and provided a powerful boost for a CDMA-driven industry. The lesson was that manufacturing capabilities were relevant to the extent they served as a catalyst for the creation and launch of new technologies; but it did not follow that Qualcomm should own those capabilities. Before refocus, the company would divest noncore properties—and what was now considered noncore used to be considered core.

Selling the CDMA Infrastructure Business to Ericsson

As Qualcomm resolved its patent litigation with Ericsson, it signed important agreements that paved the way for making CDMA the worldwide standard. Under these agreements, the two companies were jointly supporting a single CDMA world standard, while entering into patent cross licenses. As part of the deal, Ericsson purchased assets of Qualcomm's CDMA wireless infrastructure business in San Diego, California, and Boulder, Colorado. As far as Qualcomm was concerned, the objective of the infrastructure business had been met: It had driven CDMA forward into new markets. Ericsson was better equipped to enter CDMA markets worldwide and to take the business to new levels. In turn, Qualcomm could refocus on what it did best—innovation. In the early 1990s, it had struggled to make CDMA known; by the end of the decade, it was making $343 million in license, royalty, and development fees.

Selling the CDMA Phone Business to Kyocera

Another milestone in Qualcomm's refocusing followed in December 1999. To further improve operations and focus on its core competencies, Qualcomm reviewed the status of its phone manufacturing business. Amid the record peak of the mobile industry, Qualcomm's senior executives were already anticipating reverse developments: "As carriers consolidate, the price they charge for phones goes down. We expect this to put additional downward pricing pressure on manufacturers. We therefore determined the timing was right to seek buyers for QCP."[17] In December 1999, the company announced an agreement with Kyocera Corp. to transfer its phone manufacturing operations and customer commitments to this leading CDMA phone supplier in Japan, which, over-night, became positioned as a major supplier in North America and other markets worldwide. Concurrently, Qualcomm's market capitalization soared to $109 billion. Half a year later, the downward pricing pressure that Qualcomm had predicted did materialize. Driven by the massive 3G license-related debts by the operators, industry consolidation put substantial pressure on manufac-turers. As Qualcomm's old rivals rushed to outsource, initiated joint ventures in Asia, or shifted their manufacturing capabilities to low-cost players, most of them engaged in tactical actions without effective strategies. On the other hand, Jacobs and his senior executives used a purposeful strategy to refocus on core competencies.

Chips Without Fabs

By mid-2000, the company also made plans to spin off its semiconductor subsidiary, Spinco, to the public (even though the IPO was cancelled a year later, due to unfavorable environmental conditions). Donald Schrock, president of Qualcomm CDMA Technologies, built CDMA chips. While Qualcomm competed with Intel, Motorola, TI, and other chipmakers, it competed differently by not building its own chips. By 2000, Qualcomm was the world's second-largest "fabless" semiconductor manufacturer and hoped to become the largest. Rather than spend billions of dollars to build its own chip plants, Qualcomm designed the chips and contracted with other companies, principally IBM, to make them. The fabless approach allowed Schrock to focus on designing new chips, with the assistance of some 800 engineers. Oki Electric, LG Electronics, and Sony had made their own CDMA chips for their phones, but they soon favored buying chips from Qualcomm.[18]

By July 2001, Qualcomm was reconsidering plans it had made only a year ago to spin off its chipmaking unit, keeping the division internal. In a company statement, Jacobs explained that, originally, the spinoff was necessary to avoid legal conflicts that could arise from selling mobile phone chips that worked with both CDMA technology and the rival GSM technology that dominated the global mobile phone market. Now, Jacobs said, the threat of those conflicts had abated.[19] Qualcomm's chip business also faced a new challenge from Motorola, which announced plans to license blueprints of the mobile phone technology developed by the semiconductors products division. That move may give upstart mobile phone manufacturers another place to go for their chipsets other than Qualcomm.[20]

When it was still the only company backing and developing CDMA, Qualcomm served as a full-service house, supplying chips, phones, and infrastructure equipment. With CDMA success came the manufacturing pains. It could beat the rivals in technology developments but not in high-volume production. In infrastructure, it could garner only a niche against Nortel, Lucent, and others. So it sold its infrastructure business to Ericsson. In handsets, Qualcomm had built its business with Sony and sold a great number of phones, but kept losing money. So it sold that business to Kyocera. These divestitures boosted its focus, which rehabilitated its stock.

Return to R&D

The selling off of Qualcomm's businesses had been so extensive that one analyst, John Sullivan of Phillips Business Information, questioned whether Jacobs had taken up the Japanese poetic form of haiku to express his ambitions. In a widely circulated report, Sullivan imagined the chief executive's musings might look like this:

> Many business groups
> Mundane thoughts weigh down my soul
> Spin off everything[21]

Those analysts and industry practitioners that wondered about the validity of Qualcomm's strategic posture in 1999–2000 were in for a surprise. With the tech consolidation in the United States and Europe's 3G birth pains in 2000–2001, Qualcomm's "spin off everything" tactic suddenly did not look too bad at all. Unlike the hurried joint ventures and divestitures of manufacturing capabilities among second- and third-tier vendors, Jacobs's company engaged in similar efforts well before the flood. In fact, spinning off noncore properties was only part of the story; it *enabled* Qualcomm to focus; but it was *R&D* that the company would focus on. And at the end of the 1990s, it was the combination of mobility and the Internet that drove the U.S. maverick. The spin-offs were not the story; what was left after the spin-offs *was*.

In the 1980s, only a few visionaries thought that the requirements of the mobile phones and the Internet could be reconciled. As an AT&T executive put it: "We don't like where this Internet stuff is leading."[22] From the standpoint of a centrally controlled national network, a distributed network did pose a threat because, it shifted power to users. Yet it was this shift that engaged Qualcomm in 1998, when Jacobs began to streamline the company by bundling its interests in telecom carriers—including Cricket Communications and a Mexican company, Pegaso—into a holding company named Leap Wireless International. At about the same time, it formed Wireless Knowledge, a joint venture with Microsoft to provide products and services for Internet access from portable PCs (compare Chapter 14).

Qualcomm was also commercializing solutions, which aspired to provide 3G benefits with 2.5G capabilities. If speed and bandwidth were the key to data and Internet applications, it expected the High Data Rate (HDR) technology and 3G technologies to break that speed barrier wide open with chipsets and software. HDR served as a "wireless data solution right now to offer 3G benefits sooner."[23] Supported by Ericsson, Lucent, Hitachi, and others, HDR worked in existing CDMA networks but required cellular companies to add costly equipment at each cell site. In the rivalry for the next-generation technologies, Nokia and Motorola had teamed up to push for the standardization of Motorola's 1Xtreme technology over Qualcomm's HDR format for 3G networks. As far as Qualcomm was concerned, it was all in the family. 1Xtreme was based on its own CDMA patents.[24]

Qualcomm's revenue flows had four kinds of product sources: CDMA technologies, wireless systems, technology licensing, and other sources. CDMA technologies were the most important revenue source, accounting for 39 percent of total sales in 2000.[25] Technology licensing and wireless systems each accounted for 22 percent of the total sales.[26] Other products covered 17 percent of sales, ranging from digital motion picture delivery systems and e-mail software (Eudora) to government wireless communication systems. Qualcomm also had a number of subsidiaries and joint ventures with companies such as Microsoft and Kyocera.[27]

Having absorbed the lessons of i-mode's success in Japan, Qualcomm designed a standard for custom mobile-phone software (BREW) and initiated the development of a digital distribution system for cinemas worldwide. In the past, the company had served California's defense industry; now it was turning to California's major civilian industry, Hollywood. In turn, BREW—Binary Runtime Environment for Wireless—was its open, standard applications execution platform for wireless devices.[28]

Qualcomm's Focused Internationalization

In the late 1980s, Qualcomm had been a technology development start-up. Through most of the 1990s, it persisted in a growth and leadership strategy. At the close of the decade, it got back to basics again. The focus on innovation came naturally to the company, but it was also one of the few remaining viable strategic options. In the 1990s, Ericsson dominated infrastructure products, while Nokia came to dominate handsets. If Qualcomm could not dominate any of the key 2G products and services, it could still dominate the innovation that made possible these products and services. That required overthrowing the foundation that the Euro-Nordic companies had pioneered for their industry leadership—the GSM standard.

Qualcomm was too small to accomplish this objective on its own. It would have to leverage its operations worldwide and accomplish the task rapidly. Global leverage became critical to the U.S. company's strategic triumph. With the 2G transition, Qualcomm's international sales grew from 13–14 percent at the turn of the 1990s to 36 percent in 1996. In the end of the decade, the refocus refined its business concentration, but actually expanded the role of international sales, to 47 percent in 2000. Regionally, the early phase was dominated by U.S. sales (almost 90 percent), while the remaining revenues originated from South Korea and certain other geographic segments. After the first half of the 1990s, the U.S. sales accounted for two thirds of the total, while the remaining revenues came from South Korea and other countries. By 2000, the U.S. proportion was less than a half of the total, while Korean share was less than that of other countries, due to the spin-offs (see Exhibit 11-3 for more details on Qualcomm's internationalization efforts). Concurrently, Qualcomm's

Exhibit 11-3. Qualcomm's international revenues (1990–2001).

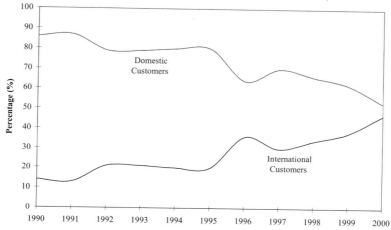

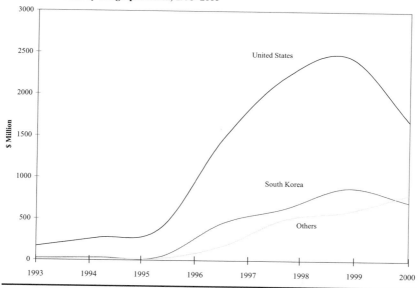

(continues)

Exhibit 11-3. (Continued).

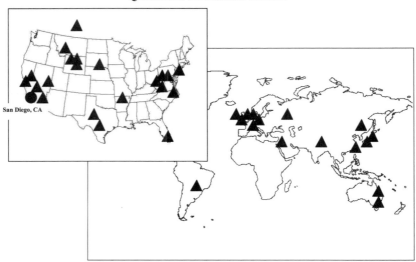

Qualcomm's Locations in 2001

San Diego, CA

Headquarters
San Diego

In the United States:	**International Locations:**
Atlanta, Georgia	Beijing, China
Bethesda, Maryland	Breda, Netherlands
Boston, Massachusetts	Drummoyne, Australia
Boulder, Colorado **(5)**	Farnborough, England
Campbell, California	Gladesville, Australia
Concord, Massachusetts	Haifa, Israel
Irving, Texas	Moscow, Russia
Kansas City, Missouri	Munich, Germany
Las Vegas, Nevada **(3)**	New Delhi, India
Miami, Florida	Sao Paulo, Brazil
Pittsburgh, Pennsylvania	Seoul, Korea
Portland, Oregon	Sophia Antipolis, France
Richardson, Texas	Thame, England
Salt Lake City, Utah	Tokyo, Japan **(2)**
San Jose, California	Toronto, Canada
Santa Clara, California	Veldhoven, The Netherlands
Scotts Valley, California	
Washington, D.C.	
Waynesburg, Pennsylvania **(2)**	

Note: Bolded, parentheses: # sites in a single location.

SOURCE: Company reports.

presence had rapidly proliferated from the San Diego base to key locations in Western Europe, Asia-Pacific, and Latin America.

This was an extraordinary feast under the most adverse circumstances. It did not happen "automatically," but through shrewd strategic measures, obstinate persistence, and ceaseless fervor for CDMA. In the U.S., Jacobs and his executives had to sell the standard to an industry that had pretty much locked in its future standard. In Europe, they were faced with the EC decision to make GSM mandatory in all European countries. In Asia-Pacific, they had to push CDMA in countries where incumbent players had cultivated market development for years, and promote the standard tirelessly, despite skeptics. From Qualcomm's point of view, the world was against the company, which was effectively under siege:

> There's no doubt in my mind that the Europeans are consciously blocking CDMA to protect the European manufacturers. At the same time, they're pushing to support their manufacturers all around the world. They do a heck of a job. We don't do anything like that. The U.S. government doesn't have any policy to push U.S. standards. When I go to meetings at the Commerce Department, Ericsson, Nortel, and Nokia are sitting at the table. No one invites us to meetings with the government in Stockholm. Ericsson's reply is that they have more employees in the U.S.A. than we do. I don't think that's true, but they do have a lot of employees in this country. It's a difficult thing for the government to deal with. But in the final analysis, the technology choices will really affect trade balances and when APC built its system in Washington (Sprint Spectrum), all the equipment was made in Europe or Canada. The phones were made in Finland and Sweden. They did have some Motorola phones, but they also had Ericsson and Nokia phones. The infrastructure was basically Ericsson or Nortel, but it was all manufactured outside the United States. No other country in the world would let people do that. We can't go over to England or France and put in our system. All we want is a chance to show what we can do. We are making some headway now. I've certainly explained to the government that they should say to other governments: "Look, these are nontariff trade barriers. It's wrong for you to say you have to use a particular technology to provide a service." [29]

Regional Objectives

Qualcomm's internationalization had different objectives regionally. In the United States, the objective was to overthrow the existing 2G standards. In Western Europe, it could do little to interfere with the GSM triumph, but it could intervene in the setting of the 3G standard. In Asia-Pacific, it would have to compete years after its rivals—Motorola, Nokia, and Ericsson—had established substantial footholds in the key markets, including Japan and China. Unlike these incumbents, Qualcomm established a foothold in Korea, which evolved into a substantial CDMA base. The Korean R&D and manufacturing capacity served as a shop window for future customers in Japan, where market access would be difficult, and China, where Qualcomm, like its rivals, lobbied hard to sell technology in exchange for market share.

From a Domestic Technology Developer . . .

At the turn of the 1990s, internationalization solidified Qualcomm's growth and leadership strategy in two ways. The company formed partnerships with prominent domestic and international communications companies, which would help it to define, fund, and validate new products and services. To enter promising international markets, it sought strategic alliances with major telecom companies, which enjoyed significant international presence. With Omni-TRACS, for instance, it established alliances with Alcatel and Koning en Hartman in Europe, C. Itoh and Nippon Steel in Japan, Canadian Satellite Communications, and others. With cellular telephone products, it established a strategic alliance with Alps Electric Corp. to facilitate the development and manufacture of cell products.

As the Japanese and the European operators and vendors moved into the 2G era in 1992, Qualcomm accelerated its internationalization through licensing, cooperation, test demonstrations, and the protection of intellectual property rights. It announced significant license agreements with Nokia in Europe and Nortel in Canada, as well as CDMA support agreements with Matsushita and Mitsubishi in Japan. These major foreign players validated Qualcomm's CDMA domestically. The first license deals were followed by others with AT&T, Motorola, Oki, Alps, and Sony as major equipment manufacturers signed support or license agreements with the company.

International cooperation escalated with increasing interest in CDMA. Qualcomm approached the Asian market through its continued CDMA joint development effort with Korea's ETRI (Electronics and Telecommunications Research Institute). As part of the agreement, it would license Korean manufacturers designated by ETRI to make CDMA infrastructure and subscriber equipment. CDMA's triumph made Korea a strategic CDMA development cluster worldwide, which was also conveniently close to China's massive potential market. In addition to licensing and international research cooperation, Qualcomm's field demonstrations triggered interest and initiated new business relationships worldwide, including those with the Deutsche Bundespost Telekom in Germany and the Swiss PTT. Finally, Qualcomm placed strong emphasis on filing and obtaining both U.S. and foreign patents and other forms of intellectual property protection for its technology. In 1992, it had been issued twenty-one patents and had twenty-nine applications pending in the United States.

. . . To a Global Technology Leader

As Qualcomm's CDMA was adopted as the U.S. digital cellular standard, it was also selected by Korea for its system. In 1993, four carriers in the United

States announced orders for CDMA, while rollouts accelerated by mid-decade in the United States and Korea. At the same time, one of the two nationwide cellular carriers in the Philippines announced a plan to implement a CDMA system by 1995. Furthermore, Qualcomm was now pursuing the international wireless local loop (WLL) market, in which radio substituted for copper wire "loops" to connect telephone switching offices to homes and offices.[30]

With OmniTRACS, Qualcomm was already operating in the United States, Canada, Mexico, Japan, and (as EutelTRACS) in several European countries (including Germany, Italy, the U.K., France), as well as in emerging markets (Brazil, Turkey, Russia). With CDMA, system orders had been placed in the United States, Korea, and the Philippines. Field trials were in progress in Australia, Germany, Korea, and Switzerland, while MoUs (memorandums of understanding) had been signed in Asian countries (e.g., China, India, Malaysia, and Pakistan), Chile, and Russia. By 1993, Qualcomm increased its focus on China (see Chapter 2). Whereas the United States averaged fifty-five phones for every one hundred people, China's average was less than one per one hundred people. With such low phone-to-population ratios, Qualcomm expected China and developing countries to provide vast markets for its wireless technology. By the mid-1990s, the largest U.S. cellular carriers had embraced CDMA, as had international phone companies, including Hutchison Telephone in Hong Kong and South Korea's two cellular carriers. Meanwhile, commercial trials were planned or underway in Canada, Latin America, and Southeast Asia. In fiscal 1996, international sales accounted for 36 percent of the company's total revenues.

In 1998, Qualcomm considered itself "truly international." It had offices in eighteen countries. As partner in the Globalstar low-earth orbit satellite communications system, it had installed preproduction and commercial gateways on four different continents. It was pushing infrastructure products to establish the company as a worldwide supplier for CDMA digital wireless systems, while phones and wireless data products were beginning to garner international customers, contributing to Qualcomm's nascent global brand. The internationalization, however, did not proceed smoothly. In 1998, the world's largest CDMA subscriber base remained in South Korea, which was impacted by the Asian financial crisis. Overall revenues from international customers accounted for 36 percent, 30 percent, and 34 percent of total revenues for fiscal 1996, 1997, and 1998, respectively. In 1999, Qualcomm refocused its strategy, which had substantial implications worldwide. As the company refocused on its core competencies, it sold the key assets of the infrastructure and phone businesses to the Swedish Ericsson and the Japanese Kyocera, respectively. Concurrently, these two companies repositioned as major suppliers in North America and other markets worldwide, overnight.[31]

After the spinoffs (infrastructure, phones), Qualcomm's revenues declined from $3.9 billion to $3.2 billion in 1999 and 2000. At the same time, Korea's portion of total sales decreased to 22 percent. In worldwide terms, the refocus strategy did not translate into full-scale de-internationalization. In 1990, overseas revenues had accounted for only 14 percent of Qualcomm's total sales. Through the first half of the decade, the technology development phase, these revenues were around 20 percent. As the company began to commercialize CDMA and reap the benefits of deployment, the proportion of international revenues grew accordingly, more than doubling to 47 percent by the year 2000. Worldwide demand was about to exceed domestic demand.

By the summer of 2001, SK Telecom, the Korean carrier, announced that it would delay the introduction of the 3G services for a year. Qualcomm aligned with SK Telecom to jointly invest some $5 million in start-up companies using Qualcomm's CDMA. Amid the transition to the 3G era, Qualcomm's headquarters and home base remained in the United States. It had substantial presence in South Korea and was rushing to expand its role in China. It also had offices in Australia, Canada, China, Brazil, Germany, France, India, Israel, Japan, the Netherlands, Russia, and the U.K. In 2000, the company generated $3.2 billion in revenues. Of the total, 53 percent originated from the United States, 22 percent from South Korea (primarily Samsung), and the remaining 25 percent from other countries.

Licenses and Royalties as Engines

By 1992, Irwin Jacobs and Harvey White, president of the company, left no doubts about their ultimate objective: "We are committed to making Qualcomm's CDMA technology the platform for wireless communications systems for this decade and the twenty-first century."[32] A decade later, that objective was accomplished. But in the early 1990s, few had taken it seriously. Toward the late 1980s, Qualcomm had been a little-known technology start-up, a defense contractor that most cellular observers had never heard of. At worst, it had been ridiculed by the leading mobile vendors; at best, it had been ignored by the industry giants. In the United States, Motorola was about to enjoy half a decade of rising profits. The Swedish Ericsson was an old telecom player that had evolved in the footsteps of the Bell invention. Even the Finnish Nokia, the latecomer in the business, had diversified into electronics in the late 1950s and joined the mobile pioneers in the 1970s. Qualcomm was a small player that enjoyed none of the high-volume manufacturing capabilities of the Japanese challengers. Nor did it have a great brand, such as Sony's Walkman or Apple's Macintosh, which might have paved its way into the cellular business. Unlike the incumbents, however, Qualcomm had CDMA, and that made all the difference. All mobile vendors nurtured one or another technology, but none had pioneered CDMA. All mobile vendors cooperated with partners, but none had CDMA-specific partners. All enjoyed worldwide leverage, but in no other case was that leverage built upon the CDMA foundation.

At the turn of the 1990s, the benefits of CDMA included greater capacity, higher quality, and several technical advancements that were attractive to operators and users.[33] Not only could CDMA systems carry up far more phone calls than current analog systems, but they were also three times as efficient as TDMA systems. CDMA was further in the productivity frontier than any alternative. Like Nokia in Western Europe in the late 1980s, Qualcomm partnered with ambitious operators in the United States. As new bands of radio spectrum were auctioned off for cellular use, new attackers challenged the incumbents. These operators did not fail to see the technology advantages that CDMA provided. PacTel Cellular (later AirTouch) became the first to sign on, in 1993. Sprint and others followed soon thereafter. Also, Qualcomm's executives thought in worldwide terms. Theirs, however, was a more focused approach. In the past, Motorola's internationalization was sequential and took decades. Qualcomm internationalized in parallel and very rapidly (see Exhibit 11-3). Motorola built its internationalization upon three to four decades of domestic expansion, whereas Qualcomm solidified its U.S. triumph with its increasing international leverage. Motorola stepped its internationalization after four decades of domestic operations; Qualcomm built its domestic bargaining power upon its worldwide expansion. Typically, the first commercial system to deliver CDMA was not located in the United States, but in Hong Kong, in 1995.

Despite its intense efforts to globalize, Qualcomm never enjoyed a comparable policy support as its overseas rivals. At the end of the 1990s, an anonymous company representative identified several key issues for conducting business in foreign markets. In each case, Qualcomm believed itself to be disadvantaged in comparison to the Euro-Nordic rivals. It believed it had:

- Difficulty in establishing positive relationships with national, regional, and local bureaucracies
- Difficulty obtaining type approvals and rural specifications, etc.
- Difficulty obtaining U.S. visas in a timely manner for foreign dealers requiring training at U.S. factories
- Difficulty in getting the U.S. to increase its influence in regional and standards bodies to ensure standards neutrality.
- Difficulty in obtaining recognition of the importance of having government officials represented at exhibitions[34]

Compared to its rivals, Qualcomm had not only developed CDMA; it was obsessed with the technology. The nature of the standards war forced Jacobs to become a public evangelist for CDMA. In contrast to contemporary wisdom, it was not a role that came naturally.[35] When Qualcomm came up with its CDMA, most of the key standards decisions had already been made. Jacobs and his senior executives could not play by the rules; they had to *redefine* the rules. At the close of the 1980s, a better mousetrap was no longer enough; rather, that mousetrap had to be far better, more efficient, and more innovative.

As the marketplace was already crowded, one had to raise hell to be heard. That was certainly not to the liking of the incumbents, nor was it politically correct. But when a company is intent on redefining the rules of the game, controversy comes with the territory.

By 2001, Qualcomm no longer saw high-volume manufacturing capabilities as vital to its strategic advantage. Its core competencies were in R&D. It would build necessary core capabilities on a more opportunistic and entrepreneurial basis. After a decade of struggling to internalize cost-efficient production capabilities, Qualcomm excelled in technology development. It could have mastered high-volume manufacturing as well, but that was not its core competency. Or as the company now saw it:

> The secret to our success is simple. We innovate new technologies with large market potential. Then we build markets for our ideas, sometimes by becoming a major manufacturer or by investing in ventures that support growth. And we try to take advantage of many opportunities for revenue growth along the way. We currently earn revenues through the sales of our own products and we earn royalties from licensing our growing patent portfolio to wireless manufacturers worldwide. As the wireless industry moves to the third generation, we believe high-speed, high-capacity wireless data is a key driver to future growth....[36]

At the close of the 1990s, Qualcomm's focus strategy reflected a return to basics. The company's revenue engine was built on innovation, which translated to dollars. Technology licensing was not Qualcomm's greatest direct source of revenues, but it was the great engine of these revenues. By mid-2000, the company had almost 330 patents and nearly 850 pending.[37] The broader and the more critical the patent portfolio, the more it attracts licensing deals. Licensees paid a one-time fee for access to the patent portfolio and then royalties based on the value of the CDMA products that they sold. For cell phones, analysts estimated the royalty averages 4.5 percent of the sales price. In 1999 the average sale price of a CDMA phone was $245. Each sale made Qualcomm $11 richer. In the fourth quarter of 1999 alone, Qualcomm took in $177 million in patent royalties, a 140 percent increase from 1998. The long-term significance of these patents, however, was not as clear as the initial profits they brought.[38] Also, the long-term predictions of the market bulls ignored the reality of still another technology transition. By 2010, the mobile industry was expected to shift into the 4G era; and if it were up to NTT DoCoMo, perhaps even earlier. That transition could mitigate the significance of current technologies, just as the emergence of CDMA nullified the Euro-Nordic dreams on a GSM-driven 3G standard. By spring 2002, the post-Enron environment led Qualcomm to an accounting debate as its shares fell to a low of $34.59, after a research firm raised concerns about accounting issues in the company's fourth-quarter and full-year financial reports.[39]

Qualcomm, of course, favored CDMA2000 over W-CDMA, the standard developed in Japan with the company's CDMA technology. Its royalties and licensing fees stemmed from its ownership of the broad 1G and 2G CDMA patents.[40] Jacobs argued that there were simple reasons for the preference: "You have to ask which is earlier to market, has the best technology, and is cheaper to roll out. My answer is CDMA2000. . . . [Many operators] have been told [W-CDMA] is an evolution of GSM, but that's not right. They think it'll be out in 2001, but it may be later. Now that the license auctions are over, operators have to think what is the fastest way to move ahead. I think CDMA2000 is the better one."[41] While Qualcomm had already signed up Hitachi, Toshiba, and Sanyo to license intellectual property (IP) related to W-CDMA, several key players—including Nokia and Motorola—had not licensed Qualcomm's W-CDMA. Similarly, Ericsson, which settled a two-year legal battle with Qualcomm by cross-licensing patents, suggested that Qualcomm's hold in 3G CDMA patents was not as strong as that in the older-generation portfolios.[42] At the end of the 1990s, almost all leading mobile vendors had signed patent licenses with Qualcomm. These covered CDMA products and products that incorporated W-CDMA, the European technology path into the 3G era. By 2001, Nokia was the only missing link. While it paid royalties on Qualcomm's CDMA, it had not signed a W-CDMA agreement. In July, Nokia expanded the terms of its CDMA cross-licensing agreement for wireless communications gear with Qualcomm. Under the "multimillion dollar" expansion, Qualcomm granted the Finnish vendor a royalty-bearing license to make and sell infrastructure gear for all CDMA wireless systems, not just handsets.[43]

The industry players formed the 3G Patent Platform, which appeared to promote Euro-Nordic pooling aspirations. The tradeoff involved reduced patent windfalls for singular pioneers.

Success Drivers: Shifting Core Capabilities

As a technology start-up, Qualcomm grew rapidly. But when Jacobs formulated its growth and leadership strategy, this expansion turned explosive. Most important, the transformation built on globalization (see Exhibit 11-4). Unlike Ericsson, Qualcomm did not have century-long multinational roots; it was a relatively new player. Unlike Nokia, Qualcomm, at least initially, did not enjoy regional political support. And unlike Motorola, Qualcomm had a limited operating history and was barely known in its home base. Initially, Jacobs tried to engage Qualcomm in a full-scale internationalization. But incumbents dominated in this game. Compared to them, Qualcomm suffered from relative cost disadvantages. Just like Motorola, Ericsson, and Nokia had struggled to build high-volume production facilities in the late 1980s, Qualcomm struggled

Exhibit 11-4. Qualcomm: drivers of wireless growth.

THE TRANSITION ERA

Products
- Qualcomm founded after the Bell breakup in the mid-1980s.
- Aggressive R&D until CDMA established in the U.S.; aggressive building of manufacturing capabilities.
- In short-term, CDMA fragments the 2G standard in the U.S.; in long-term, it provides a technology lead to U.S. innovators.

Operations
- Qualcomm's growth and leadership strategy (OmniTRACS in transportation, CDMA in cellular).
- Explosive growth with the acceptance of CDMA.
- Strategy driven by San Diego–based innovation, which is leveraged rapidly worldwide.

Markets
- Primarily a domestic entreprise, even though FDI accelerates quickly in South Korea.
- In comparison to rivals, Qualcomm is new, smaller, and more focused.
- After Tiananmen, lobbying begins in China.

THE COMPETITIVE ERA

Products
- CDMA becomes the core of the 3G standard.
- In mid-1990s, R&D expenditures decrease; investments into manufacturing and product portfolio pick up.
- Before tech slowdown in the U.S. and 3G downturn in Europe, Qualcomm spins off cellular segments and focuses on R&D.

Operations
- Before spin-offs, aggressive internationalization; after spin-offs, decreasing internationalization.
- Transition to refocus contributes to globalization of license and royalty revenues.
- Manufacturing in ancillary role to R&D operations.

Markets
- Before spin-offs, aggressive search for foreign markets; afterward, strategic posture closer to that of a global software player.
- Qualcomm's international focus translates to license and royalty fees instead of FDI.
- Heavy lobbying and long talks for access into China succeed in 2001.

through the 1990s in similar efforts until the company gave up—or found its way. Instead of trying to beat the incumbents in their game, Qualcomm refocused on *its own game* by spinning off all noncore activities.

The Transition Era

Qualcomm was founded only after the breakup of the Bell System in the mid-1980s, during the transition era. It invested aggressively into R&D until CDMA was secure in the U.S. cellular marketplace. It built manufacturing capabilities aggressively. The United States had enjoyed a unitary standard through the 1G era (AMPS), and industry practitioners expected comparable continuity in the 2G era (TDMA). To the industry, Qualcomm was a troublemaker. In Washington, it redefined the competitive field and served as a role model for American innovation.

The transition phase paralleled Qualcomm's growth and leadership strategy, which—as the terms reflect—aspired to boost the growth of the company and its technology capabilities while establishing industry leadership (with OmniTRACS in transportation and CDMA in cellular, for example). At first, Qualcomm had a highly entrepreneurial structure, but it grew explosively with the acceptance of CDMA, first in the United States and then elsewhere. Qualcomm's strategy was thoroughly driven by San Diego-based innovation, which the company sought to expand rapidly and worldwide.

Through the transition era, Qualcomm was primarily a domestic enterprise, even though FDI increased quickly in South Korea. That was not a result of a market choice, but a bold industrial policy decision designed to boost the fortunes of Korean-based vendors in the 2G era. Compared to rival vendors, Qualcomm was newer, smaller, more focused, and driven to foreign markets by innovation. In China, it began lobbying after the Tiananmen crisis.

The Competitive Era

Defying the expectations of the GSM leaders, Qualcomm managed to make CDMA the core of the 3G "single flexible standard." In the mid-1990s, R&D expenditures decreased at the expense of investments in manufacturing capabilities and a full product portfolio. But even before the tech slowdown in the United States and the 3G downturn in Europe, Qualcomm divested its cellular segments and focused entirely on R&D.

Before spin-offs, Qualcomm aggressively expanded its internationalization. After spin-offs, its internationalization decreased accordingly. Transition from growth and leadership to refocus strategy contributed to a shift from organizational internationalization to the globalization of Qualcomm's licensing and royalty flows. Manufacturing capabilities were now ancillary to R&D operations. Before spin-offs, Qualcomm aggressively sought access to foreign markets. Afterwards, its internationalization was replaced by globalization of revenue flows, and its strategic posture was comparable to Microsoft's smaller, cellular version. Qualcomm engaged in a "purer" globalization strategy, in which the primary offering was packaged R&D, and international operations were more about international licensing and royalties than FDI. Toward the end of the 1990s, Qualcomm lobbied heavily for access into China, which materialized only after roller-coaster negotiations in 2001.

Focused internationalization allowed Qualcomm's innovation to be leveraged worldwide, through licensing and royalties. Production had become a cost game. Nokia had handsets. Ericsson dominated infrastructure equipment. Qualcomm could not compete with them. But it could beat them indirectly, through focused innovation. It was no longer necessary to globalize the company. The trick was to globalize a value activity through the company. In Qualcomm's case, focused internationalization meant concentration on R&D, which was leveraged in specific worldwide markets.

Chapter 12

From "Board Stuffers" to Electronic Manufacturing Services

In the summer of 2001, *Business Week* released its annual list of world's leading IT firms. Between 1995 and 2000, it seems investments had been driven by the efforts of these efficient giants to create revenues as well as preemption or differentiation strategies. By 2000 and 2001, capital expenditures were legitimized by cost-cutting and cost-leadership—or focus strategies. The IT 100 list abounded with thriving outsourcing companies. "This is the best of times because no one ever wants to do their own manufacturing again," said Michael E. Marks, CEO of contract manufacturer Flextronics International Ltd., whose best year in the past decade had been 1992, the year after a tech slowdown. "2002 is going to be just a huge year for our industry."[1]

Industry downturns have often been upturns for outsourcers. Due to their slim margins, these companies go to great lengths for efficiency. Where a PC manufacturer or a mobile vendor might never be able to earn a decent return on investment, contract manufacturers have received a payback in short order. While a PC or mobile equipment maker tends to be increasingly focused, the contract manufacturer tends to work for many different companies. As a result, the former may use production machinery only part of the time, whereas the latter can keep it humming longer. Vendors seek to employ geographic scope to compensate for the low business scope, whereas contractors may exploit scope over business *and* geographic segments. The first tend to approach the productivity frontier via differentiation, the second via cost. In the old days, contractors had been a small cottage business. In the 1990s, they became big business. And amid the 3G transition, many have been consolidating into diversified, global giants. The top-four companies—Solectron, Flextronics, Celestica, and Sanmina-SCI—already dominated more than 50 percent of the market pie. As their customers were changing, so were they. The old competitive logic no longer applied. What did?

Value System and Contractors

Contract manufacturing became all the rage with the Internet revolution. Because of this fast-growing trend in consumer electronics, PC manufacturers, in the late 1990s, increasingly farmed out the fabrication of most components, from motherboards to disk drives to the very boxes on which they affixed their company logos. "Contract manufacturing is very prevalent across the board for all electronics, but consumer-electronics companies are particularly heavy users of contract manufacturing," said Susan Wang, then–senior VP and CFO at Solectron Corp., a leading maker of printed circuit boards for computers. "It's been a very helpful strategy for the OEMs to compete."[2] The industry trend originated from computers and peripherals, but by the end of the 1990s, it had swept through the wireless business. Actually, it was not a trend at all, but a "new deal" in the value system in which contractors had previously played an insignificant support role.[3]

Growth, Internationalization, and Co-Evolution: A Finnish Tale

Once upon a time, two Finns, Elsa and Pekka Aakula, founded a small telco called Pohjanmaan Tele in Ylivieska.[4] In 1970, they employed fifteen people. The Aakulas' first customer was Televa, an important telecom manufacturer that belonged to the Finnish government but would be acquired by Nokia a few years later. In 1972, the customer base increased with ITT and Siemens, two overseas giants. After a plant extension, the start-up faced new challenges. As Finland was hit by worldwide recession, the couple had to lay off ten employees. Aakula operated in a Finnish region known for the stubborn persistence of its inhabitants. But spirit did not suffice when bread grew thin. As they pondered the sale of the plant, the city of Ylivieska intervened by granting a longer loan period. The Aakulas gained some breathing space as rampant inflation drove many ventures to bankruptcy.

The Subcontractor Whose Name Nobody Could Pronounce

At the turn of the 1980s, the small Pohjanmaan Tele entered a new era as it began subcontracting for Nokia, which still generated most of its revenues in cable. It would soon enter a radical growth period, but the future mobile subsidiaries had not yet been launched. Telecom activities played a relatively minor role in aggregate revenues. But the Aakulas were lucky with their timing. During the first half of the 1980s, their firm manufactured cable coils and co-evolved with Nokia, which was about to engage in a slate of M&A activities. Concurrently, the number of the firm's employees increased to almost thirty. As the couple sought to increase and diversify their customers, they also initiated contract manufacturing for Nokia's NMT standard in 1987. This deal precipitated many others by Nokia, but only amid national turmoil. In the early 1990s, Finland experienced the worst recession since the Great Depression, but somehow the tiny Pohjanmaan Tele survived through these difficult years. As people despaired for jobs and the welfare state saw soup lines for the first time since the 1930s, the Aakulas worked harder than ever before. When the old Cold War order fell apart, Finland was swept by European integration.

As Jorma Ollila captured strategic leadership at Nokia, the vendor focused its operations on the mobile business and divested all noncore units. This turnaround was manna from heaven for the Aakulas, who now initiated GSM contract manufacturing for the Finnish vendor. As the contractor rushed in Nokia's footsteps abroad, the old corporate name no longer reflected its new international status. By the mid-1990s, the Finnish roots of Pohjanmaan Tele were a historical relic. The Aakulas' firm was not a telco. It was not a rural start-up. Besides, how does one negotiate business deals in Estonia, England, or China when the client can barely mutter the odd Finnish name? No foreigner could pronounce "Pohjanmaan Tele" without a serious stammer! So the growing contractor changed its name to Wecan Electronics. It had a cool, high-tech sound.

Wecan's World Travels

Manufacturing backplanes, cables, and modules, Wecan launched plants, units, and factories in Pärnu, Estonia, Dallas, Texas, and Suzhou, China while partnering in Milton Kaynes, England. In each case, the contract manufacturer co-evolved with its lead customer. By 1999, its turnover amounted to FIM 185 million, and the estimate for 2000 soared to FIM 285 million. After the extension of the Finnish plant, Wecan's surface area grew tenfold. Where Nokia went, Wecan followed. Conversely, where Nokia divested (e.g., Nokia Networks' base station factory in Dallas, Texas), so did Wecan.

At the end of the 1990s, the Aakulas took their firm public in the Helsinki Stock Exchange. By 2000, Wecan was an international contract electronics manufacturer that produced and sold telecom products and services to telecom system suppliers, particularly to manufacturers of wireless network systems. Like Nokia, it continuously measured customer satisfaction. To increase flexibility, efficiency, and speed and to widen its technology base, it built up a network with its own suppliers and strategic partners. It had production plants in Finland (Ylivieska), China (Suzhou), and Estonia (Pärnu) and a service unit in Helsinki. Its turnover was EUR 47 million and it employed 557 people in Finland, Estonia, and China. While Nokia Networks still accounted for more than 40 percent of Wecan's net sales, the contractor also delivered to Marconi Communications and cooperated with Oshino in Europe. Diversification of customer base meant protection. The greater Wecan's dependence on a single client, the fewer would be its chances to survive should its lead customer suffer from adverse conditions. Meanwhile, Wecan's marketing resources and organizational capabilities had been strengthened in both China and Europe. The share of foreign deliveries in turnover had grown to 42 percent. Now Wecan's objective was to become an international key supplier of the leading telecom systems manufacturers. To achieve its goal, it relied on flexibility, agility, and customer orientation. It expected to grow fast by going even more global and by playing a major role in contract manufacturing for 3G wireless products. The future, as the Nokians put it, seemed to have "no limits"—until the promise and hype of 3G was swept by the realities and birthpains of the new standard. Dependence on a single client reinforced risks; diversification of customer base lowered them.

Nokia's Supply Chain

Since the beginning of the Ollila era, Nokia had patiently built a sophisticated supply chain that contributed to its global leadership and ensured the rapid growth of its suppliers. By 1996, the chain was in place, and the glitches had been eliminated. In 1999, the company had an estimated 15,000 subcontractors in Finland alone, where the number of Nokia's own employees was at 21,000.[5] The subcontractors possessed little strategic flexibility. Business models were customized according to Nokia's requirements. Most relied on cost focus strategies in which margins were highly dependent on high volumes.[6] As the vendor accelerated technology standardization, cost pressures increased accordingly.

Nokia's subcontractors consisted of electronic contract manufacturers, component suppliers, software and product development companies, production equipment suppliers, as well as service firms that were indirectly dependent on Nokia. To some extent, the sources of competitive advantage among suppliers emulated those of their lead customers consisting of price (annual price erosion amounted to 20–30 percent in base station products), quality, flexibility and responsiveness, customer service, and globalization. Subcontractors struggled to manage the growth (i.e., internationalization and consolidation). Furthermore, logistics had to be highly efficient. In practice, partnerships required the *suppliers* to take greater risks for relatively smaller rewards in servicing their lead customers, which benefited from the fragmentation and the lower degree of imagery power of these connections.

Toward the end of the 1990s, consolidation accelerated among contract manufacturers, in particular. U.S.-based SCI Systems purchased Nokia factories in Oulu, Finland and Motala, Sweden, while Flextronics bought Kyrel and Sweden-based Essex acquired Finland-based Enviset. As big players concentrated on mass production, small ones were specializing and midsize competitors were squeezed out of the markets. "The pace is frenetic and the competition is tough," said Antti Jokitalo, the marketing chief of Essex. "During the past two years, international big manufacturers have arrived in the Nordic countries, where they have bought factories and subcontractors of their lead customers."[7] It was a textbook example of the sequence of excessive growth and the subsequent shakeout. It was surprising only to those who had bought the inflated dreams and the grandiose expectations.

Consolidation

When Nokia stumbled, Wecan and other small to medium-size suppliers were left with little strategic flexibility. While they sought to diversify risk, most remained dependent on Nokia's fortunes and had to endure greater volatility amid strategic inflection points. "Your Global Partner in Electronics Manufacturing" was the slogan of Wecan Electronics. It applied equally to most of Nokia's lead subcontractors. By February 2002, the autonomy of Wecan ended as well, when it signed an agreement to merge with Scanfil. Through the deal, the two hoped to create an internationally significant, vertically integrated systems supplier with production in Finland, China, Estonia, and Hungary. The merged entity's pro forma turnover for 2001 was EUR 257 million. The companies employed 1,600 people. With the merger, Wecan's name would change to Scanfil Oyj.[8]

In the 1990s, Wecan's story was a rule rather than an exception in Finland, where several successful subcontractors grew and internationalized with Nokia, and the stories of the contractors of the global mobile and IT leaders were no different in terms of fundamental industry trend. In Finland, each of these subcontractors, including Elcoteq Network Corp., JOT Automation, Eimo, and Perlos, followed its lead customer while expanding its customer base and new market potential. These symbiotic arrangements had a common denominator in mobile phones and infrastructure equipment. Eimo and Perlos manufactured molded plastic covers, Elcoteq produced mobile phones and phone parts, and JOT Automation—which some observers called a "baby Nokia" until a profit warning in spring 2000—built the equipment that Elcoteq and Nokia Mobile Phones used to manufacture the phones. Many of these firms earned 80–90 percent of their revenues from mobile phone–related products. All of them served as subcontractors for Nokia as well as Ericsson.

As Nokia and Wecan co-evolved, they also co-adapted. Like hummingbirds and Hamelia flowers in the rain forest, Nokia and Wecan shared a symbiotic relationship (i.e., a business ecosystem).[9] But the two were *not* equal. As the dominant handset vendor worldwide, Nokia enjoyed absolute and relative bargaining power. It had similar symbiotic relationships with hundreds of contractors. From the 1970s through the 1990s, the largest contractors became diversified, global players. Most of them originated from the PC and Internet revolutions, but all benefited when the wireless leaders began to outsource manufacturing capabilities at the end of the 1990s. At the same time, the support industry consolidated worldwide and acquired substantial bargaining power. In the process, the symbiotic arrangements changed as well. Some Hamelia flowers were no longer content with listening to hummingbirds; they had grown hungry.

OEMs and Outsourcing

Leading mobile vendors are original equipment manufacturers (OEMs). Through the 2G era, the second- and third-tier producers were not OEMs or were only partially OEMs. Many leading OEMs had started as a supplier, contractor, or outsourcer of sorts. Motorola built its earliest capabilities in battery eliminators. It overcame entry barriers only through R&D and as a defense contractor when it took advantage of the disruptive role of FM communications in World War II. Lars Magnus Ericsson's start-up was a simple repair shop until the Swede entered telecom manufacturing and services. Nokia used joint ventures in Asia and the United States to internationalize, but it also served as a supplier well into the mid-1990s. And Qualcomm started as a defense contractor and supplier (Linkabit) for the transport industry before it began to build manufacturing and marketing capabilities in the mobile business. One can recall similar narratives about the old European mobile giants, such as Siemens in Germany and Alcatel in France, or their more recent Asian counterparts, such as Sony and Matsushita in Japan, Samsung in Korea, and Huawei in China. In new and emerging industries, every supplier dreams of becoming an OEM. Some seize the opportunity; few succeed. In more established and mature industries, such dreams are not as realistic due to relatively high entry barriers, investment levels, and cost structure.

By 2002, a growing number of the world's leading OEMs—including Solectron, Flextronics, Celestica, and Sanmina-SCI—outsourced substantial chunks of their manufacturing capabilities to electronic manufacturing services (EMS) providers. These OEMs were once small, entrepreneurial, and fragmented. But they were transformed first with the PC revolution in the 1980s and again with the Internet revolution in the 1990s. As growth gradually stabilized in the computer markets, mobile communications provided new opportunities. In the summer of 2001, consolidation in the wireless business prompted many OEMs to increase outsourcing. It also boosted joint ventures between the vendors as well as second- and third-tier producers in the Asia-Pacific region, while resulting in divestitures of manufacturing capabilities elsewhere.

The drivers of outsourcing include continuous and long-standing market pressures to shorten time-to-market and enhance asset utilization. With the 3G transition, the leading contractors became increasingly driven by technology innovation and globalization. Through the 2G era, outsourcing had enabled the contractors' customers to focus on their core competences, particularly R&D, sales, and marketing. With the emergence of multimedia cellular services, the very role of the OEMs shifted. As these players highlighted downstream capabilities, many downplayed upstream functions (e.g., manufacturing, logistics, and operations) that were most vulnerable to price erosion, cost pressures, and commodification.

Since the 1990s, outsourcing has exhibited few or no signs of decline. The faddish notion of "core competence" legitimized the idea of retaining value activities that matched the strengths of the company while outsourcing those that were identified with its weaknesses:

> The most powerful way to prevail in global competition is still invisible to many companies. During the 1980s, top executives

were judged on their ability to restructure, declutter, and delayer their corporations. In the 1990s, they'll be judged on their ability to identify, cultivate, and exploit the core competencies that make growth possible—indeed, they'll have to rethink the concept of the corporation itself.[10]

In the course of the 1990s, stock exchanges worldwide rendered even greater support to the notion of core competence, or the older idea of "sticking to the basics." As institutional investors diversified portfolios on their own, diversified businesses became less attractive investment options than thriving and highly focused businesses that could be leveraged worldwide. Vendors such as Nokia and Qualcomm were attractive in the stock markets, which in turn allowed them to focus on core activities or, in the case of the U.S. manufacturer, to spin off everything that did not support the key operations. By 2000, the orchestration of subcontracting and the entire supply chain was one of the cornerstones of Nokia's operations and provided a benchmark for aspiring challengers. It was based on close cooperation with the suppliers at the product design stage, which Nokia described as early supplier involvement (ESI). Still another subcontracting segment pertained to the quality design of components. The Finnish vendor had some 300 primary producers worldwide supplying it with components. When the logistics worked smoothly, that allowed rapid response to problems. In 2000, for instance, the lack of a key component caused problems for many of Nokia's rivals but not for Nokia itself, due to its ability to react quickly to the situation.[11]

At the height of the 1990s, the Finnish vendor was often portrayed as a "network company" whose supplier network participated in the strategic advantages of cooperation, including revenue growth, geographic expansion, and technology innovation.[12] This assessment rested on and relied exceedingly upon the expansionary years of the Finnish vendor, ignoring the dynamic underlying that expansion. Once the dynamic had peaked, contraction followed, and the contractors carried their share of the pain, as was the case with other mobile and IT leaders. New theories of organization were not necessary; old realities of business and management were. In reality, Nokia's greater capabilities (e.g., agility and flexibility) vis-à-vis rivals had more to do with its process organization, IT systems, and able senior executives than with any new organizational arrangements. Except for the largest contractors, most of these suppliers lacked diversification and were thus highly dependent on Nokia's revenues and profitability. In addition, their geographic expansion was less about global strategies than about serving the vendor in requisite locations. And due to their upstream role, innovation was often confined to those stages of the value chain that were most vulnerable to long-term price erosion. As Asian producers caught up with technological innovation, the Finnish suppliers could not compete in local responsiveness, and they had even lesser capabilities to respond to the Asian cost-efficiencies. In other words, as long as Nokia continued to grow, the suppliers benefited, *if* they could manage the hypergrowth. But even if they could master the growth, many became overly dependent on Nokia and therefore were the first to suffer the pain in the 3G transition. These vulnerabilities were about the low degree of bargaining power and diversification among the fragmented suppliers. They were discernible in the organizational structure through the 2G era, but became—as one could expect—a subject of debate only during the 3G transition, when growth stagnated.

In several industries, OEMs heard the new battle cry and tried to adapt to new value systems and value chains by outsourcing noncore capabilities. Among EMS leaders (see Exhibit 12-1), this wave of outsourcing pertained to computers and peripherals in the early 1990s. By the end of the growth decade, it was mobile businesses' turn to capture the spotlight. According to industry estimates, the EMS industry was valued at $58 billion in 1998 and was expected to grow almost 29 percent per year, which would translate to a $203 billion market by the year 2004.[13]

In the aftermath of the Internet revolution, consolidation in the U.S. technology sector and 3G birth pains in the European wireless business only contributed to the acceleration of outsourcing. According to a 2000 survey by Bear, Stearns & Co. Inc., 90 percent of OEMs, including the market share leaders, answered yes to this key question: "Do you intend to increase your use of an electronic manufacturing services provider over the next twelve months?" Though less sexy and visible than many high-profile OEM industries, the EMS sector had evolved into one of the world's most dynamic industries in just a decade or two, with an average growth of 25 percent per year. Despite consolidation, the upside was solid. Bear, Stearns estimated the total available market at $500 billion, based on the assumption that only 15 percent was outsourced in 1999.

Toward Consolidation

Until the late 1980s, the wireless business was a niche segment. Plants were small, markets were fragmented, and product variety was high. With impending growth, nothing would remain the same. Plants expanded and markets unified. Product variety was reduced to key categories and segments. As the business shifted from the 1G era to the 2G era, it also moved from high-cost and low-volume production to low-cost and high-volume production. This shift subverted the value system—the intertwined value chains of contractors, subcontractors, and original equipment manufacturers—from within. At first, OEMs struggled to master the new production techniques, process organization, and logistics. But at the same time, they began to outsource noncore assets in the value chains. Take, for instance, Ericsson, the Swedish vendor, which by the late 1980s had coupled its infrastructure business with that of mobile

Exhibit 12-1. The EMS leaders: market share, CAGR, and customer concentration.

EMS Leaders: Market Share (2000)

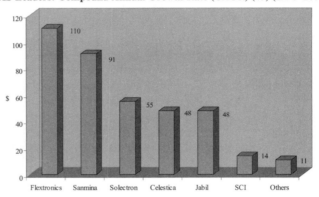

EMS Leaders: Compound Annual Growth Rate (CAGR) (%) (1996–2000)

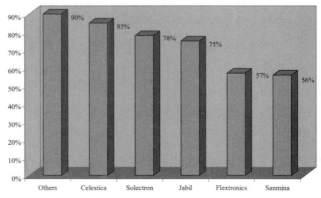

EMS Leaders: Customer Concentration (2000)*

*The revenue proportion accounted by the top-10 customers.

Source: Company reports; industry data from Manufacturing Market Insider.

phones. In Kumla, Sweden, Flemming Örneholm expected the factory to make 43,000 phones annually. However, the new manager of the plant brought the number down to 37,000. After a wave of restructurings in 1991, Kumla produced about 200,000 phones. The market signals were clear: The Swedish vendor required more capacity to focus on narrower product variety but in far greater volumes. In the absence of low-cost manufacturing capabilities, rising volumes necessitated subcontracting. Like other OEMs, Ericsson began to outsource components. This was hardly new at at the Swedish company. But as growth was about to explode, so was outsourcing, which went hand in hand with globalization. Classic outsourcing built on cost advantages (i.e., subcontracting), which globalization made possible worldwide (through cost leaders in Asia-Pacific and elsewhere). Still, such decisions required considerable debate within the firm because of the relatively high bargaining power of the unions. Eventually, Ericsson's mobile handsets were outsourced for cost reasons (see Chapter 9).[14]

A new managerial mind-set was needed to master the shift to low-cost and high-volume production with the transition to digital cellular. Amid the 3G transition, volume and cost requirements were coupled with those of technology novelty and systemic complexity. On one hand, the leading vendors began to divest those parts of the value chain that were most vulnerable to price erosion and commodification. In these areas, the vendors could no longer compete against focused low-cost players, nor did they want to, due to slim margins. However, the vendors also felt a powerful pull from those parts of the value chain where price premiums were still possible and which provided a differentiation base. In these high-margin areas, the vendors did not have to worry about low-cost players, which lacked requisite technological capabilities, did not possess the necessary intellectual property rights, or had an unfamiliar brand.

Today's diversified and highly capital-intensive global EMS leaders originate from the tiny entrepreneurial shops of the 1970s, the so-called board stuffers. During the 1980s, the largest pioneers developed into contract equipment manufacturers (CEMs), which in turn evolved into electronic manufacturing services (EMS) in the 1990s. By 2002, some of the latter pioneers were getting into original design manufacturing (ODM). At the broadest level, these phases tend to coincide with the cellular platforms: pre-cellular, analog, digital, and multimedia cellular (see Exhibit 12-2).

"Board Stuffers" (1970s)

The earliest contractors co-evolved in the 1970s with the expansion of the technology sector in the United States. These firms operated in domestic, primarily local markets. They held a support function only. As niche businesses, they concentrated on components or assembly. The tasks were highly labor-

Exhibit 12-2. From components to original design manufacturing
(1970s–present).

	Cluster/ Industry	OEM's Value Chain	Product/ Services	Financial Resources	Customer Portfolio	Risks/ Rewards
Pre-Cellular (1970s)	U.S. Domestic market	Support	Components, assembly; "board stuffers"	Insignificant; highly labor-intensive	One to few	Insignificant
1G (1980s)	U.S., Pioneering FDI	Supply	Contract manufacturing services	Growing	Few	Low
2G (1990s)	Regional, Triadization	Cooperation	Electronic manufacturing services	Capital-intensive	Many	Increasing
3G (Present)	U.S., Asia-Pacific	Strategic partnership	Expanding EMS	Globally capital-intensive	Diversified	High

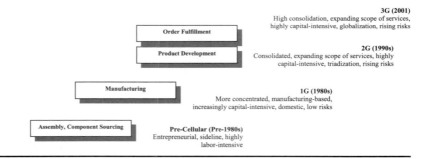

3G (2001)
High consolidation, expanding scope of services,
highly capital-intensive, globalization, rising risks

2G (1990s)
Consolidated, expanding scope of services, highly
capital-intensive, triadization, rising risks

1G (1980s)
More concentrated, manufacturing-based,
increasingly capital-intensive, domestic, low risks

Pre-Cellular (Pre-1980s)
Entrepreneurial, sideline, highly
labor-intensive

intensive. The shops had minimal financial resources and few customers. Risks
were low.

Celestica

Many of the EMS veterans launched their operations in the pre-cellular
era. Some have even older roots. Take, for instance, Celestica, Inc., a world
leader in electronics manufacturing services for industry-leading OEMs, primarily in the computer and communications sectors. With facilities in North
America, Europe, Asia, and Latin America, Celestica provided a broad range of
services, from design and prototyping to supply chain management, worldwide
distribution, and after-sales service. Its history stems from 1917, when the then
recently founded IBM created a Canadian subsidiary. As part of IBM Canada,
the plant made casings for IBM products. Decades later, the role of the supply

chain would be perfected, after the Toronto factory missed being closed during IBM's 1980s cost-cutting drive. As head of the Toronto operation, Eugene Polistuk raised the plant's profile by expanding the unit's offerings to include circuit boards, memory devices, and power supplies. This upgrading moved Celestica toward the EMS business.

Flextronics

Most EMS leaders originate from the early computer industry or from computer peripherals, networking, telecommunications, and other industries. Take Flextronics, an EMS leader that is considered the strategic giant of the lot. Joe McKenzie, a manufacturing engineer, launched the company as early as 1969, but he certainly did not expect it to turn into a global giant. In the early 1970s, McKenzie and his wife offered Silicon Valley's pioneers very basic services. While the customers provided the parts and boards, Flextronics turned them into printed circuit boards. It was a growth business, but hardly sexy. Even the McKenzies acknowledged that they were in the less-glamorous business of "board stuffing."

In 1981, Flextronics became the first U.S.-based manufacturer to go off-shore. When it launched the Flextronics Singapore facility, it triggered the rise of a new industry segment—the pioneering contract manufacturers in Singapore, which later gave rise to indigenous players such as NBL, Omni, and Venture. A year later, Flextronics was sold to Bob Todd, Joe Sullivan, and Jack Watts. As CEO, Todd pioneered automated manufacturing techniques, which meant the end of the labor-intensive and relatively cost-efficient assembly era. He saw Flextronics as a contract manufacturer, thus naming the nascent industry. With board-level testing, the company also began to implement quality and yield targets. Manufacturing capabilities provided an inadequate base of differentiation for these early pioneers. In the long term, industry consolidation required massive M&A waves, which did not occur until the 1990s.

Solectron

Roy Kusumoto had worked for computer game maker Atari and co-founded Optical Diodes before the launch of Solectron Corp. in 1977. At first, it served as an electronics assembly job shop, offering peak-period manufacturing services for Silicon Valley's growing electronics industry. As the name suggests, the company also intended to get into solar energy, but this objective did not materialize. Kusumoto brought in Winston Chen as EVP. The Taiwan native and IBM veteran became president and CEO in the early 1980s. He combined Japanese total quality management with American principles of entrepreneurial innovation. When Kusumoto left Solectron, Chen's former boss at IBM, Koichi Nishimura, joined as COO in 1988. A year later, the company went public. Determined to improve performance, Chen and Nishimura adopted the Malcolm Baldrige National Quality Award guidelines. By 1991, Solectron won the award. Soon thereafter, Nishimura became Solectron's president and, a year later, co-CEO with Chen. Such insistence on quality has contributed to contractors' capabilities in handling increasing novelty and complexity, which in turn has benefited both vendors and contractors.

Contract Manufacturers (1980s)

The "board stuffers" were followed by contract equipment manufacturers (CEMs)—or contract manufacturers (CMs)—in the 1980s. These firms provided manufacturing services to the leading OEMs while growing in their footsteps. CEMs first operated in the United States, but as their lead customers internationalized, so did the contractors. At the same time, the contractors were building their competences and capabilities while trying to avoid overt dependence by diversifying with several lead clients. Risks were still relatively low. CEMs did not have branded products. Ideally, they were product- and customer-agnostic. In practice, they focused first on computers and later on communications, just as they continued to depend on a selected few customers. The CEMs worked on a fee-based revenue model and did not assume inventory risks. Customers provided product designs while the CEMs possessed the manufacturing process engineering capabilities. The customers innovated; the CEMs executed. Most CEMs sourced from component suppliers, but some—such as Flextronics—used a vertical model with component manufacturing capabilities. Some EMS pioneers launched their operations before the 1980s, but most began as CEMs. Others, such as Sanmina, integrated from component manufacturing contracting. Conversely, some OEMs started as CEMs, including Nokia-Mobira, which lacked an umbrella brand until the early 1990s.

By the mid-1980s, rising volumes and declining costs contributed to turnkey solutions. Customers created product specifications, which were sent to the contract manufacturer. In practice, this meant the partial migration of value activities to the contract manufacturer (from manufacturing capabilities to parts purchases). In the process, original equipment manufacturers became less original. At Flextronics, for instance, OEMs would still come up with the plan, but they no longer determined the process; that was up to the CEM. With their strategic flexibility, the CEMs had a new base for differentiation. Increasing autonomy was a powerful incentive to make things faster, better, and cheaper. Flextronics, for instance, embraced computer-aided design (CAD). The company went public in 1987 and moved toward building complete, working, shippable products (i.e., "full box assembly"). These products ranged from the Hayes modem to Sun Microsystems' disk and tape subsystems in its workstations. At Flextronics, the changes in the value system and activities went hand in hand with increasing internationalization. CEMs followed the footsteps of their most valuable customers, the OEMs, which were building a presence in the lead markets worldwide. In 1988, Flextronics, with sales at $200 million, launched the first U.S.-managed contract electronics plant in China.

Electronic Manufacturing Services (1990s)

By the 1990s, the CEMs were succeeded by the EMS firms. Many EMSs were former CEMs that focused on consumer electronics, computers, and communications. As they expanded the scope of supply chain services from mass production and material sourcing toward product development and order fulfillment, they also grew increasingly capital-intensive and international through triadization. Risks increased with potential rewards. While the firms did not provide branded products, they did try to differentiate themselves vis-à-vis service strategies. The EMS leaders, in particular, were aggressive in expanding product and customer portfolios in efforts to diversify risks and to reduce customer dependency. By the end of the 1990s, they embraced the new Internet technologies and moved toward communications. Reliance on IT among EMS leaders provided a catalyst for highly efficient organizational capabilities. Flextronics, for instance, believed that its strongest competitive advantage lay in the ability to gather and analyze supply chain information. "Information flow is the real value of what we're doing," said Flextronics CFO Robert Dykes. "Aggregating information isn't enough. Getting it from one end of the supply chain to the other is what we're pushing."[15]

As growth declined in the computer markets, EMS leaders moved toward communications. With global telecom reforms, markets had become more competitive, while the rise of the wireless business translated to growing outsourcing among mobile leaders. More recently, several EMS leaders have also become original design manufacturers (ODMs) as they have increasingly participated in in-house product designs and marketed products to potential OEM customers. In this case, expansion of scope resulted in increasing risk, as ODMs' revenue flows were built on production volume and unit selling price. While ODMs were typical in PC-related segments (especially in Taiwan), their role has not been significant in the wireless business, in which products are more complicated and extensive outsourcing has been more recent.

The decade of the 1990s, however, began with the U.S. recession, which led to the decline of the high-volume technology market. Pain rippled from Silicon Valley to Asia.

Flextronics

Loaded with debt and poorly integrated operations, Flextronics was forced to divest its manufacturing operations in the United States while laying off 75 percent of its employees. To pay its debts, a new management team divested the healthy Asian operations, which resulted in the formation of Flextronics International in 1990. The company was almost bankrupt when it was taken private through external funding. Michael Marks, a former manager who became Flextronics's chairman and CEO, assembled a coalition of Silicon Valley venture capitalists in 1993. Based in Singapore, the new and improved

Flextronics expanded in Asia and the United States and went public in 1994. Marks and his team turned the company around to rebuild its presence in America. After a net loss of $6.5 million in fiscal 1992, Flextronics showed a net profit of $6.2 million only three years later. Concurrently, revenues nearly tripled, rising to $237 million in 1995.

Between 1993 and 1998, Flextronics acquired more than twelve operations, built a global infrastructure for high-volume manufacturing, expanded purchasing and engineering capabilities, grew from 3,000 employees to more than 13,000, and upped the revenue target to $5 billion. External growth and globalization went hand in hand with acquisitions in the United States (nChip in 1996), Asia-Pacific (FICO Plastics of Hong Kong in 1997), and Europe (Austria's Neutronics in 1997 and Finnish EMS company Kyrel in 1999). These two frenetic drivers boosted consolidation, which served as an entry barrier against new companies. By 1997, Flextronics completed final assembly for cellular phones, personal computers, and printers. With the Asian economic crisis, the company faced new problems. Marks considered selling the operation to Sanmina or Solectron. Instead, Ericsson decided to outsource some of its wireless switching equipment and awarded a $300 million deal to Flextronics (whose revenues at the time were only $400 million). "That launched us in Europe almost overnight," says Marks. "There was no other contract manufacturing going on there, so we were able to move very quickly with other acquisitions."[16] In particular, Flextronics relied on four tactics to drive its high revenue targets: design and engineering centers, industrial parks, product introduction centers, and regional manufacturing operations (see Exhibit 12-3). From the EMS standpoint, these revenue drivers ensured operational flexibility and customer responsiveness. Because OEMs have configured *their* value activities worldwide, leading EMS players must succeed in the same task. Throughout the world, these facilities design, test, and launch new products, shortening critical time-to-market. The 3Com PalmPilot and the Microsoft Mouse, for instance, were designed and built by Flextronics.

Between 2000 and 2001, the EMS leaders entered a new era of consolidation because of the slowdown of the U.S. technology sector and the birth pains of the 3G transition in Europe. Along with Solectron, Flextronics dictated the pace with new M&A activities. In 1994 (when it doubled its workforce through foreign acquisitions), the Denver-based DII Group, a firm that had been through several incarnations, initiated an aggressive acquisition wave. Finally, after six years of devouring other CEMs, it was DII's turn to be devoured. In April 2000, Flextronics acquired the company in a deal valued at more than $2 billion, which propelled the company to the fourth position in contract manufacturing. The contractor then expanded in Asia by acquiring JIT Holdings, a Singapore-based EMS, at about the same time Microsoft selected Flextronics to build its Xbox video game console.[17] In December 2000, Ericsson's top leadership threw a fiftieth-birthday dinner for Marks in Stockholm, where Marks suggested that Ericsson should jettison all its mobile phone operations.

Exhibit 12-3. Flextronics: operational flexibility and responsiveness to customer needs.

Michael Marks: Flextronics's Business Model

Prior to joining Flextronics, Michael Marks led Metcal, Inc., a precision heating instrument company. He has been CEO of Flextronics since 1994 and its chairman since 1993. Under his leadership, Flextronics grew from $93 million in 1993 to $12 billion in 2001.

Prior to the 1990s, Marks helped to transform the business model of the contract electronics manufacturing (CEM) industry from serving OEMs on an overflow basis to serving as a primary supplier of Electronics Manufacturing Services (EMS).

By 2002, Flextronics and other EMS leaders not only ensured increasing worldwide cost-efficiencies, but also signaled increasing capabilities in global differentiation.

Flextronics International Ltd.

Design & Engineering Centers

The Americas
Bothell, WA
Dallas, TX
Irvine, CA
Niwot, CO
Oak Ridge, TN
Wake Forest, NC
Salt Lake City, UT
San Diego, CA
San Jose, CA

Europe
Althofen, Austria
Brno, Czech Republic
Cork, Ireland
Eliat, Israel
Gdansk, Poland
Karlskrona, Sweden
Milan, Italy
Oslo, Norway
Paderborn, Germany
Solothurn, Switzerland
Stockholm, Sweden
Tampere, Finland
Treviso, Italy
Visby, Sweden
Zalaegerszeg, Hungary

Asia
Singapore
Senai, Johor, Malaysia

Industrial Parks

The Americas
Guadalajara, Mexico
Sorocaba, Brazil

Europe
Brno, Czech Republic
Gdansk, Poland
Nyiregyhaza, Hungary
Sárvár, Hungary
Zalaegerszeg, Hungary

Asia
Doumen, PRC

Product Introduction Centers

The Americas
Dallas, TX
Raleigh, NC
San Jose, CA
Tyngsboro, MA

Europe
Althofen, Austria
Karlskrona, Sweden
Kyröskoski, Finland
Malmö, Sweden
Milan, Italy
Paderborn, Germany
Solothurn, Switzerland
Stockholm, Sweden
Vasteras, Sweden

Asia
Doumen, PRC
Johore, Senai, Malaysia

Regional Manufacturing Operations

The Americas
Binghamton, NY
Chambersburg, PA
Dallas, TX
Elk Grove Village, IL
Garland, TX
Greeley, CO
Kingston, PA
Longmont, CO
Manaus, Brazil
New Braunfels, TX
Palm Harbor, FL
Parsippany, NJ
Puebla, Mexico
Raleigh, NC
Rochester, NH
San Jose, CA
Smithfield, NC
São Paulo, Brazil
Wake Forest, NC
Tlalnepantla, Mexico
West Columbia, SC
Zebulon, NC

Europe
Althofen, Austria
Avellino, Italy
Cork, Ireland
Grolleau, France
Hamilton, Scotland
Haapajarvi, Finland
Kannus, Finland
Karlskrona, Sweden
Katrineholm, Sweden
Kindberg, Austria
Kyröskoski, Finland
L'Aquila, Italy
Limerick, Ireland
Lovsjo, Sweden
Madrid, Spain
Malmö, Sweden
Migdal Haemek, Israel
Oslo, Norway
Oulainen, Finland
Paderborn, Germany
Pandrup, Denmark
Skillingaryd, Sweden
Sievi, Finland
Solothurn, Switzerland
Tab, Hungary
Tullamore, Ireland
Udine, Italy
Vaggeryd, Sweden
Västerås, Sweden
Visby, Sweden

Asia
Bangalore, India
Beijing, PRC
Changzhou, PRC
Melaka, Malaysia
Samuprakarn, Thailand
Senai, Malaysia
Shanghai, PRC
Singapore
Suzhou, PRC
Tampoi, Malaysia
Xixiang, PRC

Ten days later, Ericsson agreed to get out of the cell phone manufacturing business. "It turns out that, increasingly, companies want not just a supplier but someone to run a part of their business for them," said Marks. "The Ericsson deal was our big breakthrough."[18]

The larger the scale economies, the more extensive the efforts at operational flexibility. And the more far-reaching the attempts at customer responsiveness, the more EMS leaders such as Flextronics were driven to differentiate their strategies from those of the rivals.[19] The evolution and acceleration of branding was the most obvious side of this competitive logic. In turn, continued upgrading and innovation, along with the acquisition of manufacturing capabilities, turned the EMS leaders into potential long-term threats in the wireless business. As the leading vendors were divesting, joint venturing and partnering their manufacturing capabilities, the leading EMS players were integrating forward in the value system.

Solectron

During the first half of the 1990s, Winston Chen retired and Koichi Nishimura took over as CEO at Solectron, which built and bought a series of foreign manufacturing facilities in Malaysia (1991), Japan (1992), France (1992), the U.K. (1993), Germany (1995), and China (1996).[20] More acquisitions followed—Solectron bought Fine Pitch Technology and custom manufacturing services by Texas Instruments in 1996, entered an alliance with Ericsson in 1997, and later acquired a factory from NCR Corp. in 1998. When Solectron defeated SCI Systems as the leading contract manufacturer in 1999, it only intensified the hectic pace of merger and acquisition activities, which resulted in accelerating globalization (see Exhibit 12-4).[21] The M&As peaked two years later with the acquisition of Canadian electronics manufacturer C-MAC Industries for about $2.7 billion. "We don't just want to be the biggest, but the best, from end to end," said Nishimura, who ran Solectron. "There is no one else who has the entire chain covered—who designs, makes, and services the products."[22] Indeed, Solectron patterned its strategic moves according to changing OEM needs and outsourcing of core competences. It built strategic capabilities to sell total solutions. It concentrated on cost advantages, but it could not ignore differentiation and innovation either.

Celestica

In 1993, Celestica's sales reached nearly $1.5 billion. The following year, IBM made the operation a wholly-owned subsidiary. Three years later, it was spun off as an independent contract manufacturer, with Eugene Polistuk as CEO. IBM sold Celestica, which operated a million-square-foot factory, to Toronto-based Onex Corp. for about $750 million. This sale initiated a new growth phase at Celestica, which soon purchased Design to Distribution, Europe's largest EMS company, and acquired two U.S.-based facilities from Hew-

Exhibit 12-4. Solectron's globalization.

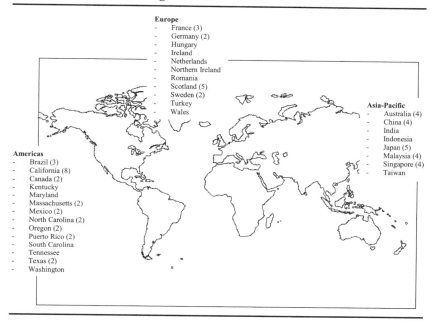

Europe
- France (3)
- Germany (2)
- Hungary
- Ireland
- Netherlands
- Northern Ireland
- Romania
- Scotland (5)
- Sweden (2)
- Turkey
- Wales

Asia-Pacific
- Australia (4)
- China (4)
- India
- Indonesia
- Japan (5)
- Malaysia (4)
- Singapore (4)
- Taiwan

Americas
- Brazil (3)
- California (8)
- Canada (2)
- Kentucky
- Maryland
- Massachusetts (2)
- Mexico (2)
- North Carolina (2)
- Oregon (2)
- Puerto Rico (2)
- South Carolina
- Tennessee
- Texas (2)
- Washington

lett-Packard, a major client. After a $361 million IPO in 1998, Celestica acquired Silicon Graphics' printed circuit assembly operation. It had now become a major force in two of three Triad regions, operating some twenty factories in North America, the U.K., and Ireland. To participate in the global chessboard, it moved into Asia by acquiring International Manufacturing Services, a California-based EMS concern with operations in China, Hong Kong, and Thailand. After these purchases, Celestica's sales reached $5 billion. By 2000 and 2001, acquisitions continued and intensified as the company took advantage of market downturns in the United States and Europe.[23]

Sanmina-SCI

Sanmina was created by Bosnian immigrants Jure Sola and Milan Mandaric in 1980 to provide just-in-time manufacturing of printed circuit boards (PCBs). At the turn of the 1990s, the company upgraded and joined the leading industry players by shifting production to higher-margin components, such as backplane assemblies and subassemblies. After Mandaric left, the company went public in 1993. Following the technology and telecom leaders as well as the leading contract manufacturers, Sanmina began to push for M&As and globalization. It purchased manufacturing plants from Comptronix (1994), Assembly Solutions (1995), Golden Eagle Systems (1996), and Lucent Technologies (1996). When it bought electronics maker Elexsys International (1997), it also opened a plant in Ireland. Loyal to the pattern of the EMS leaders, Sanmina's hunger grew toward the end of the 1990s.[24] This wave of M&As peaked in 2001, when Sanmina bought rival SCI Systems, Inc., one of the world's largest contract manufacturers. In the $4.5 billion deal, Sanmina also assumed $1.5 billion of SCI's debt.[25] The deal followed eight weeks of bargaining, during which the two companies recognized that only by merging could they compete against larger rivals Solectron and Flextronics. With $9.1 billion in sales in 2000, SCI assembled PCs and telecom gear, using relatively low-paid labor in countries such as Mexico and Malaysia. Sanmina manufactured more complex switches, routers, and optical networking equipment for the likes of Cisco, Alcatel, and Motorola, often using skilled labor or factories equipped with robots and lasers.[26]

Changing EMS Leaders

In the 1970s, the board stuffers were a tiny niche segment, a labor-intensive side-business for small entrepreneurs. In the 1980s, the PC revolution provided a powerful boost to contract manufacturers, which professionalized business practices, even if the industry remained fragmented. In the 1990s, the Internet revolution and wireless explosion served as growth catalysts to the dramatic expansion and consolidation of the EMS sector, which embraced these new technologies through new and highly efficient organizational capabilities. This IT-driven growth went hand in hand with accelerating globalization, which offered the contractors still another opportunity to reconfigure and coordinate value chains across locations worldwide.

The Logic of EMS Rivalry

By 2000, the industry had become capital-intensive and more concentrated. In just a year, the market share for the top-six EMS leaders climbed from 42 percent to 55 percent. Due to the acquisition of SCI by Sanmina, the four largest players now dominated more than 50 percent of the entire business. Membership had its privileges, but the EMS business was no longer fragmented. A market share in excess of 10 percent was required to gain membership in the top league. The growth rate, largely a function of mergers and acquisitions (often coupled with supply agreements), reflected the rapid pace of consolidation. During the latter half of the 1990s, the most aggressive players, such as Flextronics and Sanmina, enjoyed annual growth of 90 percent to 110 percent, whereas the industry average was an estimated 25 percent to 30 percent and the smaller players barely achieved 10 percent. Big was beautiful and size mattered. Strong financial resources boosted capital-intensive operations (typically via IT), while size multiplied with scale and scope economies.

Product diversification and broader service capabilities as revenue sources ensued. Conversely, estimates of customer concentration indicated that the most aggressive players exploited diversification against risk, whereas the smaller players—and even some of the big ones—continued to generate some 80 percent to 90 percent of their revenue from a single lead customer.

Industry Consolidation

In the 1990s, the revenues of EMS leaders soared from less than $100 million to almost $19 billion. Take, for instance, the largest player, Solectron. Between 1992 and 2001, its revenues climbed from $407 million to $18.7 billion, versus Flextronics ($7.2 billion), Celestica ($9.8 billion), and Sanmina-SCI ($3.9 billion). During that time period, Solectron's market capitalization rose to $9.9 billion, which was higher than that of Flextronics's ($7.2 billion), but not as high as Celestica's ($11 billion) or Sanmina's ($14.3 billion). Meanwhile, the number of EMS leaders' employees soared from a few thousand to tens of thousands, even as all engaged in extensive cost-cutting measures to retain operational flexibility. Between 1992 and 2001, the number of Flextronics employees climbed from more than 2,000 to 75,000, in comparison to Solectron (60,000), Celestica (31,000), and Sanmina (24,000).

Excluding the most volatile negative declines, most EMS leaders achieved their success with relatively narrow margins, especially compared to those of their lead customers in the wireless business or even the PC business. At Solectron, for instance, the net margin trend remained at 3.5 percent to 4.3 percent through most of the 1990s. The margins of Flextronics and Celestica were even slimmer at 1.4–2.8 percent and 1.4–2.1 percent, respectively. Only Sanmina demonstrated a higher margin trend, at 4.9–10.6 percent.

Product Portfolios

The projected 25 percent to 30 percent growth for the industry was substantially higher than the underlying demand for electronic products as a whole. In addition to consolidation, the industry was driven by increasing outsourcing (due to a broadening customer base and service portfolio) and broader technology consumption (due to the convergence and digitalization of computers and communications). In terms of their customers, all EMS leaders built balanced and diversified product portfolios. But some emphasized traditional computer segments (e.g., Solectron, Celestica) whereas others focused on communications (e.g., Sanmina-SCI, Flextronics). From the standpoint of products and services, Solectron still built 74 percent of its revenues on printed circuit board assembly and 18 percent on systems builds. At Flextronics, telecom (32 percent) and networking (20 percent) accounted for most revenues, versus servers, peripherals, and PDAs (29 percent). At Celestica, most sales originated from computer businesses (servers 33 percent, workstations 15 percent, storage 14 percent, PCs 7 percent), as opposed to communications (31 percent). However, Sanmina, which enjoyed the highest market cap, obtained 72 percent of its revenues from communications.

Triadization of Operations

By 2001, *all* EMS leaders had essentially "triadized" their operations worldwide (see Exhibit 12-5). Most had pioneered their operations in the United States, and the original emphasis remained in America. In most cases, U.S. sales still represented the majority of sales. By the same token, the greatest growth opportunities were in Asia-Pacific.[27] Solectron garnered 49 percent of its sales in the United States, but 33 percent originated from other regions, particularly Asia-Pacific. Its client roster included the "who's who" of electronics giants, including Ericsson (13 percent of sales), Cisco Systems (12 percent), and Nortel Networks (12 percent), as well as Apple Computer, Hewlett-Packard, and IBM. Similarly, Flextronics obtained some 44 percent of its sales in the Americas, 38 percent in Europe, and already 20 percent in Asia. Its customers covered most leading OEMs, including Cisco Systems, Compaq, Hewlett-Packard, IBM, Lucent, Nokia, Philips, Sony, and WebTV. At Celestica, North America accounted for 61 percent of sales, Europe 28 percent, and Asia 11 percent. Sanmina still obtained 81 percent of its sales in the United States, but SCI—which it had acquired—garnered only 49 percent of its revenues in the United States and 51 percent in foreign markets.

Shifts in Bargaining Power

The top-four EMS leaders shared many customers, but Flextronics's vertical integration of value chain activities and coordinated globalization made it unique. Reportedly, CEO Marks almost flunked the only manufacturing course he ever took at Harvard Business School, but he made up for it by understanding the force of globalization earlier than most of his peers.[28] To initiate its rapid-growth track, Flextronics focused its venture capital on building a low-cost manufacturing network not just in Asia, but *worldwide*. The most advanced operations, which made routers for Cisco and wireless base stations for Ericsson, were in the most sophisticated locations, such as Silicon Valley and Sweden. The most labor-intensive operations were in China, where the EMS company made its least advanced electronic products, from Dell's PC parts to cell phones for Nokia, Motorola, and Ericsson. Marks would use *both* operations.

Flextronics's strategy reversed conventional industry wisdom, which favored simple cost-cutting measures through production transfers from developed to less-developed country markets. Instead, the EMS firm moved mass-order production to high-wage countries, such as Austria and the Netherlands, while strengthening design and services.[29] This globalization of low-cost manufacturing locations across the world allowed the company to offer to its Triad

(text continues on page 351)

Exhibit 12-5. The EMS leaders: profits, revenues, and globalization.

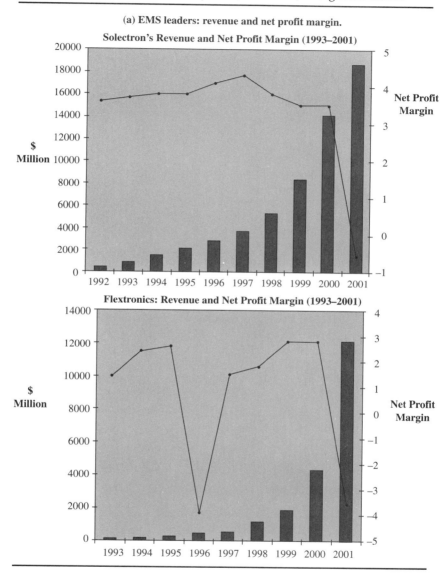

(a) EMS leaders: revenue and net profit margin.

Solectron's Revenue and Net Profit Margin (1993–2001)

Flextronics: Revenue and Net Profit Margin (1993–2001)

(continues)

Exhibit 12-5. (Continued).

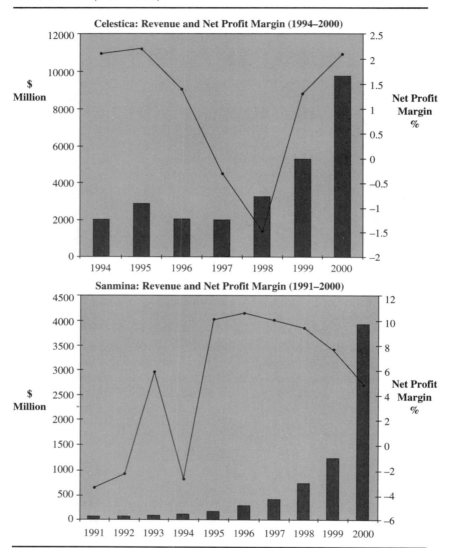

(b) EMS leaders: revenue sources (2001).

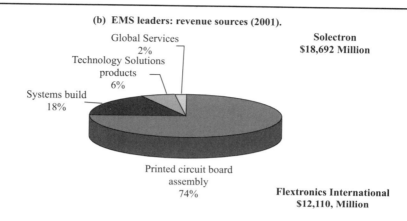

Solectron
$18,692 Million

Global Services
2%
Technology Solutions
products
6%
Systems build
18%
Printed circuit board
assembly
74%

Flextronics International
$12,110, Million

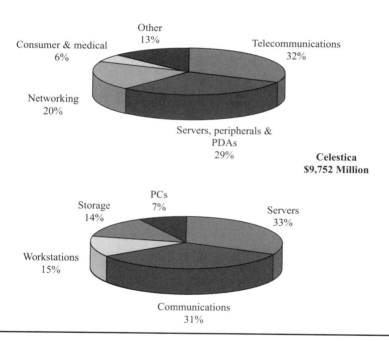

Other
13%
Consumer & medical
6%
Telecommunications
32%
Networking
20%
Servers, peripherals &
PDAs
29%

Celestica
$9,752 Million

PCs
7%
Storage
14%
Servers
33%
Workstations
15%
Communications
31%

(continues)

Exhibit 12-5. (Continued).

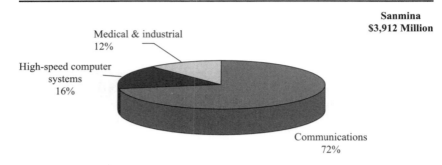

Sanmina
$3,912 Million

Medical & industrial 12%

High-speed computer systems 16%

Communications 72%

(c) EMS leaders: degree of globalization (2001).

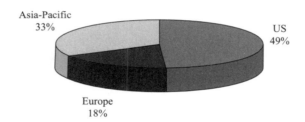

Solectron
$18.7 Billion

Asia-Pacific 33%

US 49%

Europe 18%

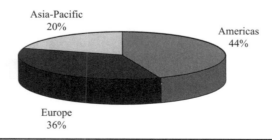

Flextronics
$12.1 Billion

Asia-Pacific 20%

Americas 44%

Europe 36%

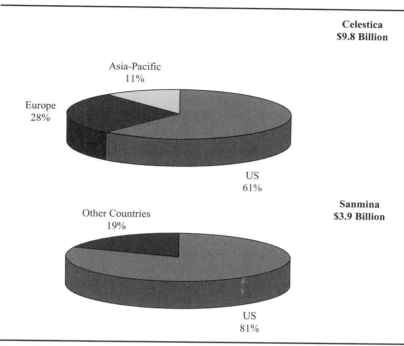

Celestica
$9.8 Billion

Asia-Pacific
11%

Europe
28%

US
61%

Other Countries
19%

Sanmina
$3.9 Billion

US
81%

SOURCE: Company reports.

customers inexpensive manufacturing in relatively close proximity. It was not just (and no longer) traditional migration to low-cost locations, but exploiting IT to coordinate global supply chains vis-à-vis key locations. Similarly, classic outsourcing strategies have historically struggled with poor infrastructure in less-developed nations. Insulating itself, Flextronics built campuses on all major continents. Not only did these campuses shorten the distance between the supplier and its customers, they also relied on standardized designs and high-level coordination through enterprise resource planning (ERP), which ensured consistency across different factories.[30]

Marks envisioned Flextronics as a one-stop, vertically integrated shop that would provide everything from engineering and product design to manufacturing and distribution. "We are a variable-cost manufacturer," explained Marks. "We share the infrastructure among a bunch of customers, so when demand for one product dries up we can switch to something else and we don't get stuck with an idle factory." For instance, if the market for handheld computers takes a dive, the same assembly lines can be used to produce a product of similar size, like a cell phone. Such efficiency was not possible for a company that only made handhelds.[31] By the same token, Flextronics did not rely on just singular advantages. It excelled in cost advantage, but it also exploited differentiation through local responsiveness, just as it had to engage in ceaseless innovation to respond to the changing requirements of the volatile environment.

In 2001, Flextronics still obtained 85 percent to 90 percent of its revenue from traditional outsourced manufacturing. Globalization of the low-cost manufacturing base, along with campus developments, prepared Flextronics to absorb even larger slices of its customers' supply chain. As some observers have noted, this logic provided OEMs with short-term cost-efficiencies, but it complicated differentiation in the long term:

> In some ways, the name brands—not only the Microsofts and Nokias but also the Kodaks and Gaps—are making a devil's bargain. If some entrepreneur has a revolutionary idea for a videophone or an instant tooth flosser, all he has to do is get Wal-Mart to agree to sell it and then get Sanmina to design and build it for him. Consider Donna Dubinsky and Jeff Hawkins, the brains behind the ubiquitous PDA, the PalmPilot. They left Palm three years ago and started Handspring with a scheme for a competing PDA, the Visor. Within fifteen months, Handspring was shipping its new Visors, thanks to Flextronics and Solectron. And now the Visor has 7 percent of the $4.3 billion global PDA market.[32]

In November 2001, Microsoft's Xbox hit retail shelves nationwide in the United States. Without Flextronics, the gaming device would have remained just another great idea without appropriate execution. "We talked to Michael Dell, and the guys at Gateway and Compaq," said J. Allard, whose foresight contributed to Microsoft's Internet strategy in 1995. "They said, 'Wait, you want to make 50 million of the same exact thing? That's not what I do.' Dell said, 'I don't want to be in the razor business if I can't get in on the blades. You're talking to the wrong guy.'"[33] With Flextronics, razors could be turned into blades. With its industrial parks, the company was able to manufacture in low-cost regions, which translated to 75 percent cuts in labor price. Traditional offshore cost-cutting, however, was only part of the story. Take, for instance, an HP printer, a typical product that might have cost an OEM $100 to build.[34] A typical OEM might pay $8 in overhead (for maintaining a factory and equipment); $4 in freight (for delivery to the retailer); $6 in sales, general, and administration (SGA) costs; $4 in labor; and $2 in finance (for expenses associated with maintaining an inventory). Flextronics, however, cut in half the combined costs of finance, SGA, and overhead because of its extensive customer portfolio, management of operations on one ERP system, factories running to 90 percent efficiency, and allocation of common supplies across its customer base. By making many components and housing suppliers on-site, it minimized delivery times and expenses. It could save in manufacturing expenses by cooperating with customers on product design to decrease the number of parts.

Finally, the $12 billion in supplies it purchased annually gave it significant bargaining power. Overall, it could reduce $8 out of the presumably fixed $76 cost of materials.

Until the 1990s, the CEM players had focused primarily on manufacturing (e.g., prototyping, material sourcing, mass producing, and final testing). In the early 1990s, digitalization and the Internet revolution prompted closer customer cooperation in product development and order fulfillment. In the process, the scope of CEM firms expanded from classic assembly to manufacturing and, in the 1990s, toward upstream (product development) and downstream (order fulfillment) activities. By 2001, these EMS firms were far more than suppliers. (Exhibit 12-6 summarizes the evolution of these contractors.)

Consider the leading handset vendor. From the standpoint of Nokia, these EMS firms incorporated critical elements of the value activities (e.g., productization, manufacturing, distribution, and services), which allowed the Finnish firm to focus on its core competencies in R&D, branding, and to some degree, manufacturing. The expanding scope of strategic capabilities among EMS leaders required financial resources and scale economies, which necessitated

Exhibit 12-6. Contractors: fragmentation, globalization, and consolidation.

MONOPOLY ERA

The earliest contractors co-evolved in the 1970s with the expansion of the technology sector in the United States.

- These firms operated in domestic, primarily local markets.
- As niche businesses, they concentrated on components or assembly.
- The tasks were highly labor-intensive.

The "board stuffers" were followed by contract equipment manufacturers (CEM) – or contract manufacturers (CM) – in the 1980s.

- These firms provided manufacturing services to the leading OEMs, while growing in their footsteps.
- CEMs first operated in the United States, but as their lead customers internationalized, so did the contractors.
- They focused first on computers and later on communications.
- They worked on a fee-based revenue model and did not assume inventory risks.
- Customers provided product designs, while the CEMs possessed the manufacturing process engineering capabilities.
- Most CEMs sourced from component suppliers, but some – such as Flextronics – used a vertical model with component manufacturing capabilities.

By the mid-1980s, rising volumes and declining costs contributed to turnkey solutions. Customers created product specifications, which were sent to the contract manufacturer. In practice, this meant the migration of value activities to the contract manufacturer (from manufacturing capabilities to parts purchases).

TRANSITION ERA

By the 1990s, the CEMs were succeeded by EMS.

- As they expanded the scope of supply chain services from mass production and material sourcing toward product development and order fulfillment, they also grew increasingly capital-intensive and international, through triadization.
- While the firms did not provide branded products, they did try to differentiate themselves vis-à-vis service strategies.
- By the end of the 1990s, they embraced the new Internet technologies and moved toward communications. Reliance on IT among EMS leaders provided a catalyst for highly efficient organizational capabilities.
- More recently, several EMS leaders have also become original design manufacturers (ODMs).

COMPETITIVE ERA

In the 1990s, the Internet revolution and wireless explosion served as growth catalysts to the dramatic expansion and consolidation of the EMS sector, which embraced these new technologies through new and highly efficient organizational capabilities.

- IT-driven growth went hand in hand with accelerating globalization, which offered the contractors an opportunity to reconfigure and coordinate value chains across locations worldwide.
- By 2000, the industry had become capital intensive and more concentrated. The four largest players now dominated more than 50 percent of the entire business.
- Big was beautiful and size mattered. Strong financial resources boosted capital-intensive operations (typically via IT), while size multiplied with scale economies.
- Product diversification and broader service capabilities ensued. The most aggressive players exploited diversification against risk, whereas the smaller players remained dependent on a single lead customer.

M&A waves, promoted consolidation, and raised entry barriers. The arrangement turned the two groups into strategic partners: Vendors were forced to engage in higher differentiation strategies, while EMS leaders had to excel in low-cost strategies. Historically, outsourcing had been pervasive in PCs and peripherals. But in the wireless business, it accelerated only with consolidation starting in 2000 and 2001. Consequently, the strategic implications were ignored or misunderstood.

In traditional outsourcing, the EMS provider made a part of a product for the customer, who then incorporated it into the final product. In the new outsourcing arrangement, customers entrusted the entire manufacturing process to the EMS provider. Customers concentrated on product design and marketing, and the EMS player did the rest. However, by the end of 2001, the leading EMS companies were getting into design for some customers as well. Ideally, this arrangement allowed both parties to focus on their core competences. But it also enabled the EMS leaders to incorporate increasingly sophisticated value activities and engage in forward integration, whereas their customers were left with design and marketing and, at times, only marketing. As long as the EMS leaders were unable to innovate into marketing and distribution, and as long as the vendors dominated these downstream activities, all parties benefited. However, when one party failed at the expense of the other, or when third parties (e.g., Microsoft in the case of operating systems and application software) eroded vendors' bargaining power, ideal efficiencies could turn into a value system in which the mobile leaders might be squeezed out. After all, through greater vertical integration, Flextronics would look more like a traditional manufacturer, but it could use each of its new vertical capabilities, such as design or logistics, for many different customers, not just one. Then again, industry giants like Intel and Microsoft could do the same in mobile chips and software applications, respectively. Such activity actually intensified competition at Ericsson, whose infrastructure segments would be attacked by IT leaders and challengers. Furthermore, it could result in the "boxification" of Nokia's handsets, if the Finnish vendor were to fail in fighting the low-cost pressures.

Chapter 13

Mobile Vision

By the turn of the millennium, the mobile equipment manufacturers—including Ericsson, Nokia, Motorola, and Qualcomm—hurriedly prepared for an impending industry convergence as traditional handsets acquired Internet capabilities, whereas IT leaders were quickly developing traditional voice capabilities. Both rushed to exploit the digital convergence.

Digital Convergence

The mobile vision offered a roadmap from voice to data. It evolved from a single standard in Europe and multiple standards in the United States. In contrast, the data vision was relatively standards-independent, which had significant implications for industry competition. In the 1990s, the GSM debate was often framed in terms of standards and industrial policies, whereas the issues that pertained to the 3G shift and the concomitant transition from voice to data communications originated as much from technology innovation and digital convergence.

From Vertical Integration to Horizontalization

In the early 1950s, U.S. telecom and computer sectors were dominated by two *de facto* monopolies, AT&T and IBM, respectively (see Exhibit 13-1). Telecommunications was highly regulated; computers were not. But in both cases, these corporate giants controlled the full industry value chain from infrastructure to software and distribution. AT&T had full command of local, long-distance, and equipment markets. Its engineers had already developed the cellular concept and were cultivating the first mobile services, albeit slowly. Initially, the computing industry was synonymous with IBM (and its superior sales force), which dominated retail sales, distribution, application software, operating systems, computers, and chips. IBM's power originated from its strength in mainframes. Big Blue's rivals were, for all practical purposes, small niche players.

In the early 1970s, U.S. telecom and computer sectors were still dominated the two monopolies, but their power was on decline. In computing, IBM's mainframe era had been challenged by minicomputers (DEC, Sperry,

Exhibit 13-1. The transformation of IT-producing industries
(1950s–present).

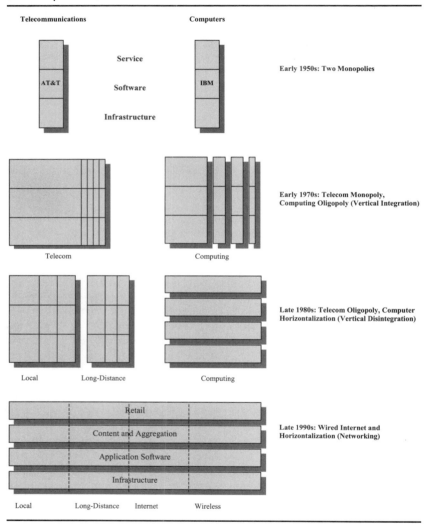

Univac, Wang). In telecommunications, AT&T's dominance had been challenged by new long-distance carriers (first MCI and later others), which seized
new technologies and questioned the rationale underlying the old natural monopoly. In both cases, the two giants *and* their new rivals continued to control
the full value chain from infrastructure to software and distribution. Through
its command of the entire value system, AT&T dominated local, long-distance,
and equipment markets; eventually, it also launched the first mobile consumer

service and prepared for the introduction of the analog cellular. The dominant carriers and telcos were vertically integrated. Similarly, in computers, IBM continued to command infrastructure, software, and distribution, even though it was challenged by new rivals. In both industries, the leading players remained vertically integrated. While IBM missed the emergence of minicomputing, the new IT paradigm did not challenge the existing industrial organization; DEC and other new challengers were vertically integrated. Telecommunications and computers were still distinct industries, even though industry visionaries had been predicting convergence since the end of the 1960s, when digitalization and data communications arrived.

By the late 1980s, AT&T's monopoly ended with the antitrust decision. A long-standing antitrust suit may have weakened IBM as well, but the erosion of its bargaining power originated from the PC revolution. In telecommunications, the breakup decision left AT&T a role in long-distance, telecom equipment, and computers (where it failed), whereas half a dozen "Baby Bells" took over local telecom segments. While the central players remained vertically integrated, new technologies increased horizontal pressures, which began to threaten both carriers and local telco monopolies. The Baby Bells acquired mobile properties, engaging in long-standing M&A activities.

Meanwhile, the PC revolution effectively ended IBM's monopoly in the computing sector. Instead, each horizontal level of the value system gave rise to a single dominant firm or an oligopoly of a few firms. The industry was de-verticalized into several horizontal layers. No longer could any one rival dominate the entire value chain. Instead, each horizontal layer gave rise to a dominant firm making chips, operating systems, or application software, or *de facto* oligopolies (PC manufacturers and retailers). While Intel dominated microprocessors, the PC clone manufacturers comprised a half dozen major players, including Compaq, Dell, Packard-Bell, Hewlett-Packard, and IBM. In operating systems, Microsoft captured dominance through its DOS and Windows-based systems, whereas Apple Computer (Macintosh), IBM (OS/2), and network-based solutions (i.e., UNIX) remained niche players. In retail and distribution, IBM's classic sales force was replaced by dealers, retail stores, superstores, and mail-order houses. Through the PC revolution, Intel and Microsoft dominated three horizontal layers (chips, OS, applications), while exercising indirect control over others (PC vendors, sales outlets). The *de facto* duopoly, Wintel (named for the *Win*dows operating system and applications coupled with In*tel's* chips), steered the industry until the mid-1990s. Wintel began to crumble only with the rise of the Internet.

Mobility and the Internet

By the mid-1990s, the PC revolution gave way to the Internet revolution. This "network of all networks" originated from the efforts of the U.S. defense forces to respond to the challenge of the Soviet Sputnik launch in 1957. These efforts were soon coupled with research on distributed computing as a way to ensure the sustainability of national information security, even in the case of a centralized nuclear attack.[1] The Internet can be traced to ARPANET, a network developed in the late 1960s with funding from the Advanced Research Projects Administration (ARPA) of the U.S. Department of Defense. The number of computer users seeking to connect to this experimental network grew rapidly.[2] While most of the funding for ARPANET came from military sources, the project was developed for the most part at universities and research-oriented government contractors.[3]

In 1986, the National Science Foundation (NSF) initiated the NSFNET, a series of high-speed networks connecting the NSF's supercomputers from various regions. With this new network backbone, the term "Internet" was formally adopted. Three years later, the World Wide Web made its debut at CERN (Conseil Europeen pour la Récherché Nucleaire), based in Geneva.[4] As Internet use in the United States became more commercial, which was inconsistent with NSF policies, the U.S. government decided to get out of the business of funding commercial networking. Concurrently, the Clinton-Gore administration stimulated the coming Internet revolution with new policy initiatives. The development of the browsers (Netscape Navigator, Microsoft Internet Explorer) allowed the commercialization of the Web, starting with the explosion of Internet advertising.[5]

In the 1980s, Apple's Steven Jobs had promised a "computer in every American home." By the end of the 1990s, Jorma Ollila, CEO and chairman of Nokia, went further with a new battle cry: "A mobile phone in every pocket!" Natural progression of this vision would lead to a handheld computer that would serve as a wireless terminal. Today, the Internet economy comprises four horizontal layers; infrastructure, applications, content and aggregation services, and retail. Through "mobilization" (see Exhibits 13-2 and 13-3), the horizontal layers of the digital economy were expected to become unplugged.

- **Mobile Infrastructure.** With the mobilization of the digital economy, a new infrastructure would emerge, comprising operators, wireless Internet service providers (ISPs), access firms, and security companies. In this layer, network operators and mobile handset and systems vendors played a central role.

- **Mobile Applications.** Similarly, wired applications were about to give rise to wireless applications. These required software products and services to facilitate web transactions, transaction intermediaries, and consultants and service companies to design, build, and maintain mobile websites, from wireless portals to mobile e-commerce sites.

- **Mobile Content and Aggregation.** In the third layer, the wired content and aggregator businesses were about to be augmented by their mobile

Exhibit 13-2. Mobilization of IT-producing industries.

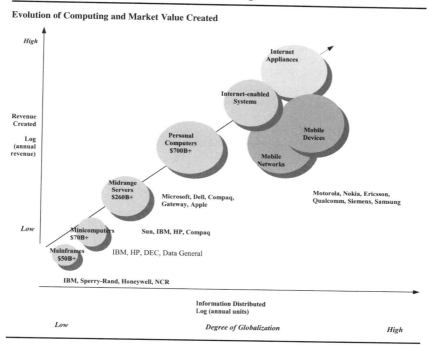

Evolution of Computing and Market Value Created

counterparts (e.g., mobile trading, mobile portals, aggregators, content providers, and ad brokers) who also sought to generate revenues indirectly, through advertising, membership subscription fees, and commissions. Some would be purely web content providers, whereas others would become mobile market makers or intermediaries. In the long run, these "mobile infomediaries" were expected to have a significant impact on the efficiency and performance of mobile e-markets.

■ **Mobile E-Commerce.** The fourth layer, wired retail, was expected to give rise to mobile e-retailers, which would enable web-based commerce transactions and cross a wide variety of vertical industries.

In the pre-cellular era, mobile voice service had been a status symbol and prohibitively expensive. In the 1G era, these services still appealed primarily to affluent individuals or corporate-sponsored business users, particularly "road warriors" and other sales professionals with great need for car phones. It was the 2G era that brought about the "mass consumerization" of mobile markets, with lower prices on services and devices, more competition, greater geographic coverage, and the advent of prepaid services. With the succession of the cellular platforms, competition has steadily intensified. Until the 2G era,

Exhibit 13-3. Mobilization of the digital economy.

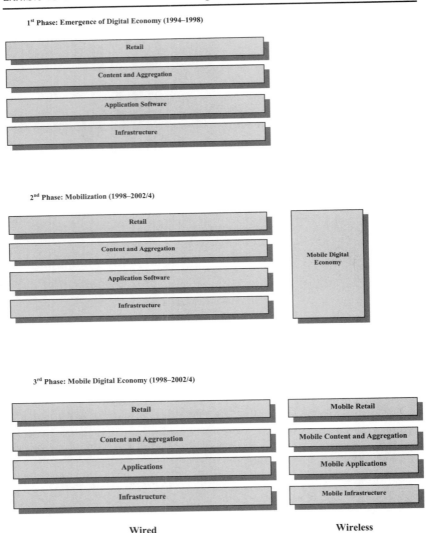

1st Phase: Emergence of Digital Economy (1994–1998)

Retail

Content and Aggregation

Application Software

Infrastructure

2nd Phase: Mobilization (1998–2002/4)

Retail

Content and Aggregation

Application Software

Infrastructure

Mobile Digital Economy

3rd Phase: Mobile Digital Economy (1998–2002/4)

Retail	Mobile Retail
Content and Aggregation	Mobile Content and Aggregation
Applications	Mobile Applications
Infrastructure	Mobile Infrastructure

Wired   **Wireless**

the penetration figures remained relatively low in larger lead markets. There was only one market, that of *original demand,* that made the GSM explosion so powerful. As long as original demand reigned, growth was explosive. Before the 3G transition, there was not only a new sales market, but also a rapidly expanding upgrade market for users who were replacing their old handset models with new ones. In the most developed cellular markets, a third market had emerged for multiple handset ownership. In 1999, upgrades accounted for some 40 percent of unit sales. The share was expected to rise to about 50 percent in 2000 and to 70 to 80 percent in the next few years.[6] Despite new service innovation (and extraordinary hype!), marketing was hard in a maturing marketplace. And as the number of rivals was extensive and most offered the "next big thing," aggregate growth was impressive, yet firm-level profitability proved depressingly low.

From "Bricks" to Smart Phones

In the long term, industry visionaries saw a world of a singular standard that would be available to single-mode terminals worldwide. In the short term, the industry needed multimode, multiband, and multinetwork wireless devices. At the heart of the 3G terminal experience, mobile leaders also saw a new way of using the phone—or what used to be called a phone. Users would not just talk to it anymore. They would be able to view multimedia images, watch video clips, listen to music, shop, book a restaurant table, and surf the Net. The handset was becoming far more than just a *hand*set.

The evolution of terminal types can be depicted on the basis of two modes of communications: data and voice (see Exhibit 13-4). Voice turned into data; data turned into voice. At the end of the 2G era, both provided relatively few offerings. In contrast to the pre-cellular and 1G "bricks," both the voice

Exhibit 13-4. From voice to data: product strategies.

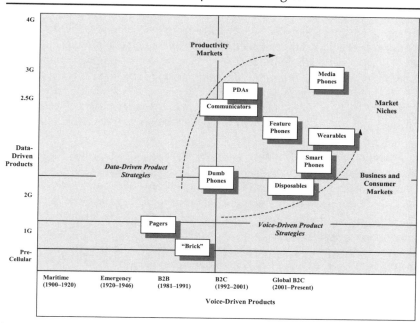

and data paths had generated ever smaller, lighter, and more user-friendly terminals that enabled rudimentary text messaging capabilities, or short message service (SMS). In future terminals, some users were expected to trade off high voice capabilities for data performance, just as others would exchange high data capabilities for voice performance. Concurrently, 2G mobile phones would evolve—vis-à-vis regional development paths—toward the voice-oriented terminals of the future: smart phones.

In the mobile business, each new cellular platform has meant new technologies, functionalities, and markets, which have given rise to increasingly specialized services. In the pre-cellular era, the early wireless technologies allowed a very primitive, simple, and homogeneous service concept. It was only with the arrival of the digital cellular standards that rudimentary data services (e.g., SMS) became possible. With 2.5G/3G technologies, providers could craft more sophisticated and heterogeneous service concepts. In the emerging value chain, enablers dominated application software, whereas network operators and service providers ruled over access to customers.

3G Services: A $320 Billion Pie by 2010

From the 1920s to the 1990s, mobile communications was dominated by voice communications, whereas the new value chain was based on "always on" data communications that enabled anytime, anyplace connectivity to content on the Internet (see Exhibit 13-5). With analog and digital cellular, voice reigned over data and the offerings were simple. With multimedia cellular, data reigned over voice and the offerings were more complex. Sensitivity to increases in the data rates made all the difference in mobile messaging, browsing, and rich voice calls. In the past, services were driven by voice communications and GSM enabled only simple short message service. With multimedia cellular, new services represented three dimensions of capabilities: *voice communications* (i.e., rich voice, including videophone), *Internet access* (i.e., mobile Internet and mobile intranets/extranets), and *mobility* (i.e., content, communications, and location-based services).

Around 2001–2002, industry professionals did their utmost to promote the mobilization of e-commerce. Still, the fact remained that only NTT Do-CoMo in Japan was actually making substantial revenue on new (but still pre-3G) mobile services, whereas consolidation in the U.S. technology sector and the downturn in the European mobile sector effectively constrained new mobile tests and experiments. Amid the 3G transition, the early estimates indicated that the worldwide revenue for 3G services would soar from $1 billion in 2002 to $321 billion in 2010. That implied annual growth of 37 percent and a steadily rising adoption curve (see Exhibit 13-6). But there were wide variations in terms of business and geographic segments.

Through the first decade of the twenty-first century, simple voice and content were emerging as the strongest service offerings. The former would

Exhibit 13-5. Changing mobile value system: toward multimedia services.

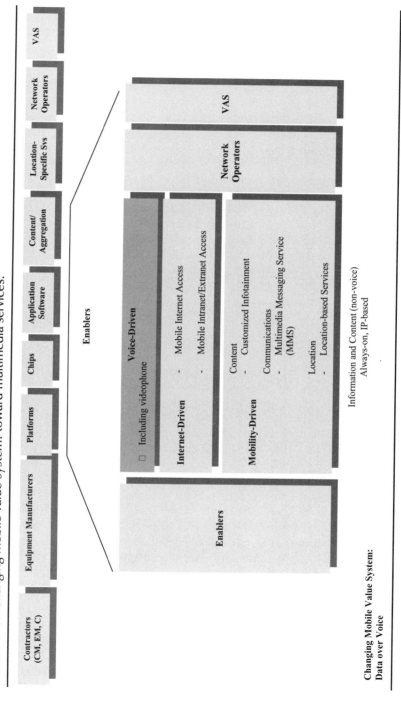

| Contractors (CM, EM, C) | Equipment Manufacturers | Platforms | Chips | Application Software | Content/ Aggregation | Location-Specific Sys | Network Operators | VAS |

Enablers

Voice-Driven
☐ Including videophone

Internet-Driven
- Mobile Internet Access
- Mobile Intranet/Extranet Access

Mobility-Driven
Content
- Customized Infotainment
Communications
- Multimedia Messaging Service (MMS)
Location
- Location-based Services

Network Operators

VAS

Enablers

Information and Content (non-voice)
Always-on, IP-based

**Changing Mobile Value System:
Data over Voice**

Exhibit 13-6. Worldwide revenue and demand estimates for 3G services.

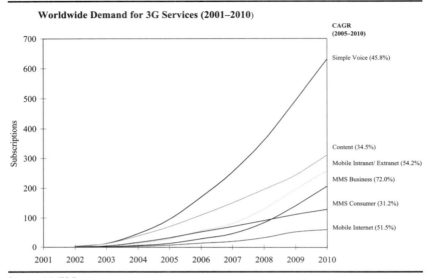

Source: UMTS Forum.

climb from $423 million to $88 billion in estimated worldwide revenues for 3G services, while the latter would increase from $306 million to $86 billion. Mobile intranet/extranet access would be the most critical offering in the business markets. It would grow even faster (44 percent in terms of compound annual growth in 2005–2010) than simple voice (31 percent) or content (33 percent) services. All other services—multimedia messaging service (MMS) business, MMS consumer, mobile Internet, and location-based services— would remain less than $25 billion, respectively. Rich voice, however, was expected to soar faster than any other offering (95 percent), but only in the latter half of the decade. Overall, demand paralleled revenue, but the dominant role of simple voice was even more apparent in subscriptions. It was expected to soar from 2.6 million in 2002 to 630 million in 2010, which translated to 46 percent in annual growth. Content (311 million in terms of estimated worldwide subscriptions for 3G services) and mobile intranet/extranet access (258 million), coupled with MMS for business users (207 million), would demonstrate strong growth as well, followed by consumer MMS and mobile Internet.[7]

After September 11, 2001

When the hell broke out in New York City and live images from downtown Manhattan were broadcast across the world, anxious anticipation swept through the headquarters, production centers, and sales outlets of mobile vendors, IT leaders, and contractors. At the same time, the unfolding nightmare triggered an explosion in emergency services and mobile consumer demand in the United States. As a massive black cloud hovered over the financial district, every New Yorker who had a cell phone was using it. The unexpected demand strained the existing capacity of all network operators and service providers, carriers, and telcos in the United States. Two months later, *Fortune* asked Pekka Ala-Pietilä, president of Nokia, how these horrible events affected the industry. The Finn's comments reflected the views of many across the industry value chain:

> The business environment—the psychological part of business—has been challenging for a while. Now the world is challenging in a different way. The tragic events have cast additional elements of uncertainty in our lives and caused anxiety over the future. So it's not easy to focus on the positive developments, and it's harder than usual to have a strong faith in the future. Yet this is just the time to keep building systems that will help people connect to each other for better understanding. And it is time to build a basis for the next phase of growth. So even though it is a moment of great uncertainty, this is exactly when we as an industry must make critical decisions about the future.[8]

In the globalizing industry, Nokia's supply chain was disrupted only for a few days, and the factory output was not affected. Like all industry players, Nokia initiated philanthropic programs to assist the victims of the terrorist attacks in the United States. Verizon Wireless struggled to set up a mobile wireless network in lower Manhattan after all communications systems had been shattered by the World Trade Center collapse. Meanwhile, temporary cell sites were quickly set up in the heart of New York City, just as "cows" ("cell on wheels") became familiar sights. These fully functional, generator-powered mobile cell sites enhanced coverage and capacity in a given area while accommodating both voice and CDMA data services.

While the attacks on the World Trade Center and Pentagon were dramatic and significant, the UMTS Forum, in February 2002, concluded that they did not materially change the 3G forecast made back in August 2001, which assumed slow adoption for the first five years.[9] However, they did highlight the weaknesses and vulnerabilities of all weaker players. Furthermore, predictions of slower subscriber growth and reduced capital spending by the carriers, accompanied by the continued meltdown of the global telecom sector, had many investors worried. 3G technology would be adopted by less than 30 percent of the worldwide mobile-subscriber base by 2010. But this was customary for any new technology, particularly one that required new end-user behavior and new business relationships across the industry value chain. Negative market conditions earlier in the year had already reduced the short-term revenue forecast for 3G services by 17 percent for a total reduction of

$10 billion by 2004. Through 2010, that was less than a one percent reduction in the overall service revenues predicted for 3G. Service revenue from 3G networks still represented a substantial market opportunity of $320 billion in 2010, $233 billion of which was expected from the new mobile data services.[10] Because of announcements by a number of global operators regarding handset shortages and other technical problems, the 3G commercialization dates for many countries had changed. In Western Europe, early 3G offerings would not begin in 2001 and 2002, but in 2002 and 2003. In the United States, the time frame assumed commercialization in 2004 because of the lack of 3G spectrum.

Despite the gloom-and-doom sentiments between fall 2000 and spring 2002, multimedia cellular was about to transform mobile communications for decades to come. Simple voice would fade out, rich voice would thrive. Rudimentary data communications would be replaced by advanced mobile Internet services, as well as mobile intranet and extranet services. SMS would give way to MMS. Content would be mobilized. Location-based services were emerging. The change was inevitable and irreversible. And as the markets would catch up with industry fundamentals, the deflated valuations would be swept by inflated valuations, once again, until the next consolidation. It was this $320 billion market pie that served to intensify the growth strategies of the mobile leaders while accelerating the entry strategies of the IT leaders—thus pushing the two strategic groups into a collision course.

Mobile Vision: Vertical Coordination

The industry landscape was changing dramatically and irreversibly. The transformation stemmed from R&D efforts that began around 1987, both in the mobile and the PC business. In one case, that year marked the launch of the Newton project; in the other, it augured the first R&D efforts in digital GSM and the future CDMA. "Nokia is ideally placed to bring the benefits of the convergence of Internet and mobility to the markets," argued Nokia's CEO Jorma Ollila in 1998.[11] Two years later the "twin drivers of the Internet and mobility" formed the foundation for Nokia's vision of the "mobile information society."[12] This vision, in turn, originated from its first efforts to manage digital convergence, soon after Ollila took charge at the Finnish vendor.

Converging Forces: The Communicator Project[13]

Around 1992, Nokia hatched a telecom project with the code name "Responder."[14] A secret unit of some twenty-five researchers, managers, and scientists gathered discreetly in Tampere, a bastion of high-technology research and one of Nokia's R&D concentrations in Finland. The Finns were given a broad mission: "Look at the next challenge." The task was to tap the future of wireless communications by coupling the Internet, computer, and telephone to produce a *portable* machine that could use each technology equally. Nokia's top management pressed the engineers to move quickly in order to preempt the perceived key rivals, Motorola and Ericsson. The first result of these development efforts, the Nokia 9000, or Communicator, hit American stores around 1996 and 1997.

As the Communicator project progressed, the focus became to create the world's first movable, pocket-size office. This device would enable users' conference calls, just as it would allow them to receive and send faxes, handle e-mail, and cruise the Internet from a moving car, a train, or a sidewalk cafe. It would, said Yrjö Neuvo, Nokia's chief technologist, "turn one-plus-one into more than two," which he called a credo of Nokia's corporate culture.[15] Nokia worked hard to globalize the product, which was featured in Paramount Pictures' action movie, *The Saint,* in April 1997. With their convergence initiatives, the pioneers, mobile leaders, and IT leaders were so driven by similar technologies, products, and services that their offerings were becoming indistinguishable. By 2001, even Handspring's Treo targeted Nokia Communicator's market space.

Following the release of the Communicator, Nokia stepped up its technology development efforts in relevant industry forums and arenas. Developing necessary capabilities took too long, and buying these capabilities was too expensive. Furthermore, the novelty and complexity of new technologies no longer permitted full control, and this was most obvious with new platforms. Consequently, even the mobile leaders engaged in technology coalitions to develop appropriate platforms. The trade-off was they would no longer be able to *control* the future, even if they could *influence* it. As data communications substituted for voice communications, mobile leaders increased R&D in Internet technologies and software M&As while collaborating with and building subsidiaries in the technology sector in the United States. Concurrently, IT leaders increased their R&D in mobile technologies and wireless M&As while boosting cooperation with developed units in the Euro-Nordic mobile clusters.

Toward Product Leadership: Managing Development Capabilities[16]

In the turbulent mobile business, superior management of development capabilities was the key to competitive advantage. Around 1992, Ericsson, for instance, would develop a new product and then do a trial production run of a few hundred mobile telephones to debug the design and the production process. In 1997, time-to-market imposed a first production run of at least a couple of thousand phones. As a result, product design, production process, and logistics had to be close to perfect when the phone left the production facilities.[17] In the 2G rivalry, Nokia had been triumphant because it had successfully integrated upstream and downstream processes. At the broadest level, development projects (i.e., product and process) tend to fall into one of five types:[18]

- **Applied research or advanced development projects** aim at inventing new science or capturing new know-how for application in specific development projects.

- **Alliance or partnered projects** (e.g., Symbian, Bluetooth, WAP) occur when the firm "buys" a newly designed product and/or process from another firm; by subcontracting a development project to a partner, a firm can leverage in-house effort, but this type of project requires some resources for coordination and integration.

- **Breakthrough development projects** (e.g., Nokia's WAP phone and Communicator) involve creating the first generation of an entirely new product and process and are "breakthrough" in the sense that their core concepts and technologies break new ground for the organization.

- **Platform or generational development projects** (e.g., Nokia's digital GSM platform phones) typically have a design life of several years and establish the basic architecture for a set of follow-on derivative projects.

- **Derivative development projects** (e.g., Nokia's digital GSM phone accessories, niche product lines, etc.) tend to be substantially narrower in scope and resource requirements than platform projects; reflecting "incremental" advancements, they tend to refine and improve selected performance dimensions to better meet the needs of specific market segments.

Mobile leaders considered critical technological capabilities embodied by highly skilled people as the key to long-term success. In many industries, acquirers seek ownership of physical assets and brands. In the technology sector, successful acquisitions tend to focus on people, not just products. Of course, long-term success depends on the sustained ability to build on excellent products, but because of rapid product life cycles, first movers can easily lose their leadership in future product generations if they are unable to develop new and critical capabilities.[19] Technologies are quickly commodified; human capital counts. Hence, the effects to diversify risks and costs through coalitions.

Technology Coalitions[20]

At the broadest level, strategic coalitions can be launched to perform any activity or set of activities in the value chain. These alliances tend to arise when performing an activity with a partner is superior to performing it internally, or externally in arm's-length transactions, or through a merger with another firm.[21]

In the wireless business, strategic coalitions were first popular in early internationalization efforts. For instance, long before the 1990s, mobile operators and vendors have entered foreign markets via joint ventures. In these cases, U.S. or European mobile players have had superior upstream capabilities (e.g., manufacturing and new product development), whereas local partners have possessed useful downstream capabilities (e.g., distribution, marketing, and service). Since the digital cellular era, technological novelty and systemic complexity have contributed to new kinds of strategic coalitions that focus on upstream rather than downstream activities. In the past, these coalitions diversified the risks and costs of internationalization. Since the 2G era, they have diversified the risks and costs of technology development. In the former case, coalitions speeded entry into markets; in the latter, they have accelerated building technology capabilities.

Through technology coalitions, mobile players hope to gain benefits that share a common denominator. They focus on technology capabilities (in the 3G era, primarily Internet-driven technologies and functionalities) that—because of prohibitive costs, risks, time, or lack of necessary competencies—cannot be created in-house, bought, or acquired.

Access to Know-How

Technology coalitions have enabled their participants to acquire, pool, or sell access to the knowledge or ability to perform activities. These coalitions have grown out of first-mover effects (e.g., one competitor is significantly ahead of others on the learning curve), comparative advantage effects (e.g., a specific country is a preferred location for performing an activity), the desire for local ownership (e.g., a specific location is preferred for performing an activity), or a combination of these three motivations. In first-mover circumstances, coalition partners have hoped to level the playing field (making the coalitions more attractive to those who are catching up compared with the first movers). In situations of comparative advantages, participants have used coalitions to benefit from national or locational advantages, which have often been coupled with foreign direct investment (FDI) in technology clusters. Finally, coalitions have been attractive when the key technologies are no longer proprietary but exclusive to coalition partners. These motivations have attracted mobile leaders to Silicon Valley and other U.S. technology clusters. Conversely, similar motivations have attracted IT leaders to the Euro-Nordic mobile clusters.

Scale Economies and Learning

Strategic partners have also hoped to gain economies of scale or learning. Pooling volume has served to raise the scale of the activity or the rate of learning compared to that of each firm operating separately. For instance, the introduction of Internet-linked mobile phones (the first version of WAP) in Finland in the fall of 1999 boosted scale economies and learning among the first movers. At first, these developments were hyped as highly attractive. "Finnish firms," reported *The Wall Street Journal* in September 1999, "lead wireless revolution as vanguard companies capture market."[22] Unfortunately, the technology was primitive, the services were limited, and the business model was weak. This example underscores the pitfalls of coalition benefits. Even the diversification of costs, risks, and time is not sufficient if alliances do not provide the right capabilities or if they offer the right capabilities in the wrong way (e.g., technologies are too rudimentary, services are too few, or the business model is not attractive). Despite the extraordinary mob-com hype in Europe (which was not that different from the dotcom hype in the United States), the demise of the first-generation WAP products and services harvested a great number of mobile start-ups that had been paraded as Europe's mobile response to America's Internet leadership. One of these was Wapit, which had been depicted as one of Finland's fastest-growing high-tech firms in international business press. After some twenty years as a rock singer with the underground Finnish band the Leningrad Cowboys, Mato Valtonen diversified into cell phones. What if, he thought, standing in the rain at a bus stop, you could find out when the next bus was scheduled just by calling a number? That led to Wapit. During the first round of financing, "there was a line of investors hoping to talk to us," said Valtonen. After two years, the start-up failed to secure a second round of financing and ultimately filed for bankruptcy. Instead of a new mob-com, Valtonen returned to his job—he took care of the brakes of a roller-coaster in a Finnish tivoli.[23] A highly symbolic end to Europe's mob-com over-population perhaps?

Shaping Rivalry

Strategic coalitions have been used to influence the basis of competition as well as the competitors. Viewed in narrow terms, such motivation can be framed in terms of facilitating collusion. Viewed in broader terms, firms employ coalitions to facilitate entry of other firms into an industry to develop a technology, to affect competitors' cost structures, or to otherwise shape competition in their favor. At the end of the 1990s, Microsoft's increasing activities in mobile Internet signaled its rising intent to embrace a new potential revenue base and extend its existing capabilities into this space. Conversely, Nokia's embrace of an open platform served as a counter-move to contain the threat. In the first case, Microsoft used coalitions to boost its operating system (OS) and application software for the mobile Internet while relying on others to scan the environment and keep abreast of new technologies. In the second case, Nokia created coalitions proactively to counter Microsoft's entry and rising bargaining power. With Microsoft, a coalition augmented existing competitor intelligence; with Nokia, a coalition served strategic and R&D needs to network and internalize relevant external know-how. In both cases, coalitions were used competitively to solidify the strengths of one's own company while exploiting the weaknesses of the rival.

Risk Reduction

All technology coalitions seek to reduce risk and uncertainty through diversification. Because no single firm can any longer control the entire value chain, strategic coalitions have become necessary instruments even for the largest players. For instance, when Ericsson, IBM, Intel, Nokia, and Toshiba founded the Bluetooth alliance in 1997, they did not just create a forum to enhance the Bluetooth specification and provide a vehicle for interoperability testing. These founding companies were also diversifying risk while ensuring extensive development activities *and* keeping an eye on each other. Technology coalitions are less about boosting revenues than about the rising costs of doing business. They tend to raise entry barriers against potential challengers that rely on sustaining technologies. (However, they cannot contain the threat of startups or challengers that rely on disruptive technologies.) Qualcomm, for instance, did not achieve its success by competing against the GSM incumbents, but by redefining the competitive terrain with its own standard, CDMA.

Technology Standardization

Due to the increasingly prohibitive costs of managing in-house technology novelty and complexity, as well as the rapid diffusion and subsequent imitation of new technologies, strategic coalitions have contributed to technology standardization since the early 1990s. Take, for instance, the proactive role of Nokia in technology coalitions, which is partly about its astute scanning of the competitive environment, but even more about the fact that coalitions have weakened its rivals while strengthening the Finnish vendor. Compared to its mobile rivals, Nokia's strengths have been in branding, segmentation, and design. By promoting open standards, it has weakened the strengths of its competitors (which have invested relatively more in technology innovation) while enhancing its own strengths (which reflect marketing innovation). Open specifications have mitigated the technology advantages of its rivals and have been good business for Nokia.

Proliferation of Technologies

In the United States, the handheld pioneers struggled to secure proprietary standards through which they hoped to translate first-mover advantages into more sustainable strategic advantages. Apple, Palm, Handspring, and other pioneers evolved from the PC revolution, which horizontalized the old industry value chains into layers of chips, operating systems, manufacturers, and application software. In contrast, mobile leaders evolved with the telecom revolution, in which the industry giants—particularly the former national PTTs—were less willing to reduce their vertical control of the value system and did so only under the force of new public policies (i.e., privatization, liberalization, and deregulation).

Preparing for the 3G transition, these differences in origins pushed the key strategic groups into very different directions. Mobile leaders initiated a slate of technology coalitions through which they hoped to diversify risks and costs. The rapid proliferation of new wireless technologies had resulted in dramatic novelty and complexity, which these leaders struggled to overcome and manage. But as witnessed by the early experiences of these coalitions, the task was not easy, whether it was a question of operating system, application software, or connectivity. After a number of disappointments, mobile leaders recrafted their strategic postures in late 2001—but in a manner that was more reminiscent of the vertical dragons they had once fought than the horizontal tigers they were supposed to be.

Managing Novelty and Complexity

Beginning with GSM, the transition from voice to data has meant increasing technological novelty and systemic complexity. With the 3G transition, the proliferation of technologies, coupled with industry globalization and the increasing number of rivals, has resulted in novelty and complexity of entirely new proportions. In the 2G era, GSM served as *the* winning coalition. In the 3G era, *multiple* coalitions were required for a winning combination. At the end of the 1990s, Nokia, for instance, engaged in a handful of major coalition activities, including WAP, Bluetooth, Symbian, SyncML, and a host of others. By 2002, the number of Nokia's major international alliances and cooperation projects had increased to almost twenty.

Through these capabilities, mobile leaders have sought to establish a foothold in emerging technologies that had a critical role in the changing wireless value chain. During the 2G transition, mobile leaders in the United States and Western Europe had been most concerned about the Japanese challenge. During the 3G transition, the Japanese—or, more broadly, the attackers in Asia-Pacific—were no longer the only threat. In 1995, Microsoft opted for a strategic U-turn to "embrace and extend" into the Internet. As far as the mobile leaders were concerned, it was only a matter of time until Microsoft, along with Intel and America Online, would enter the mobile Internet in full force. Consequently, mobile leaders used technology coalitions to respond to potential challenges by the IT leaders. Over time, however, they found the coalition strategy fragile. Take, for instance, three key coalitions that were designed to manage mobile operating systems, applications, and connectivity: Symbian's EPOC (which led to the rise of the open mobile architecture), WAP (which resulted in the launch of m-services), and Bluetooth (which prompted the emergence of 802.11b). Despite a promising start, each stumbled, moved to a new direction, or found itself challenged.

Operating Systems: From Symbian to Open Mobile Architecture

Symbian Ltd. originated in 1980, when David Potter launched a company named Psion to develop computer games and business software. In 1991, it released a palmtop computer that featured the EPOC operating system. To mobile leaders, this was a critical move at a critical time. EPOC grew in Europe and became the heart of Psion's software division, which was spun off as a subsidiary in 1996. Two years later, mobile leaders reintroduced Psion Software as Symbian. The objective was to speed up the evolution of wireless information devices. In Europe, Psion's palmtop computers were bestsellers (60 percent of the market). Nicholas "Colly" Myers remained Psion's CEO, but it was now dominated by a coalition of mobile leaders, particularly Ericsson, Nokia, and soon Motorola, as well.[24] Symbian's singular task became to develop, promote, and license EPOC for wireless devices. Another important step followed in 1999, when Symbian incorporated Sun Microsystems' Java technology into the EPOC system. Strategically speaking, mobile leaders could now leverage their OS with Java's supporters while Sun could leverage its Java with the supporters of the mobile OS. As the Symbian front leveraged development communities, it recruited new heavyweights, including Matsushita.[25] A year later, Ericsson shipped the first Symbian-based product, the Ericsson R380. Symbian's EPOC provided an OS, but it failed to establish a dominant design and adequate scale economies. By 2001, Symbian's developer community comprised 55,000 member organizations. Its objective was to make Symbian's EPOC operating system *the* standard for wireless devices. In practice, EPOC ranked third after the Palm OS and Microsoft Windows CE.[26]

In mid-November 2001, leading mobile operators (AT&T Wireless, Cingular Wireless, NTT DoCoMo, and Vodafone), vendors (Motorola, NEC, Nokia, Samsung, Siemens, Sony, and Ericsson), and consumer electronics players (Matsushita, Mitsubishi Electric, Sharp, and Toshiba) agreed to an open mobile architecture (OMA) initiative, which was to develop a common set of software and applications that would be used in future handsets. Led by Nokia, the initiative marked an important milestone as industry stakeholders began to promote new, interoperable mobile Internet access and visual contents downloading services worldwide, relying on 2G and certain intermediate technologies (e.g., GPRS) and coming 3G networks (e.g., W-CDMA). The OMA initiative was designed to enable a "nonfragmented global mobile services market." Following global and open standards, these industry leaders hoped to provide consumers with a wide selection of different yet interoperable terminals and services. The objective was to accelerate growth and to ensure requisite economies of scale throughout the industry.[27] The coalition, especially NTT DoCoMo's participation, was a coup for Nokia. Symbian offered an idea, but this initiative provided more muscle, even if did not attract the U.S. IT leaders. By late spring 2002, Nokia was no longer just funding Symbian PLC, but virtually running the show. Some observers even expected the Finnish vendor to buy Psion's stake. Nokia's Series 60 platform was based on the Symbian OS; it needed *de facto* control to secure its strategic positioning.

Applications: From WAP to M-Services

The WAP Forum was formed in September 1997 by Motorola, Ericsson, Nokia, and Phone.com (formerly Unwired Planet, the U.S. developer of microbrowser technology). It soon expanded to include more than 200 members, including operators, infrastructure suppliers, software developers, and content providers. The Wireless Application Protocol (WAP) standard was widely backed by the mobile leaders supporting Internet content access and wireless functionality for small-screen mobile devices. In Western Europe, WAP services were expected to take off in 2001, but a number of factors inhibited its upsurge there.[28] To mobile industry leaders, WAP was not a temporary stage or just another transitional technology, but an open standard for the Internet era. Through WAP, they saw themselves pushing a new value chain.

The protocol remained critical, but its commercialization would require time. Between 1997 and 2001, the WAP standard was under fire because it came late to market, it was too slow and cumbersome for most subscribers, and very few worthwhile services were made available. The problems stemmed partly from the technology and partly from the absence of a dominant design. In 2000, after months of industry hype and inflated expectations, several Nordic operators considered WAP, less politely, a bug-infested pilot experimentation. By the summer of 2001, the situation had become intolerable to most major operators. The confusion that surrounded the introduction of WAP threatened to derail mobile Internet via GPRS, said Mauro Sentinelli, managing director of Telecom Italia Mobile. "There were 165 different versions of WAP, and at a conference in Cannes . . . we had a developer from [handheld computer maker] Psion crying because he said he couldn't support them all."[29] That summer, the leading mobile vendors and operators and the industry body, the GSM Association, unveiled a new industrywide initiative, the Mobile Services (m-services) Initiative, to replace the widely criticized WAP and provide a more effective open software standard for the mobile Internet. With a common standard, these key players hoped the market for mobile Internet would grow more quickly and that new service providers would be attracted. The standard was based on a software platform made available on a royalty-free basis by the Californian software house Openwave Systems Inc.

The genesis of m-services reflected a subtle shift in the bargaining power among the key players, the vendors, and the operators. In the early days of WAP, mobile vendors had been the initiators of the mobile Internet. As WAP failed to meet expectations, operators became more willing to exercise their power. Both strategic groups, however, hoped m-services would contribute adequate revenue streams to cover investment costs in new systems. In Western Europe, the adoption of m-services was designed to boost GPRS,[30] which was expected to sell the mobile Internet experience with a simple graphical interface and to allow users to download high-quality color images, audio, and even video files. These capabilities, of course, had already been introduced in Japan, with the i-mode service of NTT DoCoMo.

Connectivity: From Bluetooth to 802.11b

By summer 2001, wireless local area networks (WLANs) provided a new cost-efficient alternative to deploying full 3G networks. The competing WLAN technologies included IEEE 802.11b, HomeRF, and Bluetooth. Of these, IEEE 802.11b appeared to be the strongest alternative with a clear upgrade path to higher-speed IEEE 802.11a.[31]

Nokia had colaunched a new consortium for wireless connectivity called Bluetooth in 1998. The moniker referred to King Harold of Denmark, a.k.a. Harold Bluetooth, who unified his empire under Christianity in the year 986. The thinly veiled reference underscored the might of Nordic leadership in the mobile Internet. At the end of the year, the Bluetooth consortium consisted of more than 250 active members; by early 2000, there were more than 1,200. The Bluetooth special interest group was led by a nine-company promoter group, including 3Com, Ericsson, IBM, Intel, Lucent Technologies, Microsoft, Motorola, Nokia, and Toshiba.[32] The consortium aimed to create an open standard for short-range communications between different electronic devices. By forming an intuitive wireless network to connect various devices, Bluetooth replaced traditional cables and interfaces. This enabled the creation of completely new applications, such as personal devices that could synchronize information without user intervention. Early evidence indicated that high wireless usage and Bluetooth attractiveness went hand in hand.[33]

Starting with the introduction of the Bluetooth protocol version 1.0 in the second quarter of 1999, mobile leaders predicted that Bluetooth chips would be the "next big thing" in wireless. In February 25, 2000, Cambridge Silicon Radios first demonstrated the wireless transfer of text between BlueCore01 integrated circuits (ICs) embedded in two PC notebooks. But unlike Harold Bluetooth, who had unified his empire, the Bluetooth standard had a difficult time between 1998 and 2001, not least because of the arrival of new alternatives. In December 5, 2001, Cahners-In-Stat group predicted that 13 million Bluetooth chipsets would be shipped in 2001. That figure was roughly double the actual number of 802.11b chipsets shipped that year. As skeptics argued, slow shipments, short-term competition from 802.11b networks, and long-term competition from 3G raised questions of Bluetooth's ability to capitalize on its buzz.[34]

Struggle for Industry Power

In the 2G era, the horizontalization of the industry in mobile communications resulted in a new generation of mobile challengers. The winners were vendors, such as Nokia, and operators, such as Vodafone, that first focused their operations and then leveraged them worldwide. Conversely, the failure to engage in such focus strategies proved costly to industry leaders, which were broken by horizontalization. The losers were former PTTs that failed to adapt to the new environment with appropriate strategies and, instead, struggled to reestablish industry control with vertical integration. The losers also included vendors, such as Motorola, which stuck to a dated electronics strategy that rested on diversification rather than focus. Instead of competing well in a clearly defined segment and adapting rapidly to a new industry environment, they competed in a mediocre manner in a broadly conceived field and embraced change slowly. The winners aligned focus with globalization; the losers fell captive to old domestic glory.

Nokia's Open-Source Base Station Initiative

In February 2002, Nokia used the 3GSM World Congress to announce an initiative aimed at making it easier for operators to mix hardware and software from different vendors in their base stations. The vendor argued that its standardization effort would help stimulate the development of easy-to-use wireless data applications—the key to generating user demand for 3G services. Without such standardization, argued Nokia, operators would not accomplish the five- to tenfold increase in wireless data revenues they expected to achieve in the next few years. The objective of Nokia's Open IP Base Station Architecture initiative was to define the base station architecture for use in next-generation, all-IP radio access. The vendor anticipated the project to lead to modular base stations with open internal interfaces. However, whether it would obtain the support of other vendors for its initiative became quickly a matter of debate.[35] It was the vendor's first open-source base station design. By the same token, never before had Nokia engaged in a struggle for the industry value chain, either. Aside from the vendors, the operators' role remained a question mark. Despite their proactive role in the GSM launch, these players had been more reactive with the 3G issues.

Under the old GSM model, operators worked with vendors to define a single set of standards for the entire network, not just the air interface. This contributed to the GSM triumph. In contrast, American standards bodies allowed multiple technologies to evolve in the name of free-market competition, which contributed to market fragmentation. The debate over air interfaces and network standards mimicked the debate over WAP only a year or two before. After the first generation of WAP devices proved to be a flop, operators intervened with m-services.[36] Now the scope of debate was broader. Many operators, behind closed doors, demonstrated little excitement over 3G networks. They saw the "wireless Web" hype as the result of country-based industrial policies and vendor strategies. They would have preferred to have bargaining power back to ensure they would not be forced to undergo massive network upgrades again.

Vertical Coordination or Horizontal Layering?

Perceptive industry practitioners and observers understood the potential of horizontalization in global strategies even *before* to the 2G era. At Nokia, for instance, the theme evolved in the research of Matti Alahuhta, a senior executive and a member of the group executive board, whose views were shaped by the global mind-set paradigm of Jean-Pierre Jeannet, a well-known academic researcher of globalization.[37] In changing environmental circumstances, the old-style vertical giants—the "vertical dragons" in Jeannet's terminology—have been descending, while the new-style horizontal focusers—the "horizontal tigers"—have been ascending. By Jeannet's own testimony, "At Nokia I formed the idea of global focus that resulted in the concept of the 'horizontal tiger.'"

> The future is with the horizontal tigers, and companies will have to carefully pick the businesses they desire to globalize while finding ways to reduce their exposure to others by divesting or floating them off. As we observe the changes among large, traditional corporations through reorganization, we are witnessing a wholesale shift from the broad-based, unfocused business to the focused niche company with their superior promise to accommodate the global imperative.[38]

Building a beachhead in most markets demanded considerable financial and managerial resources. In practice, both Nokia and Coca-Cola leveraged their limited resources by narrowing business focus while maximizing coverage of international markets. To Jeannet, that was the most important lesson. To stretch limited resources around the globe, companies would have to concentrate on fewer businesses but expand those businesses into all relevant parts worldwide.

Until the 1980s and the 1G era, the wireless business had been controlled by vertical dragons. With the 2G era, horizontal tigers stepped in. Not only did they transform the industry, they also subverted telecommunications from within by promoting competition.

Vertical Dragons?

The transition to digital cellular was not just about technology innovation. New challengers overthrew the old players and transformed the industry value system. That meant the crumbling of old vertical value chains and the emergence of new horizontal value chains. These changes were irreversible. Just like IT giants no longer despair for IBM's vertical leadership in mainframes, new mobile players have no interest in a return to the old AT&T days of full vertical integration. Instead of the old national PTTs and their exclusive suppliers, the 2G era favored world-class equipment manufacturers, competitive network operators, globalizing contractors, and agile resellers. It did *not* favor old-style efforts to vertically control the entire industry value chain. Of course, horizontal players could "stimulate" activities in various *phases* of the value chain and thereby accelerate the functioning of the *full* system.[39] Furthermore, the full impact of horizontalization would endure into the 3G era and beyond. As Jorma Ollila, Nokia's CEO, argued at the peak of the 2G era:

> The convergence of Internet to mobile phones will not lead to one single player becoming master of the universe. You're likely to see the horizontal value chain, like in computers. You've got to find your place in the value chain. Our special edge will be in voice and data terminals, where the radio link is a crucial element. Voice terminals, to a major degree, will be wireless. That will mean that our weight in the industry will grow.[40]

This strategic posture was perfectly in line with historical trends in the wireless business and with the logic of convergence. Only three years later, however, it seemed to be reversed.

In the fall of 2001, as Nokia struggled to retain its mobile leadership, it launched an open software coalition that served as a *de facto* alliance against Microsoft. The coalition announcement was soon followed by Nokia's Capital Markets Days in November 2001, where CEO and Chairman Jorma Ollila argued that, in the future, Nokia's business model would be in software, hardware, and services. "[The] PC business model is not the right reference," he noted. The mobile business was not the PC business, where hardware and software had been horizontalized into low-margin equipment manufacturers (e.g., Dell, Compaq, IBM) as well as high-margin software and microprocessor developers (e.g., Microsoft, Intel). The mobile business was different because "mobile phones are becoming intelligent devices with a lot of value-added coming from software. Value-added remains within the mobile operators and the vendors." Open competition would prevail in component chips and there would be differentiation on multiple layers, but the business would be typified by "total product concepts, end to end."[41] The implication was that the degree of novelty and complexity was inherently so high in the mobile business that making phones was far more difficult than assembling PCs because cell phones were not stand-alone devices. To be successful, a mobile vendor had to understand not only novel technologies and the complexity of the phone, but also the wireless network and the software that linked the two.

Soon thereafter, Microsoft's Bill Gates spoke publicly *against* these propositions. His argument was that, sure, the business was complicated, but it was not *that* complicated. "Nokia's primarily a hardware company. They can't afford to spend zillions—I'm the one spending zillions, five to be exact."[42] In one interview after another, Gates said that Nokia's mobile terminal was a box, and that, to paraphrase Gertrude Stein, *A box is a box is a box.* As the Nokians argued that hardware and software cannot be separated in the mobile business, they had to ensure that they controlled the business end-to-end. Such control was impossible in-house, so they employed the software coalition. But at the same time, they rendered themselves vulnerable to the argument that their "A box is not a box is not a box" strategy was really "Apple *déjà vu.*" Instead of focusing on its magnificent software in the 1980s, Apple had struggled to control the entire vertical value system. In the end, Microsoft cloned Macintosh when it introduced Windows, while PC clone manufacturers captured cost leadership, turning Apple's Macs into a niche product. In mobile communications, Nokia controlled hardware—the "box." From Gates's standpoint, the Finnish vendor resembled IBM in the pre-PC days. With the first IBM PC, Microsoft provided the OS and the software, while Intel offered the processor. IBM was the manufacturer and packager—like Nokia in the mobile business. From Ollila's standpoint, the software giant looked like, well, Microsoft, which sought to extend its dual dominance of OS and applications in the PC business into the mobile business. Yet that left an open issue: Even if Microsoft's motives were not exactly disinterested, did it really follow that hardware and software are not separable in the mobile business as well?

In the United States, the emergence of the digital economy from 1995 to 2000 illustrated the benefits of a horizontal Internet vision. In this scenario, the layers cumulatively accounted for the end-to-end services, yet each evolved independently. These arrangements built on the very nature of the Internet as a global, distributed, and highly differentiated, cost-efficient medium. In Europe, the mobile information society was evolving in a very different direction at the end of the 1990s. Instead of horizontal autonomy, it stressed vertical coordination. In this scenario, the layers would not evolve independently, but were tighter and less autonomous. Such arrangements, argued the advocates of the Internet vision—primarily U.S.-based IT leaders such as Microsoft, Intel, and AOL—would not generate comparable globalization, distribution, differentiation, or cost-efficiencies.

Besides, had not Ollila himself spoken for the very horizontalization that he was now rejecting? In a 1998 *Business Week* interview, he had noted that no single player could dominate the converging mobility and Internet value chains. Instead, there would be a "horizontal value chain, like in computers." Nokia's strategic advantages had been in voice and data terminals throughout the 2G era. If that trend continued, Nokia's bargaining power in the industry would grow. Conversely, if software were to grow separate from hardware, Nokia would suffer a double whammy. In hardware, it would be stuck with the "boxes" in which the Asian producers possessed a long-term cost advantage. In software, it would have to match the popularity and sophistication of Microsoft's products and services and overcome switching costs. Ollila saw Nokia growing bigger and better; Gates saw Nokia shrinking and failing. As Ollila had argued in 1998, a company had to find its place in the value chain.

In the 3G era, the "single, flexible standard" enabled several alternative development paths that were not mutually exclusive. But, in the long term, only those paths that optimized efficiency and effectiveness would ensure sustainable advantages. As a result, it was more than likely that Nokia would stick to its coalition strategy—not necessarily because it was the ultimately winning proposition, but as a countermeasure against Microsoft. And it was as likely that Microsoft would stick to its horizontalization principle to attack the bargaining power of the mobile leaders where they were most vulnerable.

At the end of the 1990s and the 2G era, the wireless business was dominated by horizontal tigers. Through competition, they had globalized the industry. But with the 3G era, they offered a vertical roadmap for the industry—in contrast to Microsoft and IT leaders, which employed a horizontal roadmap.

In the light of the 3G dawn, the old horizontal tigers looked more and more like new vertical dragons.

Chapter 14

IT Vision

Since the end of the 1990s, the most recent layer of the wireless value chain (i.e., enablers and services) has been the terrain of two conflicting visions of convergence—one vision has been promoted by the mobile leaders, another by the IT leaders—that is, the "Wintel" giants (Microsoft and Intel) and America Online. The mobile vision has a roadmap from voice communications to data communications. These industry leaders argue that the mobile business is inherently different from the IT business. This vision stresses *vertical coordination* in which the dominant players provide end-to-end solutions. Among other things, a single vendor (e.g., Nokia, Ericsson or Motorola) performs activities that include:

- Segmenting the customer relationships
- Providing access devices to dealers, operators, or resellers
- Structuring service opportunities on its own and in cooperation with smaller players
- Developing necessary software in-house, typically in collaboration with small tech firms or via coalitions
- Creating platforms or developing them in-house through international committees, trade associations, or strategic coalitions
- Developing, designing, manufacturing, and delivering tens of millions of mobile phones, switches, or base stations
- Cooperating with multiple contract manufacturers, component suppliers, and electronic manufacturing services, which in turn have their own subcontractors

From the standpoint of mobile leaders, this vertical system is efficient, works smoothly, and matches the requirements of increasing technology novelty and systemic complexity. The mobile leaders also prefer this industry system because it has made them rich.

The IT vision has been advocated by the U.S.-based IT leaders. Their vision has a roadmap from data to voice. These leaders say that the mobile business is not inherently different from the IT business; rather, it is morphing *into* the IT business. From their standpoint, the mobile business is just another PC industry. The IT leaders cultivate a vision that emphasizes *horizontalization* rather than vertical coordination. This vision depicts the same industry stages as the mobile vision (i.e., customer relationships, operators and resellers, service developers); but, in contrast to the mobile leaders, the IT leaders stress market transactions rather than administrative mechanisms as the driving force in the new industry value chain. In the past, the old monopoly PTTs controlled the full value chain, say the IT leaders. Why should mobile vendors control it today? From the standpoint of the IT leaders, the horizontalized system provides the optimal match between increasing novelty and complexity. As a result, each industry layer—customer relationships, distributors, services, enabling software, platforms, manufacturing, contractors, and subcontractors—will become far more competitive. The IT leaders also prefer this industry system because it has made *them* rich (see Chapter 13 for a discussion of IT-producing industries).

Through the late 1990s, these two visions co-evolved and co-specialized. By the end of 2001, they were on a collision course (see Exhibit 14-1). Historically, the IT developments originate from the late 1980s, when Apple initiated the development of the "monster in a box."

The IT Empire Strikes Back: First Phase—PDA Pioneers

The IT roadmap has been punctuated by two phases. In the first one, the emphasis was on R&D and the first stand-alone personal digital assistants (PDAs), without fully-developed Internet capabilities. From 1987 to the mid-1990s, it was dominated by Apple's Newton project and the subsequent PDAs; in the latter half of the 1990s, Palm and its rivals, including Handspring and RIM, reigned in this space. A very different phase followed after the year 2000. It started with the collaboration of Microsoft and Compaq (introducing the iPAQ Pocket PC) and climaxed with a full-scale Wintel counterattack in February 2002. In the first phase, the industry was still emerging and in the early-growth stage. The dominant design was absent. Many companies entered the business. All tested with a broad variety of technologies, products, and services. Prospects for industry expansion were extraordinary, but few firms made profits. With concerted efforts at the dominant design (basically, PDAs with Internet capabilities), the IT leaders entered the business. Industry thrust provided a powerful push for standards, which reduced variety concentrating on the most popular forms. Industry expansion accelerated, pioneers were harvested, and leaders began to enjoy profitability. The first stage of the IT roadmap (i.e., Apple's Newton, Palm products, and services) *preceded* the chasm between the narrow early-adopter markets and the mainstream markets. The second stage (i.e., Wintel products and services) emerged *after* the IT leaders managed to cross the chasm into lucrative mainstream markets.

Exhibit 14-1. Two evolutionary trajectories.

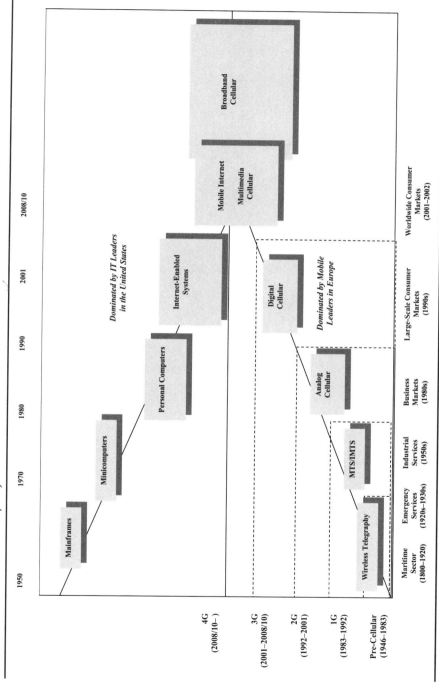

From Newton to PDAs

In 1987, Jerry Kaplan embarked on an entrepreneur's dream and formed a startup, GO Corp., to develop a handheld computer that was to be operated with a pen instead of a keyboard. Six years later, hundreds of jobs and $75 million invested to get the company off the ground were gone. Behind the numbers, he saw a "perpetual high-stakes game of creation":

> The goal is to establish new companies, magical engines of prosperity that spawn products, jobs, and wealth. The price of admission is a radical idea, one powerful enough to motivate people, attract investment, and focus society's energy on improving the way people work and play. But there is also a darker side to the story, a cautionary tale about what can happen to a young company when its timing is wrong, its technology too speculative, and its market not yet ready.[1]

The scenario is familiar to many start-ups that have evolved in the U.S. technology sector since the late 1960s and 1970s. It is even more familiar to the software and development houses that proliferated with the PC revolution in the 1980s and the Internet revolution in the 1990s. And it is most familiar to those dreamers and visionaries who foresaw the convergence of mobile voice and data a decade or two ago, but failed to bring it about.

The "Monster in a Box"

In 1982, Joseph Canion and two other former Texas Instruments engineers in Houston launched Compaq Computer to manufacture and sell portable IBM-compatible computers. The success of the (immobile) IBM PC prompted a host of companies to investigate the idea of a *mobile* computer. Over the next several years, both incumbents and start-ups struggled to develop a device that was small but still could offer real functionality. The laptop took too much space; the developers were after a handheld computing device.

By 1995, approximately $1 billion had been spent and lost in this pursuit.[2] Half of these investments may have been burned at Apple. After college dropouts Steve Jobs and Steve Wozniak founded the company in 1976, sales jumped from $7.8 million in 1978 to $117 million in 1980. By 1983, Wozniak left the firm and Jobs hired PepsiCo's legendary marketer John Sculley as president.[3] At the soft-drink firm, Sculley had turned Pepsi into the number-one brand in the cola wars. Jobs hoped Sculley could do the same for Apple in the PC business. Apple did rebound from failed product introductions by unveiling the Macintosh in 1984, but Jobs left the company after tumultuous struggles with Sculley. After a fifth of Apple's workforce was sacked, Sculley began another effort at the first handheld.

From Knowledge Navigator to the Newton and the MessagePad

Sculley introduced the idea for a personal digital assistant in 1987, the same year Jerry Kaplan launched GO Corp. and the Nordic mobile vendors initiated R&D efforts in 3G technologies. An elite team of Apple engineers began work in a research lab in Cupertino, California. Initially slated to retail at a prohibitive $8,000, the price was later reduced to $4,000 and then to a high-end PC price of about $2,000. The product soon earned a new nickname: a "monster in a box."[4]

The Newton project began in 1990, when Product Marketing Manager Michael Tchao and engineer Steve Capps decided to reconfigure the product into a compact, consumer-oriented device. Sculley was fascinated by Tchao's proposal, in which he saw a consumer version of a portable product he had envisioned some four years before, a notebook-size machine he had called the "Knowledge Navigator." The price and size of the Newton categorized it as a PC. Sculley sketched out a downsized version and listed a few key features on the cover of a *New York Times Magazine* during a flight to Tokyo in February 1991. Along with his drawing, Sculley jotted down technical, marketing, and manufacturing goals: "Pen-based, pager frequency, Mac-capability."[5]

Sculley expected the convergence of computer, consumer electronic, entertainment, and information-based industries to result in a $3.5 trillion dollar market. No single company could control such a new and undefined market. In the past, the proprietary Macintosh decisions had contributed to Microsoft's growth. Sculley wanted to "build a completely different financial model . . . a value-chain model, which says that you've got to look at the entire value chain, in terms of where you can make your profits along the way."[6] Sculley was after an international *keiretsu* between U.S. software innovators and Asian hardware manufacturers.

In the early 1990s, Apple was relieved by a spurt of revenues from the recently released Macintosh PowerBook, which garnered more than $1 billion in first-year sales and became the best-selling laptop in the market. Sculley's developers dreamed of comparable success with Newton, whose prototype was introduced in 1992 (see Exhibit 14-2). As the keynote speaker at the Consumer Electronics Show that year, Sculley regaled the crowd with optimistic predictions of the "mother of all markets" that would foster a new class of products that he called personal digital assistants (PDAs). The publicity alerted rivals, which quickly embraced Sculley's concept of PDA. Concern mounted after rumors that Microsoft had a development team working on WinPad, presumably a "Newton killer." In reality, the threat was elsewhere. Having already released a digital organizer called B.O.S.S., Casio joined with Tandy to announce the development of the Zoomer, a Newton clone developed by Jeff Hawkins, the man who would create the first PalmPilot.

Exhibit 14-2. From Newton to PDAs.

The precursors of the PDAs: from Knowledge Navigator to Newton and MessagePad.

In 1987, John Sculley (then the president of Apple Computer) wanted to show what it might be like to use personal computers in the future. So Doris and Hugh Dubberly created a short film that showed a "typical" college professor accessing data in remote locations, video-phoning a colleague, and creating an interactive multimedia document in a shared workspace.

The "Knowledge Navigator" was basically a concept for a navigation through information with a pilot's controls. This concept triggered that of Newton.

It took Apple more than six and a half years to develop the first Newton MessagePad. When it was finally released it had impressive specifications. 20 MHz processor, pressure-sensitive LCD-display, LocalTalk port, infra-red beamer. However, all these features were overshadowed by the Newtons handwriting recognition, which failed to deliver the promised 95% accuracy.

After more than six years of developing the original Newton, it took Apple over a year to upgrade it. The first upgrades were Newton MessagePad 100 and 110.

The Newton MessagePad 2000 was a complete mobile computer with a wide range of software like web-browser, email-client, word processor, fax software, calendar, address book and it was even able to record speech for up to one hour on its 4 MB memory card. However, the major advantage to its predecessor (MP 130) was its new processor. The 160 MHz StrongARM processor speeded up all operations of the Newton MessagePad 2000.

The MP 2000 was later re-launched as MessagePad 2100, the first Newton with an Ethernet networking card. It became the last Newton ever.

The eMate 300 was the only Newton with built-in keyboard. It looked like a PowerBook rather than a Newton Message Pad, but ran Newton OS. Apple predicted that the eMate 300 would sell well so it limited the eMate 300 to the educational market. It sold brilliantly and once the eMate gained positive press the other Newtons started to sell well, too.

SOURCE: Apple Online Museum (MessagePads); Doris and Clancy, Ltd. (Knowledge Navigator ad).

After a disastrous debut as a consumer product, the Newton found some success as a strategic platform in vertical markets. After two years of product development roller-coasters, Steve Jobs discontinued the Newton OS and OS-based products, including the MessagePad 2100 and eMate 300. Newton was now an estimated $500 million flop. Apple had pioneered the first real PDA in the niche markets, even if it failed to sustain the product into broader mass markets. It found the innovator and early adopter customer segments; it never managed to cross the chasm to mass consumer markets. The monster in the box had outlived its creators. Amid the rising desperation at Apple, the initiative shifted to a new start-up called Palm, Inc.

Palm's Vision

Starting with Compaq's portables and Apple's Newton concept, the fledgling Palm handheld business had several false starts. Newton crumbled. The early PDAs died. Only with the arrival of the PalmPilot, a handheld device with an elegant user interface and character-recognition system, did the nascent PDA market hit pay dirt. By 2001, Palm, Inc. had sold more than 7 million of its Palm and older PalmPilot models. But Palm was no longer the only game in town. Reminiscent of the PC market, the battle between handheld computer makers centered on disparate operating systems. In the short term, Palm suffered from attacks by Handspring, Inc. In the long term, devices from Casio, Compaq, and Hewlett-Packard that ran Windows software posed an even greater threat to Palm's dominance. And, as if to herald the final Wagnerian *Götterdämmerung*, Microsoft entered the game.

The Dynamic Duo

In 1992, when Apple revealed the Newton prototype, inventor Jeff Hawkins and marketers Donna Dubinsky and Ed Colligan joined forces to launch Palm Computing. The historical linkages to Apple and Newton went through Dubinsky and Colligan.[7] An industry veteran with nearly twenty years of technical expertise, Hawkins was the inventor of the Pilot and PalmPilot products. He had founded Palm Computing, which initially was an arm of U.S. Robotics, but became part of 3Com through the buyout of U.S. Robotics. An architect of the post-Newton handheld market, he held patents for handheld devices and features.[8] Hawkins used his research into the nature of human intelligence to create a new type of handheld computer. In 1994, he invented the Graffiti text-entry method. It solved the handwriting-recognition problem, where the Apple Newton had failed, by asking users to learn a simple method for making letters recognizable by software. That same year, Hawkins defined a short list of design goals for what would become the first PalmPilot. In addition to incorporating Graffiti, the new idea was to "keep it small, simple, affordable, and connected." The new device should:

- Fit in a shirt pocket
- Be designed for desktop synchronization
- Deliver instant performance
- Be easily affordable[9]

The early years were not easy. Palm almost went under in 1994. At first, Hawkins and Dubinsky saw their company as a software developer, working with OS and hardware companies. That strategy proved disastrous. When the Casio Zoomer—the first product featuring Palm applications—hit the market, sales were abysmal and the forced interdependence between Palm and its various partners frustrated all. Hawkins and Dubinsky understood that for Palm to succeed, it would have to build a full product, *including applications, OS, and hardware*. With the handheld computing industry awash in failed attempts, few investors were eager to jump in. In September 1995, U.S. Robotics recognized the PalmPilot's potential and purchased Palm Computing for $44 million.

The first PalmPilot-connected organizer shipped in April 1996. Because of the widespread post-Newton cynicism about handheld devices, the first five months of sales were flat. But when sales took off in the 1996 holiday season, the business grew at an extraordinary pace. The PalmPilot became the most rapidly adopted new computing product ever introduced. But just as the Newton initiative never really found an independent position within Apple, Palm was swept by the changing fortunes of its parents. When 3Com purchased U.S. Robotics, Palm became its subsidiary, which led to an internal controversy on Palm's strategy. The following year, 3Com sold 1.2 million Palms, but Hawkins, Dubinsky, and Colligan left to form their own company, Handspring, which would launch its Visor line in 1999.

Palm in Yankowski's Hand

In 1999, 3Com released the Internet-ready Palm VII and launched a Palm.net Internet service for handheld devices. By December, shares of 3Com soared 13 percent after its Palm, Inc. unit filed for an IPO as part of its planned spinoff. As the rapidly growing Palm discovered the twin drivers of mobility and the Internet, it aggressively entered the convergence game. Concurrently, America Online, Motorola, and Nokia took stakes in the handheld leader, while the mobile vendors were also pioneering the Symbian alliance. Positioning for the 3G era, the mobile leaders were hedging their bets. Meanwhile, 3Com wanted to transform Palm from a hardware vendor to a software developer, which, within three years, would derive most of its revenues from licensing software code. With its Windows CE operating system and trimmed-down versions of popular applications, Microsoft established inroads on Palm's segment. Both had products that were maturing, with features that went far beyond the standard calendar and address-book capabilities. With Internet and corporate database access, as well as wireless capabilities, analysts expected the corporate market for these devices to grow dramatically in the near future.

In December 1999, Carl Yankowski took over as Palm's CEO. After earning a degree from MIT, Yankowski had held marketing and strategic leadership positions at technology and consumer-products companies, including Reebok, Sony, Polaroid, General Electric, Pepsi, and Procter & Gamble. His charter was to build on Palm's worldwide leadership in the handheld computing market. Timing was critical. Handhelds were rapidly gaining wireless capabilities, whereas cell phones were quickly building computing capabilities. Palm could not fall behind. Before Yankowski's arrival, the company's Palm VII system, which featured wireless connectivity to the Internet, had received a lackluster reception because it had limited access to websites and was prohibitively expensive. In March 2000, 3Com sold a minority stake in Palm to the public, in an offering worth about $875 million. Unfortunately, Palm initiated expansion and acquisition initiatives amid the impending downturn.

Globalization

By 2001, Palm defined its mission in worldwide terms. Domestic market leadership and the IPO served as catalysts for Palm's "triadization" as it rushed to establish a foothold in the key markets of Western Europe and Asia-Pacific. Its mission was to be the global leader in mobile information management by:

- Providing innovative handheld computing solutions to businesses and consumers
- Working with world-class licensees and 130,000-plus software developers to create the industry-standard platform for handheld information management
- Putting the power of the Internet into every Palm handheld[10]

By the end of 1998, Palm Computing products were distributed in thirty-five countries. For 2000, revenues outside the United States accounted for 35 percent of Palm's total revenues, compared to 29 percent for fiscal 1999. With a 75 percent market share of the worldwide personal companion handheld device market, Palm was the leading global provider of handheld computers (see Exhibit 14-3).[11]

The Palm Economy—a community of Palm OS licensees, 130,000-plus registered developers, and others committed to advancing the platform and its offerings—had created more than 7,000 software applications and more than 100 add-on devices. Palm's strategy was to develop a leadership position in the broader mobile devices and services market by providing wireless Internet solutions to all of its four handheld devices. It also sought to establish its Palm platform as the leading OS for the next generation of handheld computing devices, mobile information appliances, mobile phones, and handheld devices for entertainment, such as games and music. Like mobile leaders, Palm struggled to excel in vertical coordination, whereas Compaq was the creation of and

Exhibit 14-3. Palm, Inc. worldwide (2001).

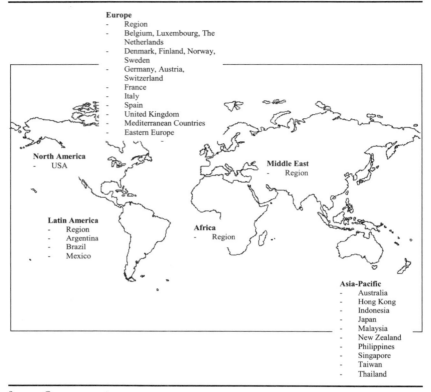

Europe
- Region
- Belgium, Luxembourg, The Netherlands
- Denmark, Finland, Norway, Sweden
- Germany, Austria, Switzerland
- France
- Italy
- Spain
- United Kingdom
- Mediterranean Countries
- Eastern Europe

North America
- USA

Latin America
- Region
- Argentina
- Brazil
- Mexico

Africa
- Region

Middle East
- Region

Asia-Pacific
- Australia
- Hong Kong
- Indonesia
- Japan
- Malaysia
- New Zealand
- Philippines
- Singapore
- Taiwan
- Thailand

SOURCE: Company reports.

advocate for horizontalization. The victory march of the PC maker heralded Microsoft's entry.

The Pioneer's Dilemma

As the segment pioneer, Palm saw itself as the leader of the "handheld revolution," despite increasing competition. Undoubtedly, it was the market leader in the key Triad nations—the United States, the U.K., Western Europe, and Asia-Pacific. Operating in growing markets, it stood to benefit from large opportunities, especially in wireless handhelds. Instead of providing homogeneous T-Model products and services, it segmented its offerings very early, first for enterprise, education, and consumer markets—then within these markets. While its OS share seemed to be growing, the market share of Pocket PC and EPOC appeared to be on the decline. It created quickly a wide development community, yet one that paled in comparison with Microsoft's multimillion-dollar developer community. Through its mobile portal, it entered location-specific services relatively early. But nothing in this pioneership included strategic advantages that would be *sustainable*. Even before the Wintel counterattack, competition began to nibble away at Palm's dominant share.

After Palm founders Jeff Hawkins, Donna Dubinsky, and Ed Colligan left to form Handspring. They launched the first Visor handheld only a year later. With the Visor product family, the core team that had developed and marketed the PalmPilot upheld its philosophy, but used Springboard modules to create an open platform for a handheld with limitless potential. As Handspring saw it, its history *was* the history of PalmPilot: "Jeff Hawkins invented it. Donna Dubinsky built the company that sold it. And Ed Colligan marketed it. Now they're doing it all over again . . . even better . . . with Handspring."[12] In effect, after the resignation of Palm's chief executive, Carl Yankowski, the affinities between Palm and Handspring prompted several money managers and analysts to urge the two pioneers to merge in order to beat the tough market. While each unveiled turnaround plans, a recombination was not in the picture—at least in early 2002. Initially, Handspring's Visor handhelds, which ran the Palm OS, provided features that differentiated it from Palm products, including colorful plastic housings, lower prices, and expansion bays for add-on modules.[13] Handspring, too, thought globally and stated its commitment to:

- Build a world-class team: A given, but you can't succeed without one.
- Battle complexity: If it's not simple, no one will use it.
- Think about the future: Build a platform that offers unique functionality, expanded possibilities, and flexibility and personalization for consumers and developers alike.
- Never rest on our laurels: Innovate, innovate, innovate.[14]

Just as the PalmPilot established an open software architecture for handheld computing, the Visor introduced a new hardware and software platform with its Springboard expansion slot. Internationalization took off in the first half of 2001, when Handspring boosted its presence in the key worldwide markets, following in Palm's footsteps. Soon it was seconded by Research In Motion Ltd. (RIM) and its BlackBerry in the corporate markets—and they were emulated and imitated by still other potential rivals. All of these pioneers excelled in pioneering the PDA space. But while the leading players were selling millions of units, the mobile vendors dominated a marketplace of 400 million units. Simply put, PDA pioneers were pre-chasm heroes; they created markets, but skimming the cream in the post-chasm markets belonged to far larger operations. It was then that the IT empire struck back. By the spring of 2002, Palm executive Michael Mace testified in Microsoft's antitrust trial that the software giant exploited its alleged monopoly power against Palm's handhelds by making its software incompatible.

The IT Empire Strikes Back: Second Phase—Wintel Counterattack

As Palm, Handspring, and a slate of new rivals (RIM and others) engaged in a rivalry of their own, the mobile and IT leaders absorbed the handheld's "look and feel." But through the 1990s, they had not worked alone. In the United States, the IT leaders had struggled feverishly to catch up. In Western Europe and the Nordic wireless clusters, the mobile leaders had done their utmost to stay close to the productivity frontier. Both were driven by digital convergence, but each offered a different roadmap. Mobile leaders moved from voice to data stressing vertical coordination. IT leaders moved from data to voice emphasizing horizontalization. At the eve of the 3G transition, the two groups were on a collision course.

Microsoft's Vision: Horizontalization

In the beginning of 1995, Microsoft seemed to be so far behind Internet upstarts that many analysts wondered if the giant whose software had dominated the PC era might be sidelined in the Internet era, although revenue growth illustrated none of these concerns.[15] In the summer of 1995, Microsoft engaged in a strategic shift, which had been in preparation for months. Under Bill Gates's leadership, the software giant adopted an "embrace and extend" strategy. The fundamental objective was to integrate the OS and the application software, both of which it dominated, with the Internet. It relied on the Microsoft Internet Explorer 1.0, the company's first browser program. The strategy also included Microsoft Network (MSN), an online community whose launch coincided with Windows 95.[16]

Unlike Palm, which made $1.6 billion in revenues and whose market cap was some $2.1 billion in 2001, Microsoft generated $25.3 billion in sales and had a $393 billion market cap, making it a formidable competitor. It earned the majority of its revenues from applications (38 percent) and platforms (32 percent), although a substantial amount was generated in enterprise software and services (20 percent). These revenues were associated with the *wired* desktop. This was Microsoft's greatest strategic strength and, by the same token, its singular vulnerability. Like the U.S.-based mobile vendors, Microsoft competed on the global chessboard. It made 38 percent of its revenues in the South Pacific and the Americas. The rest came from Europe, the Middle East, and Africa (19 percent, collectively), as well as Asia (12 percent). With Microsoft, mobility was subject to its Internet strategy. Full-scale entry into the mobility business was a question of timing.

Early Efforts to Dominate the Handheld Market

As network operators and mobile vendors prepared for the 3G era, Microsoft was well known for Pocket PC and other Windows CE-derived OS software. But historically, CE was not its first effort to attack the handheld OS market. Already in 1992, Microsoft had announced Pen Windows, perhaps to deter a pen-centric system later used in EO, an offshoot of Jerry Kaplan's startup Go Corp. Without support, however, it had been forced to drop the OS. Given the novelty and complexity, no single company could control the entire value chain in handhelds.

WinPad and Compaq Companion. As Hawkins, Dubinsky, and Colligan launched Palm Computing and Nokia initiated the "Responder," the WinPad project was secretly introduced at Microsoft headquarters in 1992. A kind of Windows 3.1 "lite," it was designed to run on an Intel 386 chip called the "Polar" and would have first shipped in a device called the "Compaq Companion." The device was supposed to launch at the 1994 Comdex and would have cost about $1,200, far more than the $500 Microsoft had targeted. Microsoft and Compaq quietly killed the project in late 1994.[17] Soon thereafter, Palm Computing shipped its first Palm Pilot, the first-ever successful pocket computer, which captured the early market.

From Pulsar and Pegasus to Windows CE. But Microsoft had not hedged all its bets on WinPad. In March 1993, it launched the Pulsar project, which seemed to be aimed at the consumer market for wireless pagers. Reportedly, many of the WinPad and Pulsar people were combined into Pegasus in late 1994. This became the basis for Windows CE (for "consumer electronics"), which was introduced in September 1996. A "lite" version of its Windows 95 OS for consumer devices, CE shipped later that year. Even as it continued to "mobilize" platforms and applications, Microsoft attempted to influence the wireless value chain through coalitions and partnerships of its own. In the CE effort, Microsoft dedicated particular attention to garnering third-party hardware and software support. It was not alone in the handheld space. Ranging from a "smart" wireless telephone to personal organizers with communications capabilities, devices were on the way from at least eight major computer and consumer electronics companies, including Hewlett-Packard, Casio Computer, and Philips Electronics.

From Intel to Small Processor Players. WinPad relied on Intel's Polar chip, but Microsoft made Windows CE portable to many different processor architectures. That opened the door for cooperation with many smaller semiconductor companies, while demolishing the "special" relationship with Intel, which Microsoft thought had neglected a growing market. In the mid-1990s, the microprocessor giant had forged a strong mobile and embedded architecture strategy, which included the i960 family of processors. As part of a legal settlement, Intel purchased Digital Semiconductor and its StrongARM technology from Digital Equipment Corp. (DEC) in 1998. This acquisition enabled Intel to make inroads into the Windows CE, but not into the palm-size PCs. Microsoft's Windows CE strategy promoted competition among processor manufacturers, which resulted in faster, cheaper chips that used less power. The fragmented supply chain ensured Microsoft's bargaining power at the expense of the processor firms. Windows CE supported processors from at least fifteen manufacturers, including ARM, Cyrix, DEC, Hitachi, IBM, Intel, MIPS, AMD, Motorola, NEC, Philips, and Toshiba. In the long term, it hoped that this competition would threaten the Palm OS, which was supported only by the Motorola DragonBall.[18]

By late 1997, Microsoft seemed to focus on at least three palmtop areas. The Gryphon project was a pocket-size, handwriting-recognition device aimed at the 3Com PalmPilot market; these products appeared in 1998. Mercury II was a more powerful handheld PC (HPC) product, a CE 3 of sorts. Apparently, there was also a larger form-factor project known as Jupiter. While Windows CE 2.0 shipped in late 1997, the company seemed to pull most of the upgrades into the Pocket PC range, competing against Palm.

Pocket PC. In 2000, Windows CE had only about 10 percent of the market for handhelds, according to IDC. In January, Gates outlined a new version of Windows CE while unveiling the Windows Media Player for Palm-size and Pocket PCs, giving consumers access to CD-quality music on handheld devices. Despite Microsoft's hopes to gain a footing in the fast-growing market for handhelds—and its marketing heft and predictions that its arrival into the market would decimate rivals—Windows CE failed to gain substantial momentum. In April, the company launched Pocket PC (formerly code-named Rapier), its new OS for handheld devices, which was intended to carve a place for Microsoft in a market dominated by Palm. Later, Compaq and Microsoft announced collaboration to make it easier for handheld devices to connect wirelessly to corporate networks. Just as with the Internet, the two anticipated growth of mobile business markets to precede that of consumer mass markets in the mobile Internet. By the next summer, Microsoft made the source code of its Windows CE 3.0 OS available to developers in a bid to compete with the "open source" software development model.[19]

In addition to Apple and Palm, Microsoft prepared to take on far more powerful players—including mobile leaders such as Nokia, Ericsson, and Motorola.

Hedging Bets: Real Options in Mobility

In the past, Microsoft had demonstrated an almost uncanny precision in timing. It did not pioneer new markets, but it often turned emerging niches into full-scale mass markets. In the early 1990s, many senior Microsoft executives had felt that the company moved too slowly toward the Internet. Toward the end of the decade, similar sentiments prevailed with regard to the mobile Internet. By the end of the 1990s, mobile hype swept markets in Europe, the United States, and Asia alike. In March 2000, eight former high-ranking Microsoft executives and two veterans of Craig McCaw's wireless empire joined forces in Ignition Corp. Their dreams of rapid wireless explosion, however, never materialized.[20] At Microsoft, mobility was only one of many concerns. In 1998, the U.S. Justice Department, backed by nineteen states, filed antitrust charges against the company, which faced similar challenges in Europe as well.

As Gates turned over the president's job to longtime Microsoft executive Steve Ballmer, the company was reorganized in 1999 along customer groups instead of product lines. That summer the company formally abandoned the PC-centric motto espoused by Gates in 1975: "A computer on every desk and in every home." The new vision statement, crafted by Ballmer, had been broadened to include Internet-based software and services, non-PC devices such as handheld computers, and TV set-top boxes: "Empower people through great software anytime, anyplace, and on any device."[21] Concurrently, Microsoft was expanding its investments from computing to communications by investing $5 billion for a minority stake in AT&T as part of the carrier's move to acquire cable operator MediaOne. In 2000, Gates named Ballmer CEO, while retaining his chairmanship and adding the title of chief software architect.

All of these developments—industry and firm turmoil, the antitrust struggle, and the reorganization of Microsoft—set the context for the software giant's efforts to "mobilize" its desktop applications and platforms between 1998 and early 2002. Instead of a visible strategic turn, it approached the mobile Internet through a number of different initiatives, which cumulatively served as a real options strategy of sorts. At first, there were efforts at joint ventures (Wireless Knowledge), strategic partnerships (Microsoft-Ericsson), and strategic alliances (Microsoft-Nokia).

Wireless Knowledge. Wireless Knowledge was launched in November 1998 to provide businesses with secure wireless access to data on Microsoft Exchange servers via mobile devices across any wireless network. It debuted with support from the wireless service provider community, but technology trials and product development met obstacles. The carriers were reticent to deploy the Wireless Knowledge service because of an industrywide anti-Microsoft and an anti-Qualcomm attitude. In the United States and Europe, many corporate customers sought to keep Microsoft out of the wireless industry. In the United States, Qualcomm was considered difficult to negotiate with, while overseas, the company was considered a threat to European-pioneered mobile communications. Besides, the mobile leaders were still pushing the WAP coalition, in which Phone.com was engaged in comparable efforts.

Microsoft and Nokia: Cooperation or Competition? In July 1999, a high-tech retreat took place in Sun Valley, Idaho. Far from the spotlight, Microsoft's Bill Gates spoke with Nokia chairman Jorma Ollila. According to Gates's e-mail after the meeting, which later became a U.S. government exhibit in the Microsoft antitrust case, the two leaders discussed the coming mobile

Internet and how their companies were preparing for it. Reportedly, Gates held out hope that the Finnish cell-phone giant might eventually incorporate Microsoft application software in its phones. "How come we don't merge our effort with Nokia?" he wrote to his colleagues. The strategic alliance never materialized. Two years later, *Business Week* speculated on the reasons of the failed "magic match-up": "Ollila and his colleagues saw long ago how Microsoft virtually took over the personal computer industry, helping itself to a heaping share of the profits. So the Finns were moving, even as Gates and Ollila chatted, to keep the Redmond behemoth at bay. This meant that if Microsoft was going to make its way to hundreds of millions of mobile users, it would get precious little help from Nokia. Now, even as the mobile Net lurches through a crisis of confidence and funding, a *mano a mano* struggle between the two giants is under way."[22] Indeed, many stories of courting and fighting between Nokia and Microsoft surfaced toward the end of the 1990s.[23]

Like most technology companies, the Finnish vendor certainly eyed Microsoft warily as a strategic partner because the software giant had a reputation of being difficult. The two companies had different roadmaps. To Microsoft, Nokia was just another chip in the global chessboard. If the Finnish company did not cooperate with Microsoft, it would have to compete with it. To Nokia, the showdown with Microsoft was a matter of life and death.

Microsoft and Ericsson. In December 1999, Microsoft and Ericsson announced a strategic partnership to develop end-to-end solutions for the wireless Internet, based on "a shared vision of convenient and fast access to information any time, anywhere, from any device." Through the partnership, Microsoft learned more about the Wireless Application Protocol (WAP) while Ericsson learned more about Microsoft Mobile Explorer (MME).[24] That same month, Microsoft joined the Bluetooth Group. The software empire was hedging its bets. Even as it led the IT front, it co-opted the tech coalitions of the mobile leaders. By spring 2001, the momentum behind the Microsoft-Ericsson alignment had largely dissipated, and the partnership fell apart.

By the close of the 1990s, all of these efforts and initiatives had accelerated Microsoft's activities in the mobile space, but none had resulted in high-profile success stories. Because of the industry downturn, Wireless Knowledge moved ahead slowly. A strategic alliance with Nokia had not only failed, but resulted in a collision course. The partnership with Ericsson was history. However, as the pressure of the antitrust case began to lessen and mobile leaders were swept by the European 3G birth pains, Microsoft's wireless options looked more promising, and it began repositioning in the mobile Internet.

Microsoft's Wireless Strategy

By 2001, Microsoft's wireless strategy comprised its efforts toward an end-to-end wireless solution that included client software, back-end servers, and end-user services. In the phone categories, Microsoft engaged in a three-pronged strategy—smart phones, features phones, and pagers. While the latter represented only one leg of the full strategy, it was the most visible one. In smart phones, Microsoft opted for in-house development, tight relationships with few mobile vendors, and cooperation with major mobile operators. In feature phones, it cooperated with the key technology coalitions that had been created by the primary mobile vendors, operators, and consumer electronics giants.

Next Generation Windows Services. In addition to Mobile Explorer and its Pocket PC handheld OS, Microsoft's wireless strategy included the yet-to-be-unveiled Next Generation Windows Services (NGWS) initiative, an effort to tie its OS with web-based applications and services. In June 2000, Gates said he expected the PC to remain the center of the computing universe, whereas the desktop would be complemented with wireless pads and devices. Microsoft anticipated that all of these devices would be linked by *its* NGWS. Said Gates of the NGWS development budget:

> We will spend more than three times what it cost to put a man on the moon. . . . It can drive the market for these devices to a whole new level. There won't be dozens and dozens of devices, but a few select ones. The digital set-top box, the phone with the screen, the electronic book—these will sell in huge quantities.[25]

Microsoft.Net. Soon thereafter, Microsoft announced a new business strategy, Microsoft.Net. The objective was to connect every computing device, from desktop PCs to cell phones, and tie them to the Internet, irrespective of the device used. In this scenario, software would be offered over the Web as a service. But it was at least two years away from delivering on its vision of Microsoft.Net. By late July 2000, Microsoft announced plans to invest $4.4 billion in R&D in high-growth markets, such as web development, wireless, and gaming, as well as its MSN network and consumer services. "The Internet plays the same role that the PC does (today). It's the Internet plus the devices, the new set-top boxes, new PCs, small-screen devices," Gates said.[26] Outside of its own development efforts, Microsoft continued to drive mobile products for 3G wireless networks, through mobile coalitions such as Bluetooth, WAP, and W3C.

The Feature Phone Platform: Microsoft Mobile Explorer. In December 1999, Microsoft launched a new mobile phone platform, Microsoft Mobile Explorer. Modular, customizable, and flexible, MME enabled handset manufacturers and wireless carriers to provide their customers with the choice of a broad line of applications and services on data-enabled telephones (or "feature phones") and next-generation smart phones. Unlike WAP, MME *could* display

HTML web content. Web developers would not have to create specific versions of their sites for cell phones. Over time, wireless network bandwidth would increase and technology would improve, which would make streaming audio and video and more robust web content feasible on cell phones. MME was a key component of Microsoft's end-to-end wireless strategy to provide mobile Internet solutions (more specifically, Microsoft Exchange Server, the BackOffice family, and MSN Mobile Services). It was a *mobilized* Internet Explorer. Through corporate customer trials, it led to Microsoft's business relationships and joint ventures with British Telecommunications, Deutsche Telekom's mobile subsidiary, NTT DoCoMo, as well as Korea Telecom Freetel.

The Smart Phone Platform: "Stinger." To Microsoft, mobile devices were personal tools. Different kinds of users preferred different kinds of tools. Some people preferred telecom options and were comfortable with a phone. Still others favored data options available with a PDA. Some might prefer a single device that could do it all—small enough to carry but big enough to meet data needs. As Microsoft hedged its bets in 1999, it began a smart phone development project, code-named "Stinger." The objective was to combine the best PDAs and the best phones to create a platform that would keep people intelligently connected any time, anywhere, by voice, e-mail, or other means. The platform was designed to include a web browser that offered multiple support (for HTML, WAP, WML, and XML formats). The Stinger had four key objectives:

- To be a great phone
- To offer remote control for communications management
- To be up and running in five minutes without support
- To offer personal information manager (PIM) and mail synchronization[27]

With its customer-driven approach, Microsoft sought to provide everything—quality, ease of use, convenience, personalization, and synchronization—that the engineering-driven vendors and operators habitually ignored. Bigger than a feature phone but smaller than a Pocket PC, Microsoft's smart phone would offer both voice and rich wireless data capabilities in a singular device. The first handset manufacturers to design a range of phones using the Microsoft smart phone platform consisted of four companies: Samsung Electronics, Mitsubishi Trium, Sendo, and HTC, the Taiwanese company that designed and built the Compaq iPAQ Pocket PC. Additionally, several mobile operators—including VoiceStream, Vodafone, Telefonica, Telstra, and T-Mobile—had agreed to provide service for the "Stinger"-based smart phones.

In August 2000, Microsoft Vice President Ben Waldman, who had left

Apple for Microsoft and now headed the company's mobile devices unit, showed off the first working prototype of Stinger, its next-generation web-enabled cell phone. Stinger was expected to compete with a range of phones developed by the members of the Symbian consortium. "Mobile devices are a key part of Microsoft's new, extended vision," Waldman said referring to Microsoft's .Net initiative. "No one can agree on the single ideal device," he said. "We're focusing on a broad range of devices."[28] By summer 2001, Microsoft began consumer tests of its smart phone in the United States, Europe, and Asia, including the Sendo model (see Exhibit 14-4).

Intel's Vision: Delivering Technology and Building Blocks

In 1971, when the Bell engineers formulated their cellular proposals, the microprocessor had barely been invented. A decade later, digitalization and miniaturization enabled the PC revolution, even though the first cellular platform was still analog-based. As the microprocessor became the "brains" of the personal computer, miniaturization would extend this revolution to cell phones as well. In 1979, Lucent invented the world's first single-chip digital signal processor (DSP). Only four years later, Texas Instruments introduced a single chip DSP that functioned at more than five million operations a second; two decades later, this figure had multiplied to thirty-five million operations per second. The entry of Texas Instruments into the DSP business precipitated the potential of large-scale production and use of the new technology.

By the 1980s, AT&T in telecommunications and IBM in computers—two vertically integrated giants—were no longer in control of these new and emerging technologies; their suppliers were. In microprocessors, OS, and software, relatively new players, such as Intel and Microsoft, captured industry leadership. In wireless communications, Motorola enjoyed the edge in the analog cellular, but because of its domestic cellular focus, it was slower to globalize. By 1997, 65 percent of the cost of an Ericsson mobile phone stemmed from integrated microelectronic circuits, or chips.[29] The components were manufactured by specialized houses in the United States, Europe, and Asia-Pacific. As industry horizontalization led to greater specialization and higher production volumes, and as the emergence of smart phones led to the demand for greater intelligence, Intel, which still dominated 80 percent of PCs worldwide, had not developed the wireless segment in a timely manner.

Building Wireless Capabilities

"The wireless world is moving into Intel's natural domain, which is data computation and data communication," said Ron Smith, senior vice president of Intel's Wireless Communications and Computing Group, in summer 2000. "And to this domain we bring semiconductor technology . . . our experience with computers and computing devices . . . our flash memory . . . our networking capability, and communications technology as well as the ability to influence and help create industry standards."[30]

Along with Microsoft, Intel had served as a catalyst to and thrived with the PC revolution. Through these years—roughly from 1984 to 1994—the *de facto* Wintel duopoly enjoyed the greatest bargaining power in the computing value system. Whereas Microsoft dominated OS and application software, Intel had more than 80 percent of the microprocessors. Among PC manufacturers, Compaq and Dell Computer failed to achieve such dominance, as did the great

Exhibit 14-4. IT leaders: mobile devices.

Microsoft's Mobile Devices

By the spring of 2002, Microsoft's Windows powered mobile devices comprised pocket PCs, handheld PCs and mobile phones.

Compaq's iPAQ Pocket PC

You want to do more with life? The iPAQ Pocket PC H3870 is designed to ride along on the voyage of life – in your pocket or mounted to your mountain bike. It's not much bigger than a calculator and comes standard with applications like Microsoft Pocket Word™, Excel™, Outlook™, Internet Explorer™, and Windows Media™ Player. (Compaq Corp., January 2002)

Sendo's Mobile Phones

Founded in August 1999, Sendo was a new mobile phone company with development, manufacturing, marketing, sales and distribution activities worldwide. It sought to produce high-performance, feature-rich mobile phones for the mass consumer market. Primary customers were network operators, distributors, and retailers throughout Europe and Asia. With headquarters in Birmingham, UK, Sendo had sales and distribution centers in Hong Kong, Italy, France, Spain, Germany, United Kingdom, Taiwan, Netherlands and Australia

sendo P200

"The Sendo D800 is only 68g and 69cc making it one of the lightest and smallest GSM phones in the world. The Sendo D800 offers all the latest features from predictive text to graphic equalizer and animated graphics."	*"Be an individual and own the fantastic Sendo P200 with 'Out of this World' features. Downloadable ringer tones, SMS smileys, games and terrific graphics make this phone an absolute must have."*	*"The J520 offers the perfect combination of style and features for the fashionable professional. This phone outshines all other phones in its class with its features and competitive price."*

SOURCES: Microsoft Corporation, Compaq Computer Corporation, and Sendo International Ltd.

retail chains, such as CompUSA. But even before the Internet revolution, the rise of the PDA market heralded the decline of the Wintel duopoly. Industry circumstances that made Microsoft and Intel the driving forces of the PC revolution eroded a decade later. When the two tackled the PDA market in 1992, the idea was that Microsoft's WinPad would run on an Intel 386 chip (Polar) and first ship in a device called the "Compaq Companion." Two years later, Microsoft and Compaq killed the project. Intel's processor, thought Microsoft, contributed to WinPad's hefty price tag. In contrast to WinPad, which relied on Intel's Polar chip, Windows CE was portable to many different processor architectures. And that meant the demise of the old relationship with Intel's x86—at first.

Starting in 1995, Intel, along with Microsoft, had "embraced and extended" into the Internet space. The global microprocessor giant remained a key player in the computing industry. Between 1997 and 2001, Microsoft, through trial and error, crafted a set of strategic options that it used to "mobilize" its software dominance into the nascent wireless value chain. Intel followed in Microsoft's footsteps.

Targeting "Road Warriors": Mobile Data Initiative. Intel's first major wireless project—Mobile Data Initiative—originated in August 1997, when the company announced a coalition of telephone, mobile phone, hardware, and software companies that intended to bundle their services to give PC users a simple wireless connection to the Net or corporate intranets. The members included Pacific Bell, Microsoft, Toshiba, IBM, Nokia, and the North America GSM Alliance. "The initiative seeks to provide business users with access to data anywhere, anytime, without compromising notebook PC performance and capability," said Stephen Nachtsheim, vice president and general manager of Intel's mobile and handheld group.[31] Intel targeted "road warriors"—highly mobile business professionals. This category accounted for only 5 percent of Internet users, but it was attractive. Business travelers who needed reliable online service were willing to pay a price premium.

Toward New DSP Architecture: Cooperation with Analog Devices. Intel's existing competencies and capabilities rested on the wired desktop, not on the wireless. As a result, it began to build some of these competencies in-house via R&D and venture capital activities. It also cooperated with Analog Devices, Inc. (ADI) in a joint engineering project and developed a low-power DSP core. During the past two decades, the convergence of computing and communications had brought about increasing portability (think of laptops, notebooks, handhelds, pocket PCs, and of course, digital cellular phones), multimedia (from CD-ROM to digital audio and video), and connectivity (network computing and the Internet). From 1999 to 2000, annual semiconductor sales grew 35 percent to nearly $400 billion. The Intel-ADI cooperation sought to combine Intel's microcontroller leadership with ADI's signal processing leadership in a new "Micro Signal Architecture." The objective was a new DSP architecture that would process data and signals and allow the products of the two companies to run the same software, while optimizing them for Internet and wireless appliances.

Acquisition of DSP Communications. Intel rushed into wireless Internet applications and planned to supply the high-volume, standards-based building blocks needed for rapid global deployment. Diversification intensified after the chipmaker's primary market—microprocessors—met declining PC prices. In October 1999, Intel acquired DSP Communications, Inc.,[32] a maker of wireless chipsets, software stacks, and reference designs, in an offer valued at approximately $1.6 billion. It was Intel's second-largest acquisition ever and its largest all-cash purchase. The buy followed a $500 million deal to purchase e-commerce software maker iPivot. In just two years, Intel had spent more than $6 billion on a dozen communications acquisitions. "Our vision is that the Internet will increasingly go wireless," said Craig Barrett, Intel's CEO, in a conference call. "You should look at this as a beachhead into wireless communications over the Internet using a variety of devices."[33] In spring 2002, DSP merged its IP licensing business with the Dublin-based Parthus Technologies. The $600 million deal was designed to exploit the industry trend toward the licensing of open-standard IP architectures for the digital economy.

Before the acquisition by Intel, DSP Communications had used Texas Instruments—Nokia's supplier—as a manufacturer. Following the acquisition, Intel used DSP's designs to manufacture chips. In the long term, that precipitated a conflict of interest for Nokia. As Intel integrated forward to ensure a position in the emerging wireless value chain, Nokia struggled to manage its wireless chipmakers. Initially, both focused on stimulating the new marketplace. In the long run, this cooperation was likely to shift into competition.

Intel Communications Fund. At the end of the 1990s, Nokia launched a venture firm to stimulate the growth of new wireless markets and technologies. Similarly, Intel teamed with key companies in the wireless arena and expanded the charter of the Intel Communications Fund (ICF) to support its wireless communications and computing efforts along with its networking and communications strategies. By 2002, the ICF was a $500 million equity investment fund that invested in technology companies developing innovative networking and communications solutions worldwide.

International Cooperation. To acquire the necessary competences and build the requisite capabilities, Intel targeted the key mobile clusters worldwide (see Exhibit 14-5). By 2000, the processor giant had manufacturing plants in the United States as well as China, Costa Rica, Ireland, Israel, Malaysia, the Philippines, and Puerto Rico. It also had sales offices in more than thirty countries worldwide. Somewhat like Motorola, it obtained more than 40 percent of its total sales from the United States, 24 percent from Europe, and 9 percent from Japan. Like its domestic activities, the overseas efforts rested on the wired desktop, not on wireless competencies. Consequently, Intel initiated a slate of international alliances to learn more and better position itself in the wireless. In 1998—a year after the Mobile Data Initiative—Intel co-launched Bluetooth with Ericsson, Nokia, IBM, and Toshiba. The company also speeded the cultivation of the wireless segment through strategic alliances. Meanwhile, Intel and Ericsson announced an alliance to define flash memory products that stored web pages, e-mail, voice, and music files. Intel and Mitsubishi Electric engaged in a joint development effort to build 3G chipsets. These international alliances originated from Wireless Competence Centers, which Intel established to focus on developing e-business partnerships and technology with world leaders in wireless communications. The centers were localized in the global wireless clusters in Stockholm, Sweden; Tsukuba, Japan; and Beijing, China.[34]

Exhibit 14-5. Intel's early expansion in the wireless.

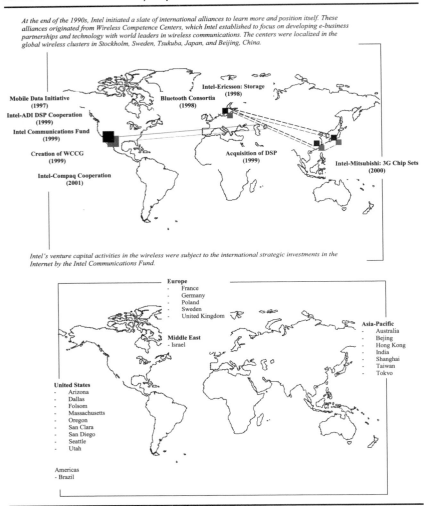

At the end of the 1990s, Intel initiated a slate of international alliances to learn more and position itself. These alliances originated from Wireless Competence Centers, which Intel established to focus on developing e-business partnerships and technology with world leaders in wireless communications. The centers were localized in the global wireless clusters in Stockholm, Sweden, Tsukuba, Japan, and Beijing, China.

Mobile Data Initiative
(1997)

Intel-ADI DSP Cooperation
(1999)

Intel Communications Fund
(1999)

Creation of WCCG
(1999)

Intel-Compaq Cooperation
(2001)

Bluetooth Consortia
(1998)

Intel-Ericsson: Storage
(1998)

Acquisition of DSP
(1999)

Intel-Mitsubishi: 3G Chip Sets
(2000)

Intel's venture capital activities in the wireless were subject to the international strategic investments in the Internet by the Intel Communications Fund.

Europe
- France
- Germany
- Poland
- Sweden
- United Kingdom

Middle East
- Israel

Asia-Pacific
- Australia
- Bejing
- Hong Kong
- India
- Shanghai
- Taiwan
- Tokyo

United States
- Arizona
- Dallas
- Folsom
- Massachusetts
- Oregon
- San Clara
- San Diego
- Seattle
- Utah

Americas
- Brazil

Rise of Intel's Wireless Subsidiary

In December 1999—only weeks after the DSP purchase—Intel's entry into the wireless was completed. It was time to consolidate the properties into the Wireless Communications & Computing Group (WCCG). The group focused on cellular and wireless communications, providing building blocks for computing and wireless communication devices and data applications in the growing cellular market. Intel was now working on *integrated chips for cell phones* that would combine most of the necessary silicon—flash memory, DSPs, and microprocessors—into a single package. Such an offering was expected to be less expensive than current chips, while allowing Intel to bring its StrongARM processor cores and a yet-to-be-released DSP core to the wireless market.

Intel's wireless strategy built on its core businesses and the Internet.

Extending Desktop Internet

In 2001, Intel generated $33.7 billion in revenues, with margins in excess of 30 percent. With $3 billion in cash and a market cap of $202 billion, it remained a flagship of the technology sector. But like Microsoft, it had to struggle to retain its dominance. Operational and strategic stumbling coincided with efforts to diversify into businesses beyond chips, as well as the tenure of CEO Craig Barrett, Intel's legendary chief of manufacturing, who had launched companywide initiatives to refocus on execution. As mobile leaders prepared for the 3G era, Intel battled against smaller archrival Applied Micro Devices, Inc. (AMD), whose Athlon processor had taken the market share away from Intel's Pentium. Intel spent billions developing the powerful 64-bit Itanium microprocessor with Hewlett-Packard.

Intel was pursuing a similar platform architecture strategy with its processors for handheld wireless devices and network backbone equipment. As far as Intel was concerned, the growth of the wireless Internet meant the convergence of computing, communications, and networking—that is, a distributed extension of the desktop Internet computing experience. In addition to high-volume production, new technologies, and increasing complexity, the wireless revolution resulted in new types of consumer applications, as well as diverse types of devices that delivered wireless Internet content to users, including PDAs, notebook and desktop PCs and networked peripherals, web pads, e-books, and other Internet appliances. Intel expected this trend to soar as wireless network standards and industry specifications (e.g., 802.11, HomeRF, and Bluetooth) transitioned from development into products. For years, all of these aspects—high-volume production, complex computing products, and diversity of devices—had been an inherent part of Intel's core competencies, first in desktop computing and thereafter in the desktop Internet. Now industry prospects seemed equally attractive in mobile Internet computing.

Intel's Internet Architectures. Like Microsoft, Intel saw the wireless strategy as the central leg of a broader Internet strategy. Said Craig Barrett in the summer of 2001, "The Internet is the growth engine of the future. It's the center of innovation. It encompasses communication, information, and commerce."[35] In 2001, the processor giant had committed some $7.5 billion in capital expenditures. At the same time, it invested $4.3 billion in R&D, more than ever before. It planned to invest a substantial amount of these funds into the wireless. As Intel reorganized its R&D operations, engaged in internal venture capital, and focused on core activities while downplaying others, it was also developing four architectures for the Internet.

- The PC platform, particularly Intel's IA-32 bit family, embodied by the Pentium 4 processor and the extended PC concept
- The Intel Personal Client Architecture (PCA) for handheld computing and communication devices
- Get Exchange Architecture, or the networking family of products
- Servers characterized by the Itanium processor family

Whereas its initial capabilities evolved from the PC architecture, Intel's future growth went hand in hand with the Internet. From the mobile standpoint, PCA was the door in. The company saw that it was poised to deliver the technology and building blocks necessary for device manufacturers, content providers, and operators.

Intel's Building Blocks. In late August 2001, Intel and Compaq announced that they would collaborate to speed the development of wireless handhelds and applications used to access and transmit data over the Internet. Concurrently, Compaq announced its support for the Intel PCA initiative. Compaq's iPAQ had quickly evolved into one of the industry's leading Pocket PC offerings, which, in turn, reinforced Intel's focus on handhelds, to maximize innovation and efficiency. In the changing wireless environment, Intel, by the turn of 2002, saw itself as a key building block supplier and whole solution provider for the wireless Internet, particularly in three areas: wireless wide area networks (WANs), wireless local area networks (WLANs), and wireless personal connectivity.

StrongARMing Into Wireless. To meet the needs of 2.5G and 3G cellular phones and other handheld devices, Intel's building blocks included a wide range of technologies, such as the Intel StrongARM processor, Intel XScale Microarchitecture, Intel flash memory chips, cellular communications baseband chipsets, and Micro Signal Architecture (DSP core) capabilities. In October 2001, six top PD makers selected Intel's StrongARM SA-1110 processor to power their next generation of communications products. These realignments reflected the second incarnation of PC leaders (Microsoft, Intel, and PC vendors) in the new wireless space.

Intel's building blocks formed a three pillar architecture—the Intel Personal Internet Client Architecture (PCA)—which was expected to simplify and speed wireless product development. Essentially, it separated the computer and communications functional blocks of a wireless device. It defined the interface between these two blocks, allowing their development to proceed in a parallel manner and saving valuable development time for hardware and software developers. Additionally, Intel was involved in wireless technologies that provided high-speed and reliable network connections using radio frequencies in place of wires and cables, including WLANs based on the IEEE 802.11 standard.

"Internet on a Chip"

In May 2001, Intel created the "Internet on a chip" through the union of a processor core, flash memory technology, and a digital signal processor. It would allow devices such as handheld computers to access the Internet and run applications twice as quickly as was previously possible. "This is a break-through in silicon technology manufacturing," said Al Fazio, principal engineer for wireless in Intel's Technology and Manufacturing Group.[36] The concept of combined processor core, DSP, and memory in a single chip was not new. The "system on a chip" concept had been first launched by Texas Instruments. TI's equivalent chip was part of the Open Multimedia Applications Platform (OMAP), an effort to create hardware and software building blocks for the next generation of cell phones and handhelds. TI was not just a leading DSP maker and Intel's main competitor in the handheld and cell phone markets; it was also Nokia's prime supplier.

Despite the inherent differences in the mobile and IT visions, Intel's relationship with Nokia was not as adversarial as that between Nokia and Microsoft. First, Nokia's emphasis on the open 3G software platform conflicted *directly* with Microsoft's. Second, Nokia's relationship with TI could mean several things to Intel—a challenge to match and transcend, a threat to neutralize through replication (e.g., the Mitsubishi deal), or an opportunity (by redefining the Nokia relationship). Still, Nokia and Intel disagreed on the most fundamental question: Are mobile phones commodities? Intel's response was affirmative. The cellular business was maturing, and product differences were disappearing, while the "phone on a chip" concept reflected horizontalization. Nokia's response was negative. Mobile terminals were about to thrive in a new era of innovation, and differences proliferated via new product categories, while the role of software was rapidly increasing.[37]

By the end of November 2001, Intel acknowledged that its objective was to generate almost one-third of its revenue from communications products in the future, even if the road ahead was murky. The new chip architecture was gaining acceptance, and the company had moved into the top ranks among communications chip makers in terms of revenue. In 2001, Intel planned to spend $1.2 billion on R&D in communications, or nearly one-third its corporate total of $3.9 billion, although its third-quarter revenue on wireless and communications products accounted for just a sixth of the total at $1.09 billion. Hans Geyer, general manager of Intel's cellular communications division, expected that it would take three to seven years for sales to approach the same sort of ratio now seen in R&D. Still, there would be more than one processor architecture for cell phones for at least the next five years. "You see a lot of things happening in the cellular industry that were seen in the PC industry ten years ago."[38] Intel's expectations were a polite way of saying to the Finnish vendor: "You can play the vertical game for a few years, if you like. But you're just playing time. A box is a box is a box. In the past, you got your position by being there first. Now you can get there first, but you must earn that position through competition. Just keep in mind that your old cost advantage is no longer an advantage. Forget full vertical coordination; it's history. Horizontalize fast unless you want to be squeezed out. And if you manage to find a position, then you'd better lead, or follow—or get the hell out of the way." By March 2002, Intel incorporated Internet-enabled cell phones and PDAs into corporate IT environments. This allowed companies to access corporate data anytime, anywhere. "Broadband access to the Internet is the next critical step we have to take," said Intel chairman Andy Grove. "The United States should leapfrog the world, and become the first region to make data the lead application to wireless."[39]

America Online's Vision

Through the 1990s, Stephen Case navigated America Online and its users toward the digital economy. At the end of the growth decade, AOL and Time Warner took a big step into the future through a merger that was designed to create the "world's first truly global media and communications company for the Internet century." Because of AOL Time Warner's flagship role in content and communications, its mobile initiatives were bound to shape the wireless industry. In March 2000, Case, now chairman of AOL Time Warner, argued that the company was ready to tackle the challenge of mobility, which he understood very broadly, through multiple access devices:

> AOL Time Warner will be well positioned to get a jump on wireless. Already, roughly 70 percent of AOL households own a cell phone, pager, or both—twice the penetration of the population at large. And we bring the leading brands in online mapping, local city guides, and Instant Messaging, among other valuable features and information for mobile users—with AOL's hallmark convenience and ease-of-use. . . . Like interactivity and convergence, mobility is a critical piece of the new networked world. Once people get a taste of it, they will expect even more. We believe that our AOL Wireless strategy will allow us to truly "grow the pie"— driving increased consumer demand, higher use of existing services, and a range of new services based on these technologies. At every level, this is a win-win-win opportunity for AOL, for our partners, and for consumers.[40]

In the late 1990s, winning was all about leveraging the PC and modem. Case thought that the years 2000 to 2005 would be all about cell phones and wireless devices across a range of platforms. But these phones and devices would have to be designed to bring all the benefits of the Internet to consumers in a *seamless* way. "Consumers are driving these trends—but they shouldn't have to be systems integrators to figure them out," Case said. "So the companies that will lead in this new world will be those that listen to consumers and connect the dots for them."[41]

Wired Web: Quest for Ubiquity and Personalization

Soon after America Online went public in 1992, Stephen Case became its CEO. The online service provider spent heavily on marketing in an effort to pass rivals Prodigy and CompuServe, while rejecting the old proprietary community model and unveiling a Windows-based version of its online software. After the IPO, Case and Jan Brandt, AOL's marketing director, devised the hardest sell that had ever been attempted by an online service.[42] They sent out software disks by direct mail to millions of PC users, offering them free trials of AOL. Like America's largest consumer marketers, AOL wanted to be anywhere, anytime, anyplace—as omnipresent as Coca-Cola. "My job," says Brandt, "was to give new meaning to the word ubiquity."[43] As a result of the direct marketing campaign, AOL's membership soared from 155,000 to 4.6 million at the start of 1996.

During the 1990s, America Online changed its marketing mix several times, often abruptly. These changes were dictated by the dynamics of the Internet evolution, just as they were enabled by AOL's flexible organizational capabilities. Far faster and more responsive than its rivals, AOL periodically reviewed and remolded its product portfolio, rebuilt and rechanneled its distribution avenues, repositioned its promotional tactics, repriced its products, and restructured its organization. Rapid changes did not take place without debate. As the leading online service provider, AOL would often be the first to break traditional ways of doing business (e.g., the decision to open chat rooms to online ads). By 1997 and 1998, it offered mass customized products and services and could boast *targeted* and desirable upscale user demographics. Unlike TV networks and cable television, AOL was neither about *broad*casting nor about *narrow*casting. Rather, the online service provider offered personalized software, aggregated content, and retail.

Unlike the older IT leaders, AOL grew with and through the Internet and, therefore, had an extraordinary industry foresight. As the service provider prepared its growth strategy, it predicted that wired Internet would evolve through four ages. Each era represented greater technological novelty and complexity, expanding markets, increasing functionalities, and more sophisticated service propositions. In the cellular space, these eras had barely begun (see Exhibit 14-6). The Iron Age, for instance, had been initiated in the Nordic lead markets in the mid-1990s, which witnessed the SMS explosion. The Bronze era would ensue with NTT DoCoMo's Freedom of Multimedia Access (FOMA) model in late 2001 and with capabilities in northern Europe barely a year later. In the United States, these developments began later, but as the

Exhibit 14-6. Ages of Internet and Mobile Internet.

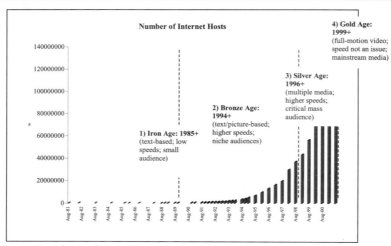

SOURCE: Network Wizards (Feb 2002).

1) Iron Age: 1985+	2) Bronze Age: 1994+	3) Silver Age: 1996+	4) Gold Age: 1999+
- Member-generated content - Branded, repackaged content - Reference database - Icons for info, logos for ads - Rudimentary transactions	- Channel creation, new content - Packaged content streams - e-com malls (with text and photos) - Interactive marketing as info providers - Celebrity events and vertical communities - Connected properties - Pointing to Web sites	- Original content - Less "repurposed" content - Programmed e-commerce - New channels for new markets - Shows - Member-generated content - New HTML content areas - Few partners; better service; increased promotion	- Cable and telephony and datacom and Hollywood blended together - Advertiser/marketers-supported - More consumers using PCs in prime time than TVs - Fully interactive services

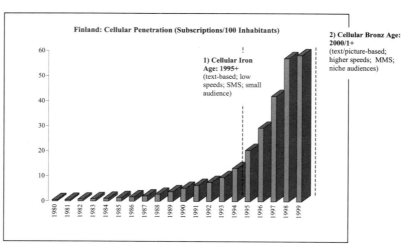

SOURCE: Finnish Company Reports.

game of catch up proceeded, they also proceeded more rapidly. From AOL's standpoint, the mobile Internet represented a natural extension of its proper scope of activities. Because the brand offered ubiquitous services, the provider would follow its users' footsteps. Furthermore, the new mobile space allowed for even greater personalization through location-based services. Last, but certainly not least, mobilization eliminated old industry boundaries, provided new opportunities for challengers, and threatened incumbents. It was also a potential instrument against Microsoft.

Wireless Web: "AOL Anywhere"

In 2000, AOL generated $7.7 billion in revenues. Most sales originated from subscription services (62 percent), but advertising and e-commerce played an increasing role (26 percent). In the long term, AOL naturally hoped to embrace mobility and extend its capabilities into the wireless business, in order to "mobilize" a substantial amount of its subscription services, as well as advertising and e-commerce. This objective evolved around 1998 to 2001.[44] In the past, AOL had thrived with user-friendly online services; now it intended to do the same in mobile services. In 1998, Barry Schuler, president of AOL's Interactive Services, portrayed mobility as a great opportunity:

> With technologies converging, we see the beginning of an era of new interactive appliances with online features, such as TV attachments, wireless phones, hand-held computers, and smart phones. We think people will want to have a single e-mail address and set of customized features across all of those devices. That's the idea behind our "AOL Anywhere" strategy.... Our goal is to be wherever people can be connected.[45]

AOL Anywhere did not come about just because PC markets were becoming saturated. It also reflected the impact of globalization. In the United States, PC penetration was relatively high. As a result, mass users accessed the Internet through desktop PCs. That was not the case in many European and Asian markets, where mobile penetration was relatively high, but PC penetration was relatively low. In these country markets, mass users accessed the Web through mobile devices. AOL wanted to ensure its strategic position in Europe's lead markets. As it diversified beyond the desktop PC, it also gained stakes in the Java and Linux development communities. With the acquisition of Netscape Communications, it gained ownership of software deals with Java developer Sun Microsystems and an equity stake in Red Hat, the largest Linux vendor. These events triggered substantial industry speculation—was AOL really after a Windows alternative? After all, it was in cooperation with Sun—

one of the most persistent Microsoft rivals—that it had launched AOL Anywhere.

Under its AOL Anywhere' strategy, AOL began to make the services, features, and content of the AOL service and other properties available through multiple connections and devices. In addition to PCs, TV sets, wireless telephones, handheld and pocket devices, and specialized Internet appliances could be used. By the end of 1999, AOL claimed 45 million Instant Messenger users, although there were other comparable applications, including the AOL-owned ICQ, Yahoo! Messenger, and Microsoft's MSN Messenger Service. At the same time, the online service provider engaged in two acquisitions. First, it purchased Tegic Communications, a company specializing in text entry for wireless devices. The online map and navigation provider MapQuest.com was then acquired in a stock deal worth $1.1 billion. In early 2000, AOL organized its wireless properties into a wireless division, which would develop interactive services for wireless devices, while striking partnerships with other technology providers to carry these services. Knowing that some 43 percent of members accessed their accounts away from home, AOL recognized the need to make it easier for members to stay in touch. In particular, the effort sought to provide value to members and partners. In the first case, the company mobilized AOL features, making them ubiquitous and integrated. In the second case, it delivered retention and increased usage. AOL's mobile strategy saw four keys to success: brands, content, functionality, and user interface.[46]

AOL announced deals with Motorola, BellSouth, Sprint PCS, Nokia, RIM, and Arch Communications to extend its Internet products to cellular telephone and pager services. As Net companies rushed into wireless to hold onto their existing customers, AOL had to provide non-PC access to its services. In addition to providing content, AOL unveiled "OL Mobile Messenger, a wireless version of its popular e-mail and AOL Instant Messenger products. Hedging bets, it joined the WAP Forum, in which Excite@Home had already enlisted. With these moves, AOL joined several Internet players—including Yahoo!, Amazon.com, Microsoft, and Excite@Home—that were aggressively developing wireless services.

In September, AOL engaged in a slate of new deals, including acquisitions, multiyear alliances, and minority stakes. New licensing and marketing agreements accelerated as it initiated cooperation with two major operators, NTT DoCoMo and AT&T Wireless. AOL and NTT DoCoMo agreed to jointly develop a range of Internet services. As a first step, DoCoMo would pay $96 million for a 42 percent stake in America Online's Japan unit. DoCoMo would later invest another $53 million. An alliance with AOL was expected to assist DoCoMo increase its global presence as a leader in wireless Internet access. Conversely, it allowed AOL to learn more about the NTT DoCoMo's service concept in Japan, which the U.S. provider hoped to incorporate with its own to globalize even faster. Mobile Internet developed more quickly in certain European and Asian locations, argued Lisa Hook, president of AOL Mobile. "Primarily, these markets are being driven by mobile instant messaging, which is one of AOL's core competencies, along with ring tone and cartoon downloads. Overall, AOL is moving very aggressively in the wireless space throughout the world, through partnerships with major wireless providers."[47]

At AOL, globalization went hand in hand with mobilization.

Shifts in Bargaining Power

As the industry boundaries that once were clearly defined no longer separate the mobile and IT leaders, their technologies, products, and services were becoming similar. Both offered end-to-end solutions, but each employed very different means to its objective. Led by Nokia, the mobile leaders cultivated a vision of vertical coordination, which conflicted with their past strategic success but was designed to reaffirm their leadership in a new era. Led by Microsoft, the IT leaders advocated a vision of horizontalization, which emulated the PC revolution and was crafted to reinforce their positioning in the mobile business.

From the postwar era until February 2002, the mobile leaders had served as the industry catalysts. This period of triumph and success peaked at the end of the 2G era. In effect, worldwide mobile phone sales between 1996 and 2000 experienced a compound annual growth rate of close to 60 percent. But in 2001, for the first time in history, the mobile phone industry posted a drop in unit sales. Worldwide sales totaled nearly 399.6 million units in 2001, a decline of 3.2 percent from 2000 sales.[48] A few weeks later, Nokia said its first quarter net sales would be slightly lower than previously expected because of a decline in sales of network equipment. As markets slumped, the response was no longer just a temporary disappointment. Rather, some saw the writing on the wall. The Wintel counterattack had begun.

The Wintel Counterattack

With the 3G transition, the mobile value system was changing, which meant substantial shifts in bargaining power. Though its core capabilities were in equipment manufacturing, Nokia sought to migrate toward the downstream side of the value chain, stressing software capabilities. Coupled with its strength in handsets and networks, vertical power and coordination made it an influential mobile leader. The new challengers were horizontally more focused. For instance, Intel concentrated on the "building blocks" in the mobile space, which made it less threatening as a potential coalition leader and more attractive as a potential coalition partner. Despite some overlapping interests with Microsoft, AOL, for the most part, focused on its core competencies in content and communications, which made it a desirable partner on the downstream side of the business. Some challengers were horizontally focused but vertically ambitious. Led by Palm, all major handheld makers, including Handspring and RIM, had harbored dreams of industry leadership. But by the end of the 1990s, each had been humbled by competitive realities. In the long term, only Microsoft, through its strength in OS and applications, and possibly NTT DoCoMo, through its capabilities in applications, equipment, and network operations, possessed adequate horizontal strengths and vertical power to challenge the mobile leaders.

Struggle for Developer Communities

In the long term, the control of developer communities was a critical driver of enablers' success (see Exhibit 14-7). Through its Open Mobile Architecture Initiative coalition, Nokia was, in effect, triadizing developers. Building upon its in-house base (including the Nokia Forum) and mobile coalition (with and through control of Symbian), Nokia employed the OAI coalition to "divide and rule" the U.S. developers (in cooperation with Java) while containing NTT DoCoMo's threat through collaboration in Japan. It was a classic effort at scale through scope—but hardly invincible.

In the early days of the 3G transition, the U.S. camp remained fragmented. Through Windows CE, Microsoft enjoyed extraordinary leverage, but it was also viewed as an unreliable strategic partner. Handheld players pos-

Exhibit 14-7.

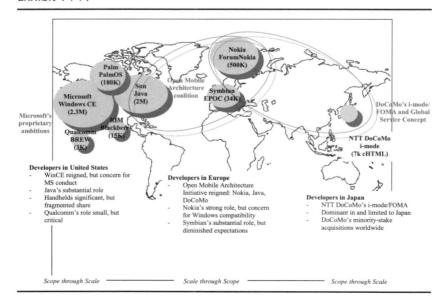

sessed substantial developer communities (including those of Palm, RIM, and others), but these contributed to market fragmentation, and cooperation between Microsoft, Intel, and Compaq challenged their early power. With the BREW development platform, Qualcomm had a small but strategic role. In the past, the R&D maverick had used its manufacturing capabilities to extend and leverage its might in enabling technologies. But after spin-offs, Qualcomm's bargaining power declined significantly. And while competition for the future was often perceived through a Microsoft-Nokia opposition, it was really about strategic coalitions among several industry leaders that represented various core clusters and lead markets.

In this competition, a significant role belonged to NTT DoCoMo, through its 3G pioneership in Japan (from i-mode to FOMA) and the subsequent efforts to translate these benefits into more sustainable advantages. The Japanese operator had a role in the Nokia-led coalition, but it also cooperated with Microsoft and America Online. And while it collaborated with both European-based mobile leaders and U.S.-based IT leaders, it purchased stakes in all central Triad locations and had a significant (but ultimately costly) stake in AT&T in the United States. It was no longer a coalition partner; it could make or break coalitions with its presence or absence. In the long term, Do-CoMo might prove to be a major player in building worldwide developer communities.

In the short term, the rivalry would be between Microsoft and Nokia. These two industry giants both were eager to control more than one horizontal layer in the emerging mobile value chain. In the 1980s, Microsoft and Intel had managed to overthrow IBM's leadership and gather the bulk of the profits in the desktop industry. Now they hoped to replicate their business model in high-end mobile phones. Competitive intensity accelerated by an order of magnitude in late 2001, when Microsoft's CEO Steve Ballmer began overseeing the Mobility Group. As a result, group leaders—vice presidents Juha Christensen and Ben Waldman who led the group—reported to Ballmer. The group was in charge of products, such as the Pocket PC 2002 handheld operating system and the Smartphone 2002 OS. Concurrently, Microsoft targeted about 110 of its 5,000 partner companies, including hardware and software developers, to become part of its new Mobility Partner Advisory Council, which encompassed firms such as Compaq, Hewlett-Packard, SAP, PeopleSoft, Siebel Systems, J. D. Edwards, and Synchrologic. Microsoft's aggressive platform promotion tactics and the accompanying cultivation of relationships with developers have been central to the software giant's success since the 1980s. An OS is only as good as the number of applications and developers that support it. Members of the council were also included in the Microsoft Global Partner Program, which included more than 750,000 developers for other Microsoft products, including Windows XP and Microsoft.Net. Reportedly, the pool of partner companies was growing at a rate of 200 to 300 per month.[49]

In early February 2002, Microsoft launched mobile versions of its MSN

Internet portal in Europe. These were specifically designed for the small color screens of handheld computers. By mid-month, Microsoft and Intel joined forces at a telecom-industry conference in Cannes, France. They were working together to design a "template" for a high-end phone that they intended to license to mobile phone makers. Mimicking the old desktop concept, this template included software from Microsoft and chips from Intel. Seeking to transition from data to voice, it aspired to extend the Wintel duopoly from the old desktop world. The announcement was far more than just a daily corporate news release. In the past, they had tried to push their products to mobile equipment makers, but with limited success. For the first time, they now appeared in public as a team—and talked tough. "A lot of the big manufacturers have approached us. They are looking to get an alternative to Nokia," Waldman commented at the 3GSM World Congress, Europe's largest wireless trade show. With its massive installed base of software on desktop computers, Microsoft hoped to achieve huge benefits from using software that looked the same and worked well together, just as Intel expected similar advantages with its building blocks. "We do not believe in separate sets of standards for the mobile world, such as WAP or picture messaging. Nokia is shortchanging the mobile user when it says there are two Internets, one for PCs and one for cell phones. That's garbage," Waldman said.[50]

However, neither Microsoft nor Intel had the requisite competences to develop a complete cell phone. Even the promised template would not include the radio chip that allowed the cell phone to connect to the network. A phone template that Microsoft had developed with TI included such a chip, as did similar designs by Motorola and Ericsson. The absence of requisite capabilities was not a barrier to full-scale industry entry. With their extraordinary financial resources, both Wintel partners could buy most competences and capabilities they did not already possess. Similarly, they argued that desktop competences provided them an advantage in transforming cell phones into terminals that could run video clips, download Internet pages, and complete other complex tasks. But to make horizontalization work, the two would need vertical industry cooperation.[51]

Microsoft had done its utmost to push MME between 2000 and 2001. It had been in talks with a slate of carriers. Since February 2002, it had been working with several European operators, including mmO2 PLC, Orange, Singapore Telecommunications (SingTel), Telefonica, Telstra, TurkCell, and the powerful Vodafone Group. Through operator deals, the software giant got its MSN brand right on the handset through tie-ins with carriers. But it needed more partnerships, including a foothold in Europe's largest and most lucrative market. On March 13, the software giant announced one of its most wide-ranging mobile deals ever, adding Deutsche Telekom (DT) to its growing list of carrier partners. In Europe, Germany was *the* lead market, just as DT was Europe's largest telecom company. The DT partnership was announced at the start of the CeBIT trade fair in Hanover, Germany. It was *the* Trojan horse

Microsoft required in smart phone segment. The software giant had to crack the higher end of the mobile phone market, which had been dominated by the mobile leaders, in order to participate in the struggle for wireless data services and enterprise customers. DT was the way to do it.

The Collision Course

Betting heavily on the emerging market for smart phones, Waldman aimed to have Microsoft's software on 100 million mobile phones in just three to five years. Translated to existing market shares, that meant almost a 25 percent share from a zero market position. In the past, Microsoft's clout had made most mobile players uneasy. Now Waldman could depict Microsoft's entry as a competitive alternative that would please both top-tier mobile vendors and operators. Vertical coordination contributed to the existence of two parallel systems, but so did Microsoft. The software giant remained the key absentee in the open standards software initiative for mobile phones that Nokia had set up. Challenged by analysts, Nokia agreed that Microsoft should be included in the alliance to ensure interoperability between different mobile phones and the Internet.

It was Symbian's failure to generate compelling software applications that had contributed to Microsoft's increasing efforts to enter the mobile business. Slow to market, Symbian and mobile leaders had not provided a counterweight against Microsoft. So Waldman portrayed it as an OS (and one that had failed). Beyond the Symbian coalition, Nokia was developing its own applications for smart phones. It had to rush. Although it still garnered three fourths of its revenues from handsets, it wanted to evolve into a software giant that could compete against Microsoft. Waldman argued that Nokia's ambitions represented more than a shift in business. He depicted the Finnish vendor as a monopolistic competitor (validated by its vertical posture) that was eager to control several stages of the value chain (software in addition to hardware). Nokia seemed like a rival that was eager to become a wireless Microsoft, a 1980s Apple *déjà vu*. Microsoft would do to Nokia what it had done to Apple—crush it.

As the rivalry intensified between Microsoft and Nokia, the mobile leader struggled to integrate forward into software. Concurrently, the software giant struggled to partner backward into handsets. A year before, Microsoft had announced its partnerships with Samsung, Mitsubishi, and Sendo. They were major industry players, but the software giant still needed deals with first-tier leaders, such as Motorola or Sony Ericsson. In fact, Microsoft's smart phone software was Nokia's dream: an OS with all key applications in one package, including e-mail, messaging, and calendars. As it pursued the wireless, Microsoft sought to standardize the upstream side of the business to accelerate horizontalization. It would sell its software integrated with semiconductors from

Texas Instruments and Intel as ready-to-use technology blocks. This interplay demonstrated the erosion of Nokia's vertical control. TI was the Finnish vendor's key supplier, which was eager to have its cake and eat it, too—that is, to serve both Nokia and Microsoft. This strategic posture worked for horizontalization, but against Nokia's vertical leadership.

An Odd Outcome

Following the high-profile Wintel attack, U.S. and Asian chip players rushed to purchase 2.5G/3G wireless capabilities in Europe. Acquiring the remaining stakes in Germany-based Condat AG, which made GSM and GPRS software, TI joined the game, even as it intensified cooperation with Nokia. The two joined forces to provide handset makers a full range of software and processor technology for smart phones. With other partners, they also formed a company in China to develop software, chips, and 3G wireless devices to put them in. This alignment was coupled by another important development as IBM declared it would challenge Intel head-on, which virtually forced Intel to make more acquisitions to retain its credibility.

While Intel kept hunting for intellectual property rights for the chip, Hewlett-Packard turned to TI for the key chips for the Jornada 928 wireless digital assistant (WDA), its first personal organizer with a built-in phone. These arrangements illustrated, in effect, the early competitive realities of horizontalization. TI supplied the chips, HP manufactured the personal organizer with its first built-in phone, the organizer would rely on Microsoft software, and it would be resold by Orange, the mobile unit of France Telecom. Each layer had its dominant players. Service innovation would ensure the genesis of new industry participants in the 3G era. It would bring together simple voice with rich voice communications, new Internet offerings (e.g., mobile Internet, intranet, and extranet), communications (e.g., multimedia messaging), content (e.g., *The Wall Street Journal* in your pocket), and location-based services (e.g., wireless push promotion as you walk by a retail store). Over time, each horizontal layer would be the site of intense rivalry. According to the age-old laws of innovation dynamics, the number of rivals would proliferate in the emergent phases. With the institution of dominant designs, only the fittest would survive. Ultimately, each of these segments would give rise to up to half a dozen major players, and hundreds of specialist producers.

If horizontalization was the future, it had two implications for Microsoft and Nokia. First, Nokia's vertical coordination was a tactic dictated by competitive circumstances, not a strategy. The idea was to gain time to built appropriate software capabilities that would be comparable to those of Microsoft. Second, Microsoft's horizontalization was the winning industry strategy, but it would not necessarily translate to a Wintel triumph. The mobile world was not a replica of the desktop world in which the bargaining power of Wintel emanated from the control of three horizontal layers. Intel owned chips, while

Microsoft ruled over operating systems and application software. It was a powerful combination. But the wireless Wintel was still more talk than substance. Intel had rapidly built a remarkable presence, but unlike the specialized European producers, it was not a major player in wireless chips. Microsoft had been building its strategic position for longer. It had a role in handhelds and was building one in mobile phones, but it owned neither mobile OS nor software.

No industry player objected to the idea of wireless OS and application software that would be compatible with comparable wired offerings. But many players in both the mobile and the IT camp *did* object to the idea of the Wintel pair controlling the full system of value activities, from contractors to service providers. And if Nokia were to demonstrate Microsoft's inclinations in the wireless space, it would soon be "disciplined," as well. End-to-end solutions required vertical coordination, but not vertical integration or vertical control. In that sense, the future did not belong to Nokia, even if the vendor proved to be a major kingmaker in the new value chain. Marrying mobile capabilities with Internet competences would transform the mobile business into a segment of the worldwide electronics sector. But the more it resembled computing, an industry that is characterized by minimal regulation, dynamic innovation, and intense competition, the less it would resemble telecommunications, an industry that used to be characterized by maximal regulation, static innovation, and no competition. With the convergence of voice and data and the first 4G tests, industry rivalry was bound to accelerate as companies and governments prepared for a broadband competition over first-mover advantages (see Exhibit 14-8).

The future belonged to horizontalization. But it did not necessarily follow that the Wintel pair would succeed in appropriating the benefits of their strategy. They were late. Skimming the cream requires the guests to arrive in time. Microsoft and Intel would have to pay a costly price to ensure strategic leadership. And as the two players had matured, they were not as willing to throw money around as in their more youthful days. They would also have to deal with guests who had not forgotten the Wintel pair's conduct in the previous parties (namely, the PC and Internet revolutions). Hence the odd outcome. On one side was a Finnish vendor that had a losing tactic, but kept improving its position. On the other side, two U.S. vendors had a winning tactic, yet failed to translate it to a dominant position. Perhaps this is what Nokia's chief Jorma Ollila meant when he once said that the mobile "future is all full of question marks and surprises. That's part of the fun in this industry."[52]

Exhibit 14-8. From 2G to 3G: GSM, WCDMA, and broadband: cellular platforms and rate of information.

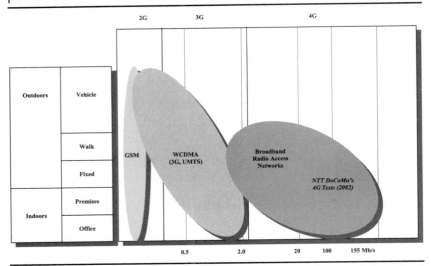

SOURCES: I. N. Kriaras, et al. (2000), ''Third-Generation Mobile Network Architectures for the Universal Mobile Telecommunications System,'' *Bell Labs Technical Journal* (Summer, 1977); D. Steinbock, ''Wireless R&D,'' unpublished manuscript (2002).

Part IV
Epilogue

Chapter 15

Geography, Strategy, and Globalization

Starting with Guglielmo Marconi's experiments with wireless telegraphy, the geography of mobile competition has shifted in several phases from the close of the nineteenth century to the early twenty-first century (see Exhibit 15-1). While the invention of the wireless first emerged in the centers of higher learning in Western Europe, the innovation migrated with Marconi to the United States, which enjoyed singular leadership from the 1920s to the 1990s. During the postwar decades, AT&T was the most powerful and innovative PTT worldwide. American vendors and operators enjoyed the most advanced products, the most efficient operations, and market leadership. This long triumphant era lasted until the early 1990s when—after the eclipse of analog cellular—the United States lost its competitive advantage. The eclipse of the U.S. advantages was self-inflicted, the result of turmoil and delays associated with the breakup of AT&T, public policies, and innovation systems. But it also demonstrated the long-standing effort by rivals to catch up, as innovation drifted to Western Europe, particularly Nordic countries, with the rise of digital cellular.

The third value migration emerged in the late 1990s. This migration—the current one—is different by nature. It does not reflect a shift of a national competitive advantage from one nation to another. Rather, it is more about the deepening of specialization and globalization of these strategic advantages. Because globalization drivers shun geographies and national boundaries, the current migration proceeds according to the dynamic imperatives of clusters and strategies. In Europe, mobile leaders and innovators have struggled to retain leadership amid growing competition, while in Japan, NTT DoCoMo initiated service innovation in next-generation technologies. In the United States, the wired Internet revolution, coupled with the convergence of mobility and the Internet, prompted the entry of the IT leaders into the mobile business. By the spring of 2002, the resurgence of the Wintel duopoly (i.e., Microsoft and Intel), coupled with other new entrants such as America Online, were boosting the resurgence of U.S. competitiveness in the cellular business. Concurrently, high-volume market growth migrated to China, where two decades of foreign direct investment (FDI) by mobile and IT leaders resulted in a

Exhibit 15-1. Value migration.

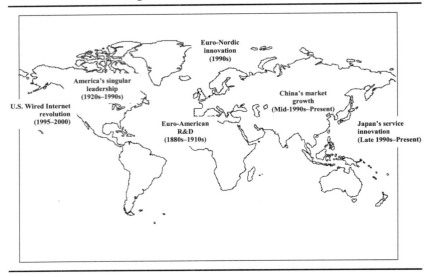

substantial technology infrastructure in the coastal regions' special economic zones (SEZs). Because of the low penetration rate, high-volume expansion was expected to characterize market development in China for years.

For a century, the quest for the wireless horizon has animated evolution in mobile communications. Triangle drivers illustrate the forces that have shaped the value migration of strategic advantages through the eras of monopoly, transition, and most recently, competition (see Exhibit 15-2).

Triangle Drivers:
From Monopoly to Competition

In the wireless industry, the business has been driven not only by a domestic productivity frontier but also by a *globalizing* productivity frontier. Since the days of Marconi, this quest for global leverage has permeated the industry, even if the old public policies kept it suppressed for almost a century. As the triangle drivers have demonstrated, technology innovation has had a critical but not an exclusive role in industry evolution. In the monopoly era, the macro drivers (i.e., the domestic PTTs, their research labs, and old public policies) determined the winners. Geography was destiny and leaders achieved scope through scale. Strategic advantages were national by nature. In the era of dynamic competition, the micro drivers (i.e., globalizing clusters, global R&D networks, and new public policies) make and break the winners, which must

(text continues on page 428)

Exhibit 15-2. Triad Plus leadership.

The Monopoly Era: America's Singular Leadership

United States

☐ AT&T has monopoly power from late 1880s until breakup of 1984. Private-sector monopoly; vertically integrated supply chain. Rise of cellular platforms coincides with turmoil caused by changing public policies.

☐ From 1930s to AT&T breakup, U.S. industry leadership rests on mobile innovation at Bell Labs (later at Motorola and other vendors as well). Reign of insular "Big Science." Innovation takes place within firms.

☐ Regulation ensures AT&T's monopoly until the "land-mobile crisis" of 1968, while broadcast and defense interests dictate spectrum policies. Rise of independent operators (RCCs); breakup of the supply chain (1956); mistaken mobile policies (roaming, CPP, and licensing).

1880s - 1984

Western Europe

☐ National PTTs rule from the 1880s to the 1980s. Public-sector monopoly, though some Nordic countries favor competitive local telcos. In large European countries, vertically integrated supply chain; in Nordic countries, vendors more competitive. Rise of cellular platforms coincides with deregulation and European integration.

☐ Starting in the 1970s, Nordic innovation promotes open and market-driven specifications. Innovation takes place within firms and in public and private research centers.

☐ PTT monopoly until EC directives in the late 1980s. Broadcasting is regulated, defense interests minimal; spectrum policies dictated by commercial interests and public mission. Large-country PTTs favor closed specifications, Nordic players advocate market-driven mobile policies. Nordic vendors first to internationalize.

E 1870s - 1981/98   N 1870s - 1987

Japan

☐ NTT's public monopoly from 1880s to 1985. Vertically integrated supply chain but cooperative supply-chain arrangements (exclusive family of suppliers).

☐ Japanese mobile innovation at NTT's highly centralized research labs and in the supply chain. In the 1970s, catch-up with U.S. innovation; emphasis on research.

☐ Regulation ensures NTT's monopoly until 1985. Broadcasting is regulated, defense interests are minimal; spectrum policies dictated by public mission. NTT favors roaming, pricing CPP and licensing policies crafted for domestic market. NTT pioneers proprietary standards for analog cellular. It is forbidden to internationalize.

1877 – 1985

China

☐ Until 1979, national PTT is subject to absolute rule of the Communist Party. A new, but cautious era begins with the economic reforms of 1979.

☐ Level of mobile innovation low until the arrival of first U.S. and European vendors in the 1980s. Mobile innovation takes place within the national PTT, and a handful of multinational vendors. Policymakers hope joint ventures will cultivate an indigenous base of suppliers.

☐ Tight monopoly arrangements until mid-1990s. Broadcasting tightly regulated, spectrum policies dictated by the military. At first, roaming and pricing (CPP) policies confined to most prosperous cities and SEZs. Coordination of national licensing policies in 1995. At first, TDMA-based standards; with Nordic vendors, GSM becomes the choice of policymakers.

1980s–mid-1990s

(continues)

Exhibit 15-2. (Continued).

The Transition Era: Euro-Nordic Pioneership

United States

- Between 1984 and 1996, transition to competition; vertically disintegrated value system. Triumph of 1G coincides with privatization, but rests on pre-1984 developments; CDMA overthrows consensus on a unified standard.

- Turmoil of Bell Labs in the post-breakup era, stabilization in early 1990s. Leadership in mobile innovation migrates to Motorola and other vendors. Rise of market-driven, decentralized and international R&D. Innovation takes place within firms, as well as public/private partnerships, tech coalitions, and academia-industry alliances.

- Deregulation over regulation; in spectrum policies, role of defense interests and broadcast lobby declines. Breakup of AT&T; accelerating competition. Analog cellular suppresses roaming; CPP is not overthrown; licensing struggles continue.

1984 – 1996

Western Europe

- Between 1981 (UK) and 1998, privatization of Euro PTTs promotes competition and deregulation. Vertically disintegrated value system; fewer new challengers and start-ups than in U.S. Rise of 2G coincides with deregulation and privatization; EC's decision to make GSM mandatory; CDMA fails to penetrate Euro fortress.

- Turmoil of PTT labs less tumultuous than in U.S. Leadership in mobile innovation migrates to Nordic countries, whose R&D starts in the 1990s as domestic and centralized. Innovation takes place within firms, and through public/private partnerships, tech coalitions, and academia-industry alliances.

- Deregulation reigns over regulation; in spectrum policies, the role of financial interests increases. Triumph of GSM boosts telecom reforms. EC directives nurture the growth of a new generation of international operators (Vodafone); large-country vendors emulate the best practices of Nordic vendors.

E Late 1980s – 1998   N 1981 – 1995

Japan

- NTT's privatization in 1985; incorporation of NTT DoCoMo in 1992. Vertically disintegrated value system; new industry players proliferate, but NTT controls industry evolution. Standard for digital era remains proprietary. Starting with Motorola, overseas players begin to seek market access.

- Principles of mobile innovation do not change. Vendors diversify to internationalize. R&D still domestic and centralized. Despite its digital pioneership, NTT does not exploit its tech edge via commercialization. Innovation takes place within firms, even if international activities accelerate.

- Deregulation accelerates; spectrum policies subject to public mission. Policies still crafted for domestic market; internationalization discouraged; closed specifications.

1985 – 1991

China

- Starting in the mid-1990s, breakup and new ownership arrangements with China Telecom. Vertical disintegration initiated; new industry players emerge; regulators control developments. Adoption of GSM. Acceleration of FDI by foreign vendors, which consolidate infrastructure and handsets markets; services highly fragmented.

- Through mobile vendors' FDI, diffusion spills over into indigenous suppliers and contractors. Innovation takes place within firms, but Chinese authorities participate increasingly in international activities.

- As the role of MPT lessens, that of Ministry of Information industry (MII) increases. Deregulation; spectrum policies dictated by military, but commercial considerations grow. Roaming, pricing, and licensing policies remain crafted for domestic market. CDMA enters China as an alternative standard. Internationalization remains low.

1995 – 2001

The Competitive Era: Triad Plus Leadership

United States

☐ Due to standards issues and domestic focus, U.S. operators internationalize slowly; overseas operators' FDI grows in the U.S.; Motorola loses leadership in the 2G transition. Convergence developments prompt the entry of IT leaders into the mobile. CDMA becomes the core of the 3G standard.

☐ Market-driven innovation proliferates. Leadership in innovation splits between the European mobile leaders and U.S. IT leaders. Mobile innovation increasingly externalized, vis-à-vis tech coalitions.

☐ Deregulation; the role of defense interests continues to constrain spectrum allocations. FCC promotes and DOJ permits increasing consolidation (which compensates for appropriate policies in roaming, CPP, licensing). Clinton and Bush administrations' efforts to promote 3G transition.

1996 – Present

Western Europe

☐ Due to GSM triumph, Euro operators and vendors best positioned for 3G era, but not as well prepared for mobile Internet (early WAP debacle). A defensive posture against the entry of U.S. IT leaders. With CDMA as core of 3G, Euro players retain competitive lead, not technology edge.

☐ Market-driven innovation proliferates through the sector; leads to globally networked innovation among the leading Nordic players. Innovation becomes increasingly externalized, vis-à-vis tech coalitions.

☐ Deregulation sweeps through mobile markets; inflated financial stakes in spectrum allocations lead to industry slowdown. Slowdown promotes increasing consolidation, at terms of the large-country players. Importance of EC regulators declines, while that of EC competition policy authorities increases.

E 1998 – Present   N 1995 - Present

Japan

☐ After NTT's incorporation, new leadership opts for new managerial approaches. Deregulation intensifies competition. DoCoMo becomes best positioned for mobile Internet. Efforts to leapfrog into 4G.

☐ DoCoMo's new leadership focuses on marketing- rather than technology-driven innovation; emphasis on low prices, high quality, large volumes; buys of minority stakes in Triad locations. Efforts at a "global service" strategy.

☐ Deregulation; spectrum allocations become subject to commercial considerations; no license taxes, no industry slowdown. Through W-CDMA, open specifications arrive in Japanese market, while new public policies permit increasing FDI by foreign players. DoCoMo and other players driven by new public policies; internationalization. NTT tries to capture corporate control at DoCoMo.

1991 – Present

China

☐ China's subscriber base becomes the largest worldwide (July 2001). Competition accelerates among old and new operators. China's vendors capture 10% of the market. GSM dominates China's path to 3G, while challengers opt for CDMA.

☐ Trading technology for access, vendors build upon the Chinese mobile industry, which accelerates diffusion. New R&D centers, networks and science parks proliferate. First price wars reflect tests with managerial innovation. R&D increases in Chinese suppliers which begin internationalization.

☐ Deregulation intensifies competition; spectrum allocations become subject to commercial considerations. Increasing FDI and new public policies results in progressive decline of centralization.

2001 – Present

E = European large-country operations
N = Nordic small-country operations

excel in products, operations, and market leadership. Business is destiny and leaders increasingly achieve scale through scope. Strategic advantages are globalizing by nature.

The Monopoly Era

At its peak, America's leadership in the wireless business covered the entire value system, which initially coincided with AT&T's value chain. This leadership extended from public policy (first the FRC then the FCC, as well as the antitrust division of the Department of Justice) and industry (AT&T, RCCs, and vendors such as Western Electric and Motorola) to innovation (Bell Labs, Motorola, GE) and markets (MTS in 1946, IMTS in 1964, and AMPS in 1983). But in each case, there were countervailing forces as well. In public policy, the objectives of the federal regulators and the DOJ's antitrust division did not work in parallel, but often conflicted. This was inevitable. The federal regulators promoted equity (which justified the perceived need for natural monopoly), while the concern of the DOJ was efficiency (which justified the promotion of competition). As long as regulators reigned over antitrust authorities, the monopoly system remained intact. When the roles were reversed, the monopoly system fell apart. These tensions were defused with consent decrees (in 1913 and 1956), but ultimately undid the Bell System (1984). In other developed Triad markets, effective competition policy, as well as the U.S.-style conflicts between regulators and competition policy authorities evolved only later—with the 2G transition.

The timeline marks the key shifts with innovation as well. Bell Labs was created in 1911, in part to deter antitrust investigations. Research on the wireless stayed within the walls of AT&T's R&D arm, which produced the breakthrough cellular concept in 1947. By demonstrating its superiority in cellular technology, Bell Labs' open publication policy was designed to keep potential challengers at a distance. The tactic was justified by its domestic focus; domestic players were regarded as primary potential attackers. By the same token, it increased the diffusion of wireless core competences worldwide, especially in a handful of advanced telecom markets. Broadly speaking, the early movers—Nordic countries and Japan—were best positioned to catch up, even though there were substantial differences between large- and small-country players in Asia and Western Europe. Until the economic reforms of the 1980s and the arrival of massive FDI flows, China was far behind the learning curve in the wireless business—but the investments by the mobile leaders were initiated soon thereafter.

In addition to the postwar catch-up effort and the diffusion of mobile R&D, America's leadership suffered from two constraints that did not pose comparable obstacles to Japanese and Euro-Nordic players—namely, flaws in regulatory policies and limited spectrum allocations.

In the United States, flaws in regulatory policies (including roaming, CPP, and licensing) served as a self-inflicted wound to the nation's wireless developments. To some extent, these issues could be traced back to the conflicts between regulators and competition policy authorities. Take, for instance, roaming. The idea of intercountry roaming came about naturally in northern Europe, where Nordic countries, with their similar cultures, promoted open exchange of capital, products and services, and ideas. In contrast, roaming proved an extraordinary policy challenge in the United States. Though technically realizable, it conflicted with long-standing public policies to avoid the centralization of power. Eventually, consolidation followed, but only after regulatory delays had deteriorated the nation's international competitiveness in the wireless industry, similar drivers have caused comparable reviews of past policies.

America's wireless leadership has also suffered from long-standing spectrum issues. Unlike broadcasting in Western Europe and Japan, American broadcasters have not been heavily regulated and broadcast interests have dominated large chunks of spectrum. The success of U.S. networks has contributed to scarcity in the U.S. spectrum policy, as far as mobile interests are concerned. Also, America's military interests have played a substantial role in the nation's spectrum policy. These constraints have been almost nonexistent in Western Europe and Japan. Only in China did the military play a greater role in spectrum policy until the 1990s, but with progressive liberalization, this influence, too, has rapidly faded into history. In contrast to other Triad regions, the U.S. contributions to the Cold War and, more recently, the war against terrorism have consumed substantial resources to ensure the security needs of the "world's only remaining superpower." For decades, these interests have limited the uses of spectrum policy, just as they have steered R&D allocations for noncivilian purposes. Neither Western Europe nor Japan has suffered from similar self-imposed duties.

Coupled with the postwar catch-up of Nordic countries and Japan, these drivers—diffusion of mobile R&D, flaws in regulatory policies, and limited spectrum allocations—all contributed to the erosion of U.S. wireless leadership after the early analog cellular era. Building on indigenous industry developments and the increasing diffusion of knowledge, Japanese and Nordic operators and vendors caught up with U.S. developments by the late 1970s. Even though Japan's NTT was the first carrier to launch an analog system in 1979, the Nordic players achieved penetration far more quickly and extensively. Unlike NTT, with its proprietary standard, the Nordic counterpart (NMT) was based on open specifications. Whereas Nordic PTTs favored competitive and internationally oriented vendors, NTT's family of suppliers was more cooperative by nature, just as the entire value system was domestic, like those of the inefficient large-country PTTs in Western Europe. As a result, NTT failed to translate its pioneership into more sustainable advantages in the analog cellular.

The Transition Era

In Western Europe, the country markets that were the first to implement new telecom policies (i.e., liberalization, privatization, and deregulation) went through a great transition in the late 1980s and early 1990s. These players were primarily in the U.K. and the Nordic countries. For many late movers (primarily large-country PTTs), developments took longer, ending only around 1998, which was the EC deadline for telecom reforms. While privatization reinforced vertical disintegration, new challengers were fewer in Western Europe than in the United States. The rise of the digital cellular standard coincided with new public policies but rested on the EC decision to promote competition while making GSM mandatory in Europe. These directives exploited wireless technology to crack down on the old European monopoly PTTs, even as they unified the fragmented market. This development path was based on U.S. lessons (i.e., America's unitary AMPS standard), but employed different instruments to bring about change (i.e., using mandatory standards to make markets rather than innovation-driven markets to make standards). Not only was the Euro-Nordic transition less tumultuous than the one in the United States, it relied more on externalized R&D. Because there was no singular AT&T-like entity, but a variety of different national PTTs, wireless innovation had been more fragmented to start with. Also, there was far more cooperation through public-private partnerships, technology coalitions, and academia-industry alliances. Whereas Nordic vendors captured leadership in equipment manufacturing, the internationalization of operators took longer, given the nature of the downstream business as well as strategic opposition by the former national PTTs.

In contrast to industry wisdom, Nordic countries did not succeed in Europe's analog cellular because they were among the first pioneering the market, but because, additionally, they developed the market with open specifications and internationally-oriented strategies. Unlike AT&T and European PTTs, they sought scale via scope, not scope via scale.

In the United States, the transition ended almost a century-long calm in the telecom industry. With the breakup of the Bell System, AT&T focused on long-distance service, equipment, and computing businesses while retaining most of the old Bell Labs. In the wireless business, the divestiture meant an entirely new era because wireless operations now shifted from AT&T to the Baby Bells (who received part of Bell Labs and rolled it into their Bellcore R&D unit). Meanwhile, the successors of the radio common carriers (RCCs) and new start-ups struggled to survive the counterattacks by these regional giants. To make matters worse, the demise of the Bell System also meant the eclipse of the old Bell Labs system. Restructuring and reorganization paralyzed Bell innovation in the late 1980s, a critical moment in history that shaped the digital transition and witnessed the fertile cooperation between the EC and the Euro-Nordic mobile leaders. And if things were not chaotic enough, Qualcomm developed its new CDMA standard, which contributed to market fragmentation. While old regulatory policies continued to suppress growth, industry consolidation allowed the business to reconcentrate what the Federal Communications Commission had refragmented in the 1980s—by rejecting national licenses and more efficient roaming solutions, and by disenabling high-volume penetration strategies that could have led to low-cost tariffs.

In Japan, NTT had introduced analog cellular well before Euro-Nordic pioneers and was among the first movers in digital cellular. But the privatization of NTT did not promote competition as quickly or as extensively as the breakup of AT&T did in the United States or the development of GSM in Europe. New industry players proliferated, and NTT's market share declined. Foreign players, including Motorola, struggled to access the Japanese market. Meanwhile, NTT launched a proprietary digital standard that confined the potential scale to the national market. The national monopoly and its exclusive club of suppliers reigned over wireless innovation, which remained domestic by nature. NTT did not and could not internationalize. The true transition in Japan began only with the incorporation of NTT DoCoMo in 1992, which resulted in new strategic objectives. Under the leadership of Kouji Ohboshi, managerial practices were practically reversed. That contributed to the market explosion in the latter half of the 1990s.

In China, market evolution remained far behind these industry leaders, but a decade of FDI flows in exchange for access to the world's most important future marketplace soon generated results. By the mid-1990s, government policymakers split up the old national PTT, China Telecom, which also gave rise to regulators (i.e., the Ministry of Information Industry). With vertical disintegration, the bargaining power of the Ministry of Posts and Telecommunications (MPT) lessened and new players surfaced. As long as American players dominated the landscape, the Chinese operators had embraced standards developed in the United States. But after the Tiananmen events, Euro-Nordic players seized the opportunity to expand their presence in China. By the mid-1990s, Chinese policymakers and regulators opted for GSM as the *de facto* national standard. Qualcomm did manage to open doors for its CDMA technology in China, but the role of this alternative standard did not increase until the 3G era. While the military continued to control spectrum policy, regulatory policies emulated the Euro-Nordic solutions.

The Competitive Era

Under Kouji Ohboshi, NTT's DoCoMo thrived in deregulation. Instead of NTT's high tariffs and low volumes, Ohboshi implemented low tariffs and high volumes. While deregulation intensified competition, DoCoMo's market share increased and the operator became best positioned for the mobile Internet opportunity. Unlike Euro-Nordic leaders, the Japanese operator saw the wireless and the Internet as complementary sides of a unitary vision. By the end of the 1990s, it began to push its i-mode service internationally by purchasing minority stakes in the Triad core clusters and lead markets. Unlike the Euro-Nordic players that sought to prolong their lead in the 3G era, DoCoMo was inclined to treat multimedia cellular as a transitional stage. It pushed for the 4G era. The ultimate objective was to establish pioneership and sustainable strategic advantages. Unlike the Euro-Nordic countries, Japanese policymakers and regulators supported these aspirations by not resorting to license taxes and thereby avoiding the industry slowdown that suppressed advancements in Europe around 2000 and 2001. Through W-CDMA, open specifications arrived in the Japanese market, while new public policies allowed for increasing FDI by foreign players. Policymakers and regulators proved less successful in the issue of corporate control—a potentially destructive struggle for governance that divided NTT and DoCoMo amid the 3G transition.

Digitalization arrived very late in the United States, where AT&T's new pricing policy in 1998 had provided a powerful boost in the marketplace. These developments followed those in the leading Euro-Nordic country markets by some four years. At the turn of the 1990s, the Baby Bells had been the pioneers of internationalization worldwide, but the lucrative home base and late arrival of digitalization suppressed the globalization of U.S.-based operators amid the 3G transition. Still, there were positive signs. Qualcomm's CDMA technology had been made the core of the multimedia standard. Even more important, the convergence of mobility and the Internet resulted in the entry of America's powerful software, electronics, and online service giants in the wireless business. As the single flexible standard began to mitigate the old technology-based advantages (i.e., the GSM strengths), the market-oriented strategies of U.S. vendors, operators, and particularly IT leaders demonstrated great potential in the 3G space. Yet the relics of the old public policies continued to haunt all innovative efforts to increase the strengths of the U.S. mobile cluster and innovation. Efforts at public-private partnerships underscored a new spirit of cooperation rather than adversity, to avoid past regulatory stalemates. Despite seemingly irreconcilable differences, industry and military views on the spectrum and wireless security were perhaps not that far apart at all. Most important, the renewed cooperation between Microsoft and Intel signaled a resurgence of U.S. strength in the cellular arena—while providing strategic nightmare scenarios to the Euro-Nordic mobile leaders.

In Western Europe, vendors and operators were best positioned in the GSM path to migrate to multimedia cellular. Some of this lead was lost with misguided efforts to sell new technologies rather than new service propositions (e.g., the early WAP debacle). At the end of the 1990s, Euro-Nordic players seemed to enjoy absolute and relative superiority in the business, thanks to what many termed the "twin drivers of mobility and the Internet." By 2002— with the consolidation in the U.S. technology sector and the 3G birth pains in

Europe—this superiority had eroded rapidly, and the twin tornado looked more like a double whammy. Now Euro-Nordic leaders found themselves eyeing suspiciously to the right and left. In one direction, there were the U.S.-based IT leaders eager to capture sizable chunks of worldwide markets. In the other direction was NTT DoCoMo, which had sold multimedia cellular by pushing services rather than technologies and was now eager to "transitionalize" the 3G era. As market-driven innovation swept through the sector, technology development was no longer internal but external involving technology coalitions, venture capital and corporate innovation, and global R&D networks. In the short term, that system worked for the Euro-Nordic leaders, which were more familiar with cooperation than American-style competition. In the longer term, these mobile leaders would find out that externalizing strengths reduced their impact, just as it was bound to result in the diffusion of competences and capabilities. In the 1950s and 1960s, the old Bell Labs had diffused its technology leadership with an open publication policy; now European operators and vendors were promoting diffusion through networking. What made perfect sense in the short term amounted to digging one's grave in the long term. And as license taxes contributed to the industry slowdown in 2000 and 2001, old first-mover advantages rapidly dissipated as well.

In China, industry expansion took off soon after 1995, but penetration remained at a single-digit level even in 2002. As competition picked up among old and new operators, China's subscriber base became the largest worldwide in July 2001. Concurrently, indigenous suppliers captured 10 percent of the marketplace (which foreign vendors had consolidated) while engaging in internationalization strategies of their own. Meanwhile, the composition of service revenues indicated that the Chinese market remained highly fragmented. GSM dominated China, but CDMA was used by old challengers and new attackers alike to nibble market shares via low-tariff strategies. Having traded technology for access, the world's largest mobile vendors practically built China's wireless innovation base between 1979 and 2001. As deregulation intensified competition, spectrum allocations shifted from the military to more commercial interests. Concurrently, rapidly rising FDI and new public policies contributed to the decline of centralization in the industry. The result was the world's largest subscriber base, but one that had barely penetrated one-tenth of the population.

Core Clusters

This triangle dynamics illuminates the past century in the wireless industry. The monopoly stage emerged with Marconi, and the pre-cellular era lasted until the early 1G era. In this era, the national PTT enjoyed a natural monopoly in telecom services in most country markets. Public policies guided industry developments, which were restricted to domestic markets. In the next stage, the national PTT lost its natural monopoly in most markets. During this great transition, regulators were isolated from national PTTs, which were privatized. As liberalization resulted in deregulation, public policies and firm strategies guided industry developments and domestic competition turned international, first by vendors and later by operators and other industry players. In the most advanced country markets, the competitive stage emerged at the end of the 2G era in the late 1990s. With this third stage, strategies began to guide industry developments, which were expanded and leveraged worldwide (see Exhibit 15-3).

After the "booming nineties," Nokia had its share of direct rivals, such as Ericsson and Motorola. Furthermore, the rankings among the second- and third-tier players were rapidly changing as even major players outsourced their manufacturing capabilities to Asia-Pacific countries. These mobile competitors shared the Finnish vendor's vision, but had a will and determination of their own. Indirect rivals, particularly the IT leaders, such as Microsoft, Intel, and America Online, had a comparable will and determination but a very different vision. Whereas the first group of firms was transitioning from voice to data, the second strategic group was migrating from data to voice. In the past, mobile leaders had been the industry innovators. But as value migrated from hardware to software, this role was changing. With the new industry thrust, the IT leaders argued that *they* had the appropriate roadmap for the industry. It would not be based on vertical coordination but horizontalization. The past bespoke for the mobile leaders; the future worked for the IT leaders; both would engage in opportunistic strategies through the 3G transition. Finally, new and sophisticated challengers were emerging in Europe, the United States, and Asia-Pacific. As Japan's NTT DoCoMo questioned the validity of old strategic approaches, South Korean players inspired bold start-ups across Asia. Concurrently, the cost-advantage strategies of China's emerging suppliers promised to shift the productivity frontier drastically in the mobile business and the technology sector at large. Like the Japanese challengers in the 1970s and 1980s, Chinese companies would reconfigure value chains and redefine cost advantages worldwide, across numerous industries—including wireless communications.

In the past, vendors and operators competed through gradual globalization. Today, most players are forced to globalize in order to compete, except for the downstream end of the value chain. New "born global" strategies promise great opportunities; but the dynamics of innovation, and the increasingly high entry barriers, virtually ensure that most new startups and challengers will be absorbed by the industry leaders.

According to Jagdish Bhagwati, a prominent proponent of the trade, "capitalism is a system that, paradoxically, can destroy privilege and open up economic

Exhibit 15-3. Industry value system: evolution and specialization.

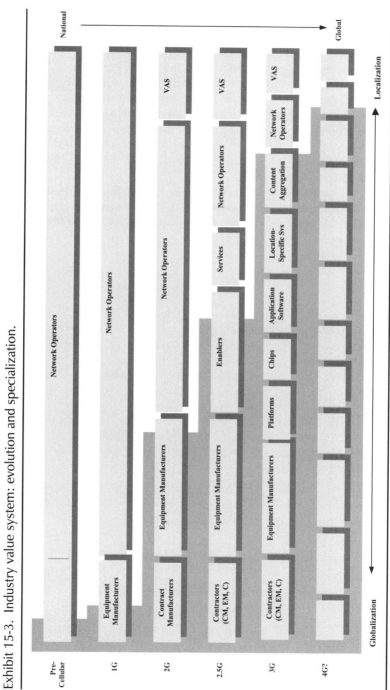

opportunity to many—but this fact is lost on most of the system's vocal critics."[1] A century of mobile evolution, especially the last decades of this history, certainly lends abundant evidence to such statements. Far from being an external manifestation of internal struggles that doom capitalism, globalization has been boosted by an internal logic of competition occurring in geographies that vitalize capitalism. Hardly identical with capitalist exploitation of weak nations, globalization actually allows smaller nations to participate in the global chessboard through focus and scope. It was the quest for global leverage by the small-country players that transformed the mobile industry, just as it was their ability to achieve scale through scope that mitigated the monopolistic benefits of the large-country players.

What a century of wireless evolution and its future prospects demonstrate is that capitalism can destroy privilege and provide economic opportunity to many—but only as long as that system is open, accessible, transparent, and potentially global.

Glossary

1G First-generation systems, which are analog and were designed for voice communications.

2G Second-generation systems, which are digital and capable of providing voice/data/fax transfer as well as a range of other value-added services, including SMS.

2.5G Evolving second-generation systems that are intermediary options before the introduction of multimedia cellular.

3G Third-generation systems, which enable multimedia and are standardized under 3GPP.

3G harmonization Harmonizing of UTRA and CDMA2000 (3G in the United States).

3GPP Third-Generation Partnership Protocol

4G Fourth-generation systems. In early 2001, Alcatel, Ericsson, Motorola, Nokia, and Siemens founded the Wireless World Research Forum (WWRF), whose "vision of the wireless world" was identified as that of 4G systems.

AM Amplitude modulation.

AMPS Advanced Mobile Phone System.

Analog Transmission of voice and images using electrical signals.

ARIB Association of Radio Industries and Businesses in Japan.

ARPU Average Revenue Per User.

ASIC Application-Specific Integrated Circuit.

ATM Asynchronous Transfer Mode.

AXE Ericsson's open-architecture system for computer-controlled digital exchanges that constitute the nodes in large public telecom networks.

Bandwidth Measure of the carrying capacity or size of a communication channel. In analog systems, bandwidth is measured in terms of hertz (Hz) and in digital systems in bits per second (bps).

Base station A radio transmitter/receiver and antenna used in the mobile cellular network.

Bluetooth   Short-range radio technology that expands wireless connectivity to personal and business mobile devices.

BREW   Binary Runtime Environment for Wireless. This Qualcomm development platform was designed to speed and simplify the development of new applications.

Broadband   Also called wideband. High-bandwidth channels are referred to as broadband, which typically signifies data rates of 1.5 or 2.0 Mbps or higher.

CDMA   Code Division Multiple Access. A technology for digital transmission of radio signals based on spread spectrum techniques.

cdmaOne/IS-95   A digital cellular standard, which applies CDMA to realize large volume traffic and enables numerous users to access a limited bandwidth.

CDMA2000   A radio transmission technology for the evolution of narrowband cdmaOne/IS-95 to 3G. It is an approved 3G standard.

CDMA2000 1X   A 3G technology that provides voice and data capabilities within a standard 1.25 MHz CDMA channel for spectral efficiency and flexibility. Doubles the voice capacity of cdmaOne systems and also supports high-speed data services.

CDMA2000 1xEV-DO   An evolution of CDMA2000, this "data optimized" version is also an approved 3G standard providing peak data rates of up 2.4 Mbps in a standard 1.25 MHz CDMA channel for fixed, portable, and mobile applications.

Cell   The geographic area covered by a single base station in a cellular mobile network.

Cellular   A mobile telephone service provided by a network of base stations, each of which covers one geographic cell within the total cellular system service area.

Cellular Mobile Telephone System   A system where each geographic area is covered by a base station (i.e., a cell).

CEM   Contract Electronics Manufacturing. *See also* EMS.

Channel   One of a number of discrete frequency ranges used by a base station to transmit and receive information from cellular terminals (such as mobile handsets).

Churn   Turnover in the number of subscribers to a network, typically measured monthly.

Circuit   A number of electrical elements and devices that have been interconnected to perform a desired electrical function.

Circuit-switched service   A data transfer communication service that applies circuit-switching for each call, to establish a circuit with the other party, and then disconnects that circuit upon call completion. Standard telephone service is based on circuit switching.

CM Contract Manufacturer. Also Contract Manufacturing. *See* EMS.

CMRS Commercial Mobile Radio Services. A U.S. definition of competitive voice- and data communications industries. The FCC releases annual reports on the state of CMRS competition in the United States.

Component An individual part or combination of parts that, when together, perform a design function or functions.

Continuous improvement The ongoing improvement of products, services, or processes through incremental and breakthrough improvements.

Core competences Those activities that a company believes it does best, should focus on, and are in its best interest for long-term success and growth.

Coverage The range of a mobile cellular network, measured in terms of geographic coverage (i.e., percent of the territorial area covered by a mobile cellular network) or population coverage (i.e., percent of the population within range of a mobile cellular network).

CPP Calling Party Pays. Billing option whereby the person making the call is charged.

CTIA The Cellular Telecommunications and Internet Association. An international U.S.-based organization that represents all elements of wireless communication.

CT1 Cordless Telephony Generation 1. Popular in Europe.

CT2. Cordless Telephony Generation 2. CT1 for digital age, primarily in UK.

D-AMPS Digital Advanced Mobile Phone System. *See* TDMA and TDMA/IS-136.

DCS-1800 GSM networks using the 1800 MHz frequency.

DECT Digital Enhanced Cordless Telecommunications. A standard for cordless telephony originally established by the ETSI.

Digital Representation of voice or other information using digits 0 and 1. Digital cellular networks (e.g., GSM, CDMA, and TDMA) allow for higher capacity, greater functionality, and improved quality.

Digital cash Generic term for new types of electronic currency being used over the Internet.

Dual band Mobile phones that can work on networks that operate on different frequency bands.

Dual mode Handsets that can work with more than one standard and/or at more than one frequency. Also called trimode or multimode.

Duplex   Mode of operation permitting the simultaneous transmission and reception of signals.

E-commerce   Electronic commerce. A broad definition of the new phenomenon of remote commercial transactions using telecommunications and the Internet.

EDGE   Enhanced Data rates for GSM Evolution. An alternative route for GSM operators who will not have 3G licenses.

EMS   Electronics Manufacturing Services. The production of electronic equipment on behalf of an original equipment manufacturer (OEM), in which the design and brand name belong to the OEM. *See also* CEM and CM.

End-product   An individual part or assembly in its final completed state.

EPOC   An operating system that turns voice-oriented handsets into media phones and wireless information devices. EPOC has been developed by Symbian.

Equity-based subscribers   *See* proportionate subscribers.

ETSI   European Telecommunications Standards Institute

Exchange   *See* switch.

FCC   Federal Communications Commission. Regulatory body governing communications technologies in the United States.

FDMA   Frequency Division Multiple Access. A cellular technology that has been used in 1G analog systems.

Fixed line   A physical line connecting the subscriber to the telephone exchange. Typically, a fixed-line network refers to the PSTN to distinguish it from mobile networks.

FM   A modulation technique in which the carrier frequency is shifted by an amount proportional to the value of the modulating signal.

Footprint   The total geographic area in which a wireless provider offers service or is licensed to offer service.

Frequency   The rate at which an electrical current alternates, usually measured in hertz (Hz). Also used to refer to a location on the radio frequency spectrum (e.g., 800, 900, or 1800 MHz).

Frequency hopping   A spread spectrum approach where both units (the base and subscriber or handset and base) hop from frequency to frequency in a simultaneous fashion.

Frequency reuse   The ability to use the same frequencies repeatedly across a cellular system. A key concept that enables a cellular system to handle a large amount of calls with a limited number of channels.

GPRS   General Packet Radio Service. An enhancement for GSM, GPRS provides packet-switched data primarily for GSM-based 2G networks.

GPS   Global Positioning System.

GSM   Global System for Mobile Communications. European-developed digital mobile cellular standard.

GSM 1800   GSM-based cellular system operating in the 1800 MHz frequency band (also referred to as PCN or PCN 1800 or DCS-1800).

GSM 900   Digital cellular network operating in the 900 MHz frequency band.

GSM 1900   GSM-based cellular system operating in the 1900 MHz frequency band (also referred to as PCS 1900 and DCS-1900).

H.323   A protocol for the transmission of real-time audio, video, and data information over packet switching–based networks.

Hand-off   In cellular communications, a telephone call is switched by computers from one transmitter to the next, without disconnecting the signal, as a vehicle moves from cell to cell.

HDML   Handheld Devices Markup Language. Now called the Wireless Markup Language (WML), it allows portions of HTML websites to be presented on cellular mobile phones and personal digital assistants (PDAs) via wireless access.

HDR   High Data Rate. A cost-effective, high-speed, high-capacity wireless technology developed by Qualcomm.

HSCSD   High Speed Circuit Switched Data. An intermediary upgrade technology for GSM based on circuit-switched technology.

HTML   Hypertext Markup Language. A script language used to describe the text content and format of a web page.

Hz   Hertz. The frequency measurement unit equal to one cycle per second.

IC   Integrated Circuit.

ICT   Information and Communication Technology.

iDEN   Integrated Digital Enhanced Networks. A Motorola 2G technology.

IEEE   Institute of Electrical and Electronics Engineers.

i-mode   A wireless service launched in Japan in spring 1999 by NTT DoCoMo. The service is accessed by a wireless packet network and the contents are described in a subset of the HTML language.

IMT-2000   International Mobile Telecommunications. IMT-2000 is the successor to the ITU's original concept of a single global 3G technology, known previously as the Future Public Land Mobile Telecommunications System (FPLMTS).

IMTS   Improved Mobile Telephone Services. An enhanced version of MTS. Pioneered by AT&T in the United States in 1964.

Interconnection   The physical connection of telephone networks owned by two different operators.

Internet   The collection of interconnected networks that use the Internet Protocol.

IP   Internet Protocol. A communication protocol commonly used by communication hardware comprising the Internet.

IPR   Intellectual Property Rights.

Iridium   Prior to its bankruptcy, the Motorola-led Iridium consortium comprised a constellation of sixty-six low-earth-orbiting (LEO) satellites. Iridium Satellite purchased the $5 billion communications system for $25 million.

ISDN   Integrated Services Digital Network.

ISO   International Standards Organization.

ISP   Internet Service Provider.

ITU   International Telecommunication Union.

Java   A computer programming language developed by Sun Microsystems that embodies many newer software development productivity and security features, such as object-oriented design and reuse.

M&A   Mergers and acquisitions.

MC-CDMA   Multi-Carrier Code Division Multiple Access. Typically, the combination of three IS-95 carriers to form one wideband carrier.

M-commerce   *See* mobile e-commerce.

MMS   Multimedia Messaging Service. A new standard for use in advanced wireless terminals for sending messages with text, photos, sounds, and/or video. The service concept is derived from SMS.

Mobile   A shorthand for mobile cellular systems.

Mobile e-commerce   A hybrid of e-commerce, mobile e-commerce is the ability to conduct monetary transactions via a mobile device, such as a WAP-enabled cell phone.

Mobile portal   A mobile destination site for accessing services from a mobile phone.

MTS   Mobile Telephone Service. First consumer mobile services. Pioneered by AT&T in the United States in 1946.

Modem   Abbreviation for modulator/demodulator. The modem converts digital computer signals into analog form for transmission over analog telephone systems.

NMIT Nokia Mobile Internet Technical Architecture. It is Nokia's global initiative that aims to provide seamless interoperability among any interaction modes, network environments, and types of access.

NMT Nordic Mobile Telephone system.

Number portability The ability of a customer to transfer an account from one service provider to another without requiring a change in number.

ODM Original Design Manufacturer. In the typical ODM model, the manufacturer designs the complete product.

OECD Organization for Economic Cooperation and Development.

OEM Original Equipment Manufacturer. The company behind the "brand name" of a product that traditionally designed, manufactured, marketed, and provided customer support for its products.

Operator A company that operates a telephone network—for example AT&T, Vodafone, and British Telecom (BT).

Outsource To hire an outside company to perform manufacturing or other services.

Packet-switching service A communication system whereby data is divided and transmitted in packets of set size.

Paging Single-direction radio service for alerting subscribers and leaving messages.

PCN Personal Communications Network. A digital telephone standard adopted mainly in urban areas of Europe.

PCS Personal Communication Services. In the United States, it refers to digital mobile networks using the 1900 MHz frequency. In other countries, it refers to digital mobile networks using the 1800 MHz frequency. Sometimes called PCN.

PDA Personal Digital Assistant. A generic term for handheld devices that combine computing and communications functions.

PDC Personal Digital Communications. A digital cellular standard used in Japan.

Penetration Telecom access, typically calculated by dividing the number of subscribers to a particular service by the population and multiplying by 100. Also referred to as teledensity (for fixed-line networks) or mobile density (for cellular networks).

Peripheral Any device used to process data for entry into or extraction from a computer.

PHS Personal Handyphone System. PHS incorporates a unique Japanese standard that melds the advantages of the European DECT and CT2.

PIN Personal Identification Number. A code used for all GSM-based phones to establish authorization for access to certain functions or information.

PMR Private Mobile Radio.

Portal Commonly refers to the starting point, or a gateway, through which users navigate the World Wide Web, gaining access to a wide range of resources and services such as e-mail, forums, search engines, and shopping malls.

Proportionate subscribers The number of subscribers of a mobile cellular operator based on ownership. It is calculated by multiplying the mobile cellular operator's share of ownership (i.e., equity) in a particular subsidiary by the total number of subscribers.

PSTN Public Switched Telephone Network. Switch-connected type telecommunications circuitry provided by communication service operators.

PTO Public Telecommunication Operator.

PTT Historically, the Ministry of Post, Telecommunications, and Telegraph. Nowadays PTT is used as a term to describe the incumbent, dominant operator in a country, many of which are being or have been privatized.

Radio link Makes it possible to wireless connect a base station to telephone switches and other units in an infrastructure.

R&D Research and Development.

RF Radio Frequency. All broadcast transmissions, from AM radio to satellites, fall into this range, which is between 30 kHz and 300 GHz.

Roaming Service that enables subscribers to use a mobile phone over the network facilities of another provider, and outside the service area of the communication service operator to which they actually subscribe.

Semiconductor An electronic conductor (e.g., silicon, selenium, or germanium) with a resistivity between metals and insulators.

Service provider A company that provides services and subscriptions to telephone, mobile phone, and Internet users.

SIM Subscriber Identity Module card. *See also* smart card.

Six-Sigma Quality A term used generally to indicate quality and process that is well-controlled (i.e., ± 6 sigma from the centerline in a control chart). In the mobile business, Motorola was the first major vendor to embrace Six Sigma, responding to the Japanese quality challenge.

Smart cards The original GSM SIM cards provided an individual identity for each mobile user, handling issues such as authentication and providing storage for basic user data and network information.

Smart phones GSM terminals with enhanced display capabilities and new functionalities. Smart phones have larger displays, often a QWERTY or touch-sensitive keypad, and specialized built-in software linked to specific services and applications.

SMS Short Message Service. A text message communication service prescribed by the ETSI. A single "short message" can contain a maximum of 160 characters.

Spectrum Most often used in the context of frequency allocations, the term refers to the frequencies allowed for a type of service out of the total available.

Spread spectrum A technique to reduce and avoid interference by taking advantage of statistical means to send a signal between two points.

Streaming One-way transmission of video and audio contents over the Internet. Streaming is also possible over advanced wideband wireless networks.

Switch Part of a mobile or fixed telephone system that routes telephone calls to their destinations.

Symbian A company created jointly by Psion, Nokia, Ericsson, and Motorola in June 1998 with the primary aim of developing and standardizing mobile phone operating systems. *See* EPOC.

TACS Total Access Communications System. An analog cellular communications system derived from AMPS.

TD/CDMA Time Division/Code Division Multiple Access.

TDMA Time Division Multiple Access. A digital cellular technology that divides frequency into time slots.

TDMA/IS-136 A digital cellular standard earlier referred to as D-AMPS.

Telematics Refers to a wireless communications system designed for the collection and dissemination of data. Applications include vehicle-based electronic systems. Static applications include stock control (e.g., automatic ordering) and monitoring of utilities meters.

Triband Refers specifically to handsets that will operate on three different frequencies, depending on the available network.

Triple mode A combined analog and digital mobile phone.

Trunk A telephone circuit or channel between two central offices or switching entities.

Turnkey A type of outsourcing method that turns over to the subcontractor all aspects of manufacturing, including material acquisition, assembly, and testing.

UMTS Universal Mobile Telecommunications System. Based on WCDMA-DS, UMTS is the European term for 3G mobile cellular systems. Data rates offered by UMTS are vehicular (144 Kbps), pedestrian (384 Kbps), and in-building (2 Mbps).

Unified messaging In the mobile environment, a service that provides an individual user access to all the recognized messaging formats, including voice mail, facsimile, pager, SMS, and e-mail, through his or her mobile terminal.

US-TDMA/IS-136   US Time Division Multiple Access/IS-136. A 2G system used in the United States.

UTRA UMTS   Terrestrial Radio Access.

VoIP   Voice over Internet Protocol. A technology for transmitting ordinary telephone calls over the Internet using packet-linked routes.

W3C   World Wide Web Consortium. A sector-wide body that promotes standardization of WWW technology.

WAP   Wireless Application Protocol. The *de facto* worldwide standard for providing Internet communications and advanced telephony services on digital mobile phones, pagers, digital assistants, and other wireless terminals.

W-CDMA   Wideband Code Division Multiple Access. Also known in Europe as UMTS. *See also* CDMA.

WCDMA-DS   Wideband Direct Spread Code Division Multiple Access. A radio interface for UMTS that is characterized by the use of a wider band than CDMA (maximum data rate of 2 Mbps).

WLL   Wireless Local Loop. A wireless connection of a telephone in a home or office to a fixed telephone network.

WML   Wireless Markup Language. An extensible markup language developed specifically for wireless applications.

World Wide Web   (1) Technically refers to the hypertext servers (HTTP servers) that allow text, graphics, and sound files to be mixed together. (2) Loosely refers to all types of resources that can be accessed.

WWRF   Wireless World Research Forum. *See* 4G.

WTO   World Trade Organization.

Notes

Preface

1. J. Dwyer and K. Flynn, "A Nation Challenged: Firefighting Inquiry; Before the Towers Fell, Fire Dept. Fought Chaos," *The New York Times* (January 30, 2002).

2. Quoted in H. M. Petrakis, *The Founder's Touch: The Life of Paul Galvin of Motorola* (Chicago: Motorola University Press/J. C. Ferguson Publishing Press, 1965), p. 159.

3. On the *Titanic* tragedy and wireless communications, see R. Minichiello, "Titanic Tragedy Spawns Wireless Advancements" at http://www.marconiusa.org; L. Lessig, *The Future of Ideas: The Fate of the Commons in a Connected World* (New York: Random House, 2001), Chapter 5.

4. See Morgan Stanley Research, The Technology IPO Yearbook, Annual Editions.

Chapter 1

1. Here, innovation is understood broadly. It may refer not just to any aspect of the value chain, from manufacturing and R&D to marketing and sales.

2. In cost strategies in particular, effectiveness includes but is not limited to efficiency.

3. Here, productivity frontier is defined as the joint function of three broad determinants: differentiation, cost position, and innovation. In an influential article, Michael E. Porter has defined productivity frontier as a joint function of only two determinants: differentiation and cost position. That may be illustrative of competitive, mature markets, but not of dynamic, emerging markets. Thus a broader notion of productivity frontier is vital. On Porter's definition, see M. E. Porter, "What Is Strategy?" *Harvard Business School Review* (November–December, 1996).

4. On regulatory regimes and antitrust authorities in the U.S. cellular prior to the great transition, see J. W. Berresford, "The Impact of Law and Regulation on Technology: The Case History of Cellular Radio," 44 *Business Lawyer* 721 (May 1989).

5. On the harmonization of national and supranational competition policy laws, see Leonard Waverman, William S. Comanor, and Akira Goto, *Competition*

Policy in the Global Economy: Modalities for Cooperation (New York: Routledge, 1997).
See also F. M. Scherer, *Competition Policies for an Integrated World Economy* (Washington, D.C.: The Brookings Institution, 1994), Chapter 3.

6. J. M. Stopford and J. T. Wells, Jr., *Managing the Multinational Enterprise*
(New York: Basic Books, 1972).

7. "Top 20 Mobile Cellular Operators—Ranked by 1999 Subscribers," ITU
(International Telecommunications Union), 2001. Vodafone Group includes the
1999 results of both Vodafone (U.K.) and Mannesmann (Germany).

8. This account on globalization, strategic management, and organizational
capabilities is indebted to C. A. Bartlett and S. Ghosal, *Managing Across Borders: The
Transnational Solution*, 2nd ed., (Boston: Harvard Business School Press, 1998). See
also M. E. Porter, ed., *Competition in Global Industries* (Boston, MA: Harvard Business
School Press, 1986); J. P. Jeannet, *Managing with a Global Mindset* (London: Prentice-
Hall, 2000).

9. G. A. Garrard, *Cellular Communications: Worldwide Market Development* (Boston: Artech House, 1998), p. 251.

10. At that point, the 3G networks were expected to start picking up mass
customers, which would translate to an increase in infrastructure and handset sales
to Nokia, thus adding pressure to keep the company in Finland.

11. See R. Luostarinen, "Internationalization of the Firm," *Acta Academiae Oe-
conomicae Helsingiensis*, Series A:30, 1980; and R. Luostarinen, "Internationalization
of Finnish Firms and their Response to Global Challenges" (UNU/WIDER, 1994).

12. M. Alahuhta, *Global Growth Strategies for High-Technology Challenges*. Acta
Polytechnica Scandinavia, Electrical Engineers Series No. 66 (Espoo: The Finnish
Academy of Technology, 1990). Dan Steinbock, *The Nokia Revolution* (New York:
AMACOM, 2001), Chapter 6; see C. A. Bartlett and S. Ghoshal, "Going Global:
Lessons from Late Movers," *Harvard Business Review* (March 1, 2000).

13. K. Ohmae, *Triad Power: The Coming Shape of Global Competition* (New York:
The Free Press, 1985), pp. 27 and 121, respectively.

14. Quoted in "Global Wireless Competitiveness Study," International Technology Consultants *Global Wireless Competitiveness Study* (June 14, 1998), p. 22.

15. In every region, the average revenue per user was expected to peak
around 2002 and 2003. In Asia-Pacific, for instance, the ARPU would climax at
$862 and then decline steadily to $517 in 2010. Although Asia-Pacific and Europe
(particularly the leading Western European nations) would lead in terms of revenue and demand, North America (especially the United States) would have the
most valuable country markets. Despite its laggard role in worldwide revenue and
demand, the U.S. would have the highest ARPU in 2010 ($528).

16. With only one mobile phone for every ten of China's 1.3 billion people,
and tariffs falling by an estimated one-fifth that year, China was likely to sustain
the pace of growth for some time. By contrast, four in ten Americans and half of
Europeans were already using mobile phones. These facts heightened China's allure for mobile vendors, such as Nokia, Ericsson, and Motorola, which faced flat
sales in Europe and North America. Sales estimates in China are from the Ministry
of Information Industry; sales estimates in the U.S. are from the Cellular Telecommunications & Internet Association.

Chapter 2

1. On the Marconi invention of the wireless telegraph, this account is indebted to G. Masini, *Marconi* (New York: Marsilio Publishers, 1995). See also S. Parker, *Guglielmo Marconi and Radio* (New York: Chelsea House Publishers, 1995); G.R.M. Garratt, *Early History of Radio: From Faraday to Marconi* (New York: IEE, 1994); P. R. Jensen, *In Marconi's Footsteps: 1894 to 1920* (Cincinnati, OH: Seven Hills Book Distributors, 1995).

2. Here disruption is defined broadly, in terms of disruptive *business* models. The latter are discontinuous and radical, and offer a new and different value proposition. They are not confined to technology development alone, but can affect any activity or set of activities in the value chain. For a *technology*-driven definition, see C. M. Christensen, *The Innovator's Dilemma.* (Boston, MA: Harvard Business School Press, 1997).

3. On the national innovation systems in the United States, the U.K., and Germany, see R. R. Nelson, ed., *National Innovation Systems: A Comparative Analysis* (New York: Oxford University Press, 1993).

4. However, most inventors and developers concentrated on wireline telegraphy—that is, conventional telegraphy carried over wires. A better understanding of the basic principles of radio emerged after the theoretical work of Scottish physicist James Clerk Maxwell, who demonstrated "physical lines" of electromagnetic force in the 1860s.

5. To overcome the mismatch, the military continued to explore different types of wireless communications. These included ancient techniques, such as semaphore signaling and heliography, which were used widely as late as World War I and could transmit codes but not deliver voice over great distances without using wires. See R. Calhoun, *Digital Cellular Radio* (Norwood, MA: Artech House, 1988), p. 24.

6. Quoted in "Real Radio Inventor Always Ignored," *The Raleigh Register,* September 7, 1976.

7. On David Hughes and many other early pioneers, see E. Hawks, *Pioneers of Wireless* (New York: Arno Press, 1974).

8. With primitive equipment, Heinrich R. Hertz established the basic concept of spark transmission, which was used in radio equipment until 1915 and remained widely used in other devices until the 1930s. His experiments also inspired worldwide excitement and stimulated other scientists, including Chandra Bose in India, Nikola Tesla in the United States, and Aleksandra Popov in Russia.

9. From Marconi's speech at the Royal Academy of Sciences in Stockholm in 1909, as quoted in G. Masini, *Marconi* (New York: Marsilio Publishers, 1995), p. 48.

10. British physicist Oliver Lodge, a contemporary of Marconi's, had succeeded in transmitting detectable Morse signals over a range of 150 meters, but this was an academic exercise for which he envisaged no commercial application.

11. R. Calhoun, *Digital Cellular Radio* (Norwood, MA: Artech House, 1988), Chapter 2.

12. L. P. Lessing, *Edwin Howard Armstrong* (New York: Charles Scribner Sons, 1956), pp. 208–210.

13. After decades of legal battles, Edwin Armstrong, who was already ill and drained of resources, committed suicide in 1954. By the late 1960s, FM was established as the superior system, and 2,000 FM stations spread across the nation.

14. S. Ostry, *The Post-Cold War Trading System* (Chicago: The University of Chicago Press, 1997), pp. 2–3.

15. The original Mobile Telephone Service (MTS) operated on six channels in the 150 MHz band with a 60 kHz channel spacing. Relying on many incremental enhancements, such as full-duplex, direct dialing, and FM channel bandwidth of 25 to 30 kHz, the Improved Mobile Telephone Service (IMTS) triggered a race toward mobile consumer markets. See A. C. Peterson, Jr., "Vehicle Radiotelephony Becomes a Bell System Practice," *Bell Laboratories Record* (April 1947). See also "Telephone Service for St. Louis Vehicles," *Bell Laboratories Record* (July 1946).

16. E. F. O'Neill, ed., *A History of Engineering and Science in the Bell System: Transmission Technology, 1925–1975* (AT&T Bell Laboratories, 1985), p. 408.

17. See Calhoun, *Digital Cellular Radio*, especially Chapter 3. The logic of the story, as the author acknowledges, derives from Kenneth Hardman, "A Primer on Cellular Mobile Telephone Systems," *Federal Bar News & Journal*, Vol. 29, No. 11 (November 1982), pp. 385–391.

18. This account of the cellular concept is indebted to D. Roessner, R. Carr, I. Feller, M. McGeary, and N. Newman, "The Role of NSF's Support of Engineering in Enabling Technological Innovation: Phase II," Final report to the National Science Foundation (Arlington, VA: SRI International, 1998). Roessner *et al.* cite the original memo describing cellular as "Mobile Telephony—Wide Area Coverage," Bell Laboratories Technical Memorandum, December 11, 1947.

19. W. R. Young, "Advanced Mobile Phone Service: Introduction, Background, and Objectives," *Bell System Technical Journal* (January 1979).

20. "Analog cellular radio," notes one industry observer, "is not so much a new technology as a new idea for organizing existing technology on a larger scale." See Calhoun, p. 39.

21. Among other things, these technologies allowed miniaturization, which has proved vital to the expansion of mobile communications since the 1980s.

22. Solid-state electronics provide the sophisticated processing required for handoff. They led to low-cost, low-power, high reliability units, especially portable units.

23. Some research on propagation and further development of the cellular concept continued, but because of the FCC's action, there was little impetus for rapid development. Bell's mobile radio research focused on further development of its existing mobile radio products, propagation studies, and so on.

24. Compare W. D. Lewis, "Coordinated Broadband Mobile Telephone System," Bell Telephone Laboratories, *IRE Transactions* (May 1960), p. 43; H. J. Schulte and W. A. Cornell, "Multi-area Mobile Telephone System," Bell Telephone Laboratories, *IRE Transactions* (May 1960), p. 49.

25. J. Collins, "Spectrum for Rent," *Telecom* (May 1, 2001).

26. Quoted in "Wireless execs point to spectrum woes," CNET News.com (March 21, 2001).

27. The work of the two inspired the "frequency hopping" form of spread spectrum, which served as a precursor for direct sequence, or CDMA.

28. See Young (January 1979).

29. J. L. Funk, *Global Competition Between and Within Standards* (London: Palgrave, 2002).

30. As early as 1983, Minister Esko Ollila had discussed the matter with France's Minister of Industry and Research. If a common cellular infrastructure were to be built in the mid-1980s, argued Ollila, the launch of a European-wide system would not have to be postponed until the next decade.

31. In the long term, data communications was expected to increase at the expense of voice communications. In the process, usage rather than penetration rates would provide a more appropriate predictor of future developments.

32. D. Steinbock, interview with Dr. Gordon Moore, chairman of Intel Corp., March 24, 1999. On the prospects of speech recognition, see also R. D. King and S. Kang, "Speech Recognition Technology: Who Says Talk Is Cheap?" *JP Morgan H&Q* (January 16, 2001).

33. D. Roessner, *et al.* (1998).

34. Initially, International Mobile Telecommunications-2000 was called Future Public Land Mobile Telecommunication Systems (FPLMTS).

35. With 3G, users were expected to have a minimum speed of 2 Mbps when stationary or walking and 348 Kbps in a moving vehicle. Among other things, that meant far faster access to the Internet.

36. For the full story, see D. Steinbock, *The Nokia Revolution* (New York: AMACOM, 2001), Chapter 8.

37. While W-CDMA would be used for wide-area applications, TD-CDMA would be used mainly for indoor applications that required little mobility.

38. The IMT-2000 radio interfaces would have to work with both of the major 3G core networks under development. Qualcomm and Ericsson settled the bitter dispute over the use of CDMA as an industry standard when they signed a cross-licensing deal. In turn, Qualcomm sold its phone manufacturing operations to Japan's Kyocera.

39. Not coincidentally, the alliance was announced only two days after the announcement of the "global and open mobile software and services market" by Nokia, NTT DoCoMo, and the world's leading mobile vendors, operators, and consumer-electronics giants.

40. World Cellular Review 2000–2005, EMC (May 24, 2001).

41. The following account is based on D. Steinbock, "The Globalization of Mobile R&D Capabilities," Unpublished Manuscript, 2002.

42. Quoted in Motorola Museum of Electronics, *Motorola: A Journey Through Time and Technology* (Schaumburg, IL.: Motorola University Press, 1994), p. 53.

43. The respective roles of R&D, however, differed at Nokia Mobile Phones (NMP), which dominated global handset competition, and Nokia Networks (NN), which was among the top-tier global vendors. At NN, R&D amounted to more than 13 percent of net sales; at NMP, it was barely 6 percent.

44. On these developments in global R&D, see Walter Kuemmerle, "Building Effective R&D Capabilities Abroad," *Harvard Business Review* (March–April 1997).

45. "Researchers Outline Vision of Next-Generation 4G Wireless," *InfoWorld* (March 31, 2001.)

46. These notes on the "Vision of the Wireless World" are from Wireless World Research Forum (WWRF), The Book of Visions 2001—Version 1.0 (December 2001).

47. These reflected regional interests (the Japanese Telecommunications Technology Council, the IST initiative influenced by the EU), efforts at international (the ITU working party) and technical harmonization (the 4Gmobile Forum). Other activities were more technically focused, including various forums and task forces.

48. Japan's Telecommunications Technology Council (TTC) had been established as a private standardization organization as early as in October 1985, with the privatization of NTT DoCoMo, to serve as a catalyst in telecom developments. By the end of 2001, the TTC's member list consisted of dozens of Japanese industry leaders in IT, telecom, and mobile businesses, including key foreign interests in Japan.

49. Quoted in "3G Licensees Court Suppliers for Cash," *Electronics Times* (April 12, 2001).

50. "Nippon Ericsson Exec: 4G Spectrum Allocation May Begin '05," *Dow Jones Newswires*, December 14, 2001.

Chapter 3

1. On the nineteenth-century technology revolution in the United States, see A. D. Chandler, Jr., *The Visible Hand: The Managerial Revolution in American Business* (Cambridge, MA: Harvard University Press, 1977), especially Part Two.

2. In 1878, the first regular telephone exchange was introduced in New Haven, Connecticut. In 1880, there were 47,900 telephones in the United States; in 1900, 1,356,000; by 1930, there were 20 million. In business, the telephone provided the means for coordinating the large, geographically dispersed, multidivisional corporations that began to emerge in the late-nineteenth century.

3. On the evolution of U.S. mass marketing, see R. S. Tedlow, *New and Improved: The Story of Mass Marketing in America* (Boston, MA: Harvard Business School Press, 1990), Chapters 1 and 6.

4. J. Newman , ed., *Wiring the World* (Washington, D.C.: *U.S. News and World Report*, 1971).

5. H. Kargman *et al.,* "Land Mobile Communications: The Historical Roots," in R. Bowers, A.M. Lee, and C. Hershey (eds.) (Beverly Hills: Sage, 1978), p. 24.

6. G. A. Garrard, *Cellular Communications: Worldwide Market Development* (Boston: Artech House, 1998), Chapter 1.

7. See R. Minichiello, "Titanic Tragedy Spawns Wireless Advancements" at http://www.marconiusa.org.

8. G. Masini, *Marconi* (New York: Marsilio Publishers, 1995), Chapter 10.

9. Lee de Forest was the inventor of the Audion vacuum tube, which made possible live radio broadcasting and became the key component of all radio, telephone, radar, television, and computer systems before the invention of the transistor in 1947. In 1902 he and his financial backers founded the De Forest Wireless Telegraph Company.

10. Garrard, *Cellular Communications: Worldwide Market Development*, p. 8.

11. The first transportable phone was documented in 1889, primarily for railroad and canal works and military purposes. During the Boer War from 1899 to 1902, Ericsson also sold a large number of transportable field telephones and so-called cavalry telephones to South Africa. See A. Attman, J. Kuuse, and U. Olsson, *L. M. Ericsson 100 Years* (Stockholm: Ericsson, 1976).

12. J. Meurling and R. Jeans, *The Mobile Phone Book: The Invention of the Mobile Phone Industry* (London: Ericsson Radio Systems/Communications Week International, 1994), p. 43.

13. On the Detroit Police Department, Motorola, and the Prohibition era, see Bowers et al. (1978); and A. Affrunti, *A Personal Journal: 50 Years at Motorola* (Rolling Meadows, IL: Motorola University Press, 1994), pp. 42–47. K. S. Dobson, "How Detroit Police Reinvented the Wheel," http://www.detroitnews.com/history/index.htm/.

14. D. Noble, "The History of Land-Mobile Radio Communications," Proceedings of the IRE, Vehicular Communications, May 1962, p. 1406.

15. Quoted in Dobson, "How Detroit Police Reinvented the Wheel," The Detroit News, available at http://www.detroitnews.com/history/index.htm/.

16. *Ibid.*

17. See H. Kargman *et al.*, "Land Mobile Communications: The Historical Roots," in Bowers et al. (1978).

18. Motorola Museum of Electronics, *Motorola: A Journey Through Time and Technology* (Schaumburg, IL: Motorola University Press, 1994), pp. 6–31.

19. D. Noble, "The History of Land-Mobile Radio Communications," p. 1408.

20. A. Affrunti, *A Personal Journal: 50 Years at Motorola* (Rolling Meadows, IL: Motorola University Press, 1994), p. 45.

21. Quoted in K. A. Brown, *Critical Connection: The MSS Story* (Rolling Meadows, IL: Motorola University Press, 1992), p. 25.

22. *Ibid.*, p. 40.

23. The Federal Radio Commission (FRC) made its first reference to two-way mobile radio in a 1932 annual report. Compare Motorola, Inc., "Reply Comments," Formal submission to FCC Docket 18262, Motorola, Inc., Schaumburg, IL, July 20, 1972, p. A-1.

24. Noble, "The History of Land-Mobile Radio Communications," p. 1406.

25. On the WWI developments, see Garrard, *Cellular Communications: Worldwide Market Development*, sections 1.3 and 1.4.

26. M. K. Simon, *et al.*, *Spread Spectrum Communications* Vol. I (Rockville, MD: Computer Science Press, 1985), p. 49.

27. See Walt Halt quoted in Brown, *Critical Connection: The MSS Story*, p. 66.

28. Noble, "The History of Land-Mobile Radio Communications," p. 1410.

29. Motorola Museum of Electronics, *Motorola: A Journey Through Time and Technology*, p. 88.

30. On the PMR systems and Pye's dominance in the U. K. market, see Garrard, *Cellular Communications*, pp. 15–19.

31. Kneitel, *Tune In Telephone Calls*.

32. E. F. O'Neill, ed., *A History of Engineering and Science in the Bell System: Transmission Technology (1925–1975)* (New York: AT&T Bell Laboratories, 1985), p. 408.

33. W. C. Y. Lee, *Mobile Communications Engineering* (New York: McGraw-Hill, 1982).

34. S. W. Gibson, *Cellular Mobile Radiotelephones* (Englewood Cliff: Prentice-Hall, 1987), p. 8.

Chapter 4

1. B. M. Friedman, *Day of Reckoning: The Consequences of American Economic Policy* (New York: Random House, 1988), p. 211.

2. M. K. Simon, J. K. Omura, R. A. Scholtz, and B. K. Levitt, *Spread Spectrum Communications, Vol. 1* (Rockville, MD: Computer Science Press, 1985) p. 49.

3. In 1940, New York Telephone made the first connection to vehicles in establishing an emergency radiotelephone service. In 1946, the first overseas telephone call was made from a moving vehicle in St. Louis to Honolulu. And in 1948, a fully automatic radiotelephone system was introduced in Richmond, Indiana.

4. Between 1959 and the early 1970s, the number of CB licensees soared from 49,000 to almost a million. (From FCC Docket No. 8658, April 1949; and Motorola, Inc., "Reply Comments.")

5. In practice, Edwin Armstrong's first FM broadcasts required five times the spectrum of conventional AM stations. See L. Lessing, *Edwin Howard Armstrong: Man of High Fidelity* (Philadelphia: Lippincott, 1956), p. 211.

6. The basic frequency allocation to these early systems remained at approximately 40 MHz until FCC Dockets 18261 and 18262 were initiated in 1968. See *U.S. Advisory Committee for Land Mobile Radio Services Report* (Washington, D.C.: FCC, 1967).

7. R. Calhoun, *Digital Cellular Radio* (Norwood, MA: Artech House, 1988), Chapter 3.

8. With the FCC's Docket 8658, Bell suggested the launch of 150 two-way channels, using 100-KHz channel spacing, but the proposal was not acted upon. In 1949, Bell offered a more elaborate plan (Docket 8976), but the FCC refused to allocate any portion of the spectrum to mobile telephony. Instead, the Commission created 70 UHF TV channels.

9. M. Nadel, E. E. Glanville, and P. L. Bereano, "Land Mobile Communications and the Regulatory Process," in R. Bowers, A. M. Lee, and C. Hershey (eds.),

Communications for a Mobile Society: An Assessment of New Technology (Beverly Hills, CA: Sage 1978).

10. Courtney, J. (1974), "FC Docket 18262—Due Process of Law," *Communications,* September.

11. Clay T. Whitehead, writing to Hon. D. Burch in Memorandum, Office of Telecommunications, Executive Office of the President, Washington, D.C. (August 17, 1973), pp. 2, 6, 8.

12. J. Meurling and R. Jeans, *The Mobile Phone Book: The Invention of the Mobile Telephone Industry* (London: Communications Week International, 1994), p. 69.

13. Automatic dialing may have been initiated in Richmond, Indiana, where the first fully automatic radiotelephone service was introduced in March 1948—some fifteen years before AT&T's automatic dialing for mobiles in 1964.

14. Aside from sales, the RCCs excelled in litigation, often tying up telephone companies (and each other) in regulatory proceedings for years. See J. W. Berresford, "The Impact of Law and Regulation on Technology: The Case History of Cellular Radio," 44 *Business Lawyer* 721 (May 1989).

15. R. W. Garnet, *The Telephone Enterprise: The Evolution of the Bell System's Horizontal Structure, 1878–1909* (Baltimore: Johns Hopkins University Press, 1985), p. 173.

16. In 1919, Western Electric's wholly owned subsidiary, International Western Electric (IWE), began to run its overseas interests. Six years later, International Telephone and Telegraph Company (ITT) took over IWE, which was renamed International Standard Electric Corporation (ISE) and became a subsidiary of ITT.

17. H. G. Fischer, and J. W. Willis (eds.), *Pike and Fischer Radio Regulations, 2nd Series,* Vol. 33, (Silver Spring, MD: Pike & Fischer), pp. 457, 466–468.

18. The competition concept may have first surfaced in a 1973 report of the Office of Telecommunications Policy (OTP), which kept in close touch with the FCC. The OTP asked explicitly whether "increased availability of mobile communications services is best achieved by a regulatory technology or by the creation of a diverse competitive environment." See M. Nadel *et al.* "Land Mobile Communications and the Regulatory Process," in Bowers *et al.* (1978).

19. J. B. Murray, Jr., *Wireless Nation: The Frenzied Launch of the Cellular Revolution in America* (New York: Perseus Publishing, 2001), p. 286.

20. Metropolitan Service Areas (MSAs).

21. Dynamic Adaptive Total Area Coverage.

22. Meurling and Jeans, *The Mobile Phone Book: The Invention of the Mobile Telephone Industry.*

23. Limitations of AMPS included low calling capacity, limited spectrum, inadequate data communications, limited privacy, and poor fraud protection.

24. The NAMPS system coupled voice processing with digital signaling, which reportedly increased the capacity of AMPS systems threefold. By the end of the 1990s, some thirty-five American and non-U.S. markets used NAMPS worldwide.

25. Affiliated's $12 million stake in McCaw Communications was eventually raised to $85 million (or 43 percent of McCaw).

26. Quoted in O. C. Corr, *Money From Thin Air* (New York: Crown Business, 2000), pp. 90, 167.

27. *Ibid,* p. 139.

28. *Ibid,* p. 77.

29. Quoted in International Technology Consultants, "Global Wireless Competitiveness Study" (June 14, 1998), p. 17.

30. One of the first strategic decisions C. Michael Armstrong made on arrival at AT&T in late 1997 was to shelve an ambitious plan to employ wireless technology, code-named Project Angel, for local service. Still, cable remained AT&T's primary path to the local markets. See "AT&T's Wireless Path to Local Service: 'Project Angel' will back up Ma Bell's cable forays," *Business Week* (December 28, 1998).

31. Statement by the President, Office of the Press Secretary, The White House, October 13, 2000.

32. Bill Clinton and Al Gore, *Putting People First* (New York: Times Books 1992), pp. 9–11. Many of these principles stemmed from the studies of the "new Democratic" Progressive Policy Institute (PPI).

33. U.S. Government, "The National Information Infrastructure: An Agenda for Action," Information Infrastructure Task Force, September 15, 1993; U.S. Government, "Global Information Infrastructure: An Agenda for Cooperation," March 1994–February 1995; U.S. Government, "A Framework for Global Electronic Commerce," December 1996–July 1997.

34. Statement by the President, Office of the Press Secretary, The White House, October 13, 2000.

35. See International Technology Consultants, "Global Wireless Competitiveness Study" (June 14, 1998).

36. A. Petersen, "Battered Wireless Sector Is Seized by the Increasing Urge to Merge," *The Wall Street Journal* (March 25, 2002).

37. B. Wasserstein, *Big Deal: Mergers and Acquisitions in the Digital Age* (New York: Warner Books, 2000), see especially Chapters 12–13.

Chapter 5

1. A. R. Bennett, "The Telephone Systems," 1895.

2. H. Johansson, *Lars Magnus Ericsson: A Brief Biography* (Stockholm: Telefonaktiebolaget LM Ericsson, 1996), p. 21. The memoir is based on a manuscript by Hemming Johansson, Ericsson's business associate and personal friend for more than three decades.

3. *Ibid.,* pp. 25, 27.

4. Later, Teli sought to establish an international position, but failed. Decades of domestic monopoly certainly did not help.

5. Ö. Sölvell, I. Zander, and M. E. Porter, *Advantage Sweden* (Stockholm: Norstedts Juridik, 1991), p. 174.

6. At the end of the 1960s the Nordic countries attempted to set up a Nordic

economic union (NORDEK), but this effort was halted by Denmark's accession to the EEC in 1973. For all practical purposes, the other Nordic countries implemented all the measures planned for NORDEK without a formal alliance. Furthermore, they created a framework for closer cooperation by founding the Nordic Council of Ministers in 1971.

7. The report recommended the use of a cellular configuration.

8. See J. Meurling with R. Jeans, *A Switch in Time: An Engineer's Tale* (Chicago: Telephony, 1985), p. 158.

9. M. Eriksson, "From Vision to Reality," *Contact* (June 22, 2000).

10. Åke Lundqvist further recalls, "When NMT was finally launched, the stage was set, and Sweden and the Nordic countries could then take the lead in the development of mobile telephony." See M. Eriksson, *ibid.*

11. G. A. Garrard, *Cellular Communications: Worldwide Market Development* (Boston: Artech House, 1998), pp. 51–52.

12. Eriksson, "From Vision to Reality."

13. D. Steinbock, *Finland's Wireless Valley* (Helsinki: Finland's Ministry of Transport and Communication, 2000–2001).

14. J. Meurling and R. Jeans, *The Ugly Duckling: Mobile Phones from Ericsson—Putting People on Speaking Terms* (Stockholm: Ericsson Mobile Communications AB, 1997), Chapters 8–9.

15. *Ibid.,* p. 50.

16. *Ibid.,* p. 56.

17. These directives were initiated by the Commission under Article 90 of the Treaty of Rome. Issued in May 1988, the first directive—Competition in Markets for Telecommunications Equipment, 88/301/EEC—ensured liberalization of the customer premises equipment (CPE) market, including mobile phones. Issued in 1990, the Services Directive ensured the separation of telecom operation and regulation. Four years later, the Green Paper built on the idea that licensing a second operator did not ensure effective competition.

18. Eriksson, "From Vision to Reality."

19. D. Steinbock, "Assessing Finland's Wireless Valley: Can the Pioneering Continue?" *Telecommunications Policy* (January, 2001). See also D. Steinbock, *The Nokia Revolution* (New York: AMACOM, 2001), Chapter 11.

20. D. Steinbock, *The Nokia Revolution* (New York: AMACOM, 2001), Chapter 5.

21. In support functions, such as finance and administration, new operators and Nordic PTTs were not that different (14 percent and 13 percent, respectively), but both differed from typical PTTs (18 percent).

22. See G. A. Garrard, *Cellular Communications: Worldwide Market Development* (Boston: Artech House, 1998), Chapter 10.

23. Soon thereafter, the Vodafone Group profit-share scheme was launched to enable all U.K. employees to participate in the company's success. In July 1998, the operator also announced the Millennium Share Options scheme, which meant that all U.K. employees received share options to the value of half their basic salaries.

24. In 1996, it became the first network operator in the U.K. to launch a prepay analog package that required no contract and no credit check. Similarly, it introduced per-second billing on the digital network, as well as options to enable customers to purchase "bundled" minutes and make off-peak local calls to fixed-line phones.

25. Through its international investments, AirTouch had more than 40 million total customers, while ownership interests amounted to 19 million subscriber accounts. With $5.2 billion in revenues, its market capitalization amounted to some £90 billion, which made it one of the top-25 companies in the world.

26. Vodafone Group, web site, March 2002.

27. Like the British operator, Mannesmann's Mobilfunk was a challenger; it had been set up only in 1989. Five years later, operating the D2 network, it became the first private network in Germany to post a profit. At about the same time, a new strategic leadership took over. A 1994 news story alleging that the firm's chairman, Werner Dieter, had committed fraud led to his resignation that year. Dieter agreed in 1996 to pay a massive fine to avoid a trial.

28. As part of the deal, Vodafone negotiated an agreement for France Telecom to acquire Orange, which was purchased as a part of the Mannesmann Group.

Chapter 6

1. On the NEC joint venture episode, the following account is indebted to H. Arisawa, ed., *Nihon Sanggyo Hyakunenshi* (*100-Year History of Japanese Industry*) Vol. 1. (Tokyo: Nihon Keizaisha, 1967); M. Mason, *American Multinationals and Japan: The Political Economy of Japanese Capital Controls, 1899–1980* (Cambridge, MA: Harvard University Press, 1992), pp. 27–28. By 1885, government labs produced 252 telephone sets based on the imported models, but the quality and technical sophistication lagged behind the Western models, and manufacturing could not keep up with the rising demand. Although smaller Japanese firms, such as Oki & Co., sought to match the foreign pioneers, they were only a little more successful in terms of quality or volume.

2. See Mason, *American Multinationals and Japan: The Political Economy of Japanese Capital Controls*, pp. 27–28.

3. M. Fransman, *Japan's Computer and Communications Industry: The Evolution of Industrial Giants and Global Competitiveness* (Oxford: Oxford University Press, 1995), Chapters 1, 2, and 4.

4. On Japan's technology catch-up and licensing policies, see T. Ozawa, "Japan: The Macro-IDP, Meso-IDPs, and the Technology Development Path (TDP)," in J. H. Dunning and R. Narula, *Foreign Direct Investment and Governments: Catalysts for Economic Restructuring* (London: Routledge 1996), pp. 142–173.

5. The Japanese government had disbanded the Ministry of Communications in 1949 and created two new ministries, the Ministry of Postal Affairs and the Ministry of Telecommunications. Concurrently, an Advisory Council was launched to explore the reconstruction of telecommunications in the postwar

Japan. A year later, the Council proposed that Japanese telecommunications should not be run by a government monopoly but by a public corporation.

6. K. Kobayashi, "The Past, Present, and Future of Telecommunications in Japan," *IEEE Communications Magazine* (May 22, 1984).

7. K. Kobayashi, *The Rise of NEC* (Basil Blackwell: Oxford 1991), p. 35.

8. Between 1939 and 1967, the portion of NTT/government sales in NEC's revenues declined from 75 percent to 50 percent. The steady erosion continued until NTT's privatization in 1985, when it accounted for a mere 13 percent of NEC's revenues.

9. See F. Ikegami, "Mobile Radio Communications in Japan," *IEEE Transactions on Communications* (August, 1972).

10. T. J. Pempel, "Land Mobile Communications in Japan: Technical Developments and Issues of International Trade," in R. Bowers, A. M. Lee, and C. Hershey, eds., *Communications for a Mobile Society: An Assessment of New Technology* (Beverly Hills, CA: Sage Publications, 1978), Chapter 13.

11. K. Araki, "Fundamental Problems of Nationwide Mobile Radio Telephone System," *NTT's Electrical Communications Laboratories Technical Journal*, Vol. 16, No. 5.

12. See D. Roessner, *et al., The Role of NSF's Support of Engineering in Enabling Technological Innovation: Phase II Final report to the National Science Foundation* (Arlington, VA: SRI International, 1998).

13. Bell Laboratories, "High Capacity Mobile Telephone Service Technical Report," unpublished document, Bell Laboratories, Holmdel, N.J., December 1971.

14. S. Ito and Y. Matsuzaka, "800 MHz Band Land Mobile Telephone System—Overall View.," *IEEE Transactions on Vehicular Technology*, Vol. VT-27, No. 4 (November 1978).

15. Between 1965 and 1975, Japan's telephone service expanded from 11 million to nearly 43 million.

16. In comparison to the public sector (8 percent), the nascent business services (manufacturing and sales, 3 percent) as well as civil engineering and construction (2 percent), played a minimal role.

17. On the exclusion of non-Japanese mobile vendors in the early Japanese market, see C. B. Bean, "How American Companies Can Capture the Overseas Market," *Communications* (May, 1975). On the opportunities in the Japanese market, see L. Kraar, "Japan Is Opening Up for Gaijin Who Know How," *Fortune* (March 1974); Ministry of Foreign Affairs, *Keys to Success: Foreign Capitalized Corporations in Japan* (Tokyo: Ministry of Foreign Affairs, 1973).

18. Quoted in *Electronics* (August 7, 1975), p. 12.

19. T. J. Pempel, "Land Mobile Communications in Japan: Technical Developments and Issues of International Trade," Chapter 13.

20. *Ibid.*

21. OECD, *Government Purchasing in Europe, North America and Japan* (Paris: OECD, 1966).

22. See M. E. Porter, H. Takeuchi, and M Sakakibara, *Can Japan Compete?* (Cambridge, MA: Perseus Publishing, 2000). These authors stress the distinction

between competitive Japan and the Japanese government model. As such, it is not applicable to Japanese mobile communications; its story is more complicated.

23. M. Fransman, *Japan's Computer and Communications Industry: The Evolution of Industrial Giants and Global Competitiveness* (Oxford: Oxford University Press, 1995), Chapter 6.

24. Quoted in D. Steinbock, *The Nokia Revolution* (New York: AMACOM, 2001), Chapter 4.

25. Essentially, the Telecommunications Business Act established different forms of regulation for different types of carriers. The more dominant the carrier, the more regulation it faced. Privatization resulted in a dramatic proliferation of rivals.

26. JTACS is a Japanese version of the TACS analog standard operating in the 800 MHz band.

27. In the early 1990s, DDI had 225 companies as shareholders, including Kyocera, which held 25 percent of the company, and Sony, which held 5 percent.

28. In 1994, Japan's mobile market had created an estimated 60,000 jobs while revenues amounted to ¥2.8 trillion. The stakes, however, were rising rapidly. In 2000, these estimates were ¥8.5 trillion and 236,000 jobs, respectively. And by 2010, Japan's Ministry of Posts and Telecommunications expected market size to be about ¥17 trillion, with 562,000 jobs. See Japan's Ministry of Posts and Telecommunications (http://www.yusei.go.jp).

29. M. Fransman, *Japan's Computer and Communications Industry: The Evolution of Industrial Giants and Global Competitiveness*, Chapters 1 and 4.

30. Steinbock, *The Nokia Revolution*, Chapter 4.

31. This analogy of a flight formation of wild geese to industrial development was originally conceptualized by a Japanese economist Kaname Akamatsu in the early 1930s. See T. Ozawa, *Japan's Technological Challenge to the West, 1950–1974: Motivation and Accomplishment* (Cambridge, MA: The MIT Press, 1954).

32. According to the NTT Corporation Act, Article 1, NTT "shall be a limited company whose purpose is to operate a domestic telecommunications business."

33. Even in 2000, NTT DoCoMo's sales to overseas customers were not prepared or disclosed, "since sales to overseas customers are not significant in relation to consolidated sales (less than 10 percent)." See NTT DoCoMo Annual Report 2000, p. 51.

34. NEC Corporation, Annual Report 2001.

35. *Ibid.*

36. DoCoMo also launched a satellite-based mobile phone system that year to serve customers beyond the range of cell sites, reaching ships and mountainous regions.

37. Two more licenses were issued for digital operators, Digital Phone Group (DPG) and Tu-Ka, operating in the 1500 MHz band. Like the proprietary systems of the 1G era, PDC was developed and launched in Japan and has been used exclusively there since 1994. Initially called JDC (Japan Digital Cellular), PDC was based on the TDMA technology, like GSM and TDMA IS-136, and operated in the 800 and 1500 MHz frequency bands.

38. PHS proved attractive in heavily populated areas where cellular technology encountered problems. While the initial base grew rapidly, cellular tariffs caught up with PHS prices, and the PHS quality disadvantages caused a rapid decline in subscriber figures. In 1999, DoCoMo took over NTT's unprofitable unit and rolled out a high-speed data service over the PHS network.

39. "Japan's NTT Fights to Keep Control of Its Rapidly Growing DoCoMo Unit," *The Wall Street Journal* (December 18, 2001).

40. Quoted in "Standardien sota ratkaisee miljardien tilaukset: Maailmankannykän kisa alkaa," *Talouselämä* No. 3, 1999.

41. Revolution Next: 3G and Wireless Internet Conference, Credit Suisse/First Boston Equity Research, Asian Telecom Services, March 19, 2001.

42. With a migration path from 2G CDMA to the CDMA 1x EV network, KDDI believed it could leverage most of its existing 2G infrastructure and lower the investment for 3G. In comparison to rolling out its separate W-CDMA network, KDDI anticipated it could save 50 percent by upgrading its network to CDMA2000 1x.

43. Jim Rohwer, "Today, Tokyo; Tomorrow, the World," *Fortune* (September 18, 2000).

44. J. L. Funk, *The Mobile Internet: How Japan Dialed Up and the West Disconnected* (Kent, UK: ISI, 2001), p. 2.

45. NTT DoCoMo adopted other key standards as well, including GIF, Java, MIDI, and HTTP.

46. Quoted in "Japan's NTT Fights to Keep Control of Its Rapidly Growing DoCoMo Unit," *The Wall Street Journal.*

47. *Ibid.*

48. K. Obuchi, *The NTT DoCoMo Phenomenon: Leading the Broadband Revolution* (New York: Halsted Press, 2001).

49. Furthermore, NTT DoCoMo provided technical support for Hong Kong–based carrier HTCL's "Orange World," an i-mode-like mobile Internet service. DoCoMo gave its partners the flexibility to customize 80 percent of the content they delivered, so they could tailor i-mode applications to the needs and tastes of their local customer base.

50. "Japan's NTT Fights to Keep Control of Its Rapidly Growing DoCoMo Unit," *The Wall Street Journal.*

Chapter 7

1. The leader of the reformist faction, Deng Xiaoping had struggled for party control after the failure of the Great Leap Forward.

2. For an introduction to the issues of China and WTO, see Sylvia Ostry, "China and the WTO: The Transparency Issue," 3 *UCLA Journal of International Law & Foreign Affairs* 1 (1998).

3. K. Ohmae, "Profits and Perils in China, Inc." *Strategy + Business* 26 (First Quarter 2002).

4. See E. Eckholm, "China's Inner Circle Reveals Big Unrest," *The New York Times* (June 3, 2001).

5. Y. Luo, *How to Enter China: Choices and Lessons* (Ann Arbor, MI: The University of Michigan Press, 2000), Chapter 3.

6. H. Y. Zhang and D. Van Den Bulcke, "China: Rapid Changes in the Investment Development Path," in J. H. Dunning and R. Narula, *Foreign Direct Investment and Governments: Catalysts for Economic Restructuring* (London: Routledge, 1996), pp. 380–422.

7. C-Y. Cheng, *Behind the Tiananmen Massacre: Social, Political and Economic Ferment in China* (Boulder, CO: Westview Press, 1990).

8. H. Ma, "China's America Problem," *Policy Review* No. 111 (February–March 2002).

9. For a critical view of SEZ developments, see Y. Zhao, and D. Schiller, "Dances with Wolves? China's Integration into Digital Capitalism," *Info* Vol. 3, No. 2 (April 2001), pp. 137–151.

10. *China Statistical Yearbook,* various issues 1979–2000. Between 1979 and 1996, FDI by developing-country businesses in China was more than three times that of developed-country firms. Hong Kong and Taiwan investors focused on labor-intensive and simple industrial processing for export markets, whereas U.S. and European (e.g., U.K., Germany) firms concentrated on capital- or technology-intensive manufacturing sectors to gain access to the growing Chinese domestic market.

11. The Tiananmen crisis occurred in 1989. Nordic players pioneered digital cellular two to three years later. In the United States, Motorola's analog triumph endured until the mid-1990s, when the mobile leaders in Western Europe first began to reap the benefits of their GSM investments in the home base and the foreign lead markets.

12. "Bush's Tricky High-Wire Act," *Business Week* (April 16, 2001).

13. The experiences of the mobile leaders illustrate foreign corporate investment strategies in which evolutionary entry, growing risk, and rising entry barriers have gone hand in hand. First movers were not assured sustainable advantages; late movers were bound to face higher entry barriers.

14. In Europe, AT&T also faced difficulties accessing the market, which was dominated by local vendors, such as Siemens, Ericsson, and CIT-Alcatel. These firms enjoyed long-standing ties with their respective national telecom administrations.

15. Quoted in "AT&T Entering Asian Market for Telecommunications," Dow Jones News Service (August 22, 1983).

16. Of the U.S. players, ITT and GTE had been involved in China for years, whereas the more recent Japanese and European suppliers were supported by their governments' export-financing policies.

17. Instead of defined joint venture investments, the memorandum of understanding (MoU) established a "long-term comprehensive partnership" between AT&T and China by identifying ten areas in which the two parties might jointly pursue business opportunities. By May 1994, AT&T signed an agreement to invest

$150 million in China over the next two years. In the process, the company launched three more joint ventures, including switch-manufacturing facilities in Qingdao and Chengdu. The Qingdao facility was the largest outside of the United States.

18. Quoted in J. McGregor and J. J. Keller, "AT&T, China Set Broad Pact on Phones, Gear: Firm's Role of Outsider, Tied to 1989 Ban, Ends; Rivals Are Formidable," *The Wall Street Journal* (February 24, 1993).

19. Quoted in J. J. Keller, "AT&T Selects Warwick as Chairman of Its New Unit for Business in China," *The Wall Street Journal* (June 16, 1993).

20. In practice, AT&T struggled to move from an international division to global matrix, while skipping over the intermediary stages. That was possible only under certain conditions. Either foreign sales would account for a significant proportion of total sales or foreign product diversity would be relatively high. With AT&T, neither condition applied.

21. Despite the stated goal to derive half of AT&T's revenue from overseas operations by 2000, foreign sales accounted for just 24 percent of about $65 billion in total annual revenue in late 1993. As a result, then CEO Allen extended the 50 percent mark to 2003. Virtually all major decisions were made in the United States, requiring foreign proposals to snake their way up through myriad departments before getting approval. See J. J. Keller, "AT&T to Give Foreign Units More Autonomy: Each Is to Get Own CEO Under Plan to Increase Revenue From Overseas," *The Wall Street Journal* (December 13, 1993). As part of the new reorganization, AT&T began consolidating its overseas facilities, which included thirty-nine plants in twenty-four countries, into three regional hubs.

22. In 1999, competing with Cisco, Lucent engaged in a $24 billion acquisition of networking hardware maker Ascend Communications. Lucent also formed alliances with Motorola to develop cable TV infrastructure equipment and with Qualcomm to build wireless network equipment. In June, Lucent signed a technology partnership with China Unicom to address opportunities in the market for next-generation networking.

23. Lucent Technologies 2000 Annual Report.

24. M. Brick, "FBI Says Lucent Workers Stole Secrets for China," *The New York Times* (May 3, 2001).

25. K. Schoenberger, with M. Warner, "Motorola Bets Big on China," *Time* (May 27, 1996).

26. If Motorola's right to access the Chinese market may have been granted only after the government failed at reverse engineering.

27. K. Schoenberger, with M. Warner, "Motorola Bets Big on China."

28. In July 1998, President Jiang Zemin ordered the People's Liberation Army (PLA) to divest itself of commercial operations, which blurred the future of China Great Wall Co., a company that was half-owned by the PLA and that controlled the CDMA frequency. Great Wall's rival was the Ministry of Information Industry, the country's powerful telecom regulator. The Ministry, in turn, controlled China Telecom, the leading phone company and owner of the largest GSM network. Minister Wu Jichuan was opposed to any CDMA rollout.

29. The internal working title for Accompli was "TaiChi."

30. Motorola, November 9, 2001.

31. Telefonaktiebolaget LM Ericsson, Annual Report 1985, p. 6.

32. Telefonaktiebolaget LM Ericsson, Annual Report 1986, p. 6.

33. Telefonaktiebolaget LM Ericsson, Annual Report 1987, p. 4.

34. Telefonaktiebolaget LM Ericsson, Annual Report 1988, p. 6.

35. Telefonaktiebolaget LM Ericsson, Annual Report 1993, p. 5.

36. Telefonaktiebolaget LM Ericsson, Annual Report 1993, p. 9.

37. Lars-Olof Pehrsson had worked for Anders Wall, a well-known Swedish financier, in Sri Lanka, while traveling in Japan, China, and the Far East. He had studied at Stanford and worked for a U.S. data company, a steel manufacturer, and a Swedish steam-roller seller.

38. Quoted in J. Meurling and R. Jeans, *The Ugly Duckling: Mobile Phones from Ericsson—Putting People on Speaking Terms* (Stockholm: Ericsson Mobile Communications AB, 1997), Chapter 20.

39. With seventeen suppliers in the market, Pehrsson considered a 15 percent share a major success, but even 5 percent to 6 percent was regarded as outstanding. To achieve its objective, Ericsson formed a joint venture with Marubeni, a Japanese trading house.

40. Telefonaktiebolaget LM Ericsson, Annual Report 1997, p. 5.

41. Telefonaktiebolaget LM Ericsson, Annual Report 1997, pp. 20–21.

42. This account draws from D. Steinbock, *The Nokia Revolution* (New York: AMACOM 2001), especially Chapter 6.

43. Quoted in "Nokia vetää ohjelmistoyritykset Kiinaan," *Talouselämä* (February 4, 2000).

44. D. Steinbock, Interview with President Martti Ahtisaari, New York City, May 2001.

45. Furthermore, to make learning as efficient as possible and unify its training processes across the company, it established the first four Nokia Learning Centers. These offered a way to transfer knowledge throughout the company. In addition to those in Finland, Italy, and Singapore, a learning center was built in China.

46. D. Steinbock, Interview with President Martti Ahtisaari, New York City, May 2001.

47. The invasion of Finnish firms accelerated late in 1999, when the United States and China agreed on the terms of China's membership in the WTO. A year later, F-Secure established a sales organization in Bejing and a subsidiary in Hong Kong. Stonesoft sought resellers in Bejing and founded an office in Hong Kong. Nedecon and Nixu were preparing to enter the Chinese market, while other Finnish players—Comptel, Elektrobit, Jutron, Aldata, and Opus Capita—explored the market. Even earlier, Nokia's suppliers, including Elcoteq, Perlos, and Ojala, had established themselves in the new market. The list of entrants also included Novo (IT), Teleste (cables), and JOT Automation (production automation). See Steinbock, *The Nokia Revolution*, Chapter 6.

48. The establishment of the Hangzhou R&D center built on Nokia's long

experience of cooperation in technology development with Chinese partners and universities. Nokia and Zhejiang University had already started cooperation. Nokia expected to recruit well-educated personnel in Hangzhou and surrounding areas.

49. For a year already, CDMA had been a bargaining chip in China's WTO negotiations with the United States. Some observers thought that Chinese leaders were unhappy with the terms of their Qualcomm deal and wanted to rewrite it. Central to the deal was Qualcomm technology that would make phones work on both CDMA and GSM networks.

50. Matt Forney, "China Postpones Project to Build Mobile Network," *The Wall Street Journal* (February 24, 2000).

51. Estimates are by The Strategis Group, a Washington D.C.–based telecommunications research firm.

52. Lucent and Motorola said they were awarded contracts valued at more than $400 million. A Nortel executive said his company won a $275 million deal, while Ericsson won a $200 million contract. The other companies could not be reached for comment. See M. Pottinger, "China Unicom Signs CDMA Contracts, In Victory for Patent-Holder Qualcomm," *The Wall Street Journal* (May 16, 2001).

53. "CTIA Signs Agreement with Chinese Counterparts," CTIA News Release, Washington, D.C., June 15, 2001.

54. P. Wonacott, "U.S.'s Qualcomm Unveils Its First License Deals in China," Dow Jones Newswires, July 3, 2001.

55. The figures cited are from the author's exchanges with China's Ministry of Information Industry.

56. Intervendor roaming was put in place with IS-41 links. This was a complex task—not technically, but due to negotiations with multiple regional operators.

57. Most of China's administrative authorities continued to employ TACS, while some in the poor northwest region used low-cost second-hand AMPS systems from AT&T. See G.A. Garrard, *Cellular Communications: Worldwide Market Development* (Boston: Artech House), pp. 387–389.

58. Compare Y. Xu, D. C. Pitt, and N. Levine, "Competition Without Privatization: The Chinese Path," in S. Macdonald and G. Madden (eds.), *Telecommunications and Socio-Economic Development* (New York: Elsevier, 1998), pp. 375–292, and Y. Xu and D. C. Pitt, "One Country, Two Systems—Contrasting Approaches of Telecommunications Deregulation in Hong Kong and China," *Telecommunications Policy*, Vol. 23, No. 3–4 (1999), pp. 245–260.

59. The northern company took in branches in Beijing, Tianjin, Hebei, Shanxi, and the Inner Mongolian Autonomous Region, while branches in the rest of the country belong to the southern company.

60. China Telecom.

61. "China Telecom Starts Unlicensed Mobile Trial," *Financial Times* (December 2, 2001).

62. Since March 2001, China Mobile Communications has provided international roaming service with the cooperation of 120 operators in sixty-six countries and regions.

63. China Mobile.

64. X. Yan and D. C. Pitt, "Competition in the Chinese Cellular Market: Promise and Problematic," in D. G. Loomis and L. D. Taylor, *The Future of the Telecommunications Industry: Forecasting and Demand Analysis* (Newark, N.J.: Kluwer, 1999), pp. 249–264.

65. H-Y. Zhang and D. Van Den Bulcke, "China: Rapid Changes in the Investment Development Path," in J. H. Dunning and R. Narula, *Foreign Direct Investment and Governments: Catalysts for Economic Restructuring* (London: Routledge, 1996), pp. 380–422.

66. Telefonaktiebolaget LM Ericsson, Annual Report 1997, pp. 20–21.

67. K. Ohmae, "Profits and Perils in China, Inc." (2002).

Chapter 8

1. Quoted in B. Avishai and W. Taylor, "Customers Drive a Technology-Driven Company: An Interview with George Fisher," *Harvard Business Review* (November–December 1989).

2. H. M. Petrakis, *The Founder's Touch: The Life of Paul Galvin of Motorola* (Chicago: Motorola University Press/J. C. Ferguson Publishing Press, 1965), p. 26 and pp. 23, respectively.

3. A. Affrunti, Sr., A Personal Journal: 50 Years at Motorola (Rolling Meadows: Motorola University Press, 1994).

4. Affrunti, *A Personal Journal: 50 Years at Motorola*, pp. 17–19.

5. Quoted in *Motorola: A Journey Through Time and Technology* (Schaumburg, IL: Motorola Museum of Electronics, 1994), p. 10.

6. Petrakis, *The Founder's Touch: The Life of Paul Galvin of Motorola*, see Chapter 9.

7. *Ibid.,* Chapter 13.

8. *Ibid.,* p. 159.

9. *Ibid.,* pp. 160–161 and 206–207, respectively.

10. Quoted in *Motorola: A Journey Through Time and Technology,* p. 53.

11. K. Brown, *Critical Connection: The MSS Story* (Rolling Meadows, IL: Motorola University Press, 1992).

12. In 1956, Robert W. Galvin became president, and in 1964, he became chairman and CEO. He had joined the company as a stock clerk in 1944, without having completed his college degree.

13. For more on Bob Galvin's view of leadership, see "A Speech by Bob Galvin on Leadership," in J. L. Cogan, G. Schuck, and S. Zuboff, "Motorola Corporation: The View from the CEO Office," Harvard Business School Case (October 20, 1994).

14. In the 1970s, Robert Galvin and William Weisz served together, and the addition of John Mitchell in the 1980s resulted in a triumvirate. When Elmer Wavering retired as COO, Weisz was elected to that post and continued as president. Robert W. Galvin continued as chairman of the board and CEO.

15. In the 1970s, Motorola developed the Participative Management Program (PMP) as a means to enhance productivity and employee involvement in the company.

16. Motorola Inc., Annual Report 1973.

17. Quoted in *Motorola: A Journey Through Time and Technology*, p. 68.

18. In 2000, the consortium of investors in Iridium declared bankruptcy to liquidate its $5 billion satellite communications system, which was designed to allow paging and wireless telephony anywhere in the world.

19. Industry competition in consumer electronics was rapidly intensifying because of attacks by new Japanese challengers and shifts of power in the value chain, particularly the rise of large U.S. wholesalers and retailers.

20. In 1981, the Motorola Training and Education Center (MTEC)—which became better known as the Motorola University by 1989—began to provide employees with instruction and coaching in the quality process and participative management skills. By 1986, Motorola invested more than $40 million in employee education.

21. Quoted in *Business Week* (March 29, 1982), p. 129.

22. Quoted in M. Y. Yoshino and U. S. Rangan , *Strategic Alliances: An Entrepreneurial Approach to Globalization* (Boston, MA: Harvard Business School Press, 1995).

23. Quoted in *Motorola: A Journey Through Time and Technology*, p. 85.

24. Yoshino and Rangan, *Strategic Alliances: An Entrepreneurial Approach to Globalization*, pp. 34–35.

25. G. Herman, "Competing with the Japanese," *Nation's Business* (November 1982).

26. M. Gentile and T. D. Jick, "Bob Galvin and Motorola, Inc. (A)," Harvard Business School Case, March 27, 1989.

27. *Motorola: A Journey Through Time and Technology*, p. 85.

28. Motorola Annual Report 1982, p. 5.

29. Motorola Annual Report 1984, p. 8.

30. Avishai and Taylor, "Customers Drive a Technology-Driven Company: An Interview with George Fisher."

31. D. Roth, "Burying Motorola," *Fortune* (July 6, 1998).

32. Herschel Shosteck Associates, news releases in 1994.

33. Motorola Annual Report 1988, pp. 2–3. In 1990, Robert W. Galvin stepped down as chairman of the board after fifty years of service to become chairman of the executive committee of the board. Consolidating his strategic leadership, George Fisher was elected chairman of the board and continued as CEO. Meanwhile, Gary L. Tooker was elected president and continued as COO, whereas Christopher B. Galvin, the future CEO of Motorola, joined the chief executive office as senior VP and assistant COO.

34. Motorola Annual Report 1980, p. 30.

35. Motorola Annual Report 1988, pp. 18.

36. Avishai and Taylor, "Customers Drive a Technology-Driven Company: An Interview with George Fisher."

37. Galvin became president and COO, and William Weisz was elected chairman of the board.

38. Roth, "Burying Motorola."

39. Previously Government Electronics Group (GEG).

40. Previously Automotive and Industrial Electronics Group (AIEG).

41. P. Coy, with R. Stodghill, "Strategies—Is Motorola a Bit Too Patient?" *Business Week* (February 5, 1996).

43. Herschel Shosteck Associates, news releases in 1998.

44. As part of the deal with Flextronics International (the largest outsourcing contract ever announced as of 1999), Motorola took a 5 percent stake in the company. Motorola also cut staff to reduce costs amid slow sales of semiconductors and mobile phones.

45. N. Tait, "Motorola to sell mobile stakes," *Financial Times* (March 5, 2001).

46. "Motorola can catch up, but we have established market share," said Anders Torstensson, general manager of cellular phones for Ericsson's U.S. subsidiary. Although Motorola once dominated the U.S. analog market and retained a clear if shrunken lead, Torstensson thought it would end up no better than neck and neck with Nokia and Ericsson in the digital market. See B. J. Feder, "Motorola: Not Invincible but Don't Write It Off," *The New York Times* (October 13, 1996).

47. On the restructuring debate, see R. O. Crockett, "A New Company Called Motorola," *Business Week* (April 17, 2000).

48. R. Crockett, "Q&A with Motorola's Galvin," *Business Week* (August 10, 1998).

49. Q. Hardy, "Motorola Unveils Its Plans for a Major Reorganization," *The Wall Street Journal* (July 10, 1998).

50. Crockett, "A New Company Called Motorola."

5. That spring Iridium went out of business, leaving Motorola to oversee the deorbiting and destruction of its satellites. At the end of the 1990s, Motorola was moving ahead in another satellite venture, Teledesic L.L.C., which aspired to deliver voice, data, and high-speed Internet access to handheld devices. In addition to Motorola, the $9 billion initiative included industry heavyweights such as Microsoft Chairman Bill Gates, cellular pioneer Craig McCaw, and Boeing.

52. These feuds led to the departure of Merle Gilmore, the number-three executive and a thirty-year Motorola veteran. The triumvirate of the CEO office shrank to Galvin and Robert L. Growney. Key executives had been replaced, and many key actors were no longer Motorola insiders. Bo Hedfors had left Ericsson to run Motorola's network infrastructure; Ed Breen, a General Instrument executive, reigned over Motorola's broadband group; and Mike Zafirovski had left General Electric to take charge of handsets.

53. R. Crockett, "Galvin on the New Motorola: 'Fast, Smart, Quick, Agile—Go," *Business Week* (April 17, 2000).

Chapter 9

1. This section is indebted to *Lars Magnus Ericsson: A Brief Biography* (Stockholm: Telefonaktiebolaget LM Ericsson, 1996), based largely on a manuscript by

Hemming Johansson, Ericsson's business associate and personal friend for more than three decades.

2. Later, Teli sought an international position but failed. Decades of domestic monopoly certainly did not help.

3. In 1896, Ericsson transferred the business of L. M. Ericsson & Co. to Aktiebolaget L. M. Ericsson & Co.

4. R. Lundström, "Swedish Multinational Growth Before 1930," in P. Hertner and G. Jones, eds., *Multinationals: Theory and History* (Aldershot: Gower, 1986).

5. In 1950, Ericsson delivered to Finland the first automatic exchange based on its crossbar system. In 1954, a subsidiary was formed in Australia and an R&D lab in Darmstadt, Germany. A year later, a factory was launched in São Jose dos Campos, Brazil. By 1956, the company turned out its first automatic mobile telephone system (MTA) and introduced its first "all-in-one" telephone. Two years later, it launched its first speakerphone. On the postwar positioning of the Swedish multinationals, see I. Zander and U. Zander, "Sweden, A Latecomer to Industrialization," in J. H. Dunning and R. Naural, *Foreign Direct Investment and Governments: Catalysts for Economic Restructuring* (London: Routledge, 1996), Chapter 4. See also B. Swedenborg, *The Multinational Operations of Swedish Firms—An Analysis of Determinants and Effects* (Stockholm: The Industrial Institute for Economic and Social Research, 1979).

6. Historically, Sweden has been more important as a home country than as a host country to multinational companies. Sweden, like Finland and other Nordic countries, is small and therefore not very attractive as a location for market-seeking foreign direct investment (FDI). In addition, regulations on inward FDI have been restrictive, even as outward FDI has been promoted. See M. Blomström and A. Kokko, "Sweden," in J. H. Dunning (ed.), *Governments, Globalization, and International Business* (New York: Oxford University Press, 1997), pp. 359–376. U. Olsson, "Securing the Markets: Swedish Multinationals in a Historical Perspective," in G. Jones and H. G. Schröter, eds., *The Rise of Multinationals in Continental Europe* (Cheltenham: Edward Elgar, 1993).

7. Compare M. Blomström and A. Kokko, "Sweden," (1997), and U. Olsson (1993), "Securing the Markets."

8. Much of the Swedish investment has been attracted abroad to avoid formal and informal trade barriers, to get closer to foreign customers, or to reduce transportation costs. Ericsson, however, belongs to those Swedish companies that have not been motivated by market access alone, but for which foreign production has been a fundamental requirement of doing business.

9. On the evolution of ITT's early telecom properties, see M. Deloraine, *When Telecom and ITT Were Young* (New York: Lehigh Books, 1974). See also R. Sobel, *ITT: The Management of Opportunity* (Washington, D.C.: BeardBooks, 1982). For a critical ITT study, see A. Sampson, *The Sovereign State of ITT* (New York: Stein & Day, 1973).

10. R. Shaplen, *Kreuger: Genius and Swindler* (New York: Knopf, 1960), p. 126.

11. In the early-twentieth century, both ITT and Ericsson had acquired operating concessions in Mexico, which were consolidated in 1948 into the jointly

owned Telefonos de Mexico. Although both companies sold out to Mexican interests a decade later, each continued as a major supplier of the market, with large manufacturing facilities in Mexico. During the 1940s Ericsson sold its domestic telephone services to focus on telecom equipment manufacturing.

12. U. Olsson, "Securing the Markets."

13. Until the late 1960s, outward FDI had not been restricted by government policies. In the 1970s, exchange regulations were introduced, but these did not hinder the growth of outward FDI. Between 1960 and 1985, the aggregate outflows doubled during each successive five-year period. At the same time, the geographical pattern of Swedish FDI flows changed. During 1978 and 1986, the value of the production by Swedish subsidiaries in the United States grew by a factor of eight. See M. Blomström and L. Ohlsson, *Economic Relations Between the United States and Sweden* (Stockholm: Svenska Handelsbanken, 1989).

14. Zander and Zander, "Sweden, A Latecomer to Industrialization," Chapter 4.

15. Hans Sund, who was formerly in charge of the Defense Division, replaced Fred Sundqvist as the head of X, which was about to shift from electromechanics to electronics. See J. Meurling with R. Jeans, *A Switch in Time: An Engineer's Tale* (Chicago, IL: Telephony, 1985).

16. The first orders of AKE 13 were booked at the end of the 1960s. Unlike its predecessor, which used discrete semiconductor components, it used integrated circuits and the control system used a multiprocessor configuration.

17. Most relied on crossbar, reed relay, or some similar electromechanical switch technology. The true stored program control (SPC) market remained small but high profile and was discussed at trade events. In France, CIT-Alcatel had introduced a digital E10 system (Nokia later competed successfully with digital switching systems based originally on the CIT-Alcatel design). Though it was designed for small applications and installed only in rural areas, Ericsson's team was intrigued by the combination of digital transmission with digital switching, which held significant potential to reduce investments required by telephone networks.

18. The team engaged in technology forecasting, but that failed often (except for the crossover point of 1984).

19. Ericsson Annual Report, 1981, p. 28.

20. B. Svedberg, "1980—A Promising Introduction to a New Decade," Ericsson Annual Report, 1980, pp. 142–143.

21. *Ibid.*, pp. 4–5.

22. Ericsson Annual Report, 1981, p. 4.

23. Ericsson Annual Report, 1982, p. 8.

24. *Ibid.*, p. 7.

25. As Bartlett and Ghoshel have shown, it is this dialectic of centralized innovation and local responsiveness that has animated Ericsson's tensions ever since. See C. A. Bartlett and S. Ghoshel, *Managing Across Borders: The Transnational Solution* (Boston: Harvard Business School Press, 1988).

26. By 2000, the company operated in over 140 countries worldwide, while its sales had soared to more than $29 billion. Concurrently, sales in Sweden had declined to just 3.2 percent of total.

27. J. Meurling and R. Jeans, *The Ugly Duckling: Mobile Phones from Ericsson—Putting People on Speaking Terms* (Stockholm: Ericsson Mobile Communications AB, 1997), p. 3.

28. In 1983, the division was split into land-mobile radio, systems, and terminals, which was taken over by Ulf J. Johansson. At the time, the Public Telecommunications Business, still another part of Ericsson, developed and produced the switches for the mobile systems. ERA (Ericsson Radio Systems AB) was responsible for mobile telephone systems. SRA was in charge of mobile radio, mobile telephony, and personal paging.

29. Ericsson Annual Report, 1982, p. 20.

30. The farmer's son had been one of the first technology PhDs to join Ericsson. His first boss was Dag Åkerberg, who developed pagers. Another boss, Olle Ulvenholm, had been responsible for marketing the paging systems. The first taught him to build microchips, the other to control product costs.

31. At first, Ericsson used an outside consultant for the industrial design of its regular telephones and early wireless models. Starting with Olivia, however, Nils Rydbeck brought in Richard Lindahl in Malmö, a designer who has been responsible for most of the ensuing models.

32. Meurling and Jeans, *The Ugly Duckling: Mobile Phones from Ericsson*, p. 28–29.

33. Because of differing technical standards, ERA (Ericsson Radio Systems AB) was in for some rough times. To comply with the U.S. specifications for the AMPS system, the AXE switch required substantial software development. On April 2, 1984, the new system was successfully inaugurated. The first nonwireline U.S. cellular network was followed by many more.

34. J. Meurling and R. Jeans, *The Ugly Duckling: Mobile Phones from Ericsson*, p. 65.

35. These divisions were Mobile Systems, Multi Services, Networks, Consumer Products, Data Backbone, and Optical Networks, Global Services as well as an additional unit for specific business operations.

36. Ericsson supplied solutions for all existing mobile systems as well as future 3G mobile systems, broadband multiservice networks, and broadband access. The solutions included network infrastructure, access equipment and terminals, application enablers, and global services to support both business and private communications.

37. Quoted in C. Brown-Humes and R. Budden, "Sony Ericsson talks big about ambitions for its new baby: The joint venture is hoping to dislodge Nokia from top position," *Financial Times* (March 7, 2002).

38. Ericsson corporate news release, February 8, 2002.

39. For more on Ericsson's mission and vision, see http://www.ericsson.com.

Chapter 10

1. The chapter at hand draws from D. Steinbock, *The Nokia Revolution* (New York: AMACOM, 2001).

2. Nokia's founders included several luminaries of the aspiring nationalist Finland, including Carl Gustaf Emil Mannerheim, the legendary Finnish freedom fighter; Carl Enrooth, a prosperous industrialist; and Alfred Kihlman, a legendary politician and educator.

3. Nokia's emphasis on differentiation originates from ad brochures in the 1880s. Idestam exhibited a talent for marketing and advertising. Nokia was dependent on overseas revenues, which required the firm to engage in differentiation earlier and more extensively than those Finnish mills that dominated domestic markets.

4. Political realities rather than market forces dictated the surge of the seller's market. Of the estimated $300 million of Finland's war reparations to the Soviet Union, cable products covered some $25 million.

5. Finnish historians have stressed the beneficial nature of Soviet trade from Finland's standpoint. This argument ignores the fact of resource dependency— something that Nokia's electronics division sought to balance with exports to the West. In contrast to the United States and its Western allies, the Soviet Union was not a sophisticated customer; it ensured trade, but not necessarily innovation.

6. Sylvia Ostry, *The Post–Cold War Trading System* (Chicago: The University of Chicago Press 1997), pp. 28–30.

7. In the PMR networks, three leading domestic players (Salora, Televa, and Nokia) each held a 25 percent market share, while the remaining proportion consisted of Swedish and Danish imports.

8. On the failed socialization and nationalization (the so-called Valco debacle) efforts, see Nils Eriksson, *Operaatio Valco-Salora* (Saarijärvi: Kustannuspiste Oy, 1979), Chapter VI.

9. D. Steinbock, Interview with Harri Holkeri, United Nations, New York City, May 10, 2001.

10. See Marco Mäkinen, *Nokia Saga: kertomus yrityksestä ja ihmisistä jotka muuttivat sen* (Helsinki: Gummerus, 1995), especially Chapter 6.

11. Kari Kairamo, "Puhe Suomen Ulkomaankauppaliiton vuosikokouksessa," Nokia, May 1987.

12. The Soviet government first presented the idea of a European security conference in the mid-1950s. Despite reservations, the United States joined the Commission on Security and Cooperation in Europe (CSCE) process when the Soviet Union indicated its readiness to start negotiations on the reduction of conventional forces in Europe. In the short term, Finland's role in the organization of the CSCE process was regarded as pro-Moscow. Hence the hawkish notion of Finlandization.

13. "The KGB had become the channel of communication between Finnish political parties of the left and the right and the Soviet Union," argues Timo Vihavainen, a Finnish foreign policy commentator. "The KGB's top official in Finland was always the Finnish president's confidant from the time of President Kekkonen to that of President Koivisto." See T. Vihavainen, *After the War: Finland's Relations with the Soviet Union (1944–91)* (Helsinki: Virtual Finland, 2000) (virtual.finland.fi). The system worked routinely through the Cold War.

14. See Viktor Vladimirov's memoirs in Finland. Viktor Vladimirov, *Näin se oli: muistelmia ja havaintoja kulissientakaisesta toiminnasta Suomessa 1954–84* (Helsinki: Otava, 1993).

15. M. Saari, *Kari Kairamo: Kohtalona Nokia* (Helsinki: Gummerus, 2001), pp. 108–109.

16. Stephen D. Moore, "Nokia Has Vexing Problem with Image: Outside of Finland, It Doesn't Have One," *The Wall Street Journal* (April 21, 1987).

17. Equipment that conformed to Consultative Committee on International Telegraphy and Telephony (CCITT) standards.

18. Quoted in "Vuorineuvos valvoo elektroniikkaa," *Talouselämä* No. 33/1984. In 1980, Nokia's electronics unit invested some FIM 180 million in product development—12 percent of all Finnish R&D. By the mid-1980s, these investments had increased to around FIM 400 million.

19. In 1984, electronics generated approximately FIM 1.7 billion, while revenues at Salora-Luxos climbed to FIM 1.8 billion. The figures, noted Kairamo, "reflect the structural changes that have taken place within the Nokia Group, with a growing emphasis toward high-technology and electronics. . . . As the size has grown, the issues of electronics have become increasingly important to group leadership. They are now strategic issues." See "Vuorineuvos valvoo elektroniikkaa," *Talouselämä* No. 33/1984.

20. Moore, "Nokia Has Vexing Problem with Image."

21. Saari, *Kari Kairamo*, p. 129.

22. By the mid-1970s, Nokia used an American license to manufacture manpack phones in Oulu, which led to the transfer of the radiophone factory from Helsinki to Oulu as well. Over time, these strategic decisions led to the rise of Nokia's subcluster of cellular activities in northern Finland.

23. Kurt Wikstedt, "Electronics," Nokia's Annual Report 1982, pp. 42–44.

24. "Autopuhelin kansainvälistyy," Mobira, Fall 1982. Quoted in Koivusalo, Kipinästä tuli syttyy, p. 55.

25. M. Pulkkinen, *The Breakthrough of Nokia Mobile Phones* (Helsinki School of Economics and Business Administration, 1997), p. 133.

26. A. J. Lagus, P. Lillrank, and K. Helin, *Managing Change: Developing Performance Excellence* (Helsinki: Center for Excellence, 2001), pp. 48–59.

27. *Ibid.* During the critical year of 1992, Nokia Mobile Phones received the Finnish Quality Award, which was followed by the introduction of a wide variety of quality methods and tools, including continuous process improvement (CPI) and the Nokia 7 problem-solving methodology. These methods were coupled with more structured measurements of customer satisfaction in 1996 and the introduction of advanced quality tools based on Six Sigma methodology a year later.

28. This odd view of Kairamo has been advocated by Martti Häikiö, the author of Nokia's official corporate biography. In Finland, Häikiö's official account was heavily touted in late fall of 2001, whereas Matti Otala's account was practically ignored. Häikiö based his view of the events leading to Kairamo's suicide on interviews with the bankers, not on a more comprehensive analysis. Compare M. Häikiö, *Nokia Oyj:n historia* [3 volumes] (Helsinki: Edita, 2001); and M. Otala, *Uskalla olla viisas* (Helsinki: Ajatus, 2001).

29. Quoted in S. D. Moore, "Finnish Electronics Firm's Bold Strategy May Be Unraveling Since Two Acquisitions," *The Wall Street Journal* (December 29, 1989).

30. Even as Nokia's revenues were reduced, Simo Vuorilehto did not sell or disinvest in those businesses he considered strategic—in particular consumer electronics, data communications, and mobile and telecommunications.

31. D. Steinbock, Interview with President Martti Ahtisaari, New York City, May 2001.

32. Stephen Baker, with Roger O. Crockett and Neil Gross, "Can CEO Ollila keep the cellular superstar flying high?" *Business Week* (August 10, 1998).

33. Justin Fox, "Nokia's Secret Code," *Fortune* (May 1, 2000).

34. *Ibid.*

35. R. Jacob, "Nokia Fumbles, But Don't Count It Out," *Time* (February 19, 1996).

36. J. Ollila, "Review by the President and CEO," Nokia Annual Report 1992, pp. 4–5.

37. Nokia Annual Report 1998.

38. Quoted in M. Specter, "Industrial Arts: The Phone Guy," *The New Yorker* (November 26, 2001), pp. 62–72.

39. In the long run, the segmentation strategy was just as vulnerable as the old mass-market strategy. As GM engaged heavily in segmentation and product differentiation, it was bound to lose some of the high-volume benefits of a pure cost leadership strategy. Conversely, it would never be as good in tailoring the products to ever-smaller customer segments as a niche rival.

40. Specter, "Industrial Arts: The Phone Guy."

41. Pulkkinen, *The Breakthrough of Nokia Mobile Phones*, p. 147.

42. In consumer markets, both Nokia and Ericsson, supported by the advanced Nordic country markets, anticipated trends better than their rivals did. But unlike its rivals, Nokia truly listened to its key corporate customers, such as AT&T, who wanted their customers to be able to communicate across frequency bands used by different formats. Such service capabilities posed complex challenges in innovation. However, successful solutions paid off in the downstream activities as products moved from business markets to consumer markets.

43. At the International Institute for Management Development (IMD), Matti Alahuhta had cooperated closely with professor Jean-Pierre Jeannet to conceptualize appropriate growth strategies for ambitious European SMEs (small and medium-size enterprises). In changing environmental circumstances, the old-style vertical giants—the "vertical dragons" in Jeannet's terminology—have been descending while the new-style horizontal focusers—the "horizontal tigers"—have been ascending.

44. J. Ollila, and P. Ala-Pietilä, "To Our Shareholders: Making best execution an asset," Nokia Annual Report 2000, pp. 4–5.

45. Quoted in "Optioiden kirjaaminen kuluiksi heikentäisi selvästi Nokian tulosta," *Helsinkin Sanomat,* (February 16, 2002).

46. Corporate News Release, Nokia, October 29, 2001.

47. J. Ollila, "Suomelta loppuu vauhti," *Helsingin Sanomat* (January 27, 2002); and J. Alkio, "Suomi on yhä Nokialle tärkeä," *Helsingin Sanomat* (January 27, 2002).

48. See Steinbock, *The Nokia Revolution* (New York: AMACOM, 2001). Ollila's term "market-making strategies" is reminiscent of recent literature in strategic management. See D. F. Spulber, *The Market Makers: How Leading Companies Create and Win Markets* (New York: McGraw Hill/Business Week Books, 1998).

49. J. Guyon, "Nokia Rocks Its Rivals," *Fortune* (March 4, 2002); A. Cowell, "Not in Finland Anymore? More Like Nokialand," *The New York Times* (February 6, 2002); and D. Steinbock *et al.*, "ICT Clusters in the Greater Helsinki Region," OECD, July 2002.

Chapter 11

1. E. Nee, "Qualcomm Hits the Big Time," *Fortune* (May 15, 2000).

2. See Qualcomm, Inc., website.

3. After holding various executive positions at Linkabit and its later reincarnations, Dr. Andrew Viterbi served as vice chairman of the Qualcomm board from its inception in 1985. A cofounder of Qualcomm, he served as chief technical officer and was the inventor of the Viterbi decoder. In the late 1990s, he also became a member of the United States President's IT Advisory Committee.

4. Q. Hardy, "Qualcomm CEO's Innovation Has Telecom Giants on Edge," *The Wall Street Journal* (September 6, 1996).

5. In 1999—some thirteen years later—General Instrument's set-top box business was acquired by Motorola, Qualcomm's rival through most of the 1990s. The $17 billion deal was finalized in January 2000.

6. Hardy, "Qualcomm CEO's Innovation Has Telecom Giants on Edge," *The Wall Street Journal*.

7. Quoted in Nee, "Qualcomm Hits the Big Time," *Fortune*.

8. InterDigital Communications Corp., which held many of the patents for the rival TDMA technology, cast a cloud over the CDMA standards-setting process by filing still-pending lawsuits that alleged patent infringement earlier that year.

9. That same year (1991) witnessed Qualcomm's IPO, as well as the introduction of e-mail software Eudora (named for "Why I Live at the P.O." author Eudora Welty), which it licensed from the University of Illinois.

10. In the short term, Ericsson and Nokia were transitioning into the "right" technology (GSM for 2G) and struggling to build the relevant production capacity. Motorola, the only producer that really possessed the required manufacturing capabilities, focused on a lucrative technology that was rapidly turning obsolete (AMPS for 1G).

11. At the end of the year, the Qualcomm/Sony joint venture Qualcomm Personal Electronics (QPE) had produced more than 400,000 CDMA handsets for U.S. and international customers and was on course to a planned production capacity of 300,000 phones per month.

12. Qualcomm, Inc. Annual Report 1996, pp. 2, 4.

13. Hardy, "Qualcomm CEO's Innovation Has Telecom Giants on Edge," *The Wall Street Journal.*

14. *Ibid.*

15. Qualcomm, Inc. Annual Report 1998, p. 6.

16. Qualcomm Inc. Annual Report 1999, p. 1.

17. Qualcomm, Inc. Annual Report 1999, p. 7.

18. Unlike its rivals, Qualcomm has been able to add features, such as geographic-positioning circuits and MP3 music-playing capability, sooner than anyone else had. Furthermore, Qualcomm's "chipsets" used fewer chips than those of competitors, making possible cell phones that were more compact and that needed less power. The chipsets also cost less to produce, giving Qualcomm the freedom to cut prices or make higher margins.

19. The move led to the resignation of COO Richard Sulpizio, who was to head up the chip unit once it had gone solo.

20. A. Hesseldahl, "Qualcomm Shifts Gears, Again," *Forbes* (July 25, 2001).

21. Romero, "Qualcomm's Shrinking Act Could Pay Off Big," *The New York Times*, October 23, 2000.

22. "There were a lot of arguments, saying that TCP-IP was too complex for cellular and the Internet was only used by geeks," recalls Phil Karn, who, in 1991, engineered the inclusion of a TCP-IP protocol stack in Qualcomm phones. Quoted in G. Gilder, *Telecosm: How Infinite Bandwidth Will Revolutionize Our World* (New York: The Free Press, 2000), Chapter 8.

23. Qualcomm, Inc. Annual Report 1999, p. 26. "We can actually do full-motion video with HDR," said Jeff Jacobs, the CEO's son and senior vice president of business development. Quoted in E. Nee, "Qualcomm Hits the Big Time: The Future Is Data," *Fortune* (May 15, 2000.)

24. By 2000, Qualcomm accelerated building applications for the wireless Internet and acquired SnapTrack, a major player in wireless position location technology. It also formed a joint venture with Ford Motor Co. called Wingcast, whose mission was to create in-vehicle wireless services for cards and trucks. Finally, the company solidified Wireless Knowledge, the venture with Microsoft, by forming an alliance to develop multimedia devices based on the Microsoft Mobile Explorer platform and wireless Pocket PCs.

25. CDMA products included integrated circuits (e.g., baseband chips, intermediate-frequency chips, power amplification chips, radio frequency chips) and systems software.

26. Qualcomm Technology Licensing (QTL) generated fees and ongoing royalties from the sales of CDMA products manufactured by the company's authorized suppliers. By the end of 2000, Qualcomm had signed licenses with more than ninety companies for cdmaOne and CDMA2000 1x and with more than forty companies for W-CDMA and other CDMA standards. In turn, Qualcomm's wireless systems included network infrastructure, handset, and modem products (Globalstar), as well as satellite and terrestrial-based two-way data messaging, position reporting, equipment, and services (such as LINQ, OmniExpress, OmniTRACS, and TruckMAIL).

27. These ventures include Qualcomm Personal Communications (a 51 percent stake in telephone handsets, with Kyocera Corp.); Qualcomm Spinco (CDMA integrated circuit and software design); Wingcast (15 percent stake in wireless services for automobiles with Ford Motor Co.); and Wireless Knowledge Inc. (50 percent ownership in security products for mobile Internet usage, with Microsoft).

28. The BREW development platform was portrayed as a very thin, standardized platform that resided in handsets, from inexpensive, mass-market phones through high-end, multipurpose wireless devices. It covered a wide variety of applications.

29. Quoted in International Technology Consultants, "Global Wireless Competitiveness Study," (June 14, 1998), p. 18.

30. Wireless local loop (WLL) technology fit Qualcomm's objective to offer highly cost-efficient services because, by eliminating the need for cabling, substantial cost-savings could be achieved in both installation and maintenance.

31. With CDMA demand escalating internationally, Qualcomm expanded its foothold in the strategic Japanese market. In Japan, two carriers, DDI and IDO, joined forces to launch the first nationwide all-digital network, while planning to merge, along with KDD, to form a unified carrier. Qualcomm was first to market with the chips that enabled Japanese handset manufacturers to surpass the specifications and facilitate an on-time launch of the national network.

32. Qualcomm, Inc. Annual Report 1992, p. 1.

33. The benefits of CDMA, argued Qualcomm, included increased capacity (to more than ten times) within the allocated frequency; higher quality; soft handoff; greater range for portables per unit of out power (which leads to lower cost, longer battery life, and smaller units); simplified frequency planning; enhanced privacy; easy transition from analog to digital with lower system cost; and a platform for new services. See Qualcomm, Inc. Annual Report 1991, p. 6.

34. International Technology Consultants, "Global Wireless Competitiveness Study," p. 18.

35. "In college, the one course I did poorly in was public speaking," Jacobs acknowledged. "But if I know what I'm talking about, I'm okay." As he won followers for CDMA, critics accused the ex-professor of combativeness, exaggerating the technology's virtues, and being unwilling to compromise. He has denied all of these charges. "People have referred to it as a religious war. I always tried to keep it rational." Quoted in Nee, "Qualcomm Hits the Big Time," *Fortune.*

36. Qualcomm, Inc., Annual Report 2000, p. 3.

37. By 2001, Irwin Jacobs and Qualcomm cofounder Viterbi, owned some twenty patents. Paul Jacobs—the son of Qualcomm's CEO/chairman, the executive vice president of wireless data, and a PhD in electrical engineering and computer science—had twenty-seven patents. Steven Altman, Qualcomm's general counsel and a tough negotiator, was in charge of the licensing deals that transformed the inventions and innovations into a growing stream of revenues.

38. Price erosion and enforcement issues worked against Qualcomm's patent power.

39. In contrast to the report by the Rockville, MD–based Center for Financial

Research and Analysis, Qualcomm said its accounting practices were in line with industry guidelines and that concerns raised by a research firm about the wireless technology firm's financial reports were taken out of context. See Qualcomm's news releases and CNET, February 8, 2002 (www.news.com).

40. Qualcomm's lock on W-CDMA was not as solid because dozens of companies had contributed to intellectual property rights, which could easily dilute the revenue stream Qualcomm collected from CDMA royalties. Qualcomm's rivals argued that because they had developed critical pieces of W-CDMA on their own, Qualcomm was not entitled to the same royalties and fees. Qualcomm disputed the allegations, arguing that its CDMA patents were broad enough to cover crucial elements of W-CDMA.

41. See "Newsmaker Q&A," *Business Week* (December 20, 2000).

42. As Nokia, Ericsson, and NTT DoCoMo challenged the validity and breadth of Qualcomm's CDMA patents, Japanese and European intellectual property (IP) courts upheld all of Qualcomm's patents. Motorola challenged Qualcomm's patents in Korea, where the vast majority of the patents were also upheld. As long as Qualcomm could collect royalties and licensing fees, revenue continued to grow with the demand for cellular communications. But if Qualcomm's broad CDMA patents were not adopted globally and upheld by IP courts, royalty and licensing revenue would be harder to come by in the long run. See L. DiCarlo, "Qualcomm's Royalty Revenue In Question," *Forbes* (July 26, 2000).

43. The deal allowed Nokia to start shipping wireless equipment that used the CDMA infrastructure worldwide. Previously, Nokia's CDMA license was limited to handsets. In turn, Qualcomm got the rights to market and sell Nokia's CDMA components, including multimode integrated circuits.

Chapter 12

1. Quoted in "IT 100 Overview: The Era of Efficiency," *Business Week* (June 18, 2001).

2. Quoted in "Chips, boards, boxes to go," *Industry Week* (July 4, 1997).

3. The author is indebted to an OECD working group presentation on the vendor/contractor relationships by Hannu Bergholm, president of Elcoteq, on September 28, 2001.

4. On the story of Wecan Electronics and Nokia's suppliers, see D. Steinbock, *The Nokia Revolution* (New York: AMACOM, 2001), Chapter 9.

5. "Nokia jakaa kasvun ja kivun," *Helsingin Sanomat* (August 1, 1999). The numbers were estimated on the basis of Nokia's lead subcontractors in Finland and thus were not precise. Not all subcontractor employees worked in Nokia-related projects. On the other hand, the aggregate number did not include all Nokia subcontractors. Finally, the number of overseas subcontractors was accelerating rapidly.

6. Tomi Alkula, "Nokia Networksin tukiasemasopimusvalmistajan kilpailutekijät: Case Wecan Electronics Oyj," Unpublished MBA Thesis (Manuscript), De-

partment of Marketing, Helsinki Economics and Business Administration, 2000. Alkula's study illustrates excellently the strategic strengths and vulnerabilities, as well as the unique dependencies, of Nokia's small and midsize suppliers.

7. "Nokia jakaa kasvun ja kivun."

8. For more, see http://www.wecan.fi and http://www.scanfil.com. For more information, see http://www.scanfil.fi.

9. On competition and cooperation in business ecosystems, see J. F. Moore, *The Death of Competition* (New York: HarperCollins, 1996).

10. C. K. Prahalad and G. Hamel, "The Core Competence of the Corporation," *Harvard Business Review* (May–June 1990). The advocates of core competence—C. K. Prahalad and Gary Hamel—illustrated success and failure examples with NEC and GTE, respectively. The two companies, however, have very different histories and have engaged in very different industries. Moreover, measuring success drivers on the basis of isolated revenue figures seldom illustrates fundamental developments.

11. On quality management at Nokia and with its suppliers, see A. J. Lagus, P. Lillrank, and K. Helin, *Managing Change: Developing Performance Excellence* (Helsinki: Center for Excellence, 2001), pp. 48–59.

12. J. Ali-Yrkkö, *Nokia's Network—Gaining Competitiveness from Co-Operation* (Helsinki: ETLA, 2000).

13. Technology Forecasters, an independent analyst, estimated the EMS industry at $73.2 billion in 1999 with a forecast of $149.4 billion for 2003.

14. J. Meurling and R. Jeans, *The Ugly Duckling: Mobile Phones from Ericsson—Putting People on Speaking Terms* (Stockholm: Ericsson Mobile Communications AB, 1997), p. 56.

15. C. Koch, "Yank Your Chain," *Darwin* (October 2001).

16. "You Name It, We'll Make It," *Time.com Global Business,* August 2001.

17. In late 2000, Motorola and Flextronics agreed to one of the largest outsourcing deals, valued at $30 billion, that would last over half a decade. With the industry slowdown, the Motorola deal unraveled, which led Flextronics to repurchase Motorola's 5 percent stake in the company.

18. "You Name It, We'll Make It."

19. To cut costs, Flextronics announced it would reduce its workforce by some 10 percent, and later by another 15 percent, even as it continued acquisitions in 2001 (e.g., acquiring Telcom Global Solutions, Xerox facilities in several countries, and a majority stake in a spinoff of Swedish Telia).

20. The sellers were computer and consumer electronics giants, such as IBM, Hewlett-Packard, and Philips Electronics. In some cases the sales included multi-year supplier deals for Solectron.

21. Solectron's hunger showed few signs of exhaustion by 2000, when, among other things, the company acquired Alcatel's operations in Puerto Rico and Texas. In 2001, these M&A activities continued, even as the company cut 25 percent of its workforce.

22. "Valley peers honor Solectron CEO today," *San Jose Mercury-News* (October 25, 2001).

23. Like Solectron, Celestica now made larger deals and benefited from the slowdown in the U.S. technology sector and the 3G post-auction hangover in Europe. In both cases, industry consolidation resulted in outsourcing, divestitures, and migration of manufacturing capabilities—typically to EMS leaders. More factory acquisitions were coupled with billion-dollar supply agreements.

24. Sanmina's other acquisitions included Massachusetts-based Altron, a leading competitor in backplane manufacturing, and assets from Nortel Networks and Devtek Electronics Enclosure, a designer of enclosure systems for the telecom and networking industries. In 2000 Sanmina acquired PCB maker Hadco for $1.3 billion, expanding its global presence. This was followed by the purchase of Swedish contract manufacturer Essex AB, a joint venture with Siemens to manufacture complex PCBs, and plant acquisitions from Nortel and Lucent.

25. Founded in 1961 by Olin King, a former NASA engineer, SCI Systems evolved into a major manufacturer of PCs and then, under A. Eugene Sapp, Jr., who became CEO in 1999, diversified into optical and wireless technology. At the nadir of the technology slump, the company bought Nokia factories in Finland and Britain, and announced that it would triple the capacity of a factory in China that made optical devices for Hitachi. However, SCI missed the boat when networking and telecom companies such as Cisco Systems became the largest customers for the EMS industry. Leading competitors such as Flextronics and Sanmina grew at a faster pace and pursued diverse acquisitions while SCI tried to add optics and networking companies to its PC and cell phone business.

26. This groundbreaking deal to buy SCI Systems was followed by another major acquisition. Sanmina acquired Alcatel's facility in Texas and signed still another multiyear supply agreement with the French telecom giant, which was divesting its manufacturing capabilities.

27. In the computer sector, Taiwanese and Japanese CEMs had historically done the outsourcing for most leading PC vendors. In the mobile business, electronic products were more complicated and outsourcing was a more recent phenomenon. It was dominated by the EMS leaders, which had started their operations in the United States. On the other hand, many of them were pushing their regional headquarters in Asia-Pacific, particularly in Singapore, where Flextronics had launched operations in 1981.

28. "You Name It, We'll Make It."

29. "Flextronics benefits from crisis," *Wirtschaftsblatt* (November 13, 2001).

30. Koch, "Yank Your Chain."

31. "You Name It, We'll Make It," *Time.com*.

32. *Ibid.*

33. J. M. O'Brien, "The Making of Xbox," *Wired* (November 2001).

34. *Ibid.*

Chapter 13

1. On the genesis of the Internet, see K. Hafner and M. Lyon, *Where Wizards Stay Up Late: The Origins of the Internet* (New York: Simon & Schuster, 1996); and M. Meeker and C. DePuy, *The Internet Report* (New York: Morgan Stanley, 1996).

2. In 1972, the first documented e-mail message was sent across the ARPANET, and in 1973, ARPA developed other, nonterrestrial networks.

3. Basic ARPANET services for remote connectivity, file transfer, and electronic mail appeared in the mid- to late-1970s.

4. The World Wide Web was developed for scientists, primarily by Tim Berners-Lee, at CERN's nuclear supercollider facility. It would facilitate research by allowing authors to reference other documents, all of which are available on the Internet. At its inception, the system was text-based (using hypertext); CERN did not start publicizing the development until about 1992.

5. See U.S. Government, "The National Information Infrastructure: An Agenda for Action," Information Infrastructure Task Force. 15.9.1993; U.S. Government, "Global Information Infrastructure: An Agenda for Cooperation," March 1994–February 1995; U.S. Government, "A Framework for Global Electronic Commerce," December 1996–July 1997. Compare also D. Steinbock, *The Birth of Internet Marketing Communications* (Westport, CT: Quorum Books, 2000).

6. D. Steinbock, "The 3G Transition: From Original Demand to Replacement Demand," CITI 3G Conference, October 25, 2001.

7. See UMTS Forum (Exhibit 13-8). Subscription numbers for rich voice and location-based services and unified messaging are not included because these service revenues reflect a summation of several components, some of which are not calculated on a per-subscription basis.

8. "The New Future: Pekka Ala-Pietilä on Terror," *Fortune* (November 26, 2001).

9. "The UMTS Third Generation Market Study Update," Report No. 17, UMTS Forum, August 2001.

10. These predictions are based on a report titled "Long-Term Potential Remains High for 3G Mobile Data Services," UMTS Forum, February 2002.

11. J. Ollila, "To Our Shareholders," Nokia's Annual Report 1998, pp. 6–7.

12. J. Ollila and P. Ala-Pietilä, "Letter to Our Shareholders," Nokia's Annual Report 1999, pp. 6–7.

13. On the Nokia Communicator story, see D. Steinbock, *The Nokia Revolution* (New York: AMACOM, 2001), Chapter 9.

14. Y. M. Ibrahim, "Cell Phones Make Nokia a World Player," *The New York Times* (August 13, 1997).

15. *Ibid.*

16. See D. Steinbock, *The Nokia Revolution* (New York: AMACOM, 2001), Chapter 9.

17. Compare J. Meurling and R. Jeans, *The Ugly Duckling: Mobile Phones from Ericsson—Putting People on Speaking Terms* (Stockholm: Ericsson Mobile Communications AB, 1997), p. 116.

18. On the characteristics of these five basic development projects, see Wheelwright, S. C., and Kim B. Clark, (1992), *Revolutionizing Product Development: Quantum Leaps in Speed, Efficiency, and Quality* (Boston, MA: Harvard Business School Press, 1992), especially Chapter 4.

19. On successful and unsuccessful acquisitions in the U.S. technology sector,

see Saikat Chaudhuri and Behnam Tabrizi, "Capturing the Real Value in High-Tech Acquisitions," *Harvard Business Review* (September–October 1999).

20. See Steinbock, *The Nokia Revolution,* Chapter 9.

21. On value chains and the general characteristics of coalitions, see Michael E. Porter and Mark B. Fuller, "Coalitions and Global Strategy," in Michael E. Porter, ed., *Competition in Global Industries* (Boston, MA: Harvard Business School Press, 1986), pp. 315–343.

22. See Almar Latour, "Finnish Firms Lead Wireless Revolution As Vanguard Companies Capture Market," *The Wall Street Journal* (September 10, 1999).

23. News release, Wapit Ltd, June 5, 2001. See also M. Valtonen, *Noh, sano naakka ku nokka katkes* (Helsinki: Tammi 2001).

24. At first, Psion retained 40 percent in the company. In 1998, Motorola joined the mobile leaders with a stake in the company. As a result, Psion's stake fell to 31 percent, while the then–top-three vendors split 69 percent of Psion evenly among each other. The strategic alliance between Nokia and Palm, which had been Symbian's top rival, precipitated discussions of cross-licensing agreements between Symbian and Palm.

25. Matsushita acquired a 9 percent stake in Symbian, which reduced Psion's stake to 29 percent and that of the top-three vendors to 63 percent. In 2000, Symbian also added Sanyo and Kenwood to its list of EPOC licensees.

26. Mobile players were hedging their bets as well. Motorola, for instance, had acquired stakes in both Palm and Symbian, while Nokia manufactured devices that relied on both Palm and EPOC software. Symbian itself intended to develop applications to access IBM's enterprise software through wireless devices, including Symbian smart phones.

27. "Industry leaders announce commitment to open mobile architecture enabling a nonfragmented global mobile services market," Press Release, Nokia Corp., November 13, 2001.

28. These factors included handset replacement requirements, growth in short message service (SMS), the move from time- to data-driven pricing for WAP services, lack of adequate content, the introduction of GPRS, and network providers' potential problems with technical issues. Although some of these factors were expected to drive WAP use, IDC thought that, in many respects, the market was not yet ready. "WAP Is on the Way, but Is Europe Ready?" IDC, London, August 27, 1999.

29. "To replace maligned WAP: Industrywide push for common standard unveiled," *Financial Post-Canada* (June 14, 2001).

30. GPRS replaced GSM, offering always-on Internet access. It was a stepping-stone to faster and costlier 3G mobile services. Because of license and infrastructure investments, the industry despaired over revenues.

31. At the time, WLANs could provide data connectivity at up to 11 Mbps per access point (IEEE 802.11b). Within one to three years, they were expected to provide access speeds of up to 54 Mbps (IEEE 802.11a and HiperLAN/2), and looking beyond three years, this data rate was expected to reach 100 Mbps. In contrast to WAP, WLANs did not require any new content creation or application

development to attract users. See D. Alven, *et al.,* "WLAN: Hotspots—Connect the Dots for a Wireless Future," Final Report for Ericsson Business Innovation and Telia Research, (Stockholm: Royal Institute of Technology/Stanford University, May 2001).

32. "Bluetooth Special Interest Group to be Led by 3Com, Ericsson, Intel, IBM, Lucent, Microsoft, Motorola," Press Release, The Bluetooth SIG, December 1, 1999.

33. According to a Strategy Analytics study, cell phone users who consumed more than 120 minutes per week demonstrated a high interest in Bluetooth, whereas users who made fewer than twenty minutes of calls per week indicated the lowest level of interest. Cellular veterans indicated a willingness to pay a considerable premium for a handset offering Bluetooth functionality. See "Strong Interest in Bluetooth from High-Usage Cellphone users," *Apendig,* Issue 1 (November 2001).

34. C. J. Kennedy, "Bluetooth Reaches the Market," *Unstrung* (December 7, 2001).

35. The only exception might have been Siemens. Recently, Siemens and Nokia had declared their support for a global open standard for broadband wireless networks, while Nokia announced its base station initiative. The proposed standard combined elements of the IEEE's 802.16 broadband specification and the Broadband Radio Access Networks (BRAN) standard from the ETSI.

36. The M-Services Initiative was a carrier-defined template for data applications that 3G handsets should support; the list of approved services included multimedia messaging service (MMS) and the latest versions of WAP and the Bluetooth wireless connectivity protocol.

37. See Steinbock, *The Nokia Revolution,* Chapter 6.

38. J. P. Jeannet, *Managing with a Global Mindset* (London: Financial Times-Prentice Hall, 2000), pp. xiv, xxi, 14–15, 164–166.

39. For example, Nokia's efforts at global branding and segmentation did not just benefit the company vis-à-vis price premiums and category dominance. They also provided a boost to the industry as a whole.

40. Richard S. Dunham, "Q&A: Nokia's Ollila on CEO Profiles and the Company's Future," *Business Week* (August 10, 1998).

41. J. Ollila, "Opening" speech at Nokia's Capital Markets Days, New York Sheraton, November 27, 2001.

42. See "Gates' Vision of the Future: A Home Operated via the Fridge," *Financial Times* (December 8, 2001).

Chapter 14

1. J. Kaplan, *Startup: A Silicon Valley Adventure* (New York: Penguin Books, 1994), pp. 1–2.

2. Accurate cost estimates are still difficult to obtain. Many industry assess-

ments, however, put the figure at $1–$1.2 billion. See Handspring's website at http://www.handspring.com/company/background.htm.

3. For Sculley's views and visions, see J. Sculley, with J. A. Byrne, *Odyssey: Pepsi to Apple* (New York: HarperTrade, 1987).

4. See M. Kounalakis, *Defying Gravity: The Making of Newton* (Hillsboro, OR: Beyond Words Publishing, 1993).

5. *Ibid.*

6. *Ibid.*

7. Colligan had been vice president of strategic and product marketing at Radius Corp. (a maker of Macintosh clones). The company's initial product was Graffiti input software for handheld devices. Before joining Palm Computing as CEO in 1992, Dubinsky had been a senior manager in a variety of logistics, sales, and marketing positions at Apple Computer and Claris Corporation. See E. Corcoran and D. Doan, "Encore!" *Forbes* (May 5, 1999).

8. Hawkins previously had served as vice president of research at GRiD Systems Corporation, which brought to the market the first pen-based computer. He had also held technical positions at Intel Corp. after studying electrical engineering at Cornell University. The GridPad had some success in professional markets.

9. See Handspring's website at http://www.handspring.com/company/background.htm.

10. See Palm's website at http://www.palm.com/about.

11. IDC, June 2000.

12. See Handspring's website, http://www.handspring.com/company/background.htm.

13. Over time, Palm was forced to play defensive catch-up with Handspring. Palm's entry-level m100 product matched the prices of Handspring's base model, and Palm offered colorful faceplates for the device.

14. See Handspring's website, http://www.handspring.com/company/background.htm.

15. Between 1990 and 1993, right before the Internet revolution, Microsoft was growing explosively, tripling sales to $3.8 billion, and increasing payroll from 5,600 to 14,400. For more on Microsoft and the early years of the Internet, see D. Steinbock, *The Birth of Internet Marketing Communications* (Westport, CT: Quorum Books, 2000), Chapter 2.

16. See K. Rebello, with A. Cortese and R. Hof, "Inside Microsoft: The Untold Story of How the Internet Forced Bill Gates to Reverse Course," *Business Week* (July 15, 1996). For more information on Microsoft and its Internet strategy, see B. Gates, with N. Myhrvold and P. Rinearson, *The Road Ahead* (New York: Viking, 1995); and J. Wallace, *Overdrive: Bill Gates and the Race to Control Cyberspace* (New York: John Wiley & Sons, 1997).

17. Early betas of Windows 95 contained a desktop version of WinPad, which would have been used for synchronization. The WinPad ran an operating system called Microsoft At Work, a scaled-down version of Windows 3.1. WinPad and At Work died on the vine, and Intel's Polar processor soon followed. The Intel processor was thought to contribute significantly to WinPad's hefty price tag.

18. On the pros and cons of the new alignment, see S. G. Bush, "Intel (not) Inside," Brighthand Consulting, Inc., October 1999.

19. There were strings attached to sampling the Windows CE source code, though. See M. Broersma, S. Shankland, and I. Fried, "Microsoft Releases Windows CE Code," CNET, July 23, 2001.

20. "Why the Wireless Internet Is for Real," CNETNews.com, July 5, 2000. When the 3G downturn hit the wireless sector just three months later, the visionaries adopted a different tone.

21. Quoted in "Microsoft Broadens Vision Statement to Go Beyond the PC-Centric World," *The Wall Street Journal* (July 23, 1999).

22. S. Baker, "Clash of the Titans: Microsoft and Nokia," *Business Week* (July 9, 2001).

23. See R. Buckman, "Microsoft, Advertisers Target the Wireless Web," *The Wall Street Journal* (July 24, 2000).

24. See "Microsoft, Ericsson Announce Strategic Partnership to Drive Mobile Internet Market," Microsoft Corp. Press Release, December 8, 1999.

25. Quoted in M. Kanellos, "Gates Talks Up Net Appliances," CNET, June 13, 2000.

26. Quoted in W. Wong, "Microsoft Taps $4.4 Billion for Web, Wireless Research," CNET, July 27, 2000.

27. For more on the "Stinger" project, see Microsoft's website, http://www.microsoft.com/mobile.

28. Quoted in S. Miles, "Microsoft Abuzz Over Web-Enabled Cell Phone," CNET, August 9, 2000.

29. J. Meurling and R. Jeans, *The Ugly Duckling: Mobile Phones from Ericsson— Putting People on Speaking Terms* (Stockholm: Ericsson Mobile Communications AB, 1997), p. 115.

30. Ron J. Smith, "Building Blocks for the Wireless Internet," Keynote Address at Wireless 2000, Tsukuba, Japan, July 11, 2000.

31. Quoted in "Wireless Initiative Bundles Services," CNET News.com, August 5, 1997.

32. Headquartered in California, but with most of its engineers in Tel Aviv, DSP Communications made chips and software for several varieties of digital cellular phones (including TDMA and PDC), especially the types used in Korea, Japan, and the United States. It was developing smart phones with Internet capabilities when it was acquired by Intel.

33. "Intel Agrees to Purchase DSP For $1.6 Billion in Cash Deal," *The Wall Street Journal* (October 15, 1999).

34. "Intel Establishes Wireless Internet Technology Center in Sweden," Intel Corp., News Release, November 12, 1999.

35. Quoted in Intel Developer Forum Conference, Intel Corp., Tokyo, Japan, April 17, 2001.

36. "Intel to unveil its 'Internet on a chip'," CNET News.com, May 16, 2001.

37. J. Ollila, "Opening" remarks at Nokia's Capital Markets Days, New York Sheraton, November 27, 2001.

38. "Intel: Cellular Chips Big for Future Sales," Reuters, November 28, 2001. See http://www.reuters.com.

39. "Intel demonstrates wireless access to enterprise IT systems at CTIA Wireless 2002," Intel Press Release, March 18, 2002.

40. S. M. Case, from a speech given at the CS First Boston Global Telecom Conference, March 8, 2000.

41. S. M. Case, from a speech given at the Goldman Sachs Communicopeia Conference, September 28, 2000.

42. On America Online's growth strategy, see D. Steinbock, *The Birth of Internet Marketing Communications* (Westport, CT: Quorum Books, 2000), Chapter 5.

43. Quoted in Marc Gunther, "The Internet Is Mr. Case's Neighborhood", *Fortune* (March 30, 1998).

44. These changes were first reported in April 1998, when AOL prepared to offer services to Internet-connected devices, eliminating the need for PCs. In effect, it is difficult to find any meaningful reference to mobile or wireless business in AOL's annual reports and 10-Ks before 1998.

45. AOL Annual Report 1998.

46. On the depiction of "AOL Anywhere" initiative, the author is indebted to Jenna Fiorito, vice president/general manager of AOL Telecom, and her presentation, "AOL Anywhere," October 25, 2001.

47. See "Talking with Lisa Hook," Interview, AOL Time Warner, May 9, 2001.

48. According to Dataquest Inc., a unit of Gartner, Inc.

49. "Microsoft Expands Mobile Program," CNET, January 29, 2002.

50. Quoted in "Microsoft Talks to Major Cell Phone Makers on Software," Reuters, February 21, 2002.

51. See D. Pringle, "Microsoft, Intel to Create 'Template' for Phone That Competes With Nokia," *The Wall Street Journal* (February 19, 2002).

52. Richard S. Dunham, "Q&A: Nokia's Ollila on CEO Profiles and the Company's Future," *Business Week* (August 10, 1998).

Chapter 15

1. J. Bhagwati, "Coping with Antiglobalization: A Trilogy of Discontents," *Foreign Affairs* (January/February 2002).

2. See Nokia's social objectives at http://www.nokia.com/aboutnokia/social/index.html, where there are links to the company's policies on corporate citizenship, employee commitment, and health and safety. See also http://www.nokia.com/aboutnokia/inbrief/nokiaway.html for more information on The Nokia Way and the company's ethical conduct commitment.

3. The seven principles of eco-efficiency defined by the World Business Council for Sustainable Development, combined with life-cycle thinking, are of primary concern in developing, producing, and marketing Nokia's products and solutions.

4. The DJSGI consist of 236 companies from sixty-one industries in twenty-seven countries and represented the "top 10 percent" sustainability companies worldwide. The total market capitalization of these companies is approximately $5.5 trillion (as of August 31, 2000). See http://www.sustainability-index.com/.

5. See http://www.FTSE4Good.com.

6. Bhagwati, "Coping with Antiglobalization: A Trilogy of Discontents."

Index